University Textbook Series

May, 1993

Especially Designed for Collateral Reading

HARRY W. JONES
Directing Editor
Professor of Law, Columbia University

---

[i]

CORPORATE TAXATION, FEDERAL, Second Edition (1990)
Howard E. Abrams, Professor of Law, Emory University.
Richard L. Doernberg, Professor of Law, Emory University.

CORPORATIONS, Second Edition (1971)
Norman D. Lattin, Professor of Law, University of California, Hastings College of the Law.

CORPORATIONS IN PERSPECTIVE (1976)
Alfred F. Conard, Professor of Law, University of Michigan.

CRIMINAL LAW, Third Edition (1982)
Rollin M. Perkins, Professor of Law, University of California, Hastings College of the Law.
Ronald N. Boyce, Professor of Law, University of Utah College of Law.

CRIMINAL PROCEDURE, Third Edition (1993)
Charles H. Whitebread, II, Professor of Law, University of Southern California.
Christopher Slobogin, Professor of Law, University of Florida.

ESTATES IN LAND & FUTURE INTERESTS, PREFACE TO, Second Edition (1984)
Thomas F. Bergin, Professor of Law, University of Virginia.
Paul G. Haskell, Professor of Law, University of North Carolina.

EVIDENCE: COMMON SENSE AND COMMON LAW (1947)
John M. Maguire, Professor of Law, Harvard University.

JURISPRUDENCE: MEN AND IDEAS OF THE LAW (1953)
The late Edwin W. Patterson, Cardozo Professor of Jurisprudence, Columbia University.

LABOR RELATIONS THE BASIC PROCESSES, LAW AND PRACTICE (1988)
Julius G. Getman, Professor of Law, University of Texas.
Bertrand E. Pogrebin, Member, New York State Bar.

LEGAL CAPITAL, Third Edition (1990)
Bayless Manning.

LEGAL RESEARCH ILLUSTRATED, Fifth Edition with 1990 Assignments Supplement
J. Myron Jacobstein, Professor of Law, Emeritus, Stanford University.
Roy M. Mersky, Professor of Law, Director of Research, University of Texas.

LEGAL RESEARCH, FUNDAMENTALS OF, Fifth Edition with 1990 Assignments Supplement
J. Myron Jacobstein, Professor of Law, Emeritus, Stanford University.
Roy M. Mersky, Professor of Law, Director of Research, University of Texas.

PROCEDURE, THE STRUCTURE OF (1979)
Robert M. Cover, Professor of Law, Yale University.
Owen M. Fiss, Professor of Law, Yale University.

PROPERTY, PRINCIPLES OF THE LAW OF, Third Edition (1989)
John E. Cribbet, Dean, Chancellor, Professor of Law Emeritus, University of Illinois.
Corwin W. Johnson, Professor of Law Emeritus, University of Texas.

TAX, FEDERAL INCOME, Second Edition (1992)
Douglas A. Kahn, Professor of Law, University of Michigan.

[ii]

UNIVERSITY TEXTBOOK SERIES—Continued

JURISPRUDENCE

MEN AND IDEAS OF THE LAW

By
EDWIN W. PATTERSON
Cardozo Professor of Jurisprudence
Columbia University

First Printed Edition

Brooklyn
THE FOUNDATION PRESS, INC.
1953

ISBN No. 0–88277–362–3

Patterson Jurisprudence F.P.Inc.
13th Reprint—1993

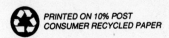

PRINTED ON 10% POST CONSUMER RECYCLED PAPER

TO
MY WIFE

*

PREFACE

To present concisely and clearly the ideas of the legal order and the general theories about law which have been and are most influential on the law of the United States of America is the primary purpose of this volume. The assumption that such ideas and theories have effects on the legal profession and, more broadly, on the social order, is verified by observation; in this sense the present treatment approaches that of cultural anthropology, extended to mature societies. Yet the method of the book is not primarily the sustained observation of effects but rather the analysis and appraisal of theories. For ideas may need no better claim on our interest than that they illumine the thoughts and gladden the hearts of individuals seeking the true and the good. In large part, then, this is a selective treatise on the philosophy of law. Since influential ideas came from men who shaped them and gave them expression, a sketch of the personality and social setting of most of the ones who have contributed to contemporary legal thought is included, with frequently a critical commentary upon the enduring part of his work.

In selecting the men and ideas of the law to be here set forth I have tried to be guided, not by my personal preferences but by the criterion of explicit or implicit acceptance in American thought directed toward action. Yet such a selection can hardly be quite objective. In some instances, as in bringing in Kant and the Neo-Kantians, I have included what I deemed *worthy of being* influential. In choosing the men and the ideas to be discussed, I have emphasized constructive contributions rather than destructive criticisms. The author's views can scarcely be left out of a survey of legal philosophy, and they have frequently been stated or suggested. In so far as the author has a coherent theory, it is "axiological realism," that legal evaluations should always be determined on the basis of facts. Still, the chief aim has been to interest rather than to indoctrinate the reader by giving some problems and some views with which he may begin thinking for himself.

As an introductory treatise on jurisprudence, this book goes far beyond the conventional limits of English analytical jurisprudence, as represented in such important treatises as those of Austin, Holland, Salmond and, more recently, Paton. The major part of this work is devoted to the realm of legal philosophy, which has chiefly to do with logical and ethical theories about

v

law. Since legal philosophers (or at least, the ones here discussed) have not contributed all of the philosophy in the law, this book provides at the outset a brief tour of philosophy in relation to some basic legal conceptions. As the scope of the book ventures only a little way into political philosophy and legal sociology, the brief chapter on the social and physical sciences is merely a thumbnail sketch.

The novice on jurisprudence is often baffled when he finds that every book or article on the subject presupposes the reading of a dozen others. Hence the implications of a writer's ideas are here spelled out to an extent that some professional jurisprudence or philosophers will find oversimplified and even distorted. For the same reason, one will find repetitions, frequent cross-references to other parts of this book, and frugality in footnoting. During some thirty years I have gathered concrete illustrations of jurisprudential ideas, chiefly from English and American law. Selections from my file of specimens are explained or at least cited. It is hoped that these devices will help to make the book readable.

The establishment of a required course in Jurisprudence at the Columbia Law School in 1938 called for a short textbook which would diminish the student drudgery of note-taking and the wear and tear on the library. The first mimeographed edition of this work, published in 1940, was expanded in later mimeographed versions of 1946, 1949 and 1951. As a student textbook this work has had a thorough try-out. During the first ten years of the required course Professor Hall's Readings in Jurisprudence was used as the basis of class discussion, and the footnotes of this work often cite Hall. To these have been added some citations of the more recent selection of readings by the late Morris R. Cohen and his son, Dr. Felix Cohen.

To my former teacher, Professor Roscoe Pound, I am deeply indebted for the inspiration of his ideas, and to my former colleague, the late Professor John Dewey, for the sane guidance of his philosophy. From my former collaborator, Professor Karl N. Llewellyn, I gained many valuable insights into the legal ordering of society. I am also grateful to Mr. Bertram Harnett of the New York bar for a thorough study of Federal cases following state law (Erie v. Tompkins) which was used in preparing my brief comment on that topic (§ 3.33).

Columbia University EDWIN W. PATTERSON
March, 1953

vi

TABLE OF CONTENTS

*

xi

JURISPRUDENCE

MEN AND IDEAS OF THE LAW

Part I

THE PROVINCE OF JURISPRUDENCE

Chapter 1

THE MEANINGS OF JURISPRUDENCE

§ 1.00—An Invitation to Jurisprudence

The present volume is an invitation as well as an introduction to jurisprudence. Before accepting the invitation the invitee may well ask, why should I give any of my time and energy to the study of jurisprudence? To this question several answers may be given. One, that this is itself one of the profoundest questions of jurisprudence, since different reasons for the value of jurisprudence are given by different jurisprudential theories, and the value of a particular jurisprudential theory may be a subject of warm controversy. A second is that the answer to this question cannot be completely given until one has explored the province of jurisprudence, and then it will be needless. A third is that different reasons will appeal to different invitees of different motivations and interests.

But to a doubting-Thomas invitee all these reasons for not answering appear to be palpable evasions of a plain man's simple question. "You are flattering," says he, "when you tell me that I have asked a profound question and that my motivations are mysterious, and you are guileful when you suggest that I accept your invitation on faith; but unless jurisprudence is an occult bog of speculation I am entitled to be told at the outset what I am likely to gain by venturing into this realm." So, at the risk of misinterpreting the invitee's interests and of misinterpreting jurisprudence, an answer will be given.

Jurisprudence consists of the general theories of, or about, law. By the use of these two prepositions one can designate roughly two types of juristic theory and analysis. The one is *internal* to the law, the other *external*. The former assumes or creates a delimitation of the field of law and explores the concepts, terminology and relations of the various parts of the law. It cuts across contracts, torts, property, procedure, etc., and provides an analysis of the general conceptions which are explicitly or implicitly involved in these parts of the law. Theories *of* law are designed to produce generalizations which will conserve knowledge and energy and furnish a guide for the use of a current legal system to meet new situations. They are like the road maps by which the traveler by automobile is guided to the sign posts which point him to his particular destination. Into the *organization* of a practical treatise, encyclopedia or digest of law go some of the theoretical considerations with which jurisprudence has to do. These include questions as to the meaning of law, the sources and forms of law, and particularly in the Anglo-American system, the significance of judicial decisions for the settlement of future questions of law. The courts strive to maintain orderliness and equality of treatment as between litgants and to that extent, at least, the individual litigant has to be concerned with the systematic aspects of the law. Jurisprudence in this sense is included in the "analytical jurisprudence" of John Austin and his English followers (infra, § 1.05).

General theories *of* law include in more recent times generalizations about the basic policies of a system of law or of some major part of that system. Can one derive or detect implicit postulates of the law of torts, of contracts, of property law, of administrative law, and do these postulates contain with respect to each other compatible or contradictory propositions, harmonious or conflicting tendencies? For instance, is the principle that legal liability is based upon fault a dominant or a recessive characteristic of the law of torts? To what extent has this principle been, and should it be, modified because of the rise of the comparatively recent institution of liability insurance? Or, how does the rise of the modern industrial corporation, with its hundreds of thousands of stockholders who are legally "proprietors" of the corporation's property, affect the traditional legal conception of "ownership" of property? Or, in the making of administrative regulations affecting a limited class of economic interests, should the procedure conform to the analogy of adjudication, in which all interested parties are entitled to be heard before a decision is reached, or to the analogy of legislation, in which no such procedural limitation applies? These are questions which have to be discussed in the respective fields of torts, corporations and administrative law. Yet they have far-reaching implications for the whole body of law, and in this sense they belong to jurisprudence. Furthermore, the exploration of such questions takes one beyond the *internal* relations of legal rules and norms into the *external* relations of the legal system to government and society, to ethical, economic, political and social beliefs and practices, to things that are analytically distinct though not causally separated from the law.

Jurisprudence in this wider sense includes the body of general theories *about* law which have been, through the various stages of Western civilization (i. e., such is the scope of this volume), put forth, accepted, and carried forward as a part of the cultural tradition. It includes, for example, ideas about the relations between law and government, law and society. Is law dependent upon government for its "existence," or can law "exist" independently of government? Is such a question merely a verbal one of definition, or does one's choice of definitions have some significant effects on one's interests and one's intellectual operations? Does law merely reflect the prevailing beliefs of a majority of the individuals in a given society, or is it an instrument of social control through superior generalizations imposed by some dominant group or derived from some outside source? Or some of each? Is justice an inherent, necessary characteristic of law, or is it an external standard by which the rightness of particular laws, or of particular actions pursuant to laws, is to be measured? What are the basic criteria of the rightness or wrongness, goodness or badness, of laws? Some of the extensive literature on these questions will be discussed in this volume.

The relations of law to philosophy is another part of the subject matter of jurisprudence. Is law a branch of ethics or morals, and so are all legal problems necessarily moral problems? Is it accurate to speak of a law as "existing" (as we have done above) when existence is considered a basic concept of metaphysics? To what extent, if at all, does legal reasoning conform to the requirements of logic, and what kind of logic? These questions are partly verbal, yet this does not make them trivial. To understand what some writers mean when they praise or deride "logic" or "metaphysics" one needs to understand some of the traditional meanings of those terms. These general theories *about* law are less legally-specialized in character and are therefore of greater interest to non-lawyers than the *internal* analyses above mentioned; the nonprofessional reader may thus find Parts I and IV of this book the most accessible ones.

That all such questions will be finally answered in this volume is not guaranteed. Jurisprudence, like philosophy, contains many more basic questions than it can settle. They recur again and again because they are basic and because they cannot be so answered that a new generation of inquiring minds will not raise them again. Aside from the practical usefulness of some parts of analytical jurisprudence, the hard-boiled practitioner may on occasion need to know the significance of principles and conceptions derived from such laymen as John Locke and John Dewey. To these vocational inducements one more may be added. Why should one enter the profession of the law unless one seeks, in addition to a means of livelihood, a lifelong opportunity to pry beneath the welter of statutes and decisions and to see the law as a part of a larger whole? Not since the eighteenth century (in the English speaking world, at least) has the literature of jurisprudence been more seething with ideas. Some of these ideas will help to shape the law and the society of the future. Through jurisprudence you may look at life in society and, like O. W. Holmes, you may catch an echo of the infinite.[1]

§ 1.01—A Basic Organization of Jurisprudence

Jurisprudence, like philosophy, deals with the problems of maneuvering an army corps rather than those of drilling a corporal's guard. Like philosophy and science, it gives no final solution of practical problems, but rather the articulate grounds for a measured conclusion. From the examples given in the preceding section it is apparent that jurisprudence, in the widest sense, tends to scatter in all directions, to become diffused and thereby confused. For an orderly presentation of the subject matter some basic classification and organization is needed. That which has been adopted in this volume, and which will here be outlined, has two objectives: to group together the common basic themes of jurisprudential literature, thus revealing basic similarities and divergences; and to simplify these basic groupings for those who are beginning the study of jurisprudence. For these reasons the three basic divisions are: *What is law?* (Part II). *What is the*

---

[1] Holmes, Collected Legal Papers (1920), 202. See infra, § 4.55, n. 40.

law? (Part III). *What should be the law?* (Part IV). To these are added the scope of jurisprudence (Part I) and a supplementary part on the judicial process (Part V).

The initial problem of jurisprudence is the determination of its own scope. The primary consequence of such a determination here will be the delimitation of the scope of this volume. A secondary, though by no means less important consequence will be, it is hoped, that the student of jurisprudence will learn to recognize the limitations of his own knowledge and to respect the knowledge of other disciplines. A good deal of pain has been caused to lawyers by non-professionals who have philosophized about law (occasionally with surprisingly useful results). A good deal of pain has been caused philosophers when jurisprudents have based their arguments wittingly or unwittingly upon philosophical assumptions. Legal theorists often use such terms as "actual," "real" and "existence" in a way to make a metaphysician raise his eyebrows. Jurisprudents sometimes rush in where philosophers fear to tread. Now and then they put in circulation pregnant aphorisms such as Holmes': "The life of the law has not been logic; it has been experience." [2] Two eminent philosophers, John Dewey[3] and Morris Cohen,[4] have taken many pages to expound the theme of this bold utterance. The introductory part of this volume therefore endeavors to present summarily the relations of jurisprudence to the branches of philosophy and to the social sciences. Since jurisprudence is itself divided into camps, a brief summary of the schools of jurisprudence (§ 1.05) is presented at the outset. Thus, rather than by relying upon a formal definition, is the province of jurisprudence delimited.

The second part discusses the nature and distinguishing characteristics of law: What is law? Here is the crossroads of jurisprudence, the Armageddon of jurisprudential controversy. Many a battle has been waged over the essential meaning of law. To change our metaphor, the meaning which a particular writer ascribes to law is often a key to the understanding of his ju-

---

[2] Holmes, The Common Law (1881), 1.

[3] Dewey, "Logical Method and Law," (1924) 10 Cornell L.Q. 17; partly reprinted in Hall, Readings in Jurisprudence (1938), 343 (hereafter cited as "Hall") and in Cohen and Cohen, Readings in Jurisprudence and Legal Philosophy (1951), 552 (hereafter cited as "Cohen and Cohen").

[4] Cohen, "The Place of Logic in the Law," (1916) 29 Harvard L.Rev. 622; Hall, 369; Cohen and Cohen, 540.

risprudential theory. A good many writers disdain or neglect to give a comprehensive definition of law; the sense (or senses) in which they use the term can be gathered only from the context. The questions discussed in Part II are thus basic to all jurisprudential literature. Moreover, it is of basic significance in the practical application of the law. Holmes tells of a Vermont Justice of the Peace who refused to give the plaintiff a judgment for the breaking of a churn, because he had looked through the statutes and could find nothing about churns.[5] A judge who understands that a law is a generalization which extends beyond the particulars to which it has heretofore been applied would not stop with the concrete wording of the statute book. Again, does the "law" of the United States guarantee to every state a republican form of government, or is the pronouncement of the Federal Constitution only a hortatory political principle? Understanding the meanings of law is basic to law and to jurisprudence.

In Part III are discussed the sources, forms and systemic relations of a body of developed law: What is *the* law? Here the examples used are almost exclusively those of Anglo-American law. The sources and forms of law, the different types of legal norms, the significance of judicial precedents, the meanings of terms, and the classifications of law are here summarily discussed. These are the materials used in legal reasoning.

In Part IV are presented the chief types of jurisprudential theory which have a bearing on the question: What *should* be the law? Oldest of these is "natural law," which has undergone several transformations in the course of its history and still has its followers in several different forms. Other jurisprudential writers have emphasized the freedom of the human will and the dignity of man as ultimate criteria of the rightness of law, or have sought to make the chief objective of law the promotion of happiness. Even philosophers of law who do not purport to tell us what it should be, but only what it is, have had considerable influence upon legal development (Austin, Kelsen, Savigny, Ehrlich, the American legal realists) and some of these are included.[6]

---

[5] Holmes, "The Path of the Law," (1897) 10 Harvard L.Rev. 457, 474; Collected Legal Papers (1920), 167, 196.

[6] Similarly, Prof. Castberg (Oslo) divides the main problems of legal philosophy into: 1. What the law "really is". 2. Problems of legal reasoning. 3. Problems of legal valuation. Castberg, Problems of Legal Philosophy (Bergen, c. 1948), 5.

The last part presents some aspects of the judicial process, a favorite theme of American writers, especially since the publication of Cardozo's book on the subject in 1921. How do judges arrive at their decisions? How much are they influenced by legal rules or concepts and how much by hunches? Does the opinion of an appellate court speak the "good" reasons for the decision and not the "real" reasons which motivated the judges (or a majority of them) to decide as they did? These are somewhat less exciting questions than they were a decade or two ago, yet they still hold a place in American jurisprudential theories.

§ 1.02—Etymology and Usage of "Jurisprudence"

The word, "jurisprudence," is derived from a Latin word (*"jurisprudentia"*) meaning originally, "knowledge of law." It then signified a practical knowledge of law and its application.[7] This meaning of the term is still given in dictionaries; for instance, Murray's New English Dictionary lists as its first meaning: "knowledge of or skill in law." [8] In this sense the word is hardly ever used today except in the use of "jurisprudence" as a synonym for law. Murray lists two other meanings of "jurisprudence": "the science which treats of human laws (written or unwritten) in general, the philosophy of law";[9] and "a system or body of laws, a legal system." The first of these is assigned to the term in this volume. The second makes "jurisprudence" an honorific synonym for "law," as in the examples given below.

The term "jurisprudence" has become even more particularized in meaning. In French law it refers to the body of judicial precedents, as distinguished from statutes and expert opinions on law. In the United States we find other special meanings. Thus treatises on "Medical Jurisprudence" deal with that part of medical knowledge which is useful in applying legal doctrines;[10] and Wait's "Architectural and Engineering Jurisprudence" is a similar conjunction of legal and non-legal informa-

---

[7] Holland, Jurisprudence (10th ed., 1906), 6–7.

[8] Funk and Wagnall's New Standard Dictionary (1930), an American dictionary, lists this meaning as third—which it is in importance.

[9] The New Standard Dictionary (supra, last note), gives the primary meaning of "jurisprudence" to be: "the philosophy of positive law," which probably means "analytical" jurisprudence. Infra, § 1.05.

[10] A recent example is Jurisprudence for Nurses, by Scheffel and McGarvah (3d ed., 1945), reviewed (1945) 31 A.B.A.J. 429.

tion. Law book publishers have sometimes sought to make their compilations of bread-and-butter law more imposing by giving them the name, "jurisprudence"; thus one finds "California Jurisprudence" and "Ohio Jurisprudence." One cannot on etymological grounds deny them the right to the use of this euphemistic polysyllable. The term "equity jurisprudence" (Pomeroy) has a peculiar justification in Anglo-American law. Because of the traditional separation of "common law" and "equity" it was unpalatable and even contradictory to speak of "equity law." That the rules and principles of equity are "law" in the broadest sense is not to be doubted. Fortunately one will seldom have difficulty in determining from the context whether "jurisprudence" is used in the broad or the narrow sense.

A word is needed to refer to a writer on jurisprudence. In this volume the term, "jurisprudent," which has the blessing of the dictionaries [11] but is rarely found in current usage, will be assigned to this meaning.

§ 1.03—Jurisprudence and Philosophy of Law

The law-trained reader who enters the realm of jurisprudence may well ask for some terminological guides to its literature. One recurrent phrase is "philosophy of law," or "legal philosophy." Is this term a synonym for jurisprudence, or something wholly distinguishable or overlapping? Neither etymology nor usage gives a clear answer. In its linguistic origin philosophy meant "love of knowledge and wisdom"; in its usage it came to embrace all knowledge of all things, if systematic and reasoned in character. In this sense to speak of "philosophy of law" is self-contradictory, "knowledge-of-all-things of law," unless law embraces all knowledge, which makes law a meaningless term. As the special sciences broke away from philosophy (§ 1.10), the latter retained as its domain only the most general theories about things human and divine. Thus "philosophy of law" means broadly "general theory of law," a term roughly equivalent to "jurisprudence" as here used. In the older literature philosophy of law was usually the work of a philosopher who was not a lawyer, and who therefore did not purport to discuss the internal structure of a body of law (theories *of* law) but rather the relations of law and the legal order to a general system of philosophy: theories *about* law. In this sense Hegel, whose treatise is

---

[11] E.g., the two cited above, this section.

entitled "philosophy of law"[12] as well as Aristotle, Hobbes, Kant, etc., were philosophers of law. Such writers bring to bear upon law in general a set of ideas about government or society or justice, or the universe in general. In this sense jurisprudence includes "philosophy of law," but the latter does not include that part of jurisprudence which consists of general theories *of* law (§ 1.00). Yet this usage is by no means uniform. One of the leading works on the theory *of* law (analytical jurisprudence) is John Austin's "Jurisprudence, or the Philosophy of Positive Law." Another important work, Pound's "An Introduction to the Philosophy of Law" (1924) has much to say about the analysis of legal terms, though it is also concerned with the societal aspects of legal institutions. An interesting and valuable work by Dabin, a law professor at Louvain, "The Philosophy of the Positive Legal Order,"[13] consists partly of what is here called theories of law (analytical jurisprudence) and partly of the relation of law to Catholic principles of morality. As lawyers have become philosophers and have thus become equipped to write on both the internal and external aspects of a system of law, "philosophy of law" has become more nearly a synonym of "jurisprudence" as here used. In Germany, on the other hand, a distinction is more clearly maintained between analytical jurisprudence ("Rechtswissenschaft") and legal philosophy ("Rechtsphilosophie"). The latter is reserved for the most abstract (and often abstruse) theories about law.

"Philosophy of law" may also be taken to include studies of legal concepts or of the methods of the legal order by the use of criteria developed in the traditional branches of philosophy: metaphysics, logic, ethics and, occasionally, esthetics. Thus John Dewey and Morris Cohen, in the articles cited above,[14] have examined some of the relations of logic to the law. Such essays are not intended to provide a systematic philosophy *of* law but rather to discover the significance of philosophy *in* the law. This relation of law to philosophy is further explored in Chapter 2.

An aversion to both "jurisprudence" and "philosophy of law," as somewhat pretentious titles, may explain why many jurispru-

---

[12] Grundlinien der Philosophie des Rechts (1821).

[13] Dabin, La Philosophie de l'Ordre Juridique Positif (1929).

[14] Supra, § 1.01, notes 3, 4. See, also, Tourtelon, Philosophy in the Development of the Law (Read trans. Modern Legal Philosophy Series, 1922). Professor Morris Cohen's Editorial Preface to this volume is a valuable discussion of the relations of philosophical conceptions to law.

dents have chosen other names for their works. Aside from the Korkunov translation,[15] more recent works are Jones' "Historical Introduction to the Theory of Law" (1940) and Friedman's "Legal Theory",[16] each a survey of legal philosophy. Stone's "The Province and Function of Law" [17] is a commentary on jurisprudence, legal philosophy and legal sociology. Paton's "Textbook on Jurisprudence" [18] and Cairns' "Legal Philosophy from Plato to Hegel" (1949) follow the older usage. An incursion into jurisprudence is always an adventure in ideas, in which the adventurer must pick his way among incongruent terminologies.

§ 1.04—Jurisprudence and "Science of Law"

The term "science of law" has been in the forefront of jurisprudential discussion during the past three decades, and the implications of that term have colored a good many legal writings which do not purport to be jurisprudential. Yet the use of the term is by no means new. One need go only as far back as Amos' "Science of Law" [19] to find a book containing chiefly jurisprudence as above (§ 1.00) defined. More recent examples of similar usage (though with widely varying content) are Kocourek's "An Introduction to the Science of Law," [20] C. J. Keyser's article, "On the Study of Legal Science" [21] and Drake's earlier article, "Jurisprudence: A Formal Science." [22] In these instances "science of law" is substantially equivalent to analytic jurisprudence, the analysis of the internal structure of the law and its more pervasive concepts,[23] the German "Rechtswissenschaft."

But this classificatory or analytic science of law, which takes legal concepts and rules as given and seeks to bring order and

---

[15] Korkunov, General Theory of Law (Modern Legal Philosophy Series, 1909).

[16] First ed., 1944; 2d ed., 1948.

[17] First ed., 1946. So Shartel, Our Legal System and How It Operates (1951) is a work on jurisprudence.

[18] 1st ed., 1946; 2d ed., 1951. See also Reuschlein, Jurisprudence: Its American Prophets (1951).

[19] Amos, Science of Law (D. Appleton & Co., New York, 1874).

[20] 1930.

[21] (1929) 38 Yale L.J. 413; Hall, 648.

[22] (1914) 13 Mich.L.Rev. 34; Hall, 647.

[23] Except Keyser's article (supra, note 21) which is an application of mathematical logic to legal reasoning.

clarity into their meanings, does not satisfy a militant group of writers who seek to develop an *empirical* science of law. They seek a body of knowledge about law, or a theory of law, which will have the same kind of validity possessed by the natural sciences: physics, chemistry, biology, etc. The primary purpose of this movement was to obtain for legal procedures the same kind of control over the future that the natural sciences have given the engineer. O. W. Holmes, who was one of its earliest protagonists, emphasized the view of law as a body of predictions of what courts will decide, the study of legal history as an anthropological investigation, and the use of statistics to determine the social consequences of legal rules.[24] Pound, more cautiously, criticized "mechanical jurisprudence" as a blind application of traditional legal concepts (e. g., of master-and-servant law) without regard to their consequences in an industrial society.[25] With Cook the tendency emerged as a new movement, subsequently called "American legal realism," [26] whose adherents frequently, ignoring the traditional conception of law, regarded legal rules and principles as generalizations descriptive of the behavior of judges.[27] From this point on the movement branched in various directions, and took on varying hues of heterodoxy. It produced, or helped to produce, importantly useful consequences in legal education, in legislation and in the judicial process, some of which will be mentioned later on. Here we are concerned with the meaning of "science of law" in relation to the traditional conception of jurisprudence. In one of the most recent and careful expositions of the objects of this new science, "jurisprudence" is "defined provisionally as the study of human behavior as a function of disorder." [28] This "social science" jurisprudence has, the author admits, "been baptized before it was born." [29] Legal propositions (that is, legal norms or precepts) are a part of the subject matter of such a science "in the sense that the conduct of the jurists in relation to the tasks illuminates and ac-

---

[24] See Holmes, "Law in Science and Science in Law," (1899) 12 Harvard L. Rev. 443; Hall, 672; "The Path of the Law," supra, § 1.01 n. 5; Hall, 670.

[25] Pound, "Mechanical Jurisprudence," (1908) 8 Columbia L.Rev. 605, relies for its philosophical base upon James' pragmatism.

[26] Discussed more fully, infra, § 4.63.

[27] Cook, "Scientific Method and the Law," (1927) 13 A.B.A.J. 303, 308; Hall, 784.

[28] Cairns, Theory of Legal Science (1941), 1.

[29] Ibid., 3.

counts for the structure of the system of law prevailing in a particular area."[30] In so far as this infant science has to do with the legal system and the legal order, it is included in the term jurisprudence as above defined (§ 1.00).

The term, "science of law," has an emotional appeal which, in its influence upon jurisprudential theory, is itself a proper study of jurisprudence. Formerly science was the cold Latin term, while "philosophy," the warm Greek term, signified the passion for discovery. Today the emotive effects are just reversed. Only the faithful few look up to, and worship, philosophy; the great majority admire and revere science. The scientists have made possible inventions which promote our material comfort and will preserve us (we hope) in time of war. The reasons are not wholly materialistic. Scientists have cleaned house better than philosophers. They have chucked out ruthlessly the vestiges of alchemy, astrology and witchcraft. They have shown their willingness to acknowledge their mistakes, they have developed an accurate terminology and, in the physical sciences, a mode of testing hypotheses which other scientists all over the world can verify or disprove. It is well, then, that jurisprudence should emulate the methods of the natural sciences. Yet the extent to which this is possible, because of the inescapable differences in the subject matters, respectively, of law and the natural sciences, is itself a fundamental question of jurisprudence. (Ch. 3).

To recapitulate: "Legal science" has an older meaning, which equates it with an orderly analysis and synthesis of legal norms and concepts (to which may be added a descriptive account of their origins and effects); and a newer meaning, an empirical science of human behavior in society. The latter is sometimes called, "sociology of law" (§ 1.20).

§ 1.05—Schools of Jurisprudence

Man has been characterized as a rational animal, a humorous animal, and an animal touched with divinity. He may also be called a classifying animal, an attribute with respect to which, as in the other instances, some men are more touched than others. The capacity to group things in classes is an inherent part of the human intellectual makeup. Classifying and labelling by groups is a necessary mnemonic device and a necessary means of the communicating of complex bodies of knowledge. Thus ju-

---

30 Ibid., 81.

risprudents and their ideas have been classified into groups called "schools." A good classification is one which grounds a reliable inference that because Jurisprudent X is classified under a certain heading, his ideas or theories about law have a certain significant characteristic or characteristics which are designated by that heading. Unfortunately not all designations of schools of jurisprudence have this inferential quality. The designation of a school of jurisprudence by the name of the founder—Kantian, Hegelian, Austinian, etc.—indicates that the members of the school have *some* characteristics in common with the founder, but does not tell *which* of many characteristics. Since the followers or members of a school usually differ among themselves on many questions, the task of interpreting a classification is to discover *what* characteristics the members of the class have in common. These, traditionally, are more likely to consist of certain basic assumptions or definitions which they hold than in the harmony or compatibility of the conclusions which they reach. Thus Hegel's theory of historical evolution was used to justify the Nazi state and also, through the writings of Karl Marx, the Soviet state to which the former was ideologically opposed. The classification of schools of jurisprudence by the names of their founders is a rough and uncertain guide to the beliefs of their followers.

The present introductory section is intended to group schools of jurisprudence into types by reference to certain broad characteristics. What aspect of law does the writer deem the most important? It is by no means easy to make such a classification, since a fruitful jurisprudent will ordinarily deem several aspects of law important, and simplification requires that some aspects be ignored. Three basic relations of law provide a simple and comprehensive basis of classification: 1. Its relation to the government, the political organization of the state; 2. Its relation to the institutions of its society (societal institutions); 3. Its relations to some ideal or set of ideals, such as justice, freedom of the will, or happiness. On this basis jurisprudential theories and systems can be grouped into three major schools: positive (imperative), institutional (historical or sociological) and philosophical. At this point a brief account of each must suffice.

1. *The Positive or Imperative School.* Those writers on jurisprudence who regard law as an imperative (command or norm) emanating from the government, or from the state as the political organization of a society, and who treat the relation of law to the state as its most important aspect, may be grouped in the *impera-*

tive school of jurisprudence. They are chiefly concerned with the definition of law, so as to differentiate it sharply from other (non-political) imperatives (morals, customs, manners, etc.) and so as to identify with certainty the political imperatives which have the characteristics of law. This task will be taken up in Part II of the present volume. The imperative jurisprudents were also concerned with the analysis of the basic concepts of a legal system, with theories *of* law (§ 1.00). Hence they are sometimes referred to as *analytical* jurists. In England the leading exponent of this school was (and still is) John Austin (1790–1859), who set forth in his "Province of Jurisprudence Determined" (1st ed., 1832) the view that a law is a command of the sovereign, and took pains to distinguish positive law from the norms of morals, which he called, "positive morality." For more than a century controversy has raged around the positions which Austin took in this volume and in his lectures on jurisprudence, delivered at University College, London, which, published posthumously, constitute Austin on Jurisprudence. After clarifying such fundamental terms as law, sovereign and sanction, Austin devoted the greater part of his lectures to the analysis of basic legal terms: right, obligation, injury, right in rem, right in personam, and the chief concepts of torts and contracts. In this respect he was emulated by later writers of this school, including Amos, Markby, Holland and even Salmond, who partly rejected Austin's mode of defining law. A good deal of analytical jurisprudence (another name for this school) is text-book law on a high level of generality. The present volume does not cover all of this analysis, for much of it has been absorbed in special branches of the law. Thus Holland, building on Austin, developed the expectation ("objective") theory of contracts, which now belongs in the course or treatise on contracts. In this sense every teacher of law is, or should be, a teacher of jurisprudence.

A more recent influential imperative or positive jurisprudent is Hans Kelsen, whose "pure theory of law" has attracted a wide following in Europe and even in the Western Hemisphere. Kelsen sought to develop, on the analogy of Kant's "Critique of Pure Reason," a conception of law purified of all extraneous elements. And what did he deem "extraneous"? On the one hand, natural science, social science, and especially sociology; on the other hand ethics, ideals of justice, ideas as to what the law *ought* to be. The pure theory of law must seek to determine the *validity* of law, and must thus "delimit law from nature and the science of law as a normative science, from all other sciences.

which aim at explaining causal, natural, processes."[31] Law is a body of norms that emanate, in a hierarchy of political authority, from the sovereign, which Kelsen regards as a basic presupposition of a legal system. Kelsen's theory will be discussed at various places further on.[32]

The imperative school is quite commonly called the "positive" school because its adherents are *chiefly* concerned with law "as *is*" (positus) rather than with law as it *ought* to be. To conclude from this that these writers are *not at all* concerned with what the law ought to be is an easy step, but a fallacious one. That Jurisprudent X believes "A," does not ground an inference that he believes "A *and not* B." Thus Corbin, whose excellent analysis of legal terms[33] was based on the imperative theory of law, has always been warmly devoted to improving the law. The term "positivist" has often been used as a term of reproach by critics of the imperative theory of law who gave it the implication above mentioned. Furthermore, "positivism" has another meaning when it refers to the philosophy of Auguste Comte, a French contemporary of Austin, who sought to found an empirical science of society, "sociology," with methods like those of physics and chemistry. A legal science of this kind (§ 1.04) would be vastly different from that of Austin or Kelsen. Despite these ambiguities, we shall use "positive," "positivism" and "positivists" to refer to the imperative school and its followers.[34]

2. *Institutional Schools: Historical and Sociological.* The institutional school of law includes those who take as their base lines the institutions of man in society, meaning thereby not merely the churches and clubs and business organizations, etc., but also the customs, mores and habit patterns of individuals and groups. The historical school takes the social institutions in a time sequence, with primacy given to the *primitive* legal institutions of the society. The sociological school takes *contempo-*

---

[31] Kelsen, "The Pure Theory of Law," (trans. by Chas. H. Wilson, 1934) 50 L.Q.Rev. 474, 480; Hall, 425, 429. Kelsen's views are fully presented in his General Theory of Law and State (Wedberg trans., 20th Century Legal Philosophy Series, 1945).

[32] Especially in §§ 2.04, 2.31, 3.22. For a valuable survey of the development of this school, see Kocourek in 2 Law: A Century of Progress (1937), 195.

[33] Corbin, "Legal Analysis and Terminology," (1919) 29 Yale L.J. 163; Hall, 471.

[34] On the origin of the term, "positive law", see Radin, "Early Statutory Interpretation" (1943) 38 Ill.L.Rev. 25.

rary institutions as its base line. The German historical school of Savigny [35] and Puchta [36] developed a conception of the origin and growth of law on the analogy of language. The common language of a nation binds its members together in a union; its laws express their common conviction of right, peculiar to them. In the early stages of national development law *is* the common conviction of right; in its later stages, when experts have taken over the technical development of the law, by a kind of inward necessity the national characteristics of the primitive laws must not be departed from, else the nation will die. No arbitrary will of the legislature can make law—true law; hence legislation can be at most declaratory and clarificatory. For the true meaning of a contemporary legal concept or doctrine must one not go to its historical antecedents? The historical school gave a theoretical justification for those vast studies of legal history which, in Europe, England and even America, were consummated during the nineteenth century. Not every legal historian is an historical jurisprudent, but most of them are accessories after the fact. The historical school tended to romanticize primitive legal institutions, to promote the growth of nationalism (which, however, needed no help), to hinder changes in the law through legislation and to perpetuate outmoded traditions. The values of this school will be discussed later (§ 4.31).

The sociological school is chiefly concerned with the relation of law to contemporary social institutions. It is still in the making, and one must be wary about ascribing basic positions. Eugen Ehrlich presented the sociological point of view in its most extreme form. The "living law" consists of the customary ways of acting together of men in society; the law of the state, "Legal Provisions," is contrasted with it, to the latter's disparagement.[37] The essential characteristic of law is that it shall *prevail*, that it shall actually represent the common interactions of men in their daily lives. "True" law is spontaneously observed and needs no enforcement. Thus enforceability by the state is not (as under the imperative theory) a necessary characteristic of law. Hence one can properly designate as law the rules of conduct

---

[35] On the Vocation of Our Age for Legislation and Jurisprudence (Hayward's trans., 1831; first published in 1814) was an argument against the adoption of the Napoleonic Codes in Germany.

[36] Puchta, Outlines of Jurisprudence as the Science of Right (Hastie's trans., 1887); Hall, 89–91.

[37] Ehrlich, "Sociology of Law," (trans. by Isaacs; 1922) 36 Harvard L.Rev. 130; Hall, 812–825.

which prevail among the members of a trade association, a labor union, or a baseball club. This and other sociological theories will be more fully discussed further on (§ 2.03).

3. *Philosophical.* The philosophical school includes all those writers on jurisprudence who were chiefly concerned with the relations of law to some set of ideals or ideas "outside the law," or at least outside the law as conceived by positivists.[38] Among such ideals are: that the purpose of society is to make men virtuous, and such is the purpose of the law; that the end of the law is to maintain justice (variously defined) in society; that legal restrictions can be justified only in so far as they promote the freedom of individuals in society (Kant); that the end of law is to promote the greatest happiness of the greatest number (Bentham). These are epitomes of theories as to what the law ought to be. Here may be included, too, Herbert Spencer's view that the law ought not to interfere with the "survival of the fittest." Even theories about law which do not purport to give a criterion as to what the law ought to be, usually do so by indirection. Thus the Marxian thesis (grounded on dialectical materialism) that the rules of law were formulated by, and promoted the selfish interests of, the dominant class in society, was aimed at revolutionary change in the law. The American legal realists, while primarily interested in method, intended that law should thus be made a better instrument of justice. The "philosophical school" is a classifier's limbo. There are many philosophical schools, having in common only the exploration of ideas somehow relevant to law. However, the significance of philosophy for the law of an Occidental state is wider than is indicated by the several schools of philosophy of law. This broader significance will be discussed in the next chapter.

The threefold division of jurisprudence into positive, institutional and philosophical schools provides a rough classification of ideas, and an even rougher classification of men. Each jurisprudent has borrowed some things from his predecessors, and in so doing has transformed that which he borrowed. Thus there are many combinations and overlappings of ideas. Men who accept the same definition of law may diverge widely as to what they deem it most important to say about law. Thus Bentham and Austin, his disciple, have substantially the same conception

---

[38] This use of "philosophical" is derived from Pound's usage; e.g., Pound, "Law and the State—Jurisprudence and Politics," (1944) 57 Harvard L.Rev. 1193, 1198.

of law; the former was primarily interested in developing the principle of utility as a guide to law making, the latter, to an analysis of mature legal systems. With others, as will be pointed out later, the writer's theories about law enter into and modify his conception of law.

Patterson Jurisprudence F.P.Inc.

Chapter 2

PHILOSOPHY IN THE LAW

§ 1.10—The Significance of Philosophy for the Law

In a popular sense philosophy includes any subject matter, and a man's "philosophy" is his slant or bias, or his aggregation of slants and biases, on a particular subject matter. Thus a judge's "philosophy" of business enterprise, or of labor union practices, may have a decisive influence on his decisions applying particular governmental regulations of business, or of labor unions. In such a case the judge's philosophy may be developed from some articulate scheme of economic or political philosophy—such as that of Adam Smith or of Montesquieu—or it may be a "common sense" philosophy which he has not fully organized and articulated. Here we are not using "philosophy" in this loose sense.

Philosophy originally included the natural and biological sciences, as well as such subjects as poetry, rhetoric and political theory. These subjects have become specialized and have broken away from philosophy. As a subject of academic study, philosophy now embraces: 1. Logic and scientific method. 2. Ethics. 3. Metaphysics. 4. Epistemology. 5. Aesthetics. Briefly stated, the subject matter of each of these branches is, respectively: truth, value, being, knowledge and beauty. To these has been added more recently semantics (or semiotics), the theory of meaning. Since law has to do in some way or other with these pervasive ideas, philosophy has some things in common with law and with jurisprudence. In the present chapter we shall try to explain each discipline and give examples of its relation to law.

The reasons for such an exploration may be briefly stated. Historically, a good many generations of lawyers and judges were trained in academic philosophy, and what they learned in philosophy has found its way into the law. Secondly, a good many writers on jurisprudence, or even on legal questions of narrower scope, have invoked philosophical concepts in their arguments, sometimes without being aware of the implications of their words. A student of jurisprudence needs a good enough map of philosophy to find his way around without falling into the quagmires. The present chapter is chiefly intended to furnish such a map. Finally, philosophy has more than once in the past provided

19

constructive guidance for the development of the law. Whether it will continue to do so depends upon the fruitfulness of philosophy.

§ 1.11—Logic and Scientific Method

To most people who are not professional philosophers "logic" means the rules of straight thinking. In this broad and simplified sense logic is an indispensable instrument of the creation, understanding and use of law, as that term is here used. This statement, which will be further supported later on, is based partly upon this writer's experience and observation of the legal thinking of lawyers, judges and law teachers over a period of many years, and partly upon a conception of law which regards it as a human creation designed to utilize the advantages of straight (logical) thinking. This view would be rejected, presumably, by those who treat logical thinking as necessarily mechanical and who glorify the "hunch" conclusion as one not genuinely derived by, or even justifiable by, any logical process. At the other extreme, formal logicians, to purify their discipline of empirical contingencies, have restricted logic to mean the science of validating forms, a science which has no direct relation to mental processes. Some of these controversies can be clarified, if not settled, by considering, first, what logic purports to be, secondly, the usefulness of logic for law, and thirdly, some of the limitations on its usefulness for law.

1. *The Scope of Logic.* The scope and subject matter of logic are matters of dispute among logicians. Their differences turn on whether logic is a formal science having to do solely with the validating forms of inference, or is concerned also with the reasoning process of reaching dependable conclusions. Formal logic shows whether or not a chain of reasoning, cast in a certain form, is valid, by axioms and theorems which constitute the subject matter of that logic. The classical example of such a form is the syllogism, an argument consisting of a major premise, a minor premise and a conclusion. Once an argument has been cast in this form, the rules of the syllogism will enable one to determine whether or not it (the conclusion in relation to those premises) is logically valid. Elsewhere I have given some examples of the ways in which the syllogism may be used to test the significance of judicial precedents in Anglo-American case law.[1] The useful-

---

[1] Dowling, Patterson and Powell, Materials for Legal Method (1946), Ch. IX; Patterson, "Logic in the Law," (1942) 90 U. of Pa.L.Rev. 875, 879–880, 898–902. Other examples are given by Treusch in Hall, 539–560.

ness for legal thinking of this kind of formulation is that it calls for close attention to the meanings of terms and to the material import of the premises, rather than that it exposes formal logical errors. Lawyers and judges rarely make such errors in their public arguments. While it takes a good deal of ingenuity and skill, and some knowledge of the rules of the syllogism, to transform an argument into syllogistic form so that its validity can be tested by the rules of logic, experience indicates that most lawyers and judges, and most advanced law students, can with a little reflection *recognize* a formally invalid syllogistic argument even if they cannot say what rule of logic makes it invalid. From this it might be argued that the rules of logic contribute nothing to legal thinking. On the contrary, it seems that they are so ingrained in the pattern of legal reasoning that one well trained in that reasoning intuitively applies them whenever the occasion arises. This is not to say that the rules of formal logic are inborn (as distinct from cultural) characteristics of the human mind; nor that lawyers consciously use syllogisms in framing their arguments. Perhaps formal logic has as much to do with (articulated) legal reasoning as Euclidean geometry has with building houses.

In the twentieth century formal logic became increasingly abstract and complex by the extension of its concepts on the analogy of mathematics. Symbolic or mathematical logic has increased the range and complexity of logical relations, but thus far these discoveries have had little or no application in law.[2] Until the law acquires a more exact and stable terminology and a more dependable mode of verification (or authentication) of its norms, it is unlikely that the more complex symbolic forms of argument will be useful to it. On the other hand, the simpler forms—the categorical and the hypothetical syllogism—are useful devices to exhibit, by explicit formulation, the meanings and ambiguities of legal terms and the legal rules or principles to which one must commit oneself in accepting certain reasons for a conclusion.

The chief type of *material* logic which has significance for law and for jurisprudence is the instrumental logic of Professor John Dewey.[3] This logic is an account of the dependable methods of the process of inquiry. It is chiefly concerned with prob-

---

[2] See 90 U. of Pa.L.Rev. 877–883.

[3] See Dewey, Logic: The Theory of Inquiry (1938); 90 U. of Pa.L.Rev. 889–894.

lematic situations, rather than with routine or stereotyped ways of acting. It recognizes that men can and do arrive at conclusions by intuition or "hunch," yet it asserts that decisions will be better in the long run when they are "reasoned," that is, arrived at by deliberation and reflective inquiry. Men do not begin thinking with premises; these only gradually emerge from the total problematic situation. "The problem is to *find* statements, of general principle and particular fact, which are worthy to serve as premises." [4] In legal administration this means that the finding and selection of the rules to apply to a set of facts is more difficult and important than is formally subsuming the facts under the rule. Instrumental logic rejects the notion, often ascribed to formal logicians, that there is a ready-made premise for every situation. It de-emphasizes the reliability of pre-existing knowledge and emphasizes the creative function of reasoned inquiry. Formal logic is primarily relevant to the *structure* of a body of law; instrumental logic is primarily relevant to the *process* of reaching decisions. Instrumental logic has influenced a generation of lawyers, judges and law teachers, and has thus had considerable influence on twentieth century American law, especially upon the judicial process (Part V).

2. *Logical Characteristics of the Law.* The lawyer, the judge and the administrative official have recourse for the solution of their problems to a body of legislation and precedents which constitute the law. This body of law has some *structural* characteristics which are formal-logical in character.[5] The chief ones are as follows:

a. *Generality.* A law is a general rule, principle or norm. Its generality consists in the general terms in which it is phrased. These general terms have the quality of logical universals, that is, they are capable of extension to, and logically may include in their meaning concrete instances which were (mentally) unknown when the rule was formulated. Thus a court may properly, and does frequently, apply the terms of a statute to a situation which the legislators could not possibly have thought of when they passed it; the law is fortunately not limited by the imaginations of legislators.[6] This quality of law is one of its most

---

[4] See Dewey, "Logical Method in Law," (1924) 10 Cornell L.Q. 17, 23; supra, § 1.01, n. 3.

[5] See Cohen, "The Place of Logic in the Law," (1916) 29 Harvard L.Rev. 622, supra, § 1.01, n. 4.

[6] Thus the business of communicating by the electric telegraph was deemed to be "commerce" within the meaning of the commerce clause of the Federal

valuable characteristics for the social order. The generality of law makes possible (though it does not guarantee) equality and impartiality in administration, the fulfillment of expectations, and control of the future. While not peculiar to law, it is on the whole the most important characteristic of the law (Ch. 5).

b. *Classification.* Classification is the logical division of a subject matter. "As the law has its excuse for being in the need to regulate future conduct, it must express itself in terms which exclude the possibility of a case falling in both or neither of two classes which it may set up." [7] Although the logician's counsel of perfection is only partly realized, the efforts of legislators and judges are best adapted to attain this end when they give careful consideration to classification. Classification of legal terms and propositions serves as a mnemonic device, it makes them findable and usable. It also serves as a basis of inference: Whether a given type of conduct is "tort" or "contract" often makes a difference in the legal consequences. Classification compels the making of distinctions, the explication of essential characteristics, and the formulation of complete or partial definitions. It leads to system.

c. *System.* A perfect logical system is one in which all of the theorems (rules) can be deduced from a definite set of axioms and definitions. "The law, of course, never succeeds in becoming a completely deductive system. It does not even succeed in becoming completely consistent. But the effort to assume the form of a deductive system underlies all constructive legal scholarship." [8] An example of system-building is the development of the law of torts during the nineteenth century out of what was, at the beginning of the century, only a set of isolated rules. By system-building concepts and norms of greater inclusiveness are developed. An example is the tendency of courts to extricate and enunciate basic policies of the law, which reveal by their apparent conflicts the fundamental issues of a decision. In a recent case the Supreme Court of the United States divided sharply on whether to apply the policy of maintaining the stability of government contracts or to apply the principle

---

Constitution (Art. I, sec. 8) although its framers could not have had this specific device in mind. Field, J., wished to confine the scope of such provisions to the experiences of the men who framed and adopted the Constitution. See Frankfurter, The Commerce Clause (1937), 45, 54.

[7] Cohen, op. cit. supra, n. 5.

[8] Ibid. at p. 624; Hall, 371; Cohen and Cohen, 542.

that the government should be protected against paying exorbitant prices; the majority rested the decision on the former.[9]
While system-making does not provide infallible guides, it can reveal basic issues in terms of which a reasoned answer to practical questions can be given.

3. *Some Limitations on the Usefulness of Logic.* In twentieth century jurisprudence, both American and European, one
finds many instances of revolt against the complacent "certainty" of nineteenth century law. In substance these revolts (American legal realism and the "free-law" movement in Europe) were
attacks on the justice or wisdom of particular legal rules and
concepts; in form they were often attacks upon the value of logic
in the formulation and administration of law. One can extricate
from these attacks on logic three principal objections:

a. *Logic does not guarantee the material correctness of its
premises.* The use of logic in legal administration does not guarantee that the premises chosen are authoritatively correct (in
the prevailing body of law) or materially just and wise. The truth
of this statement is vouched for by the more recent types of formal logic, and by instrumental logic. An example of the former
is the little book by Keyser, a mathematician, on "postulation-
al" thinking.[10] However, it is true that excessive reliance on
the formal logic of the syllogism led to the conviction that, since
deduction proceeds from precise premises, *there must be* fixed
antecedent premises in the law which are uniquely and inescapably applicable to every possible situation.[11] Even so, it seems
that logic was made the whipping boy for the faults of nineteenth
century political beliefs. At all events, logic cannot and does
not purport to guarantee the material correctness of its premises. For the judgment in any litigated case can be formally supported by any number of syllogisms having trivial premises.[12]
Nevertheless, in current critical writings on law one sometimes
encounters statements that a certain conclusion is not "logical"
because the writer disagrees with the material correctness or
appropriateness of the premises by which it is logically support-

---

9 Muschany v. U. S., 324 U.S. 49, 65 Sup.Ct. 442, 451 (1945).

10 Keyser, Thinking About Thinking (1926), especially 17–23.

11 See Dewey, op. cit., supra, n. 4.

12 E.g., "Any plaintiff named Smith suing a defendant named Brown is
entitled to judgment.
"This plaintiff is a plaintiff named Smith suing a defendant named Brown.
"Therefore, this plaintiff is entitled to judgment."

ed. Thus Professor Williston criticized certain common law doctrines as bad logic when he merely disagreed with the appropriateness of the analogies on which they were avowedly based.[13] Later, Professor Fuller, reviewing Professor Williston's treatise on contracts, contrasts the application of fixed rules, which he designates as "logic," with the application of "policy," the underlying principles of the law of contracts.[14] Yet surely the application of "policy" can be just as logical as the application of "rule." The criticism is really aimed at the material content of the treatise. The statement made at the beginning of this paragraph is a warning against the loose use of "logic" and "logical."

b. *Logic makes the law stereotyped and unadaptable.* "Mechanical jurisprudence" was the phrase used by Roscoe Pound a generation ago to designate this defect of the law and its administration.[15] He particularly criticized the continued application to a suit by employee against employer, for personal injuries arising out of and in course of employment in a factory, of common law rules (such as "assumption of risk") developed for the earlier face-to-face relation of master and servant. What he was criticizing, however, was not the logic of the judges but their failure to adapt the law to changing conditions, to make new law. The legislatures subsequently did make new law—the workmen's compensation laws. Yet such criticisms have a logical aspect, in that they show the logical characteristics of a body of law, its generality and system, as constituting a limitation on the adaptation of law to new conditions. Stability and predictability of the law are incompatible with change in the law. The reconciliation is a recurrent problem of legal method. Here again logic is not to blame. Each solution of such a problem can be logical in relation to the materials of the inquiry.

c. *Logic makes no distinction between vague terms and concrete terms.* So far as formal logic is concerned, "due process of law" may serve as a term of a premise of a syllogism just as well as "horse" or "chair" or any other common noun. One characteristic criticism made by American legal realists was that lawyers and judges used such vague terms (often called "weasel words") as "prudent," "negligent," "freedom of contract," "due

---

[13] Williston, Some Modern Tendencies in the Law (1929), 15–23; see 90 U. of Pa.L.Rev. at p. 903.

[14] Fuller, "Williston on Contracts," (1939) 18 N.C.L.Rev. 1, 8–9.

[15] Supra, § 1.04, note 25.

care" and "due process" as if they had definite meanings, to create the illusion of certainty.[16] This criticism, whether aimed at formal logic or not, illustrates one of its limitations. Formal logic is not concerned with the material correctness of its premises (supra, a.) nor with their effectiveness as means of communication. Most treatises on logic contain, however, some analysis of the meanings of terms. A common distinction is that between the *denotation* of a term, the class of things to which it refers, and its *connotation*, the characteristics which each member must have in order to qualify for membership. The usefulness of this distinction will be discussed elsewhere (§ 3.26). Still this distinction is not directly concerned with the effectiveness of terms; "due process" has connotations, and it is no concern of the logician that it is hard to find out what they are. Dewey's instrumental logic is, however, much more concerned with the effectiveness of terms. Both are supplemented by semantics (§ 1.12).

Scientific method is an extension of logic and reasoning-method which has been included in philosophy during the past century. It aims to discover what are the facts, to formulate and reformulate its conclusions objectively and unflinchingly on the basis of the facts and to communicate them in such terms that they can be verified or disproved by competent scientists anywhere. The achievements of the physical scientists have been envied by jurisprudents who have sought to use like methods in law. Scientific method in the social sciences brings in probability and statistics and the problems of inductive method. These topics are discussed elsewhere (§§ 1.21, 3.17, 3.30, 4.54, 4.63). The relation between factual (scientific) social theories and normative social theories has become an important theme of philosophical discussion.[17]

§ 1.12—Semantics

"Semantics" is here used to mean the body of theories about the meanings of words, terms and symbols. In its latest reincarnation it has been re-christened, "semiotics"; the older term will be retained here. The boundaries of the subject are hard to find, since various theories overlap logic, metaphysics, psychology, sociology, rhetoric, etc. Semantics is concerned with the mental effects of symbols and their effectiveness as means of communication. Since the law of a state is "not a brooding omnipresence in

---

16 See Frank, Law and the Modern Mind (1930), 26.

17 Northrop. The Logic of the Sciences and the Humanities (1947).

the sky, but the voice of an articulate sovereign," the law needs effective symbols, and is therefore concerned with semantics. We may mention here three types of semantic theory which have significance for the law.

1. *A Psychological Theory of Meaning.* One theory of meaning gives an analysis of communication into four factors: the utterer, the symbol (e. g., word), the thing to which it refers (called the "referent") and the utteree. A term is an effective means of communication if it causes the utteree to have in mind the same referent that the utterer had in mind.[18] From this analysis the conclusion was drawn that many terms in the law, and even more in jurisprudence and in politics, are vague and meaningless. What precisely is the referent or the mental image [19] elicited by such terms as "justice," liberty" or "unreasonable restraint of trade"? Yet it has to be recognized that the utterance of such terms has effects upon the utteree materially different from the utterance of such nonsense terms as "abracadabra" or "brillig and the slithy toves." This difference was explained by saying that "justice" and "liberty" are *emotive* terms, they express and arouse emotions.

This theory of meaning has had considerable influence on legal writing in the United States during the past two decades, and we shall have occasion to consider it elsewhere. For the present we may suggest: First, that it has had a beneficial influence in causing legal writers and government officials to employ a more exact and concrete terminology. Judicial precedents sometimes, and administrative regulations of business activities more often, substitute concrete measurable criteria for such terms as "reasonable" and "fair." Secondly, it is recognized that language has a dual function, as shown by two distinguishable types of patterns, patterns of reference and patterns of expression.[20] The law may strive to become "reason without desire," yet it cannot wholly escape this duality of its means of communication. Thirdly, the psychological theory is inadequate to explain the logical function of legal symbols, their ability to enable us to make inferences or

---

[18] See Ogden and Richards, The Meaning of Meaning (2d ed., 1927), especially 205. For a more recent comparable treatment of semantics, see Morris (C. W.), Foundation of the Theory of Signs (1938), infra, § 3.26, n. 58.

[19] For an account of the relation between mental images and meaning, see Boring, Langfeld and Weld, Psychology: A Factual Textbook (1935), 352.

[20] See Sapir, "Language" in 9 Encyclopedia of the Social Sciences (1933), 158.

applications to referents which the person or persons uttering them did not "have in mind." The legal meaning of "promise" for instance, is not exhausted by all promises heretofore made, or which any judge or legislator has heretofore had in mind. This theory remains on a primitive level of meaning.[21]

2. *The Operational Theory: Logical Positivism.* A second theory of meaning sought to take scientific meaning as the test of all meaning. To a physicist, it was said, a statement has no meaning (for physics) unless it can be verified or tested by operations on or with material objects. Then any statement has meaning only if it is possible to deduce from it propositions about present or future perceptions.[22] This or a similar theory has had a good deal of influence upon contemporary legal analysis. For instance, the Hohfeld-Corbin legal terminology, developed during the second and third decades of the present century, is an effort to give operational meaning to such basic legal terms as "right," "duty," etc. A legal right of A against B is defined as "the legal relation of A to B when society commands action or forbearance by B and will at the instance of A in some manner penalize disobedience."[23] This analysis has proved highly useful in clarifying legal thinking and legal language. It recognizes that the primary function of law is to guide one in making predictions, that is, inferences for future operations. However, it rests upon the imperative concept of law and has the limitations of that concept.

3. *The Contextual Theory of Meaning.* Another theory of meaning is that words do not have fixed meanings for all contexts, but rather their meanings depend upon their contexts and vary from context to context. From this the extreme conclusion is sometimes drawn that a word has a different (wholly or significantly different) meaning in every context in which it occurs. Now the elements of this theory are commonplace. Anyone who has used a dictionary knows that several different meanings are frequently assigned to the same term, and that he has to determine from the context of his problematic term which meaning is appropriate. In many instances this is easy. Thus a law student

---

[21] For a valuable discussion of this and other theories of meaning, displaying rare insight and good sense, see Williams, "Language and the Law", 61 L.Q.Rev. 71 (with bibliography at p. 72, n. 1), 179, 293, 384 (1945), 62 id. 387 (1946).

[22] See Carnap, Philosophy and Logical Syntax (1935), 13–14.

[23] Corbin, "Legal Analysis and Terminology," (1919) 29 Yale L.J. 163, 167; Hall, 476. See also Holmes, infra, § 2.20, n. 9.

would have no difficulty in recognizing the appropriate meaning of "battery" in the two statements: "A committed an assault and battery on B" and "A has a new battery for his car." These two statements signify different realms of discourse, the one legal, the other mechanical. Greater difficulty arises when the same word has conventionally different meanings in the same realm of discourse, such as the legal realm. For example, "contracts" in the constitutional provision that no state shall pass any law impairing the obligation of "contracts" [24] includes grants, such as a corporation charter, whereas these are not included in the term as used in the Restatement of Contracts, which restricts "contract" to "a promise or set of promises." [25] Such examples should suffice to dispel the illusion, sometimes apparent in judicial utterances, that a legal term has and must have a fixed meaning in all legal contexts.[26] On the other hand, to say that legal terms are mere "labels" for factual situations and therefore it makes no difference which one a court applies, is fallacious where the wrong label may lead someone to deal wrongly with the contents of the labeled package.[27] For this reason an English court recently felt constrained to give the word "proceeding" the same meaning in one section of the Road Traffic Act that it clearly had in another section.[28] The well-known practice of construing a statute as a whole so as to give effect to all parts of it expresses the principle that there should be continuity or sameness of meaning when necessary to avoid contradiction or absurd diversity in operational effects. Moreover, unless a legal term has a common core of meaning in different legal contexts the usefulness of law as a means of guidance and control is impaired or negated. Whether and how the common meaning of a legal term is limited by a particular context [29] is a question of law rather than of semantics. Theories

---

[24] U. S. Const., Art. I, sec. 10(1).

[25] Restatement, Contracts (1932), § 1.

[26] An Indiana court once argued that, "on principle", if a contract is indivisible for one purpose (e.g., applying the Statute of Frauds), it must be indivisible for all purposes. Smith v. Lewis, 40 Ind. 98 (1872). But Corbin found fourteen meanings of "divisible." 3 Corbin, Contracts (1951), p. 737.

[27] See De Mott v. National Bank of New Jersey, 118 N.J.Eq. 396, 179 A. 470 (1935) ("trustee" or "bailee").

[28] Cross v. British Oak Ins. Co., [1938] 2 K.B. 167; comment in 2 Modern L.Rev. 313.

[29] E.g., the limitation of the term "any felony" by the context, in U.S. v. Weil, 46 F.Supp. 323 (D.C.Ark. 1942). For further discussion, see infra, § 3.26.

of meaning have no gospel that will save lawyers the pain of thinking.

§ 1.13—Ethics and Value-Theory

Ethics consists of the theories about human conduct regarded as good or bad, right or wrong, virtuous or vicious.[30] Although not all ethical discussions terminate in commands or prohibitions, in admonitions as to how men ought to behave, the practical end of ethical theory is to provide, or to account for such motivators of human conduct. In this way ethics has a common objective with morals, with religion and with law. The terms "ethics" and "morals" are often loosely used interchangeably. Yet the two are distinguishable: "Ethics" refers to the system of theoretical norms which should guide human conduct, "morals" to the attitudes and practices which prevail in any given society or class of society.[31] Thus one can speak of the ethics of Aristotle or Spinoza or Kant, and of the morals of the Eskimos or of New York millionaires. This distinction between ethics and morals is implicit in the following passage:

> "Sound thinking requires us to perceive that moral propositions do not become authoritatively established legal precepts whenever a jurist succeeds in demonstrating to his own satisfaction that they are ethically well taken." [32]

The "unifying thread" of ethical theory is said to be:

> "Moral conceptions and processes grow naturally out of the very conditions of human life." [33]

Likewise, moral conceptions provide a good deal of the content of any body of law (infra, § 3.16).

By some writers ethics is taken to include law and jurisprudence. We do not accept this classification because there are important values in the law which are political, administrative or peculiarly legal in character. We may indicate the relations of ethics to law and jurisprudence by mentioning some of the chief similarities and differences.

1. *Virtuous Character.* One type of ethical theory is concerned primarily with an appraisal of the virtues and vices which

---

30 This tripartite summation is based on Dewey and Tufts, Ethics (rev. ed., 1932), 193–196, 342–344.

31 T. V. Smith in Encyclopedia of the Social Sciences, *sub. tit.* "Ethics."

32 Pound, Law and Morals (1924), 40.

33 Dewey and Tufts, 342.

make up a man's moral character. This type is found in Aristotle; it likewise finds expression in a jurisprudential theory that it is the end of the law to develop a society of virtuous people. In the Aristotelian system justice is a virtue, "that kind of state of character which makes people disposed to do what is just and makes them act justly and wish for what is just." [34] A recent ethical philosopher takes "virtue" to mean "all commendable qualities of moral character." [35] The notion of commendation or approval [36] of moral virtues has its counterpart in the rule of law which permits proof of a person's character by proof of his reputation in the community. Commendation is praise, and its contrary is blame; the notion of individual fault is pervasive of ethical theory as it is of morality and of many parts of the law. Yet virtues are mere potentialities, hence character evidence has limited probative force to show that a particular act was or was not done. A prudent man will act imprudently once in a while. For reasons of policy modern legal systems make the bad act rather than a bad character the criterion of conviction of crime. Yet character is the basis of the reform and treatment of those convicted. Moreover, "good moral character" is in some legal provisions decisive, as in the American statute prescribing the requirements for naturalization. A recent decision applying this statute referred to the prevalent attitude, which condones marrying a man who has obtained a Mexican divorce, to support its conclusion that a female applicant for citizenship was of "good moral character." [37] In the internal structure of the law—the conceptual criteria of legal consequences—character is of relatively minor importance. It is vastly important in the relation of law to society: The best system of law would be relatively ineffective if the members of the society (and the men who administer the laws) were not predominantly men of good character.

2. *Motive or Intention.* The motive or intention of the actor is the primary criterion of the rightness or wrongness of an act in some ethical theories. The outstanding modern example is that of Immanuel Kant, who thus sharply differentiated ethics and law: To perform one's promise when no compulsion can be

---

[34] Aristotle, Nichomachean Ethics (Oxford trans.), Bk. V, I, 1129a.

[35] Laird, An Enquiry into Moral Notions (1936), 13.

[36] Dewey and Tufts, 193, 260.

[37] Petition of R——, 56 F.Supp. 969 (D.C.Mass. 1944). However, Judge Wyzanski cited Ehrlich (supra, § 1.05) rather than an ethical philosopher.

applied to enforce it is a virtuous action, since the actor's motivation is to perform an ethical duty; to perform because motivated by the external compulsion of law is to perform a juridical duty.[38] From this it can be seen how a particular type of ethical theory leads to a particular jurisprudential theory about the relation between ethics and law. However, the motive or intention of the actor is significant in most ethical theories, and so it is, too, in many parts of the law. Such terms as "malice," wilfulness," "good faith" and "knowingly" in legal prescriptions signify the relevance of motive or intention to legal consequences. It is not true, then, as Holland and Kant have suggested, that the law is concerned always and solely with the *external* aspects of conduct. Yet the *legal* criterion of motivation is not just the "conscience" of the actor, his feeling that he is acting rightly; it is rather an external standard which is frequently the same as the standard of the community; it may be "higher" than that of the actor whose conduct is in question, and is lower than that of the saint of ethical perfection.[39] Moreover, the law gives more pervasive importance to the harmful consequences of the act than to the motive or intention of the actor. Thus the doing of acts that have, or are likely to have harmful consequences to others is often made criminal even though the actor did not "intend" to do harm. For example, the Federal Food, Drug and Cosmetic Act has been construed to put "the burden of acting at hazard upon a person otherwise innocent but standing in relation to a public danger," [40] as against the contention that "guilt is personal" and should not be imputed to one who "has no evil intention or consciousness of wrongdoing." [41] This is a recurrent problem of statutory construction, especially as to regulations of business and vocational activities. On the other hand, merely having a wicked intention or thought, however ethically wrongful, is not a violation of (modern) law unless it eventuates in conduct of commission or omission that causes or is likely to cause

---

[38] Kant, The Philosophy of Law (Hastie trans., 1887), 23; Hall, 129; infra, § 4.22.

[39] E.g., Gerseta Corp. v. Wessex-Campbell Silk Co., 3 F.2d 236 (C.C.A. N.Y. 1924), discussing the "good faith of the purchaser of a negotiable instrument."

[40] U. S. v. Dotterweich, 320 U.S. 277, 281, 64 Sup.Ct. 134, 136 (1943) (Frankfurter, J., speaking for the Court).

[41] Same case, dissenting opinion by Murphy, J., joined by Roberts, Reed and Rutledge, JJ., 320 U.S. 286, 64 Sup.Ct. 139.

results deemed harmful. In this sense the law's standard is external.

3. *Harmful Consequences.* Most ethical theories take account of the good or bad consequences of human conduct in determining its ethical character. They differ widely as to how they take account of this factor. One example is the utilitarianism of Jeremy Bentham, who said:

> "He who adopts the principle of utility esteems virtue to be a good only on account of the pleasures which result from it; he regards vice as an evil only because of the pains which it produces." [42]

Such an ethical theory may be called "teleological" because it emphasizes the end or purpose of human action. One important task of such an ethical theory is to find or create some unifying single criterion of the goodness or badness of consequences. Many teleological theories would not agree with Bentham that producing pleasures and avoiding pains is the ultimate criterion; "the good" is defined in various ways, or is regarded as undefinable. In the law one finds many parallels with teleological ethical theory. In modern legal systems conduct is of no significance unless it has *some* outward consequences which are actually or potentially harmful to others. Foreseeability of possible harm is frequently a test of the actor's legal responsibility. Moreover, the law has its own teleology; one problem of philosophical jurisprudence is to explore the ultimate end or ends of the law, such as the greatest happiness of the greatest number, the common good, etc. Another is to explore the relations between facts and values, between what is and what ought to be. On the whole teleological theories of ethics have more frequently direct relevance than the others to the specific content of the law.

4. *Intuitive vs. Reflective Evaluations.* If we turn our attention from standards of value to methods of evaluation we find another interesting parallel between ethics and law. How should one determine that a particular type of conduct is right or wrong, good or bad? According to some ethical theories one should recognize intuitively what is ethically right or wrong; according to others such evaluations should be made by a careful calculation of the actual or potential consequences of such conduct, together with a weighing of alternatives. This is only a relative difference. On the one hand, no ethical *theory* worthy of the name (as distinct from popular morals) admonishes one to rely *wholly* upon

---

[42] Bentham, The Theory of Legislation (Ogden ed., 1931), 3; Hall, 170.

one's unreflective intuitions of rightness or wrongness; on the other hand, every ethical theory has at least one intuition,[43] such as the conception of the good. The difference is between judging that something is "obviously" right or wrong, and judging that it is right or wrong because of some "reasons" which rest upon matters of fact or of belief and can therefore be tested either by observation or by fitness and compatibility with other beliefs. One finds similar differences of method in legal evaluations. Sometimes a court says that a particular type of conduct is obviously wrong or bad; other times it takes care to explore the consequences and gives a reasoned evaluation. During the past fifty years there has been increasing insistence that the content of legal rules or precepts shall be determined by their ends: How do they work? [44] To say that a legal rule is right "inherently" or "in the nature of things", and no more, does not satisfy the legal profession nor the public.

5. *Sanctions.* Turning now to the differences between ethics and the law, we find that the chief difference is in their respective sanctions. The sanction of a rule or principle of conduct is something which motivates individuals to conform to it, ordinarily something other than the individual's conviction that the rule or principle is ethically right. Sanctions, then, are external or added motivations. In ethics these may be either rewards for conformity or penalties for non-conformity. The sanctions of legal norms are, according to the terminology here chosen, always penalties or other consequences harmful to the violator. Some laws, such as those offering bounties to the killers of certain noxious wild animals, seek to motivate conduct by rewards; yet to call such a reward a "sanction" is contrary to the traditional way of regarding the consequences of conformity to law (infra, § 2.32). The sanctions of legal norms are political sanctions backed by the force of the state. No mere ethical philosopher has any such sanction for his precepts. The sanction of moral rules is approval or disapproval of conduct in the group or society in which the rules prevail. The political sanction lays, or threatens to lay, a heavy hand upon the individual. To make conduct a violation of a legal obligation involves much more than merely adjudging it to be morally wrong or bad; it involves adjudging it to be so bad as to require the laying upon it of a political sanction, with all the

---

[43] Broad, Five Types of Ethical Theory (1930), 151, quoting Sidgwick.

[44] Pound, "How Far Are We Attaining a New Measure of Values in Twentieth Century Juristic Thought?" (1936) 42 W.Va.L.Q. 81, 90.

consequences which that sanction may have for the individual violator, for the community, and for the officials who are called upon to enforce it.

6. *Non-ethical Values in the Law.* Unless ethics embraces all values—a position rejected here—the law has to be concerned with many values that are not ethical in character. In Anglo-American law one of the chief examples is the independence of the judiciary, and the corresponding limitation of the scope of the judicial function in making new law. These we may call political values, since they implement the political principle of the separation of powers. Many rules of case law have remained outmoded because of judicial deference—often too slavish—to this principle. Another limitation lies in the difficulties and dangers of proof. The reluctance of many courts to allow the recovery of damages for mental fright or shock unaccompanied by physical harm is due in part to the danger of simulation. A similar example is the abolition, by some states in recent years, of the actions for damages for breach of promise of marriage or for alienation of affections.[45] The enactment of such a law did not signify legislative approval of promise-breaking or of stealing other men's wives. It was based upon experience indicating that these legal remedies were used chiefly by adventurers for purposes of extortion; the genuinely injured fiancée preferred to bear in silence injuries which the procedure of legal proof would serve only to aggravate. These we may call administrative values. Finally, a good part of any modern system of law, especially the law of real property and commercial law, is designed to canalize transactions, to provide definite and economical ways of carrying on activities. Many of these legal rules are in their specific provisions ethically indifferent. For instance, why should one be required to drive on the right side of the road rather than on the left? Yet two things must be noted: The establishment of one rule *or* the other is necessary to carry on the orderly processes of society; and those who act in reliance upon such a rule, once established, can justly claim to have their expectations fulfilled. The law has to take account of more values, Horatio, than are dreamed of in your philosophy.

Since ethics as here defined does not embrace all value-theory and since the law expresses judgments based partly on values

---

45 E.g., N. Y. Civil Practice Act, Art. 2–A (enacted 1935). Other statutes are referred to in (1945) 158 A.L.R. 617.

which are not ethical, some term is needed to designate this more inclusive value-theory. To signify any type of general theory of value we propose to use the term, "axiology." The value-theory peculiar to law we call "legal axiology." [46]

7. *Law as a Compromise.* Another striking contrast between ethics and law is the compromise character of legal rules. For example, a municipal building code is primarily designed to compel builders to erect buildings which will be healthful, safe, and comfortable. Its specific provisions, however, are compromises between this objective and others, such as the need for using such materials and labor as are practically available and not too expensive, and the need for concrete, precise rules to guide officials and builders. The passage of controversial legislation frequently reveals a series of compromises between competing values. Many rules of case law express similar compromises. To the ethical philosopher the law seems often a sorry compromise of his ethical ideals.[47] The law as an instrument of social control has the function of prescribing ways by which men can live together in society for ends which the law cannot (fruitfully or justly) compel them to seek or to attain. The highest ethical function of the law is to make possible the maintenance of an ethically good society.

§ 1.14—Metaphysics

Metaphysics is that part of philosophy which has to do with the ultimate nature of being or existence. For most philosophers it is the core of philosophy. Its relation to such practical disciplines as law is controversial. On the one side are those philosophers who assert that metaphysics is "the sovereign science," "competent to judge every other human science, rejecting as false every scientific hypothesis which contradicts its own results." [48] On the other hand to many jurisprudents and social scientists metaphysics is an abstruse, obscure and futile body of speculation which has no significance for their problems. These criticisms

---

46 Bentham's term, "deontology", meaning the ethical theory appropriate to law, has not caught on. The word, "axiology", has regrettably been adopted by some ethical writers to mean an ethical theory of inherent or intrinsic values.

47 Cf. Cohen, "Positivism and the Limits of Idealism in the Law," (1927) 27 Columbia L.Rev. 243.

48 Maritain, An Introduction to Philosophy (1933), Ch. VI, p. 111. Maritain is one of the chief representatives of scholastic philosophy.

are partly justified by the terminology of metaphysics, which is vague because of the comprehensiveness of its subject matter. On the whole, metaphysics is the part of philosophy that has given it a bad reputation with the uninitiated.

Nevertheless, the jurisprudent, anyone who tries to express a fundamental view of law and legal method, can scarcely avoid encountering metaphysical questions; for metaphysics is, as William James said, an obstinate effort to think clearly. The assumption that there are some things which have "reality" or "existence" underlies all serious intellectual activity; no one wants to believe that his most serious reflections are mere shadow-boxing. Yet a lawyer or a judge can do a good professional job of legal thinking and writing without becoming involved in a choice between one metaphysical view and another. When he strives to present a theoretical justification, to place his views in a larger framework, he may take positions about the nature of reality which are metaphysical in character. For jurisprudence, then, the chief importance of metaphysics is to know enough about it to avoid its pitfalls. Three examples of basic metaphysical problems are: the status of universals, the status of the "ought," and the nature of causation.

1. *The Status of Universals and of Universal Propositions.* What is a rule of law? What is a legal duty? Do such things *really* exist or are they merely figments of the imagination, like the hobgoblins that were once used by ignorant parents and nursemaids to frighten children? Do legal rules and legal duties have the same kind of existence as the sheet of paper on which I am writing this or the paper on which (I hope) someone will be reading it? If not, what kind of a status do they have with respect to existence? Does a legal duty have any existence (or any meaning) apart from the marks on paper (or the uttered sounds) which symbolize it *and* apart from the ideas, the conscious thoughts, of those human beings who think of its meaning? Are any of these questions worth asking or answering or even discussing in twentieth century jurisprudence?

The reason why such questions are still worthy of some reflection and discussion is because writers on jurisprudence during the present century have raised such questions, or have used language which seems to raise them. Some of the American legal realists (infra, § 4.63) are here to be included. Professor Joseph W. Bingham was among the earliest to assert that the law consists of individual decisions and that the so-called rules of law are mere

subjective ideas in the minds of those who think about the law.[49]
More recently he explained that he believed that in legal education and in some legal philosophies "the mechanical trappings of
the law, its logical tools of thought," have been overstressed at
the expense of "its vital substance and the multifarious causes
which have determined its concrete details and consequences." [50]
From rules as mere subjective ideas in the mind to rules as tools
of thought is a significant transition from metaphysics to method.
Still, he retains the "actual decision" concept:

> "We American realists contend to the contrary that the
> cases in all their concreteness of causes and effects are the
> very substance of the law. . . ." [51]

As indicated in the foregoing quotations from Bingham, the attacks on legal rules or on legal conceptualism are usually incidental to some criticisms of the methods of law teachers or of
judges, and these may be appraised independently. Nevertheless,
such positions lead to a kind of terminology which it is awkward
to maintain; and unless unconsciously corrected in the process
of judgment, they will lead to erroneous conclusions. To return
now to Professor Bingham's position, the concrete decisions of
courts (excluding here their opinions, as he insists) are mere individual judicial orders which have no meaning for the work of
the lawyer and judge without some generalization which connects
them with other decisions, past and future. These generalizations
(for clearly several are always possible) enable the work of lawyers and judges to become reason-controlled experience; the
sense of sameness is the substantial part of reasoning. As to erroneous conclusions, I have seen lawyers cite (unsuccessfully)
precedents which had superficial factual resemblances to their instant case because they did not understand that the legal significance of a precedent depends upon the generalizations that it
supports within its legal system (infra, §§ 3.30–3.32). The
"black-horse case" mode of citation is partly a result of naïve
realism.

---

49 Bingham, "Legal Philosophy and the Law," 9 Ill.L.Rev. 96, 114 (1914);
same, "What is the Law?" 11 Mich.L.Rev. 109 (1912). The somewhat similar views of Scandinavian jurisprudents—Hägerstrom, Olivecrona, Ross—
are explained and criticized in Castberg (Professor, Oslo), Problems of Legal
Philosophy (c. 1948) Ch. II. See Ross, Towards a Realistic Jurisprudence
(1946) 78.

50 My Philosophy of Law (Symposium, 1941) 12.

51 Ibid., 13.

But in the realm of metaphysics rather than of legal method, the objections to the view that a legal rule, a legal duty, even a contingent remainder are merely ideas in somebody's mind is that all science, learning, and communication of meaning depend upon the "reality of the universals that enter into all meaning." [52] While the ideas produced in two different minds by the same symbol may vary, the common experience that communication does result tends to refute the view that this is a series of lucky accidents. Logical universals are used with common meanings because they provide the basis for reliable inferences.

Four positions may be noted with regard to the relations of: 1. Symbols. 2. Ideas in the mind. 3. Objects in the existential world outside the mind. According to *Nominalism*, the symbol ("horse") stimulates an idea in the mind; it is a convenient notation for a string of singulars (all the horses you have ever seen), but beyond the symbol, the singulars, and a concrete mental image, there is nothing else. How can one explain to another, as not wholly capricious, the inclusion of a new and doubtful item in the class? Nominalism explains communication but is weak on reasoning.[53] At the other extreme *Realism* (Platonic) conceived of ideas or conceptions as the only real existences; singulars (this horse "Count Fleet") were only manifestations, pale shadows, of them. The chief merit of this view is that it helps one to think in the grand manner, to see all things in the guise of reflections of eternal essences, to see forests rather than trees. Its demerit is that one overlooks changes in meaning as new experiences challenge interpretation. When anyone speaks of a legal concept as if it were an indestructible thing, a brooding omnipresence, he uses, or abuses, Platonic realism. When the Federal inheritance-tax laws came to be interpreted in the present century, some of the sanctified real-property distinctions had to be modified or rejected in order to prevent evasions of the statutes. A third position is *Conceptualism,* which in its modern form assumes that logical universals ("chair", "horse", "mammal") express characteristic traits which have no existence independently of the individual items in which they are embodied, and that by means of these traits one identifies any conjectural item as belonging or not belonging to the class designated by the conceptual

---

[52] Cohen (Morris R.), "Justice Holmes and the Nature of Law," 31 Columbia L.Rev. 352, 361 (1931); Cohen, Law and the Social Order (1933) 208; Cohen and Cohen, 693.

[53] See Lerner, "The Shadow World of Thurman Arnold" (1938) 47 Yale L.J. 687, 692, commenting on Arnold's strain of anti-rationalism and nominalism.

symbol. This is a moderate position for common sense thinking. If a tariff act imposes a 50% duty on "chairs" but not on "stools", one has only to assemble the characteristics attributed to chairs in standard usage and apply it to the conjectural item. The criteria of judgment are grounded in usage and in observation of objects. While I am not saying that this would be the *only* method to be used in applying the tariff law, it is a common and a permissible one in many legal contexts. However, for most (if not all) legal reasoning a more complex and abstract method is needed. This may be called *Instrumentalism*.[54] The traits of things or events which ground *legal* inference cannot plausibly be regarded as qualities or attributes of the things or events themselves; they are in part ascribed to them by legal conceptions which function as subject terms of legal propositions. For instance, "walking on land" has direct existential reference but "trespassing on land" has only *indirect* existential reference since one cannot determine that the human act one sees is a trespass unless one knows that another person has the exclusive right to possess the land; and only a set of legal propositions (and some more facts) can tell that. Legal propositions are *universal* propositions because they are guides to action. One may conclude, then, that legal rules do not have the same kind of existence as sheets of paper; yet they have several distinct references to the existential world (infra, § 2.12). I prefer to believe that they "subsist" but do not "exist". Yet surely Professor Corbin may properly speak, as he inveterately does, of legal relations being "created" and "existing",[55] since he clearly treats legal concepts and propositions as instrumental. The arrangement of legally relevant events in a time-sequence is useful to lawyers because such temporal factors as causation, foreseeability and expectation are highly important in many processes of legal evaluation. In such a sequence (e. g., the delivery of a conveyance of land) one can say that A's right to the land is "created" at a specified moment and B's right to it then no longer "exists".

2. *The Status of the "Ought".* The metaphysical status of *legal* rules or principles is further complicated by the circumstance that they are, besides being generalizations employing logical universals (as do the laws of physics), statements of what "ought" to be, or what "shall" or "shall not" be, rather than of what "is". The acceptance or rejection of this last statement, and

---

54 Dewey, Logic (1938) 262–280.

55 Corbin, Contracts (1951) §§ 622, 623; Corbin, "Conditions in the Law of Contracts", (1919) 28 Yale L.J. 739, 749.

its significance if accepted, are recurrent and fairly important issues of jurisprudence. At this point we hope merely to explain the issues. The view that law, or rather a legal generalization, is a *normative* statement rather than a merely *descriptive* one will be more fully discussed later (§ 2.20). Let us take the law of gravitation, as expressed in the formula

$$F = \frac{M_1 M_2}{D^2}$$

where F is "force", M_1 and M_2 are two separate bodies of matter, and D is the distance between them. This statement is under-stood to mean not only that it is a reliable guide (subject to modification in detail) to calculations, observations and other operations but also because it can be verified anywhere on the earth, and in that sense expresses a direct existential relation between two material bodies, a relation grounded in some attributes of the bodies as material bodies. We need not say that the above equation is "absolutely" or "eternally" true but we do assume, I believe, that if it be shown to be untrue, wholly or in part, the demonstration will be dependent upon observation leading to inference of other or different attributes or relations of the material bodies—some things that are discoverable.

Now compare a legal statement:

Any person who shall trespass on another's land shall be liable to pay damages to the owner.

On the one hand this statement cannot be verified at every point on the earth's land surface merely by observing, and inferring from observations of persons and land (without reference to some political or at least societal norm); on the other hand the statement is not, in its meaning and application, nor even in its authority or justification, wholly independent of observation and inference. The dilemma apparently is that either legal propositions (rules) are "inherent" in the "facts" to which they apply, or they are mere arbitrary figments of official imaginations having no justification in fact. The former view has been stated both in ethics and in law. Blackstone's position that judges never "make" law but merely "find" it seems partly dependent on this view. More recently the blending of fact and value has been supported by a German school of metaphysicians known as the "phenomenologists", who insist that the separation of the two is a useless myth.[56] Now one must concede that primitive men did,

---

[56] See Brecht, "The Myth of the 'Is' and the 'Ought' ", (1941) 54 Harv.L.Rev. 811; Koehler, The Place of Value in a World of Fact (1938).

and many laymen today do, evaluate certain situations as so inherently "right" or "wrong" that there can be no argument about them. Such a view is, I believe, ethically benumbing, likely to lead to arbitrary "hunch" decisions and to the stifling of free inquiry into the justification of morals and law. One of the great contributions of the German philosopher, Immanuel Kant, was his separation of "reality", the realm of science, from value, the realm of ethics (infra, §§ 4.20, 4.24), to the great benefit of both intellectual disciplines. The scientist makes his knowledge universal by consciously striving to keep out his prejudices. The ethical philosopher becomes more objective and more tolerant by being conscious of the leap from fact to value, and the law-maker, with a variety of means at his disposal, is even more aware of the evaluative theories at his disposal.

The distinction has logical significance. An "ought" proposition cannot be deductively derived from two "is" propositions; at least one "ought" proposition must be in the premises of the syllogism.[57] No matter how many elderly people were inadequately cared for in the United States in the 1930's, the conclusion that there *ought* to be a law establishing governmental compulsory old age pensions could not be explicitly deduced from the factual proposition. From it one might, for instance, merely conclude that the schools should teach children the importance of saving up money for old age. Nor can this logical difficulty be avoided by formulating legal propositions as "is" propositions: "A contract is a promise or a set of promises that the law will enforce." As M. R. Cohen pointed out, such a statement functions in a legal system which gives normative (i. e., imperative) meaning to conclusions derived from such propositions.[58] Thus in a realm of legal meanings (logical syntax) logical operations can be (and are) carried on by lawyers and judges without explicit statement of the normative character of the propositions. The difference may be further exemplified by comparing the meaning of the phrase "man walking on land" with "man trespassing on land". The former refers directly to an existential event. The latter also refers to *some* event (human act) but it does so only by the circuitous route of a set of legal prescriptions, including those which determine who owns the land. In Dewey's logic "trespass"

---

57 See Castberg, op. cit., supra, n. 49, Chap. III, § 1.

58 Cohen (M. R.), "Law and Scientific Method" in Law and the Social Order (1933) 240–241 ; Hall, 805.

has an *indirect* existential reference.[59]   Trespass, then, has a different kind of reality from walking.

Yet normative statements, as premises of law or as ethical premises for creating law, come from somewhere: They are not self-evident moral truths intuited independently of experience; they are evaluative conclusions derived by their formulators from personal or vicarious experience, and capable of being understood only as applicable to further experience (human conduct and its situations). Take one of the most self-evident of legal principles: No man shall be unjustly enriched at another's expense. The adoption by jurists of this principle, both in Roman law and in English law, came after numerous instances of unjust enrichment had come before tribunals.[60] Hence it is erroneous to classify such a legal principle with the axioms or theorems of logic or mathematics,[61] except in the sense that all subsist in an interconnected realm of meaning. Legal meanings are derived from experience (including, for instance, judicial precedents) and are always limited in meaning by their origins.

But where, says our skeptical realist, do legal rules exist? Not merely in the symbols on stone, parchment or paper in which they are expressed, but also in the minds of those who are trained to understand them. Not merely in the minds of those who are now thinking of them, but in the minds of those who are capable of understanding them, and in the attitudes of those who believe in their having objective meanings capable of logical application. These attitudes have resulted from accumulated traditions. They are important social realities.[62]

3. *Causation.* Metaphysics is concerned with causation, and so is the law. Yet the problems considered by each are substantially different. Both the metaphysical and the legal conception of cause originated with the common sense observation that for any given event an indefinite number of but-for causes can be discovered. For instance, this seller-promisee would not have

---

[59] Dewey, Logic (1938) 271.

[60] See Dawson, Unjust Enrichment (1951); Jackson, History of Quasi-contract (1936).

[61] See Frank, "What Courts Do in Fact", (1932) 26 Ill.L.Rev. 645, 648–650; Hall, 1104–1105.

[62] See Castberg, op. cit., Chap. III. Hence a statute may have meanings (apply to situations) which the draftsman never even imagined. This assertion is supported by present writer's experience in interpreting statutes that he had drafted several years previously.

made these goods but for the act of the postman in delivering the perfidious buyer's offer; should the postman be held liable? The question whether all events are predetermined by inevitable causes, or some of them arise by chance or by the exercise of man's free will, is a metaphysical question on which, I think, an answer in favor of the latter alternative is given by all legal systems which impute individual responsibility for harmful acts.[63] Even if culpability (e. g., negligence or malice) is eliminated as a criterion of legal responsibility (as under Workmen's Compensation Acts), some causal relation, however slight, must be found between the conduct of the person to be held responsible and the harm for which compensation is to be made (e. g., "arising out of and in course of the employment"). Further than this, however, metaphysical conceptions of cause merely muddy the legal waters. The law's standard of "proximate cause" involves evaluations that are peculiarly legal. In legal history "cause" has another role, which is not identical with physical cause. Thus "cause" in history has been broken down into three classes: precipitant, incentive, and responsible agent.[64] Cause is one of those pervasive concepts which needs investigation to determine its significance in the context of a particular inquiry.

§ 1.15—Epistemology

If, how, and what the human mind is capable of knowing are among the questions of epistemology, the theory of knowledge. This body of theory, sometimes included by philosophical writers with metaphysics, has attained a separate though not independent status since the searching study of knowledge contained in Kant's Critique of Pure Reason (1781). Kant's assumptions about the inherent qualities of the human mind have been somewhat modified by later experience and theorizing. Two eminent American philosophers have rejected epistemology as a distinct body of theory, on the ground that all of its valid or useful contributions are embraced within logic,[65] or within logic and psychology.[66]

---

63 See James and Perry, "Legal Cause", (1951) 60 Yale L.J. 761, 792.

64 MacIver, R. M., Social Causation (1942), Chs. 6, 7, 8.

65 Dewey, Logic (1938), 465–469. While Dewey here refers the so-called epistemological problems of modern science (e. g., how does one through a large telescope "see" a star-cluster in Hercules which is 30,000 light-years away and how does one "know" it is "now" "there") to logic and scientific method, he would recognize the relevance of psychology to other questions of knowledge.

66 Cohen (Morris R.), Reason and Nature (1931), 223, n. 38.

The latter view seems to be substantially correct. In this brief survey we shall try to show that basic assumptions about knowledge are involved in legal procedures.

Knowledge for what? If one asks this pragmatic question in response to any general question about the nature, basis or reliability of human knowledge, the inquiry will be diverted into a quest for dependable methods of building observation and reasoning into a stable system adapted to the ends of the particular discipline, be it astronomy, physics, geology, or even sociology. In this way the gross generalities of epistemology become implemented in a particular discipline. The standards of reliable knowledge in sociology are in this way notably different from those in physics. Two questions remain: 1. Do not the methods of the particular disciplines require (presuppose, or in mental process involve) some basic assumptions about knowledge or knowing? 2. Does not the over-all and non-specialized objective of satisfying human intellectual curiosity call for a general theory of knowledge above and beyond the methods of the several disciplines? This last question is one that we cannot attempt to answer, except to say that any theory of knowledge that would purport to develop conclusions *independently* of the modern scientific disciplines would seem doomed to end in mystical or emotive terms without existential reference.

The basic assumptions made by those who administer and guide legal procedures include the assumption, similar to that of all practical disciplines, that the human mind is *capable* of knowing with sufficient reliability to warrant the conclusions drawn and to justify the legal and social consequences. This does not mean, of course, that legal procedures are infallible in fact or are always right in their results. On the contrary, the continuous efforts to improve (i. e., to *change*) legal procedures implicitly assume what is stated above: We do not "give it up" merely because we discover errors or inadequacies in the legal procedures of ascertaining knowledge and using it to arrive at legal consequences (ultimately, official conduct). The assumption above stated would be negated by any one who believes that the external world is all illusion and hence the most atrocious murder is only an illusion. While such a person should be disqualified for jury service, he could scarcely object to the legal procedure which ended in electrocuting the guilty one, for would not that also be an illusion? Such an extreme position is rarely if ever found in occidental cultures. The belief that disease is an illusion is found among some religious sects, who object to the enactment and enforcement of certain public health laws. Occasionally one finds among the jurisprudents a "realist" or a "vitalist" who seems to be questioning the underlying assumption of legal procedure, yet is only pointing out its inevitable limitations. The late Professor Max Radin, in his Yale lectures on jurisprudence, asked some mildly provocative but rather naïve questions. Supposing the case of a commercial agreement about which the judge hears the testimony of the parties and of other persons and reads documents, he continues:

> "What does he know about it? . . . Such things do not constitute the agreement but merely some of the impresses that the act of agreeing has made on the environment, its reverberations, its effluvia. And with the best will in the world he cannot get into his courtroom, much less before his eyes, even so much as all the impresses of all the events that went to the making of the agreement".[67]

By its overtones, at least, this passage suggests that there is something living, vital, about this commercial agreement that escapes the process of acquiring knowledge through legal procedure. What these "vital" aspects are Professor Radin barely suggests. Surely one of the great advantages of legal procedure is that it tries to sift out the *legally* irrelevant facts. The commercial agreement may have had many aspects that a novelist or a dramatist or Mrs. Grundy would have remarked upon. Perhaps it was the first triumph of a new sales manager and enabled him to buy that sailboat that Jimmy wanted;[68] perhaps the buyer on the other side first realized when he was talked into this agreement that he was slipping, that the tragedy of old age was approaching. Let us rejoice that we lawyers can take our law and our literature separately! These dramatic details would in the litigation supposed (action to recover damages for breach of contract) be quite irrelevant. What is "vital" for the law is determined by the ends and means of the law. Radin's discussion continues by pointing out (quite properly) the fallibility of judicial modes of proof and the inevitable narrowing of legal issues for the sake of economy of time and energy.[69]

A second assumption of legal procedure is that an individual witness obtains the knowledge of direct observation not merely by the use of his senses but also by means of his perceptions, that

---

[67] Radin, Law as Logic and Experience (1940), 48–49.

[68] Cf. Marquand, Point of No Return (1950).

[69] Op. cit. supra, n. 67, 49–50.

is, the concepts or selectors of his prior experience. What the witness observed is not used except in so far as he can communicate it to the tribunal by symbols, ordinarily the common nouns and adjectives with their class-meanings. The rule of evidence that (normally) excludes from judicial proof laymen's opinions is designed to keep the witness' language at the neutral descriptive level and to exclude his erroneous or biased inferences; and the exceptions to the rule show recognition that the language of common nouns and adjectives is inadequate to communicate to a jury the data from which it can infer that, for instance, a voice heard by the witness was X's voice. Hence the witness is allowed to state directly that the voice he heard was X's voice.[70] Even this statement involves placing the observation in a class consisting of one member.

The monumental efforts of Anglo-American law to minimize bias (as well as inaccurate observation and faulty memory) in witnesses and in jurors have produced rules upon rules (e. g., the hearsay rule and the fourteen (?) rules that constitute its exceptions) until critics of the system argue that all should be swept away—including even all or most of the jury trials. Judge Jerome Frank has persuasively argued that the greatest uncertainties of the judicial process are not in the law-finding but in the fact-finding part; or at least, primarily in the witness-jury part.[71] He points out that the assumption that a fact-trial is intended to bring out "the truth" is contradicted by the "fight" theory, that the best way to get the truth out is to have two skilful advocates hammering away at each other's witnesses; the contradiction comes when in their partisan zeal the advocates distort or cover up the truth.[72] Judge Frank's remedies call for more extended discussion than can be given them here (see § 4.63).

Since Judge Frank has accused me of believing in "legal magic"[73] (i. e., that judicial trials somehow magically produce the truth), let me add two further comments which may or may not signify my magic-addiction. No other practical discipline having the high degree of intellectual subtlety and systematic clarity that the law has is as dependent in its application upon as chancy and unreliable a method of obtaining facts, in so many of its opera-

---

[70] See pungent comments by Judge Learned Hand, on the lay-opinion rule, in Central R. Co. of N. J. v. Monahan, 11 F.2d 212, 213–14 (C.C.A.N.Y. 1926).

[71] See Frank, Courts on Trial (1949).

[72] Ibid., Ch. VI.

[73] Ibid., 60–61.

tions, as is the law. What happened when two cars collided, or when a shooting affray occurred, is left to the casual observations of chance witnesses (if any), often with no training in observation and none in narration save that given by a partisan advocate. The wonder is that in some types of cases we do not get worse results. Judge Frank has suggested no way of getting a well-trained, reliable witness to be conveniently present in a choice observation post when every operative fact occurs. In short, one of the basic troubles is ineradicable. Something could be achieved, I think, by teaching the child even in grammar school the civic duty of being a fair and reliable witness in judicial trials.

The second comment is that virtually all knowledge acquired in a court-room is *inferred* knowledge, and hence the layman's distrust of conclusions drawn from circumstantial evidence (as compared with eye-witness testimony) is unwarranted.[74] Inferences can be wrong but so can witnesses. On the other hand, some judicial trials, for example, those involving monopolies and restraint of trade, bring out the most reliable evidence obtainable of the operations of some industrial giants and their economic consequences. Neither the social scientists nor the journalists have invented any better engine for the discovery of truth than the non-jury judicial trial at its best. While fact-finding by legislative committees has produced some reliable results, the performances of some have been far more inadequate and biased than any contemporary judicial trial. Methods of acquiring reliable knowledge are important in most governmental processes.

§ 1.16—Aesthetics

Aesthetics as a part of philosophy is the theory of beauty, or of the beautiful. It has less importance for law and jurisprudence than any of the other philosophic disciplines. Some possible objections may be noted. Law requires literary communication, and is therefore to be judged by literary standards. The literary style of such men as Maitland and Holmes lends charm and persuasiveness to what they have to say. The manner, however, is less important than the matter. Another example of the supposed influence of aesthetic appreciation upon law is suggested in the following passage from Cardozo:

"I am not to mar the symmetry of the legal structure by the introduction of inconsistencies and irrelevancies and artificial exceptions unless for some sufficient reason. . ."[75]

---

[74] See comment, infra, § 5.02 and n. 24.

[75] Cardozo, The Nature of the Judicial Process (1921), 32–33.

While Cardozo was speaking of *logical* development, his language suggests an aesthetic motivation. Professor Morris R. Cohen has said that aesthetics has played a considerable part in law, and that "the regard for logical simplicity of the legal system" is an example of aesthetic influence. He says:

> "Whenever judges use such expressions as—'It would be absurd,'—or 'It would be monstrous to suppose,' they are generally using this aesthetic principle."[76]

With all due respect to an eminent philosopher it seems to me that such judicial utterances express rather alarm at some proposal which challenges the judge's deep convictions on some matter of politics, ethics or professional practice, or which threatens the judge with the tedious work of overhauling a long line of precedents. Professor Llewellyn is another who has taken up the cudgels for an aesthetic theory of law. "Beauty" to him includes "functional beauty, the beauty of dam-race and turbine." [77] A craftsmanlike judicial opinion is to him a thing of beauty. Of course it gives one a pleasurable sense of satisfaction to read such an opinion, but so it does to read a well-drafted section of the Internal Revenue Act. I should not call either of them "beautiful" except as a slang way of praising them. That the sense of aesthetic appreciation has some influence upon men of the law is not to be denied; but aside from *that* aesthetic theory, it is hard to see how aesthetic theory has much to do with law, that is, with legal theory in general.[78]

---

[76] Cohen, "The Process of Judicial Legislation" in Law and the Social Order (1933), 112, 143.

[77] Llewellyn, "On the Good, the True, the Beautiful in Law," (1942) 9 U. of Chicago L.Rev. 224, 228.

[78] I. e., apart from special instances, such as the recognized use of the taxing power to support art museums, public education in art and music, etc., and the absence of such avowed recognition of the use of the police power for purely aesthetic purposes.

Chapter 3

JURISPRUDENCE AND THE SCIENCES

§ 1.20—Jurisprudence and the Social Sciences

Whether jurisprudence and law are members of the family of social sciences depends upon one's conception of law, and of social science. A social science, broadly speaking, is any science having as its subject matter the conduct, attitudes and relations of men living in society. The separate social sciences have to do with particular types or aspects of group activity. For the present purposes we shall consider four: political science, economics, sociology and anthropology. Each of these is, or purports to be, primarily a body of knowledge or theory which is based upon and verified by observation of man's social conduct, and which is so systematically interrelated that inferences can be drawn or at least comparisons can be made. In this sense the social sciences mentioned consist of propositions about matters of "fact." The question remains whether they also have to do with "normative" statements, that is, with statements as to what human conduct "ought" to be. In general the answer is a negative one: Social scientists insist upon rigorous observational techniques, and do not go beyond statements that can be verified by observation and inference; they do not purport to prescribe what men ought or ought not to do. Whether an "oughtness" is implicit, or even explicit, in some of their conclusions, is a question to be discussed below. On the other hand, if one takes the view (which is adopted in Part II of this volume) that law is essentially a body of norms or prescriptions, then law is not a social science. For instance, the statement that men *are* (or have been) imprisoned for committing perjury on the witness stand in New York is one which can be verified or disproved by observation and investigation of facts. The statement that men *ought to be* or *shall be* imprisoned for committing perjury on the witness stand is one which cannot be verified or disproved by observation and investigation of facts. For even if no men are or have been so imprisoned, it may still be that they ought to be, and that the law of New York states that they shall be. Hence to introduce law into the family of social sciences is to bring the ghost of Banquo into the feast of Macbeth.

But law, even in the strict sense here assigned to it, has certain vital relations to matters of fact, and therefore in part to the social sciences. First, a law is an authoritative pronouncement of the state, the state acts through government, and therefore law is dependent upon government. Thus one has to ascertain by reference to factual matters, the actions of legislative and other officials, whether or not it *is* the law of New York that perjurers shall be imprisoned. Secondly, the content of laws is influenced and partly determined by what goes on in society. More strictly, the law-maker is influenced in making law by what has occurred in society, as a basis for inferring what will occur in the future. Thus a law that motorists must stop before crossing designated traffic intersections is motivated by the fact that collisions and injuries have occurred and by the inference that they will occur in future at such intersections, unless restrained in some way. A red-light rule provides one way. It is not so easy to show the relation of matters of fact to some other legal requirements, such as the requirement that a contract have a consideration, yet there is such a relation. The question is still to be answered, what bearing do the conclusions and theories of the social sciences about social facts have upon the determination of the content of particular laws? This question cannot, it seems, be usefully answered by any general formula. Thirdly, a law has the sanction of the state, and the imposition of a sanction is a fact that can be verified or disproved. Fourthly, the making of a law has, through its actual and potential enforcement, its hortatory effects and in other ways, consequences upon the conduct of men in society that are capable of factual investigation. If one takes "law" in a broader sense to include the legal order—the structure of government, what officials do and what non-officials do in consequence—the law has directly to do with social facts. The study of facts of the kinds designated by the second and fourth kinds mentioned above is, roughly, the field of a newly emerging discipline or science known as the *"sociology of law."* Jurisprudence, in its widest sense (§ 1.00), includes the sociology of law (infra).

The dependence of law upon the social sciences is no more striking than their dependence upon it. This dependence consists not merely in the protection that law and the legal order afford the social scientist in his study or his statistical laboratory or on his expeditions to the slums; for all human activities at an advanced stage of culture are dependent in this way. Law and the legal order are presupposed by the postulates of most studies in, or are necessary conditions of the existence of institutions studied in, political science, economics and sociology. Through these basic methodological assumptions law and the social sciences (at least, the ones mentioned) are interdependent. The statements just made may be challenged by pointing to the litigation and enforcement consequences of law: Law, it may be said, comes into play only when prescribed regularities are not observed, do not occur. It is in this sense, perhaps, that Mr. Cairns defines jurisprudence, provisionally, as "the study of human behavior as a function of disorder." [1] It may even be said that we have no scientific proof—or very little—that law produces any regularities of human behavior. "What have we better than a blind guess," said Holmes, "that the criminal law in its present form does more good than harm?" [2] The answer to such questions, in so far as they are factual in character, lies in the development of a sociology of law. The challenge does not negate what was said above. The conception of disorder presupposes order; we cannot recognize the former without some conception of the latter. Thus legal disorder presupposes one kind of order, and economic disorder presupposes another. The social sciences mentioned study various kinds of order or regularity in society, and likewise the corresponding disorders or irregularities. Thus sociology studies crime and divorce, and economics studies the deviations from the regularities of supply and demand caused by monopolies. In each case law and the legal order are in some way presupposed.

A brief comment on each of the four social sciences mentioned, and upon an offshoot of sociology, social psychology, may serve to clarify some of the foregoing statements.[3]

§ 1.21—Political Science

Political science is the science of government; this usually means government in the modern state. Since modern states establish and maintain their governments by means of laws, and since law is dependent upon the existence of a state and a government, jurisprudence and political science are closely interdependent. Indeed, in their origins, they were intermingled and indistinguishable. Aristotle's Politics is a foundation book for

---

1 Supra, § 1.04, note 28.

2 Holmes, "The Path of the Law," (1897) 10 Harvard L.Rev. 457, 470; Hall, 671.

3 For an admirable extended account, see Cairns, Law and the Social Sciences (1935).

both. It discusses the various types of governments—monarchy, aristocracy and democracy—the functions and powers of officials and the nature of law. It also has something to say about the *better* and *worse* kinds of government, which belongs more properly to the realm of *political philosophy*. This fusion continued in the history of jurisprudence down to modern times. The separation of jurisprudence from the other two resulted from the intensive specialization of the legal profession, which has gone further in England and America than on the continent of Europe. Anglo-American lawyers and jurisprudents have concentrated on the work of courts of law during the nineteenth century and only grudgingly in the twentieth admitted the administrative tribunal to their precincts. To political scientists was left the structure and functioning of the other departments of government and the general theory of the state. Hence one writer mentions jurisprudence as a branch of political science,[4] and in an historical sense the classification is justified. The separation of political science from jurisprudence has left some unfortunate gaps in the education of lawyers. For instance, law schools do not (or did not until recently) give any systematic instruction in the organization of courts, a subject of vital importance to the legal profession, yet one which cannot be taught by the case method.

Is political science wholly a factual science or is it partly a value-science, a study of what ought to be done? The latter alternative seems the correct one. Political science is concerned not only with the structure of government but also with how it functions, whether efficiently or inefficiently and with what advantages and disadvantages to the citizens. Questions as to the justification of the state in its exercise of power over the individual, and as to the ends of the state, are commonly brought under the head of political science; yet because they deal with major and ultimate values of society they belong rather to political philosophy. The separation of the latter from jurisprudence is at best a convenient division of labor. It will be respected in the present volume.

§ 1.22—Economics

Economics, as provisionally defined by an eminent economist, "deals with social phenomena centering about the provision for the material needs of the individual and of organized groups."[5]

---

[4] Dealy, The State and Government (1921), 6–10.

[5] Seligman in "Economics," (1931) 5 Encyc. of Soc. Sci. 344.

It includes descriptions and statistical summaries of the processes of financing, production, marketing and transportation, etc., of goods. These processes furnish the subject matter of most lawyers' work. They have shaped the content of a large part of the law. Thus the requirement that a contract have a consideration indicates the predominance of bargain or exchange in economic activities. It is going too far, however, to state categorically that law and economics are related as form and content, for law deals with many kinds of conduct that are not economic in character. Turning to the reverse relation, economics presupposes law and the legal order, both in the sense that descriptive economics takes legal institutions for granted, and in the sense that economic theory—about prices, the distribution of wealth, kinds of income, etc.—must make some assumptions about the part played by the state in economic processes. Classic economic theory of the nineteenth century presupposed the laissez-faire state; Adam Smith's "Wealth of Nations" was regarded by its author as a work on political economy or jurisprudence.[6] However, the trend of orthodox economics is to consider only economic values, and not such ethical values as the just distribution of wealth and comforts among the members of a society. This latter is sometimes called "socio-ethical" economics [7] or "welfare economics." The problems of just distribution have been dealt with both in ancient and in modern times by ethical philosophers.[8] Economics as a social science, in its content and methodology, is thus only incidentally (or implicitly) concerned with what ought to be done about economic and social conditions. Yet most economists have decided views as to what the law ought to be with respect to such conditions, and properly so. Economics as a social science frequently furnishes the data and inferences for a reasoned judgment as to what the law ought to be, though there is ordinarily a considerable leap between the economic materials and the evaluation as implemented in law.[9]

---

[6] The Anglo-American legal doctrine of consideration fits the human propensity to barter. I, Ch. 2.

[7] Brinkmann in (1931) 5 Encyc. of Soc. Sci. 381–385.

[8] Aristotle, Nichomachean Ethics, 1130b–1131b; Dewey and Tufts, Ethics (rev. ed., 1932).

[9] E. g., the fair rate of return in public utility regulation. See R. L. Hale, "Economics and Law" in Ogden and Goldenweiser, The Social Sciences (1927), 131; Cohen and Cohen, 853.

§ 1.23—Sociology

Though conceivably broad enough to include all the social sciences, sociology is in practice the residuary legatee of the others. For example, sociology deals with folkways, but not primarily with the folkways of economic organization—of industrial corporations and labor unions—nor yet of lawyers and governmental officials.[10] Sociologists study not only the folkways or habit patterns of men and groups in society, but also their attitudes on moral questions, the *mores* of the society or social group. Sumner's "Folkways" is a classical example. Thus sociology is not concerned merely with external behavior; it is also concerned with evaluations. Yet it is only concerned with them as things that occur, not with their rightness or wrongness. Sociologists, even more than political scientists or economists, insist upon rigorous objectivity of method; the observer's personal biases or evaluations must not becloud his data. Still, the criteria by which the sociologist selects the problems and the data of his inquiry are ordinarily related to some *possible* realms of value. In studying crime the sociologist accepts as "criminal" whatever is made criminal by the laws of the society being studied.[11] It was surely no lucky accident that led sociologists to study the incidence, types and causes of crime, nor that those studies have had considerable influence upon the criminal law and its administration. The theory that some criminals are partly products of bad social environments was a significant contribution of sociology to the materials of law-making, especially to the creation of juvenile courts. Of scarcely less importance are sociological studies of marriage, divorce, family disorganization and illegitimacy. Sociology builds upon institutions of the legal order, and in turn helps to build them.

§ 1.24—Social Psychology

Social psychology is a discipline which adapts some of the methods of psychology and of sociology to the mental aspects of human life in society. In most sociological studies the mental elements in human conduct—motivations, beliefs, the inertia of habits—were taken into account implicitly, if not explicitly. William Graham Sumner (1840–1910), an eminent Yale sociologist who was also a rector of the Protestant Episcopal Church, de-

---

[10] Bain in (1939) 4 Amer.Soc.Rev. 561–562.

[11] See Boaz, Anthropology and Modern Life (1928), 123.

veloped the conception of the mores as the moral cement of mature society:

> "The mores are the folkways, including the philosophical and ethical generalizations as to social welfare which are suggested by them and inherent in them, as they grow." [12]

The conception of the mores of society became a basic one in the thinking of many American legal scholars, notably Professors Arthur Corbin and Karl Llewellyn. Corbin's remarkably profound treatise on the law of contracts (1951) is permeated with the view that the contract as an institutional device and the law of contracts, as a prediction of how courts will act (§ 2.20), function in a social medium of which the mores are an essential part. The proposed Uniform Commercial Code of which Llewellyn was the chief draftsman and protagonist continuously assumes that the legal standard of interpretation of commercial contracts shall be the mores of the merchants. Such an interpretation might, of course, be contrary to the mores of some larger competing class or group—such as the disorganized and partly inarticulate consumers—or to the preponderance of social interests (§ 4.61) in the community. Any transaction may be considered in its immediate social context and also in an increasingly wider circle of such contexts.

The legal scholar who seeks aid from social psychology will find in it a bewildering variety of subject matter, methods and terminology, with an encouraging trend toward greater unity and originality in the more recent studies and treatises. John Dewey's well known book on Human Nature and Conduct (1922) was sub-titled: "An Introduction to Social Psychology". It stressed the roles of habit, impulse and intelligence in human conduct in society. The individual "can't help" acquiring habits and attitudes, just as he acquires speech; the role of intelligence is to select and foster good habits. Dewey's book cited no statistical summaries, proposed no experimental methods, employed no novel terminology. That it is now regarded as a book on philosophy rather than on the subject of its sub-title is indicated by the absence of any reference to it in recent treatises on social psychology. Professor Floyd Allport's textbook of 1924,[13] a pioneer work

---

[12] Sumner, Folkways (1906), 17. Sumner was not only an influential sociologist but also, as a follower of Spencer, of significance in American philosophy. Schneider, A History of American Philosophy (1946) 382, 431. On the influence of Sumner's social philosophy, see Cahill, Judicial Legislation (1952) 23.

[13] Allport, Social Psychology (1924).

still referred to, stressed the physiological basis of human conduct as fundamental for its social interpretation. Social psychology studies the individual's behavior regarded either as a stimulus of or a response to the behavior of others; it also studies the *consciousness* of the individual in so far as it relates to social objects and reactions.[14] This conception does not limit the study to the methods of behaviorist psychology. The consciousness of the individual, his social attitudes and inner motivations, as well as his external stimuli, seem to be increasingly the concern of social psychology. Allport's book stressed the distinction between the *somatic* and *visceral* parts of the body, the neural connections of which were supplied by the cerebrospinal and the autonomic nervous systems, respectively. The former corresponds roughly to the intellectual activities; the latter is more directly associated with feeling, emotion and personality.[15] This information sustained the nineteenth century division of psychic functions into the intellect and the emotions; yet since the two nervous systems are not independent of each other, since the basic drives of hunger and sex, the deeper emotions of fear and hatred and anger, *may* neurally affect the cerebrospinal processes called "intellectual" or "rational" (the assumption being that there is, physiologically, no neural wall between them), the realist view of the 1920's was that a judge's decisions are determined by hunches and, on some occasions, rationalized by an opinion which comes as an afterthought (§ 4.64, 5.06). While this position seems to have been substantially overstated, its influence upon the political developments of the 1930's, especially on the selection of judicial personnel, was of considerable importance.

A more recent sampling of leading textbooks on social psychology shows that the physiological basis of behavior, while assumed, is no longer emphasized. Here we can merely give some suggestions as to what the law-trained specialists (the jurisprudent and the legal sociologist) may expect to glean. One recent treatise emphasizes the analogies between animal and human group behavior. The in-group feelings of hostility toward outsiders, as are found among ants and chimpanzees,[16] have significant analogues

---

14 Ibid., 12.

15 Ibid., 31–37.

16 Klineberg, Social Psychology (1940) 20. Another recent book employs as its chief method an exploration of conduct and attitudes in primitive communities (the Comanches, the Alorese of the Dutch East Indies) and a typical American town. Kardiner and others, The Psychological Frontiers of Society (1945).

in human families, tribes and nations. Another significance in method is the dependence of this book on the anthropology of primitive peoples. A second treatise contributes a systematic analysis of social phenomena into three levels: (a) The social behavior of the individual; (b) the behavior of social groups; (c) the operation of social organizations and institutions.[17] The third level which is the level of customs, rules and laws, is primarily the concern of the sociologist. The first is taken as the primary concern of the social psychologist, with the needs and goals of the individual taken to be the unit of motivational analysis.[18] This analysis leaves no place in the chimney-corner for that wraith of nineteenth century legal and political theory, the "group mind" or "group will".[19] At the same time the significant contribution of the older theory, that a socially interacting group of individuals *is* more than the aggregate of its members [20] receives appropriate recognition in the conception of "group dynamics".[21] One more suggestive view is that the individual man has a basic need for clarification which makes the search for facts an outstanding feature of his mental life. The *effort* to be rational is a basic character of mental processes, and even the contradictory beliefs and attitudes which the same person may carry around in his own peculiar logic-tight compartments are subjectively rational though objectively an outsider can detect or even prove their inconsistencies.[22] The tendency of men to rationalize is evidence of their inherent rationality (Cf. § 4.64, § 5.06). Still another interesting book on social psychology has valuable suggestions for the improvement of measurements of social attitudes by the question-and-answer method.[23] On the whole, social psychology has not been utilized in basic legal theory as much as it might have. Its

---

[17] Krech and Crutchfield, Theory and Problems of Social Psychology (1948) 13.

[18] Ibid., 30. This basic proposition, that man's conduct is (consciously or unconsciously) purposeful, seems related to the basic tenets of utilitarianism in legal philosophy. See infra, Ch. 16.

[19] Ibid., 20.

[20] See Laski (Harold), "The Personality of Associations", (1916) 29 Harvard L.Rev. 404, 415, 423.

[21] Supra, n. 17, at page 18.

[22] Ibid., 168–69.

[23] Newcomb, Social Psychology (1950), Ch. 5.

special techniques seem more valuable for political science than for jurisprudence as here delimited.[24]

§ 1.25—Anthropology

Anthropology is still primarily the science of human behavior in primitive societies although some studies of American communities are anthropological in methods. Eschewing the romantic generalizations about noble savages made by earlier writers, anthropologists of the generation just past have adhered to a rigorous technique of observation and reporting. The product of this cautious procedure has been a voluminous literature of (often fascinating) descriptions of the habit patterns, institutions and attitudes of innumerable primitive or barbaric tribes, with very little generalization about man. (I omit here anthropometrics, the measurement of man's anatomical characteristics.) This does not mean that anthropology is sterile; it reveals the diversities of human culture and man's amazing adaptability to widely differing material and cultural environments. This revelation has profound significance for the development of law and legal institutions (as well as other social institutions) in an advanced ("civilized") society: Those who fear that certain social changes will be disastrous because "contrary to human nature" frequently give human nature an inflexibility which is belied by anthropology. Moreover, studies of primitive societies furnish clues to the origins of the social institutions of a civilized society. For instance, the widespread prevalence among primitive tribes of exogamy, the custom which prohibits a man from marrying a woman of his own tribe, suggests the partly conventional character of some of our legal prohibitions against intermarriage by persons of certain degrees of consanguinity. Again, the efficacy of informal social pressures—ridicule, taboo and the like—in maintaining conformity to customary norms in small primitive tribes, without the use of force, shows that law in civilized societies exerts control through other means than by force, and suggests that the greater reliance on force in civilized societies may be due to the greater complexity of a civilized society and the greater demands which it imposes on its members.[25] A third example, already mentioned (§ 1.24) is the "in-group" attitude, the attitude that "our

---

[24] An interesting analysis of the "lawless" attitudes of American (U.S.A.) citizens based on the dispersal of power is given in Hurst, "Law and the Balance of Power in the Community", (1950) 22 Okla.B.A.J. 1223.

[25] See Llewellyn and Hoebel, The Cheyenne Way (1941), 239.

people" are better people than all others, which helps us to set sober limits to our conceptions of patriotism and nationalism. Thus anthropology furnishes the cynical acid in which to wash some of the cherished attitudes and prejudices of a civilized society.

But on the constructive side anthropology has much less to offer to law and to jurisprudence than the other three social sciences above mentioned. Our law-makers (by which is meant adjudicators as well as legislators) rarely, if ever, get from it materials directly relevant to the content of specific laws. For instance, it is interesting to know that among the Cheyenne Indians a husband could divorce his wife "on the drum," a public ceremony, "even without important cause." [26] Yet surely this does not go to show that a similar harsh and primitive practice should be established in civilized societies, even in Nevada. Again, to show that conventional exogamous rules have among primitive tribes greatly extended the scope of the taboos on intermarriage among members of a social group does not show that the more limited prohibitions of civilized societies on intermarriage between close relatives do not have biological, cultural and moral justification. Nor does the exposure of the "in-group" fallacy as the motivation of aggressive attempts to dominate other peoples negate the justification of patriotism and national loyalties as means of self-protection in a world which has not attained the homogeneity that some anthropologists love to dream about. The showing that some of our ideas about human nature are more limited than the evidence warrants does not support the conclusion that human nature is of unlimited flexibility over any period of time, much less that it will bear any kind of social change tomorrow. The gravitational pull of anthropology upon the content of specific laws and legal institutions seems about as remote as that of philosophy.

———

The relations of law to the social sciences is a part of the subject matter of jurisprudence. One important aspect of the relations between the social sciences and jurisprudence is the development in the former of scientific methods which are adaptable to the development of an empirical science of law, or sociology of law. In detail these methods are too technical for discussion here. In gross they rest upon the methods of the physical sciences,

———

26 Ibid., 185.

which will be referred to in the next section. What has been said in this chapter may serve to correct, if not to refute, the casual remark recently made by an eminent philosopher:

"All the important inferences outside logic and pure mathematics are inductive, not deductive; the only exceptions are law and theology, each of which derives its first principles from an unquestionable text, viz. the statute books and the scriptures."[27]

§ 1.26—Relations of Jurisprudence to the Physical Sciences

The discoveries and methods of the physical sciences have had profound influences upon the development of jurisprudence during the past century. An analysis of these influences will clarify the scope of jurisprudence. The development of an industrial society has made the discoveries and techniques of the physical sciences increasingly relevant to the subject matter of laws and legal procedures. Thus expert testimony as to the formulas and experimental findings of physics, chemistry, etc., is often used in litigation involving the validity of patents or the performance of contracts. Such use of empirical scientific knowledge does not make law, or jurisprudence, an empirical science any more than the use of expert testimony about the genuineness of an alleged Rembrandt painting, in a law suit involving such an issue, makes law or jurisprudence a branch of the fine arts. Again, anatomy, toxicology, physiology and physiological chemistry have provided items of knowledge useful in the detection and proof of crime, and some findings of experimental psychology have been found generally useful in the analysis of forensic proof.[28] Through such borrowings judicial experience in shaping the rules of proof has been corrected and supplemented.[29] These examples do not make an empirical science of law; yet they point to the need for the formulation of laws in terms which make available in legal operations all forms of human knowledge. The recognition of this need is in itself an important contribution to jurisprudence.

A more pervasive influence has been the attempts to use in jurisprudence the methods of the physical sciences. This we may

---

[27] Russell, A History of Western Philosophy (1945), 199.

[28] See, for example, the recent biography of Sir Bernard Spilsbury, an expert witness in many famous murder cases. Browne and Tullett, The Scalpel of Scotland Yard (1952).

[29] This influence is shown, for instance, when one compares the earlier editions of Greenleaf on Evidence with Wigmore on Evidence.

call the use of the physical science analogy. This analogy was used by an earlier generation of jurisprudents to justify designating analytical jurisprudence, the classification and analysis of legal concepts and doctrines, as "the science of law" (§ 1.04). Such designations expressed more than merely yearnings to give jurisprudence an honorific title; they represented a persistent attempt to give legal concepts and doctrines the kind of operational clarity—what difference does it make in what lawyers and officials do?—that was characteristic of the rapidly developing physical sciences. Such writers as Holmes, Hohfeld, Corbin and Wigmore represent this trend at its best. Yet this aspect of the physical science analogy has a good deal in common with the analogy of grammar, the science of language, which Holland used as the basis of his analytical jurisprudence.[30] Any organized body of knowledge with a technical vocabulary has certain *logical* characteristics which, as we have already seen (§ 1.11) are possessed by a developed body of law. What Holmes et al. have added to this formal-logical science of law is the requirement that legal concepts and norms must have meanings in terms of operations to be performed. For instance, to say that A has a "legal right" against B is to say that a court will give judgment in favor of A against B under certain circumstances. Yet this clarification of terminology does not satisfy those who want to find an empirical basis for answering the question, why should A have a legal right against B under certain circumstances? Or who, discarding such traditional legalisms as "right" and "duty," want to build an empirical science of the regularities and irregularities of human conduct, official and non-official (§ 1.04). The physical science analogy thus has a *logical* and an *empirical* aspect.

The emotional drive to perfect law by analogy to the physical sciences was expressed by Judge Cardozo in opening his Carpentier lectures in 1927. As a judge of the Court of Appeals of New York he frequently passed by, in his travel between Albany and the city of New York, one or more of the great bridges across the Hudson River:

> " 'They do this thing better with logarithms.' The wail escapes me now and again when after putting forth the best that is in me, I look upon the finished product and cannot say that it is good. In these moments of disquietude, I figure to myself the peace of mind that must come, let us say, to the designer of a mighty bridge. The finished product of his

---

[30] See Holland, Jurisprudence (10th ed., 1906), 9.

work is there before his eyes with all the beauty and simplicity and inevitableness of truth. He is not harrowed by misgivings whether the towers and piers and cables will stand the stress and strain. His business is to know. If his bridge were to fall, he would go down with it in disgrace and ruin. Yet withal, he has never a fear. No mere experiment has he wrought, but a highway to carry men and women from shore to shore, to carry them secure and unafraid, though the floods rage and boil below.

" . . . My bridges are experiments. I cannot span the tiniest stream in a region unexplored by judges or law-givers before me, and go to rest in the secure belief that the span is wisely laid." [31]

Without depreciating the marvelous controls of the bridge designer over the inert materials of steel and concrete which go to make up the bridge, we may point out that Judge Cardozo has abstracted one aspect of the total process of getting a great bridge built, one means toward the end-in-view of providing a safe and convenient way across the river, for the satisfaction of human wants. Before the bridge can be built a host of political and economic and sociological questions must be in some fashion answered. What will the bridge cost? Is the expenditure of public money for this purpose justified in competition with other demands upon the public treasury? Or shall the bridge be a toll bridge, and, if so, what toll charge will produce the maximum revenue for the purpose of paying off the costs? Will people use the bridge in sufficient numbers to pay for it or to justify the expenditure of public funds, or will it prove to be an unused pile of steel and concrete signifying only the skill of bridge engineers? What effects will the building of the bridge have on population trends, upon urban overcrowding or suburban growth? What wages, what hours of labor, what provisions as to personal injuries, should be prescribed for the workers who are to fabricate the bridge? These are questions which the bridge designer does not answer; they are questions calling for the application of some social science techniques but more frequently for the exercise of expert practical judgments. The bridge designer's methods are only a part of the totality of methods involved in getting a bridge built.[32]

[31] Cardozo, The Paradoxes of Legal Science (1928), 1–2.

[32] Since the above was written the struggles of the Roeblings in building the Brooklyn Bridge have been depicted in The New Yorker.

The physical science analogy thus tends to distort the relative importance of the various parts of this totality of methods. The laws or propositions of mechanics take the physical universe in abstraction from human wants or claims. They express relations of mass, energy, etc., which are independent of human desires and indifferent to the good or bad results which may be obtained by their use. They serve as well in building machines of destruction and death as in building bridges and highways and housing projects. The physical sciences attain exactness by taking in abstraction the simpler, non-human aspects of objects and events. As precepts of practical action they gain precision at the expense of narrowness and incompleteness, which becomes apparent when we view them as a part of the total process. In so far as jurisprudence takes account of theories of value, of good or bad or of better and worse, it seems likely that jurisprudence can never attain the exactness, the precision of prediction and control, that is attained by excluding considerations of value.

Nevertheless, the physical science analogy holds a good many clues for jurisprudence: 1. It suggests, for instance, that law can be a more effective instrument of prediction and control if its propositions are framed in terms of concepts which refer to practical operations of testing and proof, or, to put it differently, concepts which have existential reference. The effort in law to find "working rules" rather than "paper rules" is an expression of this objective. In Parts II and III we have occasion to consider this aspect of legal propositions. 2. The physical science analogy likewise shows the advantages of formulating relations in terms of concepts which vary continuously in quantity, as a means of precision in adjustment of legal consequences to the facts of a litigated case. Examples are found in various rules of damages (e. g., the builder's measure of recovery for breach of contract) and the use in regulatory legislation of quantitatively measurable concepts (specified percentage of butter-fat in milk, building codes, forty-hour week, etc.) as critical boundaries between compliance and violation that have often facilitated the guidance-value of such laws both to officials and to the public. Along these lines much has been done in increasing the exactness of legal formulae. 3. Again, the analogy of the physical sciences reminds us as lawyers that propositions of law, like the formulae of physical science, have meaning in the context of the structure or system of propositions of which they form a part (see Part III). 4. Furthermore, while controlled experiments are seldom possible (cf. § 4.63) in the determination of the consequences of laws, yet conjectures as to these consequences can acquire greatly enhanced reliability from the results of careful observations of such relevant facts as are available. The use of economic and other social data in the framing of legislation is an instance of "scientific method" in this sense. Thus the physical science analogy brings fruitful suggestions for the improvement of law as an instrument of control.

Part II

WHAT IS LAW?

Chapter 4

BASIC MODES OF CHARACTERIZING LAW

§ 2.00—Why Clarify Our Notions of Law?

Before he has advanced very far in his understanding of general theories about law the student is likely to ask himself, "What is law?" The answer to this question will consist of the meaning or meanings of law, that is, an account of its essential or basic characteristics, as conceived by one or many jurisprudents. This Chapter will be chiefly devoted to exploring those basic modes of characterizing law which correspond to the three basic relations of law (§ 1.05): To the state (imperative conception, § 2.04), to its society (institutional conception, § 2.03) and to justice or other ethical ideals (§ 2.02). To these will be added a fourth, the social-control conception of law (§ 2.06). The remainder of Part II of this book will present some further explorations of the imperative conception of law as the one deemed by this author most nearly representative of the usages of the legal profession (in the United States and in England, at least) and the one best adapted to professional needs. The discussions of law as a generalization (Ch. 5), law as a norm or prescription (Ch. 6) and the authority and sanction of law (Ch. 7), topics that often occupy a dominant place in books on jurisprudence, have been condensed in order to permit a fuller exposition of the sources, forms and systemic relations of the law (Pt. III) and theories of what the law should be (Pt. IV).

Why should we attempt to clarify our notions of law? Are the results likely to be worth the effort, in view of the fact that professional lawyers, including judges and legislative draftsmen, get along nearly all of the time in their professional work without resorting to any formal definition of law and apparently without having in mind, explicit in their reasoning, any basic or necessary characteristics of law? An American lawyer can understand practically all that is said about the American law of evidence (in judicial or administrative trials) in Wigmore's huge treatise, or about the American law of contracts in Williston's large text, without finding in those works any definition of law, and without having any such definition in mind. Even though numerous authors contributed to the composite and highly formalized treatise on American law, the Restatement of Law, that work does not contain any definition of law applicable to all of its parts. It does, however, give for use in the Restatement of the Conflict of Laws [1] a definition of law which bears a close resemblance to that of John Chipman Gray (§ 2.05).

Courts in their opinions rarely give definitions of law, and when they do, the whole definition, read in relation to the facts of the litigation and the rest of the opinion, seems to me more ornamental than utilitarian.[2] If a legal issue *is* raised which touches the meaning of law, it is likely to be limited to a single *characteristic* of law and to a particular *context*. Thus constitutional and statutory provisions containing the word "law" are ordinarily interpreted in relation to the context, so that no general or "universal" conception of law is explicitly relied upon. An example is the American constitutional provision, "no state shall pass any law impairing the obligation of contracts".[3] This provision has been construed not to include "judge-made law", i. e., not to prevent a state's highest court from overruling its prior decisions in such a way as to declare invalid a contract made in reliance upon them.[4] The word "pass" qualified the word "law" so as to limit its scope to legislation. In addition to these arguments, the great difficulties of formulating a definition of law and adhering to it consistently, are shown by numerous previous attempts in the literature of jurisprudence.

On the contrary, the need for some general conception of law, or a limited number of conceptions, is shown by the decision last cited. Without some general conception of law which included legislation the Court could not have given any meaning to the Constitutional provision, "pass any law." For this line of reasoning it was not necessary to set forth all of the characteristics of

---

[1] Restatement, Conflict of Laws (Amer.Law Inst. 1934) p. 3.

[2] Collections of judicial characterizations may be found in Bouvier's Law Dictionary (1914) and in Words and Phrases (West Publishing Co., 1940), sub. tit. "Law."

[3] U. S. Const., Art. I, sec. 10.

[4] Fleming v. Fleming, 264 U.S. 29, 44 Sup.Ct. 246 (1924). The opinion of the Court, by Taft, C. J., added that courts do not make law but merely correct erroneous interpretations of it.

law—a complete definition of "law". If the Court had done so it might have found that the generalization laid down by the Iowa court in its prior decision was relied upon in drafting the contract there involved, and that the expectation thus created was intended to be protected by the Constitution against impairment by state action, legislative or judicial. At least the advantages and disadvantages of such a construction might have been explored.

The reasons for exploring the meanings of law are deeper than this. By clarifying our ideas about any basic notion or conception we make or discover basic distinctions that improve our understanding of its relations to other things [5] and we add to our instruments of intellectual control over problematic situations of which it is a part. For a systematic treatise on jurisprudence a definition or a set of definitions of law is desirable both logically [6] and as a means of communication. In fact many jurisprudents through the centuries have speculated upon the nature or meaning of law and their definitions or partial characterizations have been collected and classified.[7] This book, like the ones just cited, is intended to aid the unsophisticated in understanding both classic and contemporary writings on jurisprudence; in these the meanings of law shift not only from author to author but also frequently within the same author's writings. A guide to the museum specimens will help one later to recognize the live animals. Some recent writers on jurisprudence have emphasized the importance of attaining a clear conception of law.[8] Others have omitted a definition or have avoided the use of "law".[9] A fairly clear conception of law is important in communications between the lawyers of one nation and another, and for communication in the international community.

---

[5] Cohen (M. R.), "Should Legal Thought Abandon Clear Distinctions?" (1941) 36 Ill.L.Rev. 239, reviewing Fuller, The Law in Quest of Itself (1940).

[6] I. e., the fewer undefined basic terms, the clearer the argument.

[7] See Pound, Outlines of Lectures on Jurisprudence (5th ed., 1943), 60–73; Holland, Jurisprudence (13th ed., 1924), Chs. II–IV.

[8] See Goodhart (A. L.), "The Importance of a Definition of Law" (1951) 3 Jour.African Admin. 106; King (B. E.), "The Concept of a Lawyer's Jurisprudence" (1952) 11 Cambridge L.J. 229; and the carefully reasoned critique of Prof. Alf Ross, Towards a Realistic Jurisprudence (1946).

[9] Stone, The Province and Function of Law (1946) gives no definition, and Judge Frank, in Courts on Trial (1949) has avoided wherever possible the use of "law". See ibid., 67. Since he uses the derivative, "legal", quite freely in this book, it is not clear what he gains by this maneuver.

Two formal distinctions here will serve to clarify the ensuing discussion. One is between a formal definition and an informal (partial) characterization of a thing. A formal definition includes everything to which the term defined refers and nothing else: It states a relation of logical equivalence. Holland's formal definition of law,

> "[A law is] a general rule of external human action enforced by a sovereign political authority." [10]

is equivalent to (impliedly asserts):

> "Any general rule of external human action enforced by a sovereign political authority is a law."

On the other hand, Aristotle's famous informal characterization of law,

> "Law is reason without desire." [11]

is not reversible, for it does not imply that

> "Anything which is reason without desire is law."

since mathematics, for example, is reason without desire.

A definition is a statement of all of the necessary characteristics of the thing being defined. Since many statements about law give some of its necessary attributes without purporting to be complete, one must take account of such informal characterizations.

But what characteristics are "necessary"? This leads us to outline three kinds of definitions:

1. *Nominal,* one chosen for use in a particular book, or in a particular statute. A purpose of the discussion in this chapter is to indicate the meaning of "law" which will be as consistently as possible adhered to in this book, unless a different meaning is indicated. It is sometimes said that a nominal definition is "arbitrary"; that is true in the sense that it implies a *resolution* to use the word in a particular way chosen by the definer; yet it will not serve its purpose, i. e., to communicate to others, unless it corresponds in part to conventional meanings.

2. *Conventional,* one dependent upon the meaning or meanings of a word in common usage. A definition states the characteristics which a thing must have in order to qualify as a member of the class defined. These necessary characteristics may be called the connotation of the term or its *intension.* When the definition prescribes the characteristics commonly regarded as necessary by

---

10 Holland, Jurisprudence (10th ed., 1906), 40.

11 Aristotle, Politics, Bk. III, Ch. XVII (Everyman ed., p. 101); Hall, 6.

people who use the term, the definition constitutes the *convention-al intension* of the term.[12] An unabridged dictionary gives several conventional meanings of the term, "law". By this test one who uses law in any of the given senses cannot be convicted of ignorant or capricious diction.

3. *Real,* a statement of the *essential* attributes of the *thing it-self,* as it is and must be. According to this view, there can be only one true definition. Law, for instance, is a class that be-longs to a larger class, a genus, and has, besides the essential at-tributes of the genus, the attributes that differentiate it from oth-er species of the genus. This metaphysical presupposition, which seems to have been useful in classifying and defining plants and animals, seems no longer acceptable [13] and at any rate is not use-fully applicable to define "law"; no one has discovered a one and only true definition of "law", beside which all others are false. Yet the notion of a real definition as a *preferable* one for most contexts or for a particular context, is inescapable; usage of traditional terms probably never provides a single clear mean-ing, and when a choice is made between conventional meanings, it is governed by reasons derived from a conception of the most important attributes, functions or other relations of the thing.[14] By this criterion the present writer has chosen the three basic modes of characterizing law (supra).

Since any definition of a term must use other terms, and since any definition of those terms must use still others, any definition must consist ultimately of undefined terms; and the effectiveness of the definition in conveying meaning, at least initially,[15] will depend upon the familiarity in conventional usage of the mean-ings of its constituent terms. Now conventional meanings are

---

12 Cohen and Nagel, op. cit., 30–32. Some logicians distinguish connotation from intension.

13 See Dewey, Logic (1938), 137–138.

14 In a recent careful formal analysis of political science, a "real" defini-tion is said to be one intended to "clarify established usage." Lasswell and Kaplan, Power and Society (1950), xix–xx. Clarification here seems designed to provide the *best* meaning for the author's linguistic system. To say that such a choice is "merely verbal" seems erroneous, though it is not merely factual. Cf. Williams (Glanville) "The Controversy Concerning the Word Law" (1949) 38 Archiv. für Rechts-und Sozialphilosophie 50, 59.

15 A novel term in a context of conventionally familiar terms gradually acquires meaning. E. g., Bentham's "real evidence" was an innovation of the early 1800's which had become familiar to the legal profession when, a century later, Wigmore introduced his jawbreaker, "autoptic proference".

often fluid meanderings; for the construction of a scientific linguistic system (§ 3.21) one needs unity and coherence. Hence a good scientific definition is partly nominal, partly conventional and partly real.

One logical risk of making a formal definition of law is the danger of circularity: The defining terms should not repeat, nor require that one know the meaning of, the term being defined. Thus if one purports to define a law:

"A law is a legal rule,"

the word "legal" is in turn defined as "pertaining to law". Yet the statement is not wholly meaningless, for "rule" is more inclusive than "law" and thus the meaning of law is partly explained. Another example is to be found in the numerous definitions of law in terms of "courts" or "judicial decisions":

"Law means the rules recognized and acted on in courts of justice.[16]"

An able Danish legal dialectician has recently made the point that all such definitions of law are circular, since a court (the kind of court required by the definition) is created by, and identifiable only by recognizing what is, law.[17] Indeed, it may be doubted that an imperative or positive definition of law can be made that will not incur this fault; for can one define "sovereignty" or "state" without reference to law? Yet if one leaves out dependence upon the state or the government, how does one distinguish law from moral rules, church rules, school rules, factory rules and others? This query applies to Professor Goodhart's proposal:

"I define law as any rule of human conduct which is recognized as being obligatory."[18]

In conclusion, circularity is not the worst defect of a definition of law in a book on jurisprudence. For it is not intended to enable a man from Mars to identify infallibly all things that are law and none others, the very moment he lands on this planet. Rather it is intended to present a reasoned analysis of the meanings of law for those who are already familiar with unquestioned instances of it, and of its effects.

---

[16] Salmond, Jurisprudence (1902) § 5; (7th ed., 1924) § 15. The latter was the last edition by the author.

[17] Ross, op. cit. supra n. 8, 59–70.

[18] Goodhart, op. cit. supra, n. 8, 109.

§ 2.01—Distinctions in Meanings: "Law", "a law", "the law", "the legal system", "the legal order"

The term "law" has been frequently defined or characterized in such a way that it clearly means *a* law, that is, a specimen or individual of the class, law. From the Greek Anaximenes of the sixth century B.C. Aristotle quoted:

> "Law is a definite statement according to a common agreement of the state warning how everything ought to be done." [19]

Blackstone's definition nourished several generations of American lawyers:

> "Municipal law [i. e., excluding the law of nations] is properly defined to be 'a rule of civil conduct prescribed by the supreme power in a state, commanding what is right and prohibiting what is wrong.' " [20]

Likewise, John Austin defines "law" as a "command". Thomas Aquinas gives a definition in terms of *"an* ordinance of reason" (infra, § 4.13), etc.

To this mode of defining law, commonly used by English writers of the nineteenth century, several objections have been raised, chiefly by the New Zealand jurist, Salmond, and by the late Professor Beale of Harvard.[21] One is that such a definition refers to a statutory law but not to a rule or principle of case law. Since the latter are quite commonly stated by lawyers in their briefs, by courts in their opinions and by text-writers, it seems that both kinds of rules are continually isolated for particular purposes and the qualifications imposed by the definition can be applied to any one such item. Take, for example, the statement:—

> "The donor can revoke his gift and obtain restitution of the thing given if the donee is subsequently guilty of gross ingratitude by seriously wrongful conduct toward the donor or a close relative."

One can show that this qualifies as law under the German Civil Code,[22] perhaps under the late Roman law, but one cannot (as I write) show that it so qualifies in New York. A second objection is that in professional usage lawyers do not speak of a rule of

---

[19] Pound, Outlines, 60–61.

[20] 1 Blackstone, Commentaries, 44.

[21] Beale, A Treatise on the Conflict of Laws (1935), §§ 3, 4 (Hall, 411) quoting Salmond, Jurisprudence (4th ed.) 10.

[22] § 530(1) is substantially the same.

case law as "a law". That usage, I suspect, goes back to a time when the common law was conceived to be the "unwritten law", or the "custom of the realm" or some other mystery; legal rules and principles were merely emanations or expressions of the invisible law. Still, it is a disadvantage to use language in a sense contrary to even a wrongly established usage. The third objection is that in defining "a law" one overlooks the totality or system of laws. This is a weighty objection, since neither as to a statutory law, nor as to a case law can one either ascertain its validity (i. e., its legality) or its meaning without reference to other laws, such as those prescribing the authority of officials or those prescribing remedies for violations. Still, "a law", meaning a statement or proposition of law can be isolated in thought from the residue of its system, without implying that it is in operation self-sufficient.

Some able writers have defined "law" as an aggregate of "a laws":—

"The sum of the rules administered by courts of justice."[23]

"The ensemble of precepts, rules or statutes which govern human activity in society, the observance whereof is sanctioned in case of need by social constraint, otherwise called public force." [24]

This aggregate of laws of any particular state I shall call "the law". Since a law in isolation from the system of which it is a part is incomplete and since I believe that all bodies of law of advanced societies (at least in the West) have a systemic character, "the legal system" will be used to designate such a body. Still, being systematic, like being rational and being just, are attributes of *good* laws but not necessarily of all laws. Since some laws are bad, or rather since people will disagree as to their goodness or badness, it seems preferable in our analysis to differentiate validity from goodness.

Sometimes "law" is used in its *total comprehension*, including not only its meaning in common usage but also the things associated with it, including the officials by which law is made and enforced, what they do under the law, even what laymen do under the law. This comprehensive conception will have to be broken down when one wants to ask, for instance, did this official act lawfully or unlawfully? Still the inveterate tendency to personi-

---

[23] Pollock & Maitland, History of English Law (1st ed., 1895), Introduction, XXV.

[24] 1 Colin et Capitant, Droit civil francais (1914) 1, defining "droit".

fy "the law", to speak of it as commanding or prohibiting, as having purposes and exercising coercion, makes some such usage occasionally inevitable. To designate the law and its institutions of enforcement, the Germans invented and Pound has adapted a useful term, "the legal order":

> "The legal order (Rechtsordnung) is an adjustment through coercion of the relations of human life arising in a social manner from the social nature of man." [25]

> ". . . the legal order, one meaning of 'law' in the lawyer's sense, that is, a régime of adjusting relations and ordering conduct by systematic and orderly application of the force of a politically organized society." [26]

A word of caution for students of European law and legal philosophies is this: The legal systems of Western Europe which were derived from Roman law have two words to designate what we call "law"; one of these words means both law and right, ordinarily legal right [27] but with an undefinable overtone of ethical rightness or justice; the other means statute-law. The two words are, in Latin "jus" and "lex"; in French, "droit" and "loi"; in Italian, "diritto" and "legge", in German, "recht" and "gesetz", in Spanish, "derecho" and "ley". Kelsen's somewhat rigid system of pure legal norms (§ 2.05, § 3.22) came as a welcome clarification of this confusing terminology to some European and South American jurists but was rejected by others because it took no account of ethical influences upon law-making.

§ 2.02—Ideal Conceptions of Law

An "ideal" conception of law (as that term is here used) is one which defines or characterizes law by requiring that it conform to certain ideal standards in order to be qualified for admission to the class, law. One who adopts this conception does not merely say that every law *ought* to be just or good according to my standards; he in effect asserts that any rule or enactment which does

---

25 Kohler, Einführung in die Rechtswissenschaft (1902), § 1 (trans. Pound, Outlines, 70).

26 Pound, The Task of the Law (1944), 43. For his earlier uses of the term, see An Introduction to the Philosophy of Law (1922) 20; Interpretations of Legal History (1923) 156; The Formative Era in American Law (1938) 13, 60; Outlines, 60.

27 However, when an equivalent for English "legal right" is sought, the adjective "subjective" is commonly used. Some writers have denied the "existence" of subjective right ("droit subjectif"). For a recent scholarly discussion of the question, see Dabin, Le droit subjectif (Paris, 1952), Ch. I.

not so conform is unworthy to be deemed law, and therefore is not law. Since this conception of law is most often used rhetorically, some passages from the famous Roman orator, Cicero, are chosen to exemplify it:

"Law [lex] is the highest reason, implanted in nature, which commands what ought to be done and forbids the opposite." [28]

Now "reason", which has here an ethical meaning (§ 4.12) is always praiseworthy. So what does Cicero do when confronted with an enactment, otherwise "law", which is not praiseworthy? He can either say it is not "law", or he can modify his terminology and say it is not "true law" or not "good law". He chooses the latter course:

"But since our whole discussion has to do with the reasoning of the populace, it will sometimes be necessary to speak in the popular manner, and give the name of law to that which in written form decrees whatever it wishes, either by command or prohibition. For such is the crowd's definition of law. But in determining what Justice is, let us begin with that supreme law which had its origin ages before any written law existed or any State had been established." [29]

"But in fact we can perceive the difference between good laws and bad by referring them to no other standard than Nature. . . ." [30]

"For every law which really deserves that name is truly praiseworthy . . . ".[31]

Popular usage, then, led him to recognize as laws some things that were not truly praiseworthy.

Another ideal conception is, apparently, that of Blackstone:—

"A rule of civil conduct, prescribed by the supreme power in a state, commanding what is right and prohibiting what is wrong." [32]

---

[28] Cicero, De Legibus, Bk. I, VI (Loeb Classical Library ed., trans. by C. W. Keyes, 1928), 317; Hall, 19; Cohen and Cohen, 376. Note that Cicero uses "lex" rather than "jus", which he employed in the same passage to mean "justice". For further discussion of Cicero's philosophy, see infra, § 4.12.

[29] Ibid.

[30] Ibid., Bk. I, XVI, 347; Hall, 21.

[31] Ibid., Bk. II, V, p. 383; Hall, 22.

[32] Supra, § 2.01, n. 20.

From the context of Blackstone's discussion it appears that he used "right" and "wrong" in an ethical sense, from which it could be argued that a rule prohibiting what is ethically right could not be a law. However, Blackstone did not, as far as I know, argue this way; he usually approved of all rules of English law as he found them. The ideal conception of law can be used to justify all existing laws, for if it means:—

All laws are ethically just rules,

then one can characterize some disputed enactment:

This enactment is a law.

Therefore this enactment is ethically just.

On other occasions, however, one can argue:—

This enactment is not ethically just.

Therefore this enactment is not a law.

This bit of logical analysis helps to explain why theories of natural law have sometimes been used conservatively and sometimes to justify legal change.[33]

Ideal conceptions of law are thus objectionable in that they either lead to undue complacency with laws as they are, or set up an extra-legal standard by which laws may be pronounced invalid. This extra-legal standard of valuation is either the individual conscience of every official and every citizen, which is anarchic in tendency, or is the voice of some external human authority, in which case the real rulers of the people are not their elected representatives. Of course it is quite different to use ethical arguments in persuading law-makers that a law ought to be changed.

A definition or characterization of law which merely says that it *ought* to be directed toward some ideal end or ends is not open to these same objections. The German philosopher, Immanuel Kant (§§ 4.20–4.22) presented the following conception of law (Recht):

"The sum of the circumstances according to which the will of one may be reconciled with the will of another according to a common rule of freedom." [34]

This is a statement of an ideal *end* which law ought to have, a criterion of its rightness, rather than a touchstone of its validity. A more recent statement of the same ideal, but with realistic in-

---

33 See further discussion, infra, § 4.17.

34 Kant, Philosophy of Law (1797) in Pound, Outlines, 65. See infra, § 4.22.

sight into the antinomy between law and liberty, was contained in the "Declaration of Legal Faith" of the late Wiley Rutledge, Associate Justice of the United States Supreme Court:

"I believe in law. At the same time I believe in freedom. And I know that each of these things may destroy the other. But I know, too, that, without both, neither can long endure." [35]

The law always aims to be just, said the late Gustav Radbruch. A court may always properly presume that the legislature had some beneficent intention in mind. Thus ideal conceptions of law play a part in the process of interpretation; yet the presumption is always rebuttable. In certain borderline cases, where it becomes necessary to distinguish between a law and a rule of a private power-holder (§ 2.33), it is advisable to consider that the end of the law is the public good, while this need not necessarily be so of the other rule.

§ 2.03—Institutional Conceptions of Law

By an "institutional conception" of law is meant one which treats the dependence of law upon the institutions of the society in which it operates as so fundamental that the reality of law is to be identified with those institutions or with some aspect of them. "Institution", as used here, includes not only organizations of people co-operating for common purposes (a family, a church, a school, a private corporation, a labor union) but also customs, regularities of behavior believed to be right or proper in a group, and mores, the mental attitudes, common to many people, about human conduct. Here we define "institution" rather broadly and "institutional conception" rather narrowly, in order to exclude those writers among the sociologists who accept the professional (imperative) conception of law and discuss the relations of law to the functioning of society as a whole. The social-control conception of law (§ 2.06) is thus differentiated from the identification of law with social institutions.

Institutional conceptions of law are very old, if not the oldest. The historical records of ancient societies and the anthropologists' studies of extant primitive societies indicate that customs, usages and mores produced effects in those societies which were comparable to the effects of laws in modern societies. These may be called "customary law", as Maine and many others have done; but it seems preferable to treat them here as precursors of law,

---

[35] Quoted in the memorial proceedings, 71 Sup.Ct. xxvii (1951).

which became differentiated from customs and mores only with the development of the political state.[36] The belief that established customs are inherently right is probably the oldest conception of right known to mankind. A custom is not merely a regularity or pattern of human behavior; it is such a regularity or pattern accompanied by a more or less conscious belief that the pattern is right and ought to be followed. Whenever a non-conformist challenges such a pattern of conduct, belief in its rightness becomes conscious and articulate. For example, the custom of the queue, or line-up, prescribes that each person who comes to be served at a ticket-window should take his place in line behind the persons already there. A long line may be formed by imitation and habit. But let some non-conformist try to horn in ahead of those who arrived earlier, and the belief in the rightness of the custom becomes conscious and even vociferous. Customs play an important part in modern societies:

> "But always and everywhere customs supply the standards for personal activities. . . . Every habit creates an unconscious expectation. . . . A habit, a routine habit, when interfered with generates uneasiness, sets up a protest in favor of restoration and a sense of need of some expiatory act. . . ."[37]

Historical Conception

The attitude or belief, common to the members of a social group, that certain patterns of conduct are right or wrong is one source of the material content of law (§§ 3.15, 3.16). Savigny, the leader of the German historical school, advanced the view that the common conviction of right, "the kindred consciousness of an inward necessity," the popular spirit (Volksgeist), gave to the law of a national society its peculiar national characteristics; law, language and manners were inseparably united.[38] And while law develops as a specialized discipline in the hands of the jurists, it does not cease to be "part of the aggregate existence of the community."[39] This romantic conception of law, which became even

---

[36] Such is the view consistently taken by Prof. Robert M. MacIver in Society: Its Structures and Changes (1931) 251–4, 272–7; The Modern State (1926). The English sociologist, Hobhouse, accepted a positivist conception of law. See Cairns, Law and the Social Sciences (1935), 148–49.

[37] Dewey, Human Nature and Conduct (1922), 75–76.

[38] Savigny, Of the Vocation of Our Age for Legislation and Jurisprudence (Hayward trans., 1831), 24. This little book was first published in 1814.

[39] Ibid., 28; Hall, 88.

more mystical with some of Savigny's followers,[40] had some influence on legal thought in England and the United States. Since it eventuated in a theory of what law ought to be, it will be discussed more fully later (§§ 4.31–4.33).

Sociological Conception

Where the historical school conceived of a nation's law as tied to the primitive consciousness of its people, the sociological conception of law located the real law in the present-day institutions of its society. The most influential statement of this view was put forth by Ehrlich.

Eugen Ehrlich (1862–1922) was born in Czernowitz in the duchy of Bukowina, which was then a part of Austro-Hungary but was later transferred to Rumania. Ehrlich received his doctorate in law from the University of Vienna, and in 1897 returned to his native city as professor of Roman law at the University of Czernowitz. While investigating the situations in which silence would be deemed to constitute an acceptance of an offer [41] he became interested in the factual situations rather than in the judicial decisions, and was thus convinced of the important part played by legal documents in the commercial life of the community. From this he was led to his conception of the Living Law of a community:

> "This then is the *living* law in contradistinction to that which is being enforced in the courts and other tribunals. The living law is the law which dominates life itself even though it has not been posited in legal propositions. The source of our knowledge of this law is, first, the modern legal document; secondly, direct observation of life, of commerce, of customs and usages, and of all associations, not only of those that the law has recognized but also of those that it has overlooked and passed by, indeed even of those it has disapproved." [42]

This passage sketches the sociological *method* which Ehrlich sought to apply in his studies of the family customs of the peas-

---

[40] See Puchta, Outlines of Jurisprudence as the Science of Right (Hastie trans., 1887) 26, 30–32, 57–58; Hall, 89–91. Usage merely externalizes the Right (Law) which "has arisen and is living in the members of the people." Ibid., 38–39; Hall, 91.

[41] Ehrlich, Die stillschweigende Willenserklärung (1893).

[42] Ehrlich, Fundamental Principles of the Sociology of Law (Moll trans., Harvard Univ. Press, 1936) 493. The original work was Grundlegung der Soziologie des Rechts (1913).

ants of Bukowina. Under the same concise and broad provisions of the Austrian Civil Code (of 1811) one might find a wide variety of practices with respect to marital property rights and the like.[43] The code provision was merely a shell that was filled in by the varying content of Living Law. In his last article, intended for American publication, Ehrlich argued that the Social Order in different countries rests upon certain fundamental social institutions: Marriage, family, possession, contract and succession (to property after the death of the owner), and that in these institutions, which (he said) are substantially the same in all countries, we find a worldwide law. In contrast with the Living Law is the Legal Provision, an instruction addressed to a court or an administrative official as to how to deal with a particular case. In the early stages of social development—among the Germans when Tacitus wrote about them—there were social institutions but few Legal Provisions. In a later stage, when the Legal Provisions have been embodied in numerous codes, it may seem to the jurist that they embrace everything.

"But life's content is even richer. To embrace the whole variegated body of human activities in Legal Provisions is about as sensible as trying to catch a stream and hold it in a pond; the part that may be caught is no longer a living stream but a stagnant pool—and a great deal cannot be caught at all." [44]

When Ehrlich began to develop his theory of Living Law in the early part of this century there were doubtless lawyers and judges in Austria and in Europe, as there were in the United States, who believed that individuals in society were governed by the law-in-books with which these jurists were familiar (§ 2.30). They needed to be reminded that law is only one means of social control. But it was wholly unnecessary to call these extra-legal controls by the name of "law", much less "Living Law". How many dramas and romances, from the Age of Pericles down to the latest cinema, have been based upon the struggles of young lovers or youthful adventurers against the dead hand of custom, of the very institutions that Ehrlich deems vital? Ehrlich's conception of Living Law was a useful rhetorical device to call attention to his real contribution, the sociological method of inquiry into the

---

43 An account of Ehrlich's studies of living law was given by Prof. W. H. Page (Wisconsin) before the Association of American Law Schools in 1914 (Proc., p. 46), partly reprinted in Hall, 825.

44 Ehrlich, "The Sociology of Law" (trans. by Nathan Isaacs, 1922), 36 Harvard L.Rev. 130, 133; Hall, 815.

grounds for the making and interpretation of law. In this he had marked influence on Pound's sociological jurisprudence (§ 4.60) and upon some phases of American legal realism (§ 4.63).

His conception of Living Law was naïve in several respects. He blandly overlooked the differences in social institutions in different countries of the civilized world; marriage is *not* the same in France, in England, in the United States. Secondly, he believed that social institutions arose "spontaneously" in society:

> "The great mass of law arises immediately in society itself in the form of a spontaneous ordering of social relations, of marriage, the family associations, possession, contracts, succession. . . ."[45]

The theory that any such complex institutions as those named arose "spontaneously" is thoroughly suspect; Ehrlich seems to be repeating the romantic notion of Savigny's Volksgeist. Thirdly, Ehrlich nowhere recognizes the reciprocal influence of law and custom on each other. How much of the ritual and sanctity of the marriage ceremony, for instance, was brought about by the law of property which treated the illegitimate child as no one's heir?

Another sociological conception of law was that of the Russian-trained Pole, L. J. Petrazhitsky (1867–1931), who sought to find the reality of law, its phenomena, in the minds of those who ascribe rights and the like to somebody—to themselves or other persons. Since the only kind of existence law has is psychological, that which distinguishes it from other psychic phenomena must be found in psychological analysis. Petrazhitsky then proceeds to construct a new psychology, according to which law fell in the class of attribute-imperative influences along with the rules of politeness.[46] His view that legal rules, legal rights and the like are mere mental constructs and do not correspond to reality seems to have influenced the Danish philosopher, Professor Alf Ross (§ 1.15) and the American sociologist, Sorokin.[47] These men take refuge from a rational system of legal norms, which often seems a superficial gloss on social life, in a social-psychological

---

[45] Ibid., 138.

[46] See Timasheff, "Petrazhitsky's Philosophy of Law", in Interpretations of Modern Legal Philosophies (Essays in Honor of Roscoe Pound) (1947) 736, 743. While the author's conception was stated in terms of individual psychology, it was really a social-psychological concept, as Professor Timasheff pointed out. A volume of Petrazhitsky's writings, translated into English, will soon be published by the Harvard University Press.

[47] See Sorokin's article in the Pound volume (supra, last note) at p. 668.

conception of law which thus far eludes scientific inquiry. Rational modes of thought should not be jettisoned even for a venture into an empirical science of law.

Sociological conceptions of law seem to confuse legal with nonlegal controls, and the raw material (or partly processed material) of usage and custom with the finished product of the lawyer's art.[48] The legal sociologist and the sociological jurist are often vague about the extent of the prevalence of the beliefs or practices on which they lay great stress; many individuals in any given society—infants, the very old and many other adults—have no beliefs or practices about a great many matters which concern the law, and yet the law has to consider their interests. Again, a good deal of law in the modern state is not an adaptation of custom or mores. Examples are the Internal Revenue Code, the Workmen's Compensation Acts, the Social Security Act. No doubt all such enactments have to *take account* of customs and mores as means to their ends or as obstacles to be got around. Finally, it is among the purposes of law to provide not only for the present members of society but also for unborn generations, whose customs and mores cannot be now investigated.

§ 2.04—Imperative Conceptions of Law

An "imperative" conception of law, as that term is here used, is one which ascribes to law at least three necessary characteristics: (1) of a rule or norm of human conduct; (2) of political authority; (3) of political sanction or enforcement. These characteristics will be more fully explored later (Chs. 5–7). The imperative conception is also called "positive" (§ 1.05) because it takes law as something "posited" by the state or its organs of government.[49] Positivists ordinarily define "law" by defining "a law," as is shown in Holland's short definition:

"[A law is] a general rule of external human action enforced by a sovereign political authority." [50]

This definition requires the three characteristics indicated above.

---

48 A parallel confusion between law and custom is neatly shown in Braybrooke, "Custom as a Source of English Law" (1951) 50 Mich.L.Rev. 71. See infra, § 3.15. Llewellyn's conception of law (or at least one of his) is a mixture of ideals, institutions, imperative rules, professional techniques, and possibly other things. My Philosophy of Law (1941) 183.

49 Etymologically the term "positive" includes the notion of arbitrariness or contingency, as opposed to "natural" or "necessary." See discussion of natural law, infra, Pt. IV, esp. § 4.13.

50 Op. cit., supra, § 2.00, note 10.

These three characteristics of law are old. Aristotle, for instance, recognizes all three of them: law as general rule,[51] as a command or prohibition,[52] emanating from the state and having compulsory power.[53] Yet Aristotle was not a positivist, because he ascribed other qualities to law, conformity to ideals or to custom, and never made it clear which characteristics he deemed essential when something having the positive characteristics lacked one of the others. His conception of law was less tightly drawn than that of positivism. The same may be said of the Roman lawyers of the classical period; for while their practical work in law (which was of the best quality) reveals an implicit understanding that law is a politically enforceable command or rule, when they came to philosophize about law under Stoic influences they put forth ideal conceptions of law, such as that of Cicero.[54] Historically, conceptions of law have varied in time and place, and one cannot force the earlier conceptions into the mold of positivism.

The imperative conception of law emerged in modern times concurrently with the development of the modern state. The English philosopher, Thomas Hobbes, an original thinker but not a lawyer nor even primarily interested in legal philosophy, came close to the imperative conception when he said:

> "Law properly is the word of him that by right hath command over others." [55]

The context of this passage shows that Hobbes included political authority and political sanction (implied in "command") in his conception. "By right," however, introduces a qualification, that the sovereign's right to command rests upon the social contract which is presupposed in the establishment of a sovereign. The imperative conception of law could not emerge until the question of the political justification of the state, or of sovereign power,

---

[51] Politics, Bk. II, Ch. VIII, 1269a; Bk. III, Ch. XI, 1282b; Nichomachean Ethics, Bk. X, 1180a, 21.

[52] Ibid., Bk. V, 1129b, 19 et seq.

[53] Politics, Bk. IV, Ch. 1; Bk. II, Ch. VIII; Bk. III, Ch. X; Nichomachean Ethics, 1180a, 22; Cairns, Legal Philosophy from Plato to Hegel (1949), 100–101.

[54] Supra, § 2.02, note 28. Celsus, a Roman jurist of c. A. D. 100 characterized law (jus) as "the art of what is right and equitable." ("Jus est ars aequi et boni.")

[55] Hobbes, Leviathan (first published in 1651) (Everyman Library ed.), 83; Hall, 55.

was distinguished from the question, by what criteria does one
determine, in a modern state, that a particular thing is or is not
a part of the law of that state?

The next step was taken by Jeremy Bentham, the great English
law reformer, who in 1782 produced a definition of law as follows:

> "A law may be defined as an assemblage of signs declara-
> tive of a volition conceived or adopted by the *sovereign* in a
> state, concerning the conduct to be observed in a certain *case*
> by a certain person or class of persons, who in the case in
> question are or are supposed to be subject to his power.
> . . ."[56]

Here one finds political sovereign and command included; the
notion of a general rule is not explicit. Bentham was more interested in reforming the law by statute than in an analysis of the
English legal system of his time. This task was undertaken by
one of his followers, Austin.

John Austin (1790–1859), a man of great intellectual vigor and
tenacity, though prevented by ill health from enjoying success
as a lawyer, became the founder of the English "analytical" or
imperative school of jurisprudence. Despite some distinguished
dissenters, it is still dominant in England, in Canada, in Australia
and New Zealand.[57] The Austinian theory of law is a rather prosy
one and so was Austin's life. Born in Suffolk of well-to-do parentage, he obtained a commission in the army and served there
about five years. His much criticized theory that a law is a kind
of command may have been influenced by this experience; on the
other hand, it may have been suggested by his labors as an equity
draftsman at Lincoln's Inn, the highly specialized vocation to
which he turned after his admission to the bar in 1818. An equity
draftsman was a barrister who drafted equity pleadings. In those
days (and in our Federal courts down to 1913) the bill in equity,
or first pleading, was frequently a tiresome and repetitious document in nine parts, each of which had to be very exact in its language. In its precision and formality it resembles the first six of

---

[56] Bentham, The Limits of Jurisprudence Defined (ed. by C. W. Everett,
1945), 88.

[57] This opinion is based on my reading of textbooks, periodicals and judicial opinions of, and on observations of the mental habits of lawyers trained
in, those countries. The Austinian influence is apparent in a short English
text which has gone through six editions since 1881: Wise, Outlines of
Jurisprudence (6th ed., 1948, by R. W. M. Dias, of Trinity Hall, Cambridge;
earlier revision by Percy H. Winfield, Cambridge).

Austin's lectures on Jurisprudence, which he began to deliver at London University (then newly founded) in 1832. Austin prepared for these lectures by studying in Germany. His principal objective was the development of a method of comparative law, by which the fundamental conceptions of "mature" (Western European) systems of law might be extricated from their details. At the outset he found it necessary to disentangle law from the mass of customs, morals and ethical ideas with which it had become intertwined. Thus his definition of law, which found many followers, was to be a mere overture to his study of particular legal doctrines, which he never completed. His lectures were at first heard by a small and select group of students, including the English logician, John Stuart Mill. However, the lectures were not sufficiently well attended to justify their continuance. In 1831 Austin published an Outline of his entire course, and in 1832 he published six lectures in a volume, The Province of Jurisprudence Determined. Both are included in the posthumous editions of his Lectures on Jurisprudence.[58]

Austin's first task was to separate positive law from things improperly called law and from things that closely resembled it. He therefore flatly states his own definition that a law is "a rule laid down for the guidance of an intelligent being by an intelligent being having power over him." [59] This excludes the "laws" of inanimate objects (physics, etc.) and the "laws" of plant or animal growth. Whether or not the physicists would agree with Austin that their "laws of thermodynamics" are "improperly so called", it is all right to call them that in a book on jurisprudence, since the failure to draw this distinction has caused considerable confusion. Next, Austin recognizes that the laws of God are laws within his definition; he prefers to call them Divine Law rather than the Law of Nature, a term which he regards as ambiguous and misleading. *Positive law* is the law set by a *political* superior to a political inferior. It is to be distinguished from *positive morality*, rules set by public opinion or by some non-political body for its subordinate members. Positive laws exist "by position". By this he means that its "position" as a part of a given legal system depends upon who uttered it. Positive law depends upon political authority.

---

[58] The additional lectures were made up from Austin's notes and from student notes, by the editor, R. C. Campbell. The reference below to the "Lectures" are to the 4th ed., 1873, by Campbell.

[59] Lectures, I, 88.

He next stated that "every law or rule . . . is a command." [60] Since this part of his definition has been criticized and rejected by virtually all later positivists, it is well to note what he meant by it. A command is a signification of desire by one intelligent being to another accompanied by an explicit or implicit threat of harm to the latter if the desire be not fulfilled; and because he is liable to such harm the latter is under a *duty* to obey the command. Thus "command" implies sanction and duty. Now it is certainly true, as Holland pointed out, that the laws of a modern state are not formulated in the imperative mood: "Kill not!" What Austin probably had in mind is that carefully drafted statutes often prescribe what "shall" and "shall not" be done; these he regarded as "commands". He was essentially right, I believe, in regarding (positive) law (i. e., any rule or principle of law) as a signification of a desire, i. e., of a purpose or intention, by one group of humans to another and larger group; yet he seems to have overlooked that the larger group *includes* the lawmakers themselves, who, as subject-personae, are bound by the laws they make as officials. Austin was unduly influenced by his military experience and by his implicit belief in a one-man sovereign. The view that "command" implies sanction seems far-fetched; indeed, he recognizes that a "law of imperfect obligation", though it purports to declare that certain acts are crimes, is no law at all if it lacks a sanction.[61] Finally, the notion that command (*with* threat of harm) implies duty, has seemed to some of Austin's critics a putting of the horse before the cart. Yet later positivists—Holmes, Hohfeld, Corbin—have defined "legal duty" in much the same way, (i. e., in terms of what a court will do (§ 2.05).

Austin's definition of a sovereign as the person or body of persons in a political society to whom the bulk of the population is in a habit of obedience still seems a useful conception. It serves to differentiate a habit of obedience to the sovereign generally from the habit of obeying a particular law, and thus answers the question, is an unenforced law still law? According to Austin, it is, and that is prevailing legal doctrine in English and American law and in most continental systems. Holland, whose definition (supra) requires enforcement, was "unduly influenced" by the historical school. Secondly, Austin's "habit of obedience", a crude conception, anchors law in social conduct and not, like Kelsen's

---

[60] Ibid., 90.

[61] Ibid., 101.

"basic norm", in the sky.[62]   Thirdly, Austin's conception avoids the vice of circularity, that the state is defined by law and law by the state. The sovereign rests not upon mere paper rules but upon the attitudes toward it of the bulk of the society. Still, the exact profile of this thing called "sovereign" (or "top dog", if you will) cannot be drawn without reference to something, whatever we may name it, which is law. The interdependence of state and law seems practically inescapable.

Several of Austin's ideas are discussed further on.[63]   Here we note two of the chief criticisms of Austin's theory: That he took no account of what the law ought to be; and that he placed excessive reliance on logic in the solution of legal problems. The first of these is based upon his statement, made in defining the scope of "jurisprudence":

> ". . . general jurisprudence, or the philosophy of positive law, is concerned with law as it necessarily *is*, rather than law as it *ought* to be; with law as it must be, *be it good or bad,* rather than law as it must be, if it be good." [64]

In this same passage Austin explained that general jurisprudence was not concerned with "the science of legislation", by which he meant the principles of legislation set forth by his older friend and intellectual leader, Jeremy Bentham.[65]   Bentham believed that a code of laws could be so clearly drawn as to do away with "judge-made" law (§ 4.43); hence he separated the ethical questions of law-making, which he called "deontology", or the science of legislation, from the analytical problems, which he called "jurisprudence". Austin obediently followed this division of labor set forth by his master. Yet Austin was not indifferent to the goodness or badness of laws. He devoted three of his first six (published) lectures to discussing the principle of utility (§ 4.41). At the end of his lecture notes, he recognized that it was impossible

---

[62] However, Kelsen brings in a conception similar to the "habit of obedience" in his requirement that, in order to be valid, a law must be a part of a legal order which, as a whole is "efficacious", i. e., prevalent among its subjects. Kelsen, General Theory of Law and State (1945) 118.

[63] On the law as a "general command", § 2.12, n. 38; his "command" theory is discussed, §§ 2.12, 2.20, 2.21; his conception of sovereignty is discussed, § 2.31; his conception of sanction, § 2.32.

[64] Lectures I, 33; also II, 1107–8; Hall, 335.

[65] In 1821 Austin with his wife and infant daughter occupied a house in London overlooking Bentham's garden, and Bentham was often among the brilliant company in Austin's drawing-room. I Dictionary of National Biography (Oxford Press, 1937–8), title, "Austin, John".

to consider jurisprudence as a literal interpretation of laws, apart from their conceivable causes or ends:

"It is impossible to consider Jurisprudence quite apart from Legislation; since the inducements or considerations of expediency which lead to the establishment of laws, must be adverted to in explaining their origin and mechanism. If the causes of laws and of the rights and obligations which they create be not assigned, the laws themselves are unintelligible." [66]

An interpreter who seeks the meaning of a legal norm in the ends for which it was created does not necessarily affirm that those ends are his own, i. e., that the law is what it *should* be.

As to the overworking of logic in law, Austin's endeavor to find the necessary conceptions of any mature system of law and his analysis of comparable legal doctrines in English and European civil law (as derived from Roman law) were intended to make English law more systematic, more simple in structure and clearer in scope and application. In this sense, it may be said, he made logical consistency and clarity of meaning important ideals of analytical jurisprudence.[67] Yet he did not conceive of any possible legal system as complete and gapless, with a ready formula for every legal controversy. On the contrary, he recognized that judicial law-making is "highly beneficial and absolutely necessary." [68] In criticizing a daring (and unsuccessful) innovation of Lord Mansfield, who tried to establish a rule that a promise based upon a prior "moral obligation" of the promisor to the promisee is legally enforceable, he objected, not to Lord Mansfield's "legislating" but to his doing so "under cover of vague and indeterminate phrases." [69] Austin was interested in effective meanings as much as in formal consistency. His analytical framework was intended to bring order into a body of law having a changing content.

While Austin's conception of law was partly anticipated by Hobbes and by Bentham,[70] it became the basis for a number of variations, most of them derived from Austin, and should be compared with others, such as that of Kelsen, which were developed independently.

---

66 Lectures, 1107; Hall, 335.

67 See Stone, The Province and Function of Law (1946), Ch. II, §§ 13–17.

68 Lectures, I, 224.

69 Ibid.

70 Supra, notes 55, 56.

§ 2.05—Variations of the Imperative Conception

The following are some of the important variations of the imperative conception:

1. *Actual Enforcement; Obedience.* Austin distinguished the sanction, the *threat* of an evil, from the actual enforcement or obedience of the law. While Holland speaks as if "enforcement" were a necessary characteristic of law,[71] he means no more than that "disobedience . . . is followed, or is likely to be followed, by some sort of penalty or inconvenience." [72] This is inaccurate; in American law, at least, a statutory law continues to be law even though for a long time it had been likely (more probable than not) that it would never be enforced. Nor does the Austinian conception require that a particular rule of law be generally obeyed. All that it requires, to use the late Dean Wigmore's phrase, is that a rule be "subject to realization by state force." [73]

2. *Courts Substituted for Sovereign.* Some English and American writers have substituted, for the sovereign political authority as the source of law, the courts of law. Thus Salmond of New Zealand at one time defined law as:

"The rules recognized and acted on in courts of justice." [74] Again, John Chipman Gray, long a professor of the law of real property at Harvard, defined law as "the rules which the courts . . . lay down for the determination of legal rights and duties." [75] Gray intentionally excluded legislation, which he regarded as only a *source* of law (§ 3.11). This limitation excludes a newly enacted statute which no court has as yet interpreted, from the "law that is." It also excludes certain rules or principles which legislative and executive officials administer without judicial review or intervention. Examples are state constitutional provisions directing the legislature to re-apportion representatives in Congress at certain intervals and some parts of international

---

[71] Supra, note 50.

[72] Holland, op. cit., 23. Pound ascribes the shift from "sanction" to "enforcement" to the influence of the historical school. Outlines, 69.

[73] II Wigmore, Cases on Torts (1911), Appendix A, § 3.

[74] Salmond, Jurisprudence (1902), § 5. In the last edition by the author (7th ed., 1924) he classified law into eight kinds (§ 5), of which the principal kind, "the law of lawyers and the law courts," is defined as above (§ 15).

[75] Gray, The Nature and Sources of the Law (1st ed., 1909), § 191; (2d ed., 1927), 84; Hall, 404. A similar definition is found in Restatement, Conflict of Laws (1934), § 3.

law. Whether these should be included may be debatable. However, it is scarcely debatable that if Gray were writing today he would have to include administrative tribunals, along with courts, as law-making organs. On the whole this judicentric approach to law, which is peculiar to Anglo-American writers, is an unwarranted narrowing of the imperative conception of law.

3. *Rules or Norms in Place of Commands.* Austin defined a law as a "command" of a political superior to a political inferior. The term "command" has been more widely criticized than any other part of Austin's conception. It is inaccurate with respect to a great many parts of a body of law. For instance, the statutory rule requiring two witnesses to a will, or the case law rule requiring that one who accepts an offer of a reward must be aware of it, are not worded as commands, though ultimately commands may be issued in consequence of their application to particular facts. Moreover, "command" suggests a particular order for a single occasion rather than a general command for many occasions, which is what Austin meant by it. Such terms as "rule" or, more inclusively, "norm" are more accurate to characterize what is meant by the imperative conception of law (§ 2.20).

4. *Rights or Legal Relations in Place of Rules.* Another variant of the imperative conception brings in rights or other legal relations. Thus Gray defines the law as "the rules which the courts . . . lay down for the determination of legal rights and duties." [76] This is too narrow, since other legal relations—powers and immunities, for instance—are determined by legal rules. Hohfeld recognized this and Corbin, amplifying and clarifying Hohfeld, made "legal relation" the central term in his conception of law:

> "A statement that a legal relation exists between A and B is a *prediction* as to what society, acting through its courts or executive agents, will do or will not do for one and against the other." [77]

A rule of law, "when reduced to words" is "a statement of the legal effect of operative facts" and the legal effect of operative facts is a legal relation.[78] The conceptions of legal relations have been highly useful in private law, such as property, torts and contracts; they have not been as useful in public law. They are in any event

---

[76] Supra, last note.

[77] Corbin, Legal Analysis and Terminology (1919), 29 Yale L.J. 163, 164; Hall, 473.

[78] Ibid.

subordinate to and dependent upon the conception of law and need not be included in a definition of it.

5. *Words, Rules, Predictions.* A more basic question is raised when law is defined as a set of words or signs. This was the mode of characterizing law adopted by Hobbes [79] and Bentham,[80] who took the nominalist position with respect to the status of universals. This metaphysical question was discussed above (§ 1.14). To a hard-headed man who believes only what he sees and hears it seems that when a judge decides a case he reads a set of black symbols on white paper, hears some more symbols uttered by witnesses and advocates, and writes or speaks still others. The law is one of these assemblages of symbols. All else is mere fiction or conjecture or fantasy. But neither Bentham nor the judge would be able to tell the symbols that are "law" from the others that are not, without some understanding of the meaning of the symbols, as being "declarative of a volition conceived or adopted by the sovereign," etc.; to understand and apply the particular symbols he looks at the judge would need some conception of the meanings of the terms. Moreover, taken literally Bentham's definition would seem to mean that there are as many different laws in a state as there are copies of the statute book. Of course Bentham did not go this far, nor has any other positivist. Corbin, for example, was careful to distinguish between a legal rule and its statement in words.[81] The imperative conception of law does not presuppose a nominalist metaphysics nor a mere behavioristic description of the legal order. Law must be found in symbols (mostly written or oral words) but what is found is what the symbols mean or signify. Here the positivists divide, or at least appear to. The older and orthodox view is that these symbols signify rules or norms, *prescriptions* of what ought to be or shall be done. A more recent view, dating from Holmes, is that they signify "prophecies," that is, *predictions,* of what will be done by judges or officials.[82] The prediction theory of law, an important variant of the imperative conception, will be discussed later (§ 2.20).

6. *"Basic Norm" for "Sovereign"; Kelsen.* The "pure theory of law" of Hans Kelsen, an eminent Austrian jurist of this century, was not derived from Austin, yet it ascribes to law charac-

---

[79] Supra, § 2.04, note 55.

[80] Ibid., note 56.

[81] Supra, note 78.

[82] See Holmes in (1897) 10 Harvard L.Rev. at p. 460–61; Hall, 670; Corbin, supra, note 77.

teristics which are substantially those mentioned at the beginning of § 2.04, supra. One variant found in Kelsen is that the Austinian conception of the sovereign is omitted as extraneous to the conception of law. For it Kelsen substitutes the "basic norm," which gives validity to the constitution of the state, which in turn gives validity to all subordinate legal norms. A legal justification of the state, says Kelsen, is impossible, "since every state is necessarily a legal state." [83] This simplifies the Austinian conception of law and makes sharper the division between the political philosophy of the state and jurisprudence (Kelsen's "legal science"). To many of Austin's followers and to lawyers engaged in their professional work Austin's conception of sovereignty is a mere excrescence, since they take the government of their state as something given and are not called upon, as lawyers, to determine whether people are in a habit of obedience to it. However, it seems unnecessary to purge the conception of positive law of all factual connections with the society for which it is established and maintained.

§ 2.06—The Social-control Conception of Law

The conception of law as an instrument or a means of social control brings together some of the aspects of the other ways of looking at law, and adds something to them. From ideal conceptions of law it takes the notion of the functions or ends of law, without committing law to any one ultimate criterion of value and without requiring that a "law" shall be a good law for any particular purpose in order to be a law at all. From the institutional theories of law, especially the sociological, it takes the conception of law as operating in a given society as *a* means of social control, concurrently with other means, and of law operating upon social institutions which supply much of its content and continually check or limit the range and effectiveness of its control. From the positive or imperative conceptions of law the social-control conception takes over the conception of law as a body of guides deliberately chosen by political officials, consciously formulated and having potentially a preponderance of force. To these it adds the idea that law is or should be technically implemented to operate as a means of social control.

The social-control conception of law, while by no means created out of whole cloth, emerged in the twentieth century from the

---

[83] 51 L.Q.R. 534–535; Hall, 658. See also Kelsen, General Theory of Law and State (1945), 115.

work of American sociologists, of whom the foremost was E. A. Ross.[84] The term "social control" in its wider sense includes any influence exerted by society upon the individual. It thus includes not only customs, beliefs, public opinion, taboos and ceremonies, but also organs of communication—the press, the radio—and social and economic organizations, and the law. Some of these controls are habit patterns which are not consciously operated toward a given end, while others, such as law, are. In a narrower sense "social control" means a consciously planned guidance of human conduct. The rise of this concept in the present century is partly due to the analogy of the natural sciences and mechanical technology. Their recent achievements in increasing human control over inanimate nature suggested that similar devices might be effective in controlling human conduct. The suggestion ran counter to the *laissez faire* policy of the political-economic theories of the nineteenth century, and to Herbert Spencer's theory of automatic social evolution.[85] The conception of social control thus challenges some basic conceptions of policy and politics.

American sociologists and economists have contributed further to the social-control conception of law. For some of them, at least, the legal order (law and government) is the basic analogue for the other forms of social control,[86] "the most definite and powerful agent of society," [87] and "one of the chief agencies in promoting social solidarity." [88] Yet government operates efficiently only if it has adequate support from public opinion, the mores, or social rituals,[89] from that self-imposed form of control which has been called "ethical control,[90] or from a majority of the members of society, who, though not sponsoring a particular law, are just barely willing to vote for it.[91] Analysis of the means of social control led Lumley to differentiate two methods, the physical

---

84 Ross, Social Control (1901). See Everett, "Social Control," 4 Encyclopedia of the Social Sciences (1931), 344, 345 et seq.; Pound, "Sociology of Law and Sociological Jurisprudence" (1943) 5 Univ. of Toronto L.J. 1, 2.

85 Infra, § 4.34.

86 Park and Burgess, Introduction to the Science of Sociology (1930), 786; Hall, 1001.

87 Clark, Social Control of Business (1926), 5; Hall, 1017.

88 MacIver, Community (1928), 161; Hall, 1014.

89 Park and Burgess, op. cit., supra, note 86, 786–787; Hall, 1001–1002.

90 MacIver, op. cit., supra, note 88, 158–160; Hall, 1013.

91 Clark, op. cit., supra, note 87, 5–11; Hall, 1017–1020.

force method and the human symbol method.[92] The former includes the policeman who drags the culprit to jail; the latter includes the flag as a symbol of nationality and the symbolized rules of law. The latter is quicker, more economical, more personality-respecting, more order-preserving.[93] In the writings of sociologists and economists who are not law-trained one often finds two types of error: to take "law" to mean the criminal law, social legislation, and constitutional law, the more dramatic kinds of law as presented in the newspapers and magazines; and to overlook the difference betwen regularities of conduct and norms of conduct.

In the United States Roscoe Pound seems to have been the first to bring the social-control conception to the attention of lawyers; his program for sociological jurisprudence was an outline of methods by which law should be used as an instrument of social control.[94] His phrase, "social engineering," as a designation of the problems of the legal order in satisfying individual wants and social interests with a maximum of human enjoyment and a minimum of waste and friction,[95] became a popular name for the social-control conception of law. The functional conception of law which became prevalent in the "free-law" movements of Continental Europe and among the American legal realists [96] are among the twentieth century movements in jurisprudence which were influenced in various ways by the social-control conception of law.

Is the social-control conception of law adequate to include all the law, that is, all that we usually call "law"? The enactment of a law designed to remedy a certain kind of evil, such as factories with unsafe machinery or merchants using unfair trade practices, is clearly a use of law as a means of social control by coercing those who cause the evil to conduct themselves differently (e. g., by installing safeguards), under threat of fine or imprisonment. The social-control conception fits best this preventive type of social legislation. A good part of the law in the statute book of a

---

[92] Lumley, Means of Social Control (1925), 11–16; Hall, 1010–1011.

[93] Ibid.

[94] Pound, The Scope and Purpose of Sociological Jurisprudence, III (1912), 25 Harvard L.Rev. 489, 512–516; Pound, op. cit., supra, n. 84.

[95] Pound, "A Theory of Social Interests," (1921) 15 Papers and Proceedings of the American Sociological Society, 16, 44; Hall, 246 (a revision was published in (1943) 57 Harvard L.Rev. 1); Pound, The Spirit of the Common Law (1921), 195–196; infra, §§ 4.60, 4.61.

[96] Infra, §§ 4.63, 4.64.

state—the provisions for licensing various callings and those prohibiting certain business practices—is of this type. Does it fit such remedial legislation as the workmen's compensation laws? Here the statute does not explicitly direct the employer to install safeguards against injuries to his employees, yet by imposing on the employer a duty to pay compensation, unqualified by fault, it indirectly coerces him to prevent injuries.[97] In the same way the law of torts, which imposes a duty to pay compensation for wrongful injuries to person, property or reputation, operates to some extent as a deterrent of conduct and thus as a social control.

Yet many parts of the law of a civilized society are unknown to those whose conduct may lead to the imposition of a legal duty to make compensation. The law of torts imposes liability for conduct which a jury may permissibly find to have been "negligent," though the person whose conduct was in question did not know at the time that there was such a legal rule, and could not with certainty have known that his conduct would violate it. More troublesome examples are found in the law of quasi contracts, such as the liability of the payee to make restitution for money paid and received under mistake. That rule can hardly deter a payee from innocently receiving mistaken payments, though it conceivably may influence him not to retain them after he learns of the mistake. A good deal of "private" law is designed to provide guidance in the settlement of disputes arising from conduct that was very little, if at all, motivated by the law. Can we properly designate these parts of the law as instruments of "social control"? Yes, because the peaceable settlement of disputes is itself a form of, and a means to, social control; indeed, it is among the earliest forms of social control undertaken by the legal order. To this may be added in a mature system of law the devices (e. g., patterns of transactions in real property and commercial law) by which the occurrence of disputes is minimized. Both dispute-settlement and dispute-prevention are among the objectives of social control through law. Once this view is accepted, the entire body of lawyer's law—e. g., the law of pleading, practice and procedure—becomes an accessory means of social control.

While every part of the law of a civilized society and of its legal order can usefully be regarded as a means of social control, yet

---

[97] By making insurance legally compulsory the compensation law gives rise to a set of institutional patterns of the insurance business—selection of risks, inspections of employers' premises, premium charges based on hazards of the employer's operations—which motivate the employer to reduce the chance of compensable injuries.

the social control conception of law is, like all the others, not to be taken as exclusive. As a guide to the understanding of the content of the law and legal processes, it overemphasizes the conscious creation of legal rules for definite purposes and the conscious use by officials of their official power for such purposes. The administration of the law, especially by courts but even to a considerable extent by long-established administrative officials, is governed to a greater extent by tradition and routine than the social-control conception makes allowance for. In the making of decisions rules and precedents, if they fit the case, are followed because they are there, because they are posited by the legal system. A second point is that the social-control conception of law depends upon or presupposes a conception of law by which it can be distinguished from other means of social control. The conception of law which best fits for this purpose, and the one which the originators of the social-control conception envisaged, is, I believe, the imperative conception of law.

Chapter 5

THE GENERALITY OF LAW

§ 2.10—The Generality of Law

By the generality of law [1] is meant its capacity to serve as a rule, a measure, a guide for an indefinite number of varied situations. Through its generality a body of law becomes the structural framework of orderly political arrangements which are capable of maintaining peace and justice (at least the best human approximations to them) among the population of an empire. Through its generality law provides the premises of reflective deliberations and reasoned decisions between the conflicting claims and interests of individuals and groups in society. Through its generality law can be made to further two important ends of political justice, the elimination of the personal prejudices of the official, and the equality between all claimants with respect to their claims. Because of the generality of law, men can be enabled to predict the legal consequences of situations that have not yet been litigated, and hence can plan their conduct for a future which is thereby rendered less uncertain. On the whole the generality of law is its most important characteristic. Through the ages rulers and ruled have striven to establish explicit generalizations, on stone, on parchment or on paper.

Yet the quality of generality is not uniquely an attribute of political law. The "laws" of the natural sciences, for instance, have this characteristic. The conception of law as a general rule, a measure or guide, is perhaps the oldest conception in the history of legal philosophy. Among Greek philosophers the laws of human conduct were regarded as regularities having a common attribute with the laws of nature, of the heavenly bodies and of the physical universe. Thus the arbitrary or conventional rules of local law-givers were subjected to critical scrutiny, and the conception of "natural law" resulted from an aspiration to find political or ethical laws having the same universality as the "laws" of physics or astronomy.[2] This entanglement of the gen-

---

[1] The term, "generality of law," is derived from Bentham, The Limits of Jurisprudence Defined (Everett ed., 1945), Ch. 11, 161 et seq.

[2] See Windelband, A History of Philosophy (Tufts trans., 1926), 57, 72–76; Hall, 9–14.

eralizations of natural science with political laws and ethical principles persisted throughout the development of legal philosophy
until modern times.   Cicero's conception of law [3] is an example of
its worst confusion.   For the clarification of this confusion we
owe most, perhaps, to Kant and Austin.   Whether on the basis
of historical priority Austin was justified in regarding the "laws"
of inanimate objects as "laws merely metaphorical" is a question
which need not be answered here.   There is some evidence for
the view that the attempts of early law-givers to bring about
regularity of human conduct supplied the analogy by which physical laws were discovered.[4]   Both physical formulas and political
laws are generalizations which only human beings can understand
and apply.[5]   They differ in that the latter can be disobeyed.   This
difference explains why (political) law has other attributes: political authority and political sanction.   There are other differences
(§ 1.26).   Still, both political laws and physical laws have the
characteristic of generality.

The generality of law is not an unmixed blessing.[6]   Every law,
as an instrument of social control, is an attempt to control the
future, and the future turns up unforeseeable situations which
make the law seem harsh and inadequate, when judged by that
sense of fairness which is sometimes called "equity," in the Aristotelian sense.   The generality of law makes sometimes an iron
rule from which litigants, and even judges, can find no escape.   It
sometimes fetters the social adjustments of a new generation with
rules which expressed the conflicts and compromises of older generations.   The generality of law can lead to "good" or "bad"
consequences, and is thus not an "ideal" attribute of law.   It is
one which law has, for better or for worse.   It is an intellectual
and ethically neutral characteristic of law.

Hence in all ages there have been revolts against the generality
of law.   More accurately, perhaps, there have been revolts against
the generality of particular laws, and some of these have been
grounded on the rejection of generality as a necessary attribute of
law.   To understand the bearing of any such revolt upon the
generality of law, one needs always to ask the question, is this an

---

3 Supra, § 2.02; infra, § 4.12.

4 See Holland, Jurisprudence (10th ed., 1906), 16, 19–20; Miller, Philosophy
of Law (1884), 374–5; Frank, Fate and Freedom (1945), Ch. X.   My own
guess is that the two types of generalizations were developed together.

5 See Austin, Lectures, 212–213.

6 See Salmond, Jurisprudence (7th ed., 1924), § 16.

attack upon the adequacy of *particular* legal generalizations, with a view to substituting others rather than an attack on the generality of all law?　Thus when Aristotle tells the legal advocate who finds that the conventional legal provisions lead to a conclusion adverse to the interests of his client that he should urge the jurors to base their conclusions on the eternal principles of "natural law," [7] he points to the substitution of a generalization of different content.　English equity began as a revolt against the strict generalities of the common law, for which it sought to substitute the conscience of the Chancellor; yet in the course of several centuries English equity developed a body of generalizations that supplemented, and sometimes conflicted with, those of the common law.　In the twentieth century this revolt appeared as a part of the "free law" movement in Europe and in some of the attacks made by American legal realists.　These latter attacks took the judicial process of deciding cases, or the whole governmental process, as the most important aspect of the legal order, and so made it equivalent to "law."　The following excerpts are illustrative:

"From the point of view of the judge, the law may fairly be said to be the judging process or the power to pass judgment." [8]

"This doing of something about disputes, this doing of it reasonably, is the business of the law.　And the people who have the doing of it in charge, whether they be judges or sheriffs or clerks or jailers or lawyers, are officials of the law.　*What* these officials do about disputes is, to my mind, the law itself." [9]

The notion that the law consists of what officials do, *independently of any generalizations as to what they will or ought to do,* may be called the "do-law" theory.　In this exclusive form probably no person with any professional legal experience has ever adopted it.　Certainly Judge Frank and Professor Llewellyn have

---

[7] Aristotle, Rhetoric (Ross trans., 1924), Bk. I, Ch. 15, 1375a–1375b; Hall, 7–8.

[8] Frank, Law and the Modern Mind (1930), 274, note.　In a later work, Judge Frank, while abjuring the use of "law", uses the term "legal rules" to include all of Pound's five types (§ 3.23) of legal generalizations.　Frank, Courts on Trial (1949) 56, n. 29.

[9] Llewellyn, The Bramble Bush (1930), 3.　(Compare Professor Llewellyn's later statement, supra, § 2.03, n. 48.)　See also Radin, "Statutory Interpretation," (1930) 43 Harvard L.Rev. 863, and Landis' rejoinder, ibid., 886, 892.

each given evidence that they do not believe it: the one in writing able opinions expounding legal generalizations; the other in drafting uniform statutes. Even if the "do-law" theory is only a scarecrow, it has summoned some able men—Morris Cohen,[10] Cardozo,[11] Pound—to come to the defense of the generality of law.

That law is a body of generalizations is harder to grasp in Anglo-American law than in Continental law, where comprehensive codes cover the entire field of the law. Case law does not produce formal, official exclusive texts of its generalizations. Where a number of judges write opinions in support of the judgment, as in the British House of Lords, it is hard to say which man's generalizations are to be used in determining the law of the case. Even where there is an official "opinion of the court," as in most American jurisdictions, the opinion usually contains variant wordings of the legal propositions which are involved in the decision. In the United States precedents are less strictly adhered to, it seems, than in England, and this makes the extrication of legal generalities more elusive. Moreover, the judicial process in a case-law régime frequently exemplifies John Stuart Mills' position that it is possible to reason "from particular to particular", i. e., from a precedent case to the instant case, without any articulate major premise. These and other factors of the Anglo-American legal order [12] tend to make the judgment or decision of the court seem the *real* thing and the generalizations on which it was or might be grounded, as well as those for which it may be cited in future cases, seem like ghostly conjectures. This tendency produces a fallacious emphasis upon doing, as opposed to reasons for doing, which is caricatured in the "do-law" theory. To mistake the data or the consequences of a generalization for the generalization is fallacious. It would have been fallacious for Sir Isaac Newton to say that the law of gravity consists of what apples do.

---

10 Supra, § 1.11, n. 5.

11 "Is there any law beyond the precept of isolated judgments? Must we surrender the quest for the universal, and content ourselves with what is merely a succession of particulars? Back of the changing phenomena are we to posit a substratum which gives coherence and reality?" Cardozo, The Growth of the Law (1924), 29. See Patterson, "Cardozo's Philosophy of Law," (1939) 88 U. of Pa.L.Rev. 71, 78.

12 Including, as Judge Frank has often emphasized, the uncertainty of fact-finding, especially in cases tried before a jury. See Courts on Trial (1940), and numerous earlier writings.

The generality of law is sufficiently important to call for further exploration of its functional significance in relation to government and society and of its logical aspects.

§ 2.11—Functional Aspects of the Generality of Law

Some of the functional aspects of law as a body of generalizations have been mentioned at the beginning of the last section. Here it is intended to show how all of the major functions of law in society depend for their realization upon the generality of law.

Law and government are inseparable and yet distinguishable. In the modern state, at least, government requires some form of control other than through individual commands. The generalizations which indicate the scope of each official's authority, the *kinds* of situations in which he is to act and his power to act, are prescriptions, not merely or more significantly descriptions; they are laws. Even if at the outset laws went no further than to prescribe official authority, without prescribing on what grounds officials should decide to act, the regular practice of making such decisions would lead to generalizations about the grounds of decision—to a body of case law.[13] Yet these generalizations are not the government: the people who act as officials, the acts they do, their desires, ideals and prejudices. As an institution a government has regularities of behavior and patterns of structure which are partly determined by law and partly not. This is true of the foreign policy of our State Department, for instance, and of the practices of clerks of court in filing papers. That a government should strive to become a "government of laws" is a worthy ideal, though one that it can never attain, and ought not to attain unqualifiedly.[14] That a government should strive to become "a government of laws *and not of men*," [15] is unattainable because it is self-contradictory. As a set of prescriptions for official conduct, laws without officials would be prescriptions with no pharmacist to fill them. The same people who talk about the ideal of

---

13 See Llewellyn, "Case Law," (1930) 3 Encyc. of Soc. Sci., 249.

14 I. e., official discretion and "equity" (judicial departure from law) cannot be eliminated.

15 Mass. Constitution (Michie's Mass. Anno. Laws, 1933), Pt. I, Art. XXX: ". . . to the end it may be a government of laws and not of men." Among the a-logical factors are official fact-finding and the multiple-reference of the partly-processed facts of controversies worth litigating; i. e., different combinations of the total facts will make different legal generalizations applicable. As to the latter, see Stone, The Province and Function of Law (1946), Ch. VII, especially § 17.

"government of laws" can also be heard talking about "legal red tape," that is, too much law in government. The point is worth emphasizing that law and government are not identical, and it is confusing to talk as if they were.

The generality of law is an important means of protecting the individual against official partiality and oppression. Impartiality in dispute-settling is a minimum end of law; it might be attained by the official casting of (honest) dice, or by any other form of chance decision. The use of this method to choose those who were to be drafted into the American armed forces, in 1917 and again in 1940, shows that this method is not wholly obsolete. Of course the drawing was circumscribed by an elaborate set of legal rules specifying the classes of persons who were to be subject to the draft. The chance method of decision satisfies the minimum requirement of impartiality. It is a satisfactory method only when it can be safely assumed that all the claims among which some selection must be made are of substantially equal merit. This assumption cannot safely be made with respect to the claims involved in civil and criminal litigation generally, and so officials deciding such disputes are required to pass upon the merits of the respective claims. For this purpose the official adjudicators are provided with general directions as to the merits of claims and the methods of determining their merits, which constitute the bulk of professional lawyers' law. These general directions—the law of contracts, of torts, of property, etc.—are designed to circumscribe the decision of the official so that his personal prejudices, and all other factors incompatible with the merits of the claim as indicated by the legal directions, shall have no influence upon the decision. That the law is not uniformly efficacious in attaining this end does not prove that it is not an end.

The function of law in protecting the individual against official oppression is illustrated by the principle of criminal law, "no punishment without a law." [16] By prescribing in advance what kinds of conduct shall be sufficient to invoke severe official penalties, the criminal law furnishes a safeguard to the liberty of the individual against imprisonment because of conduct not so specified.[17] In order that this safeguard be efficacious something more is required than a merely logical generality. For any law in gen-

---

16 See Hall, "Nulla Poena Sine Lege," (1937) 47 Yale L.J. 165.

17 See Radin, Law as Logic and Experience (1940), 108; McBoyle v. U. S., 283 U.S. 25, 51 Sup.Ct. 340 (1931).

eral terms, as distinct from individual terms, would satisfy the logical requirement of generality: "Any person who shall act contrary to the best interests of the state shall be guilty of a felony." [18] Yet such a provision, though enacted with the proper formalities for a statute, would not be valid law under the constitution of the United States.[19] For functional efficacy requires something more than logical generality. Does it follow that such a vague generalization is necessarily not law in any sense? The answer is negative. If the answer were affirmative, then, as a matter of usage, a good deal of notoriously vague case law—such as the doctrine of laches and the principles of undue influence— would have to be relegated to some limbo of mumbo-jumbo. A more basic reason is that to require that law be semantically effective to fulfill its functions, or any one of them, is to introduce the ideal requirement with its attendant confusions. The generality of law does not guarantee that official oppression will be eliminated; it furnishes a means by which it *may* be minimized.

The same may be said of legal "certainty," the reliable guidance for the citizen with respect to his future conduct. The effort to formulate definite rules of property and commercial law is directed toward this end. Men risk their fortunes and their hopes of security upon the reliability of rules of property law. The efficiency of such rules depends upon the semantic requirement that their terms have concreteness of reference; yet the logical generality of the terms is a necessary condition.

Any body of law is, or has in it, many compromises between conflicting claims and interests, between competing ideas of justice, policy or convenience. Almost any controversial statute, in its passage through the legislature, reveals the process of give and take which culminates in the final formula. A similar process of compromise often precedes the emergence of an appellate court's opinion in a warmly contested case, though the privacy of judicial chambers ordinarily screens the process. The formulation which emerges from the law-making process is likely not to be moulded to any one's heart's desire. Yet it provides a modus vivendi. Because of this function of law it is ordinarily not safe

---

[18] The press-censorship law of Nazi Germany contained a provision of about this vagueness. See the recent decision declaring "sacrilegious" too vague as a statutory ground for denying a motion picture license. Burstyn, Inc. v. Wilson, 343 U.S. 495, 72 Sup.Ct. 777 (1952).

[19] See the vague law declared to be unconstitutional in Lanzetta v. State of New Jersey, 306 U.S. 451, 59 Sup.Ct. 618 (1939).

to *identify* the meaning of a statute with *"the* policy" which it was intended to fulfill—for several policies may be partly given effect in a statute. Law as a generalization is capable of promoting reconciliation and peace.

A mature body of law has ordinarily continuity with the past. The legal doctrines that it carries forward from past generations may or may not be conducive to the welfare of the present society.[20] Looking upon the brighter side of it, one can see that it enables laws to survive changes in the personnel of government, and it preserves the wisdom of wise lawmakers—legislative and judicial—to live on after they have passed away. That is possible because laws are general rules or principles in communicable form. A wise man's hunches do not survive him. A body of law is thus a co-operative product, of many men in the same generation, and of men of successive generations. Law-makers may not be any wiser than law-administrators; but *if* they are, the wisdom of the few who are wise may be, through law, transmitted in part to a host of administrators who are less wise.[21] The blueprints of the inventor transmit his ingenuity to a host of mechanics who make the finished product. The two cases have basic differences (supra, § 1.26), yet they have one basic similarity. The generality of law makes possible the mass utilization of ingenuity and wisdom.

These reasons in support of the view that generality is a characteristic of law need not have been presented so fully but for the recent attempts to represent law as something that lacks this quality. It was suggested above that most of these attacks—at least the ones by men of legal experience—do not in the final analysis deny that rules or principles or policies of law play an indispensable role in the judicial and administrative processes. For the reasons indicated at the beginning of this section it is advisable to distinguish the law of a state from the totality of its governmental processes.

"Justice according to law" is used by writers on jurisprudence to mean the decision of particular disputes by adjudicators—judicial or administrative—who apply established rules and principles of law, i. e., lawyer's law. It has been said that "justice" can be

---

20 "But the present has a right to govern itself so far as it can; and it ought always to be remembered that historic continuity with the past is not a duty, it is only a necessity." Holmes, "Learning and Science" (1895) in Hall, 669. See also Salmond, Jurisprudence (7th ed., 1924), § 16.

21 For similar arguments by St. Thomas Aquinas, see infra, § 4.13, p. 350.

administered without law. "All that the judge absolutely requires," said Markby, "is authority to settle all disputes that come before him." [22] Such a statement means that judges could decide disputes without any decisional law as to the *merits* of the respective claims; they could decide them by chance or by hunch. However, in a political society of substantial size, unity and permanency, that is, in a state,[23] some general standing directions would be needed to give the judges *authority* to decide disputes. The kind of law that sets the framework of government, "structural law," is important though sometimes overlooked by lawyers, who are primarily interested in the law by which disputes are to be decided, "decisional law." This is the law referred to in "justice according to law."

Professor Roscoe Pound has listed six advantages of the administration of justice according to law. All of them are, it will be seen, advantages which were attributed above to the generality of law:

"(1) Law makes it possible to predict the course which the administration of justice will take; (2) law secures against errors of individual judgment [i. e., of the individual judge]; (3) law secures against improper motives on the part of those who administer justice; (4) law provides the magistrate with standards in which the ethical ideas of the community are formulated; (5) law gives the magistrate the benefit of all the experience of his predecessors; (6) law prevents sacrifice of ultimate interests, social and individual, to the more obvious and pressing but less weighty, immediate interests." [24]

Where Professor Pound says "secures" and "prevents," one might more safely say "makes it possible" to secure or prevent, or makes security or prevention more probable than it would be without law. For the advantages above listed are based on experience, and on that basis are only more or less probable. Critics who become impatient with the prevailing legal order—they are always with us—are likely to point to any exaggeration of the advantages of justice according to law as indicating a belief in a

---

[22] Markby, Elements of Law, § 201. ". . . the administration of justice is perfectly possible without law at all." Salmond, op. cit., supra, n. 20, § 15, p. 40.

[23] See Lowie, The Origin of the State (1927).

[24] Pound, "Justice According to Law," (1913) 13 Columbia L.Rev. 696, 709. See also Salmond, op. cit., supra, note 20, § 16.

priori or absolute principles. A more cautious view of these advantages makes it easier to see that in some situations, such as the need for administrative tribunals to adjust serious and urgent conflicts in an industrial society, the advantages of "justice according to law" may be outweighed by other advantages of social expediency and justice, with the result that tribunals are established with only a minimum of decisional rules to begin with. In the long run, however, the advantages of law as a set of decisional norms will become apparent on the basis of experience.

Many of the arguments in support of my view that the generality of law is its most important characteristic have been touched upon in discussing the reasons for studying jurisprudence (§ 1.00) and the uses of logic in law (§ 1.11) and will be further developed in explaining efforts to make law systematic (§ 3.20). Among the more mundane explanations of the human tendency to develop more inclusive generalizations is the economy of effort in remembering and recording ideas, in logical reasoning about them, and in communicating ideas, one's own or others, to other people. Intellectual curiosity about the "why" of things leads to explicit generalizations which, even though often equivocal, narrow the range of choice. Finally, as a law teacher for many years I have been impressed with the view that generalizations of or about law constitute the only knowledge about law that I can transmit to students. Along with the generalizations the students acquire examples of their operational meanings, as exemplified in adjudications or in my own experience (professor's anecdotes). This is my vocational preference. It does not mean that all of legal education need be confined to "law in books".

§ 2.12—Logical Aspects of the Generality of Law

What has been said about the importance of logic for law and about the limitations of logic (supra, § 1.11) is pertinent here and need not be repeated. The place of logical control in the operations of government is shown by Professor John Dewey's statement:

> An operation not formulated in a proposition is logically uncontrolled, no matter how useful it may be in habitual practice.[25]

The basic unit of logical analysis is the "proposition." If law is an aggregate of laws, if laws are generalizations, and generalizations are general propositions, then each proposition of law is "a

---

[25] Dewey, Logic: The Theory of Inquiry (1938), 274.

law." The chief objection to defining law by defining "a law" is the systematic character of law. However, logical theory shows clearly that a proposition (of any kind) has no *logical* function or status in isolation. The analysis of law into propositions is thus a logical device. It is an indispensable one for lawyers and judges because they have to deal at any one time with only a limited number of propositions of law—such as those involved in a particular case. Are "laws" or "rules of law" somehow different from "propositions of law"? According to the view here taken, a law is a proposition of law having a certain status, namely, that it has the authority and sanction of the state. Thus "proposition of law" has a tentative or indeterminate status with relation to these additional characteristics: It may or not be a part of the law of a particular state. This may be illustrated by taking a statement of law from a leading treatise on American law, and determining whether or not it is a rule of law in the state of New York. Take the following example:

"A promise to pay all or part of a debt of the promisor, discharged or dischargeable in bankruptcy proceedings begun before the promise is made, is binding." [26]

This is a proposition of law because it has a legal meaning; "is binding" means legal consequences, that an action is maintainable upon such a promise. But in New York a statute establishes an authoritative proposition that no action shall be maintained upon a promise to pay a debt discharged in bankruptcy unless the promise (or a memorandum thereof) is in writing and signed by the party to be charged.[27] Since the Restatement proposition means (implies) that oral promises to pay, etc., are binding and the New York statute means that they are not, the two are contradictory and the Restatement proposition of law is (partly) incorrect with respect to the law of New York.

In what sense, if at all, can it be said that propositions of law are true or false? A leading treatise on logic defines a proposition as "anything which can be said to be true or false." [28] An assertion such as "Churchill has red hair" or "Franklin D. Roosevelt died in 1945" is something that one can verify or disprove.

---

[26] Restatement, Contracts (American Law Institute, 1932), § 87, omitting an exception that is not pertinent here. In the context the proposition means that such a promise "is binding" even though not given for a consideration.

[27] N. Y. Personal Property Law, § 31.

[28] Cohen and Nagel, An Introduction to Logic and Scientific Method (1934), 27.

The same authors state, however, that a command is not a proposition, because a command "cannot as such be true or false." [29] When the boss says to the office boy, "Deliver this package to Mr. Jones," or the sheriff says to the jailer, "Lock this man up in the padded cell," nothing is asserted that can be verified or disproved. If Austin was right in calling a law a "command" (§ 2.04) then a law is not (by Cohen and Nagel's test) a proposition and law is banished from the realm of logic. This startling conclusion would merely lead some observers of the legal scene to say, "I told you so!" However, it would have shocked a good many generations of English and American judges, and it contradicts what Professor Morris R. Cohen, one of the logicians above quoted, has said about the place of logic in the law (§ 1.11). The answer is that the logicians were referring to an utterance imperative in form, and that Austin was using the term "command" too loosely. Laws are not commands, though they may eventuate in commands.

A more hopeful approach to the question of the truth or falsity of legal propositions is to ask, what significant questions can be asked about such propositions? The *legally* significant questions that can be asked about a proposition of law, such as the Restatement proposition or the New York statutory proposition above mentioned,[30] may be summarized as follows: (1) What person or persons uttered the proposition? (2) What was the exact text (symbolization) of the utterance? (3) What authority did such person or persons have to make such an utterance? (4) What is the meaning of the utterance (or, what are its meanings) with respect to the facts which it requires ("operative facts") and the legal consequences (ultimately, official conduct)? The first two of these are to be answered by observations and inferences of fact. While the procedures for answering them are not immune from logical control (e. g., the inference that a certain book accurately expresses the official text of a statute or a judicial opinion), they are not often seriously controverted in modern law. The legal historian has to worry about these questions more than the professional lawyer. The latter two are *primarily* legal questions. The authority of the persons who uttered the proposition depends in part on occurrences (election or appointment) and in part on the structural laws which prescribe the authority of such persons. The fourth question is ordinarily the most sig-

---

29 Ibid., 28.

30 Supra, notes 26, 27.

nificant one for it is the one which gives the proposition the character of a logical instrument of control over governmental operations. A body of law consists of propositions having interrelated meanings. Thus, by determining the meanings of the two propositions mentioned above one was enabled to conclude that the unofficial utterance conflicted in part with the official utterance. Most legal battles (controversies about questions of law) are waged in this realm of meanings.

A fifth question which might be asked about any question of law is: (5) Is it a just rule? Is it justified? This question is relevant to the meaning of the proposition of law in question only in so far as it points to some other authoritative proposition of the legal system which had a conflicting meaning.[31] It would be futile, for instance, to question in a law court the justice of the New York statute quoted above, unless one could point to some other authoritative proposition of the same legal system which contradicted it. However, this fifth question is commonly relevant in controversies about the meaning of case law because judges do have a limited authority to make law, and the line between extricating the meaning of an established proposition of law and making a (partly) new one is notoriously amorphous.

In what sense, then, is a proposition of law "true" or "false"? It can be "true" or "false" only in the sense that it is or is not an utterance by some person or persons having authority to make such an utterance, and even then it is only true or false to the extent of such authority. The statement: *It is the law of New York that* an oral promise to pay a debt discharged in bankruptcy is binding" can be shown to be false; but the part of this statement not italicized, standing alone, has no meaning that is susceptible of factual verification or disproof. Compare the scientific proposition, "All bodies are attracted to each other by a force which varies directly with the product of their respective masses and inversely with the square of the distance between them" ($F = \frac{MM_1}{D^2}$). The meaning of this proposition can be verified by observation and inference. Then compare the proposition: "Pure water at sea level boils at 100° C." The latter is not verified by experience; it is a conventional rule for testing thermometers, for assigning a meaning to "100° C." For more than

---

[31] The analysis here given may be compared with that of the late Professor Kantorowicz, in "Legal Science—A Summary of Its Methodology," (1928) 28 Columbia L.Rev. 679; Hall, 124.

a century this convention has been followed among scientists.[32] Legal propositions resemble the latter rather than the former. Hence it seems better to say that a legal proposition is "correct" or "incorrect" in relation to a specified body of positive law, than to call it "true" or "false." Professor Kelsen expresses a similar conception when he says that law has "validity." [33] Professor Dewey believing that even scientific propositions rest to some extent on the authority of those who affirm them, and distrusting the accumulated meanings of "truth," has substituted "warrantably assertible." [34] To say that a proposition of law is a correct statement of the law of New York is to say that we are warranted in asserting it to be authoritative in New York.

What is a "General" Proposition? The generality of a proposition depends upon the generality of its terms (or of at least one of its terms). A proposition of law is general because its terms refer to an indefinite number of individual instances, in contrast with a term which refers to an individual instance or a definite number of individual instances. Compare the two following statements:

> I.   All persons born or naturalized in the United States, and subject to the jurisdiction thereof, are citizens of the United States, and of the state wherein they reside.[35]
> II.   John was born in the United States.

The first means not merely that those persons who were born or naturalized in the United States, etc., *before* 1868, the date of the adoption of the Amendment, but that an indefinite number of persons thereafter and hereafter having the prescribed qualifications, will be citizens. The second refers only to a single individual. The general terms of propositions are common nouns. The immediate forms of individual propositions have as their subjects only proper names (such as "John") or demonstratives ("this," "that"), which are the two ways of referring immediately (without the mediation of a general term) to an individual item.[36] However, one can refer to an individual item by using a

---

32 The standardizing of thermometers is no doubt a more complex matter than is here pictured.

33 Kelsen in (1935) 51 L.Q.Rev. 517; Hall, 653. However, the "validity" of a legal proposition cannot be "purified" of factual elements to the extent that Professor Kelsen's Pure Theory requires.

34 Dewey, op. cit., supra, note 25, Ch. I, especially pp. 4–9.

35 U. S. Constitution, Amendment XIV, sec. 1.

36 This analysis is based on Eaton, General Logic (1931), 58–64.

general term, such as "this man." Proper name includes the name of a group, such as the United States Steel Corporation. Thus the following statement is an individual proposition:

III. All (present) stockholders of the United States Steel Corporation were born in the United States.

Even though the number of stockholders is several hundred thousand, it is still a definite number at any given time.

Now suppose that a statute were passed by Congress as follows:

IV. All present and future stockholders of the United States Steel Corporation shall be exempt from the payment of income taxes.

The subject of this proposition is an indefinite number of persons, since it is not impossible that everyone born in the United States may become such a stockholder. Logically, then, this is a general, not an individual, "law." In its operation, however, it would lack the impartiality of law; it would appear to be a kind of favoritism. Thus while it would be a law, it would almost certainly not be a good law, and it would probably not be a valid law because of the "equal protection" clause of the Federal constitution. The highest court of California recently held unconstitutional a California statute that barred the Communist Party, by name, from participating in primary elections, on the ground that it was a special law imposing "peculiar disabilities in the exercise of a common right upon a single person or group arbitrarily selected." [37] Since the statute would bar an indefinite number of persons (all present and future members of the Communist Party) from a certain mode of action (becoming a candidate in the primaries on the Communist ticket), it seems to be a general rule and therefore "a law." Constitutional restraints prevent legislatures from making laws which they otherwise might.

Now the term, "United States Steel Corporation" and the term, "Communist Party of U. S. A." are proper names, and therefore the propositions above mentioned (proposition IV and the California statute) are not "universal" in scope. It might therefore be argued that they are not really laws. The argument proves too much. Every positive law is limited in scope to the residents of the territory or citizens of the state that gives it authority; the class of individuals to whom it applies is thus partly defined by the use of a proper name, such as "United States of

---

[37] Communist Party of U. S. A. v. Peek, 20 Cal.2d 536, 549, 127 P.2d 889, 897 (1942).

America" or "France." Even if there were a world government with world law, it would be limited to one of the smaller planets, the Earth. The generality of positive law is not the same as the universality of physical laws. This limitation has significance for the conflict of laws.

The generality of a law depends, as was said above, upon its being applicable to an indefinite number of human beings. This seems the most significant aspect of the generality of law. However, Austin defined generality with respect to the *acts* enjoined or prohibited. He says that a command to the whole community (of a state) to do a "specifically determined" act (as distinguished from a *class* of acts or forbearances) is not a law.[38] Two difficulties with this test may be pointed out: One is that if the test is a *class* of acts, then the following (hypothetical) official enactment or order would be a law: "John Doe shall not drive any motor vehicle on a highway at a speed exceeding twenty miles per hour." On the contrary, this is not a law by the test above proposed, since it applies only to a single individual. The second objection is that one cannot conceive of a command or order addressed to an indefinite number of individuals to do or not to do a single individual act. Thus a provision of the naturalization statute requiring all applicants for citizenship, as a condition of naturalization, to take an oath to support the constitution of the United States, is applicable to an indefinite number of persons and requires an indefinite number of acts, all of the *same kind*. The same is true of a prohibition, such as: "Any person who shall deface the Washington Monument in Washington, D. C., shall be guilty of a misdemeanor and shall be punishable by, etc." An indefinite number of acts might be violations of such a provision, because it applies to an indefinite number of persons.[39] Now take an order like this: "All male inhabitants of the United States between the ages of twenty-one and forty-five shall register with Selective Service Draft Boards on October 15, 1940." The number of such persons on that date was a definite number, and the number of such acts was definite, too. This would not be a law, but rather an executive order. The Selective Service Act (of

---

38 Austin, Lectures on Jurisprudence (4th ed., 1874), 97.

39 In applying the distinction between rule-making and adjudication under the Federal Administrative Procedure Act of 1946 (60 Stat. 237, 5 U.S.C.A. § 100) the generality of persons was referred to as a test, though not exclusive. Willapoint Oysters v. Ewing, 174 F.2d 676, 678, 692 (C.A.9 1949), certiorari denied 338 U.S. 860, 70 Sup.Ct. 101 (1949).

1940) applied to all who should *thereafter* become twenty-one years of age—an indefinite number.

An enactment of a legislature that is applicable only to a named individual is not a "law" as that term is here used, though by usage such enactments are often called "private laws." Thus an act of Congress directing the Secretary of the Treasury to have a medal made and to present it to Roland Boucher for his heroism in rescuing several children from drowning [40] is not a "law" in the general sense of that term. An enactment of the legislature of Louisiana authorizing Miss Annie C. Lewis to institute a suit against the state for personal injuries sustained while she was confined in a state institution was held by the Supreme Court of that state not to be a "law," not even a "special law." [41] Although the legislature is, under the separation of powers, the primary "law-making" body, not every order of the legislature makes law. An order of a Board of Park Commissioners fixing the salary of a named individual was held not to be a "law." [42] Such decisions are not, of course, conclusive as to the general conception of law, since that conception may be modified by the context in which the word, "law," occurs.

For the reasons indicated an ordinary judgment of a court is not a "law." Such a judgment applies only to a limited number of individuals, the parties to the case. Thus a Federal criminal sentence declares that the defendant "is hereby committed" to the custody of the Attorney-General for imprisonment,[43] and a civil judgment is a declaration that the plaintiff (or plaintiffs) a named individual or individuals, "do recover" of the named defendant(s) a specified sum, etc.[44] Here I disagree with Dr. Kelsen's statement that the judicial decision itself is an individual legal norm.[45] The expression "individual legal norm" is, in the terminology here adopted, a self-contradiction. However, a prohibitory-injunction decree is a legal norm if it prohibits not only

---

[40] Act of Congress of January 20, 1942, 56 U.S.Stat.L.Pt. 2, pp. 1099–1100, "Private Laws," 77th Congress, 2d Sess.

[41] Lewis v. State, 196 La. 814, 818, 200 So. 265, 266 (1941).

[42] McCarthy v. City of Malden, 303 Mass. 563, 566, 22 N.E.2d 104, 107 (1939).

[43] For a form of such judgment, see Robinson, Cases on Criminal Law and Procedure (1941), 1216.

[44] For a form, see Scott and Simpson, Cases on Judicial Remedies (1938), 35.

[45] Kelsen, General Theory of Law and State (1945), 134. Hall, 656.

the named defendants but also all other persons having knowledge of the decree from doing designated acts. In a recent Federal case the court argued that such a decree was a law.[46] The Supreme Court reversed the decision without commenting on the generality of law.[47]

"General" and "Special" Laws. The constitutions of nearly all states of the United States contain provisions that prohibit, or limit in various ways, the enactment of "special" or "local" laws; a few refer to "private" laws. In some the term "general" law is used in opposition to "special" or "local" law.[48] Judicial constructions of these provisions show that the logical conception of generality is relevant but not always decisive; something that has the logical generality of law may be deemed to be prohibited because of its functional or operational meaning. One main objective of such provisions, it is frequently recognized, is to prevent the enactment of legislation applicable to a single municipality. Hence an enactment applicable only to a single municipality, by name, would be a "special" or "local" law, though its provisions would affect an indefinite number of individual humans, the present and future inhabitants of the named municipality. On the other hand, a classification of municipalities on the basis of population is for many purposes a reasonable classification. A recent Florida statute prescribed a peculiar method of nominating county commissioners in counties having a population of not less than 18,000 and not more than 18,500, as shown by the last Federal census *preceding the enactment of the law.* Although the formula included two counties, it was held invalid as a "local" or "special" law.[49] Since the number of counties was fixed once and for always by the Federal census already taken, the proposition in its reference to counties was individual, not general. A "class" that is closed when the statute is enacted is not a general class.[50] The enactment was not *possibly* applicable to an indefi-

---

46 U. S. v. Pendergast, 35 F.Supp. 593, 599 (D.C.Mo. 1940).

47 Pendergast v. U. S., 317 U.S. 412, 63 Sup.Ct. 268 (1943).

48 Citations in Paramino Lumber Co. v. Marshall, 309 U.S. 370, 380, 60 Sup.Ct. 600, 604, note 24 (1940); see Cloe and Marcus, "Special and Local Legislation," (1936) 24 Ky.L.J. 351.

49 State ex rel. Levine v. Bailey, 124 Fla. 241, 168 So. 12 (1936).

50 Similar statutes were held invalid in: Jones v. Methvin, 193 Ga. 17, 21, 17 S.E.2d 172, 175 (1941) ("all counties having a population of more than 21,020 and less than 21,024, according to the official census of the United States for the year 1940"); City of Fort Worth v. Bobbitt, 121 Tex. 14, 36 S.W.2d 470 (1931).

nite number of municipal corporations. On the other hand, a statute applicable to cities having a population of more than 500,000, as determined by the *present or any future* Federal census, is not necessarily invalid merely because at the time of enactment only one city has the required population.[51] Here the class was not closed; other cities might attain the required population. However, a mere possibility that others might enter the class is not always deemed sufficient; a high degree of probability that only one individual will be found to be included in the class is sometimes deemed to make the enactment "special" or "local." The New York constitution prohibits the enactment of laws relating to the property, affairs or government of cities, which shall be "special or local either in its terms or in its effect." [52] A statute studiously worded in general terms but specifying many conditions which, though they fitted the case of a particular claimant exactly, it would have been "a most singular coincidence" if they applied to even one other individual's case, was held to be invalid.[53] Cardozo, J., said:

> "An act is not general when the class established by its provisions is at once so narrow and arbitrary that duplication of its content is to be ranked as an unexpected freak of chance, a turn of the wheel of fortune defying probabilities. . . ." [54]

This New York statute was not, however, in terms applicable to an indefinite number of claims, since it was limited to claims barred within one year before its enactment. It thus did not

---

[51] E. g., Admiral Realty Co. v. City of New York, 206 N.Y. 110, 138, 99 N.E. 241, 249 (1912) (statute applicable to cities having more than one million population).

[52] N. Y. Constitution (1924), Art. XII, sec. 2 (similar provision in Art. IX, sec. 11 of the 1936 constitution).

[53] In re Elm Street in City of New York, 246 N.Y. 72, 158 N.E. 24 (1927). A similar dodge was held invalid in State ex rel. Atty. General v. Lee, 193 Ark. 270, 272, 99 S.W.2d 835, 836 (1936). The New York provision (Laws 1925, Ch. 602, sec. 1) read:
"Sec. 1. Where an award of damages has been made and confirmed by the Supreme Court in condemnation proceedings to acquire title in fee to real property for the purpose of opening, widening or extending a street in any city and said award has not been paid, but within one year last past has been adjudged by the courts of this state to have been barred by any statute of limitations, a claim for the payment of such award may . . . again be prosecuted . . . as if the same had not been barred. . . ."

[54] 246 N.Y. at p. 78, 158 N.E. at p. 26.

meet even the logical test of generality.[55] The New York constitution prescribes both the logical ("in its terms") and the operational or functional ("in its effect") test of generality.

Whether a given legislative direction is a "general law" is determined partly by the context in which the term occurs, and also partly by a basic conception of law. Enough has been said in this and the two preceding sections to show what generality means in the basic conception here adopted.

---

[55] See supra, note 53.

Chapter 6

THE NORMATIVE CHARACTER OF LAW

§ 2.20—Law as Rule, Prediction, Norm

That the law of a modern state is a body of rules is a conception of law widely accepted by writers on jurisprudence (supra, §§ 2.00, 2.01, 2.04). Even Salmond, who recognizes a half-dozen varieties of law, defines "civil law," the only kind with which he is concerned, as a body of "rules" or "principles":

> "The law may be defined as the body of principles recognized and applied by the state in the administration of justice. In other words, the law consists of the rules recognized and acted on by courts of justice." [1]

Despite his insistence upon the primacy of "the spirit of the people" among the sources of law (§ 2.03), Savigny, when he came to write a treatise on modern Roman law, defined law in terms of rules:

> "The rules whereby such boundaries [i. e., boundaries within which the existence and activity of each individual gains a secure free opportunity] are determined and through them this free opportunity is secured are the law." [2]

Here three topics will be examined: 1. The meanings of "rule." 2. The broader conception, "norm." 3. To whom are legal norms addressed?

1. *The Meanings of "Rule."* The notion of a rule appears at first a simple one, yet analysis reveals differences in meaning which are significant for the conception of law.

a. *Regularity of recurrence of phenomena.* This is a very old conception of rule, one that originally was thought to include both physical laws and political laws. More recently Salmond used law in the widest sense to include "any standard or pattern to which actions (whether the acts of rational agents or the operations of nature) are or ought to be conformed." [3] Ehrlich's conception of "living law" (supra, §§ 1.05, 2.03) is a recurrence of

---

[1] Salmond, Jurisprudence (7th ed., 1924), § 13, p. 33.

[2] Savigny, System des heutigen römischen Rechts (1840), § 52; translated Pound, Outlines (5th ed.), 65.

[3] Op. cit., § 5.

this notion; and Pound's provocative phrase, "law in action", meant primarily regularities of official behavior that did not conform to the "law in books." [4] Ehrlich referred to the regularities of conduct of individuals and groups in society; Pound, to the conduct of courts. This latter conception of law is likely to seem the real one to the lawyer who believes that the court has not correctly applied the law to his case, and to the professor who believes he can "line up" a group of decisions in some pattern which the judges unfortunately overlooked or neglected to mention. However, the view that the law *consists of* such regularities is inadequate and even misleading. A newly enacted statute is law although it has as yet established no regularities of behavior, official or unofficial. A crucial judicial decision becomes a precedent [5] binding on lower courts before it has established regularities of conduct. Moreover, the highest court has the *power* to break with its past regularities. One could draw a pattern of the Supreme Court decisions between 1890 and 1930 on the constitutionality of statutes regulating business and industry that would be quite misleading with respect to the decisions on the same subject after 1937. The sociologist of law, surveying the legal scene with cheerful detachment, may well regard the statute or the decision as merely the tentative beginning of a new set of regularities. To the lawyer and judge who have the responsibility of shaping the new regularities, the statute and the precedent are prescriptions of what they ought to do or shall do. And even if a statute ceases to produce any regularities, it does not, in most modern legal systems, cease to be law. Factual regularities are important for the efficiency or goodness of laws, but they do not adequately exemplify the conception of law.

b. *Prediction.* From regularity of occurrence in the past to a prediction of similar regularity or occurrence in the future is an almost inevitable step; and yet it is a very important one. That a line of decisions of a court, displaying a specific regularity down to the present time, is a basis for predicting what the court will do in the future, is generally accepted in Anglo-American law, and to some extent in the European systems. However, the famous and influential prediction theory of law of O. W. Holmes, Jr. was not based upon regularities of conduct but upon the rules

---

[4] Pound, "Law in Books and Law in Action," (1910) 44 American L.Rev. 12; Cohen and Cohen, 419.

[5] "Precedent" is used throughout this book to mean the "decision" (the judgment or order of the tribunal in its context of pleadings and evidence) plus the significance of the decision and opinion for future decisions.

laid down in the books. Addressing a body of law students and practicing lawyers, he stepped down from the bench for the moment to look at law from the practitioner's point of view. "When we study law," he said, "we are studying what we shall want in order to appear before judges, or to advise people in such a way as to keep them out of court." "The object of our study, then, is prediction, the prediction of the incidence of the public force through the instrumentality of the courts." These predictions are to be made, he said, by the study of the judicial reports, treatises and statutes. The most important effort of legal thought is to make these prophecies more precise and to generalize them into a thoroughly connected system. Putting them into general propositions makes them easier to understand. In this context Holmes said:

"The prophecies of what the courts will do in fact, and nothing more pretentious, are what I mean by the law." [6]

Holmes' prediction theory of law has had a pervasive influence upon legal thinking in the United States. Those who came after him have drawn from isolated passages conclusions scarcely warranted by his address as a whole. Holmes wanted to dispel two confusing notions about law: one, the confusion of moral ideas and legal ideas; the other, that the law "is a deduction from principles of ethics or admitted axioms or what not, which may or may not coincide with the decisions." [7] While the language of the law abounds in terms having moral connotations—right, duty, malice, intent, negligence, etc.—these have different meanings in law. For instance, "malice" in defamation cases does not mean actual desire to harm; one can be liable for defaming a person whom one believes to be dead.[8] To find the legal meanings of such a term we must "wash it with cynical acid and expel everything except the object of our study, the operations of the law." [9] That is the way the "bad man" looks at law; he cares nothing about ethical rules, but is likely "to care a good deal to avoid being made to pay money, and will want to keep out of jail if he can." [10] For him a judgment of a court means no more than that

---

[6] The foregoing is partly quoted and partly paraphrased from "The Path of the Law," in Holmes, Collected Legal Papers (1920), 167–169; originally printed in (1897) 10 Harvard L.Rev. 457; Hall, 670; Cohen and Cohen, 416–417.

[7] Op. cit., 172; Hall, 670; Cohen and Cohen, 417.

[8] Ibid., 176–177.

[9] Ibid., 174.

[10] Ibid., 170.

"if a man does or omits certain things, he will be made to suffer in this way or that by the judgment of the court." [11]

Holmes thus presents in a dramatic way the view that the meaning of law depends upon its operational effects, a view derived from Charles S. Peirce's pragmatism (infra, § 4.50) and resembling that of logical positivism (§ 1.12). And in rejecting the notion that law is the product of deduction from ethical principles or axioms he anchored law to decisions and other official acts. Both of these ideas were substantial contributions to twentieth century jurisprudence.

The influence of the prediction theory on legal education can be seen in the writings of such able law teachers as Walter Wheeler Cook, Herman Oliphant and Arthur L. Corbin. Corbin, following Hohfeld, defined a legal relation to be "a prediction as to what society, acting through its courts or executive agents, will do or not do for one [party] and against the other." [12] Cook, a leader among the American legal realists (infra, § 4.63), extended the prediction theory to include not only the operational effects of law on official conduct, but also its effects upon the individuals and institutions of society.[13] Judge Cardozo, whose books had considerable influence on law faculties during the 1920's, while not defining law as a prediction, accepted predictability as the test of authority of a legal doctrine:

"A principle or rule of conduct so established as to justify a prediction with reasonable certainty that it will be enforced by the courts if its authority is challenged is, then, for the purpose of our study, a principle or rule of law." [14]

Under the influence of the prediction theory, legal scholars, lawyers and judges re-examined traditional legal doctrines and punctured a good many inflated windbags.

The prediction theory was congenial to the mores of the legal profession at the close of the nineteenth century. The leadership of the bar had passed from the dramatic advocates, the

---

[11] Ibid., 169.

[12] Corbin, "Legal Analysis and Terminology," (1919) 29 Yale L.J. 163, 164; Hall, 473. See supra, § 2.05, note 77.

[13] See Cook, "Scientific Method and the Law," (1927) 13 A.B.A.J. 303, 308; Hall, 784–786. However, Pound's sociological jurisprudence had previously presented a similar view. Infra, § 4.60.

[14] The Growth of the Law (1924), 52. Further discussion of Cardozo, infra, § 4.62.

Daniel Websters, to the shrewd legal counselors who were guid·
ing the destinies of American commerce, industry and finance.
To these counselors the most important aspect of the law was its
certainty, its capacity to serve as an instrument of prediction
for the drafting of instruments and other legal arrangements.
Holmes himself did not regard certainty as the most important
function of law, for he said (rather inconsistently) that "certainty
generally is illusion." [15]　The charge that Holmes sought to banish
social ideals from the law is refuted by the latter part of the same
address, in which he urged that judges should constantly have in
mind the basic social policies of the law.[16]　However, the prediction theory emphasizes the need for narrow, precise rules in concrete terms, and stresses the semantic ineffectiveness (§ 1.12) of
statements of social policy unless they are implemented by definite legal consequences.　The "prophecies" that Holmes referred
to were the *generalized* predictions of legal rules and doctrines
from which the *individualized* predictions of the legal counselor
are derived.

The prediction theory of law is inadequate for two reasons:
first, because legal rules *alone* do not provide adequate grounds
for predicting what judicial decisions (or other official conduct)
will be.　Second, because it approaches law from the standpoint
of the practitioner, and does not adequately present that of the
judge.　As to the first, the outcome of litigation depends upon
many factors besides legal rules: the prejudices or ideas of fairness of the judges and the jurymen, their making or not making
correct findings of fact, the availability and cogency of witnesses,
etc.　Legal rules do not purport to predict the effects of any of
these factors.　Furthermore, a lawyer trying to predict the outcome of projected litigation needs information about many matters which are involved in the particular case: in a patent suit,
information about physics and chemistry, or in an automobile
negligence case the distance in which a given car traveling at a
given speed can be brought to a stop.　Not everything that a
legal practitioner needs to know is law.　As to the second, the
law does not appear to the judge as a *prediction* of what he "will"
do.　He is trying to make up his mind what he will do.　When he
turns to the law for guidance, he regards legal rules as telling

---

[15] Op. cit., supra, note 6, 181; Hall, 670.

[16] Ibid., 184: "their [judges'] duty of weighing considerations of social
advantage."

him what he "should" or "shall" or "may" do.[17] Neither statutes nor judicial opinions contain explicitly any predictions as to what officials will do. The prediction aspect of law is a derivation from its imperative or normative aspect. The latter is its more inclusive and therefore its basic aspect.

c. *Prudential prescription.* Closely related to the view that a rule is a prediction is the one that a rule prescribes a course of conduct to be followed in the practice of an art, in order to get the best results. Salmond gave these rules a separate name, "Professional or Technical Law," and included under this heading the "laws" of musical and poetical composition, the "laws" of style, the "laws" of architecture, and the rules for playing games.[18] So the law (political law) is in one sense a set of rules for the practitioners of an art: counseling, advocacy, adjudicating disputes. Bentham, taking the rules of law to be addressed to laymen, compared rules of law to prudential prescriptions of a similar sort. The sanctions of these prescriptions are "physical or natural sanctions," the harmful consequences that follow from not conforming to the admonition of the rule.[19] "You had better screen your fireplace" is a prudential prescription that *if* you do not, your house may be thereby set on fire; the hardship is a physical or natural consequence of non-conformity.

This view of law (by no means the only one produced by Jeremy Bentham's fertile imagination) has an appealing simplicity. What is the Statute of Wills to a layman but a prudential prescription that if he tries to make a will without conforming to the statutory formalities, his document will be legally ineffective? Or, if you endorse a negotiable instrument unqualifiedly (without adding some such words as "without recourse"), you may be held liable to pay it if another party does not. That is all that the "bad man" wants to know about the law; it is also, in the illustrations given, all that the "good man" wants to know. For these illustrations exemplify Immanuel Kant's view that the law deals only with the external aspects of conduct, and takes no account of motives (infra, § 4.22). Legally it makes no difference whether a man pays his income tax because he feels un-

---

[17] A trial-court judge may examine legal doctrines and precedents with a view to predicting what an appellate court will do on appeal; yet I doubt if that is ordinarily his primary conception of legal guidance.

[18] Salmond, op. cit., supra, note 1, § 11, p. 31.

[19] Austin, Lectures (4th ed., 1874), 217–219.

der a moral duty to support the government, or because he wants to keep out of jail.

However, the prudential prescription analogy is, as to the layman at least, open to two kinds of objections. The law does not always purport to give a man an option to conform or not to conform to its admonition. The penal law does not merely say, "if you choose to commit premeditated murder, you will be executed or imprisoned for life." We express this by saying that the law imposes a legal *duty* not to commit murder; the policy of the law is to prevent its occurrence. The legal policy has legal consequences other than execution or imprisonment; it invalidates agreements which tend to promote or encourage murder. On the other hand, there is no legal duty to make a will, or to endorse an instrument without recourse. The prudential prescription idea is only a partial explanation of the nature of law.

A second objection is more fundamental, namely, that the disadvantageous consequences of not conforming to law are not physical or natural consequences caused by non-conformity; they are imposed by political authority. If a man eats imprudently, his discomfort or illness follows autonomously from his imprudent act. If a man commits murder or neglects to have at least two witnesses to his will, the legal consequence follows only because the law prescribes that it shall follow. Some European jurisprudents have expressed this idea by saying that the sanction of law is heteronomous, or that the law is a heteronomous system. Again we come back to the imperative or normative conception of law as the most pervasive and basic one.

d. *Imperative or norm.* The conception of law as a body of imperatives (§ 2.04) raises some difficulties. When as lawyers we come to examine the body of law with which we are familiar, we find a good many statements that are not explicitly imperative ("shall" or "must") and that do not seem to lead to a command or prohibition. For instance, "a bid at an auction sale is an offer." Does that statement have an imperative meaning? Assuming that it is a correct proposition of the law in State X, it does. For it means that the auctioneer has a power of acceptance, and if he exercises that power a contract will be made, and if the contract is not fulfilled, an action may be maintained that will result in a judgment for damages, and any interference with the execution of that judgment may be suppressed by official force or imprisonment. The word "offer" has these implications only in the technical vocabulary of the law. "Offer" is also a term of common speech, and in that context it has no such implications. One who advertises goods for sale may say that he "offers" to sell them, and yet he may not have made a legal offer.[20] A good part of a body of law, especially case law, consists of statements that are definitional in character, that is, they explain the meanings of legal terms. Law students and teachers, legal scholars, even at times lawyers and judges, may objectify this realm of meanings [21] and treat it as if it had no relation to the realm of judicial judgments, sheriffs and jails. In this realm of meaning there are no norms but only relations of implication. Against this objectification and isolation of the law Holmes protested in his prediction theory.[22] Legal propositions and conceptions are *as such* meaningless unless they imply ultimately some consequences in the conduct (i. e. action or inaction) of political officials. Since, however, political officials are human beings with the power to act or not to act in accordance with these implications, the latter are imperative or normative; they express what "shall" be done (or omitted) or what "ought" to be done (or omitted). The difference between "shall" and "ought" is here chiefly one of emphasis. At least to the judges of a highest court the implications of the court's precedents ought to be followed unless they find cogent reasons for overruling them. That legal propositions imply that something ought to be done by officials is what is meant by their normative character. The law of a state is a body of legal norms.

2. *The Transition from Rules to Norms.* In the nineteenth century it was common, at least among Anglo-American jurisprudents, to define law as a body of rules. The word "rule" has come to mean, with many though not all writers, a rather precise and concretely worded proposition of law, such as, "a bid at an auction sale is an offer." If law consists only of such rules, then it does not include broader and vaguer statements of principle, such as, "no man shall profit by his own wrong," "no one shall be unjustly enriched at another's expense," [23] or "no

---

[20] E. g., Spencer v. Harding, L. R. 5 C. P. 561 (1870), where the circular in question read, "we are instructed to offer," yet the court held it was not an "offer."

[21] Cf. Kantorowicz, "Legal Science—A Summary of its Methodology," (1928) 28 Columbia L.Rev. 879, 882–884; Hall, 125.

[22] Supra, note 6. See also Frank, "Mr. Justice Holmes and Non-Euclidean Legal Thinking," (1932) 17 Cornell L.Q. 568; Hall, 365, 368. For a discussion of "law in discourse", see infra, § 3.00.

[23] Restatement, Restitution (1937), § 1.

person shall be deprived of life, liberty or property without due process of law." [24] Yet the latter are surely a part of the law of a good many states. A body of law also contains some basic "policies" commonly called public policies, which can scarcely be called "rules." To include these variants Roscoe Pound proposed a good many years ago the term, "norm." [25] It has considerable currency in European writings, though not in the usage of practitioners or judges.[26]

3. *To Whom are Legal Norms Addressed?* If legal norms are norms of human conduct, whose conduct are they rules of? To whom are they addressed? Are they directions to laymen, or to officials, or partly to each or both? The commands or admonitions of the Ten Commandments are addressed to laymen: "Thou shalt not kill." This is characteristic of a moral code rather than a legal code. The Code of Hammurabi (c. B. C. 1900) is typically in the "if—then" form: If a designated kind of conduct, then a designated penalty. The hypothetical legal norm directs officials as to the penalties or other sanctions to be imposed for designated kinds of conduct; it is also an admonition to subjects not to do the acts designated unless they want to suffer the consequences. It is a direction for both officials and laymen.

Austin, and probably most English writers on jurisprudence, conceived of a law as a command addressed to the subjects, laymen; such a command created a legal "duty" of the subject not to do the act prohibited. The introduction of the term "duty" as a necessary term in defining law has caused a good deal of unnecessary trouble to some English jurisprudents. "If a man makes a will without having at least two witnesses, then his will shall be a nullity." The late Professor Buckland was troubled by the thought that if nullity is a sanction, then every man must be under a duty to make a will,[27] which is obviously not correct.

---

24 ". . . nor shall any state deprive any person of life, liberty or property without due process of law." U. S. Constitution, Amendment XIV, sec. 1.

25 Pound, Outlines of Lectures on Jurisprudence, (5th ed., 1943), 75.

26 The term "legal norm" was used recently substantially in the sense defined above, while "legal rule" was used to mean a prediction derived from a legal norm. King, "The Concept of a Lawyer's Jurisprudence (1952) 11 Camb.L.J. 229, 233. This terminology is novel. Other writers use "rule" to include all norms.

27 Buckland, Some Reflections on Jurisprudence (1945), 90. The sanction of law is discussed in Ch. 7.

The Austinian view that all laws are commands is inadequate, if not inaccurate. The hypothetical imperative may or may not imply a duty to avoid the legal consequence predicated.

The question, to whom are legal norms addressed, has significance in several different ways. First, if every legal norm is addressed to officials, and if every legal norm has a sanction, then what is the sanction of the norm which obliges a judge to decide in accordance with the norm? This question will be discussed later (§ 2.32). Secondly, if a question arises as to whether a statute is so vaguely worded as not to conform to the requirement of "due process of law" of the Federal constitution, whose understanding of it is to be taken as the standard, the layman's or the judge's? In a recent case the test, applied to a statute creating a Federal criminal offense, was said to be whether it gave "a person, acting with reference to the statute, fair warning that his conduct was within its prohibition."[28]   Apparently the layman's standard was the test. That this standard is commonly applicable is shown by the use in Anglo-American law of a good many terms taken over from common speech.[29]   At least statutes defining penal offenses should be written in terms that are, to use Bentham's word, "cognoscible." Yet many rules of property law, and most rules of procedural law, are scarcely cognoscible to laymen. In this sense some legal norms are addressed primarily to laymen and incidentally to officials; while others are addressed only to officials, including the legal profession.

Thirdly, the functional aspect of law in society calls for a consideration of how law can be communicated to the individuals in society or made accessible to them through the legal profession. This question will be reserved for later discussion (§ 3.02).

§ 2.21—Negative, Permissive and Other Incomplete Legal Norms

The conception of law as a body of politically authoritative rules or norms purports to be applicable to, and to include, the entire body of law of a mature society. When one tries to apply it to any such body of things called "law" by professional usage, one encounters various kinds of difficulties. Such a body of law

---

[28] Opinion of Douglas, J., in Screws v. U. S., 325 U.S. 91, 65 Sup.Ct. 1031, 1036 (1945). See also concurring opinion of Rutledge, J., p. 1048. The court did not discuss what *level* of lay understanding should be the criterion.

[29] See Pollock, Essays in Jurisprudence in Ethics (1882), 257–259; Hall, 437–438. For a partial list of such terms, see Hall, 440–441. See infra, §§ 3.02, 3.27.

has not grown strictly within the framework of a hothouse definition; a chief purpose in trying to find an over-all accurate conception of law is to clarify significantly the somewhat amorphous data produced by historic and institutional processes. One kind of difficulty is presented here. In the authoritative statements of law one finds negative propositions of law, permissive propositions of law and definitions of legal terms, which do not seem to conform to the positive or imperative conception of law.

The Austinian conception of a law as a "command" of the sovereign is open to grave objections on this score. Thus Austin had to admit that a statute which repeals a prior statute is not a "command" of the state, and yet it is a law "properly so called"; he therefore treated it as an exception to his definition of law.[30] Salmond gave as one reason for rejecting the command theory of law, that there are many permissive rules of law which are nonimperative in character. As examples he gave, "a rule, for instance, declaring that witchcraft or heresy is no crime, or that damage done by competition in trade is no cause of action."[31] These he regarded as falling within his definition of law as "the principles acted on by courts of justice," but they are "in no sense rules of conduct enforced by the state."[32] By "rules of conduct" here Salmond means rules prescribing the conduct of subjects (laymen) rather than of officials. Either of Salmond's permissive rules is a rule for the conduct of officials, and each would be enforced by the state in the sense that a judgment of a lower court convicting a woman of the crime of witchcraft, or adjudging that damages be paid for harm done through ("fair") competition in trade, would be reversed by an appellate court, on the ground that Salmond's permissive rule is one of the "principles acted on by courts of justice." Thus Salmond's repealing statute may be taken to mean: "If a person commits witchcraft, no court shall therefor convict her of crime." This is a hypothetical imperative norm.

The conception of law as a command of sovereign to subject, sanctioned by harmful governmental action in case of disobedience, is inadequate or misleading as a characterization of many

---

30 I Austin, Jurisprudence (4th ed., 1874), 101.

31 Salmond, Jurisprudence (7th ed., 1924), 54. The view that all juridical norms are commands, including even the so-called "permissive" norms, is presented in Korkunov, General Theory of Law (Hastings trans., 1909), 169 et seq.; Hall, 415–420.

32 Ibid.

rules of positive law (§ 2.20). The statute of wills, for instance, is not a command to property owners to make wills. It merely prescribes the conduct (or some of it) necessary to create a testament which will have certain legal consequences, the transfer of ownership at death, and the consequences which follow from that. Now it may be said that if the facts are sufficient [33] to imply the transfer of ownership to the devisee, the law commands all other persons not to interfere with the devisee's enjoyment and exercise of ownership, tortiously or criminally.[34] In this indirect sense every legal norm may be taken as a command not to interfere with the legal order which it helps to establish or maintain. Yet in the example given it seems more accurate to say that the statute of wills expresses no command; the "commands" are found in the law of crimes or of torts, which are predicated upon the legal consequence—ownership—prescribed by the statute of wills. Even the norms of crimes or of torts can be stated better for professional purposes as a set of propositions prescribing the legal effects of operative facts. While the political significance of these propositions may be popularly stated in terms of command or prohibition of government to subjects, their legal significance does not involve such an interpretation.

But the rejection of the command-conception as a touchstone of law does not settle all the questions that can be raised about the status of negative propositions of law. These questions will be clarified by grouping them under three headings: logical (or methodological), ontological and political.

The logical status of negative propositions of law may be illustrated by taking a well known example, the English Statute of Frauds:

> "No action shall be brought . . . whereby to charge the defendant upon any special promise to answer for the debt default or miscarriages of another person . . . unless the agreement upon which such action shall be brought, or some memorandum or note thereof, shall be in writing, and signed by the party to be charged therewith or some other person thereunto by him lawfully authorized." [35]

---

[33] I.e., not only execution of the will in compliance with the express requirements of the statute, but also the death of the testator and the absence of fraud, undue influence or other facts negativing the validity of the will.

[34] See Bentham, The Limits of Jurisprudence Defined (ed. Everett, 1945), Ch. 2, especially pp. 61, 62.

[35] Stat. 29 Car. II, c. 3, sec. 4 (1677). Similar statutes have been enacted and are still in force in nearly all states of the U. S. A.

This statutory provision may be conveniently paraphrased as follows:

> An oral promise by the defendant to answer for the debt, etc., of another, without a written note or memorandum signed, etc., does not imply judgment against the defendant for breach of contract.

As a generalization serving to guide the conduct of judges, lawyers and laymen this proposition has useful significance because it serves to discriminate one kind of promise which is not actionable from others which are actionable. The statute would have been merely a quaint vagary of the legislature, not wholly meaningless but certainly not very useful, except upon the assumption, (1) that some such oral promises were actionable before the statute was enacted, and would be without it; and (2) that after the statute was enacted some guaranty promises (those conforming to the statute) would be actionable. Suppose, for instance, a statute were enacted:

> "An oral refusal by a person to make a promise is not actionable as a breach of contract."

Such a statute would, in any system of law, be a legislative oddity because a refusal, oral or otherwise, to make a promise does not under any circumstances imply an actionable contract; [36] that is, because it does not fit into a body of legal norms which give it significance. If such a foolish statute were enacted, it might give rise to the question whether the legislature intended to make actionable a written refusal to promise.

The effect of the Statute of Frauds, quoted above, is to add, for suretyship or guaranty promises, an additional necessary fact to those previously prescribed by the law of contracts for an action for breach of such a contract. The legislature might have acomplished the same result by stating all the previous requirements of such an action and then adding this new one, a signed memorandum; but that would have been a much more difficult legislative task, a step toward codification of the common law.

In English common law jurisdictions (including nearly all of the United States) the practice of using negative statements to modify the rules of case law has become a legislative habit, whether the purpose is to add a requirement or to abrogate one

---

[36] This statement is believed to be correct even as to "compulsory" contracts, such as insurance and collective labor agreements.

previously enforced by courts. An example of the latter is found in the New York statute intended to abrogate the distinction between mistake of fact and mistake of law, and to allow relief for the latter kind of mistake:

> "When relief against mistake is sought in an action . . ., relief shall not be denied merely because the mistake is one of law rather than one of fact." [37]

The double negative, "not . . . denied," implies [38] an affirmative proposition of this sort:

> A mistake of law, under circumstances like those of an actionable mistake of fact, is similarly actionable.

Such a proposition in statutory form would sound less precise than the negative form adopted; the latter is thus more orthodox in a legal tradition which regards statutes as precise and narrow intrusions into the body of the common law.

As an example of negative propositions in case law, let us take one familiar to most beginning students of the law of contracts:

> "An advertisement for bids or tenders is not an offer." [39]

The predicate term of this proposition, "offer," is a legal term implying legal consequences. The proposition above quoted thus serves to delimit the scope of the term "offer" by pointing to something which is not included within it, does not satisfy its requirements. The negative proposition is significant because an advertisement for bids resembles an offer, and some advertisements do have the legal consequences of an offer. The negative proposition is useful and significant for judges and lawyers only because it can be used in connection with other propositions which give legal significance to the term "offer." A good deal of a body of case law is stated in this negative form because it is easier to state what is not within the scope of a legal term than to state all of its necessary and sufficient characteristics. Since a single case for which a practical judgment is required rarely or (more likely) never involves a crucial consideration of all of these characteristics, the negative proposition provides an economical mode of reasoning in case law.

---

[37] N.Y.C.P.A. § 112–f, enacted in 1942 on the recommendation of the Law Revision Commission of New York.

[38] I.e., "shall not be denied" means "shall not be not granted"; since the court is required to act on the claim for relief (a postulate of the legal system), the only way for a court to avoid denying relief is to grant it.

[39] Williston, Contracts (rev. ed., 1936), § 31.

The practice does, however, tend to induce neglect of the affirmative grounds for judicial action, e. g., for enforcing any promises.

Negative legal propositions are those which negate the implication of legal consequences from operative facts. They have significance and usefulness when taken in a logical relationship with affirmative propositions, which affirm the implication of legal consequences from operative facts. It may seem, then, that negative propositions of law have an inferior status to affirmative ones. This is true in the sense that a claimant who desires to move an official to act in accordance with law must produce some affirmative proposition which calls for action. Yet affirmative propositions of law are dependent for the clarification of their terms, and therefore for the scope of their operation, upon negative propositions, such as the one quoted above. The relation betwen affirmative and negative propositions (in general) has been stated thus:

"(1) such propositions [affirmative and negative] are functional in resolution of a problematic situation, and are (2) conjugate or functionally correspondent in relation to each other." [40]

But if we take negative legal propositions in a different sense, if we take them as asserting the existence of negative classes of things, they become *ontologically* absurd or meaningless. Suppose, for instance, that we take the negative proposition above quoted [41] to mean:

"An advertisement for bids or tenders is a no-offer."

The statement is absurd because we do not recognize any such class of things as "no-offers." The opposite of "offer," including everything that is not an offer—sealing wax and cabbages and kings—is not a class of things, yet the the proposition last stated seems to say that an advertisement for bids or tenders is a member of such a class.

The most striking example of this kind of statement is found in discussions of Hohfeld's conceptions, "no-right" and "negative operative fact." The latter is discussed later (§ 2.22). The term "no-right" was invented by Hohfeld to fill out symmetrically his table of jural opposites and jural correlatives.[42] A "no-right" was defined as the opposite of a right, and the correlative of a privilege.

---

40 Dewey, Logic: The Theory of Inquiry (1938), 181.

41 Supra, note 39.

42 Hohfeld's table is set forth in Corbin, op.cit., supra, § 2.05, note 77; Hall, 475; also infra, § 2.22, n. 60.

As a shorthand notation used in legal analysis, in contrasting the
legal relations of one who has fulfilled the requirements for a legal
claim with those of one who has not, the term has the advantage
of brevity. However, some of Hohfeld's followers indulged in such
expressions as "the news gatherer now has no-rights that they
[readers of the newspaper] refrain from communicating to others
the news in question, so long as it is for such non-commercial purposes."[43] Such a statement too readily conjures up a picture out
of "Alice in Wonderland." First Professor Page,[44] then Professor
Fuller[45] and Professor Pound[46] have commented caustically on
this mode of statement. The statement, "A has a no-right to this
watch," is an awkward way of saying, "A has not a right to this
watch," which is (or may be under some circumstances) a sensible
and useful proposition.[47] However, Professor Fuller, in a passage
obscured by elaborate sarcasm, seems to have urged this error of
some Hohfeldians as a refutation of legal positivism, and to have
said that a decision of a court denying the plaintiff recovery is
not a "decision of law," i. e., a legal precedent for a rule of law.[48]
For the reasons given above, a judicial precedent establishing a
negative proposition of law is logically significant when used in
conjunction with affirmative propositions. If one takes negative
propositions as a part of the tools of legal reasoning, and not as
implying negative categories of being, they have a place in the
body of positive legal norms.

Thirdly, negative propositions of law may be taken to imply per-
missions or liberties conceded to subjects (citizens); this is their
political aspect. To use Salmond's examples,[49] a law abolishing

---

43 Note, "The Associated Press Case," (1919) 28 Yale L.J. 386, 389, by the
late Professor Walter Wheeler Cook. Cf. Goble, "Affirmative and Negative
Legal Relations," (1922) 4 Ill.L.Q. 94.

44 Page, "Terminology and Classification in Fundamental Legal Relations,"
(1921) 4 Am.L.Sch.Rev. 616, same in Handbook of the Association of American Law Schools (1920), 199, 209.

45 Fuller, "Legal Fictions," (1931) 25 Ill.L.Rev. 887, 892, note 208.

46 Pound, "Fifty Years of Jurisprudence," (1937) 50 Harvard L.Rev. 557,
573, 574.

47 In logical terms, the difference between these two propositions is stated
thus: "... the negative particle [no, not] ... must be taken to characterize
the copula [is, has], not the subject or the predicate" [term of the proposi-
tion]. Cohen and Nagel, An Introduction to Logic and Scientific Method
(1934), 36.

48 Fuller, The Law in Quest of Itself (1940), 40–41.

49 Supra, note 31.

the crimes of witchcraft and heresy negates the legal norm which formerly attached penal consequences to kinds of conduct designated as witchcraft and heresy, and thus negates judicial action against individuals who are alleged to have so conducted themselves. It thus enlarges the area of individual liberty, of religious freedom. Likewise, a statute abolishing restrictions on fair competition enlarges the area of freedom of trade. The Bill of Rights (first ten amendments) of the Constitution of the United States contains a number of negative legal norms which imply individual civil liberties. Thus the first amendment reads:

> "Congress shall make no law respecting an establishment of religion, or prohibiting the free exercise thereof; or abridging freedom of speech or of the press; or the right of the people peaceably to assemble and to petition the Government for a redress of grievances."

This article negates the validity of any legal norm enacted by Congress which would, for example, attach penal consequences to the exercise of freedom of speech or of the press (within the meaning of the amendment); it gives to subjects a permission or liberty against such governmental action. Such negative legal propositions are highly significant in determining the relations between the government and the individual.

But not all negative propositions of law have this kind of political significance. In the first place, one can find many negative legal propositions which merely negate a particular legal consequence, but leave others unaffected. For instance, from the New York Penal Law [50] one can derive the proposition:

> Manslaughter is not punishable by death.

Yet this does not imply that the residents or subjects of New York are conceded a permission or liberty to commit manslaughter. Again, in many states the following is a correct statement of law:

> The making of an innocent misrepresentation, even though deceptive and harmful to the representee, is not actionable by him as a tort.

Yet this does not imply a permission to utter such a misrepresentation, since it may be actionable as a basis for rescission of a transaction.

In the second place, it seems basically fallacious to conceive of all the activities of individuals in a political society as being either

---

[50] Secs. 1044, 1045, 1049 to 1053.

legalized by the permission of the government, or made illegal. Most of the daily activities of individuals in society are legally neutral; they do not bear with them the stigmata of legality or illegality. One does not draw one's breath or greet one's friends or eat one's dinner by permission of the state in which one happens to be when one so acts. Only if the legal consequences of such action are called in question does it become necessary to determine what they are. In that case a determination that the conduct was not actionable is legally significant as well as a determination that it was. The legal system contains certain methodological postulates which require a legal determination in such a case: that the judge cannot refuse to give a decision because he finds no law on the case, and (more debatably) that the law contains legal norms on which a determination one way or the other can be legally grounded. These methodological assumptions do not imply a political relation between state and subject, whereby all conduct of a subject is permitted by the state, or not permitted. Perhaps it is otherwise in the political theory of a totalitarian state. In a non-totalitarian state the legal order, as one kind of social control, is maintained for the benefit of the individual members of the society. In such a régime a "permission" from the state becomes significant only as a subtraction (as in the case of the First Amendment) from some governmental power.[51]

Negative propositions of law thus are incomplete legal norms. A legal definition is another example of an incomplete legal norm. Thus a statutory definition of murder in the first degree [52] is incomplete without a legal norm stating the consequences of the conduct so defined.[53] Likewise, a definitional type of proposition of case law is incomplete; for instance:

     A corporation is a legal person.

---

[51] Another example: A license from the state to engage in a certain vocation, such as practicing medicine, constitutes an exception to a general prohibition: "No person shall practice medicine without a license."

[52] E.g., N.Y.Penal Law, sec. 1044: "Murder in the first degree defined. The killing of a human being, unless it is excusable or justifiable, is murder in the first degree, when committed: 1. From a deliberate and premeditated design to effect the death of the person killed, or of another, or, .." [But note that "excusable or justifiable" leaves much to be cleared up.]

[53] E.g., N.Y.Penal Law, sec. 1045: "Punishment for murder in the first degree. Murder in the first degree is punishable by death, unless the jury recommends life imprisonment as provided by section ten hundred forty-five-a."

This proposition implies, for example, that a corporation can sue and be sued in its corporate name; it is a legal norm because it implies such legal consequences.

Are there any complete legal norms? Dialectically, the use of "incomplete norm" implies a class of "complete norms"; yet this class may be a null class, one having no members. Could some Marathon legal draftsman condense into one non-stop sentence all of the necessary circumstances and official acts terminating, say, in the execution of a man for murder in the first degree? This might be possible, but who would want it? The question is somewhat like, are there any complete maps? Some maps are more complete in detail than others, yet none designates every bush by the roadside. For some operations one needs a map of a large area, for others a map of a small area showing every road crossing. Each is complete for its purpose. And so of legal norms. A complete legal norm is one which designates more or less precisely the legal consequences of operative facts. The statute quoted above,[54] prescribing the consequences of first degree murder, is in this way complete, although a lawyer engaged in prosecuting or defending a first-degree murder charge would have to know a good deal more than it tells him. The legal rules and principles of a body of professional law are not built to function in isolation from all others.[55] None is complete in the sense of being self-sufficient. Yet by analysis one can separate one or more of the body of legal norms, to serve as guides in the selection of facts or as grounds of a legal argument. The law is a more or less systematic body of legal norms.

§ 2.22—Operative Facts and Legal Consequences

Whenever we find law fulfilling its basic function, to serve as a guide to official decisions or determinations, we find that one or several propositions of law mean that a set of events and things in the existential world implies a certain kind of official action or determination (including official refusal to act in a certain way). That is, the function of law in a problematic situation is to point to the official conduct (action or inaction) that should follow in reference to that situation. The existential world of past occurrences and existences is something that we cannot change and

---

54 Supra, note 53.

55 To the same effect: Brown, The Austinian Theory of Law (1931), 346–47; King, "The Concept of a Lawyer's Jurisprudence (1952) 11 Camb.L.J. 229, 234.

in this sense we call it the realm of "fact." To have a régime of governmental action at all presupposes that to some extent and in some ways the *future* realm of fact can be changed. Otherwise the régime would be futile or would at best have no more significance than the forecasts of the Weather Bureau.[56] The primary function of law is to state or imply that from certain facts it follows that a certain kind or kinds of official conduct should or shall follow. This is what we mean by a legal rule or, more broadly, a legal norm (§ 2.20). It appears in the "if . . . then" formulation of legal rules which (if we may trust the translators) is as old as the Code of Hammurabi. This basic characteristic of legal norms has long been recognized by European jurisprudents. For instance, Korkunov, a law professor of the imperial Russian régime, agrees with Zitelmann, a German jurisprudent of the last century, that "a legal rule is a hypothetic judgment as to what is to be done," and adds:

> "So, if law gives the definition of a contract or a crime, there is here only an order for connecting with human actions constituting a contract or a crime, the juridical consequences of such contract or crime." [57]

Later he refers to "hypothesis" and "disposition" as the "universal elements" of all "juridical norms." [58] Similarly Kelsen, whose imperative theory of law (§ 2.05) has had considerable influence on jurisprudential thought in the present century, regards the "Ought" of a legal rule as indicating "the specific sense in which the legal condition and the legal consequence are held together in the legal rule." [59] In American jurisprudence this basic conception of legal rules or norms has been most clearly presented in the Hohfeld-Corbin analysis of "operative facts" and "legal consequences." Using their terminology one can say that a legal rule or norm is a statement that from designated "operative facts," designated "legal consequences" shall or should follow. Since this is an adaptation rather than a literal statement of the Hohfeld-Corbin position, the latter will now be examined.

---

56 See Fuller, "American Legal Realism," (1934) 82 U. of Pa.L.Rev. 429; Hall, 994–1000.

57 Both quotations from Korkunov, General Theory of Law (Hastings trans., 1909), 169–170; Hall, 416.

58 Ibid., 176–178; Hall, 421.

59 Kelsen, "The Pure Theory of Law," (1934) 50 L.Q.Rev. 474, 485; Hall, 433. See also Kelsen, General Theory of Law and State (1945) 53.

"Operative Facts." The term "operative fact" was invented by the late Professor Wesley N. Hohfeld as an adjunct of his comprehensive table of jural (legal) relations. His primary purpose was to distinguish "operative facts" from "evidential facts." He began with the example of a "jural transaction," that is, a contract, conveyance, etc. A promissory note signed and delivered by the maker to the payee is an "operative document," since these facts operate to create a jural relation, a duty of the maker to the payee and a right of the payee against the maker. On the other hand, the signing and delivery of a receipt by the payee to the maker, reciting that the specified sum has been paid, is not operative but only evidential; the fact of payment is the operative fact which extinguishes the duty of the maker to the payee. With this illustration (which is not taken from Hohfeld but is believed to exemplify his meaning) we may quote from his article:

> "The facts important in relation to a given jural transaction may be either *operative* facts or *evidential* facts. Operative, constitutive, causal or dispositive facts suffice to change legal relations, that is, either to create a new relation, or to extinguish an old one, or to perform both of these functions simultaneously." [60]

Having derived the term from legal transactions, he then extended it to other situations:

> "Taking another example,—this time from the field of torts—if X commits an assault on Y by putting the latter in fear of bodily injury, this group of facts immediately creates in Y the privilege of self-defense,—that is, the privilege of using sufficient force to repel X's attack; or, correlatively, the otherwise existing duty of Y to refrain from the application of force to the person of X is, by virtue of the special operative facts, immediately terminated or extinguished." [61]

The meaning of "evidential fact" he stated thus:

> "An evidential fact is one which, on being ascertained, affords some logical basis—not conclusive—for inferring some

---

[60] Hohfeld, Fundamental Legal Conceptions as Applied in Judicial Reasoning (Yale Univ.Press, 1920), 32; same in (1913) 23 Yale L.J. 16, 25. In footnote 20, he acknowledges suggestions from Thayer, Holland and Bentham. The latter's conception of "investitive" and "divestitive" facts seems to have been the model. See Patterson, "Bentham on the Nature and Method of Law," (1946) 33 Calif.L.Rev. 612, 619–620.

[61] Hohfeld, op.cit., 32–33.

other fact. The latter may be either a constitutive [operative] fact or an intermediate evidential fact." [62]

Thus the operative facts of a conveyance, for instance, are that A signed, acknowledged and delivered a certain document to B as grantee; the document itself, when produced in court to prove B's title, is merely evidence that these operative facts occurred.

One merit of Hohfeld's terminology is that it distinguished between factual inferences and legal "inferences." That a signature resembling A's signature (as verified by a witness who is familiar with other specimens of it) is on a document tends to prove that A signed it; this is an inference of fact. That A signed the document, conjoined with other facts, signifies that B became the owner of the property; this is a legal "inference," that is, a process of reasoning that leads to a legal conclusion. Now if it is a *legal* inference (that is, a legally grounded inference) it is so because of some proposition of law that *such* facts shall have such legal consequence. In logical terms, the operative facts are those denoted by the *subject* term of a proposition of which the predicate term is a change in legal relations, such as:

(a) The execution and delivery by the owner of a conveyance of specified land is a transfer of ownership of the land.[63]

Such a proposition does not "solve" any problem as to the transaction between A and B; it tells what to look for, and if another proposition is established, that is, warrantably accepted as correct, then a connection is established between the A–B occurrences and a legal consequence (minor premise):

(b) A's signature and handing over to B of Exhibit 1 (describing specified land) is (was) the execution and delivery by the owner of a conveyance of specified land.

By implication from (a) and (b) the conclusion follows:

(c) A's signature, etc., is (was) a transfer of ownership of the land.

Are the "operative facts" the subject term of the major premise, or the minor premise as a whole, or the subject term of the minor premise? Hohfeld seems to have sensed this ambiguity, for while he said at one place that:

---

[62] Ibid., 34.

[63] I.e., "conveyance" is used to mean the instrument, "transfer" to mean the change in legal relations. "Ownership" is an aggregate of rights, powers, privileges, etc.—"legal relations" in the Hohfeldian sense.

> "The operative facts of real life are . . . very specific," [64]

he also said, further on:

> "It now remains to observe that in many situations a single convenient term is employed to designate (generically) certain miscellaneous groups of operative facts which, though differing widely as to their individual ingredients, have, as regards a given matter, the same *net* force and effect. When employed with discrimination, the term 'possession' is a word of this character; so also the term 'capacity,' the term 'domicile,' etc. But the general tendency to confuse legal and non-legal quantities is manifest here as elsewhere, so that only too frequently these words are used rather nebulously to indicate legal relations as such." [65]

It would be erroneous to say that operative facts are of two different kinds, specific and generic. Rather the specific and the generic are two different aspects of operative facts; the latter are legal conceptions expressed in terms which *denote* specific operative facts and *connote* legal consequences. In this sense a legal norm is a statement predicating some legal consequence of (generic) operative facts.

One merit of Hohfeld's analysis was, as has been said, that it differentiated factual inferences from legal inferences. More important than this, however, are two others: first, its emphasis on the dual aspect of legal terms as referring to facts and to legal consequences, and second, its emphasis on the crucial step taken when a determination is made that certain facts ("specific") *are to be* characterized as satisfying the requirements of a legal concept. These emphases paved the way for more precise analyses of such legal terms as "possession," "title" and "negligence," to the breakdown of what Professor Llewellyn has called "lump concept" thinking into narrower rules and more concrete terms. Tested by this analysis, some traditional legal terms were found so meaningless in reference to operative facts that they were mere labels for legal conclusions. "Privity of contract" is one example, and it seems that "waiver" is another. When "waiver" is defined as "the voluntary relinquishment of a known right," the term "voluntary" is nearly meaningless, and so a waiver is anything that will have the consequence, relinquishment of a known right. The factual grounds for attaching such labels are left obscure.

---

[64] Op.cit., 33.

[65] Ibid., 34–35.

However, the crucial step taken in characterizing facts as operative was obscured in Hohfeld's treatment and in that of some of his followers, by metaphorical language which suggested metaphysical assumptions. Hohfeld spoke of operative facts "creating" legal relations,[66] and Professor Corbin, who greatly simplified and clarified Hohfeld, defined an operative fact in terms of "existence" and "cause":

> "Any fact the existence or occurrence of which will cause new legal relations between persons." [67]

But "facts" do not cause new legal relations to arise in the same sense in which a lighted match causes a piece of paper to burn. A's striking B may "cause" B to strike back, but B's striking back is not a legal relation. Facts are not (legally) "operative" in an existential sense but only in legal reasoning. Facts are concrete and legal relations are abstract:

> "In the proposition, 'If an act of trespassing, then liability to a penalty,' the terms are abstract and the *relation* is non-temporal and non-existential, even though the contents, the ideas of trespassing and of penalty, have indirect existential reference." [68]

The risks of reasoning in saying that operative facts "cause" or "create" legal relations is that we may be misled by our own language into reifying legal relations, that is treating them as things that are just there and have only to be discovered—and once we have "found" them, they are final and immutable. This danger is akin to the dogmatism of some theories of what law should be (Pt. IV). However, the analysis of a legal situation in a temporal sequence is useful in legal reasoning (§ 1.14), and Professor Corbin elsewhere stated the logical relation of operative facts:

> "When we state that some particular legal relation exists we are impliedly asserting the existence of certain facts, and we are expressing our present mental concept of the societal consequences that will normally follow in the future." [69]

---

66 Supra, note 60.

67 Corbin, "Legal Analysis and Terminology," (1919) 29 Yale L.J. 163; Hall, 472.

68 Dewey, Logic: The Theory of Inquiry (1938), 271. Cf. the view of the phenomenologists: Brecht, in (1941) 54 Harvard L.Rev. 811. See previous discussion, supra, § 1.14.

69 Op.cit., supra, note 67; Hall, 473.

By "particular" he means "individual," as explained above
(§ 2.12): "Green is under a duty to pay Brown $100." Professor
Corbin is here stating a legal conclusion as a prediction (§ 2.20).

The Hohfeldian conception of "operative facts" has some of
the over-simplicity, or epistemological naiveté, of John Locke's
theory of knowledge which Bentham took over and used in his
earlier legal analysis.[70] Take, for example, the legal questions
raised by the collision of two automobiles at a highway intersec-
tion. The "facts" used in legal reasoning are the statements of
witnesses who apprehend and communicate the occurrence in the
generic terms of common speech, such as: "The black sedan was
going fifty miles an hour at the highway crossing." Such statements are not just raw "data"; they are taken, that is, selected
from among the various perceptions and statements of witnesses
and the selecting devices are legal rules or norms which make
them legally "operative," e. g., a rule that negligently injuring
another imposes legal liability. Thus "negligently injuring another" is, in this legal rule,[71] a "generic" operative fact; it connotes the consequence, "legal liability," and denotes the multitude
of concrete statements from which the conclusion, "negligent injury," may be drawn.

Negative Operative Facts. Hohfeld also introduced the term,
"negative operative facts." [72] For example, in the creation of a
contractual obligation of A to B, the "affirmative operative facts"
are, among others, that each of the parties is a human being, that
each of them has lived for not less than a certain period of time,
that A has made an "offer," that B has "accepted" it, etc.

> "It is sometimes necessary to consider, also, what may,
> from the particular point of view, be regarded as *negative*
> operative facts. Thus, e. g., the fact that A did not wilfully
> misrepresent an important matter to B, and the fact that A
> had not 'revoked' his offer, must really be included as parts
> of the totality of operative facts in the case already put."[73]

Apparently Hohfeld in developing the conception of a negative
operative fact was seeking to find a way of stating in one proposition all of the operative facts which a lawyer would need to

---

[70] See Patterson, op.cit., supra, note 60.

[71] Which is obviously not adequately stated. For a comprehensive statement of the elements of a cause of action for negligence, see Restatement,
Torts, § 281.

[72] Hohfeld, op.cit., supra, note 60, 32.

[73] Ibid.

consider in determining whether A was under a contractual obligation to B. The problem, then, is one of the completeness of a legal proposition. As was pointed out above (§ 2.21) no legal proposition encountered in legal literature is so complete that it can function in isolation from others. Yet some legal propositions are so incomplete that they would be customarily regarded as inaccurate:

> One who makes an offer to another is under a contractual obligation to the other to perform the offer.

This is inaccurate because "contractual obligation" connotes at least acceptance in addition to offer. That it does so is a matter of convention among lawyers. The legal definition of a term is its conventional intension, the necessary and sufficient characteristics which are conventionally regarded as justifying the use of the term. Similarly, the standard of accuracy and completeness for any legal proposition is dependent upon usage in the profession. It is also dependent, when application to a concrete situation is involved, (as Hohfeld indicated) upon whether it is "necessary" to consider additional facts. The term "negative operative fact" does not contribute anything and, following Corbin's example,[74] we may safely abandon it.

The term, "operative fact," has gained widespread usage in American legal writings,[75] and has had significant influence on the contemporary American conception of law. Such usage does not confine the term to Hohfeld's scheme of jural relations, and it is not so confined here. Indeed, "rights," "duties," "powers," etc. are convenient but subordinate terms in the analysis or condensation of legal propositions. A legal norm may express the relation of operative facts (e. g., "murder in the first degree") to legal consequences (e. g., "is punishable by death") without employing any of Hohfeld's terminology of "right," "duty," etc. As Corbin's terminology shows, these terms imply legal consequences, i. e., official conduct. And as Professor Llewellyn's argument persuasively shows,[76] the simplification of our conception of law calls for the elimination of "right" and similar terms as *necessary* con-

---

[74] Supra, note 67.

[75] A recent example occurs in the opinion of Goodrich, J., in Wallman v. United Casualty Co., 147 F.2d 636 (C.C.A., N.J., 1945). See also Murphy, J., in St. Louis Fire & Marine Ins. Co. v. Whitney, 96 F.Supp. 555, 558 (D.C.Pa. 1951).

[76] Llewellyn, "A Realistic Jurisprudence—the Next Step," (1930) 30 Columbia L.Rev. 432, 435 et seq.

stituents of law. Antecedent to rights are claims and interests which the law in various ways protects. Law is a way of ordering the relations between (a) the claims and interests of individuals in society and (b) the governmental actions which serve to implement or reject those claims and interests.

"Operative fact" includes not only human acts (or omissions) but also many events or existences beyond human control, such as the fortuitous death of a person (which may operate to transfer his property by will or inheritance or to terminate his duty to perform a contract) or the fortuitous destruction of the subject matter of a contract (which may terminate a contractual duty). The notion of a legal norm is thus broader than Holland's "rule of external human action." [77] Moreover, official conduct may be a legal consequence of one legal proposition and an operative fact of another. Thus an order of foreclosure and sale of property may be a legal consequence of certain operative facts (execution of a mortgage, default, etc.) and an operative fact in the chain of title of one who purchases at the foreclosure sale. The operative facts of procedural law include many previous judicial rulings. Since a judicial ruling on the admissibility of evidence in a trial is a legal consequence, an evidential fact, which grounds a factual inference, may also be an operative fact of a legal proposition which prescribes its admissibility (or non-admissibility) in evidence. Thus the testimony of witness A as to what B stated (out of court) to have occurred may ground a factual inference as to what occurred, and may also be an operative fact of a legal proposition that hearsay is not admissible in evidence. The conception of law here proposed thus includes procedural as well as substantive law.

Does it also embrace those broad principles and policies which have a place in a mature body of law, and yet which do not seem to state any relation between operative facts and legal consequences? For example, the principle that one who has been unjustly enriched at the expense of another is required to make restitution to the other,[78] or the policy that in property transactions freedom of alienation should be preserved? Yes, because principles and policies are legal propositions in so far as they mediately or indirectly mean a relation between operative facts and legal consequences. This they do at least in so far as they are exemplified in more concrete legal rules. For example, the prin-

---

[77] Supra, § 2.04, n. 49.

[78] Restatement, Restitution (1937), § 1.

ciple of unjust enrichment is exemplified (but not completely exhausted) in the legal rules prescribing restitution for mistake, fraud, etc. The policy of freedom of alienation is exemplified in rules limiting the duration, etc., of future interests in property.[79] Thus principles and policies, if they have any legal meaning at all, are statements of the legal consequences of operative facts.

Operative Factors. In many cases the adjudication of a legal dispute, in so far as it is dependent on the application of legal norms, turns upon whether or not some crucial term of a legal norm is found to be satisfied by the facts, and this is dependent upon an appraisal of the situation in which no one fact or combination of facts is decisive but rather one points one way and another points another way. An example is the Fair Labor Standards Act of 1938,[80] which is applicable only to an employee whose work is "necessary to the production" of goods for interstate commerce. In determining what work does and what does not fall within the meaning of the quoted term physical remoteness of the employee from the process of production, that is, the *degree* of remoteness, is a relevant factor:

> "Mere separation of an occupation from the physical process of production does not preclude application of the Fair Labor Standards Act. But remoteness of a particular occupation from the physical process is a relevant factor in drawing the line." [81]

These "relevant factors" are not quite "operative facts" in the sense in which Hohfeld and Corbin conceived the term; they do not "operate" with the decisiveness of the execution and delivery of a deed, etc. They are "operative factors" in a determination to characterize or not to characterize a given situation by a legal term. Nor are they confined to statutory rules. For example, it has been established in most American case-law jurisdictions for a generation or more that a "material" failure of performance by one party to a bilateral contract (with certain limitations) has the effect of discharging the other party from his duty of performing a promise given in exchange.[82] "Material" cannot be defined in

---

[79] See Restatement, Property, vol. IV.

[80] 29 U.S.C.A. § 201 et seq.

[81] Frankfurter, J., (for the Court) in 10 East 40th Street Bldg., Inc. v. Callus, 325 U.S. 578, 65 Sup.Ct. 1227, 1229 (1945) (elevator operators of office building held not within the Act). See also Darr v. Mutual Life Ins. Co., 74 F.Supp. 80 (D.C.N.Y.1947), applying the same statute.

[82] Restatement, Contracts (1932) § 274.

terms of logical equivalence: These kinds of circumstances are necessary and sufficient to make a breach material. One can list the "influential circumstances," the factors that should be taken account of in determining materiality.[83] The determination is to result from an appraisal of the character and extent of each factor and its probable consequences in relation to the consequences of the determination, one way or the other, and in relation to alternative ways, if any, of giving redress for the breach. What "material" means in this context is partly determined by what consequences will follow from the determination of its meaning. The factorial analysis of legal concepts may seem to have made the law less certain; on the contrary, it has made it more certain by revealing as a rational process what is otherwise concealed by the veil of judicial certitude: "We find the plaintiff committed a material breach." A similar use of factorial analysis is made in the law of servitudes.[84] Other examples might be given.

"Legal Consequences." The meaning of "legal consequences" has been exemplified in previous passages. They are, to use Professor Corbin's terms, "immediate or remote consequences in the form of action or non-action by the judicial and executive agents of society."[85] Many propositions of law express conclusions which only mediately or by implication indicate official action. Examples are the statement that a promise to pay a debt of the promisor that has been discharged in bankruptcy "is binding"[86] or a statement of the elements of a cause of action for negligence.[87] Such terms as "is binding" and "cause of action" are conventional links in the chain of implication from specific (or individual) operative facts to specific (or individual) official action. It can be shown that many other terms, such as "offer," "acceptance," "negligence," have this same analytic function. It will be noted that Professor Corbin included "the judicial and executive agents" of society. Whether a norm calling for official action of executive officials without the intervention of a court,

---

[83] Ibid., § 275.

[84] Restatement, Property, vol. V (1944), §§ 483 ("Factors in Ascertaining Extent" of an easement), 471, 478, 476. See also Restatement, Torts, I, §§ 431, 433 ("substantial factor" of "causation"). Cardozo, J., regarded the "appraisal" of such factors as a "process" rather than a "rule". Yome v. Gorman, 242 N.Y. 395, 402–403, 152 N.E. 126, 128 (1926).

[85] Corbin, op.cit., supra, note 12; Hall, 473.

[86] Supra, § 2.12, note 26.

[87] Restatement, Torts (1934), § 281.

or for the official action of a legislature, is properly to be called a law, is a question reserved for later discussion.

To avoid misunderstanding it seems necessary to add that the foregoing discussion (Chapters 5, 6) does not assume: (a) that legal rules or norms are the only factors influential in the process of official adjudication (judicial or administrative); (b) that official adjudications are mentally arrived at by mere deductions from legal norms; (c) that official adjudications are invariably consistent with the conclusions which would result from the correct application of the appropriate legal norms. The judicial process will be discussed further on, especially in Part V.

Chapter 7

THE AUTHORITY AND SANCTION OF LAW

§ 2.30—The Significance of Authority, Power and Sanction

The imperative or positive conception (§§ 2.04, 2.05) makes the authority and sanction of the state a necessary characteristic of law. Nothing which does not have political authority is law; every general rule which has political authority and sanction is law. The statement made by Sheldon Amos, one of Austin's followers, is:

> "A law . . . is a command proceeding from the supreme political authority of a state, and addressed to the persons who are subjects of that authority." [1]

If we substitute for "a command" the term "a norm of official or non-official conduct" (§ 2.20), and if "subjects of that authority" be understood to include subordinate officials as well as non-officials, the definition is nearer to the conception of law here accepted. Every legal norm must in some sense "proceed" from the supreme political authority of a state; yet how it "proceeds" is a question not simple to answer in the modern representative ("democratic") state. It cannot be said, for example, that the supreme political authority must be the *author* of every legal norm, nor that every norm must be *deduced* from general principles laid down by the supreme political authority. This relation will be explored later (§ 2.31). Moreover, the Amos definition omits the requirement of sanction: a legal norm is one having the ultimate sanction of the state. This qualification seems necessary in order to distinguish law from the many merely hortatory norms or admonitions uttered by officials of the twentieth century state. Examples are official proclamations of Mother's Day, Fire Prevention Week, etc., and the admonitions of traffic officials to drive carefully, etc. Potential though not actual enforcement of decisions made pursuant to the norm is required.

The conception of law as dependent upon political authority goes back at least as far as Aristotle (§ 2.04, n. 53). However, the conception took more definite form with the rise of the modern European state, and is intimately related to theories of the state,

---

[1] Amos, The Science of Law (1874), 48. Cf. Wigmore's definition, supra, § 2.05, n. 73.

147

of sovereignty and of government. Since these theories by a convenient and traditional division of labor (at least in Anglo-American literature) belong rather to political science than to jurisprudence, they will be treated summarily here. Law-trained persons and perhaps most laymen in a modern state are so accustomed to regarding law as dependent upon political authority that they are commonly unaware of the difficulties of maintaining this position. These consist on the one hand in clarifying the dependency in such a way that it will fit the observed facts of political practice, and on the other hand in meeting certain real or fanciful objections to it.

One line of objection is to identify political authority with the exercise of force, to identify force with arbitrariness and violence, and thus to make it appear that the imperative conception of law makes law unjust and evil. This is an idealist type (§ 2.02) of criticism. Two answers may be shortly given. One is that the imperative conception does not imply the universal or even the frequent exercise of force to compel conformity to laws (§ 2.32). That officials have the power and the privilege of using force is in many situations an inducement of conformity. Secondly, the exercise of force is not necessarily unjust or evil. Years ago John Dewey, after listening to the tiresome arguments of Russian philosophical anarchists (followers of Tolstoy), wrote a persuasive analysis of force, which is a neutral term, and "violence", which he took to mean the (ethically wrong) abuse of force.[2] The *intelligent* use of force is neither arbitrary nor unjust. The force necessarily used by a policeman to apprehend a dangerous murderer is a good kind of force. Another type of objection, perhaps more often literary than philosophic, is to contrast "authoritarian" rules with individual freedom, on the assumption that the latter is always a good.

The institutionalist attack upon the conception of state-law was vigorously stated by Eugen Ehrlich (§ 2.03) when he said:
> "The modern jurist is accustomed to seeing a world ruled by law and legal coercion."[3]

Now there may have been legal positivists near the beginning of the twentieth century, when Ehrlich wrote, who believed in this

---

[2] Dewey, "Force, Violence and Law" in Intelligence in the Modern World (Joseph Ratner ed., 1939), 486; reprinted from Characters and Events (Joseph Ratner ed., 1929), 782–789; 634–641.

[3] Ehrlich, Fundamental Principles of the Sociology of Law (Moll trans., 1936; first published in 1913), 83.

all-pervasive influence of law and its means of enforcement. Is it not marvelous, one might say, that New York City's 15,000 policemen are able to control the conduct of its population of 6,-000,000 (not to mention the commuters and tourists)?[4] However, most jurists today are well aware that law is only *a* means of social control (§ 2.06) and that non-legal controls are equally influential in maintaining peace and order in society. While John Austin (§ 2.04) wrote before "sociology" or "social science" were recognized terms, he did recognize the existence (though hardly the importance) of those social controls which he called "positive morality". One of his recent followers, Professor Manning, has persuasively suggested that Austin conceived of political coercion as being effective chiefly in the marginal case: The one in which other social pressures would be insufficient to induce conformity.[5] Today Ehrlich's objection rests upon an erroneous assumption.

The view that authority is in some sense arbitrary is correct. Authority in its lowest terms is a kind of influence on human conduct (including thinking as well as acting or not acting), an influence that leads one to accept the judgment of another as a basis for his own judgment. For instance, a newspaper reader who accepts a dramatic critic's judgment of a play that the reader has not seen, does so partly on the basis of such information contained in the play review as enables him to form his independent judgment of the merits, and partly on the authority of the critic. The "independence" of the reader's own judgment is, of course, limited and relative, since it is influenced by ideas derived from other authorities: Parents, the school, the church, his friends. What John Dewey calls "the cultural matrix" of inquiry [6] is itself a kind of authority. Thus the opposition between "authority" and "reason", while meaningful and important, is not a fixed or absolute dichotomy. Indeed, it seems that the independence of judgment from authority can be asserted only in reference to a particular authority. Even in physical or biological science, the American or English scientist, while free from the authority of Soviet-Marxist ideology, does his work in reliance (for the time being) upon the "authority" of established propositions of his science and even upon the "authority" of certain eminent scientists.

---

[4] The figures, of police and population, are much higher today.

[5] Manning, "Austin Today; or 'The Province of Jurisprudence' Reexamined" in Modern Theories of Law (1933), 180, 194.

[6] Dewey, Logic: The Theory of Inquiry (1938), Ch. III.

But the grounding of judgment on authority is not necessarily wholly unreflective or unreasoned. Reasons why a proposition derived from authority should be accepted can be adduced by pointing to prior instances in which reliance on this authority has been followed by good consequences. Moreover, the reasons of convenience and orderliness why *some* authority should be recognized are often sufficient in social affairs to justify acceptances of a definite authority which is most likely to attain those ends. To identify authority with arbitrariness is fallacious.

§ 2.31—The Kinds of Authority of Law

The foregoing brief survey of the meanings of "authority" serves to introduce our view that law has several kinds of authority which may be grouped as follows:

1. *Formal Authority or Authorization.* The proposed application of a so-called "legal norm" to a given problematic situation gives rise to the question whether or not that norm is formally authoritative. The norm may be or purport to be, the exact wording of a statute, in which case the (personified) authority of the norm is the legislative branch of government. One can ordinarily rely upon the official publication of the statute as sufficient proof of its enactment by the legislature and approval by the executive (when required); the formal power of the legislative body to enact a norm of this content is dependent upon the constitution. These two elements—power and exercise of power—constitute the *validity* of the norm. At the price of circularity we may call this "legal authority", since it is peculiarly within the province of the legal profession. The validity of a legal norm as determined by the test of its formal authorization is substantially the same as Professor Hans Kelsen's conception of validity, which is explained later (§ 3.22). The meaning of "power" here is formal power (a conception sometimes identified with authority) [7] rather than material or physical power. The latter is here reserved for political authority.

The formal authorization of case law, the law of judicial precedents, gave Austin some difficulty because England had no written constitution conferring judicial power on certain courts. The formal authorization of the English higher courts to declare law (and sometimes partly to create it) depends upon official custom

---

[7] In a recent work carefully formulating the meanings of political terms, authority is defined as formal power. Lasswell and Kaplan, Power and Society: A Framework for Political Inquiry (1950), 133.

of long standing rather than on explicit authorization by the sovereign, the Parliament (with royal assent). Nevertheless the formal authorization of the latter is genuine, as appears most clearly when the legislative body expressly negates the norms laid down by judicial precedents.[8] Under the régime of a written constitution, as in the United States and in most other nations of the world, the express recognition of judicial power *may* be taken to imply a conferring of power upon the higher courts to make some pronouncements of legal norms. As will be shown later (§ 3.22) the grant of formal authorization is not as explicit as Kelsen's theory requires it to be.

Formal authorization does not and need not go beyond the constitution of the state. It can be determined almost exclusively by consulting the books in a law library. "Almost" because the fact of election or appointment of certain persons as officials and their identification as the persons who exercised the formal power, would have to be established in order to establish the formal authorization of a legal norm.[9]

2. *Political Authority: The State.* The term "political authority" is here used to mean that the official body which gave a legal norm formal authority had the material power of the state to support it. This means not only the attitude of the subjects of the state, or of the greater and more influential part of them; it means also the attitudes of governmental officials and their physical powers of enforcement. By the prevailing imperative conception it is enough if the government as a whole has political authority, that is, the support of officials and of citizens (§ 2.04). A particular legal norm, formally valid, may lack the support of both enforcement officials and lay subjects, without losing its formal validity. The reason for this is, I suppose, partly administrative and partly functional. It would be difficult to determine *when* a legal norm had fallen into disuse (by non-enforcement and non-obedience) to such a degree as to cease to be law. Moreover, the repeal of laws should be determined by the official bodies authorized to make law, not by enforcement officials or by laymen. Could a law be repealed by desuetude in one part of a state and not in another? Yet lack of political authority does impair the *reliability of the prediction* (as to the outcome of litigation)

---

[8] See Livesidge v. Anderson, [1942] A.C. 206; infra, §§ 3.15, 3.22.

[9] Statutory presumptions, official certificates and the law of *de facto* officers which precludes collateral attack on minor defects of official status, all qualify the statement made in the text.

which may be drawn from a given legal norm. For judges, and even more so juries, will be reluctant to give effect to legal norms which are notoriously moribund. Examples are found in the decisions involving enforcement of the so-called Blue Laws, the statutes requiring strict observance of Sunday as a day of rest. The National Prohibition Act of the United States (1919-1933) provided another example. On the other hand, the political authority of law has its affirmative values. The loyalty of subjects to a governmental régime leads them to accept, even though grudgingly, decisions made and action taken pursuant to legal norms that would be unacceptable from other sources.

3. *Personal Authority or Authorship.* The expertness or wisdom of the person or persons who created a legal norm, or approved it, is another kind of authority of law. In primitive societies very often the personal authority of the chief or headman is the chief motivation of those who obey his rule.[10] Many ancient and medieval laws were revered because of the wisdom of the men who created them: The laws of Solon, the laws of Alfred, etc. Nor is this kind of authority absent in modern law. The views of Littleton on tenures, of Lord Mansfield on many phases of commercial law, of Chief Justice John Marshall on the constitutional law of the United States, have a degree of influence not attributable merely to the legal powers which those men held. The opinions of eminent text-writers on law have, in England and the United States, a kind of authority which is neither legal nor political (§ 3.14). Furthermore, the case law of one state when cited in a court of another state having a cognate system of law (e. g., a New York precedent cited in Ohio) is influential in the latter court and is sometimes followed because of the respect due to the court of the first state as interpreters of a common source of legal doctrine—the English law adopted by statute as a basis of decision in both states—and as adapters of this source material to the needs of people living under similar political and social conditions (§ 3.13). Sometimes the exceptional abilities of the judges of the first state are influential. Thus a proposition of law may because of its origin have an influence beyond the scope of its legal validity.

§ 2.32—The State, the Sovereign and the Law

What is a state? By a convenient division of labor this question has been in recent years assigned to the domain of political

---

10 See Lowie, The Origin of the State (1927) 5.

philosophy, and excluded from jurisprudence. This division of labor will be respected here because an exploration of the conception of the state is beyond the scope of this volume. Accordingly we turn for a concise definition of the state to a distinguished author who is not only a political philosopher but also and primarily a sociologist:

"A state is an association which, acting through law as promulgated by a government endowed to this end with coercive power, maintains within a community territorially demarcated the universal external conditions of social order." [11]

A state is generically a kind of association, and thus has to maintain itself in competition with other associations, such as other states, and with business associations and religious orders, and other cultural organizations. The state acts through a government endowed with coercive power and through law which the government promulgates. Both law and government are indispensable instrumentalities of a state. The "community" is the society of individuals living within a demarcated territory for whom the state maintains order. To be a state an association must maintain a minimum of social order. At least a state must repress promiscuous and continuous acts of violence; this is among the "universal external conditions of social order." Professor MacIver has given us a conception of the state's minimum function; he has avoided the temptation to idealize the state. Nor has he tried, as Austin did, to avoid the circularity of defining the state as dependent on law, and law as dependent on the state. This inter-dependence is an essential characteristic of state and law.

To this conception of law various objections have been made. One is that it leaves out customary law. Of this it suffices to say here that while custom is a recognized *source* of law, a customary norm of conduct which becomes a legal norm is transformed into something substantially different from what it was before. The status of customary law is examined later (§ 3.15). Another objection is that international law, or a good deal of it, is excluded from the domain of law, since the government of a state does not have "coercive power" outside of its own territory, or at least

---

11 MacIver, The Modern State (1926), 22. The author is careful to say that this is only a preliminary definition, and that "the whole of this volume is devoted to answering the question, what *is* the state?" (p. 3). For a valuable account of theories of the state, see Pound, "Law and the State—Jurisprudence and Politics," (1944) 57 Harvard L.Rev. 1193.

not against the "coercive power" of a stronger state. In so far as this objection is addressed to the sanction of law rather than to state authority, it will be discussed later (§ 2.35). For the present it suffices to point out that international law as we now know it is chiefly a product of the actions of state officials.[12]

Is the assertion that the state is dependent upon law, and that law is dependent upon the state, a purely dogmatic statement, derived *a priori,* or is it verified by experience? Is the definition purely nominal or partly real? Has there ever been a state (an association fulfilling the other requirements of a state) which somehow got along without law? A recent case in point is Soviet Russia. Lenin taught that with the success of the communist revolution law and the state would wither away; in a classless society they would not be needed. Yet for a time after the overthrow of the capitalist régime, law would be necessary, "until the people have been taught how to work for the society."[13] Shortly after the October Revolution, 1917, the old system of Russian courts and the laws relating to the judiciary were abolished by decrees and new courts were established with power to decide in accordance with the "revolutionary legal consciousness"; by 1920 they were forbidden to decide in accordance with the old laws, whether civil or criminal.[14] Even these decrees, it may be noted, constituted structural law, since they established the scope of official authority of the Peoples Courts; they did not, however, provide a body of decisional law. During the period between the close of 1917 and 1922 "law and order can hardly be said to have existed."[15] Between 1922 and 1938 a new legal order emerged in Soviet Russia. Law and the state became the principal instruments of the new economic régime. By 1938 the extremist followers of Lenin were denounced by Vyshinsky, the new State Commissar of Justice, as saboteurs of Soviet law. The identification of law and economics or of law and politics, he said, destroys the specific character of law, "which is the totality of rules of be-

---

[12] The chief sources of international law, as studied and practiced in the United States, are (besides treaties) the decisions of national courts and the official actions of foreign offices together with their justifications for such actions. The decisions of international tribunals still cover only small areas.

[13] Laserson, Russia and the Western World (1945), 125. This discussion of Soviet law is based primarily on the brief discussion in this book; the conclusion is supported by Vyshinsky's book, cited below, and by Gsovski, infra, § 3.24, n. 71.

[14] Ibid. 118.

[15] Ibid., 125.

havior, customs and social principles established by the state and compulsorily defended by state power." [16] Vyshinsky's conception of law is not very different from Holland's (§ 2.04). Civil and criminal law were re-introduced, both in legal education and in legislation and administration.[17] This recent social experiment supports the conclusion that not only structural law but also some measure of decisional law is necessary to the maintenance of the modern state.

Are there any examples of a régime of law without a state which promulgates and establishes the law through its organs of government? Three possible examples may be briefly mentioned. One is the kind of régime found in some primitive social groups, such as the "laws" of the Cheyenne Indians as described by Professors Llewellyn and Hoebel.[18] Since no official Censor of Jurisprudential Terminology has been or should be established to prevent anthropologists from using the term "law" to designate the mores of primitive societies, one can only say that "law" in such a context has a substantially different meaning from that which it has in the modern state. Even though there are suggestive similarities, confusion is likely to result from trying to make the same term include both types of phenomena. A second possible example is the continued validity and application of the ordinary civil and criminal law of a nation after it has been conquered by another nation. Thus the French Civil Code continued in effect, for the most part, after the Nazi conquest of France in 1940–1942. Did the French legal régime, then, continue independently of the Nazi state? Certainly not, for the Nazi state adopted and enforced in French territory all those provisions of the French code that it did not expressly abrogate. Such cases give little difficulty if one accepts the elementary distinction between authority and authorship. Obviously the Nazi state was not the author of the French Codes, but neither for that matter was the French Third Republic. The legal and political authority of the French codes has been changed several times since they were originally drafted, even though the conflict-of-laws rule of *another* state may treat them as being, for its practical purposes, continuous. A third possible example is the body of rules estab-

---

16 Ibid., 131. See Vyshinsky, The Law of the Soviet State, (1948), 50.

17 Ibid., 135. A valuable short comment is Fuller, "Pashukanis and Vyshinsky: A Study in the Development of Marxian Legal Theory", (1949) 47 Mich. L.Rev. 1157.

18 See Llewellyn and Hoebel, The Cheyenne Way (1941).

lished for the conduct of its members by a private corporation, a labor union or a religious body within a state. For reasons which will be stated further on (§ 2.34), such rules are to be called "law" only metaphorically.

Sovereignty; the Sovereign. The conception of sovereignty has been one of the trouble spots of the positive or imperative theory of law. Austin made it an essential part of his conception of law by defining law as a command of sovereign to subject. Holland substituted rule for command but retained the notion of enforcement by a sovereign political authority. Other writers have sought to eliminate the notion of sovereignty. Dr. Hans Kelsen stops with the "basic norm" of the Constitution as a necessary presupposition of a legal system. Gray and Salmond substitute pronouncement by the courts for promulgation by a sovereign (§ 2.05). Yet the conception of a sovereign political authority cannot be so easily disposed of. It continually turns up when attempts are made to establish an international legal order, whether it be called League of Nations or United Nations or a proposed World State. In such assemblages one nation after another interposes a veto or makes reservations designed to protect its sovereignty.[19] Within a state the question frequently arises whether the government or some other form of association has supreme power. To ignore the question of sovereignty in relation to law is to leave a gap between jurisprudence and political philosophy.

To fill this gap John Austin (§ 2.04) worked out a rather colorless conception of sovereignty:

> "If a *determinate* human superior, *not* in a habit of obedience to a like superior, receive *habitual* obedience from the *bulk* of a given society, that determinate superior is sovereign in that society, and the society (including the superior) is a society political and independent." [20]

So careful was he to distinguish the sovereign from the political society of which it was sovereign, that he regarded only the sovereign as being truly independent:

> "The party truly independent (independent, that is to say, of a determinate human superior), is not the society but the sovereign portion of the society: that certain member

---

[19] The United Nations "is based on the principal of the sovereign equality of all of its members." U. N. Charter, Art. 2(1).

[20] Austin, Lectures on Jurisprudence (4th ed., 1873), I, 226 (Lecture VI); Hall, 398.

of the society, or that certain body of members, to whose commands, expressed or intimated, the generality or bulk of its members render habitual obedience." [21]

Austin did not ascribe to the sovereign absolute and unlimited power, as some political philosophers had done. His crucial test of sovereignty, the "habit of obedience" of the bulk of the population, which he derived from Bentham,[22] is an empirical test much preferable to the "divine right of kings" which an earlier generation of Englishmen had discarded, and one which seems a fairly workable method of determining when a new or revolutionary government has established itself in power. If the bulk of the population (a bare majority would hardly do) are going about their private affairs without attempting to overthrow the government, then one can infer that they are in a "habit of obedience" to it, or one can conclude that the government is maintaining, to use Professor MacIver's language, "the universal external conditions of social order." [23] No such test can be applied with the exactness of a micrometer caliper, as Austin fully recognized.[24]

But Austin conceived of the sovereign as a determinate person or body of persons. Who is this person or body in a particular state? In England it was in his time the Parliament, or the king, peers and commons.[25] In the United States it has been said to be that body or combination of bodies which has power to amend the Federal constitution.[26] It does rather strain one's imagination to conceive of the bulk of the population of the United States being in a "habit of obedience" to two-thirds of each house of Congress and three-fourths of the state legislatures; and the strain becomes even greater if one tries to include the alternative methods of amending the Federal constitution, namely, by a convention, called by Congress on the application of the legislatures of two-thirds of the states, to *propose* amendments, and by conventions which may be called in the several states to ratify amend-

---

21 Ibid., 227.

22 Ibid., 240, quoting Bentham's Fragment on Government (1776).

23 Supra, note 11.

24 Lectures, 234 (Cromwellian England), 235 (Mexico).

25 Ibid., 253.

26 Austin, to preserve his definition, said that the sovereign in the United States "resides in the states' governments as *forming one aggregate body.*" Ibid. 268, note r. But the "one aggregate body" is a fiction; there are forty-eight distinct legislatures. He also overlooks the required modes of initiating amendments.

ments.[27] The "habit of obedience" conception can be applied to an individual or a single body continuously maintained, but not to such a complex set of potential and usually non-existent bodies. Bentham's looser conception of the sovereign as merely the body having highest authority in the government [28] comes nearer to accuracy. Yet even this conception of sovereignty does not quite fit the complex amending process in the United States, unless one includes the potential conventions as a part of the "government." Both Austin and Bentham failed in their efforts to locate a single unified sovereign, an individual or body of individuals having sovereign power, in many modern states.

A distinction between political sovereignty and legal sovereignty will serve to clarify the relation of law to sovereignty. Political sovereignty, according to Professor MacIver, may be divided into three stages: the general will, the loyalty and patriotism and trust which the members of a political society (a state) place in the decisions of its constituted government even when they do not agree with it; the ultimate sovereign, the power which ultimately determines the policy or direction of the state; and the government, the legislative sovereign, which has the exclusive right to make laws within the sphere assigned to it by the ultimate sovereign.[29] At no stage in this series does any one body have, *in fact,* unlimited power; for even so-called absolute dictators must have some regard for the wishes of their subjects, as is shown by the studious control which they exercise over all means of influencing public opinion. Legal sovereignty, on the other hand, is the process, including constitutional norms and official acts, by which the *validity* (§ 2.31) of any so-called legal norm of the state can be determined. Ultimately legal sovereignty depends upon political sovereignty, for a mere paper rule is not a law. Whereas political sovereignty includes degrees of power and limitations on power, legal sovereignty admits of no such degrees; there are no half-way valid laws. This does not mean, on the one hand, that legal sovereignty presupposes absolute unlimited power; nor on the other hand, that there are no doubtful cases of legal validity. All that legal sovereignty presupposes is a method by which such doubts may be eventually determined.

---

27 U. S. Constitution, Art. V.

28 Bentham, Principles of Morals and Legislation (1789; Clarendon Press ed., 1892), 218. See also Lasswell and Kaplan, Power and Society: A Framework for Political Inquiry (1950), 177: "Sovereignty is the highest degree of authority".

29 MacIver, op.cit., supra, n. 11, 21–24.

A law, then, is a norm having the authority of the state acting in the way and within the limits prescribed by the ultimate political sovereign. This is a necessary part of the conception of law, because a state in order to maintain social order among its members must first maintain legal order among its officials. Such is the connection between law and internal sovereignty. With respect to the external sovereignty, or political independence of the state, the question of legal validity is not substantially different, though it may be more difficult to answer in some cases. When a states loses its independence of external political power [30] by conquest it is the usual practice to leave most of its legal system unchanged.

The law of a state is a *unique* body of norms of conduct because the state is a unique kind of association. It is the only association having irrecusable membership. One can resign from a club or a union or a church or a political party (in most states); the rules adopted by those bodies for their members will then no longer be applicable. One cannot resign from a state without leaving its territory, and then ordinarily only by becoming a member of another state.[31] A second unique characteristic of the state is its coercive power paramount to that of any internal association or group. A state law supersedes any rule of another association or group which conflicts with it. While the continuous or complete enforcement of a state law is not essential to its legal validity, and cartels, labor unions or religious bodies may temporarily defy state law, yet the basic requirement that social order be maintained will eventually lead to the suppression of such disorders, or to their legalization through change in the law of the state.

§ 2.33—The Sanction of Law

The term sanction is of religious derivation and originally referred to the sacredness of religious requirements. To sanction a precept was to sanctify it. From this came the notion of a penalty or punishment for violation. Still later usage extended the conception of sanction to include reward as well as punishment.[32] In its broadest sense sanction includes any consequence, either of violation or of observance of a norm, which motivates men to

---

30 Professor MacIver's definition of "a state" does not require independence of external sovereign power. Supra, n. 11.

31 MacIver, op.cit., 17–21.

32 See Blackstone, Commentaries, I, 56.

conform to it. This broad usage is not, however, generally followed by jurisprudential writers, who limit legal sanction to a harmful consequence imposed by state officials. We shall examine the reasons for such a limitation, and try to determine the meaning of a legal sanction.

Are consequences harmful to the violator of a legal norm but not imposed by state officials, "sanctions" of that norm? One who murders another may incur harmful consequences in the form of reprisals by the victim's relatives and friends, or in the form of loss of reputation in the community. Are these "sanctions" of the law prohibiting murder? They are not *legal* sanctions, since they are not consequences imposed by state officials; in this sense they are not sanctions of a legal norm. One of the chief functions of law is to supplant the disorderly blood-feud of private vengeance and to re-enforce the indeterminate and ineffective repressive effects of public opinion or reputation. These consequences are sanctions of moral norms which may be partly co-extensive with legal norms. When a moral norm is taken by a law-maker to furnish the ideological content of a legal norm, it is transformed into something materially different: It is given a determinate authority and a determinate sanction, and these additions ordinarily, if not inevitably, produce differences in content. For instance, the moral norm with respect to homicide, in any community or class, is not identical, as to what constitutes unjustifiable homicide, with the legal norm. Giving a moral norm authoritative legal status is the creation of a "new" norm.[33] Of course moral sanctions, in a particular case of violation of law, may and frequently do re-enforce legal sanctions. Only the latter are, strictly speaking, the sanctions of legal norms.

A man who recklessly drives an automobile in a crowded highway incurs a grave risk of being injured by a collision with another object; is this (possible or probable) consequence a "sanction" of a legal norm that prohibits negligent driving? Certainly it is not a legal sanction, and it seems confusing to say that it is a "sanction" at all. For a sanction is a consequence imposed by someone other than the violator of a norm. Bentham introduced the confusing notion of "physical" sanction to designate this kind of consequence of the violation of a norm which it is prudent for one to obey; Austin, however, rejected it.[34] The conception of law

---

[33] Cf. Dewey, book review of Allen, Law in the Making (1927), in (1928) 28 Columbia L.Rev. 832–833, which makes a similar point as to custom.

[34] Austin, Lectures on Jurisprudence (4th ed., 1873), 217–218.

as a prudential prescription has been discussed above (§ 2.20 (c)). No doubt the effectiveness of a legal rule, that is, the probability that people will conform to it, is increased when prudent self-interest re-enforces the legal sanction. Such a motivation is not, however, a necessary characteristic of law. For instance, violations of price and rationing regulations during World War II were ordinarily profitable or beneficial to the violators, apart from legal penalties and the feeble and uncertain moral sanctions of disapproval in the community. In ethical theory the painful sense of guilt or shame caused by the violation of an ethical duty is sometimes referred to as an "internal" sanction, as opposed to the "external" sanctions of law and morals above mentioned. Here we shall confine "sanction" to external sanctions.

Why is not the giving of a reward by state officials for conformity to a legal norm also to be regarded as a sanction? In one sense, the security and social order which the subjects of a state receive as "rewards" for the maintenance of obedience to law are the principal, and the most worthy, incentives to conformity or obedience. By maintaining a social order and an economic system in which its subjects may satisfy their material wants, the state rewards them for their conformity to law. The presence of such an incentive is attested when popular indignation is aroused because some gangster or racketeer becomes wealthy by illegal activities. The state needs to suppress such activities for its self-preservation. Yet these rewards are not sanctions of the law as a whole, or of any particular law, because sanction means something added to a norm of conduct as a definite incentive. Now rewards *might* be offered for conformity to all laws; but such a scheme seems thoroughly impractical. How much conformity, and for what length of time, would be so rewarded? Jeremy Bentham presented two other arguments against such a general system of rewards: that the law cannot be as certain of creating pleasure as of causing pain; and that to reward one man, in the only general form of reward which is possible, the pecuniary reward, would necessitate taking money from others and thus causing them greater pain.[35] Whether or not these reasons are sufficient, clearly reward is an exceptional method of inducing men to conduct which the law seeks to promote or encourage.[36] One example is the type of law, found in some American states, which

---

[35] Bentham, The Limits of Jurisprudence Defined (Everett ed., 1945), 226, n. 5.

[36] See Buckland, Some Reflections on Jurisprudence (1945), 89.

directed certain officials to pay from public funds bounties for the killing of certain destructive animals. If the law of State X provides that a certain official shall pay a dollar for every wolf scalp, is this payment the "sanction" of a legal rule that the inhabitants shall or ought to kill wolves? [37] A more recent example is the Federal Agricultural Adjustment Act, which provides for payments to agricultural land-owners who abstain from using a portion of their lands for the growing of a certain crop. In both cases, of course, the payment is an inducement to an indefinite group of individuals to conduct themselves in a certain way. In a sense every citizen "ought" to conduct himself in the way that his state seeks to promote by offering rewards; he "ought" to kill wolves or he "ought" not to plant a part of his land in wheat. Yet these "oughts" signify at most indefinite duties, moral or political duties rather than legal duties. This, coupled with the rarity of specific rewards, explains why by prevailing usage a reward is not regarded as a "sanction," and that term is limited to *harmful* consequences imposed by officials.[38]

The sanction of law may be considered in gross or in particular. The sanction of the legal order as a whole is the physical power of the state, acting through its organs of government, to restrain or otherwise coerce by force those who defy its laws. This coercive power of the state within its territory is a characteristic that differentiates the state from other forms of association and the law of the state from the norms of other associations. Sanction is thus a necessary attribute of the kind of law here considered.

Can it be said that every particular law has a sanction, and if so, in what sense? Two ideas commonly associated with sanction are *duty* and *punishment*. A penal law satisfies both of these conditions: A statute providing that murder in the first degree is punishable by death has a punitive sanction, and in common usage it imposes a "duty" not to commit murder. What is the sanction of rules of private law? A statute provides that no will shall be valid unless executed by the testator in the presence of two wit-

---

37 E.g., one such statute provides that "the commissioners of each county nay cause to be paid out of the county treasury" a sum not exceeding twenty iollars for each scalp of a wolf killed in the county. Indiana Stat.Ann. (Burns, 1948), sec. 26–1101.

38 See MacIver, Society—Its Structure and Changes (1933), 248–252; Hall, 919; Austin, Lectures on Jurisprudence (1869), I, 182; Hall, 395. More recently sanctions were divided into affirmative (rewards) and negative ("deprivation of values") with the latter playing admittedly the more important ro..e, Lasswell, and Kaplan, Power and Society (1950) 48–49.

nesses. Is every subject of this state under a duty to execute a will with two witnesses? Certainly not; every subject is privileged to die intestate (as most of them do). Yet this statute establishes a legal norm which officials will conform to by refusing to recognize as a dispositive instrument any will not so witnessed. This is sometimes called the "sanction by nullity." [39] This conception of sanction, as Professor Buckland points out, seems rather strained. A better analysis of this type of legal rule is afforded by recurring to the conception of negative propositions of law (§ 2.21). The statute states in negative form one of the requirements of a valid will. If all such requirements are satisfied, then a judgment will be rendered in favor of the persons to whom the testator's property is transferred (on the death of the testator) and this judgment will be enforced by the sheriff or other executive official against other claimants. The "sanction" of such a negative legal rule is found only when we extricate the affirmative legal rule which it implies. In a similar way the rule that no promise is binding without a consideration, and similar rules of case law, imply rules of affirmative action that are sanctioned.

The sanction by nullity does seem applicable, however, to illegal transactions. A court is directed by rules of positive law to refuse enforcement to a contract which has an immoral purpose or tendency or is a gambling transaction, or is made for the purpose of defrauding others, etc. In each of these cases, it seems, there is a norm which prohibits such conduct, and which has (sometimes with additional criminal sanctions) a civil sanction of nullity.[40] Official refusal to act *may* constitute a sanction.

Are sanctions always punishments? If A converts B's chattel to his use, and B obtains a judgment against A for the value of the chattel, the court sanctions the rule prohibiting conversion of another's property, but does it "punish" A? In common usage

---

[39] Buckland, op.cit., n. 36, 90–92. The state does not seek to induce citizens to make wills, but it does seek to induce those who choose to make a will to make it in a way (writing with signature and witnesses) which will minimize uncertainties of proof, hence avoid disputes and promote public order.

[40] By this analysis legality of purpose or tendency is not a necessary element of the definition of "contract"; rather illegality is a reason (among many) why some contract claims are not given legal enforcement. This view is supported by the circumstance that some claims based on illegal contracts are enforced, e.g., where the parties are not in pari delicto. The "rules of positive law" referred to in the text include, of course, many rules of the case law of contracts; "illegality" need not be based on a statutory provision.

the damages are deemed "compensatory," not "punitive." It seems, then, that a sanction is not necessarily punitive, though it is always something disadvantageous or harmful. The orderly execution of such a judgment is a sanction. Ultimately, of course, such a rule of property is sanctioned by punitive measures, such as the penalties imposed for interfering with a sheriff in the execution of the judgment. In this sense, it seems, all legal norms are *ultimately* sanctioned by punitive measures.

Does the conception of sanction add anything to the position, taken above (§ 2.22), that a legal norm is a statement that certain legal consequences shall or ought to follow from certain operative facts? The answer is affirmative. One kind of case in which official conduct is not a sanction was mentioned above, the statute of wills, where a proposition of law states in requirement of a particular kind of claim. Another illustration of this kind of case is the requirement of the election law that all voters must be twenty-one years or more of age. The minority of an applicant implies as a consequence the refusal by election officials to permit him to vote; yet such refusal is not intended to motivate minors to grow older. Thus sanction is narrower in scope than legal consequences, and involves the notion of intention to motivate conduct.

Aside from cases of this negative kind, there are many others by which to test the statement that every legal norm necessarily has a definite sanction. A court renders a declaratory judgment that the plaintiff, a liability insurance company, is not bound to pay any judgment against the insured obtained by a certain injured party for injuries arising out of a certain accident. This judgment is a legal consequence but is not by itself a sanction of any legal norm; however, it will lead to a refusal by a court to award such a judgment if and when such an action is brought. Again, the President of the United States issues a formal proclamation declaring the fourth Thursday in November to be a national holiday, Thanksgiving Day. Is this proclamation a law? Let us assume that the President in issuing such a proclamation is acting officially, and not merely as a prominent citizen. Does the proclamation have any legal consequences? It may be that officials and employees of the Federal government are thereby privileged not to work at their official employments on that day; if so the proclamation has legal consequences. Moreover, a Federal official who attempted to compel his subordinates to work on that day might be removed from office under a statute authorizing removal for misfeasance in office. Unless the Thanksgiving

Proclamation has some such consequences, it is not a "law," whatever may be its hortatory effects.

Now take another example. Officials or employees of the United States Department of Agriculture, acting pursuant to official authorization and at public expense, prepare and publish a bulletin recommending the use of a certain preparation, say, in the treatment of poison-ivy sufferers. Clearly such a recommendation is not a law: no official consequences follow from failure to use the preparation. The officials of a modern state engage in many activities other than making or enforcing laws. These activities may, of course, have harmful consequences which are not legal sanctions. An official bulletin may recommend the use of A's product to the exclusion of B's, thereby harming B's business. That such official activity is not a law-making or law-enforcing activity is no reason why B should not have a judicial remedy, or other official remedy for the violation of a legal norm by the official who caused the harm.

The Sanction of Official Conduct. The Austinian theory of law (§ 2.04) was rejected by Salmond on the ground that the courts by whom the law of a state is administered and applied are not subject to any sanction when they fail to administer and apply the law. In Anglo-American law, at least, a judge is not personally liable to one who is harmed by his honest but erroneous failure to apply the law correctly to given facts. Probably nothing short of malice toward the losing party, or bribery or other corruption, would subject a judge to such liability. Are judges, then, under no legal duty to administer and apply the law correctly as well as honestly? Where legislative impeachment or other removal proceedings on the ground of incompetency or wilful though honest obstinacy are authorized, it is not quite correct to say that the duty of judges to apply the law correctly is not sanctioned. Nor is it any answer to say that such sanctions have less influence in determining a judge's decision to apply the law than has his sense of moral or political obligation; for the same may well be said of conformity to law by perhaps a majority of private citizens. A lower court's failure to apply the law correctly has or may have a legal consequence if an appeal is taken; yet the reversal of a judge's decision, though it may influence his conduct in future cases, is not a sanction of his official duty because that is not its chief end. Salmond's strongest point is that a court of last resort, in English and American law, has avowedly the power to overrule its precedents, and unavowedly the power to ignore them and to distinguish them on inadequate grounds. It might be answered that if the judges of a court ran amok in overruling or ignoring their case law, the legislature could impeach and remove them.[41] While removal from office by impeachment is clearly a sanction, it is not a sanction of any particular decisional norm that the court is obliged to apply, and thus does not quite meet Salmond's objection. However, if one concedes that in overruling precedents, or in establishing a new precedent in conflict with previous ones, a court exercises a law-making (not a "legislative") power, the objection disappears; for judicial law-making, like legislation, means legally authorized departure in some respect from previous law. In conclusion, the conception of sanction as a harmful consequence officially and regularly applied to a violation of a legal norm does not seem applicable to decisional norms interpreted as addressed to judges of courts. The same may be said of administrative officials acting within the scope of their discretionary powers. Yet these concessions to the independence of the judiciary (and of adjudicative administrative officials) should not obscure the fact that, in Anglo-American law at least, government officials are subject to rules of law and to legal sanctions.

Is Judicial Enforceability Necessary? Must an official norm of the state, in order to constitute a law, be one which the courts —that is, the judicial organs of government—will interpret, apply and order to be enforced? The position taken by Gray and some others that only the rules laid down by courts are law (§ 2.05) involves this point and a good deal more. One example is the requirement of re-apportionment of members of the Federal House of Representatives among districts determined in accordance with population. The Federal Constitution, supplemented by Federal legislation, contains provisions which direct the state legislatures to re-apportion their Congressional districts after each decennial census. Yet the Supreme Court of the United States has consistently refused to enforce this requirement. In a recent case the Court refused to declare invalid an earlier Illinois apportionment statute which the legislature had left unaltered in violation of the Federal requirement. The Court had power to render a declaratory judgment yet it deemed this claim "beyond its competence to grant." The opinion by Frankfurter, J., gave as a reason that "due regard for the effective working of this government revealed this issue to be of a peculiarly political nature and therefore not meet for judicial determination."[42] "The [Federal]

---

[41] E.g., U.S.Const., Art. I, sec. 1 (5, 6, 7).

[42] Colegrove v. Green, 328 U.S. 549, 552, 66 Sup.Ct. 1198, 1199 (1946).

Constitution," he added, "has many commands that are not enforceable by courts because they clearly fall outside the conditions and purposes that circumscribe judicial action." [43] Other examples mentioned by Mr. Justice Frankfurter are: The provision that a fugitive from justice "shall, on demand of the Executive authority of the state from which he fled, be delivered up to be removed to the state having jurisdiction of the crime"; [44] the provision that the President "shall take care that the laws be faithfully executed"; [45] and the provision that "the United States shall guarantee to every state in this Union a republican form of government." [46]

Are these "commands" rules or principles of law without sanctions? One kind of sanction is applicable to those which are directed to executive officials: the sanction of impeachment and removal from office. A President who neglected flagrantly to enforce the laws of the United States, or who failed to take steps to suppress a non-republican form of government in a state of the Union, might be impeached and removed. This sanction would not be applicable to legislative bodies under the present Constitution of the United States. Is the failure of the voters to re-elect to office executive and legislative officials who fail to obey these non-justiciable (or other) constitutional commands a "sanction"? No doubt this is, in a republican or representative form of government, a basic method of political control. Yet it is not a "sanction" as that term is used in reference to law. It would be applicable only to those officials who chose to become candidates for re-election; because of the many issues and motives in an election it is too uncertain a consequence to operate as a legal sanction; and it is not, as legal sanctions are, prescribed by law as a consequence of violation of a norm. These constitutional commands are primarily political admonitions rather than laws.

But to deny that they are laws is to confine the term to the realm of judicial decision in which professional lawyers customarily work. This is the realm of legal certainty, for whatever may be said of the uncertainty of judicial decisions, they are relatively predictable as compared with the vagaries of legislatures and executives. Yet to exclude imperatives or norms, addressed to

---

[43] Ibid., 556.

[44] U.S.Const., Art. IV, sec. 2.

[45] Ibid., Art. II, sec. 3.

[46] Ibid., Art. IV, sec. 4.

the latter, which courts will not attempt to enforce, is to give law a narrow meaning. The objection that there is no legal sanction applicable to officials or official bodies who refuse to obey these constitutional commands is not fatal, for, as has been pointed out, the judges, too, are not subject to any sanctions with respect to their application of particular legal norms. If and when the legislature re-apportions Congressional districts, or the chief executive of a state orders a fugitive from justice sent back, legal sanctions attach to that official act, and the judiciary will attach legal consequences: in the one case, by upholding the right of a voter to vote in a district so established; in the other, by refusing to release on habeas corpus a fugitive detained pursuant to such an order.[47] Or, if the President were to order Federal troops to overthrow by force a dictator who had established himself in a state and had overthrown its republican form of government, he would be acting within his legal authority which the courts would recognize in an appropriate case. Indeed, to exclude such provisions from our conception of law would banish beyond the pale many of the structural provisions of constitutional law in modern states; for outside the United States, the judicial branch has far less extensive powers of control over the other branches. Constitutional directives to officials are law even if the courts will not enforce them. One unfortunate consequence of the exclusive emphasis upon judicial enforceability as a necessary characteristic of law (§ 2.05) has been that other officials have often felt themselves under no obligation to conform to the law. In the United States, legislators have cheerfully voted to enact laws which they felt sure the courts would declare to be unconstitutional. To achieve its basic functions the state needs to have all of its officials under its legal régime.

Sanctions of Permissive Norms. The constitutional provisions above mentioned, and many other legal provisions, may be interpreted, not as imposing legal duties on officials, but rather as conferring legal powers and privileges. For instance, the provision that "the United States shall guarantee to every state in this Union a republican form of government" may be taken to mean that the President has power to order the United States army to suppress a dictatorship, and that he is legally privileged so to act, that is,

---

[47] The New York governor's warrant of extradition was held sufficient to justify holding a fugitive for extradition to another state despite his claim of innocence. People ex rel. Tobin v. Police Commissioner, 89 N.Y.S.2d 15 (Sup.Ct., 1949) relying on People ex rel Higley v. Millspaw, 281 N.Y. 441, 24 N.E.2d 117 (1940).

is not legally liable for harm done to others through his exercise of the power. It may also imply a prohibition that no person shall attempt to establish a non-republican form of government in any state. If so, this prohibition is a legal norm sanctioned by the President's exercise of his power, and probably also sanctioned by judicial remedies after the President acts. In this sense, it seems, every provision creating an official power to act signifies a prohibition against interference by non-officials with the exercise of the power, and this prohibition is legally sanctioned. *In conclusion,* then, it seems that every law has in some sense a legal sanction, and that sanction is a necessary characteristic of a body of law and of every legal provision.

To avoid misunderstanding we must note three other propositions which are *not* implied by this conclusion:

1. *Actual Enforcement Not Necessary.* A statute is law before it is enforced, and it continues to be law even though it ceases to be enforced. This is the doctrine adopted in most, if not all, modern states. The doctrine of repeal by desuetude, that a law ceases to be law when it has not been enforced by officials or customarily observed by subjects for a long time, gained recognition in the Roman law,[48] in the canon law [49] and in some systems of law based on the Roman law; but it has not been recognized in English [50] or American law.[51] The requirement of habitual obedience or enforcement applies only to the body of law as a whole (§ 2.32).

2. *The Sanction of Law is Not Necessarily the Chief or Efficient Cause of its Obedience.* Most people obey most laws because of habit or imitation or social pressures, rather than because of fear of legal sanctions. Yet if all law-enforcing agencies were suddenly withdrawn, one would soon discover, I believe, that legal sanctions are necessary to re-enforce other incentives to the maintenance of order. Those who find temporary advantages for themselves in social disorder are likely to break down the patterns of obedience of others.[52]

---

[48] Digest I, 3, 32 (Julianus).

[49] Decretals of Gregory IX, Lib. I, tit. IV, cap. 11.

[50] See Buckland and McNair, Roman Law and Common Law (1936), 15–16.

[51] Except in a few early nineteenth century cases. See note, "Judicial Abrogation of the Obsolete Statute: A Comparative View", 64 Harv.L.Rev. 1181 (1951).

[52] The results of the Boston policemen's strike of 1919 seemed to me to support this thesis, as did also the effects of the National Prohibition Act and of price-limiting regulations of World War II and following.

3. *The Social Effects of Law are Not Confined to the Application of Sanctions.* Laws have hortatory effects; they engender habits and customs. Automobile drivers stop at red lights even when no policemen are around, and with no thought of a penalty. Zoning ordinances and building codes have established new standards of community planning and development. Aside from these examples it is always to be remembered that the modern state furnishes many services to its members other than the protection of their interests by legal sanctions. Public health measures, for instance, have modified a good many popular habits during the past generation. Unemployment compensation and old-age pensions are other examples of benefits provided by the modern state. Yet law is a part of the means by which such benefits are provided, and none of them would be worth much without the maintenance of an orderly society through law.

§ 2.34—The "Laws" of Private Power-holders: Guardians, Corporations, Labor Unions, Contracting Parties

The rather seductive view that the rules of conduct adopted and enforced by religious bodies, employers, private corporations, labor unions, baseball leagues and other organizations, are "laws," has sometimes been espoused by jurisprudents. Certainly the rules laid down by an employer for the employees of a large industrial plant, sanctioned by dismissal from employment, are more important to thousands of employees than *some* rules of estate law, such as, for example, the rules under which a few wealthy persons create spendthrift trusts for their wayward children. The rules of the labor union to which the employees belong are often no less important for members than the employer's rules. Dismissal from employment or expulsion from the union are ordinarily more harmful sanctions than the moderate fines imposed for violations of traffic laws. Thus the rules of private organizations are norms of conduct with severe sanctions, and it may be that they consciously influence the daily activities of more people than do the state's laws. In Ehrlich's terms they might be called "living law" (§ 2.03).

Two different kinds of conclusions have been drawn as to the significance of these rules: one, that they are "laws" though not state laws; the other, that they are a part of the law of the state. As to the former but little need be said. That they are more important than state law as a whole is not true, for state law is a necessary means of maintaining social order without which these subordinate organizations could not function. Here we use "law" to mean state law; other uses of the term are metaphorical.

The other conclusion calls for fuller examination. Bentham appears to have been the first modern writer to assert that the rules laid down by a subordinate power-holder are "laws" of the sovereign. His argument is that the sovereign grants a power to a private corporation, for instance, to make rules for the conduct of its members; a member who violates such a rule may be expelled or penalized, and the law of the state will recognize such acts as legally privileged; therefore, the state adopts the rule as a part of its law.[53] Austin followed Bentham to the extent of recognizing that the rules made by a guardian for the conduct of his ward are laws of the state, since the state will hold the guardian legally privileged to punish the ward for violation of rules made within the scope of that power.[54] More recently Dr. Hans Kelsen has argued that the parties to a private contract make law for each other, since they create by authority of law norms of conduct which bind each other and for which the state provides sanctions, the remedies for breach of contract.[55] These examples will suffice to show the position taken. Since the power to make law is ordinarily a delegated power (that is, always except when the political sovereign makes it directly), and since the power to sanction a rule implies the power to make a rule, the state (or sovereign) has impliedly delegated the latter power to all holders of the former. So it may be argued.

Several reasons have been given for rejecting this line of argument. Gray rejected it on the ground that to call such rules "law" is contrary to established usage; and on the further ground that the state in permitting private organizations to act for their own purposes does not make those purposes its own.[56] This seems a sound argument. A religious organization may have a rule requiring its members to profess certain religious beliefs, and if the organization expels a member who violates the rule, the expulsion will be legally privileged and the member's rights of membership will be deemed to have ceased, pursuant to the law

---

[53] Bentham, The Limits of Jurisprudence Defined (1945; written in 1782), 104–105.

[54] Austin, Lectures, 185, note f; Hall, 397.

[55] See Modern Theories of Law (1933), 116–117; Kelsen, General Theory of Law and State (1945), 36, 90, 204, 311. This conception fits neatly into Kelsen's conception of the "gradual concretization of law," yet does not seem essential to it.

[56] Gray, The Nature and Sources of the Law (1909), §§ 332–333.

of the state. Yet the state does not thereby adopt as *its* law a rule requiring anyone to profess such a religious belief. In the United States, at least, such a conclusion would be contrary to the spirit if not the letter of constitutional provisions forbidding the establishment of a religion.[57] A similar argument applies to the rules of an employer for employees, and of a private corporation or a labor union for its members. These organizations are not required to make their rules for the promotion of the general welfare; the officials of the state are. Does this argument introduce into the conception of law an ideal qualification? (§ 2.02). By the same argument could it not be said that a rule enacted by an official state legislature is not "law" if it does not seek to promote the common welfare? Has that arch-positivist, Gray, permitted idealism to infect his conception of law? This is a difficult question for legal positivism, but the answer is still negative. The reason why, in a given state, the rules of a private corporation or a labor union, or of private contracting parties, are not law is because those who make or promulgate them do not have the authority to act for the state in so doing. On the other hand, some rules of private-power-holders may be contrary to the policy of the state, and so illegal.

The difference between state law and non-state rules of conduct needs to be maintained for another reason. If the rules of a religious body or a labor union are state law, then the legislature of the state has power to repeal them and enact other rules. On the contrary, the maintenance of a realm of individual activity within which the state does not intrude is an essential attribute of the freedom of the individual as against the state.[58] Any rule of a private power-holder may be a part of the legal justification for his act; it may be one of the "operative facts" from which legal consequences follow. To say this is not to say that it is a legal rule.

§ 2.35—The Legal Status of International Law

Ever since Jeremy Bentham invented the term "international law" to designate what had theretofore been called "the law of

---

57 E. g., U.S.Const. Amendment I (a limitation on both Federal and state legislative powers).

58 See Patterson, "Bentham on the Nature and Method of Law," (1945) 23 California L.Rev. 612, 618. On the related question of what constitutes "state action" under the "due process" clause, see, for example, Lundberg v. Chicago Great Western Ry. Co., 76 F.Supp. 61 (D.C.Mo.1948).

nations" [59] (jus gentium, droit des gens) the question whether or in what sense international law is "law" has been a subject of doubt and controversy. Bentham distinguished "internal law," the law applied by the internal tribunals of a state to individuals, from "international law," the "rules for the conduct" of sovereigns in their transactions with each other. He doubted the propriety of classifying the latter as law.[60] His follower, John Austin, probably relying upon Bentham's later definition of law (§ 2.05), as well as his own, classified international law under "rules set and enforced by mere opinion" which were "improperly termed laws" [61] and were properly called "positive international morality." [62] Rules or principles of international law, prescribing the conduct of states in their relations with each other, are not laws in the Austinian sense because they are not laid down by a sovereign political authority to persons who are in a state of subjection to it, and because no sanction is prescribed to motivate conformity to such rules or to attach punishment or redress to non-conformity. The Austinian position has been rejected by many writers, who have sought to defend the legal character of international law. The body of literature on the subject is extensive. The Statute of the International Court of Justice, adopted as a part of the United Nations Charter in 1945, and the Nuremberg Trial of war criminals, have raised anew questions as to the legal status of international law. The continuance of the controversy shows that something more is involved than merely an Anglo-American lawyer's alleged copyright on the use of the word "law." While words are symbols, they are also tools and weapons, and they can mislead as well as lead those to whom they are addressed. Here two questions will be discussed: 1. Is international law, or any part of it, a part of the positive law of a state? 2. What characteristics does international law have in common with positive state-law?

1. *International Law as State Law.* A recent and widely used treatise gives as the meaning of international law "the principles and rules of conduct declaratory thereof which nations feel themselves bound to observe, and therefore commonly do ob-

---

[59] Bentham, An Introduction to the Principles of Morals and Legislation (Clarendon Press ed., 1892), 326 (Ch. XVII, sec. 25, note 1). This book, written in 1780, was first published in 1789.

[60] Ibid., 327.

[61] Austin, Lectures (1873), 89.

[62] Ibid., 177, 188–189.

serve, in their relations with each other." [63]   International law,
then, consists of norms of which the subjects (persons obligated)
are states,[64] and of which the objects (things regulated) are
relations between states. Now a good many of these norms are
recognized and enforced by the law of the state. In the United
States the rules relating to the immunity of sovereign states
from being sued in national courts, and the rules relating to
the immunity from arrest or restraint of ambassadors of foreign states, are rules of decision for national courts and are a part
of the law of the United States. The Constitution significantly
gives Federal courts jurisdiction over "cases affecting ambassadors, other public ministers and consuls," and over controversies
"between a state [of the Union], or the citizens thereof, and
foreign states, citizens or subjects." [65]   The rule that a nation
is bound by treaties that it executes is recognized by the provision that the "Constitution, and the laws of the United States
which shall be made in pursuance thereof, *and all treaties made,
or which shall be made, under the authority of the United States,*
shall be the supreme law of the land; and the judges in every
state shall be bound thereby . . . ." [66]   Thus a treaty provision
that the citizens of a foreign state shall be permitted to acquire
and own land in the United States overrides a state statute denying aliens such a permission. In a case involving such an alien
the Supreme Court said that "the Constitution, laws and treaties
of the United States are as much a part of the laws of every state
as its own local laws and constitution." [67]   However, two limitations on this doctrine make it lack persuasion of the legal character of international law. One is that only those treaty provisions which are "self-executing" are given effect by courts; that
is, those which the courts can apply without additional legislation by Congress.[68]   A court of the United States could not enforce the vital provision of the United Nations Charter by which

---

[63] I Hyde, International Law (2d. ed., 1945), 1.

[64] However, the movement in favor of recognizing individuals as subjects.
is ably defended in Jessup, "The Subjects of a Modern Law of Nations,"
(1947) 45 Mich.L.Rev. 383.

[65] U.S.Const., Art. III, sec. 2.

[66] Ibid., Art. VI, sec. 2.

[67] Hauenstein v. Lynham, 100 U.S. 483, 490 (1890). See also Jordan v. Tash-
iro, 278 U.S. 123, 49 Sup.Ct. 47 (1928).

[68] See opinion of Marshall, C. J., in Foster v. Neilson, 2 Pet. (27 U.S.) 253,
314 (1829).

member nations are obligated to support the Security Council in maintaining peace:

> "All members of the United Nations, in order to contribute to the maintenance of international peace and security, undertake to make available to the Security Council, on its call and in accordance with a special agreement or agreements, armed forces, assistance, and facilities, including rights of passage, necessary for the purpose of maintaining international peace and security." [69]

Only the executive or the legislative branch of the United States government could give effect to this "undertaking." In what sense, if at all, is this treaty provision a part of the "supreme law of the land"? Perhaps only in the sense that *if* the executive and legislative branches act in fulfillment of the undertaking, the courts would be obliged to recognize their acts as within their constitutional powers. In this way the treaty provision is like those constitutional mandates that the courts will not enforce (§ 2.32) but with some important differences to be mentioned below. This leads us to the second limitation on the effect of treaties, that if the Congress subsequently enacts a statute in conflict with a treaty provision, the courts will give effect to the statute [70] and thus, in a sense, uphold a violation of international law. More accurately, the executive, legislative and judicial organs of the United States sometimes adopt as a part of national law norms for the conduct of individual subjects which correspond in content with some norms of international law for the conduct of nations (states).

Another part of international law, or at least of its literary sources, is the records of positions taken and acts done by the foreign office (State Department) in presenting claims and in conducting negotiations with other nations. This material, especially when systematically digested, furnishes precedents, rules and principles which the officials of the foreign office feel obliged to follow and ordinarily, perhaps, do follow. Whether they are a part of the law of the United States in the same sense that constitutional mandates are (§ 2.32) need not be determined. For even as such they are not norms enforceable against the United States.

2. *What Characteristics Does International Law Have in Common with Positive State-Law?* International law consists

---

[69] Charter of the United Nations (San Francisco, June 26, 1945), Art. 43 (1).

[70] The Cherokee Tobacco, 11 Wall. (78 U.S.) 616 (1871).

of norms of conduct for states which they are in some sense obliged to conform to through their officials. These norms have
the characteristic of generality (Chapter 5) and they prescribe
expressly or by implication official conduct that ought to follow
from operative facts (§ 2.22). Do they have a sanction like that
of a legal sanction (§ 2.32)? In my judgment, they do not.
O. W. Holmes, rejecting Austin's view that international law is
not properly designated as law, suggested that war is a "sanction"
of international law.[71] But nations do not go to war merely, if at
all, because of violations of international law; and there is not
(or was not when Holmes wrote) any rule of international law
prohibiting war for any reason or no reason. By the Kellogg-
Briand treaty of 1928 the principal nations of the world re-
nounced war as an instrument of national policy; and thousands
of peace-loving people were misled into believing that war had
been "outlawed" in the same way that national law "outlaws"
murder. In the absence of any orderly and effective machinery
to sanction this treaty, its obligations were ignored by nations
which do not respect international morality.

Another argument by analogy is drawn from constitutional
law. We have seen that certain constitutional mandates to officials are not sanctioned by judicial enforcement and do not have
any comparable sanction (§ 2.33). Similarly (it may be said)
obligations imposed on a state by international law (including an
international treaty) become legal obligations imposed on its
officials. Professor MacIver cautiously contends that this analogy "removes half the difficulty of applying the term 'law' to those
further rules which are regulative of the conduct of states in
relation to one another." [72] The half he refers to is the technical
half: Foreign office officials are obliged to follow and apply
(some) rules of international law in the same way as the President is obliged to guarantee each state a republican form of government or a state legislature is obliged to re-apportion Congressional districts. The other half of the difficulty is more serious.
Constitutional provisions are sanctioned by impeachment. International law lacks not only the legal sanctions of a world state
but also the political authority (§ 2.31) which a world state
would derive from a world community.[73]

---

[71] Holmes, "Codes and the Arrangement of the Law," (1870) 5 American
L.Rev. 1, 5; Hall, 403, 404.

[72] MacIver, The Modern State (1926), 281. He refers to English constitutional law rather than American.

[73] Dr. Kelsen's "basic norm" seems to me at best a convenient fiction.

To MacIver's analogy we may add an even more important one, that international law is created or formulated by a professional class of lawyers who have developed techniques and systemic characteristics like those of the better systems of national law.

Some further light is thrown on the nature of international law by the United Nations Charter, which includes, as an annex, the Statute of the International Court of Justice. Only states may be parties in cases before the Court,[74] and then only if they separately agree to. The decisional law of the Court is indicated by the following provision:

"1. The Court, whose function is to decide in accordance with international law such disputes as are submitted to it, shall apply:

"a. international conventions, whether general or particular, establishing rules expressly recognized by the contesting states;

"b. international custom, as evidence of a general practice accepted as law;

"c. the general principles of law recognized by civilized nations;

"d. subject to the provisions of Article 59,[75] judicial decisions and the teachings of the most highly qualified publicists of the various nations, as subsidiary means for the determination of rules of law.

"2. This provision shall not prejudice the power of the Court to decide a case ex aequo et bono, if the parties agree thereto." [76]

The reference to "ex aequo et bono" reminds us that Hugo Grotius founded the law of nations in 1620 upon "natural law," which is undoubtedly different from positive law (infra, Part IV).

Customary law is a fourth analogy by which the legal character of international law has been sustained. Professor Sheldon Glueck has recently argued that the waging or instigating of an aggressive war was a violation of an international law based on custom, as evidenced by, among other things, the Kellogg-Briand treaty.[77] Aside from doubts as to the evidence of this

---

[74] Art. 34 (1).

[75] I.e., that the decisions of the court have no binding force except in respect of the particular case—apparently a rejection of judicial precedents as "binding" law.

[76] Art. 38.

[77] See Glueck, The Nuremberg Trial and Aggressive War (1946).

"custom," custom does not become law in any sense until it has received official recognition or sanction as law (§ 3.15). The argument from custom is one way of removing the objection that Goering and his fellow-Nazis were tried for a crime (aggressive war) which was created after the deeds were done. The multinational Executive Agreement of August 8, 1945, which established the tribunal, made the law by which it operates and by which the conduct of the accused is being judged. The judgments of the tribunal were sanctioned by joint state action. The proceedings seem sufficiently "legal" in character without trying to make a dubious custom into a law. While it is unfortunate that the law here operates ex post facto, the defendants can scarcely claim unfair surprise. However, the legal status of the Nuremberg Trial will probably be debated for some time to come.[78]

In conclusion, the foregoing discussion is not intended to deprecate the value of international law; as a former student and part-time teacher of the subject I respect its intellectual qualities and its usefulness. Nor was it intended to exclude any one from using the term "law" in reference to international law. Whatever may be said about labels, an international legal order providing peace and security comparable to that provided internally by the better specimens of state legal order, does not exist.

§ 2.36—Some Conclusions

The foregoing discussion (Part II) sets forth what I consider to be the most interesting aspects of the question, What is law? As I have indicated, it is not merely a question of choosing labels. The three basic relations of law, to the state, to society and to ideal ends, still [79] seem sufficiently comprehensive and yet sufficiently divisive to serve as general guides to the various senses in which "law" is used. Of these the first seems the relation most useful in distinguishing law from other things and in characterizing lawyer's law. Law is characterized not only by its relation to the political association, the state, but also by its unique character as a legal meaning, that is, a statement meaning that from designated operative facts a certain kind of official conduct shall or should follow. This imperative or positive conception

---

[78] See review of Professor Glueck's book by Floyd E. Thompson (1946), 32 A.B.A.J. 506–7.

[79] First published in my essay in the volume, My Philosophy of Law (1941), 229–243. My chief indebtedness is to Roscoe Pound.

of law does not, as some people appear to believe, preclude the legal profession or any one else engaged in determining whether a particular meaning (of operative facts and official conduct) has validity in a certain state, from considering also both the possible and probable ends, ideal or otherwise, of such a legal norm, and its relations to various aspects of the society. This is so because clearly such relations are or should be considered in the process of law-making, adjudicative or legislative.

The imperative theory of law is far from perfect, as the foregoing discussion shows. Those who attack it usually profess to have in reserve either some immutable set of ideals, which if revealed turn out to be authoritative religious or ethical doctrines, or else some hunch about the soul of society which seems too ineffable for communication. On the other hand, the improvements in the American legal order during the past forty years (roughly the period of my membership in the bar) have been made within the framework and with the instrumentalities of legal positivism. That the formulation of the imperative theory, even the analysis and terminology, involve some evaluations, cannot be denied; even formal definitions in law or political science [80] express some choices of values. The values of the imperative conception are partly discussed above (especially in §§ 2.10–2.12) and will be further discussed in Parts III, IV and V. Briefly the principal values of the imperative theory are peace, orderliness and freedom from official tyranny.

Now for a few formal conclusions, which are to be understood by reference to the foregoing (Part II) discussion:

"Law" in its total comprehension may be taken to include legal norms, the officials who enforce them, the usages and practices of such officials, the ideals of legal norms, the mental attitudes of officials and laymen with respect to the government, and, indeed, anything related to or even analogous to "state-law", or any part or combination of the foregoing. In this volume this use of "law" has been studiously avoided.

"Law" as here used means a more or less systematic and interrelated body of legal norms.

A legal norm is a statement (a) which means a kind or kinds of official conduct shall or should follow from certain operative facts and (b) which has the authority and sanction of the state.

---

[80] See Laswell and Kaplan, Power and Society: A Framework for Political Inquiry (1950), xiii.

Part III

WHAT IS THE LAW?

(The Sources, Forms and Systemic Relations of the Law of a State)

Chapter 8

THE USES OF THE LAW

§ 3.00—"Finding the Law": The Static Aspect of a Legal Judgment

In this part (Part III) we are concerned primarily with the problem of "finding the law." The meaning of this phrase includes the routine information on the use of law books which is given at the beginning of many law school curricula. Here we shall study the same materials—the contents of a good law library in a state—at a somewhat higher level of generality. The subsequent chapters on the sources and forms of the law (Chap. 9), the systemic relations of a body of law (Chap. 10) and the significance of precedents (Chap. 11) will serve to exemplify this broader meaning. In this study our chief instruments will be logic and semantics, yet we shall not attempt to "purify" the law of its evaluations, its principles and policies and standards. One cannot "find the law" without considering whence it came and what it is for.

"Finding the law" is the static aspect of legal judgments, that is, of the reasoning process of arriving at "legal judgments." By this term is meant not merely the formal judgments of courts but also any practical decision, that someone should do this, or should not do that, in the making of which the law plays a dominant or controlling part, even though not the predominant or most important part. It may be a judicial judgment or decree, or it may be a counselor's decision that your old Aunt Clara should be advised to execute a certain will, or a counselor's decision that a manufacturing company should use a certain set of contract forms. In all such decisions factors that we may call "non-legal" will play a part, perhaps the predominant part; and in many of them choices of desire and expediency for which the law pro-

180

vides no guidance, will be predominantly decisive. For example, the contents of Aunt Clara's will may be determined, more importantly, by her affections for nephew John and her antipathy for nephew William than by anything in the law of wills. Similarly, the choice of contract forms may be influenced a good deal by the expediency of making transactions understandable by laymen, even at the sacrifice of legal precision and thoroughness. Yet in so far as the channeling of the decision is a legal one, the person who is to make the decision will have to find some kind of an answer to the question, "What is the law?"

Before examining the law in its more static, systematic and philosophic aspects, we propose to summarize briefly the more important kinds of uses of the law in American society, and to analyze these uses in relation to the problem of finding the law. Most of these uses are professional, that is, they are made by law-trained men. Yet because the law is not maintained primarily for the intellectual delight and pecuniary benefit of lawyers, officials and professors, we shall discuss briefly a somewhat unconventional topic, how do laymen find out about the law?

The extent to which legal norms or ideas about them influence the making of practical judgments has been a subject of lively discussion during the last few decades. Principally this discussion has centered upon the "judicial process," the process by which courts arrive at their judgments, and the relations to this process of the reasons given in the court's opinion. This topic is reserved for fuller discussion later (Part V). Here we merely point out some of the extreme positions in regard to it.

The prevailing conception of the judicial process at the close of the nineteenth century was, it seems, that judicial judgments were inescapably determined by the logical application of rules of law. The late Judge Cardozo, trained in law near the close of that century, admitted in 1923 that when he first began to practice law he was often surprised at the frequency with which courts missed the correct path of legal reasoning.[1] O. W. Holmes satirized this view when he referred to his anonymous colleague who believed that to give a right decision he had only to do his sums correctly.[2] Roscoe Pound, borrowing a simile from the late Herman Kantorowicz, called this the "slot machine" theory of judicial decisions.

---

[1] Cardozo, The Growth of the Law (1924), 57.

[2] Holmes, "The Path of the Law", in Collected Legal Papers (1920), (first published in 1897).

"The necessary machinery has been provided in advance
by legislation or by received legal principles, and one has
but to put in the facts above and draw out the decision below." [3]

The mechanical theory of judicial decisions assumed that they
were causally determined by legal rules rather than that legal
norms served as logical guides in the process of sifting and evaluating facts and arriving at a judgment. It identified logical implication with judgment.

A different tactic is taken in Professor Mortimer Adler's "science of law in discourse": " . . . the science of law in discourse is a purely formal science, like mathematics; its subject-
matter is entirely propositional; its only instrumentality is formal logic." [4]

"Law in discourse" is an "academic subject-matter, a body of
propositions having certain formal relations capable of analysis." [5] It is thus distinguished from "law as official action," a
term which Professor Adler uses to designate "all of the actual
processes which take place in time, the prosecution of litigation,
the advisory work of the law office, the judicial administration
of disputes, and so forth." [6] The conclusions reached by formal
logic are certain, in relation to the premises; the conclusions
reached with respect to "law as official action" are only more or
less probable, since many other factors influence official action
besides the conclusions derived from law in discourse. By sharply differentiating the formal analysis of legal arguments ("law
in discourse") from the prediction of judicial decisions ("law as
official action"), Professor Adler rejected or at least clarified the
nineteenth century assumption referred to above.[7]

The formal analysis of legal propositions or arguments is an
important and, indeed, an indispensable part of the process of

---

3 Pound, "Courts and Legislation", in The Science of Legal Method (1917),
206, citing Kantorowicz, Rechtswissenschaft und Soziologie, 5.

4 Adler, "Legal Certainty", (1931) 31 Columbia L.Rev. 91, 102; Hall, p. 390.

5 Ibid.

6 Ibid.

7 Professor Adler does explain, however, that the two (legal prediction
and formal analysis) are closely related; thus the discovery that there are
two or more rules of law which might be "expressed" by a future decision
lowers the probability that any one of these rules will be the one that decision will express. Ibid., 102, n. 17; Hall, pp. 389–390.

"finding the law." Examples are shown in a good many judicial opinions which state the reasons (justifications) for the court's decision. However, the formal analysis of legal propositions does not tell us (a) whether or not those propositions are authoritative, that is, are a part of the law of the state with which we are concerned, nor (b) the meanings of the terms of those propositions, in that they necessarily refer to facts outside the system, nor (c) that from those propositions a decision one way or the other should be given on the multiple facts (events and existences) of an individual case. "Finding the law," as the term is here conceived, includes (a) and (b) and also the use of these two in selecting and processing the facts for (c). "Finding the law" does not tell us infallibly what a court or a judge will decide; it can provide him with one or more legal grounds for his decision, or with legal grounds for alternative (incompatible) decisions.

Legal propositions may be implicit in a particular body of law though rarely or never expressed officially. One example is the rule that a court should not refuse to give judgment because it finds no applicable law. This rule is explicitly stated in the French Civil Code.[8] It is not, I believe, as explicitly stated in American case law. The Supreme Court of the United States has declared that a Federal court cannot refuse to pass upon (dismiss without prejudice to a future suit on the same claim) a claim properly brought before it (under diversity of citizenship) merely because the court finds that the state law is muddled and uncertain.[9] The litigants, both plaintiff and defendant, are entitled to have the dispute settled one way or another. That the judge must find a way of settling it has an important bearing on the relation of the legal system to judicial decisions. (The point will be developed more fully in the discussion of legal principles and policies in Ch. 10).

§ 3.01—Professional Uses of the Law

What the law-trained man finds the law to be will depend in part upon the institutional setting in which he works (what is commonly expected of one in his position) and partly upon the function which he seeks to fulfill. The three principal uses of the law by professional men are those of the counselor, the advocate,

---

[8] French Civil Code, Art. 4.

[9] Meredith v. City of Winter Haven, 320 U.S. 228, 64 Sup.Ct. 7 (1943).

and the judge or other adjudicative official. This threefold division may be compared with the three major functions or "law-jobs" of the legal order as outlined by Professor Karl N. Llewellyn in an illuminating essay: 1. Taking care of the "trouble-case." 2. Channeling conduct in advance of trouble. 3. Determining who has the official "say", the official power to make law or legal decisions.[10] While the first of these involves the work of the advocate, it also involves the work of a counselor who is trying to settle a "trouble-case" without litigation, and of the judge who wants to find or make a rule for the decision of the trouble case. Thus the classification cuts across the one proposed here.

The other professional uses of the law are subordinate or auxiliary. The non-adjudicative official has to use law in determining the scope of his powers and to some extent in determining the content of his official acts. This use of law by "executive" officials ranging from the policeman on the beat to the governor or the President, is an important one in maintaining the legal order of a society. Yet since these officials turn in doubtful cases to a counselor (e. g. the attorney-general) for guidance and are with few exceptions subject to judicial control, their use of law is subordinate. The legislator uses law in framing new law, but his use of present law as a guide is subordinate to his function of creating new law. The treatise-writer and the law-teacher use law professionally, yet obviously their uses are auxiliary to those of the officials, advocates and counselors.

The closer one comes to the diversities of uses made of the law the more likely one is to believe that there is in substance no such thing as a body of authoritative legal norms, that the sentences which pass by that name are merely conjured up from a common vocabulary by utterers who seek to give plausible reasons for their actions. When one considers the functions or purposes which are fulfilled by the use of law, this view turns out to be superficial and inadequate.

1. *The Counselor.* The counselor uses the law to forecast the consequences of conduct which has not yet occurred and which can be shaped, though not wholly determined, by the choice of the client on the advice of counsel. The creative and imaginative work of counseling-to-avoid-trouble appears most strikingly in the drafting of legal transactions. Thus the whole structure of modern corporate organization rests upon a complex sequence of

---

[10] Llewellyn, "The Normative, the Legal and the Law Jobs: The Problem of Juristic Method", (1940) 49 Yale L.J. 1355, 1373–83.

consensual acts which are guided by the corporation counselor. The late Nicholas Murray Butler said somewhere that the most important invention of the nineteenth century was the business corporation. Yet the complex and adaptable structure of corporate organization was not the product of a single mind but rather of a numberless series of creative acts of legal counselors. Similarly the forms of trust indentures are mountainous accretions of counselors' skill. The primary duty of the counselor to his client is, or at least was thought to be, to minimize his client's risks. So the counselor tries to choose his law accordingly. A rule that *might* be applied favorably to his client is to be used as a last resort; a precedent of doubtful significance is to be given its minimum value if favorable, its maximum value if unfavorable, to his client. A rule that requires the proof of facts which a jury would be reluctant to find, will be avoided. Holmes' prediction theory of law (§ 2.20) expressed the counselor's view of the law which was dominant at the close of the last century. Yet the counselor has not only the task of avoiding dispute and litigation but also the job of getting people to work together peaceably and with mutual satisfaction. He has to consider the principles and policies that the courts will regard as important when his product is brought before them.[11] Still it remains true that the counselor prefers rules that can be relied on to vague principles that can be easily deflated. The law of conveyancing is his Garden of Eden.

2. *The Advocate.* The advocate is one who presents written or oral arguments to a legal tribunal in support of, or against, a claim upon which the tribunal is to decide. In its broadest sense "argument" includes the proof of facts presented to a tribunal by witnesses. Here we are concerned only with written or oral arguments on questions of law. The prevailing assumption of the adversary method of settling disputes is that the adjudicative official can best be enlightened and informed as to the legal grounds for decision by having each advocate present the strongest argument that he can in favor of his client's position. At its best advocacy can be a dialectic exploration of the law, as one can sometimes see in the reported colloquy between advocate and judge

---

[11] With the change from advocacy to counseling as the most esteemed type of legal practice, the counselor, it is said, lost his sense of public responsibility. See Howe, review of I Swaine, The Cravath Firm and Its Predecessors (1946) in (1947) 60 Harvard L.Rev. 838–843. The history of this influential New York firm gives much evidence of the counselor's role in shaping the decisions of "big business."

in the English reports. Yet the advocate's duty to his client is to present his client's case in its most favorable aspects, whether he actually believes in them or not. Hence a lawyer as advocate will make statements of law or cite precedents in his brief which he would not rely upon in his work as a counselor. As long as he does not purport to state his personal beliefs he is restrained, if at all, only by prudence in the lengths to which he can go in argument. Indeed, the advocate is the lawyer who has given the profession a bad reputation throughout the ages. The Greek Sophists were teachers of the arts of rhetoric and disputation; skeptical of man's ability to find truth, they aimed at success in persuasion. The term "sophistry" thus comes to mean a superficially persuasive but unsound and misleading argument. The Greek tribunals to which these sophistries were addressed were enormous in size (one had 1,501 "judges")[12] and were composed of unspecialized personnel. The arguments made to a court on questions of law are today more restrained by prudence, and yet the practice of presenting only one side of a case makes the advocate's use of law sometimes a perversion of it.

The advocate, like the counselor, prefers a definite rule in his favor, a case "on all fours," if he can find one. If he cannot, he may, within the tradition of advocacy, turn to extra-legal arguments. It is no accident that one of Aristotle's brief references to "natural law" is to be found in his book on Rhetoric,[13] where he quotes from Sophocles' drama Antigone's appeal to the "eternal _aw" against the "written law." Such an argument is addressed, it would seem, to the law-creating power of the tribunal, its power to limit established law by interpretation or to create a new legal rule or principle. Bold advocates have thus from time to time brought about changes in case law. Even here, however, the prudent advocate, in addressing law-trained adjudicators, will seek to ground his argument on principles or policies having some authority in the legal system.

3. *The Judge or Other Adjudicative Official.* An adjudicative official, or adjudicator, is an official who has some discretionary power to make decisions, on individual claims and after a contentious procedure, which are recognized by other officials as having some measure of finality and which have some significance

---

12 Russell, A Survey of Western Philosophy (1945) 75, referring to the trial of Pericles.

13 Aristotle, Rhetoric (Ross trans., 1924), Bk. I, Ch. 15, 1375a–1375b; Hall, pp. 7–8.

as precedents. The definition includes judges of ordinary courts and the members of "quasi-judicial" administrative agencies. Perhaps the greater part of the lawyer's work is concerned with the adjudicator's decisions. The counselor tries to predict what the decision will be (or will not be) and the advocate tries to influence the making of the decision. The adjudicator is not trying to predict what it will be but to determine what it shall be.

The extent to which legal rules and principles influence or determine the decisions of judges has been the subject of lively dispute during the past three decades (supra, § 3.00). The theory that judges make up their minds from the facts of a case how they are going to decide it and then go to the law library to find "good" reasons for it has had and still has a considerable following. This will be discussed later (§§ 4.64, 5.06). Even if it were true (and it is partly true) that a judge in writing the opinion of the court is using legal propositions as an advocate does, still his use of them would be important. In an appellate court, where propositions of law are argued by advocates and discussed by the judges in camera, and where an opinion is commonly written, the effort to arrive at a decision by using legal propositions as guides is, I believe, typical and predominant.

However, with trial judges the situation is frequently, perhaps normally, different. Rulings must be made speedily, with little or no chance for the presentation of legal authorities. No doubt many such decisions are made by "hunch." Yet in many situations this hunch is the intuition of a law-trained man, whose education and experience have conditioned him to respond in fairly definite ways to the stimulus of certain facts; for instance, to a proposal to impeach a witness' credibility by proof that he lied on a particular occasion. Even though the opposing advocate or the judge does not bring to the level of his conscious deliberation the legal rules and precedents on such a situation, they are nevertheless operative in his decision. Now a large proportion of the decisions which a trial judge is called upon to make in the course of a trial are of this type, for the structure of legal procedure within which the lawyers and the judge operate is designed to break down the legal issues of the trial in just this way. On the other hand, those who emphasize the difference between the role of the law in the trial court [14] and its rule in the appellate court point to the uncertainty of a jury trial, the difficulty of *predicting*

---

[14] See Frank, "Cardozo and the Upper-Court Myth," (1948) 13 Law and Contemp.Prob. 369.

what will be the judgment rendered on the verdict. No doubt this emphasis is justified. The uncertainties as to how witnesses will testify (if at all), as to how the jury will "react" to the facts in giving a general verdict, as to how the trial judge will characterize the "facts" presented in proof, cannot be wholly nor substantially resolved by performing expertly the job of finding the law. Yet the decisions of the trial judge will be on the whole better if they are the products of a deliberate process in which, as in other cases, legal propositions play a controlling part (§ 3.00) than if they are the products of unreflective hunches.[15]

The appellate court, having no authority or only a limited authority to decide issues of fact, is the forum in which legal norms, the authoritative rules and principles of law, have the most decisive influence. Toward its decisions the work of the counselor, the advocate and the judge are mediately or immediately directed. Even here it would be fallacious to assume that the court's decision is determined by "pure" law, that the advocate who is the most diligent and correct expounder of "the law" is sure to win his case. Aside from the personality factors which play some part (infra, Part V) and the law-creating function of the appellate court (ibid.), the chief factor of uncertainty in appellate court decisions is, I believe, the characterization of the facts in the record by the appellate judges. For example, do the statements of witnesses (in the record) constitute "facts" which connote the legal consequences of, for instance, res ipsa loquitur, or of an offer to contract? Such uncertainties, though reducible by the skillful presentation of proof in the trial court, are not wholly escapable because legal propositions can be only one of the component factors of a practical judgment (§ 3.00).

The use of legal propositions by appellate judges has, I think, three main functions. One is to guide the process of deliberation which eventuates in a decision. A second is to justify the decision as a judgment made in accordance with law. A third is to provide guidance for the future by placing the decision, on its selected facts, in the relevant context of the legal system.

The part played by the law in the decisions of non-judicial adjudicators, i. e., administrative tribunals,[16] is even more difficult to

---

15 The frequent use by the trial judge of legal rules and policies, for which he makes his own search in a law library, is indicated by the candid discussion of an able and experienced trial judge of the New York Supreme Court. See Botein, Trial Judge (1952), especially 42, 134.

16 Arbitrators, at least those whose awards are given by statute the status of judgments, are also to be included, but are here omitted from the discussion.

determine. In the United States (at least) the powers and procedure of administrative tribunals are prescribed, more or less thoroughly, by statute, and thus the statute is the basic text (within the limits of the constitution) to which the administrative process must be referred. "Administrative law" is still made up chiefly of the norms limiting the powers and procedure of administrative tribunals (including the finality of their decisions) rather than their norms of decision. The latter are not to be ignored, however, for many administrative tribunals give opinions with their decisions and have thus developed a considerable body of case law to which they often refer for guidance or justification. One practice of administrative tribunals, which is frequently required by statute or judicial decision, is the formulation of "findings of fact" on which the decision is based. These findings of fact are statements of the legally relevant and material facts which are selected or inferred from the raw facts presented to the tribunal. They are or purport to be adequate to imply, in conjunction with some tenable legal propositions, the legal consequences of the decision. The role of law (including their own case law) in the work of many administrative tribunals is scarcely less important than it is in the work of courts.

§ 3.02—The Layman's Use of the Law

The state and the law are maintained for the good of the individuals in the community, and yet the layman's use of the law in the process of arriving at practical judgments has received relatively little attention in the literature of jurisprudence. It may be said that the law falls upon laymen like the rain or the lighting, that all they know is official action after something has happened, and that the law, as a cause or an explanation or a justification of what has happened, is ex post facto.[17] Or it may be said that laymen make their practical judgments by inscrutable hunches, partly guided by the mores and habit patterns of a family, a community, a class or an institution, except where they consult lawyers, in which case the lawyer and not the layman "uses" the law. Or it may be said that we have no techniques for obtaining reliable knowledge about the layman's use, if any, of the law. Each of these positions is true in some cases, yet none is satisfactory. In this section will be presented first, the views of some jurisprudential writers and then a partial analysis of the problem.

---

[17] See Gray, The Nature and Sources of the Law (1909), § 225; (1927), p. 100.

To writers of the positive or imperative school, the topic is peripheral or irrelevant. Peripheral to Austin, who required as a characteristic of law a "habit of obedience" of the members of a political society to its sovereign (§ 2.32), yet did not consider how the law enacted or adopted by the sovereign was made known to its subjects. Irrelevant to Kelsen, who regards the effects of law in society as a subject for investigation by the sociology of law, but not by jurisprudence.[18]

The institutional schools (§§ 1.05, 2.03) came closer to the question. Savigny's view that the primitive and basic law of a nation is something dwelling in the spirit of its people, their common conviction of inward necessity, would make the layman's use of the law as spontaneous and habitual as his use of language. One does not need to know grammar in order to use popular language, and one does not need to know the jurist's law in order to use the law of the popular spirit. This romantic conception of law may explain why the legal order governed by jurist's law causes as little pained surprise among laymen as it does, but it does not explain how the *technical* law of the jurists is made known to laymen. Early in the present century Ehrlich undertook the investigation which Savigny had neglected. His Seminar of Living Law (§ 2.03) was designed to find out the social and business arrangements by which members of a family, an association or a trade, governed their conduct. He thus came to the conclusion that the Legal Provisions, the norms of decision addressed to courts and administrative officials, had a relatively minor influence upon the daily life of the people. The fundamental arrangements of society are governed by the basic institutions of the Social Order: marriage, family, possession, contract, succession.[19] While Ehrlich in his more exuberant passages rather too conveniently minimized the influence of the law of the state in shaping the Social Order, he does give a partial explanation of how laymen learn to use the private law of the basic social institutions, that is, by growing up and participating in the numerous associations of a civilized society.

A different explanation was provided by the law-of-nature school. St. Thomas Aquinas included promulgation as a necessary element of human law, because man could not partake of law

---

[18] Kelsen, "The Pure Theory of Law", (1934) 50 L.Q.Rev. 474, 481; Hall 425, 429.

[19] See Ehrlich, "The Sociology of Law", (1922) 36 Harvard L.Rev. 130, 131; Hall, 812, 813.

as a rational being unless it was known to him; he added that the law of nature could be known to every man by the exercise of his reason.[20] The English philosopher Thomas Hobbes (1588–1679), himself a layman, believed that a command of the Sovereign was law only to those who "have means to take notice of it," and that every man has the means to take notice of the law of nature.[21] This theory may explain how men can know that murder and other crimes of violence are wrong, and therefore presumably illegal; but a man's reason and conscience would scarcely tell him that, in Hobbes' time, a decedent's real property descended to his heir while his personalty went to his personal representatives. Hobbes recognized this and declared:

"The Law of Nature excepted, it belongeth to the essence of all other Lawes, to be made known, to every man that shall be obliged to obey them, either by word, or writing, or some other act, known to proceed from the Sovereign Authority." [22]

The leader of the Utilitarians, Jeremy Bentham (1748–1832), included in his rather unwieldly definition of law the "prospect" that law would motivate those persons with whose conduct it was concerned [23] and attacked the English judge-made (case) law on the ground that its obscurity gave the lawyers a monopoly of the law.[24] His proposed remedy was the drafting and enactment of a comprehensive code or codes of law in language that all men could understand. While his dream was only partly realized, he had a wholesome influence on English and American legislation of the last century.

Three recent discussions relevant to our question must be mentioned. The late Professor Underhill Moore and his colleagues at the Yale Institute of Human Relations made an empirical investigation of the effects of certain traffic (parking) signs on automobile drivers.[25] The results of the study were summarized in a frequency distribution which expressed quantitatively the "success" of the sign in attaining its intended result. The theory

---

20 Aquinas, The Summa Theologica (trans. by Dominican Fathers, 1927), vol. 8, pp. 7–8 (Part II, Second Part, Q. 90).

21 Hobbes, Leviathan (Everyman Library ed.), 143–44.

22 Ibid., 144.

23 Bentham, The Limits of Jurisprudence Defined (Everett ed., 1945, from MS. of 1782), 88.

24 Ibid., 274–278.

25 For a summary see Moore's essay in My Philosophy of Law (1941), 203; also infra, § 4. 63, n. 48.

of behaviorism which provided some of the basic assumptions for the study will be discussed in connection with American Legal Realism (§ 4.63). While this investigation is, I believe, the most thorough and systematically methodical (i. e., explicit in its controlling assumptions) experiment yet made on the influence of law on laymen, the narrowness of its scope makes it of limited significance for the problem here discussed. The second item to be mentioned is the proposal by Professor W. F. Willoughby, a political scientist, that the state should, in furtherance of its public welfare function, assume "the burden of seeing that private rights are enforced," by establishing an office, analogous to that of the prosecuting attorney, to examine into and conduct litigation for the redress of private injuries.[26] This goes considerably beyond giving the layman information about law. The third item is the study made by Professors Clark and Corstvet at Yale of the situations in which laymen probably needed professional legal advice but did not employ a lawyer.[27] The conclusion to be drawn from this study, that the legal profession should be so organized as to make legal advice on common transactions available at moderate cost to persons of moderate means,[28] is sound and practicable.

The more one considers the broad problem of the layman's use of the law in determining his conduct, the more one wonders that laymen do not run afoul of the law more often than they do. The answer is to be found, I think. in subdividing the problem. Let us consider three main functions of law: The transactional function, the remedial function and the penal function.

The law of civilized states provides a variety of ways by which men may effectuate their transactions, by which they obligate themselves or acquire rights to property or services or dispose of their property or services. Probably the legal rudiments of a

---

[26] Willoughby, Principles of Judicial Administration (The Brookings Institution, Washington, 1929), 97. The proposed English plan is much more limited. Smith, "The English Legal Assistance Plan", (1949) 35 A.B.A.J. 453, 526. Its effective date was postponed because of the cost. (1950) 36 A.B.A.J. 31, 45.

[27] Clark and Corstvet, "Untapped Legal Business in New Haven: The Economics of the Legal Profession", (1938) 47 Yale L.J. 1272.

[28] On free legal aid to the poor, the pioneer work is Smith, (Reginald Heber), Justice and the Poor (Carnegie Foundation for the Advancement of Teaching, Bulletin No. 13, 1919); see also Willoughby, op.cit., supra, n. 26, Chs. XL–XLIV. The latest proposal, established in several cities, is: "The Lawyer Reference Plan", (1950) 36 A.B.A.J. 24.

simple transaction, such as buying and selling chattels, are learned by laymen from their parents and associates. Holmes said that
the legal requirement of consideration is only a form but it "falls
in with our common habits of thought, so that we do not notice
it." [29] This rudimentary information is often sadly deficient for
complex transactions, as the law reports often show. A course
in legal hygiene, i. e., "when to go to a lawyer," should be a part
of primary and secondary education. By the remedial function
is meant the redress of injuries. The layman who has suffered
an injury ordinarily does go to a lawyer; yet it must be confessed
that what he learns from the lawyer is often largely ex post facto
law. The penal function is the most important, for the injustice
of imposing punishment upon a man who did not know that his
conduct was illegal, is the most harsh. In the present century
this function has been extended considerably beyond the traditional crimes against person or property which were generally
recognized in the community as immoral or anti-social. For these
newer types of penal offense special techniques of communication
and admonition are necessary. For example, the provisions of
the traffic laws are communicated not only by highway signs but
by pamphlets distributed to novices who apply for driver's li-
censes. The newspapers provide a casual and often distorted or
inadequate communication of penal laws.[30] The problem is one
which deserves further effort.

Under a representative government in a liberal state the communication of the law, or of some of it, to the layman has another
purpose than that of giving him what he needs in his daily personal affairs. In a state maintaining freedom of speech, freedom
of the ballot-box and freedom to organize peaceable opposition to
the government, the citizen as a voter is, more or less directly, a
participant in the making and changing of the law. The paradox
of a "democratic" state is that it needs to inform its citizens about
the law in order that they shall conform to it and also in order
that they may change it. It seems highly improbable that a liberal state can be maintained if the government has a monopoly
of both of these functions. Hence the critical function of communication, along with the conformity function, must be carried
out by unofficial independent agencies, the press, the radio, the
movies. The misinformation they often purvey about matters

---

[29] Holmes, The Common Law (1881), 273.

[30] And of other laws. See quotation in (1947) 33 A.B.A.J. 668.

legal is a part of the price that must be paid for having a liberal state.

The need for the communication of the law to laymen calls for the statement of its rules and principles in popular language which the layman can understand. On the other hand the professional development of the law as a system adequate for the needs of a complex society with diversified interests calls for the development of what Professor Dewey has called a "scientific" or technical linguistic system, one in which the meaning of each term "is expressly determined by its relations to the other members of the language system." [31] The values of this kind of system in the law will be discussed later (§ 3.21). These conflicting needs continually create tensions in the process of formulating law, between popular terminology and professional terminology. The conflict is partly resolved by subdivision and specialization. The conduct prohibited by a traffic law should be (and usually is) stated in layman's language; the conduct prohibited by the rule against perpetuities need not be, since wealthy individuals who want to tie up their estates usually consult lawyers. Still the differences between popular language and professional language cause many difficulties in improving the communication of law to laymen.

Whatever these improvements may be, the layman's information about the law will, as far as one can foresee, always need to be supplemented by that of the specialist. The modern state has endeavored to satisfy an increasing multiciplity of human wants through an increasing complexity of governmental organization and to administer justice with an increasing refinement of legal principles and concepts. The law-trained man is a specialist not merely in the detailed information which is practically inaccessible to laymen but also in an understanding of what law is for and what are its long-range effects. The law, then, is a discipline requiring, like medicine and engineering, specialized study and training. To promote more economical and convenient availability to the layman of the specialist's services is a better objective than improvement of the layman's independent use of the law.

---

[31] Dewey, Logic (1938) 50.

Patterson Jurisprudence F.P.Inc.

Chapter 9

THE SOURCES AND AUTHORITATIVE FORMS
OF THE LAW

§ 3.10—Sources, Forms and Literary Materials

The kinds of questions that can be asked about the truth or falsity of a legal proposition were set forth above (§ 2.12) and the uses that professional lawyers make of such information was briefly summarized (§§ 3.00, 3.01). What are the lawyer's sources of information about the law? One answer is that they consist of the books and other printed matter in a good law library. This answer is superficial and inadequate because some classification of literary materials is necessary to determine what are the more reliable sources, and secondly because, in one sense, some sources of the law cannot be found in a law library. Among the latter, aside from customs and principles of morality, to be discussed later (§§ 3.15, 3.16), are the traditional techniques of problem-solving which are rarely formulated in generalizations although they are peculiar attributes of a given legal system. Thus it is said that Anglo-American common law is

> ". . . essentially a mode of judicial and juristic thinking, a mode of treating legal problems rather than a fixed body of definite rules." [1]

This statement is a rhetorical "definition" in that it emphasizes the aspect of Anglo-American law which suited the immediate purpose. Yet the author as an experienced lawyer knows that one cannot advise a client or decide a case without something more than an understanding of the "mode of judicial and juristic thinking" that is typical of the common law. One must have some more specific knowledge of the law of the jurisdiction by which the problem-solving is to be guided and, in a sense, controlled. Moreover, juristic technique is exemplified in the recorded sources of law.

The term "sources" can be clarified by pointing out that there are three senses in which it is used: Literary materials, authoritative forms, and material or contentual derivation.

Literary Materials. The literary materials of the law of any civilized state are to be found in its law libraries. A distinction

---

[1] Pound, The Spirit of the Common Law (1921) 1.

must be drawn between the "literary sources" of law and other "legal" literature, such as biographies of judges and famous lawyers.[2] The classes of literary materials are statute books (including constitutions), judicial reports, digests of case law, administrative reports, treatises, legal periodicals, and a few others of minor importance. Because of our federal system and our quantity of judicial reports an adequate American law library is much more voluminous than that of, for instance, a French lawyer, who gets along handily with a small library which he keeps at home. In either case the professional use of the literary sources is guided by a trained understanding of the relations between the authoritative sources and other sources.

In another sense the sources of the law of a modern state are the officials or bodies of officials whose acts and utterances give it validity. These are the authoritative sources of its law. In nearly all modern systems of law there are two types of officials who have this authority: legislative and adjudicative.[3] The latter includes judges of ordinary courts and administrative quasi-judges. Since some of the latter have power also to make general regulations not connected with the settlement of particular disputes, it is more accurate to divide powers, rather than officials, into legislative and adjudicative. This division leads to the recognition, in Anglo-American legal theory and to a lesser extent in other systems, of two *authoritative forms* of law: legislation and case law. These will be discussed more fully in this Chapter. (§§ 3.11–3.13)

In a third sense the sources of a body of law are the things from which the material content of its prescriptions, the ideas that they express, were derived, immediately or ultimately. Thus the Roman law of bailments was a material source of the English common law of bailments as set forth in the leading case of Coggs v. Bernard.[4] Langdell's little treatise on contracts was a material source of some parts of the law of contracts of Massachusetts or New York. In this sense, too, customs and morals are sources of

---

[2] Salmond, Jurisprudence (7th ed. 1924), § 48, n. a.

[3] On the power of particular groups to create law by creating customs, see infra, § 3.15. I say "nearly" because in Soviet Russia the principle of separation of powers is rejected as a bourgeois device, though there is a "distribution of functions" which bears a family resemblance to it. See Gsovski, Soviet Civil Law, vol. I (1948), 74; Vyshinsky, The Law of the Soviet State (Babb trans., 1948), 312–322.

[4] 2 Ld.Raym. 909 (1703). But Lord Holt tried to square his decision with the English requirement of consideration.

the law, though they are not usually included in the literary sources. Indeed, in this enlarged sense one could say that grammar and logic are sources of the law, since they are valuable instruments of exact linguistic expression; and even Dickens' novel satirizing the expensive and dilatory English Chancery system was a source of the idea that it should be reformed. Here we limit our inquiry to those sources which have more directly contributed to the normative content of some part of the law. In this limited sense we include six classes of material sources: 1. The law of other jurisdictions (§ 3.13). 2. Opinions of legal experts, including treatises and periodicals (§ 3.14). 3. Customs. 4. Principles of morality.[5] 5. Societal facts (§ 3.16). 6. Philosophical and religious ideas, discussed in Part IV. While there are some overlappings in this division, it will serve to indicate the main lines of derivation of the law.

§ 3.11—Legislation as a Form of Law

Legislation is one of the principal forms of law in the modern state. In the earlier periods of legal history, law was thought to have a divine or an immemorial traditional origin, and man dared not tamper with it. Legislation as a method of deliberately creating new law represents a later stage in the development of both Roman and English law than such ameliorative devices as legal fictions and equity.[6] Among the reasons for the growing importance of legislation during the past two centuries are the need for greater complexity of governmental organization, the need for certainty in the powers and decisional norms of officials, and the belief that men were capable of deliberately making law to satisfy these needs.

The term "legislation", as here used, includes all legal norms deliberately created in so many words by officials having power so to do.[7] It includes the written constitution of a state and in the United States both the federal and state constitutions. It does

---

[5] The first four are a part of Gray's list of "sources". The Nature and Sources of the Law (1909), Chaps. VIII–XIII.

[6] Infra, § 4.32; Maine, Ancient Law, Ch. II. See Stone, The Province and Function of Law (1946), Ch. XIX, §§ 3, 4, for a critical appraisal of Maine's thesis.

[7] "Legislation" is used as a broader term than "statute" and as a narrower term than "law-making", which includes also the creation of law by the adjudicative process. "Judicial legislation", a term used by many writers, is in this context inaccurate unless confined to the adoption of "rules of court" which govern judicial procedure.

not include those parts of a written constitution which are merely hortatory in character (§ 2.32). The United States Constitution (Art. VI, par. 2) gives treaties made "under the authority of the United States" the status of legislative authority superior to state constitutions or statutes. The hierarchy of legislation (in the United States) proceeds downward to subordinate forms, through federal statutes (which are on a parity with treaties), federal executive orders and administrative regulations, state constitutions, state statutes (the ordinary legislation of state legislatures), state administrative regulations and municipal ordinances.[8] It also includes the formal rules of procedure adopted by courts. The determination of these hierarchic relations in particular cases constitutes one of the recurrent problems of administration.

Nor is the determination of what constitutes legislation, as opposed to other official utterances, always easy. Especially in reference to the utterances of administrative officials, it is sometimes hard to tell mere advice or opinion from a regulation. For this reason, and also to provide a means of communication, it is sometimes required that official regulations be filed in a particular office (New York) or be published officially, as in the case of federal regulations.

Aside from this difficulty, three practical tests serve to mark off legislation from case law. The official or officials uttering it must have power to create legal norms in legislative form. The textual form is fixed in so many words. The literary sources of legislation are usually separated from case law.[9]

The levels of authority in a complex system of legislative norms can best be explained by Dr. Hans Kelsen's theory of law, which will be examined more fully later (§ 3.22). A superior legislative norm (one authorizing subordinate legislation) ordinarily, perhaps always, does two things: It contains *power* norms, authorizing an official or officials to make subordinate legislation; and it contains in some measure *decisional* norms, which guide the official in determining the content of the particular norms which he does make. Even the limitations on his power are partial guides. Yet the subordinate legislative power necessarily includes some free discretion.

The relations of legislation to judicial decisions have been the subject of a prolific jurisprudential literature. One view is that of

---

[8] See Dowling, Patterson and Powell, Materials for Legal Method (1946), 21–29; (2d ed. 1952 by Harry W. Jones), 7–12.

[9] Ibid., 14–15.

John Chipman Gray, who asserted that because the courts have the power to interpret and apply statutes, the latter are not law but only sources of the law, which consist of the rules laid down by courts (§ 2.05). The gist of his argument is:

> "As between the legislative and judicial organs of a society, it is the judicial which has the last say as to what is and what is not law in a community. To quote . . . the words of Bishop Hoadley: 'Nay, whoever hath an absolute authority to interpret any written or spoken laws, it is he who is truly the lawgiver to all intents and purposes, and not the person who first wrote them.' " [10]

> ". . . it is with the meaning declared by the courts, and with no other meaning, that [statutes] are imposed upon the community as Law." [11]

To the argument that courts interpret and apply a statute in accordance with the intention of the legislature, Gray replies that, in the cases in which doubt arises as to the meaning of the statute, the legislature "had no real intention, one way or another on the point in question" and

> "when the judges are professing to declare what the legislature meant, they are themselves legislating to fill up *casus omissi*".[12]

These arguments have a realistic appeal to lawyers who would never give an opinion based on a statute without looking for the judicial interpretations, if any, and especially to lawyers who have just argued (unsuccessfully) a "trouble case" in a court of last resort on a nice point of statutory interpretation.

But this view of statutes seems narrow and misleading. First, it overemphasizes the "trouble case" that leads to litigation. Statutes are law, are used as law by laymen and counselors and officials (supra, Ch. 8) in many instances without the aid of judicial interpretation. When the federal income tax law is amended, most men pay their taxes without waiting to see whether, in a test case, the court will hold that John Doe has to pay. Secondly, the suggestion, implied in Bishop Hoadley's sermon (preached before the King in 1717), that a court has "absolute authority" to

---

[10] Gray, The Nature and Sources of the Law (1909), § 369. A similar view was expressed by Salmond, Jurisprudence (7th ed., 1924), §§ 44, 49, though in § 44 he says: "What the Statute Book says becomes law forthwith and ipso jure."

[11] Ibid., § 366.

[12] Ibid., § 370.

interpret a statute, is misleading. Not only are courts officially bound to recognize the supremacy of the legislature over the court's views of what the law should be, but also a judicial interpretation may be abrogated by an amendment to the statute. Aside from this, Gray gave only passing recognition to administrative agencies, which also interpret and apply statutes.

The supremacy of the ordinary legislature over the judiciary is a basic component of modern political organizations. Gray recognizes this when he says that one rule as to the sources of the law is "clear and precise":

> "The State requires that the acts of its legislative organ shall bind the courts, and so far as they go, shall be paramount to all other sources. This may be said to be a necessary consequence from the very conception of an organized community of men." [13]

While it is possible to conceive of an "organized community" without the traditional doctrine of the separation of powers between the legislature, the judiciary and the executive, the principle of legislative supremacy is a part of that doctrine. The legislature is usually made up of popularly elected representatives, and their function is primarily to make laws which will be applied by the other two branches. The subordination of the courts to legislative norms is no less an important part of this scheme than is the independence of the judiciary from interference by the other two branches in the discharge of the judicial function.

The superiority of legislative norms to judicial norms is limited or weakened in several different ways. One is the court's power to "interpret" a statute of doubtful meaning in reference to a particular dispute, as Gray pointed out. Another is the court's power to declare a statute invalid, wholly or in part, because the legislature exceeded the powers given it by the constitution. This limitation is only rarely recognized outside the United States. A third is the limited scope of legislation as compared with case law. In England and in most of the United States, the acts of the legislature do not purport to provide decisional norms for most of the legal issues raised in judicial litigation. In Western Europe and in South America the private law, as well as penal and procedural law, is codified, that is, the legislative text is comprehensive and exclusive.

What differences in the professional use of the law under the two systems are due to the presence or absence of a comprehen-

---

[13] Ibid., § 273.

sive code? It is very difficult to say what differences, as they exist, are due to code or no code, rather than to professional traditions and historic derivation of the content of the law. Thus the state of California has a comprehensive Civil Code, as well as other codes; and yet the professional methods of the bar and bench are typically Anglo-American rather than European, due, I believe, to the Anglo-American derivations of its law and its professional traditions. The codes of Western Europe and South America have Roman backgrounds, and some of the Roman professional usages. The code lawyer begins with the code, and his conclusions must always be based upon a certain section or sections of the code. In this sense, as Gray pointed out, his method is more deductive than the Anglo-American's. Yet the language of even the best (civil) codes is broad and vague as compared with the rules stated in English and American judicial precedents, or even with the text of the Restatement of the Law of particular subjects. The deductive aspect may be more formal than real. The gap between the vague generalities of the code and the facts of a particular situation are, in Roman law countries, filled in by systematic treatises, the opinions of experts, rather than by case law. The systematic character of a well constructed code [14] tends, I believe, to make professional reasoning more abstract and deductive.[15]

The Interpretation of Statutes. On the principles or methods of interpreting statutes much more has been written than anyone should ever read. I say this because generalizations about the ways in which statutes have been or should be or will be interpreted have a low predictive value for counselors and a low guidance value for judges. For instance, one can assert with confidence that a court will, in a doubtful case, apply the statute *either* in accordance with its "plain meaning" *or* in accordance with the court's conception of some legislative policy which its language signifies; but which of these two methods will be chosen, in cases where they lead to conflicting conclusions, cannot be stated *in general* with any such confidence. The efforts of legal experts to increase predictability by new formulations of the principles of statutory interpretation have not been very successful. As one writer has said:

---

[14] The systematic character of a code diminishes as new legislation is added without being thoroughly integrated into it. See de la Morandière, "The Reform of the French Civil Code", (1948) 97 U. of Pa.L.Rev. 1, 5–6.

[15] But see a contrary view in Robinson, Law and the Lawyers (1935) 213–216.

"It must be admitted that one who essays an analysis of the judicial process in the application of statute law finds more conflict in legal literature than inconsistency in the judicial decisions." [16]

The general principles of statutory interpretation serve to provide arguments to the advocate. They also serve to indicate the range of choice open to an adjudicative official who seeks to give a reasoned judgment.

The relations of these principles to some of the chief problems of jurisprudence can be indicated by discussing two aspects of statutory interpretation: 1. "Legislative intention", and 2. "Plain meaning" vs. "Policy of the statute".

Legislative Intention. A court in interpreting a statute for the purpose of applying or not applying it to the facts of a litigated case should give effect to the intention of the legislature. This principle is accepted by all Anglo-American courts; at least I know of none that categorically rejects it.[17] This principle signifies two basic political principles: That statutory law (at least) is an authoritative utterance (§§ 2.31, 2.32), and that the ordinary legislature has superior authority to the courts with respect to law making. The latter principle was discussed above. The principle of legislative intention has been attacked as a myth or a fiction on the ground that the members of the legislature have, and can have, no common "intention" with respect to the meaning of a statute enacted by it, that the statute is necessarily applied by courts to situations which the members of the enacting body did not foresee, and that the judges do, and should, give effect to their own ideas of policy and justice in applying statutes.[18] The basis of this view is, I think, the psychological theory of the meanings of symbols (§ 1.12). Assuming that the meaning of a word is that part of its referent in the mind of the utterer which is evoked by the word in the mind of the utteree, and that legislative inten-

---

[16] Jones,"Statutory Doubts and Legislative Intention", (1940) 40 Col.L.Rev. 957, 959.

[17] The same or a similar basic principle is generally accepted in European law. For Germany, see Heck in The Jurisprudence of Interests (1948), 177 et seq.

[18] This summary of the argument represents at least a part of the views expressed in Radin, "Statutory Interpretation", (1930) 43 Harv.L.Rev. 863, and in Ehrlich's earlier views, as stated by Heck, op.cit. supra, last note, 177–178. I find it difficult to determine what Professors Radin and Ehrlich meant by their respective utterances.

tion is just that meaning, then legislative intention is always or almost always a fiction, since the mental images of all of the members of the legislature who voted "aye" on the passage of the bill could scarcely have been identical. Even if one says that their mental referents had a great many items in common because they happened to have grown up in a community having a common language, still one can say that in a great many cases (especially the difficult ones that practicing lawyers have to worry about) "legislative intention" is a fiction.[19] Yet it is not a "pure" fiction if one concedes that the common words of a language *do* manage to convey meanings which are common to utterer and utteree. The psychological theory of "intention" parallels another conception of "intention", that the intention of a statute is simply its meaning, not limited to what its utterers had in mind. Accordingly common nouns as symbols of logical universals include in their meaning (denote) many particulars which the utterer did not think of; this is the conception of the logical universal. It is rejected by those who assert that in applying a statutory term to a thing invented after the statute was enacted (e. g., the term "deadly weapon" to an atomic bomb) the court is not giving effect to the intention of the legislature but is itself legislating with a fictitious justification.[20] This view has a realistic practical appeal to many persons (including myself) because it applies the same "common sense" to legislative utterances that is applied to the daily utterances of popular speech. However, it is objectionable in several respects. First, even words of common speech are understood and applied without thought of "fiction" to new particulars. When the term "ball" was first applied to a "basket-ball", an invention of the late nineteenth century, surely no one thought of this as a fictitious use of the term, though Noah Webster never heard of such an object. Secondly, a statute is not a casual utterance, but is one deliberately made to serve as a norm of conduct, official and unofficial. The "intention" of the legislators that it shall serve as a guide for cases which they have not thought about is just as real as the intention that it shall apply to the cases they have in mind in voting "aye". Thirdly, a statute is not just an utterance of popular language; it is intended to and does enter into a highly specialized linguistic system, the legal system, and its meanings are

---

[19] See Jones, "Extrinsic Aids in the Federal Courts", (1940) 25 Ia.L.Rev. 737, 742.

[20] See Frank, Law and the Modern Mind (1930), 26 (with a caveat as to Judge Frank's later views). But see Jones, op.cit., loc.cit., supra, last note.

controlled in part by this relation (§ 3.21). The principle of legislative intention is neither a mere ceremonial nor a useless formula.

"Plain Meaning" vs. *"Policy" Interpretation.* One pair of conflicting principles of statutory interpretation is the rule that the court should give effect to the "plain meaning" of the statute, as opposed to the principle that a court should effectuate the policy of the statute, or what is apparently an equivalent term, its "purpose". The "plain meaning" doctrine signifies that the statutory language has a clear and obvious meaning and that it is the duty of the court to give effect to that meaning even though it leads to a conclusion which cannot be grounded on the (most likely) policy or purpose of the legislature.[21] That a statute can have a plain meaning in reference to some types of questions that *might* be raised about it is, I believe, correct. Speaking of the Federal statute which makes it a penal offense to transport in interstate or foreign commerce a stolen "motor vehicle", Professor Jones has said that while a judge could very well hold that an airplane was or was not a "motor vehicle",[22] he could hardly extend the statutory concept to include bobsleds or sailboats, or limit it to Chevrolets and Fords.[23] Such questions rarely or never become litigated issues.

A more serious question is whether a court can ever determine the meaning of a statute without considering "its policy". The English courts avow that they can consider the policy of a statute only when its language is ambiguous. Professor Stone has persuasively argued that they cannot help considering "policy" in finding that there is an ambiguity in the terms.[24] In some sense this is true even in ascertaining "plain meaning". At least a court *should* not apply a statute without relying upon *some* conception of what the statute was designed to accomplish. Still the opposition between "plain meaning" and "policy" interpretation does not vanish, for it usually resolves itself into a clash between an obvious meaning consonant with some conceivable policy, and

---

21 E.g., Caminetti v. United States, 242 U.S. 470, 37 Sup.Ct. 192 (1917) (holding the "White Slave" Act was not limited to commercial prostitution); McNerny v. City of Geneva, 290 N.Y. 505, 49 N.E.2d 986 (1943) (here "plain meaning" was enough, but "policy" reënforced it).

22 In McBoyle v. United States, 283 U.S. 25, 51 Sup.Ct. 340 (1931), it was held not.

23 Jones, op.cit. supra, n. 20, 739.

24 Stone, The Province and Function of Law (1946), Ch. VII, § 27 (p. 193).

a meaning required by some more likely policy. As Holmes said, the court may say:

> "We see what you are driving at, but you have not said it, and therefore we shall go on as before." [25]

A statute normally has several conceivable "policies", one of which may be to regulate the subject matter thus far and no farther, to compromise between conflicting interests. "Policy" interpretation leads to the search for clues in the legislative history of the statute. Here the psychological conception of meaning has its justification to a limited [26] extent. The English courts have, however, refused to consider extrinsic aids to the interpretation of acts of Parliament. Such aids are useful but not indispensable. Judges endowed with no less wisdom than the legislators can ascertain the most likely "policies" of a statute by considering the political and social setting of its enactment and the previous state of the law.

§ 3.12—Case Law as a Form of Law

By "case law" [27] is meant the law of judicial and other adjudicative precedents, including the precedents of administrative tribunals. Professor Llewellyn has well stated the inevitability of case law in any system of law:

> "Case law in some form and to some extent is found wherever there is law. A mere series of decisions of individual cases does not of course in itself constitute a system of law. But in any judicial system rules of law arise sooner or later out of the solution of practical problems, whether or not such formulations are desired, intended or consciously recognized. These generalizations contained in, or built upon, past decisions, when taken as normative for future disputes, create a legal system. Precedent, however,

---

[25] In Johnson v. United States, 163 F. 30 (C.C.A.Mass.1908) quoted by Frankfurter, J., in Keifer & Keifer v. Reconstruction Finance Corp., 306 U.S. 381, 391, 59 Sup.Ct. 516, 519 (1939).

[26] E.g., the undisclosed meaning which the actual draftsman of the statute had in mind is not an admissible aid to interpretation. See the opinion by Surrogate Wingate officially interpreting a statute which he had helped to draft, in Matter of Bommer, 159 Misc. 511, 288 N.Y.S. 410, 425 (1936).

[27] The use of the term, "case law", goes back at least to 1882, when Sir Frederick Pollock said: "Modern writers call it ["unwritten law"] after its source by the more convenient and accurate name of case-law." Essays in Jurisprudence and Ethics (1882), 237. His essay is entitled "The Science of Case Law."

is operative before it is recognized. Towards its operation drive all those phases of human make-up which build habit in the individual and institutions in the group: laziness as to the re-working of a problem once solved; the time and energy saved by routine, especially under pressure of business; the values of routine as a curb on arbitrariness and as a prop of weakness, inexperience and instability; the social values of predictability; the power of whatever exists to produce expectations and the power of expectations to become normative. The force of precedent in the law is heightened by an additional factor: that curious, almost universal sense of justice which urges that all men are properly to be treated alike in like circumstances." [28]

To these may be added two other reasons for case law: The conscious creation of case law by successive generations of judges, in English and American law, has preserved and utilized the techniques and some of the wisdom of the past; and the application of case law to the facts of the case gives it a concreteness of meaning and often a dramatic impact which are lacking in the abstract and pallid code. Case law is not expressed in exact authoritative formulations, as legislation is, and is therefore relatively formless. Yet it has enough distinctive characteristics to make it recognizable as a "form" of law.

For the purpose of "finding the law" (§ 3.00), two questions may be asked about case law: 1. In what sense and to what extent is it "binding" on officials and non-officials or merely a persuasive source of law-making? 2. How does one determine *what* is "binding", or persuasive, in official precedents? These two questions cannot be entirely separated, because the indefiniteness or flexibility of what is "binding" necessarily qualifies the "bindingness", or even raises the question whether any case law is "binding". Nevertheless we shall reserve for a later discussion (Ch. 11) the theories as to the interpretation of precedents in Anglo-American law.

The first question may be subdivided into a number of subordinate questions: 1. Is a single judicial precedent binding upon the court which made it and upon courts subordinate to it, that is, courts whose judgments it can correct or reverse? 2. Is a series of judicial precedents similarly binding? 3. Is a court permitted, or do its own rules permit it, to overrule or modify its

---

[28] Llewellyn, "Case Law", 3 Encyc. Soc. Sci. 249 (1930).

own precedents?   4.   What is the persuasive effect of precedents which are not deemed "binding" upon the court?

The word "binding" in this connection gives rise to considerable doubts because there is no direct sanction of the norm which binds judges to follow their case law (§ 2.33). It may be argued, then, that the "bindingness" of case law is merely a state of mind or a ceremonial utterance, and hence a fiction. On the contrary, the avowals of courts that they are "bound" by precedents are not mere shams, because the reasons for following precedent are cogent, as Professor Llewellyn has shown, and because the same argument could be made against their avowals that they are bound by legislation. If what the judges (of an appellate court) believe they are bound to do is controlling in determining their decision, it is in this sense "binding". Moreover, that a lower court may be reversed on appeal because of its failure to follow a binding precedent or precedents is a cogent indirect pressure. As to the term "precedent", it is here used to mean an adjudicative decision (judgment or order) plus the facts on which it was based and the reasons, if any were given, on which it was grounded. Whether an unreported decision, or one which the court did not intend to serve as a precedent, is one, seems to be rather a question of the extent of its authority.

In nations having legal systems derived from the Roman law, commonly called "civil law countries", the doctrine of judicial precedents as found in England and the United States is not recognized. A passage in Justinian's Codex,[29] a compilation of Roman legislation, declares that no judge or arbiter is deemed bound to follow opinions which were not rightly adjudged, but rather the judge is to follow truth, law and justice. In early Roman law the judex was a layman, "little more than an arbitrator," and it was "impossible" that his judgments could be binding.[30] The development of Roman law into a great legal system was brought about by the opinions of experts (§ 3.14). The categorical rejection of case law as "binding" was continued in civil law countries, with some modifications. Thus the provisions of the United Nations Charter with respect to the International Court of Justice are a compromise in which the civil law point of view prevailed. While the Court may resort to judicial decisions as subsidiary means of determining rules of law, the decisions of

---

[29] Codex, 7.45.13 (A.D.533), quoted by Goodhart, 50 L.Q.Rev. at 56.

[30] Buckland and McNair, Roman Law and Common Law (1936), 6: "The Romans had, in principle, no case law . . ."

the Court have no binding force except in respect to the particular case.[31]

The status of judicial precedents in French law is another example.[32] A single decision, even of the highest court, is not deemed binding ("en droit") either on that court or on subordinate courts. A statute of 1837 provides that after the highest court (Cour de Cassation) has *twice* reversed the decision of a lower court in a particular case, the lower court is bound to follow the highest court's precedent in a third trial of that particular case.[33] According to French legal doctrine ("en droit") another lower court in a substantially similar case would not be bound to follow the highest court's twice-told precedent. But in fact ("en fait") lower courts are likely to follow such a precedent; and a uniform course of decisions (jurisprudence constante) is regarded as binding in all courts in about the same way that it is binding in the United States on the highest court which rendered the decisions,[34] and is relied upon by French text-writers. A distinguished French jurist recently said that one could not find the "true" civil law in the texts of the old Civil Code; one must study also the judicial decisions applying each article.[35] Thus the French seem to maintain a formal doctrine of non-bindingness of precedent which is about as fictitious [36] as our formal doctrine of bindingness. Yet the use of judicial precedents in the two systems is, I believe, materially different, because the authoritative starting points of legal reasoning are different.

English law has the tightest system of judicial precedent. Not only is a lower court bound to follow a single precedent of one of its superior courts, but the two highest courts, the House of Lords and the Court of Appeal, are "bound absolutely" to follow their own single precedents,[37] that is, they cannot overrule them. This

---

31 Statute of the International Court of Justice (U. S. Dept. of State Publication 2349, 1945), §§ 34, 59. See also supra, § 2.35.

32 A good discussion is Goodhart, "Precedents in English and Continental Law", (1934) 50 L.Q.Rev. 40.

33 Loi du 1er Avril, 1837, Arts. 1, 2; 3 Glasson, Morel et Tissier, Traité théorique et pratique d'organisation judiciaire de compétence et de procédure civile (3ième éd., 1929), 980.

34 Ibid.; Goodhart, 50 L.Q.Rev. at 42.

35 De la Morandière (Dean of the Faculty of Law of the University of Paris), "The Reform of the French Civil Code", (1948) 97 U. of Pa.L.Rev. 1, 6.

36 A fiction may be a partial or approximate truth.

37 Goodhart, 50 L.Q.Rev. at p. 42; Goodhart, "Precedent in the Court of Appeal", (1947) 9 Camb.L.J. 349. This doctrine was finally established in the

latter rule has been the subject of much doubt and criticism—doubt as to whether the court really follows its inconvenient precedents, and criticism of the rigidity of the rule, if it does. A single precedent is binding only if "directly in point", hence the interpretation of the scope of the precedent is crucial. By limiting the scope of the precedent to other cases duplicating a large number of its detailed facts, the English court can make its formal doctrine of binding precedent less frequently applicable than the looser American doctrine is.

In the United States, in both federal and state courts, a court is bound to follow a clearly applicable precedent of a court superior to it. Indeed, it seems that lower courts regard themselves as bound to follow the next higher level of authority in its interpretations of the highest authority.[38] In a recent opinion Frank, J., said that the federal Circuit Court of Appeals is not to interpret a federal statute directly but rather to interpret the interpretations of the statute by the federal Supreme Court.[39] These statements, I believe, are commonly accepted. Though it is not easy to demonstrate by case law the binding character of case law, experience indicates that it is, subject to its inherent limitations, as controlling as any other norm of the judicial process. It is true that a contrary doctrine has gained some recognition, that a lower federal court should follow the "trend" of Supreme Court decisions, indicating that a particular precedent *will* be overruled.[40] But this practice is, I believe, exceptional;[41] at least it should be a last resort of advocates and counselors.

House of Lords in 1898, and in the Court of Appeal in 1944. However, the general doctrine of the authority of judicial precedents was established in England by the end of the 18th century. Holdsworth, "Case Law", (1934) 50 L.Q.Rev. 180.

[38] Thus the Supreme Court of New York (a court of first instance) felt itself obliged to follow a decision of the intermediate appellate court (Appellate Division) even though it deemed this decision to be in conflict with the decisions of the highest court (Court of Appeals). Sullivan v. Sullivan, 73 N.Y.S.2d 547 (Sup.Ct. Kings 1947). This rule was laid down for federal courts (under Erie v. Tompkins) in Fidelity Union Trust Co. v. Field, 311 U.S. 169, 61 Sup.Ct. 176 (1940).

[39] McComb v. Utica Knitting Co., 164 F.2d 670, 673 (C.C.A.2d 1947).

[40] E.g., Gardella v. Chandler, 172 F.2d 402 (C.A.2d 1949), relying on Parker, J., in Barnette v. West Virginia, 47 F.Supp. 251, 253 (D.C.W.Va.1942), forecasting the overruling of the prior Supreme Court decision on the "flag salute".

[41] Another "forecast" was rejected in Spector Motor Service, Inc. v. McLaughlin, 323 U.S. 101, 65 Sup.Ct. 152 (1944). The argument that a higher

On the other hand, no American court of last resort feels itself "absolutely bound" to follow its own precedents; the court
violates no constitutional or legislative provision, no oath of office
and no traditional rule of its own making when it overrules its
own precedent or precedents. Aside from expressly overruling
them, which is comparatively rare, the court can and does frequently ignore them, or distinguish them on trivial grounds.
These latter practices create more uncertainty in our case law,
I believe, than does the practice of express overruling. One supreme court has expressly stated that the rule of stare decisis is
addressed to the court's discretion and that the advantages of
overruling should be balanced against the disadvantages in order
to reach a decision.[42] While this is commendable candor, an appellate court ordinarily does not have time to assess in each case
brought before it the advantages and disadvantages of following
its precedents. The values of stare decisis hold back judicial
avulsions, though they do not prevent erosions.

The power of an appellate court to overrule its precedents, and
the power of any court to interpret precedents, led Gray to the
position that precedents are not law but merely sources of law.[43]
Yet he defined law as "the rules that the courts . . . lay
down for the determination of legal rights and duties." [44] Thus
he was led to the curious position that the rules laid down by
a court in deciding a case are "the law" for that case but are only
sources of the law for the "next case". This view would be less
objectionable if he did not also classify as sources precedents
from other common law jurisdictions, opinions of experts and
principles of morality. To place these latter on the same plane
with the case law of the highest court of the jurisdiction in
which the "next" case is to be decided, is misleading.[45]

An older view of judicial precedents was that they were "evidences" of the unwritten law. Sir Matthew Hale adopted this
view,[46] and Blackstone gave it a gloss by explaining that judicial

---

court's decision is unsound is to be addressed to that court. Aetna Portland
Cement Co. v. Federal Trade Commission, 157 F.2d 533, 570 (C.C.A.7th 1944).

[42] Amoskeag Trust Co. v. Dartmouth College, 89 N.H. 471, 474, 200 A. 786,
788 (1938).

[43] Gray, The Nature and Sources of the Law (1909), §§ 273-74.

[44] Supra, § 2.05, n. 75.

[45] Gray apparently recognized this, op.cit., § 518.

[46] Holdsworth, op.cit., supra, n. 37, at p. 183.

precedents reflected the common custom of the realm. Professor Goodhart has suggested that only the first precedent would do that; thereafter the courts follow precedent.[47] Aside from that, the notion that case law is derived from popular custom is a disingenuous fiction. Precedents reflect what Coke called "the artificial reason" of the law. In a leading case construing the doctrine of Erie v. Tompkins, the Supreme Court referred to a precedent of an intermediate state court as "a datum for determining state law"; yet it was a datum not to be disregarded by a federal court "unless it is convinced by other persuasive data that the highest state court would decide otherwise."[48] The law of a state is not to be ascertained from a single or a few items, case law or statutory, but from a judicious appraisal of the relevant portions of the whole system. For the reasons already indicated, it seems more accurate to say that the judicial precedents of an American state, or of the United States, are a part of its law.

Administrative Adjudications; Arbitration. Case law is also operative in the processes of administrative adjudication, though its status is not clear. Many administrative tribunals cite and purport to follow their precedents, which are collected and published like judicial reports. It seems that no rule of judicial review requires such tribunals to follow the decisions of their predecessors as precedents.[49] The extent to which stare decisis should be applied by such a tribunal would seem to depend upon the powers, procedure and function of the particular tribunal. Many decisions of arbitrators in labor disputes and in commercial disputes are collected and published, and are referred to by arbitrators.[50] Since one of the chief reasons for resorting to arbitration is to avoid the delay, expense and "technicality" of judicial litigation, it is to be hoped that arbitration will not become encumbered by an unwieldy apparatus of precedents. These examples show the tendency of adjudicators to create and to follow case law.

---

[47] 50 L.Q.Rev. 44.

[48] West v. American Tel. & Tel. Co., 311 U.S. 223, 237, 61 Sup.Ct. 179, 183 (1940).

[49] See Federal Communications Commission v. Pottsville Broadcasting Co., 309 U.S. 134, 60 Sup.Ct. 437 (1940); State Airlines, Inc. v. Civil Aeronautics Board, 174 F.2d 510 (C.A.D.C.1949).

[50] See note, "Predictability of Result in Commercial Arbitration", (1948) 61 Harv.L.Rev. 1022.

§ 3.13—Persuasive Authorities; the Law of Cognate Jurisdictions

The reported judicial precedents of appellate courts in the United States contain, and for more than a century have contained, citations of precedents of English courts or of other American courts. Advocates continue to cite such cases in their arguments and counselors to some extent rely on them in giving their opinions. What do these practices signify?

One answer is that English judicial precedents were a part of the "taught tradition" of American law, a tradition translated to an American context by colonial and early American lawyers who had studied law in England and later by American law schools.[51] The older English precedents have a kind of traditional authority (§ 2.31) which is compounded of reverence for the past and the inertia of habit. The citation of recent English precedents, which is today unusual, must be explained on other grounds.

The "reception statutes" of most American states give an exceptional status to English case law established before the date of reception. These statutes commonly adopt English law as of a certain time (usually 1607, the date of the earliest English settlement at Jamestown) as the rules of decision "in so far as applicable".[52] Thus English precedents decided before the reception date were, formally speaking, adopted as a part of the law of the state. They were more than "persuasive" authorities; they were "binding" precedents (§ 3.12), subject to the statutory qualifications such as "in so far as applicable"; and subject also to the powers of courts to change the law. The "safety-valve" clause was invoked whenever the pressures of American political and economic conditions, "societal facts", made adherence to English precedents intolerable. Thus the English rule that the owner of domestic animals is liable without fault for damage caused by their trespassing on the land of a crop-owner was rejected in many western states as inapplicable to their economic conditions, such as the scarcity of timber for fencing and the dominance of

---

51 See Pound, The Formative Era in American Law (1938), Ch. III, especially pp. 81–83.

52 See Pope, "The English Common Law in the United States", (1910) 24 Harv.L.Rev. 6, 19–30, discussing the varying provisions and interpretations of these statutes. The qualifying clauses varied. By means of them the courts made American law responsive to social needs. Hall, "The Common Law: An Account of Its Reception in the United States" (1951) 4 Vanderbilt L.Rev. 791, 825. See also 1 Powell, Real Property (1950) § 45.

cattle-raising as a means of livelihood.[53] Pound's explanation is that the courts determined what was or was not applicable "by reference to an idealized picture of pioneer, rural, agricultural America of the fore part of the nineteenth century".[54] This was an important factor but not the only one. Many English doctrines and devices were not carried over because of differences in political institutions: the royal prerogative, the procedures of fine and recovery as a means by which a married woman could convey real property, many doctrines of English ecclesiastical courts. These adaptations of English case law by American courts partly explain the greater looseness of stare decisis in the United States than in England. Still the "received" English case law (and ordinarily the statutes) prior to the reception date had an explicit authoritative status.

Another explanation of the citation of English and other-state American precedents is that they are the opinions of able and learned men as to what the law is, or ought to be.[55] Gray thought they could properly have no greater weight "than the opinions of equally learned non-judicial persons who have the same advantages and the same motives for arriving at a just conclusion." [56] This explanation ascribes a "personal authority" (§ 2.31) to such opinions which is supported by various facts, such as the citations of the opinions of eminent judges or of highly respected courts (e. g., those of Massachusetts and New York).[57] Still the opinions of other equally able and learned men who were judges or lawyers in France or Germany did not have the same weight. An additional and more important reason was and still is that the other-state judges were charged with the responsibility to administer a cognate legal system.

At one period in American legal history continental European law had considerable influence on the development of American law. Chancellor Kent in New York took delight in citing French legal treatises to his less learned colleagues,[58] and this practice

---

53 E.g., Seeley v. Peters, 10 Ill. 130, 138–154 (1848); Note, (1922) 7 Iowa L.Bull. 176.

54 Op.cit. supra, n. 51, 97.

55 Gray, The Nature and Sources of the Law (1909), § 523 (as to English precedents).

56 Ibid., §§ 518, 523.

57 See Pound, op.cit., 89–90.

58 See Pound, op.cit., 106.

was continued until about the middle of the century.[59] These borrowings from another legal system were not always fortunate in their consequences,[60] for a legal doctrine of one system often has peculiar conceptions and limitations that cannot without distortion of meaning be transplanted into another system. These borrowings were frequently justified on the ground that they were in accordance with "reason" and "nature",[61] a circumstance which supports Gray's explanation. However, the practice of borrowing from European law was not very widespread in the United States. It has become rare except in such fields as admiralty, marine insurance, and international law, where the need for uniformity is buttressed by many common traditions.

The principal reason why other-state precedents have an exceptional persuasive authority in American law is, I believe, because they are conclusions deliberately reached by judicial officials charged with the responsibility of administering a cognate system of law. By a "cognate system" I mean one which has similar professional traditions, similar general concepts and doctrines, and similar procedural devices. A court of State A may assume that a precedent of State B was logically deduced from basic premises of the law of State B which are the same as those of State A; if this were so then State A would be rejecting its own basic law if it reached a conclusion contrary to that of State B. Such an assumption is not fantastic but it exaggerates the inevitability of conclusions arrived at by judicial reasoning (§ 3.00).

A more modest appraisal is that the other-state decision is the judgment of able and learned men who have very similar traditional guides and techniques and who, if they extend their concepts, are aware of the same limitations upon the propriety of their doing so. The extension of the narrow common law rules of liability without fault to include the case of a potentially dangerous structure on land (Rylands v. Fletcher) was not an inevi-

---

[59] In Wheadon v. Olds, 20 Wend. 174 (N.Y.Sup.Ct.1838) the court cited Pothier and Domat on the law of mistake in transactions. See Pound, "The Ideal Element in American Judicial Decision", (1931) 45 Harv.L.Rev. 136, 137; Hall, p. 326.

[60] See Patterson, "Illusory Promises and Promisor's Options", Selected Readings in the Law of Contracts (1931), 409; and Buckland's strictures on the use of Roman law materials in the leading case of Taylor v. Caldwell, 3 B. & S. 826 (1863) in (1933) 46 Harv.L.Rev. 1281, 1287–1289.

[61] Pound, op.cit., 107.

table logical deduction, but a court could find analogies for it in the case law of England and the United States. A good many American courts followed the English precedent; others rejected the extension and applied the more pervasive principle that tort liability is based upon fault.[62] The entire discussion, in so far as authoritative legal materials were concerned, could be carried on in the same framework of concepts and doctrines. Again, when a federal court more recently was called upon to determine whether under the law of Missouri an action could be maintained for an anticipatory total breach of a 99-year lease and found no Missouri precedents "in point", it felt authorized to look to the decisions in other states and to English decisions more recent than 1607, even though at that time the action based on anticipatory breach was not recognized.[63] On the other hand a recent Kentucky case awarding a judgment payable in installments for the anticipatory breach of a disability insurance contract [64] has been rejected elsewhere.[65] The installment judgment is not a traditional common law device. A recent Massachusetts case declined to regard English precedents on legislative powers as persuasive because England has no written constitution limiting such powers.[66] These examples show the meaning of what is at best a rather elusive concept.

The need for uniformity is another reason why other-state precedents are persuasive. This reason and the next preceding one are the basis for the prediction that, in State X where no controlling precedents on a legal issue and no other clues can be found, the appellate court decision will probably follow the "weight of authority" or "majority view" in other states. The reliability of this mode of prediction is often exaggerated; yet it is, I believe, verified in a good many cases. Uniformity is especially important in the law governing commercial transactions, and uniform statutes on important parts of commercial law have become widespread. In the interpretation of these acts the courts

---

[62] Ibid., 89–90; and see a fuller discussion of this problem in Pound, Interpretations of Legal History (1923), 105–109.

[63] Hawkinson v. Johnston, 122 F.2d 724 (C.C.A.Mo.1941).

[64] Equitable Life Assur. Soc. of U. S. v. Branham, 250 Ky. 472, 63 S.W.2d 498 (1933), relying partly on the statutory analogy of Workmen's Compensation awards.

[65] Brix v. People's Mutual Life Ins. Co., 2 Cal.2d 446, 41 P.2d 537 (1935); (1936) 24 Calif.L.Rev. 216.

[66] Meunier's Case, 319 Mass. 421, 66 N.E.2d 198 (1946).

strive to maintain uniformity. The rule of statutory interpretation, that a "borrowed statute" will be interpreted as it was in the state from which it was borrowed,[67] is partly to be explained by the principle of uniformity, and partly by that of legislative intention to adopt the interpretations with the act.

Finally, the precedents of other-state courts may be regarded as evaluations made in the same (or a similar) cultural matrix. Why should any rule of the doctrine of consideration be different in New York and Illinois, since in both states bargaining is a part of daily life and arouses about the same expectations and disappointments? However, this line of reasoning is less persuasive than the two previously given. Doctrinal differences between American states are influenced very little by economic or cultural differences. The latter are much more faithfully reflected in statutes. The "taught tradition" of case law tends to ignore local anomalies.

While other-state and English precedents, and to a lesser extent those of common-law Canadian provinces, are persuasive authorities in American courts, they are not binding authorities as are those of the same jurisdiction. They may be used to narrow inconvenient precedents or even to justify overruling them. In two states (Maine and West Virginia) the precedents of another state (Massachusetts and Virginia) decided before the two were separated are deemed binding authorities. These exceptions are merely nominal. Even when a court of State A in a case before it is obliged by its choice-of-law rule to apply the law of State B, its conclusion as to the law of State B is not a part of the law of State B.[68]

Other-State Statutes. That State B has a certain statutory rule is not even a persuasive authority for a court in State A, which has no such rule; it is rather persuasive authority for the contrary view. The fact that State B found it necessary to enact a statute shows that it was not a part of the case law of State B, and hence is not a part of A's cognate body of case law. This view, which is still the orthodox one,[69] seems to be based upon two

---

67 E. g., Hoffer Bros. v. Smith, 148 Va. 220, 138 S.E. 474 (1927) (Virginia Workmen's Compensation Act borrowed from Indiana). But the borrowing-state court may reject the interpretations as unreasonable, (1930) 43 Harv. L.Rev. 623.

68 Disagreeing with the statement made in Baird v. Baird, 223 N.C. 730, 734, 28 S.E.2d 225, 228 (1943).

69 See Panama R. Co. v. Rock, 266 U.S. 209, 45 Sup.Ct. 58 (1924) denying

premises. One is that statutes are rules for specific situations; they embody no principle; they are "in the law but not of it".[70] The other is that courts have only a narrow and limited function of law-making. The former might well be abandoned. A statute of State A has been frequently used as expressing a principle that the courts of State A will apply to situations not within the operative facts and legal consequences of the statute. For example, a statute limiting the percentage of interest on a loan which could be recovered in an action at law provided the basis for enjoining a usurious loan company from doing business.[71] In this sort of situation the statute seems to be a persuasive authority in the courts of its jurisdiction. Similarly, the statutes of those states which have abolished the distinction between mistakes of law and of fact should be persuasive in the courts of other states. On the other hand, the type of legal rule that courts can adopt or create without the aid of legislation is limited. No state court could have adopted in toto another's Workmen's Compensation Act, even though all other states had such acts. It would be futile to argue that a court should add to its Statute of Frauds provisions which have been added in other states, such as the one applicable to real estate broker's commissions. Even where the judicial power of law-making is adequate, the absence of local legislation may signify a legislative policy rather than a legislative oversight.

§ 3.14—Opinions of Legal Experts; Treatises and Periodicals

In every mature or civilized system of law the opinions of legal experts are one of the sources of the law.[72] They are material sources (§ 3.10) in that from a text-writer may be derived the ideas which give material content to a formal rule or principle of law. Thus an English or American court may have taken over a legal concept or norm from one of the famous French

---

an action for wrongful death in Panama. Even Holmes' dissent tried to tie his proposed rule to the vague provisions of the Panama Civil Code. But legislative changes were deemed to show the "reason and experience" of later generations in Funk v. U. S., 290 U.S. 371, 54 Sup.Ct. 212 (1933).

70 Stone (Harlan F.) in The Future of the Common Law (1937), 133.

71 State ex rel. Goff v. O'Neil, 205 Minn. 366, 286 N.W. 316 (1939). See Pound, Common Law and Legislation, (1908) 21 Harv.L.Rev. 383, 385–6; Landis, "Statutes and the Sources of Law", in Harvard Legal Essays (1934), 213, 221, 227.

72 Gray, The Nature and Sources of the Law (1909), Ch. XI, gives a valuable discussion of this subject.

authors, Pothier or Domat, who derived it from Justinian's Digest, which in turn derived it from the praetorian edict.[73] But the opinions of experts in the legal system of a state are more than material sources of its law, in this broad sense; they are more persuasive and more nearly authoritative than the morals of the community or the ethical ideas of philosophers or of poets, dramatists and novelists, though these latter may also lend content (as well as emotive drive) to changes in the law. Legal experts provide more than the raw materials of the law. They provide, quite commonly, legal propositions fitted for adoption and use. When they are experts in the law of the same or a cognate jurisdiction, they are, we may say, "persuasive authorities".[74] The obiter dicta of judges in their opinions are also expert opinions and in Anglo-American law are (according to the orthodox academic view) merely persuasive authorities. However, the term "legal expert" is used here to mean primarily unofficial experts.

The opinions of legal experts have less influence in determining judicial decisions in Anglo-American jurisdictions than in civil law jurisdictions. This generalization may be open to question,[75] but it is in accord with the professional traditions and juridical methods of the two types of jurisdictions. Several reasons may be given for this difference: The lesser influence of judicial precedents in civil law countries (§ 3.12), the Roman law background of the civil law systems, and the specialization in professional careers of law-trained men in civil law countries. The Roman law gave great weight to expert opinions and little or none to judicial decisions.[76] In the classical period of Roman law, the jurisconsults, jurisprudentes, were unofficial experts who gave opinions for the decisions of cases pending before the judicial officers, the magistrates or judges. The latter were not bound to follow these opinions; yet in course of time some jurisconsults attained pre-eminence and their opinions were highly respected. The Emperor Augustus (31 B.C.—14 A.D.) conferred on certain persons the imperial authority to give such opinions

---

[73] See Salmond, Jurisprudence (7th ed., 1924), § 45; supra, § 3.13, nn. 59, 60.

[74] "But textbooks remain only persuasive authorities . . . ." Paton, Jurisprudence (1946), § 53, p. 199.

[75] E. g., some American state court opinions appear to be slavishly following a few sentences from a legal encyclopedia.

[76] The decreta and rescripta of the Roman Emperors are classed by Gray as "judicial acts"; at one period they were relied upon as precedents. Op. cit., §§ 429–433.

(jus respondendi) and at that time, or a little later, their opinions (responsa) were made binding on the courts. The jurisconsults thus attained a rather curious official status. Many of their responses were preserved and had control or influence like that of American judicial precedents. Besides giving responses, many jurists wrote legal treatises, and by the time of Diocletian (284–305 A.D.) the writings of the great jurists of the earlier period, both their responsa and their treatises, were deemed authoritative. The famous Law of Citations (426 A.D.) named five great jurists whose writings should be pre-eminently authoritative: Papinian, Paulus, Gaius, Ulpian and Modestinus. All of these learned jurists had been dead more than two centuries before their opinions attained this high authority. What a revolution in American law and legal education would be brought about if American courts were now required to cite and follow (apart from statutes) mainly [77] the writings of Bracton, Littleton, Coke, Hale and Blackstone! The writings of the distinguished jurists attained an even higher status when the Emperor Justinian gave statutory authority to his Digest (Pandects), which was largely composed of selections from their writings. The Digest became the principal source of authority for Roman law in the middle ages, and that law was "received" in western Europe at the time of the Renaissance largely through the influence of the learned Doctors who had mastered its texts. This brief sketch of a long and complex development [78] will suffice to indicate why the opinions of unofficial experts have such great influence in countries of the received Roman law.

The career-specialization of law teachers and authors is another reason for the position of the expert in most civil law countries. At the outset of his career, in France or in (pre-war) Germany, a law-trained man had to choose whether he would try to be a judge, or a practicing lawyer or notary, or a law teacher and legal author. The latter group was thus set apart and attained greater prestige. In the United States and in the English-law portions of the British Commonwealth, no such division of training for specialized careers is found. While the vocation of the law teacher has, in the United States, become much more dif-

---

[77] The Law of Citations did not expressly exclude the use of other authorities.

[78] I have relied chiefly on Gray, who was making a similar point (op.cit., §§ 424–434), and on Paton, who gives an excellent short account of the same development, op.cit., 202.

ferentiated than it was a century ago, law professors' *opinions*, as distinct from their summaries of case law, are still ordinarily only mildly persuasive authorities.

Yet the influence of text-writers on the long-run development of English and American law has been quite important. Five legal authors had a great influence on English law: Glanville, Bracton, Littleton, Coke and Blackstone. Their influence was greatest after they were dead. This may account for the English canon of citation that a living author cannot be cited as an "authority".[79] Pound has pointed out the considerable influence of treatises on the shaping of American law during the "formative period", from the Revolution until about 1850.[80] Blackstone, Kent and Story, among others, were used by courts and lawyers to fill in the gaps of their own case law. As precedents became more abundant, treatises declined in influence. Still later the unwieldy bulk of case law has once more increased the resort to legal treatises.[81]

What is the significance of a legal treatise (in book or periodical form) as a source of law for an appellate court? At least four types of significance may be distinguished: 1. Constructive, an expression of the author's views as to what the law ought to be. 2. Interpretative, an interpretation of legislation and case law in terms of general rules, principles and policies. 3. Terminological, an exploration and clarification of the meanings of legal terms as used in legislation and case law. 4. Summarizing, a summary or condensation of what courts have held or said in their published opinions. This analysis could be further refined, but it will serve for the present purpose.

Constructive legal treatises are still rather rare in England and the United States, as compared with those of continental Europe. Yet here their number is fortunately increasing. An outstanding example is Wigmore's monumental treatise on the law of Evidence, which also has the other three attributes referred to above. While Wigmore was more explicit than most text-writers in stating what the law ought to be, he often skilfully supported his view by showing that a contemporary rule

---

[79] Thus an English judge, Lord Wright, cited a treatise of the (then) aged Sir Frederick Pollock as "fortunately not a work of authority". Nicholls v. Ely Beet Sugar Factory, Ltd., [1936] 1 Ch. at 349; Paton, op.cit., 200.

[80] Pound, The Formative Era of American Law (1938), Ch. IV.

[81] Paton (op.cit., 199) points out a similar sequence in English law.

had originally a different meaning or purpose, or by exposing the implicit policies of the rule. In many treatises the author brings in his own constructive views under the guise of "interpretation" and thus makes them seem more objective. Yet a clear separation of the two seems more desirable.[82]

The legal expert's "interpretation", subtly affected by his own preferences, is often highly influential. An outstanding example is Professor Williston's excellent treatise on the law of Contracts.[83] Unlike Wigmore, Professor Williston rarely explores the underlying policies or values of the rules and concepts which he very ably interprets.[84] His interpretation is genetic and terminological rather than axiological. In this he follows the tradition of most American legal treatises.

A legal treatise which merely summarizes the judicial precedents under conventional headings, without critical comment and with a minimum of interpretation and reconciliation, is scarcely to be called "expert opinion", and yet it is the type most heavily relied upon by many American courts. The Brobdignagian encyclopedias commonly put out by law book publishers are of this type. The anonymity of their authorship and the impartiality with which they state conflicting rules or holdings (a feature which appeals especially to the advocates on both sides of a case) gives them an appearance of objectivity. While their widespread use has reduced the provincialism of American state law, their lack of even critical analysis makes them a hindrance to the development of American law. Their increasing bulk and their avidity for wood-pulp will probably, as in the case of the diplodocus, lead to their extinction. The late Professor Herman Kantorowicz aptly characterized most American legal treatises as "recent legal history".

The law review is the chief outlet for constructive or critical legal discussions. Here an author can present his novel insights into current legal problems and expound his proposals for change. Yet they are far less often cited in judicial opinions (even by judges who have read them) than are legal treatises in book form.[85] This seems due partly to their ephemeral and sometimes

---

[82] Besides Wigmore, another example of such separation is Cheshire, Private International Law (1935); Paton, op.cit., 205.

[83] First edition, 1920; second edition, by Williston and Thompson, 1936.

[84] See Professor Fuller's criticism in (1939) 18 N.C.L.Rev. 1, 8–9, and my own in (1939) 27 Georgetown L.J. 999.

[85] Judge Cardozo said that judges are reluctant to cite anything that is

tentative character (they are often "trial balloons") and partly to the fact that a board of student editors has more or less control over their contents. Yet the summaries of case law in student editorial notes are, in my experience, more reliable than those of the anonymous encyclopedias. The influence of law review articles on the development of American law has been greater than the citations would indicate. Thus an article by two youthful authors on "The Right of Privacy", published in 1890, helped to persuade many courts to recognize that right.[86] For law in the making, the law review often aids the imaginative reasoning of the judge and the legislator. The legal expert is often a useful gadfly.

The reasons why courts do not and should not regard the opinions of legal experts as more than persuasive authorities are threefold: First, the individual expert may express his own biases and errors, his selective or partial investigations. Second, the expert is not charged with the responsibility of making law for the immediate needs of present-day society; his opinions may be Utopian. Third, the representative form of government and the principle of legislative supremacy demand that the choice and formulation of important policies shall be made by elected officials.

The American Law Institute in preparing its Restatement of Law endeavored to overcome the first of these objections by bringing together a group of legal experts (chiefly law professors, but including judges and practitioners) whose peculiar slants were minimized by arduous criticism and discussion of proposed texts. It sought to eliminate the second objection by regularly though not uniformly [87] adhering to the rule that the text must state the preponderant view of American case law. It avoided the third by making no pretense of being "official", by limiting its subject matter to the traditional branches of private law and by minimizing its references to principle or policy. The Re-

---

not between hard covers. See Grinnell's article in (1941) 25 J.Amer.Jud.Soc. 10, rightly criticizing this tradition.

[86] Brandeis and Warren, "The Right of Privacy", (1890) 4 Harv.L.Rev. 193; Note, (1929) 43 Harv.L.Rev. 270, 302; Stone, The Province and Function of Law (1946), 514.

[87] The Restatement has sometimes adopted a "minority" view, sometimes filled a gap by extrapolation. For a short discussion of the Restatement and its influence on American courts see Goodrich, "The Story of the American Law Institute", 1951 Wash.U.L.Q. 283–305.

statement is our most comprehensive reliable treatise or. law. Its greatest values are its consistent terminology and its orderly coherent arrangements of rules, exceptions and definitions. Both of these, if used by courts, will serve to quell the Babel of forty-eight states. Most of its rules are wisely and skilfully stated. Yet its limitations, above referred to, precluded any discussion of conflicting views and of the arguments for each. It is to be hoped that the next generation of judges, familiar with its texts, will not treat them as sacred oracles. The opinions of legal experts can hinder or mislead, as well as help, the development of the law.

§ 3.15—Custom as a Source of the Law

The role of custom in society and its relation to law have been the subjects of an extensive literature,[88] most of which deals with the part played by custom in primitive societies, i. e., those which lack an integrated political organization. The institutionalist (§ 2.03) criticisms of the imperative conception of law have been chiefly based on the argument that in many societies at a certain stage customs, which had no authority and sanction of the state in the modern sense, fulfilled the function of law, and therefore should be called "law".[89] No harm will result from calling the prevailing customs of such a society its "customary law", if the difference in meaning is understood. The customs of primitive societies have more than an antiquarian interest for the legal profession of a mature state, since its officials and citizens are frequently called upon to determine the legal relations of the members of societies in which customary law prevails. An example is the case in which an American state court was called upon to determine the validity of a polygamous marriage under the customary law of an Indian tribe.[90] In such cases customary law becomes a rule of decision by virtue of the conflict-of-laws, or private international law, rule of the forum. Commercial and

---

[88] See the valuable analysis and survey of the literature of custom in Allen, Law in the Making (3d ed., 1939), Chs. I–II. A shorter discussion is found in Salmond, Jurisprudence (7th ed., 1924), Ch. IX.

[89] MacIver, Society—Its Structure and Changes, (1933) 274–276, in Hall, pp. 922–926, favors reserving the term "law" for state-law.

[90] Kobogum v. Jackson Iron Co., 76 Mich. 498, 43 N.W. 602 (1889); Hall, p. 880. Allen (op.cit., supra, n. 88) gives other examples in the English courts.

political relations with such a society also call for an understanding of its customs.

At the outset of any discussion of custom one is confronted with the obscurity of its scope and meaning.[91] In part this is due to the romantic glorification of custom by the German historical school, by English legal writers from Fortescue to Blackstone, and by many nineteenth century anthropologists.[92] This romantic fallacy is especially seductive when one looks back upon the obscure origins of customs in one's own society and one's imagination is untrammeled by sober facts. Thus the romanticists assume that custom is unchanging; whereas a careful historian, investigating the records of English customs, emphasizes the flexibility of custom.[93] Another difference is as to the origin of customs: Some writers believe that customs arise spontaneously out of the cooperation and interaction of the members of a group;[94] while others, notably Maine, have asserted that customs arise from the making of arbitral or judicial decisions in particular cases.[95] One may suspect that some of these conflicts are due to different meanings of "custom".

Those who try to define "custom" generally agree that every custom has an *internal*, or mentalistic, element, and an *external*, or behavioristic, one. The latter consists of a practice or regularity of conduct, in a certain way, of the members of a group of people. The former consists of their "conviction of inward necessity", as Savigny put it, their "opinio necessitatis", their belief that the conduct is right and obligatory, or, in a different light, the expectation of each member of the group that the others will conduct themselves in accordance with the previous practice. In this latter aspect customs are *conventions*, and give rise

---

[91] Professor Llewellyn thinks the term is "too blunt and confused to serve in careful analysis", (1940) 49 Yale L.J. 1355, 1359, n. 1. However, the widespread use of the term in jurisprudential, historical and sociological literature calls for some discussion of it.

[92] See Allen, op.cit. supra, n. 88.

[93] Plucknett, A Concise History of English Law (2d ed., 1936), 272 ff.; Hall, p. 875.

[94] Thus even MacIver says that customs grow up "spontaneously", in contrast with laws. Op.cit., 275; Hall, p. 927. Sumner's "folkways", closely related to customs, are "made unconsciously". Sumner, Folkways (1906), 3; Hall, p. 906.

[95] Maine, Ancient Law, quoted in Allen, op.cit., 115. E. Lambert, the noted French comparative-law scholar, supports Maine's thesis. Ibid., 116–117.

to claims having the same ethical basis that promises have. This aspect is, I believe, their most important one for modern law.

The mental element in customs is difficult to distinguish from morals, the prevalent beliefs and attitudes in a social group as to the rightness or wrongness of certain types of conduct (§ 1.13). Thus monogamy, the practice of having only one wife (at one time), is usual in Occidental societies; and the belief that this practice is right is a prevalent moral belief in such societies. Are fashions and etiquette to be regarded as customs, or is a belief in the moral rightness or obligatoriness of the conduct necessary to make a "true" custom? The answer is twofold: First, that customs of fashion and etiquette do not engender sufficiently serious expectations to deserve enforcement by legal sanctions; and secondly, that many customs recognized and applied by English courts were based on expediency or convenience rather than on moral conviction.[96] Hence custom and morals overlap but are not identical.

The term "custom" is also used to include, besides popular or lay customs, official customs in a modern state. Some European writers refer to case law as "customary law"; the usage is inaccurate at least to the extent that a single judicial decision can change the law. A more apt example is the custom of administrative officials in applying a statute, which may influence a court in choosing between doubtful interpretations of the statute.[97] The constitution of Great Britain is said to contain "a great deal more custom than law, in the ordinary sense of those terms".[98] The whole system of Parliamentary-Cabinet government has grown up by custom; yet if the Parliament enacts a statute conflicting with the custom, the statute will be law.[99] In the United States it has been argued that certain official customs have become a part of our constitutional law. Examples are the custom that the President shall not seek a third term of office, and the custom that a presidential elector shall vote for the candidate of his political party. Yet in recent years both customs were violated, and the violations were not deemed "illegal" by other of-

---

[96] Allen, op.cit., 94–95.

[97] The practice of state authorities in taxing public utilities was said to be "the gloss which life has written" upon the statute by Frankfurter, J., in Nashville, C. & St. L. Ry. v. Browning, 310 U.S. 362, 369, 60 Sup.Ct. 968, 972 (1940).

[98] Allen, op.cit., 71.

[99] See Livesidge v. Anderson, [1942] A.C. 206.

ficials. It is misleading to designate such customs as a part of
constitutional law.

Custom as a Source of Law in England. In England the customs of a locality or of a trade have long been recognized as a
source of particular rules of decision which are contrary to common law rules.[1] An example of local custom is Wigglesworth v.
Dallison [2] in which a tenant whose lease expired on May 1, 1776,
sued his lessor for taking crops which were planted by the tenant before that date, and offered proof of a local custom of the
parish that under such circumstances the tenant was entitled to
the crops. The jury found the custom was proved and gave a
verdict for the tenant. In upholding the custom as a "reasonable"
one Lord Mansfield pointed out that it did not contradict the
terms of the lease. Yet it did contradict the common law rule as
to emblements which would otherwise have determined the tenant's rights under the lease. Another leading English case on custom is the famous Case of Tanistry,[3] in which the English judges
rejected an Irish custom that the real property of a deceased
should descend, not to the eldest son, but to the "older and most
worthy" of the blood and surname of the deceased, on the ground
that it was too uncertain and that it was contrary to the common
law rule of primogeniture. English courts have often rejected
customs which they deemed contrary to statute or to a basic principle of the common law or "unreasonable".[4] It seems that an express agreement between private parties could derogate more
from the common law than could a local custom.

The English courts have applied various tests to determine
whether a local custom, proved to the satisfaction of judge and
jury, will be given effect, yet English writers do not agree on the
formulation of these tests. Allen lists the following: 1. Antiquity. 2. Continuance. 3. Peaceable enjoyment. 4. Obligatoriness. 5. Certainty (as to its terms). 6. Reasonableness.
7. Legality.[5] The requirement of antiquity (which does not
apply to trade customs) means that the custom must have existed
from time immemorial; this was construed to mean from 1189
A.D., but proof that the custom had existed for a very long time

---

[1] Allen, op.cit., 125–126.

[2] 1 Doug. 201 (1779); Hall, p. 878.

[3] Dav. 29 (1608).

[4] Allen, op.cit. 126, 134–140.

[5] Allen, op.cit., 126–141.

and that it *might* have existed continuously since 1189, will satisfy the requirement. These "tests" show that the English courts use customs as sources of exceptional rules which they apply to particular situations. Presumably after a custom has once been approved by the court, that decision will be a precedent for the court's later *approval* of the same (local or trade) custom in another controversy; but it seems that in a later suit between different parties the custom must again be proved as a fact.[6]

American Applications of Custom. Custom in the English or continental sense is more than, and should be distinguished from, a mere linguistic usage as to the meaning of certain words in an agreement. Such linguistic usages have been frequently proved in American courts (as well as in England) and have been deemed controlling in the interpretation of specific words in a contract.[7] In such cases the usage signifies that the words *are* used with a peculiar or special meaning, rather than that they *ought* to be; the usage is not a "genuine" custom. Wigmore correctly explained such cases as involving the adoption by the parties of a peculiar trade dictionary, in which certain terms had meanings different from those in the common dictionaries.[8] The recognition of peculiar linguistic usages is not a recognition of custom in the traditional sense.

Aside from these instances, special lay customs have rarely been given effect in American law. The English tests have scarcely been mentioned; the test of immemorial antiquity has been ignored.[9] In one case, brought in the admiralty jurisdiction of a federal court, the plaintiff had harpooned a fin-whale, which

---

6 Professor Allen, op.cit., did not mention this point, but it seems to follow from the rule that a court will not take judicial notice of special customs.

7 E. g., Hurst v. W. J. Lake & Co., Inc., 141 Ore. 306, 16 P.2d 627 (1932); Hall, p. 802. In an English case a local "custom" whereby "1,000 rabbits" meant "1,200 rabbits" was given effect. Smith v. Wilson, 3 B. & Ad. 728 (1832). For other examples, see Williston, Contracts (1936), § 650.

8 Wigmore, Evidence, secs. 2463-65. Similarly, customary practices are admissible to show negligence in tort actions.

9 The requirement that the custom be "ancient, notorious, uniform" etc., was stated as dictum but not applied in Port Investment Co. v. Oregon Mut. Fire Ins. Co., 163 Ore. 1, 94 P.2d 734 (1939). In one New Hampshire case, a local custom in favor of the inhabitants of a village was given effect upon proof of twenty years continuous use, which the court deemed sufficient proof that the custom was immemorial. Knowles v. Dow, 22 N.H. 387 (1851). This case is exceptional.

escaped and was found on the beach by the defendants, who appropriated it. The plaintiff proved a custom, acquiesced in for many years, whereby the one who first harpooned the whale was entitled to it even if it escaped. The court found that the custom was necessary to the continuance of the fin-whaling industry and gave it effect.[10] Here the custom served to interpret the common law rule that he who first takes effective possession of a wild animal is entitled to it. A trade custom whereby a buyer of goods has a right to return unsold goods in lieu of paying the price has been given effect in some cases.[11] Here the custom contradicted the legal consequences ordinarily to be inferred from the transaction in about the same way as in Wigglesworth v. Dallison.[12] In other cases American courts have rejected proof of a custom as lacking "certainty and uniformity",[13] or as contrary to the explicit terms of a written contract[14] or as unreasonable.[15] American courts seem unfamiliar with the proof of special customs, and sometimes even take judicial notice of them.[16] This unfamiliarity with the use of custom may account for its rarity.

Are Customs "Law"? The view that customs, even those of special or limited groups in a society, are a part of the law of the society ipso facto and before they have been recognized or implemented by a court or a legislature has the support of some very able and learned men. Legal philosophers otherwise as far apart as St. Thomas Aquinas[17] and Dr. Hans Kelsen[18] have recognized

---

[10] Ghen v. Rich, 8 F. 159 (D.C.Mass.1881); Hall, p. 887.

[11] Homix Products, Inc., v. Henry Pape, Inc., 274 App.Div. 648, 86 N.Y.S. 2d 648 (1949); see Gottlieb v. Charles Scribner's Sons, 232 Ala. 33, 166 So. 685 (1936).

[12] Supra, n. 2. An easement by prescription but not by custom, in favor of local inhabitants, is recognized. Gillies v. Orienta, 159 Misc. 675, 289 N. Y.S. 733 (1936).

[13] Bagwell v. Susman, 165 F.2d 412, 416 (C.C.A.Tenn.1947) (alleged custom also contradicted a provision of the Uniform Sales Act).

[14] Port Investment Co. v. Oregon, etc., Ins. Co., supra, n. 9; Albert v. R. P. Farnsworth & Co., Inc., 176 F.2d 198 (C.A.La.1949).

[15] Bankus v. State, 4 Ind. 114 (1853), Hall, p. 889 ("charivari" custom); Fuller v. Robinson, 86 N.Y. 306 (1881), Hall, p. 890 (alleged trade custom).

[16] Shipley v. Pittsburgh & L. E. R. Co., 68 F.Supp. 395 (W.D.Pa.1946), modified without mentioning "custom", 70 F.Supp. 870 (D.C.Pa.1947).

[17] St. Thomas Aquinas, Summa Theologica, Treatise on Law (II, I), Q. 97, Art. 3 (Dominican Fathers' trans., 1927), pp. 79–81. His chief argument applies only to customs which manifest the free consent of the whole people.

[18] Kelsen, General Theory of Law and State (1945), 128: ". . . custom is a law-creating procedure in the same sense as legislation."

the law-creating power of custom. Kelsen argues that the members of a custom-creating group have a kind of delegated authority to make their customs law. Moreover, Kelsen says that a rule created by custom may be binding on individuals other than those who create it.[19] The conception of delegation seems a groundless fiction, which contradicts the basic conception of a state law as a norm created by officials for public rather than private ends (§ 2.33). Another reason for rejecting this view was brought out in Professor John Dewey's comment on Allen's view that in England a proved (special) custom is, if it satisfies the judicial tests, merely "declared" by the court to be operative law:

> "In this case, a rule of law cannot be considered as the mere reduplication in formal statement of antecedent custom, for it involves an element which is additive and in a sense, as viewed from the standpoint of prior custom, creative." [20]

Brown, an English writer who follows the Austinian view that customs are not law until recognized and enforced by courts, ascribes the opposing view to the Blackstonian theory that courts do not make, but merely declare law.[21] While this dispute is not, as to special customs, of much practical importance because of their limited use, it is not a mere verbal one since it involves some basic conceptions of the legal order.

General Customs as Sources of the Law. The view that special customs are only sources of law is supported by the consideration of general or common customs. Blackstone, repeating his predecessors, described the English common law as the common custom of the realm; and followers of the historical school in the United States have repeated this view.[22] Pound has shown that the shifts and changes of English case law cannot be explained on any such simple theory.[23] However, common or general customs of a society influence the content of its law in several different ways. In a very broad sense of custom, practices prevalent

---

19 Ibid.

20 Dewey, book review, (1928) 28 Col.L.Rev. 832, of Allen, Law in the Making (1st ed., 1928).

21 Brown, "Customary Law in Modern England", (1905) 5 Col.L.Rev. 561, 582–3; Hall, 896, 903.

22 See Pound, "Juristic Science and Law", (1918) 31 Harv.L.Rev. 1047.

23 Ibid., 1049–50. See also the excellent article by Mr. E. K. Braybrooke of New Zealand, "Custom as a Source of English Law," (1951) 50 Mich.L.Rev. 71.

and approved in the society provide some basic legal conceptions, such as marriage, possession, ownership and the like. Again, many legal rules would have no meaning without supporting usages. Thus, the rule that mailing an acceptance of a mailed offer constitutes a contract is dependent upon the use of the post office as a means of communication, yet the usage would decide no controversies without an evaluation. It would have been possible to hold that the acceptance was not effective until received. Here a second point may be made, that societal practices create *needs* for new legal norms, but it remains for courts and legislatures to satisfy such needs by creating appropriate legal devices. Thirdly, the general practices of a society or of a considerable part of it may render ineffective officially created norms. If examples are needed, the fate of the Eighteenth Amendment will serve. The general practices, usages and customs of a society provide much of the raw materials of its legislation and case law.

§ 3.16—Principles of Morality as Sources

The principles of morality which are prevalent in a given society are sources of its law, in the sense that the content and meaning of its legislation and case law are materially influenced by those principles. Since the relations between law and morals have been the subject of an extensive literature,[24] we shall confine our discussion to four aspects of these relations in a mature, politically organized society: 1. The meaning of principles of morality. 2. The ascertainment and choice of moral standards. 3. The formal validation and implementation of moral principles. 4. The advantages and limitations of using moral principles as sources of the law.

1. *The Meaning of Principles of Morality.* The distinction between "ethics" as the theoretical system of principles that should guide human conduct, and "morals" as the beliefs and practices that are prevalent in a social group, has been pointed out (§ 1.13). Gray included both in his "principles of morality" that were sources of law,[25] though his discussion related chiefly to morals. Since courts and legislators are even more reluctant to implement by law the ethical principles of philosophers than the prevalent morals of a society, and since the former requires an extended discussion of philosophies of law (Pt. IV, infra), in the present

---

[24] See Pound, Law and Morals (2d ed., 1936), and Bibliography; Pound, Outline of Jurisprudence (1943), 80–83.

[25] Gray, The Nature and Sources of the Law (1909), §§ 644, 650–651.

discussion "principles of morality" will be confined to the latter. It may, indeed, be doubted that such a separation is possible, since ethical philosophers ordinarily begin their inquiries with some regard for morals and morals determines to some extent, if only by way of negation, the conclusions of ethics. Still, prevalent moral principles can be approved or disapproved by a diversity of ethical principles, and for any given society, such as that of the United States or one of its states, the prevalence of morals is more readily verifiable by empirical proof.[26] We thus exclude for the present a discussion of "moral law", a term used by some writers as synonymous with "natural law" or "natural justice".[27]

To differentiate morals from customs is scarcely less difficult. Allen, emphasizing the institutional basis of law, speaks of "positive morality" as only an invented name for "custom",[28] meaning apparently general customs rather than those local or special customs which constitute, he says, exceptions to the common law.[29] Since the traditional conception of custom includes a feeling of obligatoriness (§ 3.15), the distinction between morals and custom is to be maintained by emphasizing the mental attitude rather than the external observance. While many moral principles are exemplified in habitual regularities of conduct and are thus customary, many prevalent moral beliefs are broader in scope than verifiable customs. Thus the moral principle that one should tell the truth is more widely believed in than one would conclude from observing the usual practices with respect to truthtelling in making and breaking social engagements, selling secondhand automobiles or writing political campaign literature. A second point to be made is that custom does not necessarily rest upon a "moral" conviction of obligatoriness (§ 3.15). Many customs, such as that of driving on the right side of the road rather than the left, are rules of expediency; the contrary rule would have the same value if conformity to it prevailed. True, the belief that *some* certain rule should be observed to avoid collisions is a moral principle in the broadest sense. Yet once a rule has been established, those who observe it do so chiefly from pruden-

---

[26] See Pound, Law and Morals (1924), 101–102, on the subjectivity of ethical judgments in cases where there is no general agreement in the social mores as to the approved conduct.

[27] E. g., Salmond, Jurisprudence (7th ed., 1924), § 8. See infra, Ch. 13.

[28] Allen, Law in the Making (3d ed., 1939), 65.

[29] Ibid., 125; supra, § 3.15.

tial rather than moral motives.[30] This last distinction is at best a subtle one (is not prudence a virtue?). Hence the emphasis on the mental attitude toward conduct is the chief method of differentiation between customs and prevalent morality.

John Austin, following Bentham,[31] distinguished positive law from positive morality by their respective sanctions. "Positive morality" includes those principles of conduct that are sanctioned only by "general opinion", by the manifested approval or disapproval of the members of a social group.[32] This criterion serves to differentiate positive morality from ethical theories, yet it includes everything from village customs to international law, which Austin called "positive international morality". The positivist criterion, despite its inherent vagueness, has the merit of giving a factual status to morality. Gray included in his "principles of morality" what he called "public policy".[33] The latter will be here excluded, since the term "policy" now has become a term of legal art (§ 3.24). As to common American usage, "morality" most commonly denotes sexual morality, with sporadic extensions that include "fraud", "malice" and the like.

2. *The Ascertainment and Choice of Principles of Morality.* Considering moral principles as sources of specific legal norms, we may ask, how do officials who resort to this source determine what moral principles prevail, and, in case of differing moral principles in the same society, how do they choose between them? As to the first, the answer is that judges have no established techniques for hearing proof of "positive morality", and when they take cognizance of them the all-embracing conception of "judicial notice" accounts for such factual evidence of morality as appears in the record. Such evidence is rare. In most cases the judge derives his conception of morality from his own experience in living in the community. Thus in the case cited earlier (§ 1.13), a federal judge held that a woman applicant for citizenship was of "good moral character" although she had married and lived with a man in the honest but mistaken belief that his previous divorce was legally valid, and continued to live with him after she

---

[30] See Sidgwick, The Methods of Ethics (1930), 28, 31 (the moral "ought" is indefinable); Stone, The Province and Function of Law (1946), 681 (emotion of ethical obligation is distinctive).

[31] See Bentham, A Comment on the Commentaries (ed. Everett, 1928), 95.

[32] Austin, Jurisprudence (4th ed., 1873), Lecture V, p. 187; Paton, Jurisprudence (1946), § 16.

[33] Gray, op.cit., § 644.

discovered its invalidity.[34] The opinion discloses no evidence (other than prior judicial precedents) upon which the conclusion as to the prevalent moral attitude of the community (the "living law") was based. How could the judge have conducted a factual investigation of the prevalent social mores? Perhaps by reading assiduously in sociological literature, or perhaps by inviting interested groups to appear as amici curiae. I am not suggesting that the judge decided wrongly in this case, but I am suggesting that the judge's unproved assumptions as to the prevalent morals of the community *may* be based on nothing more than his personal moral beliefs. The *legal* issue, however, was in this case not merely one of prevalent moral beliefs but was also one of applying the policy of the naturalization statute, namely, was the applicant's conduct *so* morally reprehensible (if at all) *as* to justify denying her citizenship?

In another recent case, involving a suit by the government to confiscate imported books on nudism as "obscene" within the meaning of the federal statute, the court took judicial notice of a considerable body of literature on varying standards of decency in dress, and noted especially the reproductions of classic statuary in a leading encyclopedia, in arriving at its decision that the volumes were not obscene.[35] The dissenting judge in the same case said that the expert opinions of psychologists and sociologists "would seem relevant only if directed to what the present community conscience is, in reference to a book of this character".[36] In the absence of any such proof in the lower court, an appellate court has to make an astute guess (with due deference to the findings of the lower court) as to what is the moral sense of the community. The critical problem of euthanasia was presented in a recent case. An alien applicant for citizenship who performed euthanasia on his son, an idiot blind deaf-mute, was held to be by the community standard not of "good moral character",[37] though one judge dissented on the ground that the trial

---

[34] Petition of R———, 56 F.Supp. 969 (D.C.Mass.1944). For discussion see (1948) 16 U. of Chi.L.Rev. 138.

[35] Parmelee v. U. S., 113 F.2d 729 (D.C.App.1940). Cf. Sunshine Book Co. v. McCaffrey, 112 N.Y.S.2d 476, 481 (Sup.Ct.Spec.T.1952).

[36] Ibid., 741.

[37] Repouille v. U. S., 165 F.2d 152 (C.C.A.2 1947). Learned Hand, J., in the majority opinion, stated that the test was not his own belief but whether the moral convictions of people in this country would be "outraged". Frank, J., dissented.

court should be directed to hear evidence on the point. The ascertainment of positive morality, where relevant, still awaits a satisfactory solution.

The choice between the moral standards of different classes or groups in the society is another problem. In the case last cited, Frank, J., suggested that the standard to guide the court should be that of the "ethical leaders" of the community.[38] Yet if the ethical leaders of the society (in this case, the whole United States since a federal statute was involved) disagree, as they probably would, the court would still be confronted with a choice between moral principles, plus the policy problem mentioned above. Cardozo saw the problem of choice and felt that the law "will not hold the crowd to the morality of saints and seers"; rather it will

> "strive to follow the principle and practice of the men and women of the community whom the social mind would rank as intelligent and virtuous." [39]

The level of morality is, for ordinary private transactions, somewhat below that of the most virtuous, and considerably above that of the most vicious. Yet Cardozo applied to a "fiduciary relation", that between partners,[40] a standard of honesty and loyalty considerably above that of the "man in the street". Sometimes, indeed, the law may tolerate conduct which seems to the ingenuous morally honest, though more intelligent citizens would deem it fraudulent, as in the case involving the sale of "lucky stones" through the mail.[41] Yet an individual cannot legally justify his conduct by showing that it was morally right by his own standard and by that of the group to which he belonged.[42] The state must sometimes strive to suppress the moralities of minority groups.

Considered historically, judicial adoptions, avowed or covert, of moral principles have brought about a good many elevations of legal standards. Two examples will suffice. The standards of

---

38 Ibid., at p. 154.

39 Cardozo, The Paradoxes of Legal Science (1928), 37.

40 Meinhard v. Salmon, 249 N.Y. 458, 164 N.E. 545 (1928) (constructive trust imposed on property acquired by one partner by obtaining extension of partnership lease).

41 Cf. Dolan v. Hurley, 283 F. 695 (D.C.Mass.1922), affirmed 297 F. 825 (C.C.A.1 1924).

42 Cleveland v. U. S., 329 U.S. 14, 67 Sup.Ct. 13 (1946) (belief in plural marriage no defense to prosecution under Mann Act).

honesty imposed upon sellers of goods have, since the time of Chancellor Kent,[43] been substantially lifted.[44] Again, the scope of tortious conduct has been extended to include that which, while otherwise privileged, is done through malice. An example is the "spite fence" which a man builds on his land merely to harm his neighbor.[45] Yet even here the argument has been recently made that the law should not attempt to control a man's moral conduct.[46] This argument is similar to Kant's position (Ch. 14) that the law cannot coerce the ethical observance of a duty. However, courts can prevent or grant reparation for the external harm caused by a malicious act, even if they cannot cleanse an evil mind. The moral climate in which judges and legislators live has greatly influenced their law-making.

3. *The Formal Validation and Implementation of Moral Principles.* By what authority do state officials adopt moral principles as sources of the law that they make or administer? Here the thesis will be maintained that official authority to adopt moral principles as norms for legal implementation must be found in some superior norm except in the case of the sovereign political authority (§ 2.31). In the case of the ordinary legislature with plenary powers only the constitutional provisions legally inhibit the implementation of moral principles. Even a legislature of enumerated powers, such as the American Congress, has within those limits the power to make the maintenance of moral standards a primary objective of its statutes, as in the case of the Mann (White Slave) Act. The ascertainment and choice of positive moral standards is a task primarily for the legislature, and it can be done better through committee hearings than through prevailing judicial procedures that necessarily operate under the pressure of deciding a particular controversy. The legislative function is not merely to choose and approve moral principles; it has also to determine which ones should be implemented in order to attain the ends of the legal order, and how they should be implemented. It is now fortunately unusual to find a court declaring invalid a legislative enactment which refused to implement a moral principle that the court conceived to be paramount.[47]

---

[43] See Seixas v. Woods, 2 Caines 48 (N.Y.Sup.Ct.1804) (seller not liable for misdescription unless "warranted").

[44] See Radin, The Lawful Pursuit of Gain (1931), Ch. III; Ames, "Law and Morals" in Lectures in Legal History (1913), 438–9.

[45] See Prosser, Torts (1941), 32; Ames, op.cit., supra, 402, 449.

[46] Cohen v. Perrino, 355 Pa. 455, 459, 50 A.2d 348, 350 (1947).

[47] Cf. Heck v. Schupp, 394 Ill. 296, 68 N.E.2d 464 (1946); here the court

The thesis above stated has been accepted, with a substantial degree of uniformity, by English and American courts. In order to adopt a principle of morality as a ground for its decision, a court must find some formal validating authority in prior law. The prevalent view of the judicial function was thus expressed by Judge Wyzanski:

> "Ordinarily if Congress leaves a case to a judge to decide, it expects him to appraise the facts by technical criteria. He has not the freedom which a jury so often exercises to disregard the letter of the law and apply the sentiment of the community. But there are exceptional cases in which the judge enjoys a broader scope. By using in the Nationality Act a phrase so popular as 'good moral character' Congress seems to have invited the judges to concern themselves . . . with the norms of society and the way average men of good will will act, in short with what Eugen Ehrlich . . . calls 'the ascertainment of the living law'." [48]

Mr. Justice Black, who is surely no stickler for empty formalities, in a case involving the claim of the Federal government that a shipbuilding contract was extortionate and had been obtained by duress, said that the profits made on war contracts might justly arouse indignation—

> "But indignation based on the notions of morality of this or any other court cannot be judicially transmuted into a principle of law of greater force than the expressed will of Congress." [49]

Frankfurter, J., dissenting, said:

> "But the function of the judiciary is not so limited that it must sanction the use of the federal courts as instruments of injustice in disregard of moral and equitable principles *which have been part of the law* for centuries." [50]

He grounded his conclusion in part on the judicial precedents as to "undue influence".

The formal *authority* of courts to use moral principles as sources of the law does not necessarily impose a *requirement* that

---

referred to "moral law" but also relied on provisions of the Illinois Constitution.

[48] Petition of R———, 56 F.Supp. at 971. See supra, § 1.13, n. 37.

[49] U. S. v. Bethlehem Steel Corp., 315 U.S. 289, 308–309, 62 Sup.Ct. 581, 591–592 (1942).

[50] 315 U. S., at pp. 312–313 (italics added).

they do so nor a guide as to how they should; the formal authorization may be vague and general. A recent example is the recognition of a minor child's right to recover damages from a woman who alienated the affections of the child's father and thus deprived the child of the father's support.[51] The court rested its decision chiefly on Pound's conception of judicial empiricism [52] and on certain analogies in case law [53] rather than on an avowed moral principle, yet its moral views seem to have been the chief motivation. The court also based its decision on a provision of the Illinois constitution:

> "Every person ought to find a certain remedy in the laws for all injuries and wrongs which he may receive in his person, property or reputation." [54]

However, the Supreme Court of Connecticut, faced with a similar problem and the same constitutional language, construed "injuries and wrongs" to mean *legal* injuries and wrongs, and therefore not to require the creation of a new legal right: the right of a minor child to recover damages from a man who had alienated his mother's affections.[55]

A legal system usually contains many propositions which refer obliquely to moral principles, and thus authorize the courts to resort to them as guides for interpretation and application. The principle of unjust enrichment is one, the principle that "no man shall profit by his own wrong", is another, both drawn from case law. The Nationality Act phrase, "good moral character", is an example of statutory authority. Even such a term as "good faith" in the law of negotiable instruments law calls for some consideration of the practical morality of the commercial community.[56] In code systems there are ordinarily even broader provisions, such as:

---

[51] Daily v. Parker, 152 F.2d 174 (C.C.A.Ill.1945), followed in Johnson v. Luhman, 330 Ill.App. 598, 71 N.E.2d 810 (1947). See (1950) 63 Harv.L.Rev. 541, for other precedents.

[52] Pound, The Spirit of the Common Law (1921), 183.

[53] The analogies included inducing breach of contract and contributing tort-feasor. See (1947) 12 Mo.L.Rev. 358.

[54] Ill.Const. Art. 2, Sec. 19.

[55] Taylor v. Keefe, 134 Conn. 156, 163, 56 A.2d 768, 771 (1947). In accord: Henson v. Thomas, 231 N.C. 173, 56 S.E.2d 432 (1949).

[56] Gerseta Corp. v. Wessex-Campbell Silk Co., 3 F.2d 236, 238 (C.C.A.2d 1924). The German Civil Code (1900) contains "good faith" provisions as to all contracts, Arts. 157, 242.

"Everyone is bound to exercise his rights and to perform his obligations in accordance with the rules of good faith. A manifest abuse of a right is not protected by the law." [57]

The covert and unavowed recognition by courts of moral principles under the guise of legal techniques may seem to belie the thesis proposed above; yet it is, in effect, a recognition of that thesis. An example is the "implied condition" in a contract behind which, as Holmes pointed out, lies a judgment as to community practice or policy.[58] A New York court's failure to recognize the formal character of the implied condition led it to reject the conception of an implied condition (not evidenced by an explicit agreement) in the gift of jewelry by a man to his fiancée, that the gifts would be returned if she broke off the engagement;[59] the court excluded any "matter of ethics". Yet the moral beliefs of the community (or of at least the women) calls, I believe, for a return of the engagement ring by the jilting fiancée. The law in some jurisdictions implements this moral principle by the device of the implied condition.[60]

The recognition of a principle of popular morality as ethically sound or as a useful device of social control is one thing; its implementation by the law is quite another. The legislature or the court has to decide not merely that a type of conduct is wrong and deserves disapproval but that definite legal consequences should be attached to it. Thus in Dailey v. Parker [61] the question was whether the defendant should pay for the plaintiff's loss of support and whether the allowance of such an action would bring with it the vexatious litigation and other evils which followed the allowance of other alienation suits.[62] Questions of *legal* policy have to be, and ought to be avowedly, decided whenever a court implements a moral principle. Sometimes, it seems, courts have decided, unwisely, to deny enforcement of a contract on the ground of "illegality" or public policy. An example is the English decision which denied recovery of rent stipulated in a lease of

---

[57] Swiss Civil Code (1912) Art. 2. Similar provisions are found in German Civil Code (1900) § 226; Soviet Civil Code (1923) § 1. See I Gsovsky, Soviet Civil Law (1948), 324 ff.

[58] Holmes, "The Path of the Law" (1897) 10 Harv.L.Rev. 457, 466; Collected Legal Papers (1920) 167, 181.

[59] Rosenberg v. Lewis, 210 App.Div. 690, 206 N.Y.S. 353 (1924).

[60] See Restatement, Restitution (1937), § 58, Comments b, c, and Reporters' Notes.

[61] Supra, n. 51.

[62] See the arguments of this sort in Taylor v. Keefe, supra, n. 55.

an apartment for one year because the lessor knew that the lessee intended to live on the premises as a certain man's mistress.[63] The nature and extent of the lessor's contribution to the lessee's immoral conduct did not call for such a severe penalty.[64] Principles of morality only provide material for the jurist's art. They are not sources of the law in the same sense as the law of cognate jurisdictions (§ 3.13) or the opinions of legal experts (§ 3.14), for these latter express judgments that *legal* consequences should attach to certain conduct. That judgment must still be made as to custom and morals.

4. *Advantages and Limitations.* According to Gray, principles of morality are used to interpret the other "sources" of the law and to fill in gaps.[65] An example of the latter was the recognition of the minor child's alienation suit;[66] of the former was the interpretation of the citizenship statute.[67] The late Herman Kantorowicz, in formulating his theory of "legal science", included principles of morality, as "nascent implicit law", under "free law", which the court is free to use when "formal law" fails to provide a solution.[68] These views exemplify the necessary part which the moral convictions of a society play in the making and administration of its laws. By gradually changing case law in conformity with the moral standards of the entire community, courts are able to experiment cautiously with the recognition of novel legal rights and duties which a legislature would initially have difficulty in defining and delimiting, and which, in the pressure of urgent political demands, it would not undertake unless it had a Law Revision Commission to draft statutes.

Yet there are many limitations upon the use by courts of morality as a source of law:

1. A judge's choice of a moral principle may be only his own personal predilection and not that of the whole community, or one on which there is general agreement.[69]

---

[63] See Upfill v. Wright, [1911] 1 K.B. 506. The court cited the Book of Common Prayer of the Church of England, which declared fornication to be a deadly sin.

[64] Cf. Fineman v. Faulkner, 174 N.C. 13, 93 S.E. 384 (1917).

[65] Gray, op.cit. supra, n. 25, Ch. XIII, §§ 642–645.

[66] Supra, n. 51.

[67] Supra, notes 34, 37.

[68] Kantorowicz, "Legal Science: A Summary of Its Methodology" (1928) 28 Col.L.Rev. 679, 696.

[69] Supra, n. 26.

2. Or the court's choice of a moral principle may be that of a minority group. Even the people of the United States have many diverse and conflicting moral principles from which to choose.[70]

3. The "fusion" of law and morals is not an unmixed blessing; it may be oppressive to minority groups. Dr. Hans Frank, one of the legal spokesmen of Nazism, proclaimed:

> "For National Socialism there is no difference in content between morals and law, in that morals represents the innate norm of the community arising out of the self-help instinct of the race, while law is the life-norm of the state, expressed by the authority of the Leader.[71]

It is well to remember that a social group can have as much tyranny under moralism as under legalism.

4. The frequent introduction of moral principles into some areas of case law will create greater uncertainty, where certainty is an important end of legal policy.[72]

5. For a modern society the legislature, if supplied with expert technical assistance, can better implement new or emergent principles of morality than can the courts.[73]

§ 3.17—Societal Facts as Sources

The conception of the informal or contentual sources of the law may be extended to include "societal facts". The term is a loose one and can be more easily illustrated than defined. The law of a society as a body of authoritative normative meanings cannot be fully understood or used without a knowledge of a great many facts that are peculiar to that society. For instance, the grammar and the vocabulary of the language needs to be understood; this is not, however, what I mean by a "societal fact". The customs and positive morality of a society are societal facts which are already charged with normative meanings, with conclusions that something ought or ought not to be done. Other

---

[70] For a survey by a philosopher, see Tufts, America's Social Morality: Dilemmas of the Changing Mores (1933).

[71] Frank, Rechtsgrundlegung des Nationalsozialischen Führerstaates (2d ed., 1938), 11, n. 8.

[72] Cf. Kantorowicz, op.cit. 704.

[73] However, as was said above, in some instances the courts can gradually bring about a change through judicial empiricism. See, for example, the change in seller's liability referred to above, notes 43, 44.

practices, attitudes and occurrences in the society have normative implications only when evaluated by some people as desirable or undesirable. Usages continued through imitation and habit operate through the "normative power of the factual" [74] to preserve the status quo. As long as the practice of satisfying wants by means of bargains or exchanges continues in civilized societies, the law needs to provide some recognition and regulation of it, though not necessarily the technical doctrine of consideration. On the other hand, some societal facts provide the basis for evaluations that call for change in the law, and it is these that we are here primarily concerned with. Familiar examples may be found in the societal facts that developed with the growth of industry in the United States. When it became a fact that around seventy per cent of the employees who suffered personal injuries in industrial plants were not compensated for their injuries under the then existing law, the conclusion that some change in the law ought to be made was an initial evaluation made at first by "reformers", and eventually refined by lawyers into the provisions of workmen's compensation laws. Likewise, the fact that a large percentage of automobile accident victims are uncompensated has led to legislation making liability insurance compulsory in some states, though this process is not completed. The influence of new societal facts in producing new law is not itself new. In fourteenth century England the reduction of the population by the plague was the occasion for the enactment of the Statute of Labourers (1349), which survived to trouble later legal solutions of labor problems. Enough has been said to show what is meant here by "societal facts". It does not include mere facts of physical causation, such as the effects of particular machines, nor biological facts, such as the mortality tables and the inferences to be established by blood-test groupings,[75] however useful these may be in certain judicial procedures.

The evaluation of societal facts as calling for legal change is not the inevitable consequence of any qualities inherent in them; too often and too long have they been either ignored or accepted

---

[74] Ehrlich, Fundamental Principles of the Sociology of Law (Moll trans., 1936), 86; Stone, The Province and Function of Law (1946), 675 (Ch. XXV, § 1).

[75] But see Note (1948) 61 Harv.L.Rev. 692–702, where blood-grouping tests of paternity are discussed as "social and economic facts". This usage is misleading.

as an inevitable phase of the status quo. Much less inevitable is the evaluation embodied in any specific law or type of law. Hence it is futile to hope for the time when a group of busy workers known as "social scientists", freed from all presuppositions of value, will bring the legislator and the judge neat bundles of societal facts ready for legal processing. Of course, many of the common facts about a society or some part of it, can be usefully gleaned from non-legal books. The statistics of industry and population are sometimes relevant to judicial,[76] often to legislative problems. The investigation of societal facts by a trained sociologist with some possible and problematic legal changes in view seems on the whole the best method of legal sociology. A good many useful studies of this kind have been made during the past three decades.

The use of societal facts is primarily for the legislature since it is charged with the responsibility of saying what, if anything, should be done about them. Hence legislative committees have wide powers of investigation, and their data and findings are always practically relevant and in the United States are often judicially relevant, to the legislation, if any, that comes out of them. Preambles to statutes often set forth the societal harms which the legislature intends to remedy.

The judicial use of societal facts, apart from what has been said about custom (§ 3.15) and positive morality (§ 3.16) is best exemplified in cases where a court is required to pass upon the constitutional validity of statutes. The leading case is, of course, Muller v. Oregon,[77] in which Louis Brandeis filed a brief containing the opinions of experts and reports of committees as to the effects upon women of long hours of work, and also the statutes of nineteen states, of Great Britain and of several European countries, limiting the hours of labor for women. The court remarked that these citations "may not be, technically speaking, authorities", but

" .   .   .   they are significant of a widespread belief that woman's physical structure, and the functions she performs in consequence thereof, justify special legislation."[78]

---

[76] E. g., Miller v. Schoene, 276 U.S. 272, 48 Sup.Ct. 246 (1928), the "cedar rust" case.

[77] 208 U.S. 412, 28 Sup.Ct. 324 (1908), holding valid an Oregon statute which penalized the employment of women in factories and laundries for more than ten hours a day.

[78] Ibid., 420.

Since then the relevance of similar material with respect to such constitutional questions has seldom been doubted, and it has become a recognized part of the judicial process,[79] though the more recent presumption of constitutionality has rendered its use less important. [80]

The use of facts of common knowledge by courts in the interpretation and application of law is too well known to need extensive comment. In determining whether certain transactions were fraudulent one court said:

> "The inferences to be gathered from a chain of circumstances depend largely upon the common sense knowledge of the motives and intentions of men in like circumstances." [81]

No doubt the assumption of the court as to such "common sense knowledge" might be decisive in a particular case; yet it would not, I think, be a "source of law", but only a premise for an inference of fact to which law attaches certain consequences. Moreover, the influence of what a judge knows or thinks he knows about societal facts is not a "source" of the law which he interprets or remoulds, even though it may influence him emotionally. Not everything that influences judicial decisions is law.

---

[79] See Frankfurter, "Mr. Justice Brandeis and the Constitution" (1931) 45 Harv.L.Rev. 33, 45–48; (1930) 30 Col.L.Rev. 360; supra, n. 76.

[80] See West Coast Hotel Co. v. Parrish, 300 U.S. 379, 57 Sup.Ct. 578 (1936), upholding a Washington statute which authorized prescribing minimum wages for women and minors. Hughes, C. J., stated the social consequences of exploiting workers who have but little bargaining power. On the importance of improved methods of finding societal facts, see Cohen, (Julius), "Towards Realism in Legisprudence", (1950) 59 Yale L.J. 886.

[81] Connolly v. Gishwiller, 162 F.2d 428 (C.C.A.Ill.1947).

Chapter 10

LEGAL SYSTEM AND TERMINOLOGY

§ 3.20—The Uses and Limitations of System in the Law

The law of a modern state is always tending to become systematic and yet it never attains the form of a single perfect logical system. In this Chapter we shall discuss this thesis and the various types of order in the law. First let us note some comments upon the thesis.

The problems of orderly and systematic arrangement are somewhat more acute in a case-law system than in a code system. In 1882 Sir Frederick Pollock, writing on the "science of case-law" said:

> "The state of English case law as a whole might be not unfairly described as chaos tempered by Fisher's Digest".[1]

He argued that English case-law is made and should be made "scientific" by induction from judicial precedents, on the analogy of the inductive natural sciences. He did very little to clarify this time-honored (§ 1.26) analogy.

In 1871 Professor C. C. Langdell, in the preface to the book which inaugurated the case method of legal education, asserted that "the number of fundamental legal doctrines is much less than is commonly supposed" and added:

> "If these doctrines could be so classified and arranged that each should be found in its proper place, and nowhere else, they would cease to be formidable from their number".[2]

His selection and arrangement of cases on the law of contracts was designed to aid

> "all who desire to study that branch of law systematically and in its original sources".[3]

---

[1] Pollock, Essays in Jurisprudence and Ethics (1882), 238. But more recently an English legal author has asserted that English law is no less systematic than Continental (code) law. Lawson, The Rational Strength of English Law (1951).

[2] Langdell, A Selection of Cases on the Law of Contracts (Boston, 1871), vii.

[3] Ibid.

Numerous casebook makers, following in Langdell's footsteps, and going beyond, have furthered the systematic development of American case law.

System-building has been a primary task of philosophers, and a philosopher's work has often been judged by the originality, fruitfulness, comprehensiveness and consistency of its system. Especially logic has been concerned with system-building, since all systemic relations are in some sense logical. Two of the foremost American legal philosophers, representing diverse though rather complementary views, have commented on the systematic character of the law. The late Morris R. Cohen, opposing the "anti-intellectual" tendency of early twentieth century crusaders who denied the value of logic and general principles in law, pointed out that:

> "It is easy enough to refute these new crusaders out of their own mouths, and show that they themselves attach great value to a clear and logically consistent elaboration of the law".[4]

The following quotations state concisely his own position:

> "Like the classical Romans, we utilize . . . that most wonderful discovery, or invention, of the Greeks—rational deductive system. We try to reduce the law to the smallest number of general principles from which all possible cases can be reached, just as we try to reduce our knowledge of nature to a deductive mathematical system. This rational form also gives the law the appearance of complete freedom from arbitrary will and thus satisfies the modern demand for equality in the enforcement of law."

> "The law, of course, never succeeds in becoming a completely deductive system. It does not even succeed in becoming completely consistent. But the effort to assume the form of a deductive system underlies all constructive legal scholarship."[5]

Professor Cohen pointed out that such familiar conceptions of modern law as property, contract and tort were the result of a process of generalization and abstraction from the initial data of scattered decisions and punitive rules.

---

[4] Cohen, "The Place of Logic in the Law", (1916) 29 Harv.L.Rev. 622, 623; Hall, p. 370; Cohen and Cohen, pp. 541–542.

[5] Ibid., 624; Hall, p. 371. See also Lasswell and MacDougal, "Legal Education and Public Policy", (1943) 52 Yale L.J. 203, 235.

Professor John Dewey, contrasting the position of formal logic with that of his instrumental logic, said:

"According to the latter, logical systematization with a view to the utmost generality and consistency of propositions is indispensable but is not ultimate. It is an instrumentality, not an end. It is a means of improving, facilitating, clarifying the inquiry that leads up to concrete decisions; primarily that particular inquiry which has just been engaged in, but secondarily, and of greater ultimate importance, other inquiries directed at making other decisions in similar fields. And here at least I may fall back for confirmation on the special theme of law. It is most important that rules of law should form as coherent generalized logical systems as possible. But these logical systematizations of law in any field, whether of crime, contract or torts, with their reduction of a multitude of decisions to a few general principles that are logically consistent with one another while it may be an end in itself for a particular student, is clearly in last resort subservient to the economical and effective reaching of decisions in particular cases." [6]

While Professor Dewey emphasized the usefulness of system in reaching particular decisions, he also pointed out that "of greater ultimate importance" is the making of a logical system of law for *other* controversies that have not yet arisen. This is the task of the legislator, the appellate court of last resort and the legal scholar.

Reasons for Seeking to Make Law Systematic. The reasons why men strive to make the law systematic are ultimately as inscrutable as the reasons why we reason, but let us try to set down, in the simplest kind of "system", the principal ones:

1. The tendency of the human mind to seek the more inclusive order, to reduce scattered diversity to a simpler order by reducing to a few the number of ideas or propositions needed to identify or control them, seems to be an innate human trait. Possibly it arises from a sense of beauty (but cf. § 1.16) or a desire for power; or maybe it is solely utilitarian. Most of the reasons given for the development of case law (§ 3.12) are applicable here.

2. The utility of more inclusive concepts is that they enable us to answer more concrete questions and with less effort. As

---

[6] Dewey, "Logical Method and Law", (1924) 10 Corn.L.Q. 17, 20; Hall, pp. 345–346.

Professor Cohen said, "it is like fishing with large nets instead of with single lines".[7] Not only that such broad conceptions as property, contract and tort enable us to locate the field of inquiry for the determination of particular controversies, but also that such terms as "primary right" and "remedial right" enable us to proceed logically from one compartment of the law to another.

3. The deliberate creation of legal terms as a set of related meanings facilitates reasoning and especially the communication of reasons as justifications for particular decisions and of generalizations as guides for official and lay conduct. We shall discuss linguistic system in the next section.

4. The striving for logical consistency in the norms of the legal system is a response to the demand for equality of treatment in the administration of justice. As Professor Cohen suggested, this end cannot be perfectly attained merely by making legal rules systematic and consistent, because of the personal element in legal judgment(§ 3.00), yet the results are worth the effort.

5. The partition and limitation of power among officials of various grades and functions is a political requisite of a complex government, and serves to protect both officials and laymen against uncertainty and tyranny. This will be discussed further in § 3.22.

6. The compartmentalization of modern law has increased the efficiency of specialization of function, both of legal norms and of the jurists who use them. Thus admiralty is a special compartment, set apart from the common law because its rules apply to maritime transactions and controversies, and its practitioners are specialists. (See infra, § 3.21).

7. At the mundane level of "finding the law" in a law library the use of "system", or at least orderly arrangement, is exemplified in the table of contents of a code or a set of compiled statutes and in the headings and sub-headings of a working digest of case law. Even though the latter may obligingly list the same legal proposition under several different headings (thus failing to attain Professor Langdell's ideal), still it is developed by some logical scheme of classification.

As Professor Cohen said in the passage quoted above, the law has never succeeded in becoming a perfect system. Not even Justinian's Corpus Juris, nor Napoleon's Code, nor the modern

---

[7] Op. cit., 625; Hall, p. 372.

codes that have greatly improved upon it, are perfect logical systems. The reasons for this do not include the inability of gifted human minds to construct perfect logical systems, for logicians and mathematicians have constructed them. Euclidean geometry is close enough to a perfect logical system to serve as a familiar example. In a perfect logical system the initial assumptions would be axioms, postulates and definitions of terms, from which the theorems of the system could be logically deduced.[8] It is generally agreed that these initial assumptions must be "fruitful" in order to permit the logical development of subordinate propositions. Some genius may develop a perfect logical system for law, but I doubt that it would be workable or that we should want to live under it.

Reasons Why Perfect System Unattainable. The reasons why the law never attains complete rational deductivity and consistency, are without too much procrustean bedding, threefold:

1. *Factual derivation.* A legal system is built from, and logically depends upon, concrete factual phenomena, principally the enactment of statutes in specific language or the adjudication of specific controversies; it does not begin (temporally) with authoritative axioms and definitions. Rather these are constructed, or proposed, as interpretations of the phenomena. The use of the analogy of physical science to explain that the development of case law is "inductive" is at least as old as Pollock's essay.[9] The term may not be accurately used in a logical sense, but it serves to indicate that the process of law-making has not been logically deductive. The more general is dependent upon the less general. The higher generalizations of a legal system are usually not authoritative; they are proposed by legal experts, who differ among themselves. The legal phenomena (statutes and judicial precedents) present various possible interpretations; and they come about through the pressures of human demands and frailties. While the physical scientist must make his theories fit the results of his experiments (else some other scientist may show him up), his very considerable control enables him to avoid equivocal results. Still, the control of legal phenomena (statu-

---

[8] See Cohen and Nagel, An Introduction to Logic and Scientific Method (1936), Ch. VII, especially 133–137. In mathematical systems, the definitions of terms need not be explicit.—I use "perfect logical system" to denote such systems, in order that I may use "system" in the looser sense which is usual in law and jurisprudence.

[9] Supra, n. 1.

tory drafting and the writing of reported judicial opinions) can make the law less chaotic.

2. *Popular terminology.* Unfortunately for the system-builder, legal terminology is continually "corrupted" by intrusions from popular terminology; and the need for communicating the law to laymen, jurors, non-professional legislators and the like, prevents the development of a technical terminology which is necessary for precise system-building.

3. *Social change.* Continuous social change is another reason why the effort to make the law systematic must, like the labor of Sisyphus, continually be done over again as new inventions and new types of human associations, and new ideas about the way to deal with both the old and the new, continually emerge in society. The law, as Holmes said, is always growing at one end and sloughing off at the other.

§ 3.21—Types of Order in the Law

When Benjamin Franklin said at the signing of the Declaration of Independence, "we must all hang together or we shall hang separately", he expressed a simple but inescapable principle of political organization. The signers of the Declaration did not all hang together perfectly, as subsequent events showed; yet they hung together well enough to succeed, with others, in establishing a new political organization. Similarly, a body of law must hang together well enough to minimize contradiction and avoid chaos. Every first-rate legal philosopher, from Plato to Pound, has recognized this need; and a few of them (notably Kant and Hegel) have offered schemes for systematizing the law. Yet for the most part they have confined their efforts to the building of systems of ethics, metaphysics or theology that would serve to explain what the law ought to be.[10] Here we shall attempt the more mundane task of trying to find the types of order in legal systems as they are.

At the outset we must recognize that the law of a modern state, even after centuries of effort to make it rational, is made up of criteria that are arbitrary as well as criteria that are rational. Even the arbitrary elements are in some sense rational, in so far as they represent conventional and useful compromises. Thus the authority of the state and of each of its officials is an ar-

---

10 This is well brought out in Cairns, **Legal Philosophy from Plato to Hegel** (1949).

bitrary element in the legal order and yet it is essential to the attainment in even a moderate degree of the ends of a politically organized society (§ 2.33). On the other hand, any abstract "rational" or functional criterion of law must be ultimately reduced to concrete rules or decisions, which are in some sense arbitrary. Since authority is a pervasive criterion of legal systems, let us pass on to two other types of conventional criteria, the spatial and the temporal, and contrast these with the others, which we shall call "functional".

1. *Spatial Order.* A modern state is a political organization that operates to maintain order within a demarcated territory of the earth's surface (§ 2.32). This is not an indispensable characteristic of a politically organized society, for some have been nomadic. It is an important characteristic of the modern state. Official powers of coercion are with some exceptions, limited to acts done within the state's territory. The exceptions relate chiefly to military and diplomatic officials, and need not concern us here. This limitation on official "jurisdiction" maintains order in preventing clashes between officials of different states. A more significant aspect for the present discussion is the limitation which it places upon the range of operation of a state's legal norms. Here the implications of spatial order became more complex and controversial. The law of State A attaches legal consequences to human acts, and other occurrences, within the territory of State A, and ordinarily does not apply to (i. e., its operative facts do not denote) acts and occurrences in State B.[11] This "ordinary" law is supplemented, for civil or private law at least, by a part of State A's law commonly known as "conflict of laws" or "private international law", which says that courts of State A will with some limitations apply to litigation in State A the law of State B with respect to some of the facts connected with State B that are relevant to such litigation. This extension has long been dominated by the conception of the state's territorial power or jurisdiction, as in choice-of-law rules that the place of making a contract necessarily determined the rules to be applied elsewhere to certain legal problems arising from it; yet the place of making, or of any other act or occurrence, may be less significant than other factors in the total situation with respect to State A's choice of legal criteria. The territorial limitation on official *power* is not directly involved in such a problem; yet it must be admitted that the concept of spa-

---

[11] See Restatement, Conflict of Laws (1934), § 1.

tial order has been a dominant one. The principles that should determine the choice-of-law rules of State A are beyond the scope of this discussion. It need hardly be noted that territorial demarcation often serves to delimit the scope of official power and to mark the scope of operation of legal norms *within* a sovereign state, as in the case of the laws of the several states of the United States. This territorial limitation is, I believe, to be read into every state statute which purports in its language to have universal operation (§ 2.12). A curious example of territorial limitation of law was that which prevailed in Poland after World War II. Five different systems of civil law were in force in different parts of Poland in 1945 and down to the revisions of 1946.[12] Finally, the spatial limitation of the operation of legal norms still competes with another and older one, that of citizenship or nationality. Thus every modern state punishes a few crimes such as treason, committed by its citizens beyond its borders, and a few states, such as Italy, go further.

2. *Temporal Order.* The chief criterion of temporal order in the law is familiar: The newer law supersedes the older in so far, at least,[13] as the two conflict. To this rule there are some apparent exceptions (e. g., the new statute is usually interpreted not to apply to operative facts existing before its enactment) but as far as I know, no real ones. It applies to case law as well as to legislation. The application of the rule is often by no means simple because of the difficulty of determining whether and to what extent, the new law does conflict with the old. In the process of interpretation another temporal criterion often enters, the notion of traditional authority (§ 2.31) or the view that the older laws express the wisdom of past generations and the newer intrusions are to be construed as narrowly as possible. The rule that "statutes in derogation of the common law are to be strictly construed" was partly an expression of this view. The saner aspects of this criterion will be discussed below under "genetic system".

3. *Functional Order.* By this term is meant any type of or-der which is created or maintained so that legal norms may achieve their functions, as conceived in accordance with any

---

12 Judlowski, "Le Nouveau Droit de la Famille en Pologne", (1949) 1 Revue International de Droit Comparé 67, 68. The five were, in origin, French, pre-Soviet Russian, Austrian, German and Hungarian.

13 The interpretation of a new law as a "repeal by implication" may go further.

principles, political, ethical, logical or methodological. The systems discussed below are of this type.

The conception of system is a logical one but the conception of function is not a conception of formal logic. When we consider the efforts of legislators, judges, lawyers and legal scholars to make the law systematic, we need to note the different kinds of system that have been developed. In presenting five types for discussion I have tried to exhibit the principal uses of system in modern law. These are:

1. *Political system: The hierarchy of official authority.* This is represented by the "dynamic system" of Dr. Hans Kelsen's Pure Theory of Law. It will be discussed in the next section.

2. *The hierarchy of logical inclusiveness of legal norms.* This is represented by Roscoe Pound's hierarchy of "legal precepts", and by the recent emphasis on the difference between "rules" and "policies". It will be discussed in later sections ·(§§ 3.23, 3.24, 3.25).

3. *Linguistic system.* Any body of law that is developed by a professional class acquires a specialized terminology and in this sense it becomes a linguistic system. "Right", "duty", "remedy", "property", "contract", "trust" in that system have meanings different from their meanings in other systems, meanings that are peculiar to the legal system. Moreover, these meanings are different from those of everyday speech, which is a loose "system" in the sense that people are able to communicate with each other and to control their activities fairly harmoniously by the use of it. The latter is a system in a "practical and institutional" sense:

> "Its meanings hang together not in virtue of their examined relationship to one another, but because they are current in the same set of group habits and expectations. They hang together because of group activities, group interests, customs and institutions." [14]

"Scientific" language, on the other hand, is subject to another test, that each meaning "is expressly determined by its relation to the other members of the language system".[15] The language is constructed to serve the purpose of reasoned discourse. Its terms constitute a set of logically related meanings. In this the law is a "scientific" language system.

---

[14] Dewey, Logic: The Theory of Inquiry (1938), 50.

[15] Ibid.

That modern systems of law employ "technical" terms hardly needs to be said. Many of these terms are created for, and function as bearers of meaning only in, a legal system. Examples are "tort", "contingent remainder", "fee simple", "quasi contract", "easement", "constructive condition", to name only a few. They have no meanings in popular language or in any other language system. In the legal system to which they belong they have meanings that imply legal consequences, mediate or intermediate (§ 2.22). That is, to say that a particular situation constitutes a "tort" is to say that a number of remedial consequences follow [16] and eventually these terminate in official action. To avoid misunderstanding, let me say that it is not assumed here that either the denotations of such technical terms (the factual situations to which they refer) or the legal consequences which follow are always clear or pre-determined for "discovery" by lawyers or judges.

Among the conclusions that may be drawn from the systemic character of legal language, two may be mentioned here. While State A's legal system is always distinct from State B's, yet because of a common historical origin of the two systems the technical terms in State A's system may have meanings so nearly the same as those of the same symbols in State B's system that the judiciary of either State may properly resort to the other's meanings for guidance. This partly explains why the law of cognate systems is persuasive authority (§ 3.13) and perhaps why the statutes of another state are not regarded as persuasive. Secondly, the attempt made by Austin to discover the "fundamental conceptions" of all mature legal systems [17] could succeed only if confined to cognate systems; even if extended to Roman law systems, it ran the risk of inaccuracy.

What is often overlooked is that every legal term, as a *legal* term and therefore as a member of a legal language system, has meanings which imply legal consequences in that system. A great many traditional legal terms are symbolically identical with terms of popular language, of morality or ethics. Examples are "malice", "intent", "right", "duty", "conversion", "offer", to mention only a few. The first part of Holmes' now fa-

---

[16] I. e., not only as to the criteria of a "cause of action" but also as to defenses, e. g., what statute of limitation applies.

[17] Austin, Jurisprudence (3d ed., 1869), vol. 2, pp. 1107–1108; Hall, pp. 335–336. Austin spoke of "principles" but he apparently meant such general concepts as "right", "duty" and the like.

mous and controversial address to law students, "The Path of the Law", was devoted to warning his hearers that such legal terms as "duty" and "malice" must not be confused with their symbolic twins in morals or popular language; in order to dramatize this contrast he introduced the highly controversial metaphor of the "bad man".[18]   When Professor Wesley N. Hohfeld began years ago his admirable effort to clarify legal terminology, he insisted upon the difference between "property" in the popular sense, as denoting a physical object, and property in the legal sense, as connoting a set of legal relations.[19]   Similarly, Hohfeld, and after him Professor Corbin, reduced "right" and "duty" to definite legal meanings in terms of legal consequences,[20] i. e., actions for redress and defenses.   The effort to increase the technical precision of legal terms is a worthy effort of constructive legal scholarship; and while such effort should have other worthy objectives, such as the introduction of new legal norms (or, what is logically the same, of new meanings of old ones) into a legal system, its job is only half done if it does not indicate the meanings of its terms in the legal system.

That many legal terms are grossly ambiguous is for lawyers a trite observation.   The term "conversion" means usurpation of ownership of a chattel in the law of torts (or of chattels), and something quite different in the law of "equitable conversion". This instance of symbolic duplicity does not cause confusion because the legal propositions in which the term functions have different realms of operation.   "Consideration" has different meanings in relation to promises (contracts) and grants, as indicated by the terms "good consideration" and "valuable consideration".   The qualifiers are meaningless when taken out of context, since some "good" considerations (love and affection) may be more valuable than many "valuable" considerations.   Even symbols of popular speech newly taken over into the law, acquire meanings implying legal consequences and in different contexts may have different meanings.   The term "employee" as used in statutes designed for the protection and welfare of workers is an example.   Women who did piece work at home for compensation by a company which supplied the materials and received

---

[18] (1897) 10 Harv.L.Rev. 457, 459–462.

[19] Hohfeld, "Fundamental Legal Conceptions as Applied in Judicial Reasoning", (1913) 23 Yale L.J. 16, 19–22.

[20] Corbin, "Legal Analysis and Terminology", (1919) 29 Yale L.J. 163; Hall, pp. 471–484.

the product were held to be "employees" within the meaning of the federal Fair Labor Standards Act [21] but not under the Social Security Act.[22] The meaning of "employee" in the California Labor Code was held not conclusive as to its meaning in a group life insurance policy.[23] Such examples warn the lawyer (if he needs any warning) that legal terms do not have fixed meanings; and they warn statutory draftsmen to define in the statute its crucial and pervasive terms.

The conception of linguistic system here set forth raises two important yet difficult problems in legal method. One arises from the contextual theory of meaning, already referred to (§ 1.12). This conception has been stated by Professor Dewey as follows:

"Any word or phrase has the meaning which it has only in relation to the code of which it is one constituent." [24]

What is this "code" and how far does it extend? By narrowing legal contexts one could reduce the meaning of a legal term to its meaning in the context of a particular litigation, and it would have no meaning for any other law suit. This reductio ad absurdum of the contextual theory does not destroy it; it merely shows that sagacity in interpretation must be used to determine what legal meaning is the appropriate one in a given legal context. The other problem is that legal terms must have meanings that are ultimately (and often immediately) translatable into (or transferable from) popular terminology. The lay witnesses who recount facts cannot classify them under or translate them into legal terms; the rule against "opinion" evidence could probably be invoked against them if they tried to. The jurors who determine "questions of fact" in litigation need to be instructed as to the legal criteria of such facts. The law is dependent upon inexpert casual observers for most of its facts; it needs to be, in part, understandable by laymen who want to use it (§ 3.03); and unlike natural science it needs to be responsive in some ways to the changing mores of the society which it serves. The relation between legal terminology and popular terminology is thus a recurrent problem. (§ 3.27).

---

[21] Walling v. American Needlecrafts, Inc., 139 F.2d 60 (C.C.A.6 1943). The differences in wording of the two statutes do not seem material.

[22] Glenn, Collector v. Beard, 141 F.2d 376 (C.C.A.6 1944).

[23] John Hancock Mut. Life Ins. Co. v. Dorman, 108 F.2d 220 (C.C.A.9 1940).

[24] Dewey, op. cit., 49. Elsewhere he refers to a "constellation of meanings".

4. *Genetic System.* By "genetic system" is meant any constellation of legal meanings which cluster around a certain historical core, or which have resulted from a certain historical development, usually though not necessarily with the assumption that the older legal rules or principles have superior authority ("traditional authority", § 2.31) or persuasiveness. This last is, I think, what Professor Langdell had in mind when he said, in the preface to his path-breaking casebook on Contracts that

> "the cases which are useful and necessary for this purpose [mastering the doctrine effectually] at the present day bear an exceedingly small proportion to all that have been reported. The vast majority are useless and worse than useless for any purpose of systematic study." [25]

His selections of cases show the main lines of development of the principal doctrines of the English law of contracts during the preceding three centuries, with some additional American cases. Many early law school casebooks were constructed on the genetic plan. At about the same time in Germany legal scholars were arduously exploring the meanings of Roman law texts more than a thousand years old. A more recent example was the scholarly effort to show that the doctrine of consideration derived its meaning from the action of debt or the action of assumpsit, or both. The present meaning(s) of "consideration" can scarcely be understood without reference to its historical uses and contexts; and the doctrine of consideration is a small genetic system of rules. The Anglo-American common law has a good many such nests of genetic system.

Cardozo sensed the difference between the *necessity* of seeking and heeding the historical development of common law doctrines and the *duty* to follow them when he distinguished the "line of historical development" which he called the "method of evolution", from "the line of the customs of the community" which he called "the method of tradition".[26] The former he took to mean that the judge must accept, sometimes with resignation, that some conceptions and doctrines of the law are historical growths.

> "No law-giver meditating a code of laws conceived the system of feudal tenures." [27]

---

[25] Langdell, op. cit., supra, § 3.20, n. 2.

[26] Cardozo, The Nature of the Judicial Process (1921), 30–31. See infra, § 4.62; Patterson, Cardozo's "Philosophy of Law", (1939) 88 U. of Pa.L.Rev. 156, 161, 163.

[27] Cardozo, op. cit., 54.

The necessity of resorting to the genetic meanings of legal terms and propositions is, in substance, the same as the necessity of resorting to usage for the understanding of language. Even a statute that purports to modify or reform some traditional body of law calls for a reference to that which it modifies, in order to understand the scope of the new provisions. Moreover, genetic systems have some of the values of certainty and stability that are among the desirable ends of the law. The disadvantages of genetic system are that it hinders the development of law along rational and functional lines. One example of a genetic system in Anglo-American law is the body of legal doctrines called "equity", meaning the powers and norms of the English Court of Chancery (primarily) and its successors in America. The new federal Rules of Civil Procedure were carefully designed to avoid reference to "equity". Breaking with the past is usually a difficult but often a necessary task.

5. *Classification and Compartmentalization.* Classification is, strictly speaking, the grouping of individuals into classes,[28] but we shall use it here to include also the division of a genus into species, or of a class into sub-classes. A classification is supposed to be based upon some logical principle, some fundamentum divisionis and so the alphabetical order of names in a telephone book or of titles in a law digest, is not a classification but an "arrangement".[29] A logical classification is a step in the formation of an hypothesis or an inference, that is, it tells us something about the things classified. Numerous "classifications" of a body of law have been proposed but no one thus far adopted, as far as I know, conforms strictly to the logical requirements of classification. Most of them, according to Pound, are based on "the schemes of arrangement worked out to organize and systematize the modern Roman law".[30] That is, no single criterion explains the various classes. Thus the divisions of the German Civil Code, worked out over a period of more than twenty years, are:

    I.   General Principles
    II.   Obligations
    III.   Things

---

28 See Cohen and Nagel, An Introduction to Logic and Scientific Method (1934) 241.

29 Kocourek, Classification of the Law, (1934) 11 N.Y.U.L.Q.Rev. 319, 322; Hall, p. 615.

30 Pound, "Classification of Law", (1924) 37 Harv.L.Rev. 933, 949. Both this article and Professor Kocourek's give many examples of classification.

IV.   Family

V.   Succession.[31]

Certainly the law of succession might include parts of the law of things (property) and vice versa. Another example of "classification" in law illustrates the difficulty: Obligations are divided into contract, tort and quasi-contract. The first two are distinguishable on some criterion or principle, but the third is merely a catch-all, invented by Roman jurists, and used in Anglo-American law to include the duties of public officials as well as the duty to make restitution for unjust enrichment. It seems, then, that legal classifications are partly "logical" classifications and partly convenient arrangements.

Within various major "classes" of legal rules the process of systematization goes on. Thus the Restatement of Law has not purported to discuss the whole of American law but has stated in an orderly and systematic way the rules, definitions and principles of large compartments: Contracts, Torts, Property, Restitution, Conflict of Laws, etc. This compartmentalization makes a part of the law take on a systematic character.[32] Moreover, compartmentalization applies to larger bodies of rules. Thus in European code systems there are often a Civil Code, a Penal or Criminal Code, a Code of Civil Procedure, one of Criminal Procedure, a Commercial Code, and sometimes also special codes, such as Patent Law. Compartmentalization provides a means of stating rules having a common subject matter with conciseness and economy of effort. In some compartments, such as Real Property and Conflict of Laws, which the layman has little or no occasion to use without consulting a lawyer, the choice of unique symbols, as in the natural sciences, permits more effective control over legal reasoning, and its specialists may develop a high degree of certainty in that part of the law. But compartmentalization has its dangers, too. Aside from those mentioned above as arising from the conception of a technical linguistic system, there is the danger that specialists will overlook the common ends of law as a whole, in their zeal to make a part of it systematic.

---

31 Kocourek, op. cit., 327; Hall, p. 620.

32 I. e., the definitions of terms, the statements qualified by specified exceptions, and the effort to use a term with a consistent meaning in all contexts.

§ 3.22—The Hierarchy of Official Authority: Kelsen

Since every state has a considerable number of officials (including in that term, official bodies), it needs to have and typically does have a mode of determining the kind and extent of their authority. This leads practically to the institution of a set of relations of super-ordination and subordination between officials. In so far as these relations are determined or controllable by law, these relations constitute a hierarchy of legal authority. Among the purposes which this legal delimitation of official authority serves are the efficiency of the government in achieving its affirmative ends, the protection of subordinate officials against the tyranny of superiors, and above all the protection of the citizen against arbitrary or tyrannical official acts. This much, at least, is familiar to lawyers and need not be elaborated. The legal norms conferring authority on officials are ordinarily accompanied by norms imposing official duties upon them and by norms which confer privileges or immunities in the discharge of their official duties, such as the privilege of an officer to use reasonable force in making an arrest or the privilege of a judge to make honest errors in his decisions. The relations between officials as such are primarily relations of legal power. Some of these officials have power to make law, to create legal norms. Within the system of legal power one can, or is supposed to be able to, determine whether or not a particular official (or body) had power to create a particular norm, and thus one can determine the legal validity (§ 2.31) of that norm. Thus the legal validity of a norm can be traced to higher norms, except that eventually one comes to a norm or body of norms which are the constitution of the state. Assuming that this constitution has political authority, all of its norms and all subordinate norms created pursuant to it have legal validity.

An illustration of the meaning of this hierarchy is presented in a recent Supreme Court decision. The insurance commissioner of South Carolina ordered a New Jersey insurance company to pay a tax on its insurance premiums from business done in South Carolina, which was computed at a rate higher than the rate of taxation of similar premiums of South Carolina corporations. A South Carolina statute clearly gave or purported to give the commissioner power to make this order. The New Jersey corporation by appropriate proceedings challenged the validity of the South Carolina statute. The Supreme Court, pursuant to the commerce clause of the federal constitution, had consistently held that a state could not impose discriminatory tax burdens on interstate commerce; and it had more recently held that the doing of an insurance business across state lines fell within the power of Congress to regulate interstate commerce. However, a more recent Congressional statute had purported to confer power on the states to regulate (with some exceptions) and tax an interstate insurance business. The authority of Congress to confer a power of discriminatory taxation on the states depended upon the interpretation of the federal constitution. The Supreme Court held that Congress had such power, and therefore upheld the action of the South Carolina official.[33] The latter's power was thus traced back to the federal constitution.

The hierarchy of official power to create legal norms enables one to determine the validity of all legislation (legislative law) under the federal constitution. The validity of subordinate legislation of federal administrative tribunals is dependent upon the power conferred by a federal statute, the validity of which is in turn dependent upon the power conferred on the federal legislature by the federal constitution. The hierarchy of official power applies (in a somewhat different way) to case law. The law laid down by the federal Supreme Court within the scope of the power conferred upon it is superior to that of any other court. The hierarchy of case law, from courts of last resort to intermediate courts, is familiar and need not be elaborated. As between valid legislation and case law, the former is superior.

This account of the political system in American law is based upon, and is partly a paraphrase of, the theory of norms developed by Dr. Hans Kelsen in his Pure Theory of Law.[34] Dr. Kelsen was for many years a distinguished professor of law at Coblenz and Vienna, and he was the principal draughtsman of the Austrian Constitution of 1920. His theory of law has won many followers in European countries and in other parts of the world. It includes more than the part here referred to. He sought to distinguish law from certain other things which were continually being confused with it, such as theories of justice or ethics, and the regularities of behavior in society or the social effects of law,

---

[33] Prudential Ins. Co. v. Benjamin, 328 U.S. 408, 66 Sup.Ct. 1142 (1946).

[34] A short account is given in Kelsen, "The Pure Theory of Law", (1934) 50 L.Q.Rev. 454, Hall, p. 425 and (1935) 51 L.Q.Rev. 517, Hall, p. 653 (trans. by H. W. Wilson). A fuller and more recent account is in Kelsen, General Theory of Law and State (trans. Wedberg, 1945), in which, however, he uses the term Pure Theory of Law in the Preface but apparently not elsewhere. See Patterson, "Hans Kelsen and His Pure Theory of Law", (1952) 40 Calif.L. Rev. 5–10.

legal sociology. Both of these he called "meta-juristic". He thus adopts an imperative conception of law (§ 2.04). He partially based his theory upon Kantian philosophy, notably Kant's epistemology. Although this does not seem to be an essential part of his theory,[35] it has affected his terminology, e. g., his use of "act of will".

Kelsen's theory has added several important ideas to those of English analytical jurisprudence. Austin in his endeavor to trace all law to the sovereign was confronted with the fact that most of the English law of his day was common law created by the courts. He explained this by saying that subordinate law-making bodies or officials are "reservoirs" fed from the fountain-head of sovereignty.[36] Kelsen's analysis explains this relation schematically better, in that the courts have power to create as well as to apply law,[37] though one would still have some difficulty in applying it to English or American case law. A second contribution of Kelsen's theory was that it added to the traditional conception of a law as "a rule of human conduct" the conception of a law as conferring power to create legal norms. This clarifies the function of the constitution, and of many statutes, in the legal system. A third contribution of Kelsen's theory is his view that the difference between the law-creating function and the law-applying function is merely a relative one. Since the power of an official to create law is always based upon a legal norm, every law-creating act of the official is an application of the power norm.

"Creation of law is always application of law".[38]

This leads him to the conclusion that the judgment of a court is an "individual norm" for the parties to the suit, a view criticized above (§ 2.34). Kelsen rejects the Austinian view that a law (legal norm) must be a *general* rule. Perhaps Kelsen's contribution to positive legal theory can be best summarized by saying that he treats the law of a state as a dynamic rather than a static system, that he explains the relation between the "being" and the "becoming" of law.

---

35 See Wilk, "Law and the State as Pure Ideas", (1941) 51 Intern.J.Ethics 158.

36 2 Austin, Jurisprudence (4th ed., 1873), 526. For a criticism, see Allen, Law in the Making (1935), 3–6.

37 Austin, too, recognized that judicial legislation is an oblique mode of creating law. Op. cit., 548–9.

38 General Theory of Law and State (1945), 133.

Kelsen's theory of law has, however, been generally unacceptable to English legal scholars,[39] despite its similarity to the Austinian positivism which was commonly prevalent in England. In part this is due to Kelsen's effort to squeeze the last drop of history, sociology and axiology out of the law and make it a "pure" power system. In his effort to clarify and schematize the legal system, he has left out a good many important difficulties even of analytical jurisprudence. The following comments will present some of the deficiencies of his system, as I see them.

1. *The "Basic Norm"*. Kelsen was not content to stop with the constitution of the state as the highest body of authoritative norms. He asked, why is the constitution valid? Perhaps this may lead us back to an earlier constitution, which authorized a revision and was superseded by it. Eventually we come to a constitution that cannot be derived from an earlier one. The validity of this ultimate constitution, he says, *presupposes* a "basic norm" which vested law-creating powers in the body that adopted it.

> "It is postulated that one ought to behave as the individual, or the individuals, who laid down the first constitution have ordained." [40]

The basic norm is not itself a positive legal norm because it was not created by an official body empowered to create it. It is a necessary presupposition of our believing in the validity of the entire body of positive legal norms created pursuant to the constitution. Kelsen insists that it is not a "natural law" concept; it is not a general principle, such as, "it is best to obey the authorities in power, whoever they are." It is a norm which enjoins obedience to a particular constitution. Hence if a revolution occurs and a new constitution is adopted, a new basic norm is presupposed.[41]

Now the assumption that the constitution is valid and that laws created pursuant to it are valid, is one which lawyers and judges make in their everyday work. But this assumption depends ultimately upon the political authority not only of the officials who created the constitution but also of those who maintain and uphold that constitution at the present time. This is something outside the constitution or the norms created pursuant to it. The

---

[39] See Jones, Historical Introduction to the Theory of Law (1940), 222 ff.; Allen, Law in the Making (1935), 45–58; Paton, Jurisprudence (1946), 10–15; Stone, The Province and Function of Law (1946), 91 ff.

[40] General Theory, 115.

[41] Ibid.

political authority of a legal system (§ 2.31) cannot be determined merely by working in a law library or even by making presuppositions about the written constitution that one finds there. Moreover, the political authority of the legal system is not, except by extraordinarily reverent persons, regarded as derived exclusively from the acts of the "founding fathers" who adopted the constitution; it depends also upon the present political situation. On the whole, if one must have a simple explanation of what makes a paper power-scheme be or become a working power-scheme, the "habit of obedience" of Austin and Bentham seems better than the basic norm.

2. *Static and Dynamic Systems of Norms.* Kelsen contrasts a system of morality, which he conceives of as a "static" system, with a legal system, which he regards as a "dynamic system". The former, he says, is derived from a basic moral norm, such as "one should live in harmony with the universe", "by means of an intellectual operation, viz., by inference from the general to the particular". Legal norms "have to be created through acts of will by those individuals who have been authorized to create norms by some higher norm".[42] Now it is true that the power system outlined above is not in the form of a logical system, such as Euclid's geometry, and Kelsen has shown us a kind of legal order that is not dependent upon axioms of natural law or morality or political theory. Yet the creation and application of law involve *both* intellectual operations (e. g., interpreting higher norms) and "acts of will" (e. g., enactments or judgments). Kelsen has at this point overemphasized the creative and arbitrary element in official acts. However, he recognizes that the higher norm may function in two ways:

"As pointed out, the creation of a legal norm can be determined in two different directions: the higher norm may determine: (1) the organ and the procedure by which a lower norm is to be created, and (2) the contents of the lower norm. Even if the higher norm determines only the organ, and that means the individual [or body] by which the lower norm has to be created, and that again means authorizes this organ to determine at its own discretion the procedure of creating the lower norm and the contents of this norm, the higher norm is 'applied' in the creation of the lower norm".[43]

---

[42] Ibid., 112–113.

[43] Ibid., 133.

We shall come back to this passage when we discuss his conception of a "definite rule" (infra, this section).

3. *Subordination and Not Co-ordination.* Kelsen's conception of the hierarchy of legal norms is by its terms one of superordination and subordination, and he excludes the conception of co-ordination, that is, of governmental organs having powers on the same level to create legal norms with respect to different subject matters:

> "The legal order, especially the legal order the personification of which is the state, is therefore not a system of norms coordinated to each other, standing, so to speak, side by side on the same level, but a hierarchy of different levels of norms".[44]

On the contrary, the legal order of a modern state is based upon co-ordination as well as subordination. Kelsen needlessly tries to show that his power system is the only kind of order in the law. By the distribution of functions different bodies are given power to create legal norms with respect to different subject matters. Thus the norms of the Interstate Commerce Commission and the Federal Communications Commission are co-ordinate; if the two should ever conflict, the conflict would be resolved by determining the appropriate subject matter of each, or by the temporal order (§ 3.21) of enactment of the statutes conferring power, rather than by deciding which organ is "superior" to the other. Again, many co-ordinate law-making organs have powers territorially limited; the state governments in the United States are co-ordinate in this way (§ 3.21). This does not deny the value of Kelsen's theory as showing one kind of order in the law.

4. *"A Definite Rule".* One further over-simplification of Kelsen's theory needs to be mentioned. He says:

> "A norm is a valid legal norm by virtue of the fact that it has been created according to *a definite rule* and by virtue thereof only".[45]

The exaggeration consists in the assertion that there is *one* rule which authorizes the creation of law and that it is definite, i. e., clear as to the power conferred. One example might be the provision of the New York state constitution with respect to the principal legislative organ:

---

44 Ibid., 124.

45 Ibid., 113; emphasis added.

"The legislative power of this state shall be vested in the Senate and Assembly".[46]

This provision designates the law-creating organ, and that, in Kelsen's theory, is sufficient to make it a superior legal norm.[47] Yet Kelsen assumes that if no directions are given, the organ has power to determine "at its own discretion" the contents of the lower norm.[48] This is, of course, not so, because the legislature of New York is limited in its law-creating powers by many provisions of the Federal constitution, by historic concepts of what is legislative power, and by numerous other provisions in the New York constitution, such as the Bill of Rights (Art. I). If it be argued that these are merely "negative" limitations, it is still true that the law-creating power of the legislature is not wholly discretionary and is not determined by a single definite rule. If one turns to the norm-creating powers of courts, it is no less difficult to find "a definite rule". The New York constitution provides, with respect to the highest court of the state:

"The jurisdiction of the court of appeals shall be limited to questions of law except . . ."[49]

The corresponding provision of the Federal constitution, as to its highest court, is somewhat more definite, yet its meaning is still a matter of controversy between able lawyers.[50] If Kelsen's statement means merely that the legal validity of every official act should be traceable to at least one provision of the constitution, it has some merit, even though, unfortunately, the validity of an official act cannot usually, if ever, be determined by consulting only one "definite rule". Even though it is over-simplified, Kelsen's theory gives an analysis that is useful, for the reasons above mentioned, of one kind of order in the law of a modern state.

§ 3.23—The Hierarchy of Inclusiveness of Norms: Pound

The reasons why the law of a modern state tends to become systematic and the reasons why it never succeeds in doing so have been presented above (§ 3.20). We now venture to submit

---

[46] N. Y. Constitution (1938), Art. III, § 1. (McKinney's N. Y. Consolidated Laws Anno., 1949, vol. 2).

[47] Supra, n. 43.

[48] Ibid.

[49] Supra, n. 46, Art. VI, § 4 (as amended to take effect in 1944).

[50] See Roberts (Owen J.) in (1949) 35 A.B.A.J. 1 and Grinnell in (1949) 35 Ibid. 648.

three minimum requirements of a logical system that are commonly (though not indisputably) recognized by lawyers and judges in using the law. These are:

1. Two legal propositions of the same integrated political order [51] must not be permitted to contradict each other.

2. An apparent contradiction between two legal propositions can be eliminated by finding (or creating) some proposition(s) of greater inclusiveness that will serve to delimit one or both of the two so that they do not contradict each other.

3. Every judicial decision is (or can be) logically grounded on one or more legal norms.

The first of these statements is, I believe, the least questionable since contradictory guides would be worse than none at all. The recurring efforts of advocates in their arguments and of courts in their opinions to "reconcile" or "distinguish" judicial precedents are evidences in support of this statement. The second statement is more debatable since the reasons why a rule or a precedent is limited so as to reconcile it with another one are often not stated in a court's opinion. That is, judicial precedents are often said to be "distinguishable on their facts", without specifying what facts; or the distinguishing fact or facts are pointed out but without any indication as to the significance of those facts in terms of a higher (more inclusive) generalization or a delimitation of the rule of the precedent case.[52] In such a case, it is arguable, the judge who wrote the opinion and the others who concurred did not "have in mind" *any one* general principle which would serve to justify the distinguishing of the precedent case, and this may well be true. The distinction may be felt but not perceived. Nevertheless a court in a later case (or another interpreter) may properly explain the distinguishing in terms of an explicit generalization. In that situation several distinguishing principles may appear to be equally available. This kind of distinguishing, by the statement of alternative principles of distinction, is also fairly common in judicial opinions because judges are aware that their opinions are relied upon and do not wish to

---

51 I. e., a state or jurisdiction.

52 In some cases the court does both. Cf. Rolfe v. Hewitt, 227 N.Y. 486, 494, 125 N.E. 804, 806 (1920), where McLaughlin, J., said: "A judicial opinion, like a judgment, must be read as applicable only to the facts involved and is an authority only for what is actually decided." This extreme statement was needless (since the earlier case was adequately distinguished) and misleading.

commit themselves to a particular formula for the future. Nevertheless the statement above made is, I believe, an assumption widely held and used. It is subject to one apparent exception, that a court having power to do so may overrule one of the two contradictory precedents; yet even this implies that some superior principle justifies the overruling; and ordinarily this principle is treated by the judge as if it were already imminent in the legal system.

The third statement above made is highly controversial. It is the assumption that the law is a *complete* system with no logical "gaps" and that there are no "unprovided cases". In support of this view it may be pointed out that courts, when confronted with a novel claim for which there are no precedents either way, sometimes resort to a general principle of legislation or case law to support a decision allowing the claim, as in the case of the minor's suit for the defendant's seduction of his father; [53] and that an accumulated body of law contains a good many such generalizations. Ancient maxims such as "so use your own as not to harm another" (sic utere tuo ut alienum non laedas) have received authoritative recognition, though somewhat uncertain, in Anglo-American and Western European legal systems, and they provide at least a formal logical ground for the recognition of many new claims as legal rights. The aggregate of such generalizations may possibly be adequate to support formally recognition of any and all novel claims. The arguments against the third position are, briefly, twofold: First, that such vague generalizations as the one mentioned above are inadequate in meaning to guide a genuine reasoning process; and secondly, that there is always an alternative (at least one) ground for the *rejection* of a novel claim, namely, that the claimant has not sustained the procedural burden of producing facts and law adequate to move the tribunal to favorable action.[54] Yet this procedural rule is a part of the legal norms available for use. The first objection raises an important semantic difficulty inherent in the use of generalizations of a high level of abstraction, that any effort to justify concrete decisions on particular cases by the use of such abstractions is likely to seem (and may be) purely formal and ceremonial. The answer is that judges (and others who professionally use the law) should

---

[53] Supra, § 3.16, n. 51.

[54] As in Pyle v. Waechter, 202 Iowa 695, 210 N.W. 926 (1926) (mother denied right to recover damages from one who had alienated affections of minor son).

(and commonly do) seek to find generalizations in the legal system that are genuinely persuasive (as well as formally adequate). However, for the present discussion it is not necessary to assume that this search will always be successful. It is enough that it is made and should be made.

The three assumptions above stated, or even the first two, will serve to explain the recognition of a hierarchy of logical inclusiveness in the Anglo-American legal systems, which may appear to be made up of narrow and concrete precedents and narrow and concrete statutes. So it often appears to continental European jurists, whose codes provide them with broad, vague principles [55] as authoritative "starting points of legal reasoning"; and so it often appears to English judges, who continue to display a traditional distrust of "principles" and "policies" as reasons for their decisions. Dean Roscoe Pound, in an address before the International Congress on Comparative Law in 1932, presented a hierarchy of "legal precepts" in modern systems of law which included five types: Rules, principles, conceptions, doctrines and standards.[56] He had previously discussed three of these: Rules, principles and standards.[57] The five listed above may be explained as follows:

1. *Rules,* according to Pound, are "precepts attaching a definite detailed legal consequence to a definite detailed state of facts".[58] They were the staple of ancient codes. He takes an example from the ancient Roman law: "If the father sell the son [into slavery] three times, let the son be free from the father".[59] Even here, it may be pointed out, the rule is unintelligible out of context: one needs to understand what "sell into slavery" meant in ancient Roman law, and that "free from the father" meant the ending of the father's rights as a paterfamilias in Roman law. *In this context,* the Roman precept conforms to Pound's definition. Other common examples are found in the "tariff of compositions", rules prescribing the amount to be paid by a man or his kinsmen for doing certain kinds of legal injuries to another; these provisions were found in the ancient Code of Hammurabi, the law

[55] See citations supra, § 3.16, nn. 56, 57; Dawson, "Economic Duress and the Fair Exchange in French and German Law", (1937) 12 Tul.L.Rev. 42, 73.

[56] Pound, "Hierarchy of Sources and Forms in Different Systems of Law", (1933) 7 Tul.L.Rev. 475, 482–486; Hall, 661.

[57] Pound, An Introduction to the Philosophy of Law (1921), Ch. IV, 115–120.

[58] Pound, op. cit., supra, n. 56, 482; Hall, 661.

[59] Ibid.

of the Salic Franks and in some Anglo-Saxon laws.[60] They were designed to buy off private vengeance by providing a judicial mode of obtaining reparation, and their exactness was designed to eliminate discretion in applying them. Their narrow and episodic character may also be due to the law-makers' ignorance of logical tools for attaining a greater degree of generality.[61] While most of them were limited to intentional injuries, some prescribed rules for unintentional injuries:

"If at their common work [of wood-cutting] one man slay another unwilfully, let the tree [which fell upon the deceased] be given to the kindred [of the deceased]." [62]

A rule which limits liability for unintentional injuries to cases of woodcutting seems episodic and arbitrary; modern law has substituted broader rules of liability for negligent injuries, or for the typical consequences of potentially dangerous machinery and processes.[63]

Pound finds further illustrations of rules in the modern law of property, in commercial law and in criminal law; of them he says:

"They fix the mode of entering into the more common and significant business transactions. For example, they determine how negotiable instruments should be drawn to have certain detailed and determinate effects." [64]

The negotiable instruments law is a good example of the difference between the rules of ancient codes and modern rules. The rules as to negotiability prescribe the characteristics, such as "unconditional order or promise to pay money", "payable to order or to bearer", which an instrument must have in order that the consequences of "negotiability" shall follow; but those consequences are stated elsewhere in related rules, such as those prescribing the liabilities of endorsers and other transferors and those stating the defenses available against a holder in due course. Thus modern legal rules, while they have much broader scope than ancient ones, gain precision in meaning through being a part of a system of inter-related rules. In the same way rules of case

---

[60] For collections of these ancient laws, see Kocourek and Wigmore, Sources of Ancient and Primitive Law (1915).

[61] See Professor Morris Cohen's statement, supra, § 3.20, n. 5.

[62] Quoted from the Laws of Alfred by Salmond, Jurisprudence (7th ed., 1924), 431. Such a rule probably originated in an arbitral decision.

[63] See Ehrenzweig, Negligence without Fault (1951).

[64] Pound, op. cit., supra, n. 56, 482; Hall, 661.

law, while not capable of formulation in fixed language, gain precision in meaning through the systemic relations of precedents in the same jurisdiction. Despite the recent tendency to disdain rules as archaic and arbitrary, they serve many of the important ends for which certain parts of the legal system are maintained. As Pound says, "they are the bone and sinew of the legal order".[65]

2. *Principles* are, according to Pound, "authoritative starting points for legal reasoning, employed continually and legitimately where cases are covered or are not fully or obviously covered by rules in the narrower sense".[66] Pound thus expresses the Anglo-American judicial tradition that principles are to be resorted to where rules fail to provide a satisfactory answer. They fill in the gaps left by rules. They are also used in choosing between competing analogies or rules. Besides these uses, principles serve to explain and to extend rules. However, chronologically, rules usually come before principles. Thus many of the rules as to quasi-contractual recovery were established before the principle of unjust enrichment was used by Lord Mansfield to justify them and to cover cases not provided for by them.[67] Other examples of principles, given by Pound, are the principle of tort law that liability is based upon fault, and the principle of courts of equity that as between two persons equally innocent, one of whom must lose, the court will not interfere. Pound adds that principles often conflict, and that the conflict must be resolved by resorting to what he calls the "received ideals" of the legal order, that is, to a higher set of principles. Principles do not refer to detailed states of fact nor do they prescribe definite legal consequences. Their vagueness would make them useless as "authoritative starting points" of legal reasoning were it not that they are anchored in compartmental (§ 3.21) legal contexts, as in the three illustrations given above. Pound omits another characteristic of principles that I think important, namely, that they have a self-evident appeal to one's moral or ethical feelings (§ 3.24).

3. *Conceptions,* according to Pound, are "authoritative categories to which types or classes of transactions, cases or situations are referred, in consequence of which a series of rules, principles and standards become applicable. They are chiefly the work of law teachers and law writers." [68] Pound gives no illustra-

---

65 Ibid., 483; Hall, 662.

66 Ibid.

67 See Jackson, The History of Quasi Contract in English Law (1936).

68 Pound, op. cit., supra, n. 56, 484; Hall, 663.

tions but one can guess that he means such legal categories as "sale", "bailment", "negotiable instrument" which serve to define compartments, sub-systems in a body of law (§ 3.21). They are not *merely* labels, since the meaning of the conception implies a good many of the subsidiary rules. Thus "sale" implies "warranty" (unless negatived—such rules are not compulsory) and "bailment" implies some care by the bailee. Let me add to Pound's discussion that such a category can be a dubious tool when taken as *exclusive;* e. g., when "not a sale" means "no warranty", as in some of the earlier cases denying that restaurant proprietors were liable to their customers for nonnegligently serving injurious substances as food, because serving food was not a "sale."

4. *Doctrines,* according to Pound, "are systematic fittings together of rules, principles, standards and conceptions with respect to particular situations or types of cases or fields of the legal order, in logically interdependent schemes, whereby reasoning may proceed on the basis of the scheme and its logical implications".[69] He then refers to "doctrinal writings", the treatises of such eminent legal experts as Coke, Pothier, Savigny and Story. As no illustration of a "doctrine" is given, one may conjecture that it includes such examples as "the doctrine of consideration", "the doctrine of respondeat superior", "the doctrine of laches". These terms are often used as if they referred to a single rule, whereas upon examination of their uses one finds they are made up of a body of rules connected by some central idea. Thus the doctrine of consideration is a constellation of rules connected with the central idea that "bargained-for promises are legally enforceable". The statement in quotation implements common usages of Anglo-American society and yet it is not accurate since there are many exceptions to it. The rule that a promise to perform a pre-existing duty is not a consideration is one, and the rule requiring mutuality of obligation in bilateral contracts, I believe, is another. Neither of these is, I think, a *necessary* implication of the concept of consideration. In English law a third rule, that the consideration must come from the person to whom the performance of the promise is to be rendered, has excluded the judicial recognition of the right of a third-party beneficiary. Again, this is not a necessary consequence of the proposition above quoted (or of its negative twin, that unbargained-for promises are not legally enforceable) and American

---

[69] Ibid., 485; Hall, 664.

courts generally so hold. The proposal of the English Law Revision Committee to reform the whole doctrine of consideration is broken up into one main rule and several subsidiary rules.[70] Similarly, the doctrine of laches can be shown on analysis, which cannot be developed here, to embody several distinct rules or principles related to the idea of delay in bringing or maintaining a suit. Thus in American law "doctrine", if I have used it correctly, is a loose term which requires further analysis.

5. *Standards,* according to Pound, "are general limits of permissible conduct to be applied according to the circumstances of each case. They are the chief reliance of modern law for individualization of application and are coming to be applied to conduct [of individuals] and conduct of enterprises over a very wide domain." [71] A common example is the standard of the "reasonable prudent man" in the Anglo-American law of tort liability for negligence. It does not prescribe any definite pattern of conduct. The test has been stated thus: "What would a reasonable prudent man have done considering the circumstances that he ought to have known and the consequences that should have been foreseen?" [72] Every lawyer experienced in the trial of negligence cases knows how uncertain the verdict of a jury, charged with the application of this ancient brocard, can be. While the customs of others in similar circumstances are evidential, they are not conclusive, for the jury may permissibly find that the custom is imprudent. Thus the standard sacrifices certainty in prediction to flexibility, that is, to the evaluation ad hoc of circumstances which cannot be specified in advance. The same is true of the many other standards found in modern systems of law. Pound mentions the standard of fair conduct of a fiduciary and the standard of reasonable service in the law of public utilities. The Roman law and its modern European derivatives contain the standard of a diligent head of a family and the standard of proper use by a usufructuary.

In the United States standards fulfilled a useful function in legislation conferring adjudicative or rule-making powers on administrative agencies for the regulation of public utilities and other business or industrial enterprises. The regulation of railroad rates is an example. At first some state legislatures pre-

---

[70] Sixth Interim Report of the Law Revision Committee (1937), criticized in Hamson, Reform of Consideration, (1938) 54 L.Q.Rev. 233.

[71] Pound, op. cit., supra, n. 56, 485; Hall, p. 664.

[72] Paton, Jurisprudence (1946), § 87, p. 313; (2d ed. 1951), § 103, p. 379.

scribed maximum railroad passenger rates at so much per mile of travel. This method avoided the objection that legislative power cannot be delegated, but it proved otherwise impracticable. Hence the legislatures conferred on administrative commissions (the Interstate Commerce Commission and various state commissions) the power to determine "reasonable" rates. The non-delegation principle was generally held not to be violated by such legislation, and this cleared the way for the further use of standards in legislation regulating labor relations, such as the "unfair labor practice". That such legislation confers power on administrative agencies to make law seems hardly questionable, since many of them have established rules and precedents pursuant to their statutory powers; yet the standard is not, in the context of well drafted legislation, a semantic vacuum. It has limits, apart from specific statutory ones, that are intuitively perceived. As Pound says, standards involve a "moral judgment upon conduct".[73] The intuition to which they appeal is sometimes that of "common sense", as in the case of the reasonable prudent man in negligence cases, sometimes that of an uncommonly high sense of duty, as in the case of courts of equity determining the duties of trustees, and sometimes that of expert, trained intuition, as in the case of reasonable public utility rates.[74] While standards are useful and even indispensable legal devices in modern law, they should be clarified as far as may be feasible, in the legislation which employs them or in the administrative agency's case law, by rules which increase predictability and give effect to reasonable expectations.

Thus "rules" are the lowest level in the hierarchy of logical inclusiveness. Pound's "conceptions" and "standards" are terms of legal propositions rather than legal norms, while "doctrine" is a loose mode of reference. His distinction between "rules" and "principles" is, I think, his most valuable contribution. To these one must add "policy",[75] a type of legal norm whose meaning and usefulness are still controversial.

---

[73] Pound, op. cit., supra, n. 57, 118. But the "legal standard" has been called "a legal category of indeterminate reference". Stone, The Province and Function of Law (1946), Ch. VII, § 22.

[74] See Pound, op. cit., supra, n. 57; Pound, Administrative Application of Legal Standards, (1919) 44 Rep.Amer.Bar Ass'n 445.

[75] Pound's conception of "public policies" is discussed infra, § 4.61.

§ 3.24—Rules and Principles

During the past five or six decades vigorous and sustained assaults have been made upon legal rules and the legal concepts which are their component terms. These attacks have been motivated by diverse objectives, have centered upon different rules and concepts, and have sometimes led to bewilderingly incompatible positions. Holmes' prediction theory of law (§ 2.20) would call for precise rules that would guide the court's decision, yet his criticism of the judge who was absolutely certain of the correctness of his decisions, his comment on what judges really do when they "imply" conditions in contracts, and his proposal that judges should weigh considerations of social advantage,[76] would make judicial decisions more unpredictable. Professor Llewellyn, summarizing the points of general agreement among American Legal Realists, includes "the need for courts to face squarely the policy questions in their cases, and use the full freedom precedent affords in working toward conclusions that seem indicated"; and he also includes "a strong tendency to think it wiser to narrow rather than to widen the categories in which concepts and rules . . . are made".[77] Here is no direct contradiction but certainly a tension between opposite desires: The one to make the law more exact and scientific, the other to make judicial decisions more continuously just and responsive to contemporary social needs. The same tension appears in a good many criticisms of judicial reasoning by the purported logical application of legal rules.[78] It is not a psychopathic condition of the legal mind but a manifestation of a normal and recurrent problem of the making and administration of law.

Here we shall endeavor to determine the meaning and function in modern law of three types of legal norms: Rules, principles and policies.

1. *Rules.* The term "rule" is commonly used to designate *any* type of legal norm or legal proposition, including all three of those just mentioned.[79] Here we use the term in the narrower sense

---

[76] Holmes, "The Path of the Law", (1897) 10 Harv.L.Rev. 457 ff.

[77] Llewellyn, "Some Realism about Realism—Responding to Dean Pound", (1931) 44 Harv.L.Rev. 1222, 1254, 1255.

[78] See Stone, The Province and Function of Law (1946), Ch. VII, "Fallacies of the Logical Form in Legal Reasoning", especially §§ 12–32.

[79] A recent example is Frank, "Cardozo and the Upper-Court Myth", (1948) 13 Law and Contemp. Prob. 369, 376, n. 34, making his usage explicit.

indicated by Pound (§ 3.23), the meaning of which will be further examined below. As a tentative reformulation of Pound's definition the following is submitted: A legal rule is a statement that designated operative facts shall have definite legal consequences.[80] The discussion of legal rules will be divided into: a. The functions of legal rules in a modern system of law. b. Some disadvantages and limitations. c. Some comments on the meaning of "rule".

a. The functions that legal rules are intended to serve include nearly all of the advantages which Pound has ascribed to "justice according to law" [81] and nearly all of the reasons which Llewellyn has given for the formation of case law (§ 3.12). Legal rules are intended to serve as guides for the conduct of laymen who want to shape their conduct so as to predict and control the future with a high degree of probability that their expectations will be fulfilled. Legal rules are also intended to serve one of the basic requirements of justice, that like cases shall have like consequences in the law. That is, legal rules are intended to eliminate the effects of favoritism, corruption, bias, and even queerness of the judge (or other law-applying official). Legal rules are intended to make explicit a compromise between conflicting or competing social interests, and thus to prevent the sacrifice of ultimately more valuable interests to "pressing but less weighty immediate interests".[82] These are the functions of legal rules in reference to the public, that is, the undifferentiated members of the society. In reference to administration, legal rules are intended to economize the time and energy of officials and to speed up the process of administration by providing concretely meaningful guides for the decision of recurrent types of questions. This function is especially important in the drafting of legislation for administrative agencies: To confer official power in discretionary terms often invites needless disputes and consumes the time of more officials. The areas of discretion should therefore be limited to those in which the issues are important and cannot be satisfactorily determined by rule. To take an example from personal experience, the fees to be paid for an insurance broker's license

---

80 See Corbin, "Legal Analysis and Terminology", (1919) 29 Yale L.J. 163, 164; Hall, p. 473.

81 Supra, § 2.11, n. 24. The fourth one is not included here: "law provides the magistrate with standards in which the ethical ideals of the community are formulated". Legal rules serve to implement such standards.

82 Pound, op. cit., supra, § 2.11, n. 24.

should be numerically prescribed in the statute rather than left to official discretion by providing that a "reasonable" fee shall be paid; on the other hand, the grounds of revocation of a broker's license are "incompetent" or "untrustworthy"; [83] these legal standards confer official discretion on the question of excluding a man from his chosen means of livelihood.

One further function of legal rules has been less frequently mentioned: Their usefulness in narrowing and clarifying the legal issue or issues in litigation. Any one who reads widely in the judicial decisions on a certain subject, such as contracts, can observe how the legal rule that was problematic in one case is assumed to have been satisfied in another. The legal rules as to offer, acceptance and consideration are sufficiently detailed to enable counsel and judge to break down the controversy into such legal issues as: Was there an offer? Was the acceptance timely? Did the acceptance match the offer? These issues are worth adjudicating only on the assumption that other require- ments for a contract action have been satisfied. To take a fa- miliar example, the question whether or not the circular inviting bids for the purchase of a stock of goods was an "offer", in Spenc- er v. Harding,[84] would have been a moot question without the as- sumption that the "offer" had been accepted and that the other requisites of a contract action were fulfilled. When the spotlight of legal argument is thrown on the legal meaning of "offer", in reference to its application to the facts taken as true (on demur- rer), what appears to be a clear and simple concept is found to have blurry edges. In another case where the legal issue was whether or not there had been an "acceptance" by the mailing of a letter,[85] the assumption was that the requirement of "offer" had been satisfied. Moreover, even if both of these issues were raised in the same litigation, each would, in Anglo-American tech- nique, be discussed separately. The issue-finding function of le- gal rules is a valuable aid in making the judicial process a reason-

---

[83] See N. Y. Insurance Law (Laws of 1939, Ch. 882), § 119(6) (9). One lowly maxim from my work in redrafting the insurance law was: "Discretion costs taxpayers' money".

[84] L.R. 5 C.P. 561 (1870). The analysis is presented in Dowling, Patterson and Powell, Materials for Legal Method (1946) 11. That questions about offer or acceptance seldom arise in reported appellate litigation now seems to indicate that the rules are fulfilling their minimum function.

[85] Household Fire & Carriage Accident Ins. Co., Ltd. v. Grant, 4 Exch.Div. 216 (1879).

ing process. That function is, I believe, less adequately performed by principles, policies or standards.

How well do legal rules fulfill the function of legal certainty, mentioned above? This question calls for an opinion that cannot be tested as a scientific truth and yet can be based upon experience. My own opinion is that, at least as to litigated cases in appellate courts, legal rules provide a high degree of predictability in areas where it is needed most. Apart from this, legal rules provide a considerable degree of "certainty" in reference to questions that are not litigated. If the statute requires two witnesses to a will, an instrument with only one witness will not even be offered for probate.[86] In those situations where laymen consult lawyers (§ 3.00) this service of legal rules is an important one. Even though legal rules more often prevent unfounded litigation than predict a successful outcome, they serve a useful purpose.

b. The disadvantages of legal rules are substantially those of law in general (§ 2.10). The rule-maker tries to control the future, and in so doing he may overlook situations for which his rules provide no guidance (the "gap" problem) and situations to which the rules are applicable but in which the application will, because of additional facts of which the rule takes no account, produce a bad result (the "hardship" problem). In both of these situations a régime of rules is more likely to prove defective than one of principles or policies, which are more inclusive, less precise, and provide some guidance for novel situations. These inherent limitations make rule-law less adapted to the needs of certain areas of law, such as large portions of torts, constructive trusts, and constitutional law. Characteristically legal rules are in terms ethically neutral and thus they strike no responsive chord in the individual conscience of the reader, especially one who wants to settle matters by some standard or arbiter outside the law. One further objection to legal rules in a modern state is that the attempt to provide precise consequences for precise facts in a vast variety of situations makes the literary materials of law (§ 3.10) unwieldy, expensive and difficult to use. These are, briefly stated, the principal deficiencies of legal rules.

The critics of legal rules have ascribed to them a good many defects that are not peculiar to them. One of these is the defective terminology in which they are often stated. Professor Stone has pointed out that there are, in English case law, often many

---

[86] See Dickinson, "Legal Rules: Their Function in the Process of Decision", (1931) 79 U. of Pa.L.Rev. 833, 847; Hall, pp. 1116–17.

competing versions of the same rule, rules whose key terms have a "concealed multiple reference" (e. g., the "res gesta" doctrine,[87] which is a constellation of rules, as Wigmore showed), rules with indeterminate or circuitous reference, and the like.[88] These criticisms are doubtless justified, for one finds similar dubious rules in American law. A further objection to the rule-technique is that no statement of a rule derived from judicial precedents can ever be put forward as the single authoritative formulation of the rule (§ 3.12).[89] This is a more serious objection to the supposition that legal rules can promote legal certainty, fulfill expectations and ease the burdens of weary counselors and judges. Still my own observation is that the indeterminacy of a *body* of interrelated precedents in a single jurisdiction has been considerably exaggerated by writers seeking an unattainable degree of legal certainty. Another objection is that courts follow outmoded rules because of their traditional authority; but in American courts of last resort, at least, this is not inevitable.[90] The objection that judges can refuse or fail to apply legal rules even when they are clearly worded and clearly applicable to the facts (at least, the objector thinks so) is not a defect of rules but, if at all, of the process of judgment, including trial by jury. Finally there is the objection that on the same set of facts, two different rules may be equally applicable. Professor Stone gives a neat illustration: Should the liability of a lessor of a building, who operated a passenger elevator, for injuries resulting from such operation to a person coming to visit a tenant, be determined by the rule applicable to occupiers of realty or by the rule applicable to common carriers of passengers? [91] Professor Hall had previously pointed out a similar competition of rules, with respect to the liability of a steamship company to a passenger, between the rule as to innkeepers and the rule as to common carriers of passengers.[92] Such conflicts will inevitably arise because the law is not a perfect system. The solution suggested above (§ 3.24) is that some higher

---

[87] Op. cit., supra, n. 73, § 16.

[88] Op. cit., supra, n. 73.

[89] Stone, op. cit., § 23.

[90] See the method of overruling with only prospective (not retrospective) operation, infra, § 5.04.

[91] Haseldine v. Daw, (1941) 1 All.E.R. 525, rev. (1941) 2 K.B. 343. The lower court applied the more stringent duty of the common carrier. See Stone, op. cit., pp. 139, 144, 177.

[92] Hall, p. 577.

principle must be found (or possibly created) to reconcile the apparent contradiction in the two rules. Another way of analyzing the *Haseldine* case was that there was no case law rule applicable to elevators, and that there was thus a gap in the law which the court could fill in by principle or policy. This solution would not be as satisfactory as the first one, to conscientious judges who would rather feel they are interpreting law than making it.

c. The connotation of "legal rule" has already been indicated in stating the functions that it is intended to fulfill, and a part of its denotation has been exemplified in the illustrations above. Two further points may be made. First, a legal rule never functions in isolation from other rules; it is to be used for the determination of a legal issue which is found or created by the use of other legal rules. (See a., supra.) Hence the terms of a rule are definite enough if they can be made definite by reference to other legal rules: This is the effect of linguistic system (§ 3.21) or logical syntax. The use of this device is obviously hampered by the inconsistent usage of terms that one finds in judicial opinions. One of the chief merits of a good law treatise is to provide a consistent terminology (§ 3.14). Eventually in using this device one comes to a term that is not defined in the system, a "primitive" term.[93] Let us take as an example the rule of the Restatement of Contracts:

> "A revocable offer is terminated by the death of the offeree . . . ".[94]

By reference to another rule (§ 35) the meaning of "terminated" is ascertained; the meaning of "revocable" is likewise given by other sections; and the meaning of "offer" is defined in terms of "promise" (§ 24) which is in turn defined as "an undertaking" (§ 2). But "undertaking" is not defined, though its meaning is illustrated; it is, in this system, a primitive term. In the application of the rule above quoted the meaning of "offer" would not be in question (though it might be another issue in the same case). If the meaning of "offer" were in issue, the court would have to determine the issue by reference to analogies, or preferably by avowedly considering the consequences in the law and in society of holding *such* an utterance to be an offer or not. This would be reasoning from a policy or policies.[95]

---

[93] No system can define all of its terms "without committing the unpardonable sin of circularity". Keyser, "On the Study of Legal Science", (1929) 38 Yale L.J. 413, 420.

[94] Restatement, Contracts (1932), § 48.

[95] However, in determining whether an advertisement or a circular is an

A second point is that the meanings of legal rules are not the same as, but are not wholly separable from, their purposes or principles or policies. The rule just quoted (death terminates an offer) is incompatible with the principle that the law should give effect to the reasonable expectations of the promisee (who loses his power of acceptance even though he does not know of the offeror's death) and is compatible with the view that a contract must be a "meeting of minds", or perhaps with the principle of individual autonomy or freedom of the will. The judge who applies the rule does not have to think through these policy interpretations, yet he should be aware of them even though he disagrees with them. It is erroneous to think that the application of legal rules is necessarily or properly a mechanical process, unrelated to the ultimate ends of the legal order.

2. *Principles.* The term "principle" is often used to include "rule". Professor Goodhart, for instance, uses it to mean the holding or ratio decidendi of a judicial precedent.[96] Here it is used in the sense indicated above (§ 3.23) to designate a legal norm stated in rather vague terms and having a moral or ethical persuasiveness that is self-evident. Principles appeal to one's intuitive sense of rightness, without any argument as to consequences. Thus any one who rejects the principle, "no one should be unjustly enriched at another's expense", would be suspected of having a defective moral sense. Principles correspond to an intuitive type of ethical theory, and policies correspond to a teleological theory (§ 1.13). This distinction will be further discussed later. Principles do not indicate explicitly the operative facts or the legal consequences to which they apply. Hence it might be claimed that they are meaningless, or that they are not legal norms at all, but rather the norms of some extra-legal system such as morals or natural law. No doubt many new legal principles have been created from ideas derived from morals or ethics, for principles express the moral convictions of a society.[97] Yet as in the case of customs (§ 3.15), when a legal principle is created, it takes on a different meaning from the moral principle from which it was derived. It implies legal consequences (ultimately official

---

offer, judicial opinions far more often rely on analogies than on explicit policies.

[96] See Goodhart, "Determining the Ratio Decidendi of a Case", (1930) 40 Yale L.J. 161.

[97] See Seavey, "Principles of Torts", (1942) 56 Harv.L.Rev. 72, 74. Some of Professor Seavey's "principles" are "policies", as that term is here used.

action) and operative facts which are expressed in legal rules or precedents. The conception of levels of meaning (§ 3.25) explains how principles have meanings in a legal system. Moreover, legal principles in case law are not axioms assumed a priori but are rather generalizations derived "inductively" from rules and precedents.[98] While the meaning of a principle necessarily extends beyond its concrete applications, it is a mistake to believe that a legal principle thus derived is right for all eternity. As Pound has pointed out (§ 3.23), a principle often conflicts with another principle. Thus the principle that one should perform one's promise (pacta servanda sunt) as implemented in the law of contracts, conflicts with the literal meaning of the principle of unjust enrichment, as where a seller of property exacts an extortionate price, or an employer makes excessive profits from the services of his employees. Since it would not be applied in either of these instances, the principle of unjust enrichment is thus limited in meaning by the compartment in which it developed, that of quasi contract or restitution.[99] Similarly, "no liability without fault" is limited to tort liability; innocent and blameless promise-breakers are often held liable. Such traditional principles are more often limited by the traditional compartment in which they were first recognized than by using the "received ideals" of the legal system, as Dean Pound suggested (supra, § 3.23).

The reliability of principles as authoritative guides is generally regarded as less than that of rules. Pound has said that legal principles are in a sense "hortatory".[1] Cardozo, after discussing the "higher and broader revelations of a social order", "norms of right and justice", said:

> "I doubt whether these types or patterns, except to the extent that they are consistent with statute or decision, should receive the name of law." [2]

A Federal court under the yoke of Erie v. Tompkins was held obliged to apply a state statute of limitation rather than a principle of laches, since it was concluded that this is what a state court

---

[98] Ibid. Still, the principle that the government should not arbitrarily discriminate in favor of one citizen and against another, seems an a priori principle. See Messenger v. Pennsylvania R. Co., 36 N.J.L. 407 (1873).

[99] See Pink v. Title Guaranty & Trust Co., 274 N.Y. 167, 8 N.E.2d 321 (1937).

[1] Pound, "For the Minority Report", (1941) 27 A.B.A.J. 664, 677.

[2] The Growth of the Law (1924), 47–48. See, for example, Grobin v. Grobin, 184 Misc. 996, 55 N.Y.S.2d 32, 36 (1945).

would have done.[3] This is not to say, however, that principles are not a part of state law.

The logical function of principles in case law is threefold: To limit the scope of rules, to extend the scope of rules and to provide for the casus omissus (the "gap" problem) by creating novel precedents which eventually establish new rules.

§ 3.25—Policies; Public Policy

"Policy" has during the past few decades been a favorite term of writers who would improve upon or discard the traditional rule-technique of the judicial process and of legal education. In its etymology "policy" is a descendant of "polity" and is a close relative of "politics" and "police". Thus "policy" refers primarily to plans for governmental action rather than to moral or ethical principles; yet the distinction is not consistently maintained. During the nineteenth century English courts were, and they still are, very reluctant to accept "public policy" as a ground for decision except with respect to illegal contracts.[4] They regarded policy as a very unruly horse; once you mount it, you can never tell where it will take you. Yet throughout that century courts frequently held contracts to be illegal and unenforceable on the ground of "public policy". The emergence of policy as an overall conception in the present century signifies, I believe, not merely skepticism as to rule-technique, but a recognition that law and politics are not wholly separable and that the law should be tested by its consequences (i. e., its effects in relation to its ends). Hence "policy", distinguished from "principle" (§ 3.24), signifies a teleological axiology.[5] Yet the distinction is not a cleavage, for intuitive principles are based in some sense on past experience of consequences and policies imply some ultimate evaluations (of ends to be sought) which are partly intuitive.

---

[3] Guaranty Trust Co. of N. Y. v. York, 326 U.S. 99, 65 Sup.Ct. 1464 (1945).

[4] See Lord Wright, "Public Policy", in Legal Essays and Addresses (1939) 66, 72–75. As showing the variance in terminology, he refers to the "public policy" that a criminal shall not reap the fruits of his crime (p. 87), though this would be a "principle" in the terminology suggested above.

[5] The "public policy" mentioned in the last note seems to have been applied without a nice calculation of consequences in a case holding that the personal representatives of the insured who committed suicide while sane could not recover on a life insurance policy. Ibid., 85; Beresford v. Royal Ins. Co., [1938] A.C. 586. The beneficary, most frequently (in the U.S.A.) the insured's wife, will not profit by *her* wrong if she is awarded the proceeds of the life insurance.

The beginning of the policy-school (if it is a school) can be traced to Holmes' writings, particularly to these suggestions:

"I think that the judges themselves have failed adequately to recognize their duty of weighing considerations of social advantage. The duty is inevitable, and the result of the often proclaimed judicial aversion to deal with such considerations is simply to leave the very ground and foundation of judgments inarticulate, and often unconscious, as I have said. . . . I cannot but believe that if the training of lawyers led them habitually to consider more definitely and explicitly the social advantage on which the rule they lay down must be justified, they sometimes would hesitate where now they are confident, and see that really they were taking sides upon debatable and burning questions." [6]

Pound in 1921 listed ten paramount public policies of Anglo-American law and developed a scheme of social interests which was, in effect, a summary of policies in modern legal systems (§ 4.61). The legal realists believed that policy should play a more important part in the judicial process.[7] Professor Fuller criticized Professor Williston's monumental treatise on contracts because it resorted to policy only where "logic" failed.[8] A comprehensive statement of the significance of policy-science for legal education was published by Professors Lasswell and McDougal in 1943.[9] The policy-technique is in the ascendant in legal education and in law review writing. It has found more limited recognition in the opinions of American appellate courts.

The meaning of "policy", partly indicated above, is further amplified in the following statements:

" . . . in current case law public policy is a principle of judicial legislation or interpretation founded on the current needs of the community; . . . it may be regarded as the highest common factor of public sentiment and intelligence as ascertained by the judges assisted by the Bar; and . . . nowadays it is emphatically not an ideal standard to which law ought to conform." [10]

---

6 Op. cit., § 3.24, n. 76, 10 Harv.L.Rev. at pp. 467, 468.

7 Supra, § 3.24, n. 77.

8 Supra, § 1.11, n. 14.

9 "Legal Education and Public Policy: Professional Training in the Public Interest", (1943) 52 Yale L.J. 203.

10 Winfield, "Ethics in English Case Law", (1931) 45 Harv.L.Rev. 112, referring to his earlier article in (1928) 42 Harv.L.Rev. 76. On expert fact-

Professors Lasswell and McDougal were more definite in their statement of ends:

> *"Policy norms.* These are propositions about how values ought to be distributed, including those to which we have given special mention, like power, respect, knowledge, safety and health, comfort and convenience." [11]

These writers, along with Professor Fuller,[12] apparently regard policies as non-legal in character. Professor Pound and Professor Stone [13] treat them as a part of the legal order, as does Professor Winfield in the passage above quoted. The former seek to create an ideal philosophy of law; the latter seek to interpret the law in terms of policy. In this latter sense (the one used here) policies are derived from statutes and precedents. This version is more likely to be acceptable to a court.[14] The policy that one judge sees in a statute or judicial precedent may seem to another a mere "gloss".[15]

Since policies are derived from, or perhaps better, suggested by and grounded upon, narrower propositions of statutory law, or judicial precedents of flexible scope, policies frequently come into conflict with other policies. Indeed, it is said to be one of the merits of the policy technique that it requires one to discover (or invent?) the conflicting policies in a legal problem and solve it by a choice or a compromise between the two. A few examples from many must suffice here. The policy of preventing fraud gave way, in a case where a minor had obtained employment by fraudulently misrepresenting his age, to the policy of protecting the employee "against his own improvidence and folly" as embodied

---

finding for policy formulation, see Merton (Robert K.), "The Role of Applied Social Science in the Formation of Policy: A Research Memorandum," (1949) 16 Philosophy of Science 161.

11 Supra, n. 9, at p. 241.

12 Supra, n. 8.

13 See Stone, The Province and Function of Law (1946), Ch. XX, §§ 6–10; and also Paton, Jurisprudence (2d ed. 1951), 99.

14 "The public policy of the state or the nation is to be found in its statutes, and, when cases arise concerning matters upon which they are silent, then in its judicial decisions and the constant practice of the government officials." Quoted in Groome v. Freyn Engineering Co., 374 Ill. 113, 28 N.E.2d 274, 279 (1940).

15 Compare the opinions of Douglas, J., and Rutledge, J., in Cohen v. Beneficial Industrial Loan Corp., 337 U.S. 541, 69 Sup.Ct. 1221, 1231 (1949).

in Workmen's Compensation laws.[16] Although the policy of the statute regulating the fees of employment agencies was broad enough to include protecting employers (as well as employees) from exorbitant charges, the policy that penal statutes be strictly construed in order to protect individual liberty prevailed.[17] The public policy that contracts made by authorized government officials be reliable out-weighed a vague and unformulated policy against charging the government too high a price for land.[18] In the much-mooted sound truck decisions the policy of protecting freedom of speech against arbitrary official interference out-weighed both the policy of protecting people from distracting noises and the policy of allowing the states to choose how they shall implement policies.[19] While this last case was widely interpreted as a policy struggle, it seems on analysis to have been a struggle over the *means* of implementing a policy—in this case, by giving the chief of police the power to issue or refuse permits to use sound trucks. Thus the solution of policy problems (of legal problems analyzed by the policy technique) is not arrived at merely by voting for one policy or another. It also involves the jurist's art of implementing a policy or several policies, through legal rules and procedures.

The view that statutes signify policies that they do not express and yet that can be used in applying them has not always been recognized. A leading authority on statutory interpretation denied that statutes had an ethical basis, since the purpose of putting them in fixed language was to avoid inquiring into the "equities" of particular cases.[20] Today it might be said that this states one general policy of statutory interpretation, namely, that the legislature intended to go no further in its implementation of the ends or purposes (particular policies) of the legislation than is manifested in the literal meaning of its words. The "plain meaning" rule (§ 3.11) is an expression of this policy. To avoid such interpretations statutory draftsmen often insert statements of policy at the beginning of a statute. Such a declaration in the Na-

---

[16] Sacklowitz v. Charles Hamburg & Co., Inc., 295 N.Y. 264, 67 N.E.2d 152 (1946), quoting Cardozo, J., in Surace v. Danna, 248 N.Y. 18, 22, 161 N.E. 315, 316.

[17] Faingaert v. Moss, 295 N.Y. 18, 64 N.E.2d 337 (1945).

[18] Muschany v. U. S., 324 U.S. 49, 65 Sup.Ct. 442 (1945) (opinion of the Court by Black, J.; three dissents).

[19] Saia v. People of State of New York, 334 U.S. 558, 68 Sup.Ct. 1148 (1948).

[20] Freund, Legislative Regulation (1932), 55–56.

tional Labor Relations Act was held to bring it in conflict with a
state law regulating labor unions, which was therefore declared
invalid,[21] although the federal law contained no requirements that
the state law directly contradicted. Yet a consideration of the
policy of a statute may narrow its effect. Thus the policy of O.
P. A. price regulations of automobile sales was said to be to prevent inflation, and hence the regulation did not limit an insured's
recovery on an insurance contract.[22] Finally, in determining the
constitutional validity of a statute, the motivation of the legislature in enacting it (such as the pressure of lobbyists) is not the
same as the policy that the legislature might justifiably have intended to effectuate.[23]

While the policy approach to legal problems has considerable
merit when used by able legal scholars to expose the reasons for
legal rules and doctrines, it would lead to some hasty and bad
judgments if all judges in all cases were to discard all legal rules
and decide on the ground of a choice between competing policies.
Moreover, policies should be used by courts as aids to the interpretation of statutes or precedents, and otherwise rarely where
the latter are indeterminate.

The use of policy in Soviet Russia, expressly recognized by the
Civil Code, nominally goes no further than this. The Soviet Civil
Code, section 4, provides:

> "In the absence of legislative enactments or decrees bear-
> ing upon the decision of a case, the court shall decide the
> case guided by the general principles of soviet legislation,
> and by the general policies of the workers and peasants' gov-
> ernment." [24]

The Communist Party leaders exert a considerable influence by
directions issued to all departments of the government [25] and this
dominance follows from the Soviet conception that law expresses

---

[21] Hill v. State of Florida, 325 U.S. 538, 65 Sup.Ct. 1373 (1945).

[22] Tierney v. General Exchange Ins. Co., 60 F.Supp. 331 (N.D.Tex. 1945).

[23] See Daniel v. Family Security Life Ins. Co., 336 U.S. 220, 69 Sup.Ct.
550 (1949).

[24] Gsovski, Soviet Civil Law (1948), vol. I, p. 325. See also Berman, Justice
in Russia (1950), showing the Russian tendency to place politics beyond law
and yet to establish the protection of property and contract rights by the
judiciary. The "policy" state tends to become a "rule" state. See Schlesinger, "Justice in Russia: A Dissent", (1951) 60 Yale L.J. 976, 979.

[25] Ibid., 76–77. The extent to which this includes the judiciary is not clear.

the will of the dominant class.[26] The fusion of law and politics appears to be a characteristic device whereby totalitarian régimes break down the independence of the judiciary and thereby weaken the legal protection of individual liberty. The users of policy technique should always be mindful that the line between law and politics is still worth preserving.

§ 3.26—Theories of Meaning in Relation to Law; "Operative Factors"

Some recent and important American jurisprudential theories have taken account of, and been influenced by, recent theories of meaning.[27] We have mentioned above three types of these: Psychological, operational and contextual (§ 1.12). We have also said that, among the significant questions that can be asked about an asserted legal proposition, the most important, in the professional use of law, is one about its meaning (§ 2.12). While "semantics" or "semiotics" is a novel name used to designate theories of meaning, the concern about meanings of terms is not itself new. Theories of meaning were long ago developed by philosophers, especially logicians. Yet the intensive study of meaning-theory during the present century has contributed new insights. This study has been motivated by, or responds to, the vast increase in the mechanical means of communication between men in modern society, and the need for improving means of communication for increasingly larger and better integrated societies, including the ultimate dream of a world society. Thus theories of meaning have a social function that includes their usefulness for the political function of law.

The present section will be confined to a more modest scope, that is, theories of meaning in relation to professional uses of the law (§ 3.01). We shall begin with some of the simpler conceptions of logicians, and then move on to a more complex theory of

---

[26] Vyshinsky, The Law of the Soviet State, (Babb trans., 1948), 50, 159–160. Soviet law rejects the principle of separation of powers. Gsovski, op. cit., 24. In Yugoslavia, it is said, Communist party policy was implemented in the rules determining the amount of workmen's compensation benefits. See Choumenkovitch, "Insurance under Communism" (1950) 11 Casualty & Surety Journal 24, 25–26.

[27] American legal realism (infra, §§ 4.63, 4.64) was aided by Ogden and Richards, The Meaning of Meaning, (2d ed., 1927). In their theory of policy-science Professors Lasswell and McDougal adopted (52 Yale L.J. 235) the semiotic analysis of Professor C. W. Morris, discussed below.

semiotics. One difficulty encountered in applying logical conceptions of meaning to legal problem-solving is that many of the statements, of pleading or proof, which the lawyer or judge has to start with in arriving at a legal judgment or evaluation are narrative or adverbial in language and that these have to be translated into substantives, common nouns or adjectives, in order to fit into the mold of the traditional logical device, the categorical syllogism, which employs as its verb only some form of "to be". Thus the statement, "D invited P to come onto D's premises" must be translated into "P in coming on D's premises was an invitee of D", and the statement, "D offered to sell his Ford car to P" must be translated into "D's utterance was an offer to sell his Ford car to P". The translation changes the meaning of the statement from a narrative one to one of implication. A second point is that most legal propositions are in the form of statements that something "shall", "must", "should" or "may" be done or have legal consequences; and here again a translation into the standard subject-predicate form effects some change in meaning. These caveats apply to the long established distinction between connotation and denotation.

1. *Connotation and Denotation: Analytic Use.* Logicians have differed as to the use of the terms "connotation" and "denotation". First let us consider the analysis of Professors Cohen and Nagel.[28] They begin with Aristotle's postulate that all propositions either assert or deny something of something else, that is, they either assert or deny a predicate of a subject; these two are the "terms" of the proposition. A term may be viewed either as a class of objects or as a set of attributes or characteristics which determine the objects as members of the class. The first is the *denotation* or extension of the term, the second is its *connotation* or intension. Thus the term "qualified voter of New York" connotes the attributes, "twenty-one years old or more", "citizen of the United States", "resident of the state", etc., while it denotes all humans who now *or hereafter will* have these attributes. In this view the connotation and the denotation of a term (such as "qualified voter") [29] are inseparable and the class of objects designated by it is not exhausted by its *present* members. Thus the

---

28 Cohen and Nagel, An Introduction to Logic and Scientific Method (1936), Ch. II, sec. 2, "The Traditional Analysis of Propositions".

29 I. e., we omit here application of this analysis to terms that are proper names ("*Socrates* is a qualified voter") and indexal signs ("*This* is a qualified voter").

New York statute defining the qualifications of voters extends to persons who may qualify in the future (§ 2.12). This analysis is useful in the drafting of statutes, for very often a crucial problem is, how extensive should be the operation of a change in the law? In regulating insurance companies in a certain way or in fixing minimum wages, should one include all insurance companies, or all employees, or should one exclude certain classes? The qualifiers attached to the term "insurance company" or "employee" will determine the extension of the statutory term, e. g., "all *life* insurance companies", "all *mutual life* insurance companies" or "all employes *engaged in interstate commerce*", etc. To add to the attributes required is to increase the intension of the term; and ordinarily *an increase in intension results in a decrease of extension*. Thus "all insurance companies" is more extensive (designates a class having more present and potential members) than "all life-insurance companies". However, this is not necessarily so, since one may add a qualification that will exclude no presently known object: One would deprive no person of the voting privilege if one required that voters be less than 1,000 years old. Still, in practice, every lobbyist knows that the way to get his clients freed from the operation of a baneful statute is to insert some innocent "proviso" that will increase the intension and decrease the extension of the crucial term. Statistical estimates are often made by the Treasury Department of the number of taxpayers and the amount of revenue that will be affected by proposed changes in the terms of federal taxation statutes. From this it can be seen that "the denotation of a term clearly depends upon its connotation".[30]

How to find the connotation of a term, other than the attributes explicitly stated, is another problem. Here there are, historically, two competing versions: One, that the connotation of a term is found by considering the "essential" attributes which members of the class must by their nature have; the other that the connotation consists of the attributes conventionally assigned to the term. The former frequently leads to a "subjective intension" that varies with the interpreter. The latter points to the need, in statutory drafting, for provisions defining crucial terms. The definition of a term is thus its *conventional intension*.[31] However, this analysis stops short of a solution because, first, every definition must employ some undefined term; and secondly, case-law terms are rare-

---

30 Ibid., 32.

31 Ibid., 31.

ly, if ever, authoritatively *defined,* that is, all the attributes listed in one place. Such definitions are often supplied by unauthoritative treatises (§ 3.14). Nevertheless, it would be an exaggeration to say that case law always provides terms of indeterminate reference,[32] because the answer to a legal problem may turn upon a single attribute and the necessity of that attribute may be pretty clearly required by a series of precedents or even a single precedent.[33] A complete definition of a legal term (all of its attributes) is not necessary for the determination of any legal issue in the judicial process (except perhaps the peculiar issue of the constitutional validity of a statute). The connotation of a case law term is ordinarily to be determined by its context, its linguistic system (§ 3.21).

2. *Connotation and Denotation: Synthetic Use.* In his treatise on instrumental logic Professor John Dewey gives a different version of connotation and denotation which is significant for legal problem-solving. Whereas the older analysis began with terms as logically conditioning the meanings of propositions, he begins by considering the proposition or propositions which will yield a final judgment and regards terms as logically conditioned by propositions.[34] A quality may serve to *describe* a kind but "to become a universal it must be so defined as to indicate a possible mode of operation".[35] Legal propositions (legal norms of a given state) always indicate possible modes of operation (i. e., legal consequences) and the terms entering into them are "universal" and "abstract".[36] But how, then, can one "apply" them to existences? Here Dewey insists that there needs to be a corresponding denotative or descriptive term to connect existence with the consequence predicated:

"Existential terms are denotative; abstract terms are connotative. Every denotative term is related to a corresponding or conjugate connotative term as far as its denotative capacity is *warranted*—substantially the scholastic use of connotation." [37]

---

[32] Cf. Stone, The Province and Function of Law (1946), 186, Ch. VII, § 23.

[33] See discussion of the rule that death terminates an offer, supra, § 3.24.

[34] Dewey, Logic (1938), 349.

[35] Ibid., 353.

[36] Ibid., 279–280. See also 271, and supra, § 2.22.

[37] Ibid., 356.

While the import of this passage is hard to grasp without a fuller exposition of Dewey's system for legal problem-solving, it signifies: 1. That the "facts" of pleading or proof are statements in descriptive or narrative (denotative) terms of existences or occurrences. 2. That the leap from these descriptive terms to the connotative term or terms of a legal proposition is the crucial step in arriving at a judgment (conclusion). 3. That in deciding whether or not this step is warranted, we have to consider the meaning of the legal proposition as a whole, its consequences, in relation to its ends, in relation to other propositions and to the ends of the legal order of which it is a part. That is why I call it a "synthetic" [38] use of the distinction between connotation and denotation.

An illustration or two will help. A circular describing goods for sale to the highest bidder may be called an "offer" by witnesses, may even call itself an "offer"; these are mere descriptive terms and are not conclusive on the issue whether or not it was an offer in the law of contracts.[39] This issue may be determined by the analogies of precedents (as in the case last cited), that is, by considering the consequences of holding *such* an utterance under *such* circumstances (no minimum bid was specified) as an offer which could be accepted by a bid to pay any amount. To avoid the double use of the word "offer", as both descriptive (denotative) and connotative (implying legal consequences), it is preferable to choose another descriptive term, such as "proposal".[40] Thus in the case cited the defendant's circular was a "proposal" but not an "offer"; the plaintiff's "bid" was not an "acceptance" but only a "proposal". Similarly, in determining whether or not a "promise" (descriptive) by a news-gathering company to furnish to a radio broadcasting company a news broadcast "as far as practicable", was a legally enforceable promise, the court considered whether, in a hypothetical case not before the court, the plaintiff would be privileged to refuse performance merely by *saying* it was not practicable.[41] The court held that the plaintiff's

---

[38] Without reference to Kant's distinction between analytic and synthetic propositions.

[39] See Spencer v. Harding, L. R. 5 C. P. 561 (1870), the circular began "We are instructed to offer . . ."; yet the court held it was not an "offer" in the legal sense.

[40] Restatement, Contracts (1932), sec. 23, states that a "proposal" is essential to an offer.

[41] King Features Syndicate, Inc. v. Valley Broadcasting Co., Inc., 42 F. Supp. 107 (D.C.Tex. 1941).

"promise" (descriptive) was illusory, i. e., that it was not a promise (connotative).[42] Again, in determining whether the plaintiff, a woman in whose family a soldier, aged twenty-nine, had lived as a son for several years, was a person "in loco parentis" to him within the meaning of a statute limiting the beneficiaries of soldiers' life insurance, the court held that the term quoted was not limited to its common law meaning (which extended only to minors) and that for the purposes of this statute the plaintiff was such a person.[43] The differing interpretations of the word "employee" under the federal Fair Labor Standards Act and the Social Security Act have been referred to above.[44] This mode of determining and applying meanings has the great merit of telling the judges never to forget what legal meanings *are for*. However, it may lead to some of the disadvantages of the policy-technique (§ 3.25). Its tendency to create insulated realms of discourse in which the same legal symbol (e. g., "employee") has different referents, as in the two cases last cited, may lead to confusion and uncertainty where the one realm cannot be sufficiently insulated from the other. Yet the risks of poor reasoning on the descriptive level are shown by the tendency of courts to determine what was a "public utility" or "a business affected by a public interest" by using as the test the *physical* analogy of the common carrier rather than the economic and social consequences of the type of business involved.[45] In law as in other practical disciplines there is no royal road to perfection.

3. *Legal Fictions.* We call a "legal fiction" any affirmation that a certain symbol (word or phrase) that is connotative in a legal context has a denotative reference that contradicts the denotative reference of the same symbol in some other context, usually that of popular language.[46] Thus the affirmation that "husband and wife are one person" in the English common law had a considerable variety of legal consequences, and *in that context* it was a warranted ("true") assertion. Professor Dewey said [47]

---

42 The statement that an illusory promise "is in fact no promise" (Restatement, Contracts (1932), sec. 2, Comment b) means that it is *in law* no promise.

43 Zazove v. U. S., 156 F.2d 24 (C.C.A.7 1946).

44 Supra, § 3.21, notes 21, 22.

45 See Scott, "Judicial Logic as Applied in Delimiting the Concept of 'Business Affected with a Public Interest' ", (1930) 19 Ky.L.J. 16; Hall, p. 575.

46 On the historic role of legal fictions, see Paton, Jurisprudence (1946), 46–49; (2d ed., 1951) 42–45.

47 In our Seminar in Legal Philosophy, 1925–1930.

that *in that context* it was a "legal fact". Only when we transfer the affirmation to another context does it become fictitious; e. g., a restaurant proprietor would not feed a husband and wife for the price charged one person. Fortunately these cruder fictions have been largely eliminated from modern law. The contradiction may appear in another *legal* context, as in the case of the "implied contract" of earlier quasi-contract law. That "contract" in one realm of discourse (the law of contracts) meant "promise" or "assent" led to confusion when the same symbol was used in another context where it had no such meaning. A more subtle fiction appeared where a court held that drunkenness was an "accident or calamity" as used in a statute calling for the discharge of a juror,[48] though neither in popular speech nor under the law as to "drunken driving" would such a meaning be correct.

The case of Rosen v. Rosen [49] shows the kind of legal puzzle that arises where in two legal realms of discourse the same legal symbol has different denotative references. In a suit to obtain the dissolution of a partnership between plaintiff and defendant and to obtain an accounting, plaintiff alleged that defendant held "real property" belonging to the partnership in his name, and filed a notice of lis pendens, which would notify any prospective purchaser of plaintiff's claim. The lis pendens statute authorized the filing of such a notice in any action to recover a judgment affecting title to, possession, use or enjoyment of "real property".[50] The Partnership Act declared that any interest of a partner in partnership assets was "personal property".[51] The defendant relying on this statute moved to cancel the notice of lis pendens. The judge agreed with the defendant that this was not a property action within the meaning of the lis pendens statute, but granted the motion on condition that defendant give a surety bond to protect plaintiff.[52] The Partnership Act provision, that a partner's interest in land is "personal property", is a "legal fiction", in that in most other contexts an interest in land is "real property". The purpose of the fiction, historically, was to determine the rights of partnership creditors and of descendants of deceased partners.

---

[48] Fetty v. State, 119 Neb. 619, 230 N.W. 440 (1930).

[49] 126 Misc. 37, 212 N.Y.S. 405 (1925).

[50] N. Y. C. P. A., § 120.

[51] N. Y. Partnership Law, § 52.

[52] There were other reasons, of hardship to defendant, for this solution.

If this conjecture is correct, then the correct solution of the puzzle seems to be that the plaintiff's interest was "real property" within the meaning of the lis pendens statute.

4. *Operative Factors.* We have called attention above to "operative factors" as items relevant in the process of determining whether or not to characterize a given situation by a legal term (§ 2.22). These items are, in Dewey's conception of connotation and denotation, clues to be looked for in the litigated situation, some of which point to the affirmation and some to the denial of the conclusion that the legal term, whose meaning is in issue, properly denotes the situation. They signify, I believe, implicit conflicting or competing principles or policies, (of the legal norm in which the crucial term connotes legal consequences) which have not been and perhaps cannot be made explicit and consistent in statement. Yet lists of operative factors, like definitions, are useful to lawyers and judges in facilitating the search for relevant descriptive data. A list of the operative factors relevant in applying a legal term is not a definition of the term, and yet it is an effort to increase the order and certainty of the legal norm implicated. This is indicated by the use of such lists in the Restatement of Contracts and of Property.[53]

5. *Levels of Meaning.* The idea of "levels of meaning" has been found useful to explain the role of different types of terms in legal contexts, especially broad or vague terms. It corresponds to the difference between abstract terms and concrete terms, between "a sweet taste" as a concrete term and "justice" as an abstract term referring to something that cannot be perceived through the senses at all.[54] Yet one can perceive existential situations which one can affirm as being or not being an instance of justice. So "due process of law" in the Fourteenth Amendment is not meaningless because it calls to mind no sensations nor existences; its meaning is to be found partly in the judicial precedents applying it to concrete situations. These precedents, when stated in general terms, provide rules that exemplify but do not exhaust the meaning of the matrix term. Many years ago Judge Learned Hand wrote an article to show that the principle of unjust enrichment was not too vague and meaningless to serve as the

---

[53] Supra, § 2.22, notes 82–84. Law review notes employing this technique are (1942) 42 Col.L.Rev. 1030, 1036–7; "Factors Relied on By Arbitrators in Determining Wage Rates", (1947) 47 Col.L.Rev. 1026.

[54] Creighton and Smart, An Introductory Logic. (5th ed., 1932), Ch. IV, p. 63.

basic principle of the law of quasi contracts,[55] because its meaning would be exemplified in many propositions having narrower and more concrete meaning. Some recent semantic writings, especially those based on a psychological theory of meaning (§ 1.12), have condemned as abstract and vicious terms for which a concrete referent cannot be pointed out.[56] The correction for the abuse of abstractions is, according to Dewey, to note that "their referents are possible modes of operating"[57] as in the illustrations given. The meanings of legal principles and legal policies are to be found in the possible modes of legal operations to which they point, including those that already have exemplified their meaning.

6. *Semiotics: The Three Dimensions of the Use of Signs.* A comprehensive view of the various ways in which signs function is given in Professor C. W. Morris' theory of semiotics.[58] The process (semiosis) in which something functions as a sign may be regarded as involving four factors: 1. That which acts as a sign. 2. That which the sign refers to. 3. That effect on some interpreter in virtue of which the thing is a sign to that interpreter. 4. The interpreter.[59] From these, with the addition of relations between signs, he constructs three dimensions of semiosis which are the objects of study by three theories of meaning: 1. Semantics, the relations of signs to the objects which they designate. 2. Pragmatics, the relations of signs to interpreters. 3. Syntactics, the relations of signs to each other.[60] The careful use of language explaining these three dimensions makes summary difficult. Semantics inquires about the semantical rules which determine the applicability of a sign to a given situation under given conditions; these include rules of linquistic usage.[61] The term "pragmatics", was chosen to acclaim the work of Peirce, James and Dewey in calling attention to the relations of signs to their users; but it is not synonymous with "pragmatism".[62]

---

[55] See Hand, "Restitution and Unjust Enrichment", (1897) 11 Harv.L.Rev. 249.

[56] See Chase, The Tyranny of Words.

[57] Dewey, Logic (1938), 352.

[58] Morris, "Foundation of the Theory of Signs", in I Internat'l Encyc. of Unified Science, No. 2 (1938).

[59] Op. cit., 3.

[60] Op. cit., 6.

[61] Op. cit., 24.

[62] Op. cit., 29–30.

One of the oldest forms of pragmatics was the use of rhetoric by legal advocates. Other examples are found in the law of defamation, where the relevant meaning is the effect of the language upon its interpreters.[63] Syntactics includes as its most developed part logical syntax, which concentrates upon the logico-grammatical structure of language.[64] In this section the discussion has been chiefly about the semantic and syntactic dimensions.

A fourth dimension, which Professor Morris may have included in pragmatics, is the effect on the interpreter of *his* relation to the utterer of the language. "Who said so?" is always an important question to ask in legal discourse (§ 2.12). The "authority" of the utterer is not insignificant even in such a realm of discourse as physics or chemistry.

Theories of meaning have served and can further serve to clarify the use of legal language. The refinement of legal meanings is continually checked by the dependence of legal terminology upon popular terminology.

§ 3.27—Legal Terminology and Popular Terminology

At several points previously the relation of popular language to legal language has been discussed, especially in the discussion of linguistic system (§ 3.21). In addition to all the other pulls of policy and ethics, the law is subjected to a pull in one direction, the need to use terms that are understandable by intelligent laymen, and a pull in the other direction, the need to develop an exact, technical vocabulary as a means to professional efficiency. Sir Frederick Pollock, who recognized the need for technical language, urged that "the test of sound technical language is that it is capable of being put into sensible English . . ."[65] This is a rather surprising statement, coming from the learned author of several important legal treatises. In the context it appears that he referred to the old common law forms of action, the language of which could not be put into sensible English that would *justify* their continuance. Now it is true that all legal terms have ultimately existential reference, they refer to things and acts and events that have occurred and may or shall occur, and that a pro-

---

[63] See Philbrick, Language and the Law (1949), Ch. II—a book concerned chiefly with pragmatics.

[64] Morris, op. cit., 13–15.

[65] Pollock, Essays in Jurisprudence and Ethics (1882), 258; Hall, pp. 437–438.

fessional man can give examples in language that a layman would regard as "sensible English". But they (legal terms and propositions) cannot be transformed or translated into popular speech without some distortion or dilution of the meanings that they have in the linguistic system of the law. That is why legal counselors should accept the responsibility for advising clients as to definite courses of action, rather than merely giving them legal generalizations, and also why the giving of prudent advice calls for a good deal more than merely an understanding of the law (§ 3.01).

Jeremy Bentham, the English law reformer (§ 4.40) believed that the obscurity and technicality of English law was due to the fact that most of it was case law, and that a comprehensive code could be drafted in simple language that intelligent laymen could understand. His dream has not been realized anywhere, and yet his influence has made for greater simplicity in the drafting of statutes, especially penal legislation, in terms that laymen could understand. While courts are careful to avoid the assumption that the accused has read the statute before doing the acts that are alleged to constitute a crime,[66] the policy that penal statutes should be strictly construed [67] has its basis partly in the need for accurate communication of the scope of penal statutes. In the regulation of business activities of a complex character the need for communication extends no further than the common understanding of those who are likely to engage in the business. Thus it is sufficient if building codes and zoning laws are stated in language understandable by builders, architects and engineers; it is not necessary that they be intelligible to laymen generally. As was suggested above (§ 3.02), the baffling problem of how to communicate law to laymen appears less formidable when subdivided.

Even the technical findings of natural scientists should be communicable to the uninitiated, though the need is scarcely as urgent as in the case of law. However, the administration of law brings legal terminology into contact with popular terminology at a number of places, and thus makes the former much more dependent on the latter than in the case of the ivory-tower scientist.

---

[66] See the careful language of Holmes, J., in McBoyle v. U. S., 283 U.S. 25, 51 Sup.Ct. 340 (1931): "Although it is not likely that a criminal will carefully consider the text of a law before he murders or steals . . .". Similar cautious language is found in Screws v. U. S., 325 U.S. 91, 65 Sup. Ct. 1031 (1945).

[67] E. g., Faingaert v. Moss, 295 N.Y. 18, 64 N.E.2d 337 (1945). Cf. dissent by Frankfurter, J., in Winters v. People of State of New York, 333 U.S. 507, 68 Sup.Ct. 665, 679 (1948).

One such contact is in the proof of the facts on which judicial or administrative action is grounded. In many types of litigation, such as those involving the law of torts and penal law, the proof depends upon the casual unrecorded recollections of casual untrained observers, the witnesses; and their statements in narrative form must be processed by the adjudicator if he is to apply reflectively the norms of legal implication (§ 3.26). How the judge will "see" the facts is one of the uncertainties of trial litigation. When one adds to this the uncertainty as to how a jury will "see" the facts one has indicated two of the principal uncertainties of the outcome of trials.[68]

The communication of the applicable law by a judge to a jury is one of the least satisfactory aspects of Anglo-American judicial administration. Especially is this true where the judge is required to give general instructions, on the law only, to the jury, and to allow them to bring in a general verdict. Even where the judge is required to go beyond stating "abstract" rules of law and to state how the rules (hypothetically) apply to the facts in evidence,[69] the jurors may either misunderstand the instructions or deliberately ignore them. Now there are, indeed, three competing versions of the jury's function: One that it is to find the facts for the application of the law by the judge, a second that the jury is to find the facts and apply the law to them, and a third that they are to decide the merits of the controversy. The latter, for example, is consistent with the rule that a jury can always acquit in a criminal prosecution, but is scarcely consistent with the control of the admissibility of evidence by the judge using legal criteria of relevancy. Even in civil cases, the jury's general verdict on such issues as negligence often represents the correction of formal law by popular morals or mores. If this be an accepted version of the jury's function, they should be told of their power and their responsibility. The second version of the jury's function is closest to the general verdict procedure. If the first version of the jury's verdict be accepted (for civil cases), some more satisfactory type of jury control can be devised, such as the giving of a verdict upon special questions, framed by lawyers and given by the judge.[70] Even though most American juries now conceive

---

68 See Frank, "Cardozo and the Upper-Court Myth", (1948) 13 **Law & Contemp.Probs.** 369; Frank, Courts on Trial (1949).

69 As in Lachman v. Pennsylvania Greyhound Lines, 160 F.2d 496, 501 (C.C.A.4 1947).

70 McCormick, "Jury Verdicts upon Special Questions in Civil Cases", (1943) 27 Jour.Am.Jud.Soc. 84–88.

their function to be to decide the dispute on its merits,[71] it is not necessary that they have this illusion (for it is partly an illusion) in order that they may discharge their no less important function of deciding on issues of fact. A procedure that would more effectively limit civil juries to this function would, I believe, sacrifice very little of the genuine values inherent in a jury system, and would gain considerably in the impartiality and predictability of trial decisions. An alert judiciary can better take care of hardship cases and unprovided cases (§ 5.05) than can a casually selected body of twelve men and women.

In conclusion, the efforts to make the law more nearly systematic and to develop an exact vocabulary by means of which legal experts can communicate with each other should be continued; and legal terminology should be adapted to explanation in popular language in those areas where laymen participate directly in the administration or making of law (witnesses, jurors, voters in referendum elections) or where they directly rely on it for guidance, without the aid of a legal expert.

---

[71] Ibid., 85. See also Botein, Trial Judge (1952) 179, 208.

Chapter 11

THE LAW OF JUDICIAL PRECEDENTS

§ 3.30—Determining the Legal Significance of a Precedent

The most distinctive characteristic of English law and American law, in comparison with other modern systems, is the predominance in the former of the law of (derived from) judicial precedents (§ 3.12). Yet when one asks, how does one determine the legal significance of judicial precedents?—one finds only fragmentary answers in authoritative materials and no entirely satisfactory theory offered by the writers who have dealt with the subject. In this Chapter several of these theories, especially those of the late Professor Oliphant and of Professor Goodhart, will be examined (§§ 3.31, 3.32). The present section outlines the chief problems involved.

1. *The Political Problem.* The political problem of case law is, to what extent, if at all, are courts authorized to create law, and, if they are, how are their creations to be manifested? The older view of Hale and Blackstone was that the courts merely found and declared the law.[1] This view emphasizes the function of the judge as an expert administrator of the law made by others and denies him any creative function whatever. Despite the inroads that have been made upon this conception by jurisprudents and legal scholars from Bentham and Austin to the present time, it remains the conception of the judicial function which prevails in most of the work of judges and lawyers. The briefs of lawyers are ordinarily based on the assumption that the court will be bound by and will apply previously established law, and the opinions of courts ordinarily purport to justify their decisions as applications of previously established law. Two canons of case law construction, generally recognized by legal scholars and by courts, seem to support this view. One is that the court is authorized to decide only the case before it, and that anything which the court says about other cases is mere dictum, or obiter dictum.[2] The dis-

---

[1] See, Hale, History of the Common Law (1820 ed.) 89; 1 Blackstone, Commentaries (1765) 63–64, 68–71, and other citations in Wambaugh, The Study of Cases (2d ed. 1894) 77, n. 2.

[2] Wambaugh, op.cit., Ch. II, especially §§ 5, 13, 15, 20; Gray, The Nature and Sources of the Law (1909) § 555; Goodhart, "Determining the Ratio Decidendi of a Case", (1930) 40 Yale L.J. 161, reprinted in Goodhart, Essays

tinction between dictum and holding is elementary in legal education, though it must be pointed out that lawyers often rely upon dicta in their briefs and so do judges in their opinions. The second is that the propositions of law stated in the court's opinion, even though that opinion be unanimously adopted by all of the judges, are not in their precise language authoritative statements of law.[3] While here again practice is not wholly consistent with theory, in that lawyers' briefs and courts' opinions often contain numerous quotations from previous judicial opinions, yet it is unusual for either lawyers or courts to pick these statements to pieces, word by word, as if they were statutes. If a careful job of case law construction is done, the statements of law in the opinion are always interpreted in relation to the facts of the case before the court (and also in relation to other precedents). As further evidence of the declaratory function of courts one may point out that in England and in many American states, judges are appointed rather than elected, and that even in states where they are elected, they do not ordinarily make campaign speeches stating the policies that they will adopt if elected.

However, the view that courts do "make law" has been accepted by analytical jurisprudents ever since the time of Bentham. It is true that the declaratory theory had to take account of the power of a court to overrule its precedents; but this was explained on the assumption that the overruled precedent was contrary to reason or expediency, and was therefore found not to be the law.[4] Jeremy Bentham asserted not only that courts do make law, but also that they should not have the power to do so, because, among other reasons, judge-made law operated retroactively.[5] Most analytical jurists recognize that judge-made law is inevitable, that courts are authorized to create new law and that their doing so is not necessarily a judicial usurpation. Thus Austin believed that courts can and do "legislate", but said that they do so "obliquely", not directly.[6] Salmond distinguished between de-

---

in Jurisprudence and the Common Law (1930) (hereafter cited as "Essays");
Morgan, Introduction to the Study of Law (2d ed., 1948) 154.

3 Wambaugh, op.cit., §§ 13, 16 (but he seems to imply that, apart from the dictum rule, the opinion is an authoritative statement of the law); Goodhart, Essays, pp. 5–9. See infra, § 3.32.

4 See, Holdsworth, "Case Law", (1934) 50 L.Q.Rev. 180, 185, quoting Coke's statement that if a rule would lead to inconvenient results, it is not law.

5 See, 5 Bentham, Works, (Bowring ed.) 235, quoted in Wambaugh, op.cit., p. 78, n. 3.

6 2 Austin, Jurisprudence, (4th ed., 1873), Lecture XXIX, pp. 547–548.

claratory and originative precedents; each kind is a "source" of law; the courts are vested with "a distinct law-creating power . . . openly and lawfully exercised".[7] Gray exaggerated the law-creating power of courts so greatly that he regarded statutes, apart from judicial interpretation, as merely "sources" of the law (§ 3.11). Some very able judges, in their unofficial utterances, have recognized the law-creating function of courts. Lord Chancellor Westbury in the last century referred to the "legal fiction" that courts find in previous law the rules or analogies for the decision of every case, however novel.[8] Judge Learned Hand, recognizing that "there is a hierarchy of power in which the judge stands low", said that "nevertheless, the judge has, by custom, his own proper representative character as a complementary organ of the social will".[9] Cardozo's rather startling book on the judicial process was a cautious yet candid statement of the creative work of courts.[10] In the United States the originative theory is a widely accepted legal doctrine, at least outside of court rooms.

The problem of ascertaining (finding and constructing) case law from judicial precedents is affected by these competing versions of the judicial function in several different ways. First, if a single precedent is examined, did the court purport to apply, or to leave unmodified, previous precedents, or did it in effect modify them and thus create a new rule of law, or, what is for the present purpose the same thing, a new exception to an old rule? An example is Judge Cardozo's opinion in the well known case of De Cicco v. Schweizer,[11] in which he expressly accepted the rule established by three precedents of the same court that "a promise by A to B to induce him not to break his contract with C is void", but constructed an ingenious interpretation of the facts of the instant case (that it was a promise by A to B and C jointly to induce them not to rescind or abandon their prior contract) which made the established rule inapplicable. The declaratory theory would signify that the pre-existing duty rule was unmodified. The creative theory, noting the ingenuity used to escape from the older theory, would say that the prior precedents were at

---

[7] Salmond, Jurisprudence, (7th ed., 1924), § 55, pp. 188–190.

[8] See, Wambaugh, op.cit., 75, n. 2.

[9] Hand, "The Speech of Justice", (1916) 29 Harv.L.Rev. 617.

[10] Cardozo, The Nature of the Judicial Process, (1921), especially 103–141.

[11] 221 N.Y. 431, 117 N.E. 807 (1917).

least rendered doubtful. Secondly, the declaratory theory would seem to assume that the rule of any single precedent is logically contained in the rules or principles of prior precedents. This is not a satisfactory assumption for the reason, among others, that it ignores the fact that case law has changed, without statutory intervention, over considerable periods of time. The creative theory would recognize that every precedent (of a court of last resort, at least) contains, or may contain, new law, yet it would have the problem of explaining from what material sources the judges made this new law. For example, Salmond, who saw this problem, said at first that courts derive new principles from "the principles of natural justice, practical expediency, and common sense"; yet further on he recognized that "natural justice" is often an uncertain guide, and turned to persuasive authorities and the analogies of pre-existing law as material sources.[12] If the legal system be taken to include principles and policies (§§ 3.23–3.25), the materials for new judge-made rules are at least partly derivable from previous law. Thirdly, in the use of judicial precedents by an appellate court the assumption may be either that the precedents establish rules that *bind* the court (the strict rule of stare decisis) or that they establish principles or policies which *permit* the court to decide the instant case in accordance with a rule or principle that it approves.[13] Appellate courts, in so far as they have authority to overrule or modify precedents, are in a position to equivocate a good deal on this point, and their opinions indicate that they do so frequently.[14] The argument from precedent sometimes seeks to find a binding rule that the court must follow, sometimes to find a permissive (and persuasive) principle that it may and would like to follow. Subordinate courts, in so far as they have the time to examine case law thoroughly, are more inclined to look for binding precedents, though they have literally the power to innovate.

The distinction just made is otherwise expressed by saying either that case law is rigid or that it is flexible. Professor Goodhart has presented persuasive evidence that in the United States case law is regarded, by lawyers, judges and legal scholars, as less

---

12 Salmond, op.cit., § 61.

13 An example is Daily v. Parker, discussed supra, § 3.16, n. 51, where the court found a permissive authority in a rather equivocal provision of the Illinois constitution.

14 Seven varieties of equivocation (in this and other ways) are presented in Llewellyn, "The Rule of Law in Our Case-Law of Contracts", (1938) 47 Yale L.J. 1243, 1244–46.

rigid and binding than in England, and he suggested five reasons for this American tendency: The uncontrollable flood of American decisions; the predominant position of constitutional questions in American law (which accustoms American courts to policy arguments); the American need for flexibility in legal development (due to rapid social and economic changes); the method of teaching in American law schools (by the use of casebooks containing conflicting cases of different jurisdictions, from which teacher and student try to extract the "best" rule); and the Restatement of Law by the American Law Institute (which offers each state court a substitute for its inconvenient precedents).[15] To these may be added the habit of citing persuasive authorities (§ 3.13) from other states.

Since Professor Goodhart wrote, the rule of Erie R. Co. v. Tompkins,[16] which requires federal courts, in cases over which they have jurisdiction because of diversity of citizenship, to apply the case law of the state (whose law is the appropriate one) has revived the doctrine of stare decisis and given it a setting that it never before had (§ 3.33). While the English House of Lords and Court of Appeal are bound to follow their prior decisions, still it is they who determine whether or not they *are* following; and while subordinate state courts are bound to follow the precedents of their higher courts, still a trial court may enforce a novel claim, or even one rejected by its "binding" precedents, on the assumption that the error, if any, can be corrected on appeal to a higher state court. The federal court cannot indulge this assumption. The federal decisions under the *Erie* rule, of which several hundred have now been reported, show the difficulties of determining what the rule of stare decisis means with enough precision to apply it without the traditional safety valve, the authority of courts to create law interstitially.

2. *The Axiological Problem.* By this is meant the problem of weighing the values of stare decisis, in the strict sense, against other values in any case or type of case which calls for a departure from precedent.[17] The need for following precedents is much

---

15 Goodhart, "Case Law in England and America", in Essays in Jurisprudence and the Common Law, (1931) 65–71, reprinted from (1930) 15 Cornell L.Q. 173. He quotes numerous criticisms of the strict rule of stare decisis by American writers. Essays, pp. 58–64.

16 304 U.S. 64, 58 Sup.Ct. 817 (1938).

17 Professor Fuller describes the situation as one of continuous tension between fiat and "reason", which he describes as "natural law". "Reason and Fiat in Case Law", (1946) 59 Harv.L.Rev. 381, 392.

greater in some types than in others. This has long been recognized in respect to real property [18] and contracts, and the principle applies also to protect persons accused of crime from retroactive overruling.[19] Judge Cardozo thought the innovation of holding an automobile manufacturer liable in tort to the ultimate purchaser (ignoring the requirement of "privity") would not be likely to upset expectations,[20] and later, discussing the same theme, he said:

> "My impression is that the instances of honest reliance and genuine disappointment are rarer than they are commonly supposed to be by those who exalt the virtues of stability and certainty." [21]

In other passages of his writings, both official and unofficial, Cardozo valued highly the advantages of adherence to precedent.[22] It has other values than certainty and stability (§ 3.12). Yet American courts today show a greater willingness than English courts to treat the doctrine of stare decisis as expressing evaluations which *may* be outweighed by the values of a particular kind of claim, whenever the claim can be implemented by means within the scope of the judicial function.

This uncertainty as to the axiological status of adherence to precedent has affected the technique of determining what precedents stand for in two ways: 1. The opinions of the precedents from which one seeks to determine case law are less careful to "reconcile" prior precedents, and hence one can, fairly often, find in a given jurisdiction two or even more lines (series) of precedents, each supporting a different rule and none referring to the other or others.[23] Partly this is due to defective judicial crafts-

---

[18] Wisconsin Power & Light Co. v. Beloit, 215 Wis. 439, 254 N.W. 119 (1934); see, Dunn v. Micco, 106 F.2d 356, 359 (C.C.A.Okl.1939); Cardozo, The Paradoxes of Legal Science, (1928) 70–71.

[19] See State v. Bell, 136 N.C. 674, 49 S.E. 163 (1904).

[20] Cardozo, op.cit., supra, n. 10, at p. 146, discussing MacPherson v. Buick Motor Co., 217 N.Y. 382, 111 N.E. 1050 (1916).

[21] (1932) 55 Rep.N.Y. State Bar Ass'n at p. 295.

[22] "I think adherence to precedent should be the rule and not the exception." The Nature of the Judicial Process, (1921) 149. Mr. Justice Douglas recently suggested that, in constitutional law, "stare decisis must give way before the dynamic component of history". "Stare Decisis", (1949) 49 Col.L. Rev. 735, 736.

[23] An example is (or at least was) the rule as to the liability in tort of a promisor who makes a promise with no intent to perform it. In Massa-

manship. Partly it is due to the judge's belief that whatever he and his colleagues on the appellate bench regard as clearly right should prevail over all prior precedents. The study of precedents (whether of one's own or another jurisdiction) has at least the merit of revealing situations for which one's incipient intuitive generalizations would be inadequate, or too broad, and therefore needing modification. 2. The loosening of the conception of stare decisis has led to the interpretation of precedents as standing for (warranting the assertion of) principles or policies rather than rules (§§ 3.23–3.25). This is manifested when the court, and the lawyers who argue to it, seek to find in precedents justification (permission and persuasion) for a proposed decision, rather than rules from which it inexorably follows. Thus the technique of determining the legal significance of precedents is affected by changing evaluations of adherence to precedents.

3. *The Logical Problem.* Case law involves a number of logical problems. The primary one may be stated generally as the problem of induction, or the problem of reasoning by analogy. The first is the problem of constructing a generalization from one or more particulars; the second is that of reasoning from one particular to another. The latter will be considered first.

John Stuart Mill argued that men can and do reason from particular to particular without the use of any articulate major premise. To which other logicians retorted that there is always *some* major premise (generalization) including the two particulars, or that such reasoning, while it may lead intuitively to a correct conclusion, is logically uncontrolled. Reasoning by analogy has been analyzed as follows: From the known characteristics (a, b, c, x) of particular A, we infer that particular B, which has some of the known characteristics of A (a, b, c), also has another characteristic (x).[24] Such an inference is only a (more or less) probable inference, the reliability of which depends on fair sampling; and this in turn depends, as the same authors indicate elsewhere [25] upon sagacity in selecting characteristics. The same observa-

---

chusetts there were at one time three lines of cases, each apparently isolated from the others. Cf. Brown v. C. A. Pierce & Co., 229 Mass. 44, 118 N.E. 266 (1918); Feldman v. Witmark, 254 Mass. 480, 150 N.E. 329 (1926); Ciarlo v. Ciarlo, 244 Mass. 453, 139 N.E. 344 (1923).

[24] Cohen and Nagel, An Introduction to Logic and Scientific Method, (1936), Ch. XIV, § 4, pp. 286–288. A good account is given in Coffey, The Science of Logic, (1912) 153–158; Hall, p. 561.

[25] Cohen and Nagel 221–222.

tion applies to induction, or the process of basing probable generalizations upon particulars.[26] That inductive generalizations are only probable and not certain is generally agreed. Thus even the proposition, "all men are mortal", taken empirically (synthetically) is only highly probable, since we do not know for certain that all men now living will die.

The application of logical theories to legal propositions involves some difficulties, as has been pointed out (§ 2.12). Yet the logical analysis of reasoning by analogy and induction has direct relevance to the technique of deriving case law from judicial precedents. First, one can find in judicial opinions many citations of prior precedents as authorities without an articulate generalization connecting the precedent with the instant case; and, of course, this is even more common as to precedents that are distinguished, and are cited with the multiguous "cf". This usage may signify that the judge who wrote the opinion did not have in mind any generalization at all, or, more likely, that he had several in mind and could not choose between them, or could not get his colleagues (on the appellate bench) to agree upon one. Yet the fact that a precedent was cited in support of the decision, or even that it was carefully distinguished, gives it added authoritative recognition; and conversely, the fact that it was not cited in a case where it was clearly relevant, detracts from its authority.[27] Thus the authority of a precedent (the likelihood that it will be included as a basis for reasoning) is not settled once and for all but varies with changes in the legal system.

A second observation is that a legal norm, considered as a part of the authoritative law of a given jurisdiction, has only a more or less probable authoritative status. For authority depends upon fact, and all factual inferences are only more or less probable. The Holmes prediction theory of law emphasized this aspect and Cardozo gave it careful statement.[28] Yet the inference is not just like a statistical inference, such as the mortality table, which is based upon a very large number of particular instances. The *number* of precedents of State X in which Rule A has been approved and applied may not be as significant as the *courts* that rendered those decisions. One precedent of the highest court

---

[26] Dewey, Logic, (1938) 423.

[27] See Wambaugh, op.cit., supra, n. 1, 66, who adds that a precedent may have decided a question so elementary that it was deemed unnecessary to cite it.

[28] Supra, § 2.20, and quotation, n. 14.

may give Rule A a higher degree of authority in State X than a score of precedents in subordinate courts. For the latter are regarded as merely persuasive precedents in the former.[29] More fundamentally, a collection of precedents that support or reject a certain rule is not just a sampling process, as in the case of the selection of mortality data in constructing a mortality table; for the collection of precedents, if thoroughly done, can embrace *all* specimens, not just a sample. Hence the "weight of authority" on a legal question within the domain of the several states, determined by counting the number of states on one side (say, fifteen) and the number on the other (say, nine) is not used as a ground for inferring that in the remaining states decisions *have* been rendered in the same proportion. On the other hand, the "weight of authority", a favorite device of textwriters and law teachers, is some indication that in states having no decision of the question the "majority rule" will be adopted, more likely than not. This inference is based on the belief that the other courts will consider the need for uniformity, or that they will respect the opinions of able and learned men charged with official responsibility to determine the law. Yet the "weight-of-authority" inference has a low degree of probability unless supported by qualitative factors, such as the oldness or recency of the cases, the prestige of the courts that rendered them, and the like. The inference from weight of authority is not of the statistical type.

The chief logical difficulty in determining the ratio decidendi of a precedent is that for any decision of a court on a recorded set of facts, an indefinite number of major premises may be thought of that will logically ground the decision. This may be called the "logical indeterminacy" of a single precedent.[30] The logical problem here is essentially the same as that involved in selecting the signifying characteristics of an analogy, discussed above. Does it follow that the legal significance of a judicial precedent is wholly indeterminate and that judges who purport to apply or to reason from a precedent are relying upon an illusion? The answer is negative, for the following reasons: The possible major premises of a single precedent are ordinarily limited by the court's opinion,

---

[29] Wambaugh, op.cit., §§ 63, 88.

[30] The term is taken from Stone, The Province and Function of Law, (1946) Ch. VII, § 23, citing F. S. Cohen, Ethical Systems and Legal Ideals, (1933) 33–40; Cairns, The Theory of Legal Science, (1941). The point was emphasized earlier by Oliphant (infra, § 3.31), Hall, pp. 580–583; and by Morris Cohen, Law and the Social Order, (1933) 214. See illustrations in Dowling, Patterson and Powell, Materials for Legal Method, (1946) Ch. X.

which may state the propositions of law from which the court is reasoning or at least may state the "material" facts of the case as seen by the court.[31] The ratio decidendi or holding of a precedent may be derivable from the precedent itself. Secondly, the holding of a precedent may be derived from its relation to other precedents, as where a decision without opinion indicates a choice between conflicting rules stated by subordinate courts.[32] Even though one can derive a definite holding from a single precedent, that is, from its facts, decision and opinion, yet the legal significance of the precedent cannot be determined without consulting other precedents which may modify or limit the scope of that holding. This may be called the *systemic significance* of a precedent. While a single precedent of a court of last resort may establish or create "new law", the scope of the innovation needs always to be tested by reference to the *contemporaneous* precedents in the jurisdiction. Now this is a counsel of perfection, for it is often laborious to determine the systemic significance of a precedent. A busy court is likely to follow a single precedent as if the words in the opinion were oracular. Moreover, in finding the law of judicial precedents one has to take them one at a time, and hence guides to the determination of the holding of a particular case, such as Professor Goodhart's (§ 3.32) are valuable. Yet there is no reason why a federal court, required to follow state law should be obliged to follow mechanically a single state court precedent without regard to its legal significance in the related body of state precedents (§ 3.33).

4. *The Multiple-Ground Precedent.* Two other problems arise when there are several legal issues in a case, or where there are several concurring opinions in a case. The latter is discussed below (§ 3.32). The former has been answered in introductory texts. If the appellant has raised several legal issues, and the court affirms the decision, it disposes of both issues and the affirmance is (at least if the opinion indicates that both issues were involved on the facts) an authority for propositions of law on both issues.[33] Likewise if the court gives two or more reasons for its

---

[31] See Wambaugh, op.cit. §§ 6, 8, 10; Goodhart, infra, § 3.32.

[32] E. g., memorandum decisions, without opinion, in Sosnow, Kranz & Simcoe, Inc., v. Storatti Corp., 295 N.Y. 675, 65 N.E.2d 326 (1946), which impliedly overruled one line of lower court cases and approved another. Such a memorandum decision was followed (reluctantly) in Rosner v. Textile Binding & Trust Co., 193 Misc. 653, 84 N.Y.S.2d 441 (1948).

[33] See Wisconsin Power & Light Co. v. Beloit, supra, n. 18; Woods v. Interstate Realty Co., 337 U.S. 535, 69 Sup.Ct. 1235, 1237 (1949).

decision to reverse the lower court, the decision is a holding on each of these reasons, though any one alone would have sufficed.[34] Again, if the court rejects three alleged errors of the appellant but reverses on a fourth, its decision is a holding on the first three (as well as on the fourth) since they were deliberately passed upon by the court.[35] So when a court states the law to be applied by a trial court on a re-trial, after reverse and remand, such statements are holdings and not dicta. The conclusion seems to be that any determination as to a problematic legal proposition which the court made deliberately and as a part of its official duty in deciding a particular case, is its determination of case law. The "intent" to lay down a rule for future cases is not necessary, or perhaps is to be presumed. The question remains whether a decision can be a precedent for any proposition which the court did not have in mind when it made the decision. Oliphant would answer in the affirmative (§ 3.31), while Professor Goodhart would, with the re-phrasing to be noted later, answer in the negative (§ 3.32).

§ 3.31—The Stimulus-Response Method: Oliphant

A novel and somewhat controversial method of determining the legal significance of judicial precedents was proposed by the late Professor Herman Oliphant in his presidential address before the Association of American Law Schools in 1927.[36] That method, stated briefly, is that one should determine case law from "the battered experiences of judges among brutal facts", that the "predictable element" in judicial precedents is to be found in "what courts have done in response to the stimuli of the facts in concrete cases before them", rather than in the study of "vague and shifting rationalizations".[37] This we shall call the "stimulus-response" theory of the method of finding case law in judicial precedents (and later the "fact-decision" technique).

Oliphant's illustration of the use of this method will serve to clarify its meaning: There are (he said) two lines of cases involving the validity (legality) of promises not to compete; they

---

34 See Morgan, op.cit., supra, n. 2, 156–7.

35 Morgan, op.cit., supra, 157.

36 Oliphant, "A Return to Stare Decisis", (1928) 14 A.B.A.J. 71, 159; 1928 Proc.Ass'n Amer.L.Sch., 76.

37 Ibid., 14 A.B.A.J. 159.

are considered to be in square conflict with each other. How can we reconcile them?

"But when the opinions [of the courts] are ignored and the facts re-examined all the cases holding the promises invalid are found to be cases of employees' promises not to compete with their employers after a term of employment. Contemporary guild regulation not noticed in the opinions made their holding eminently sound. All the cases [with one exception in which it did not appear which situation was involved] holding the promises valid were cases of promises by those selling a business and promising not to compete with the purchasers. Contemporary economic reality made these holdings also eminently sound. This distinction between these two lines of cases is not even hinted at in any of the opinions but the courts' intuition of experience led them to follow it with amazing sureness and the law resulting fitted life. That is a sample of the stuff capable of scientific study." [38]

The technique thus exemplified is now fairly common in the writings of American legal scholars, in law teaching, and, to a lesser extent, in the reported opinions of courts. Let us first examine some of Oliphant's basic assumptions and then some of the implications of his theory.

Four basic assumptions may be found in Oliphant's exposition of his theory. One is that the "political virtues" of the principle of stare decisis lie in the fact that judicial decisions represent the cautious step-by-step experience of courts in dealing with concrete cases. A second is that an indefinite number of generalizations (legal propositions) can be proposed as major premises from which, consistently with the facts of a precedent, its decision may be deduced (§ 3.30). A third is that the significance of a precedent as a sample of judicial experience can be explained as the response of the court to the stimuli of the facts in the record. A fourth, suggested but not categorically stated, is that the opinion of the court is a "rationalization" prepared after the decision, which gives the "good" reasons but not the "real" reasons. The last two are psychological theories, to be further discussed in connection with American Legal Realism (§ 4.64) and the judicial process (§ 5.06).

The assumption that judicial decisions are manifestations of judicial experience in deciding cautiously concrete cases brought

---

[38] Ibid.

before courts is scarcely different from Pound's judicial empiricism.[39] The primary responsibility of a court is to make a judicial order in response to claims and facts presented to it. Unlike the legislator, who states a general rule to cover many cases that he cannot foresee (§ 3.11), the judge has a superior kind of experience in dealing with the manifold and varied concrete situations presented in litigation. What they *do* about them, charged with this responsibility, is of primary significance. It seems to follow that what they *say* about them, in giving reasons for the doing, is of secondary significance. Thus far Oliphant's critics (e. g., Pound and Goodhart) would not substantially disagree with him though they would disagree with some of his specific implications from this thesis.

The logical indeterminacy of a single precedent was one of the principal reasons why Oliphant thought it necessary to find another method of interpreting precedents. He referred to a recent decision (not cited) in which A's father had induced her not to marry B, as she had promised B to do; the court held the father was not liable to B in an action for inducing breach of contract. On this decision, a widening gradation of propositions can be built: 1. Fathers are privileged to induce daughters to break promises to marry. 2. Parents are so privileged. 3. Parents are so privileged as to both daughters and sons. 4. All persons are so privileged as to promises to marry. 5. Parents are so privileged as to all promises made by their children. 6. All persons are so privileged as to all promises made by anyone.[40] On what proposition shall we take our stand, within the meaning of stare decisis? Is not the third proposition (he asks) a mere dictum as to any of the cases it would cover? A dictum is usually defined as a statement of law, in a court's opinion, that is not "necessary" for the decision of the instant case.[41] Oliphant was trying to show that the broad generalizations which the precedent court, a later court, or legal scholars and text writers, often purported to base on a precedent were unwarranted overgeneralizations, and there-

---

[39] Pound, The Spirit of the Common Law, (1921) 1.

[40] Oliphant, op.cit., 14 A.B.A.J. 73.

[41] Wambaugh, The Study of Cases, (2d ed., 1894), § 13 ("so far as the opinion goes beyond a statement of the proposition of law necessarily involved in the case . . ."); Morgan, An Introduction to the Study of Law, (1948) 155 ("those portions of an opinion not necessary to the decision are usually called dicta or obiter dicta"). What is meant by "necessarily"?

fore to be distrusted. In this he follows a characteristic tenet of the legal realists.[42]

However, the uncertainty of precedent significance is not as great as Professor Oliphant's illustration might lead one to believe. First, any one of the six propositions, if stated in the court's opinion as a ground for the decision, could not then be ruled out as mere dictum (though it might be erroneous). A dictum is a statement of law in the opinion which *could not logically*, on the facts found, be a major premise for the selected facts and the decision. Any of the six could satisfy this test. Secondly, the sixth proposition would, in most American jurisdictions, conflict with precedents holding that, under some circumstances, inducing breach of contract is an actionable wrong, and thus would have at best a dubious significance. Thirdly, other precedents in family law and tort law might be found to conflict with propositions 2–5. Oliphant was on the right track in seeking a method of interpreting a series of precedents rather than a single precedent.

Oliphant rejected the significance of the court's opinion in applying his stimulus-response analysis of a precedent. He was influenced by the assumption of behavioristic psychologists, that introspection is an unreliable method, that the psychologist must not rely on what his subject (here, the judge) *says* about his consciousness. He was also influenced by the analogy of the conditioned reflex, a technique developed for animal psychology by the Russian, Pavlov (§ 4.64). Thus Oliphant speaks of "the response of their [the judges'] intuition of experience to the stimulus of human situations . . .".[43] Granting this assumption, we may ask, what are the stimuli and what are the responses? Oliphant said that the stimuli are *all* the facts in the record. (He was speaking primarily in reference to appellate courts.) He thus ignores the pleadings, the briefs on appeal, the arguments of counsel, the comments of a judge's colleagues, all of which are "stimuli". The only response he considers is the court's decision, its order or ruling. Why is not the court's opinion a part of the response? Here he methodically excluded it, though he reserved for further discussion the usefulness of "prior rationalizations".[44] He rejected the opinion for three reasons, I believe: Because (he thought) it was introspective evidence; because (he thought) it

---

[42] Supra, § 3.24, n. 77; infra, § 4.63.

[43] Op. cit., 14 A.B.A.J. 159.

[44] Ibid., n. 5.

was not a reliable report of a judge's mental process in deciding a case, and because his own experience as a law teacher had led him to the conclusion that opinions often over-generalize, or generalize inaccurately.

Oliphant's theory is inadequate for several reasons. The stimulus-response analysis has to be applied more broadly than he did to make it account (if, indeed, it can) for such a complex process as the argument and decision of an appellate court. He assumes (methodically, of course) that judges decide only by intuition, not by reason; or that if they do reason, we have no reliable evidence of what their reasoning was. In rejecting the opinion of the court he rejected a significant part of the traditionally conditioned response (§ 5.06).[45]

On practical grounds Oliphant's emphasis upon the fact-decision interpretation and his de-emphasis of the court's opinion has much to commend it. Holmes remarked long ago that it is easier to find fault with a court's reasons than with its decision. The decision may be right for other reasons. An appellate court, let alone a trial court, can rarely take the time to state the relevant law (and distinguish cognate propositions) as fully and clearly as it would like to. Sometimes even an appellate court opinion overlooks an important aspect of the case that was presented in the facts. Many American judges (and some English ones) are notably inept at writing opinions, though they may be wise in making decisions. By methodically narrowing the scope of the "holdings" (legal propositions) of precedents, Oliphant widens the gaps in the legal system, and leaves many "novel" cases to be decided by— what? By theories as to the policy of the law. His reconciliation of the precedents on agreements not to compete would leave undecided cases involving other types of situations than employer-employee and seller-buyer. Oliphant's theory is thus compatible with the policy technique (§§ 3.24, 3.25).

The fact-decision technique of construing precedents is, I believe, recognized and used by American courts. A single illustration will not prove this statement, but it may clarify it. A federal court, bound to apply Pennsylvania law to an insured's action

---

[45] His emphasis on "all the facts in the record" as the stimuli led to the collection of appellate records in law libraries. However, before his time, courts sometimes consulted the record in construing a precedent. E. g., Garrison, V. C., in Sullivan v. Maroney, 76 N.J.Eq. 104, 73 A. 842 (1909), affirmed on other reasoning in 77 N.J.Eq. 565, 78 A. 150. But this is obviously an added burden to an already laborious technique.

against an insurer, declined to rule that the insured's claim was barred by the insured's unreasonable delay in giving the insurer notice of disablement. The court's opinion relied upon a Pennsylvania precedent in which the facts showed similar unreasonable delay, yet the Pennsylvania court, although the point was argued in the briefs, made no mention of it in its opinion, and gave judgment for the insured.[46] If the policy to be effectuated in requiring federal courts to follow state-court law is to make it as sure as possible that on the same facts-in-the-record the same decision will follow in either court,[47] the Oliphant technique, used in construing state-court precedents, will be within the scope of that policy.

§ 3.32—The Facts Treated by the Court as Material: Goodhart

That the opinion of the court is not to be ignored, but is to be used in determining what facts the court treated as material, is the thesis proposed by Professor Arthur L. Goodhart of Oxford University.[48] From the material facts in relation to the decision one determines the ratio decidendi of a precedent. He begins by pointing out that the term, "ratio decidendi", is one of the most misleading expressions in the English language, "for the reason which the judge gives for his decision is never the binding part of the precedent".[49] From this statement and his exposition of it we can, I believe, derive his initial assumptions: First, he is primarily interested in finding a method of determining the holding of a *single precedent*. Secondly, he is interested primarily in determining what the precedent stands for as a *binding* authority, which the same court and its subordinate courts are obliged to follow. This is a typical English case law assumption (§ 3.30). Thirdly, by the "reason which the judge gives" Professor Goodhart means the arguments of principle, history, policy or expediency which the court gives for its holding. If the court states a definite rule that it is applying, that is also a reason, but that is not what Professor Goodhart means. In excluding, methodically, reasons of principle or policy as "binding", he represents the tradition of English courts (§ 3.26).

---

[46] N. Y. Life Ins. Co. v. Levine, 138 F.2d 286 (C.C.A.Pa. 1943).

[47] Excluding, of course, federal rules of procedure and federal legislation.

[48] Goodhart, "Determining the Ratio Decidendi of a Case", in Essays in Jurisprudence and the Common Law (1931) 1–26; same in (1930) 40 Yale L.J. 161–183.

[49] Essays, p. 2.

However, the reasons given by the court for its holding may be taken to limit the scope of that holding by indicating what facts are material. One of Professor Goodhart's examples is Hochster v. Delatour,[50] in which an employee was allowed to maintain an action for damages for an anticipatory breach of a bilateral contract of employment made with the defendant. One of the arguments in Lord Campbell's opinion was that since the plaintiff would, by the defendant's anticipatory repudiation, be excused from performing conditions, such as being ready and able to begin work when the time for performance arrived, he should be entitled to sue at once. Professor Goodhart regards this as a non sequitur, and not necessary to the holding of the case. Yet this reason has, in the United States, been used to limit the scope of anticipatory breach to promises which are, at the time of the promisor's repudiation or other anticipatory breach, subject to some condition of future performance by the promisee.[51] The reasons given in the opinion are frequently significant as indications of what facts the court regarded as material. Even historical reasons may indicate that the court is arguing within a genetic system (§ 3.21).

Professor Goodhart then gives a very good argument to show that the statement of the rule of law in the court's opinion is not to be relied upon implicitly. He quotes a passage from Professor Morgan's introductory text:

> "Those portions of the opinion setting forth the rules of law applied by the court, the application of which was required for the determination of the issues presented, are to be considered as decision and as primary authority in later cases in the same jurisdiction."[52]

Professor Morgan's statement is, I think, a good initial assumption: If the court in a single opinion has definitely committed itself to a clearly enunciated rule or rules as the ground(s) for its

---

[50] 2 E. & B. 678 (1853).

[51] See Restatement, Contracts, (1932) § 318; Brown Paper Mill Co. v. Irvin, 146 F.2d 232 (C.C.A.Ark. 1944). Cf. Sagamore Corp. v. Willcut, 120 Conn. 315, 180 A. 464 (1935).

[52] Citing Morgan, An Introduction to the Study of Law, (1st ed., 1926) 109. The same passage is found in the second edition (1948) at pp. 155–56. Prof. Goodhart also quotes a similar statement from Halsbury, The Laws of England, title "Judgments" (vol. 18, p. 210). Professor Morgan's norm is supported by: Hutcheson, "Status of the Rule of Judicial Precedents", (1940) 14 U. of Cin.L.Rev. 259, 262; West v. American Tel. & Tel. Co., 311 U.S. 223, 236, 61 Sup.Ct. 179, 183 (1940).

decision and if these are not dicta by the test stated above
(§ 3.31), that rule or those rules are as reliable an indication as
one can find *in that case* of what the court has held. The opinion
may show on its face that the court has purported merely to state
the rule of previous precedents, and has stated it too broadly; then
the court's rule is less reliable. We may feel sure that the court's
rule is inaccurately stated by reference to other precedents which
the court did not cite nor discuss; but that is merely to say that
case law cannot be reliably ascertained from a single precedent.
One of the arguments used by Professor Goodhart in criticizing
Professor Morgan's statement, is that a court may insert an unnecessary qualification in its rule. Thus in 1866 (he said) an
English court stated the rule of respondeat superior, that a master
is liable for every such wrong (fraud) of his servant or agent
"as is committed in the course of the service and for the master's
benefit".[53]

> "It was generally believed that this statement of the law
> was correct until, forty-five years later, the House of Lords
> in Lloyd v. Grace Smith & Co.[54] held that it was too narrow.
> The words 'and for the master's benefit' were merely de-
> scriptive of the facts in the Barwick case, and not a neces-
> sary part of the principle involved." [55]

But during these forty-five years how was any lawyer or judge
to know that these words were "merely descriptive" and not a
statement of a fact treated by the court as material? By Professor Goodhart's test, the statement in the Barwick case was an
accurate statement of the holding of the case. Its legal significance when he wrote had been modified by the later decision.

However, Professor Goodhart gives other reasons for believing that Professor Morgan's advice to beginning students is inadequate. One is that courts do not always write opinions, yet a
decision without opinion may be a significant precedent.[56] Again,
a court may state a principle, such as "no one shall profit by his
own wrong", which is obviously too broad; [57] that is, obviously
by reference to other precedents. When there are several concurring opinions, in a precedent case, one rarely finds the same

---

[53] Barwick v. English Joint Stock Bank, L. R. 2 Ex. 259, 265 (1866–67).

[54] [1912] A.C. 716.

[55] Essays, p. 8.

[56] Supra, § 3.30, n. 32.

[57] Essays, p. 7.

rule stated in each of them. Hence we must seek a more inclusive criterion than Professor Morgan's advice provides.

Professor Goodhart then rejects Oliphant's stimulus-response analysis as too simple. The significant facts are the ones that seemed significant to the judge.

"It is by his choice of the material facts that the judge creates law." [58]

Agreeing with Professor Goodhart that the court's view of the facts, especially as one finds it in the opinion, cannot be ignored, one has then to ask, how does one ascertain the material facts? Professor Goodhart offers a number of rules to guide this process. The first one is:

"All facts of person, time, place, kind and amount are immaterial unless stated to be material." [59]

This is, interpreted in his context, a good working rule for most purposes. If an attribute of the person (e.g., a foreign ambassador violating a speed law) is material, the opinion will ordinarily so state. If the time of occurrence of a material fact is itself material (e.g., the statute of limitations is a defense) the opinion will usually so state. The word "kind" is more dubious. By it the author means that a contract for the sale of a book for $10 is to be treated no differently from a "similar" contract to sell a valuable painting for $100,000.[60] Here the legal realists, with Oliphant, might differ: With a difference in kind of subject matter the contracts would in most cases be in terms dissimilar. Still in Professor Goodhart's context, it is a workable rule. It is derived, however, from the whole body of precedents, or from some basic principles and policies of our legal order, such as that courts should not discriminate arbitrarily between litigants.

If there is no opinion, or the opinion gives no facts, then all facts in the record, other than those stated in the first rule, are to be treated as material.[61] This seems to concede more to Oliphant's point of view than is necessary. A decision without opinion, and with only a *reporter's* summary of the facts (as in a "memorandum decision") may indicate clearly a holding on a legal issue on which lower courts have been divided.[62] Again, in

---

[58] Ibid., 10.

[59] Essays, 25.

[60] Essays, p. 11.

[61] Essays, p. 26.

[62] Supra, § 3.30, n. 32.

this country a court's opinion may contain statements of law indicating what facts are material, although those facts are stated only in the reporter's statement. Perhaps this rule is peculiar to English reports.

If the opinion in a precedent case does state the facts, this statement cannot be contradicted from the full record of the case.[63] Likewise all facts which the judge specifically states to be material, or to be immaterial, must be considered to be such in determining what the case stands for. Suppose a fact appears in the report of the case which *might* be material but which the court does not treat as material? Then it is impliedly treated as immaterial. An example is the famous case of Rylands v. Fletcher,[64] in which the independent contractor, who built the reservoir for defendant on his land, was negligent in not filling up disused mining shafts; yet the opinions ignored this fact and it is not regarded as a necessary part of the holding.[65] If the court's opinion omits a fact in the record, presumably it was deemed immaterial. When different concurring opinions treat different facts to be material, then all of those facts together qualify the holding. The author states significantly:

"There is a presumption against wide principles of law, and the smaller the number of material facts in a case the wider the principle will be." [66]

This brings us back to what was said above, that Professor Goodhart is discussing the "bindingness" of a precedent, rather than the principles or policies for which it *may* be taken to stand.

Professor Goodhart's rules for determining the binding rule of a case by determining the "material facts" as seen by the court, are more reliable in English than in American courts, since the latter are more inclined to seek *justifications* in precedents rather than *obligations*. While his distrust of broad generalizations in opinions is similar to Oliphant's, he uses the court's opinion to narrow the scope of the "material" facts and thus to make for a broader rule than Oliphant's, taken literally, would permit. Professor Goodhart's conception of a "material fact" seems not very different from Hohfeld's conception of an "operative fact" (§ 2.22) but is narrower in scope. Two limitations of Professor

---

[63] Essays, p. 12, p. 26.

[64] L.R. 3 H.L. 330 (1868).

[65] See, Essays, p. 17.

[66] Essays, p. 21.

Goodhart's analysis are, I believe: First, he does not expressly recognize the logical indeterminacy of a precedent, and therefore the possibility of several holdings being equally compatible with the court's opinion. Secondly, he does not expressly recognize that case law is to be determined from a system of precedents (§ 3.30).

§ 3.33—State Law in Federal Courts: Erie v. Tompkins

The requirement that federal courts shall apply the law of state court precedents in deciding cases of which the federal court has jurisdiction by reason of diversity of citizenship of the litigants was established in 1938 by the Supreme Court decision in Erie Railroad Co. v. Tompkins.[67] Among the reasons given for this decision was that the application of federal case law to this type of case had not resulted in the desired uniformity of law throughout the country, but had resulted in a discrimination in favor of non-citizens against citizens of a state in cases which would have been differently decided in state courts. The policy of the Erie case was to minimize this discrimination by adopting the requirement stated above. Dissatisfaction with the overruled decision of Swift v. Tyson,[68] which left the federal courts autonomous with respect to "common law" questions, led one to expect that the Erie rule would produce results that would meet with general approval. Yet within the first decade after its adoption it has evoked severe criticisms from some able critics. Partly these are based on procedural difficulties but mainly they relate to the implications of the Erie requirement as strictly implemented by subsequent decisions of the Supreme Court. We are here concerned only with the problems and solutions relating to the determination of case law which federal decisions applying the Erie rule have thus far presented.

---

[67] 304 U.S. 64, 58 Sup.Ct. 817 (1938). The exact scope of the requirement is not relevant here. It does not apply to "procedural" questions, nor to those involving the interpretation of the federal constitution, treaties and statutes. On the exceptions, see (1946) 59 Harv.L.Rev. 966. Federal courts are also required to apply state law in some other situations, not considered here. For a careful selection of cases and other references in this section the author is indebted to Mr. Bertram Harnett of the New York Bar.

[68] 16 Pet. (41 U.S.) 1, 18 (1843). The court construed the phrase, "the laws of the several states" (in the federal Judiciary Act of 1789, § 34) to include only state legislation (constitution, statutes, etc.).

A federal court is *required* to follow state law regardless of its own belief as to the soundness of that law, in a case where the state court has clearly spoken:

"The highest court of the state is the final arbiter of what is state law. When it has spoken, its pronouncement is to be accepted by federal courts as defining state law unless it has later given clear and persuasive indication that its pronouncement will be modified, limited or restricted." [69]

Here is recognition that a single precedent may establish a legal rule, yet its significance must always be checked by reference to *later* precedents. There is no recognition that the rule enunciated by the state court may be seen as too broad when checked against *prior* precedents of the same court, although this kind of limitation is frequently recognized.

The rule was further extended to require that a federal court shall follow a clear pronouncement of a state intermediate appellate court, unless the federal court is convinced by other "data" (presumably other decisions in the same state) that the highest state court would decide otherwise.[70] This implication of the requirement has proved more annoying to its critics than any other aspect of it. Professor Corbin thinks it absurd that the justices of the United States Supreme Court (and all other federal judges) are forbidden to use their own "reasoning" and need only have clear reading glasses to determine what the law is.[71] Perhaps there is an assumption here that Supreme Court justices are superior in wisdom and learning to state court judges. This may be so but it is beside the point. The same superior men must yield their judgment to the pronouncement of a state legislature, which may also be less wise and learned, because that is a consequence of the federal system. There are, however, other difficulties with the intermediate-court rule. One is that, construed rigorously, it would require the federal courts to follow unpublished decisions of state trial courts. This would require counsel to search for such unpublished decisions, and might require federal trial courts to follow decisions which state trial courts generally would feel

---

[69] Stone, C. J., in West v. American Tel. & Tel. Co., 311 U.S. 223, 236, 61 Sup.Ct. 179, 183 (1940).

[70] Ibid., 237 (Ohio County Court of Appeals decision); see, also Fidelity Union Trust Co. v. Field, 311 U.S. 169, 61 Sup.Ct. 176 (1940) (extending the requirement to a decision of a New Jersey Vice-Chancellor, who had original jurisdiction, state-wide).

[71] Corbin, "The Laws of the Several States", (1941) 50 Yale L.J. 762, 768.

free to reject. A recent Supreme Court decision has relieved the
federal court of these irksome implications of its earlier rulings,
although no general rule as to state trial court precedents was
laid down.[72]

Judge Clark criticizes the rule in so far as it forbids a federal
court to "re-examine state law beyond the wooden limits of a
single precedent".[73] The language of the opinion in the West
case and in other cases *might* lead a federal court to conceive that
this is what it is required to do. Yet an examination of federal
court cases indicates that they feel authorized to consider the
body of state law as a whole and draw their own conclusions as
to the scope of a state court precedent.[74] Yet the line between
finding the law and creating it is, in case law, often a narrow one,
and the federal court is at least as limited in the latter respect
as a state court, following state law, would be.

Some federal courts have apparently felt obliged to follow a
dictum of a state appellate court, in the absence of any other evidence of state law.[75] That is most likely what a state trial court
would do, though the highest state court would feel free to disregard its own dicta. A federal trial court is, it seems, in the position of a state trial court of similar jurisdiction;[76] and a federal
appellate court is required to supervise lower federal courts to the
end that they will fulfill this role. However, a dictum of the

---

[72] King v. Order of United Commercial Travelers, 333 U.S. 153, 162, 68
Sup.Ct. 488, 493 (1948), holding that a federal court was not bound to follow
a South Carolina trial court decision, where such decisions were never published nor cited in the same or other courts.

[73] Clark (C.E.), "State Law in Federal Courts: The Brooding Omnipresence
of Erie v. Tompkins", (1946) 55 Yale L.J. 267, 293.

[74] E. g., Mangol v. Metropolitan Life Ins. Co., 103 F.2d 14 (C.C.A.7 1939)
(where the highest state court based its decision on only one of two reasons
and thus did not impair a line of earlier state court precedents); Hottenstein
v. York Ice Machinery Corp., 136 F.2d 944 (C.C.A.3 1943), certiorari denied
325 U.S. 886, 65 Sup.Ct. 1573 (1945).

[75] See Blair v. U. S., 147 F.2d 840 (C.C.A.8 1943) (a statement of law by a
state court in answer to a contention of one party, even though "inoperative"
under the facts of the case); Chicago Great Western Ry. Co. v. Beecher, 150
F.2d 394 (C.C.A.Minn. 1945), certiorari denied 326 U.S. 781, 66 Sup.Ct. 339
(1946) (dicta in several Iowa Supreme Court decisions). But see Schwellen-
bach, J., in Bank of California v. American Fruit Growers, 41 F.Supp. 967
(D.C.Wash., 1941).

[76] In the King case the opinion (unanimous!) repeated the test of Stone, J.:
"rules of decision commonly accepted and acted upon by the bar and inferior
courts". 333 U.S. at p. 161, citing 311 U.S. at p. 236.

highest state court may clearly be erroneous or unwarranted when other state court decisions are studied.[77] A single precedent, and all the more a single dictum, must be validated by reference to the analogies and principles of the system.

The most troublesome situation for a federal court is when the state law is "confused or non-existent".[78] It is rare, indeed, that the entire body of state court law contains no guidance whatever as to the decision of a case within the Erie requirement. By "non-existent" is (apparently) meant that there are no state precedents "directly" in point. Here some federal courts have tried to find the policy of state court decisions,[79] to determine whether the state courts have been "strict" in applying relevant doctrines,[80] to find authority in state court "analogies".[81] Others have looked beyond state law to persuasive authorities from other states, which they treat as evidence of what the local law will be when determined by state courts.[82] Judge Goodrich has used the presumption that the state court would follow "general law" as a basis for applying the Restatement of Law.[83] Judge Frank suggested that the federal court should try to predict what the able lawyers on the highest state court, fully conversant with state law, would hold.[84] On the other hand, a few federal

---

[77] See New England Mut. Life Ins. Co. v. Mitchell, 118 F.2d 414 (C.C.A.4 1941) certiorari denied 314 U.S. 629, 62 Sup.Ct. 60 (1942).

[78] Clark, op. cit., supra, n. 73, at 290.

[79] See Bagnel v. Springfield Sand & Tile Co., 144 F.2d 65 (C.C.A.1 1944) (policy of "broad" interpretation of statute).

[80] See Cold Metal Process Co. v. McLouth Steel Corp., 126 F.2d 185 (C.C.A. 6, 1942) (Michigan cases showed "strict" view of jurisdictional requirements).

[81] Clark, J., in Huss v. Prudential Ins. Co., 37 F.Supp. 364 (D.C.Conn. 1941). So the Florida policy of freedom of contract was relied on in Ringling Bros.-Barnum & Bailey v. Olvera, 119 F.2d 584 (C.C.A.9 1941).

[82] Adam Hat Stores v. Lefco, 134 F.2d 101 (C.C.A.Pa. 1943) (in absence of Pennsylvania authority, the court followed a Massachusetts opinion by Holmes, J.); Wigginton v. Order of United Commercial Travelers, 126 F.2d 659 (C.C.A.7, 1942), certiorari denied 317 U.S. 636, 63 Sup.Ct. 28 (1942); New York Life Ins. Co. v. Rogers, 126 F.2d 784 (C.C.A.Ariz. 1942).

[83] Stentor Electric Mfg. Co. v. Klaxon Co., 125 F.2d 820 (C.C.A.Del. 1941), certiorari denied 316 U.S. 685, 62 Sup.Ct. 1284 (1942) (Restatement of Conflict of Laws); Hornstein v. Kramer Bros., 133 F.2d 143 (C.C.A.Pa. 1943) (Restatement, Judgments).

[84] See Cooper v. American Airlines, 149 F.2d 355 (C.C.A.N.Y. 1945). The "prediction" test was approved in New York Life Ins. Co. v. Bennion, 158 F.2d 260, 262 (C.C.A.Utah 1946).

courts have intimated that, in the absence of a state court decision directly in point, the federal court is free to adopt the "rule prescribed by reason",[85] or the decision "which reason dictates".[86] Such statements remind one of the "carefree days"[87] of Swift v. Tyson. This sampling of federal decisions is inadequate to reveal the care and skill with which they have reviewed state court precedents.

The policy of the Erie rule will be satisfied if, in a case to which no reported state precedent is clearly applicable, the federal court faithfully strives to apply the concepts, policies and techniques which a state court would apply. In so doing the judge must use his own reasoning and will be guided in his interpretation by his beliefs about questions of fairness, expediency or justice. Yet his beliefs are to be checked against the beliefs of others who have formulated the body of state court precedents. This calls for a wide search in the state court statutes and precedents. Obviously federal trial courts will not always find time to make such a systematic search for each case, much less to embody the results of it in an opinion. For a federal appellate court to go through the same process would be a double burden. Fortunately the Supreme Court has ameliorated somewhat the rigors of the Erie rule by adopting a presumption in favor of the finding of law by the federal district judge[88] (who is ordinarily a member of the bar of his district). This presumption maintains the policy of the Erie rule since it can be rebutted by citing state court holdings to the contrary. The Erie rule has been, I believe, ably and conscientiously applied by federal judges. Their opinions have thrown much light on the problems of finding the law in judicial precedents.

---

[85] See Powell v. Maryland Trust Co., 125 F.2d 260, 269 (C.C.A.Va. 1942) (but carefully distinguishing Maryland precedents).

[86] See New England Mut. Life v. Mitchell, supra, n. 11, 420; but the context limits this language.

[87] See Frank, J., in Zell v. American Seating Co., 138 F.2d 641, 643 (C.C. A.2 1943).

[88] Huddleston v. Dwyer, 322 U.S. 232, 236, 237, 64 Sup.Ct. 1015, 1017, 1018 (1943). See, MacGregor v. State Mut. Life Assur. Co., 315 U.S. 280, 62 Sup. Ct. 607 (1941); also (1946) 24 Tex.L.Rev. 361.

Part IV

WHAT SHOULD BE THE LAW?

Chapter 12

GENERAL SIGNIFICANCE OF LEGAL PHILOSOPHIES

§ 4.00—Positive Law and What It Should Be

The conception of law heretofore presented includes two principal ideas, that a law is a norm of conduct having the authority and sanction of the state (Pt. II) and the law of a state is a partly systematic body of norms ascertained to be authoritative by recourse to the authoritative sources of the law (Pt. III). In investigating these two phases of the conception of law the assumption was made that something is ascertainable by the methods used and that this something is positive law, or law that is. The question which we discuss in Pt. IV also presupposes that there is something which is (positive) law, that it can be different from what it is, and that if it be changed there will be a different law that is. The two questions are analytically distinct.

They are also distinct in the governmental procedures of the modern state. The maintenance of the legal order in a state requires that somebody's ideas about what the law should be must be rejected in favor of somebody else's ideas about what it should be. It requires, in short, political authority to make laws, to enforce and administer laws, and thus to determine what laws have this authority, to the exclusion (temporary or permanent) of what other people may believe they should be. The modern state is the political organization of a society that is often diverse in culture, often concentrated, often controlled in part by complex patterns of cooperation and competition, by economic and non-economic institutions. The state has the primary and unique function of maintaining order in the whole of society and as a means to this end of avoiding or adjusting conflicts of interest between individuals and groups in society by the establishment and administration of general prescriptions or norms which we call "law". Experience has shown that law is a necessary instrument of social control in the modern state (§ 2.06), no matter what the ends of the state may be. The use of law as an instrument of social control requires that law be authoritative, that some persons have authority to make or declare law which may be different from what others believe it should be.

Now the reader has doubtless encountered many arguments, in newspapers, in periodicals or books, in conversations, that some established legal norm should be changed or some new law should be enacted, or that some official action should have or should not have been taken for reasons given. Most of these arguments do not sound like the legal-philosophical ideas that are set forth in the following pages (Pt. IV). Is legal philosophy, then, so remote from life that no one ever resorts to it in practical affairs? The answer has been partly given above (§ 1.00). The reasons for studying legal philosophy are partly practical, partly to satisfy one's intellectual curiosity. In a sense, every man who gives a reasoned argument about what law should be has a kind of "philosophy of law" (§ 1.10), fragmentary and inconsistent though it be. When pressed for more fundamental reasons, he will often come up with a fragmentary idea from some of the major types of legal philosophy which are discussed below. Thus he may argue that something is contrary to the "law of nature" (§ 4.10) or that it violates a man's "inalienable rights" (§ 4.15) or that it violates a basic postulate of civilization (§ 4.61). One of the chief values of studying legal philosophy is to be able to detect and classify the types of arguments that appear in contemporary discussions of what law should be. Most legal philosophers have begun with simple and persuasive statements and have developed their systems from or within the framework of these elementary ideas. The legal philosopher is more persistent than the lay philosopher in thinking his problems through; more consistent in tying his ideas together, and more fruitful and productive for the comprehensive and long-range view of man and society. Because of these differences the ideas of many legal philosophers have been influential for many years or many centuries after their utterance. Those are the ones with whom we are primarily concerned here.

While some legal philosophies have been constructed to justify legal change, some have been put forth, or have been used, to oppose change, to justify adherence to the law as it is; and some have been used first for one purpose and then for another. For instance, the social-contract theory of Thomas Hobbes was put forth in the seventeenth century to oppose the claims of the Puritan rebels; and John Locke's social-contract thesis (§ 4.15) was published as a justification for the English revolution of 1688, was used as a justification for the American Revolution, and its theory of "inalienable rights" was invoked in the nineteenth century to resist legal changes affecting private property. Thus legal philosophies can be merely *critical* of the existing legal order or some parts of it, or *constructive* of changes in it, or *conservative* of it as it is.

Now some of the influential legal theories outlined below have not purported to discuss the question, what should be the law? Savigny's view that a nation's laws are primarily derived from the historically primitive convictions of rightness of the people (§ 4.31) was stated as if it were a description by a legal historian; yet it was used to argue that the law *should be* always consistent with those primitive convictions and that the law of Germany should not be codified. What is the use of describing law and legal institutions except as a way of influencing something to occur in the future? Again, Dr. Hans Kelsen's Pure Theory of Law, which was partly discussed above in connection with legal system (§ 3.22), was intended to influence the law of the future by greater clarity in legal thinking. Some legal philosophies have been much concerned with problems of metaphysics and epistemology; these parts we have omitted except where some explanation is necessary to understand their normative purport. Most recent philosophers of law have been lawyers or judges and have been chiefly concerned with problems of legal method, of logic and semantics and judicial reasoning. Yet it has been true of the Pragmatists, of Pound and Cardozo, even of the Legal Realists (Chaps. 17, 18), that they were ultimately concerned with improving the law and its administration.

Someone may say that the real conflicts between individuals in society are clashes between the realizations of their interests or desires rather than contradictions between their ideas of what the law should be. Hence, it may be argued, all that is required to maintain social control in a given society is a government with officials having power to make individual decisions and orders and to take individual actions for the preservation of order and the settlement of disputes. If to placate their subjects officials give "reasons" for their decisions which they call "law", that is only a ceremonial but not a necessary part of the process of social control through government. This cynical view of the state and law is inadequate and misleading (Pt. II). Here we may add that when men's acts are called in question, they ordinarily offer justifications in terms of *like* conduct of others, in terms of general rules; and they expect of others who interfere with them similar justifications of such interference. Now it is true that this giving and asking of justifications *may* be only a cultural postulate or belief of western civilization, and *maybe* it can be suppressed in a society governed by brutal power. Still even in such a society there would survive the human capacity to differentiate what is from what ought to be, to make particular judgments as to what ought to be, and even to formulate more or less articulately generalizations as to what ought to be. This capacity seems to be as common a trait of humans as is the capacity to use the multiplication table, and varies enormously as between different individuals. Because of it officials make or select or interpret laws, and subjects demand that officials govern by laws and not by caprice. Because of it, too, subjects sometimes decide that they know better than officials what the law should be, and find in this comforting thought a justification for their disobedience of law.

But the reasons just given also explain why the differentiation between what the law is and what it should be is not as easy in practice as the theory requires. The officials who administer and apply the law may well have different ideas as to what it should be from those of the legislators who enacted it or the judges who declared it; and the adjudicator's ideas may be enforced by him as law. In the judicial process, too, what the judges conceive the rule of law to be *for* may be decisive of what they "find" that it *is*. Yet every judge of recent times has wanted conscientiously to apply "the law" as it is more than he has wanted to apply his individual views of what it should be.[1] Although judges (at least, appellate judges) can, do and inevitably must change the law by their decisional opinions, yet the judicial attitude just mentioned is a desirable corollary of judicial independence.

§ 4.01—In Relation to the Judicial Process

What influence, if any, do legal philosophers have on the judicial process, upon the decisions of cases and the giving of reasons in official opinions? If one answers on the basis of the number of citations in judicial opinions, the influence appears to be slight. Even if one includes in the evidence instances of absorbed quota-

---

[1] "Judges must constantly fight against the temptation to yield to the luxury of legislating the law for the particular case". Botein, Trial Judge (1952) 142.

tions from or indirect references to a legal philosophy, as in the case of the "natural law" references (§ 4.18), the influence on English and American case law does not seem to be very great. The non-official utterances of some judges, such as Holmes (§ 4.55) and Cardozo (§ 4.62) reveal how much legal philosophers affected their thinking. Still, such judges are rare. To establish that any distinct philosophy of law had a decisive influence upon a particular judicial decision or the enunciation of any particular legal doctrine is rarely possible, for the generalizations of legal philosophy are usually too comprehensive and abstract to be decisive of legal issues in litigation. An English writer, after examining the evidences of the influence of ethical theories on English case law, concluded that while a good many legal principles "embody" ethical or moral theories, it can rarely be shown that the decision would have been different if one ethical theory rather than another had been chosen.[2]   In the United States this conclusion would have to be slightly modified, and if one adds economic and political theories in Supreme Court decisions on constitutional interpretation, the modification would have to be more substantial. The efforts of many recent American judges to set forth in their opinions not only the formal rules that justify the decision but also the principles or policies on which these rules depend eventually will lead to a search for basic guides in legal philosophy. Still it will be prudent advocacy for a long time ahead not to argue a case to a court merely on grounds derived from a philosopher of law.

§ 4.02—In Relation to the Legislative Process

The influence of legal philosophy upon legislation has been and is somewhat greater and more readily provable. Savigny's theory of the Volksgeist (§ 4.31) was influential in blocking the codification of German civil law for nearly a century. On the other hand Bentham's utilitarianism (§§ 4.40–4.43) included a program of legal and political reform that influenced English legislation for more than a century. In New York the followers of Bentham found their efforts to codify the law partly frustrated by arguments drawn from Savigny's conception of law (§ 4.33). Still it is true that the "average" legislator knows no more of legal philosophy than the "average" judge, and that in the humdrum of the legislative process there is very little direct reference to a philosophy of law.

---

[2] See Winfield, "Ethics in Case Law" (1931) 45 Harv.L.Rev. 112.

Its influence upon legislators as upon judges is likely to be indirect, through the cultural matrix as evidenced in individual and
group opinions. This kind of influence legal philosophies share
with religions, with political theories, with social science (as
known to the nonprofessional) and with the mores of society.
Indeed, if one were to include everything that influences the law
of a modern state, one would have to include novels, plays and
poems. Plato long ago deprecated the disturbing influence of the
makers of stories upon the beliefs of children in his reason-created
Republic:

> "Our first duty [he has Socrates say] is to set a watch
> over the makers of stories. . . . Thus [the nurses and
> mothers] will shape [the children's] souls with stories far
> more than they shape their bodies with their hands. But we
> shall have to throw away most of the stories they tell now." [3]

Dramatists, poets and novelists have often created their most
dramatic and moving themes by challenging some law or legal
institution. Sometimes they have prepared the way for needed
legal changes and sometimes they have only raked the muck. To
legal philosophers we turn for reasoned statements about the law.

§ 4.03—What To Look For in a Philosophy of Law

Philosophers of law differ from each other in their scope of
inclusiveness. The earliest ones, Plato and Aristotle, included a
comprehensive theory of the state, of education, of individual and
social ethics. More precisely, the earlier ones constructed general
philosophies in which these subjects were intertwined. The differentiation of philosophy from the sciences and of legal philosophy from political philosophy together with the rise of economics,
sociology, anthropology and other social sciences has led many
recent legal philosophers to limit themselves to the structural
and power aspects of the legal order, as in Kelsen's General
Theory of Law and State, or to the judicial process, as in the case
of Cardozo. How could one compare Plato with Cardozo, or
Holmes with Aristotle? It is difficult to compare men who are
talking about different things. Yet one can discover *wherein*
they are talking about the same things, and wherein about different things. When a new legal philosopher appears on the scene,
one can ask about his writings, as one can ask about the older
ones, a series of questions which will be useful in placing him.

---

[3] Plato, The Republic, II, 377 (Everyman ed.).

The following list of questions has been found useful for this purpose; even negative answers will be significant.

1. What is the writer's conception of the state and its functions in society?

2. What is the writer's conception of law: ideal, institutional, imperative, or some combination or variation of these?

3. What is the writer's conception of justice, of what it is or how it may be determined?

4. What basic assumptions about human nature does the writer make?

5. What basic metaphysical or ethical assumptions does the writer make?

6. What basic political or governmental doctrines does the writer adopt?

7. By what method does the writer purport to support his basic principles and conclusions, or by what data or other evidence does he support them?

8. What ideas did the writer derive from previous writers, and what ideas were original?

9. What circumstances in the life of the writer serve to explain some aspects of his philosophy?

10. What circumstances in the writer's contemporary social milieu serve to explain the origin of his ideas, or their influence or lack of influence?

Chapter 13

NATURAL LAW AND NATURAL RIGHTS

§ 4.10—The Scope and Meaning of "Natural Law"

The oldest and most widely accepted theory of legal valuation in Western civilization is that which is called "natural law" or "the law of nature". Its beginnings can be traced to the ancient Greek philosophers, especially to Aristotle (§ 4.11). It passed through a Stoic reincarnation and became the principles of order immanent in the universe. In this phase its most brilliant protagonist was the Roman lawyer and orator, Cicero, and its most enduring contribution was the conception of a law common to all peoples, *jus gentium* (§ 4.12). At the close of the Middle Ages, following the rediscovery of Aristotle's writings by Western Europeans, natural law was made an integral part of the philosophy of law of St. Thomas Aquinas (§ 4.13) and thus became a part of modern scholastic philosophy (§ 4.14). Natural law had also its Protestant representatives, one of whom, Hugo Grotius, became the founder of international law. Another offshoot of the law of nature was the "state of nature", transformed into the law-state by the social contract, with its reservations of "natural rights" (§ 4.15). What "natural law" means in relation to the nature of man is a question not easily answered (§ 4.16) and its relation to positive law has long been a subject of distinction and dispute (§ 4.17). The influence of natural law theory upon English and American judicial decisions has been sporadic but persistent (§ 4.18). In this Chapter we present the salient aspects of natural law theory, without attempting to comment upon all of the variations in its voluminous literature.[1]

The term, "natural law", has been used with many different meanings, for which no single definition will even roughly suffice. Not only has it been used to refer to conceptions or ideas having diverse characteristics, but also these characteristics have been referred to by other names. At the outset let us note six somewhat distinct meanings, and indicate which of these finds a place in the ensuing discussion:

---

[1] Comprehensive citations of the literature are found in: Stone, The Province and Function of Law (1946), Ch. VIII; Pound, Outlines of Lectures on Jurisprudence (5th ed., 1943), distributed through Parts 1, 2, 3. See also Paton, Jurisprudence (2d ed. 1951), §§ 26–33.

1. Any critical or constructive theory of legal valuation, or of the ideals of law. Pound has sometimes used "natural law" in this sense, in discussing judicial usage.[2] By a similar process one can include in natural law some of the utilitarian versions, including even the work of Jeremy Bentham,[3] who categorically rejected "the law of nature".[4] However, Pound has elsewhere recognized that natural law does not embrace all of the important legal philosophies, that is, theories of what should be the law.[5] This meaning of "natural law" is too inclusive to be accurate or serviceable.

2. The use of reason in the making and administration of law. Sir Frederick Pollock, following St. Germain's Doctor and Student, took the English lawyer's "reason" to be the equivalent of the civil lawyer's "law of nature".[6] A similar conception seems to pervade Professor Fuller's support of natural law as opposed to the arbitrariness of positive law.[7] This broad meaning of "natural law" is not used here because other theories of legal valuation are based upon reason.

3. Principles of human conduct that are discoverable by "reason" from the basic inclinations of human nature, and that are absolute, immutable and of universal validity for all times and places. This is the basic conception of scholastic natural law (infra, §§ 4.13, 4.14) and of most natural law philosophers. This is one of the two meanings employed in this discussion.

4. A theory of natural rights based upon a supposed "state" of nature, a pre-political society, and a supposed social compact in which men conferred limited powers on a political government, and in so doing reserved natural rights. With the logical apparatus of the "state" of nature and the social compact omitted, this theory derives natural rights, chiefly political and economic, from

---

[2] Pound, "The Ideal Element in Judicial Decision," (1931) 45 Harvard L. Rev. 136, 147–48 (Hall, p. 326), referring to "ethical", "religious", "political" natural law.

[3] See Pound, "Revival of Natural Law" (1942) 17 Notre Dame Lawyer 287, 295–296. A similar interpretation is given in LeBoutillier, American Democracy and Natural Law (1950).

[4] Bentham, Principles of Legislation, Ch. XIII, sec. 10, in Bentham, The Theory of Legislation (Ogden ed., 1932).

[5] See Pound, Outlines, supra, n. 1.

[6] Pollock, The Expansion of the Common Law (1904), 109.

[7] See Fuller, The Law in Quest of Itself (1941), e. g., pp. 103–104.

the "nature" of political society. It is here referred to as the "natural rights" theory (infra, § 4.15).

5. Norms of human conduct discoverable by experience and observation as prevalent and useful among different peoples. This empirical slant was given to natural law by some Roman jurists (§ 4.12), and by Ehrlich in explaining the "natural law" influence upon European codification.[8] Such usage is rather exceptional, since ordinarily natural law is taken to mean the a priori, intuitively perceived, principles that should govern conduct. Principles derived from systematic observation of different legal orders belong more properly to legal sociology or comparative law.

6. The capacity to perceive, or any intuitive perception of, "justice" or "equity" in concrete situations. In this sense the English Chancellors of the seventeenth and eighteenth centuries frequently based their decisions upon natural law and equity.[9] The use of such terms and judicial reliance upon such conceptions is still, to a limited extent, a part of the Anglo-American judicial tradition; and the historical origin of this tradition was, predominantly, Aristotle's conception of equity (§ 4.11). Yet the present-day use of such conceptions as justice and equity is not necessarily derived from any of the traditional theories of natural law. The followers of other legal philosophies, such as utilitarianism and sociological jurisprudence, have also a sense of justice and equity. Hence this meaning is not used here.

This analysis of the meanings of "natural law", while not exhaustive nor exclusive,[10] will serve to indicate the linguistic usage of this Chapter and some of the problems discussed in it. Two other meanings, now commonly discarded or subordinated, will be mentioned presently: The natural law of physical objects, or physical laws; and the natural law common to all animals.

---

8 See Stone, op. cit., 219; Ehrlich, Fundamental Principles of the Sociology of Law (Moll trans., 1936), 421.

9 See references in Pound, Outlines (supra, n. 1), 42–43; Stone, op. cit., 227–228; infra, § 4.18.

10 Gurvitch has listed six meanings of "natural law". See Paton, Jurisprudence (1946), 84. Haines gives eight. The Revival of Natural Law Concepts (1930), 333–338. A novel psycho-analytic conception of natural law, developed from childish emotions and nursery habits is discussed in Bienenfeld, Rediscovery of Justice (1947), Pt. I, esp. p. 48.

§ 4.11—Greek Theories of Natural Law: Aristotle

The historical origin of the concept of natural law, in the normative sense, is closely related to that of physical laws, the "laws" of natural science. According to some versions of the origin of natural law, the discovery of order and regularity in the movements of the heavenly bodies preceded, and provided an analogy for, the search for basic universal principles of human conduct.[11] That physical laws have provided influential incentives and analogies for the development of normative theories of natural law is a profound and important fact. For instance, Aristotle compared the natural or universal component of political laws with the fire that burns the same in Persia as in Greece. In so far as the physical science analogy has led to the search for empirical knowledge upon which the evaluations of law-making and law-administration should be based, it has had a wholesome influence. In so far as it has led to insistence upon the unchangeableness and eternal rightness of particular legal rules (or moral rules), it has often been a deterrent to a reasoned evaluation of legal change.

The historical primacy of the physical science conception of natural law has been denied.[12] The conception of natural law as a tradition of Western civilization originated in Greece. At a time prior to the speculations of Greek philosophers, the prevalent conceptions of a "higher" law were probably anthropomorphic, the decrees of gods who were more powerful and perfect men; and physical phenomena were likewise often ascribed to the wishes of the gods. The separation of physical laws from magic and superstition was a striking achievement of Greek philosophy; scarcely less important was the separation of *physis*, the order of occurrences and forces independent of human contrivances, from *nomos*, the variable and somewhat arbitrary rules of human conduct. This separation had been accomplished by the fifth century B. C.; thus it preceded both the Platonic and the Stoic con-

---

[11] See Windelband, A History of Philosophy (Tufts trans., 2d ed., 1926), 27, 57, 171. "The concept [law of nature] was originally bound up with that of physical laws." Jones, Historical Introduction to the General Theory of Law (1940), 98.

[12] See Frank, Courts on Trial (1949), 351. Sir Frederick Pollock states the early Greek anthropomorphic conception of nature: "To a Greek mind in the Homeric age, and probably much later, the reign of law was the same, or nearly the same, in nature and in man". Essays in Jurisprudence and Ethics (1882), 57–59.

ception of justice and natural law.[13] Since these Greek conceptions of "natural law" are not the same as the earlier notions of
divine law and since the former arose after and partly as a result of the separation of physical laws, the dependence of natural
law, as that term is here used, upon the physical law analogy
seems fairly clear. At the same time the suggestive analogy of
human laws for the search for uniformities in physical existence, the "leap-frogging" from one to the other,[14] has continued
throughout the history of natural law.

Plato's conception of justice had many facets, some of which
were similar to that of natural law. Justice according to nature
was contrasted with justice according to enactment; and thus the
"unwritten law" of ancient tradition and usage supplies the deficiencies of legislation.[15] A recent study of Plato's changing and
somewhat obscure doctrines concludes that he found two solutions of the problem of natural justice: A law of nature based
upon physical existence, and one based upon the social compact
of the founders of a society. The gulf between *physis* and *nomos,*
between the factual and the normative (to use comparable modern terms) was bridged by transforming *physis* into the Idea of
justice, which had a universal existence.[16] This idea, taken over
by the Stoics, led to some further confusion in the history of
natural law (§ 4.12).

Aristotle's philosophy contained only a few explicit discussions
of "natural law". Yet these, together with his conceptions of
justice and equity, have had profound influence upon subsequent
legal philosophy. One such passage is in his Rhetoric: The advocate who finds that the written law is against his client's case
should urge the tribunal to apply the "universal law", the unchanging law of nature. However, if the written law supports his
case, the advocate should argue that both judges and jurors are
bound by their oaths to apply the written law.[17] While some later
writers have taken this passage to express Aristotle's views, it

---

13 Morrow, "Plato and the Law of Nature" in Essays in Political Theory
(ed. Konvitz and Murphy, 1948), (Presented to George H. Sabine), 17, 19, 25.

14 Frank, op. cit. (supra, n. 12), 352.

15 See Cairns, Legal Philosophy from Plato to Hegel (1949), 46.

16 See Morrow, op. cit. (supra, n. 13) at pp. 25–28, 43.

17 Aristotle, Rhetoric (Ross trans., 1924), Bk. I, Ch. 15, pp. 1375a–1375b;
Hall, Readings, p. 7.

seems more likely that he was merely repeating contemporaneous oratory for the guidance of his pupils.[18]

Aristotle's most significant passage on natural law is the one in which he begins:

"Of political justice part is natural, part legal,— natural, that which everywhere has the same force and does does not exist by people's thinking this or that; legal, that which is originally indifferent, but when it has been laid down is not indifferent, e. g., that a prisoner's ransom shall be a mina. . . . Now some think that all justice is of this [latter] sort, because that which is by nature is unchangeable and has everywhere the same force (as fire burns both here and in Persia), while they see change in the things recognized as just . . . there is something that is just even by nature, yet all of it is changeable; but still some is by nature, some not by nature." [19]

The physical analogy (fire that burns the same everywhere) is not put forth as Aristotle's but rather as that of his imaginary critic. In his answer to this critic Aristotle seems to hedge: Even natural justice is changeable; yet some things are natural, as by nature the right hand is stronger, though some men change this and become ambidextrous. Here the analogy is man's physiological or psychic nature, rather than inanimate existence. Aristotle seems to be saying that there is a constancy in human nature which makes all human laws have something in common; yet even this constancy is sometimes subject to change. Neither in this passage nor elsewhere in Aristotle's discussions of law and justice does he subscribe to a belief in universal, immutable laws of nature which override conventional (positive) laws.[20] Aristotle's Universal Justice is an ethical rather than a legal conception.[21]

Yet in this passage Aristotle revealed a rare insight into the difference between the ends and the means of human laws. Thus the law prescribing a prisoner's ransom presumably was intended to reward the captor for his valor, to preclude him from practic-

---

[18] Wormuth, "Aristotle on Law" in Essays in Political Theory, supra, n. 13, 45, 58.

[19] Ethica Nicomachea (Ross trans., 1942), Bk. V, 7, 1134 b.

[20] See Wormuth, op.cit. (supra, n. 18), 59. Cf. Fuller's translation in The Problems of Jurisprudence (1949), 49–50.

[21] Cairns, op. cit. (supra, n. 15), 120.

ing unlimited extortion on the prisoner's relatives, and to encourage the latter to make efforts to raise the fixed ransom
money. All of these ends were good reasons for making such a
law; and after it is made they stand for the "policies" of the law,
to use a modern term. Within limits the amount of the ransom
was not vital to the working of the law; once fixed, however, it
was not "indifferent", since the captor, the prisoner and the relatives should be entitled to rely upon it. Moreover, the means
used—the amount of the ransom—might be placed so high as to
discourage relatives, or so low that captors would seek to evade
it. Aristotle's distinction between natural and conventional justice provides the starting point for present-day conceptions of
legal method,[22] and for the social-control conception of law
(§ 2.05).

Aristotle's conception of justice as a moral virtue, a state of
character and an attitude of mind, did not mean that justice was
natural to man; but rather that man is adapted by his nature
to receive moral virtue, which is made perfect in him by habit.[23]
This human capacity to acquire the virtue of justice is also a capacity to sense and to understand instances of justice and injustice; it thus provides the possibility of a common understanding
of justice among the peoples of the earth, especially among those
who have attained similar levels of civilization and comparable
bodies of law. The sense of justice can not only be perfected by
habit, but it can also be improved by reason and instruction.[24]
Apart from these environmental influences it has no content, no
norms nor principles.

A third major contribution of Aristotle to natural-law theory is
his well known doctrine that man is by nature a political (or social) animal. The family, he says, is the association "established
by nature for the supply of men's every-day wants"; but when
men aim at something more than the supply of daily needs, they
unite in villages, and eventually in the state. Since the state enables man to attain the good life, the end for which man is by na-

---

22 See ibid., 79. His distinction between distributive and commutative justice is discussed infra, § 4.23.

23 Ethics (Ross trans., 1942) Bk. II, 1103a: "Neither by nature, then, nor
contrary to nature do the virtues arise in us; rather we are adapted by
nature to receive them, and are made perfect by habit."

24 Ibid., 1103b: The legislator seeks to make the citizens good by forming good habits in them. However, Aristotle mainly reserved teaching for
the development of the "intellectual" virtues.

ture destined, the state, as an association for the perfection of his nature, is itself a creation of nature.[25] In this argument "nature" seems to mean at first basic biological characteristics and impulses (man's everyday wants) and later the inherent potentialities of development latent in mankind which enable men to attain the good life. This conception of the nature (or "natures") of man as determining the ends of the state has been accepted in many later political philosophies. It has long had to compete with other views, that the state, the political organization of society, should have the more restricted function of preserving peace and order so that man may satisfy his daily wants and perfect his nature without further aid from the state (§ 4.15). In this latter view "individual freedom" from state control may mean that freedom is an end "in itself", rather than a means employed by the wise legislator for the attainment of the individual's good life through the state.

In truth the mature individual living in a western civilized society has conflicting drives or impulses, some of which cause him to seek society and social organization, with its conventions and political contrivances, its opportunities and burdens, while others urge withdrawal into the contentment of solitude. To draw any unique and unqualified conclusions about what the political organization of society should or should not do from any one of these drives or impulses alone leads to a one-sided dogmatism, with individual anarchy at one extreme and all-embracing totalitarianism at the other. Just as the individual must, in making a deliberate choice, reconcile or compromise between his own conflicting drives, so the statesman needs to find a reasoned compromise between the conflicting drives of individuals in society. The use of "nature" or "natural" in either the individual's or the statesman's process of reasoning seems only to confuse it. Aristotle's use of those terms in his discussion of the state did not imply a "law of nature" which overrides state law, but rather a theory of what "good" laws should be like,[26] a theory of political axiology.

Aristotle's conception of equity was sometimes included in later natural law theories, although he did not expressly formulate the connection. Equity is a kind of justice superior to legal justice; the latter demands in all cases strict application of the written

---

[25] Aristotle, Politics, Bk. I, ch. 2 (Jowett trans., 1926), 27–28; Hall, pp. 4–5.

[26] The citizen "may obey bad laws as well as good". Ibid., Bk. IV, ch. 8 (Jowett trans.), 163.

law. Equity is a correction of legal justice. Since all law is "universal", i. e., consists of general statements, it will sometimes happen that a case arises which is not "covered" by the general statement; and in such a case, where the legislator has erred by over-simplification, it is right to correct the omission, to say what the legislator would have provided had he thought of this case.[27]

Aristotle conceived of equity as a principle of individual ethics (the equitable man may accept from his unfortunate debtor less than the court would adjudge him entitled to) and also as a principle of the administration of law. "About some things it is impossible to lay down a law, so that a decree is needed." [28] The individual in his ethics may be moved by feelings of mercy or generosity, which vary inscrutably from case to case. The judicial administrator ought to be governed by some principle or principles, even in his equitable decrees, which satisfy the minimum requirements of equality and impartiality if not of predictability. Hence the administration of equity from case to case will almost certainly develop generalizations which have the character of legal norms.[29] Thus the use of equity becomes eventually a means of legal change, of subtle and gradual law making (§ 4.32).

Two questions about this process of equitable law-making remain: How is the judge to know when a concrete case is covered by a settled rule and when it is an appropriate case for equity? Whence does he derive the ideas or notions about fairness which he needs in order to arrive at an equitable decision? Aristotle's discussion of equity gives no definite guidance in answering either of these questions; certainly he does not suggest that there is a storehouse of universal immutable principles from which the solutions can be drawn. His analysis of the method of discriminating the equitable correctly, by intuitive reason which perceives the universal in the particular,[30] shows that he did not regard the equitable judgment as merely an emotional hunch.[31]

Neither justice nor equity in Aristotle's view was a natural phenomenon, something which men could attain without the aid

---

[27] Aristotle, Ethics (op. cit., supra, n. 13), Bk. V, 10, 1137a–1138a.

[28] Ibid., 1137b.

[29] See Cairns (op. cit., supra, n. 15), 109.

[30] Ethics, Bk. VI, 9.

[31] Even though an equitable judgment is "sympathetic judgment about certain facts", it is a discriminating judgment. Ibid., VI, 11, 1143a–20–24.

of human artifice. The conception of "nature" in Aristotle's discussions of ethics and law is, primarily and most consistently, that of the ends toward which men should be guided by their potentialities and their needs. These three Aristotelian conceptions—nature, justice and equity—had a profound influence upon later developments in law and in legal philosophy.

§ 4.12—The Stoics; Jus Gentium; International Law

Three important ideas of modern law and legal theory were derived mainly from Stoic philosophy: The conception of a universal law for all mankind under which all men are equals; the idea of a method of deriving universal principles of law from the observation of the laws of different peoples; and the conception of a law binding upon all states, which has been called, since Bentham invented the phrase, "international law". Along with the seeds of these humanitarian conceptions Stoicism also brought in the fusion and confusion of physical laws and normative laws.

The founder of the Stoic school, Zeno, a native of Cyprus, became eventually a popular teacher of philosophy at Athens in the third century B. C. Zeno was of Phoenician origin, and most of the followers of the Stoic school came from Asia Minor or Roman Italy.[32] Stoic philosophy represents a mixture of scarcely reconcilable ideas. The Stoics sought to found a religion upon the ruins of Greek and Roman polytheism. They developed a conception of God as immanent in the universe which was close to pantheism.

"The universe is a living being, of which God is the soul, the governing intelligence, the sovereign law, the motive principle, the animating warmth." [33] More than once it has been pointed out that a thoroughgoing pantheism is incompatible with the conception of an individual's responsibility for his vicious or wrongful acts. If God is in everything and every individual is a part of God, then the individual has no one to whom he can be responsible and no moral freedom of choice.[34] However, the Stoic creeds were never thoroughly pantheistic. The Stoic ethical theory had less influence upon legal philosophy than its naïve metaphysics,

32 Weber and Perry, History of Philosophy (1925), 106–7.

33 Ibid., 108.

34 See, for example, Russell, A Survey of Western Philosophy (1945), 255; Weber and Perry, op. cit., 111.

as interpreted in the emotive rhetoric of a famous Stoic follower, Marcus Tullius Cicero (B.C. 106–43).

Cicero was a great orator, a distinguished and somewhat unstable politician, and a lawyer of somewhat doubtful legal learning.[35] As a legal and political philosopher he gave remarkably persuasive expression to the Stoic philosophy which he had learned from his teachers, but he did not draw upon the legal materials of Rome as the starting point of his speculations.[36] The fundamental conception of Cicero is that of "true law", transcending the enactments and customs of particular nations, and identified with "right reason", which is immanent in nature, in the universe and in the minds of the wisest men. The following well known passage illustrates the transition from the omnipresent universe to human intelligence:

"Law is the highest reason, implanted in Nature, which commands what ought to be done and forbids the opposite. This reason, when firmly fixed and developed in the human mind, is Law. And so [the most learned men] believe that Law is intelligence, whose natural function is to command right conduct and forbid wrongdoing." [37]

The last sentence quoted suggests Aristotle's moderate conception of the nature of a thing as its function: The function of human intelligence is to make wise commands and prohibitions. Yet in other parts of the same passage he brings in the notion of an overriding natural law which is superior to human enactments. The crowd's definition of law includes that which in written form decrees whatever it wishes. But Justice is determined by the Supreme Law which originated ages before any written law existed. Here is the notion of an unwritten law of immemorial antiquity, which was one of the favorite Greek conceptions of natural law. From this conception to that of an ancient Golden Age, or State of Nature, was an easy step.

The universality and immutability of natural law or "true" law was proclaimed in another passage:

"True law is right reason in agreement with nature; it is of universal application, unchanging and everlasting; it

---

[35] Cicero's legal knowledge is a matter of dispute. Cairns, Legal Philosophy from Plato to Hegel (1949), 161. He was not a great jurist nor an original thinker. Sabine, A History of Political Theory (1937), 161.

[36] Cairns, op. cit., 142.

[37] Cicero, De Legibus (Keyes trans., Loeb Classical Library, 1928), Bk. I VI, p. 317; Hall, p. 19.

summons to duty by its commands, and averts from wrong-doing by its prohibitions. And it does not lay its commands or prohibitions upon good men in vain, though neither have any effect upon the wicked." [38]

The meaning of "nature" in such passages is indeed elusive. Is it human nature? Then surely human nature is not always right nor reasonable. Is it physical nature? Then how can even a wicked man disobey its commands and prohibitions? The fusion of the physical and the normative, which is typical of Stoic philosophy,[39] was emphasized when God was deemed the ruler of both animate beings and inanimate things:

"Thus [the wisest men] have been accustomed to say that Law is the primal and ultimate mind of God, whose reason directs all things either by compulsion or restraint. Wherefore that law which the gods have given to the human race has been justly praised; for it is the reason and mind of a wise law-giver applied to command and prohibition." [40]

Cicero is said to have had a conception of heavenly law (lex caelestis) from which natural law was derived as the perfected reason of the wise man.[41] At the other extreme the prolific Roman jurist Ulpian, some two centuries after Cicero, included in natural law the appetites and instincts which man has in common with the lower animals.[42] Most later protagonists of natural law have rejected Ulpian's notion as carrying the idea of universality a bit too far.

Despite the semantic and syntactic confusions of Stoic legal philosophy, its conception of a universal law for all men had far-reaching consequences. First it provided a theoretical basis for the jus gentium, that part of Roman law which the Roman jurists had developed for litigation involving the claims of foreigners as

---

38 Cicero, De Re Publica (Keyes trans., Loeb Classical Library, 1928), Bk. III, XXII, p. 211; Hall, p. 18. A slightly different translation of this passage was quoted by Walsh, J., in Sodero v. Sodero, 56 N.Y.S.2d 823, 827 (N. Y.Sup.Ct.1945) (holding an Arkansas divorce invalid). But the more limited (and sensible) view that natural law was to Cicero only a critique of positive law is well stated in Wilkin, Eternal Lawyer (1947) esp. 226–227.

39 See Morrow, op. cit., supra, § 4.11, n. 13, at pp. 18–19.

40 Op. cit., supra, n. 37, Bk. II, IV, pp. 380–381; Hall, p. 21.

41 See Cairns, op. cit., 135–142.

42 The passage from Ulpian was incorporated in Justinian's Digest and in his textbook for students, the Institutes; and was adopted by Bracton. Jones, Historical Introduction to the Theory of Law (1940), 103, n. 5.

well as of Roman citizens. The latter alone were entitled to the benefits of the jus civile, or older Roman law. The jus gentium in this concrete sense consisted of a distinct body of concepts and norms which, while not derived from a systematic study of the laws of various nations, were shorn of some of the formalities and intricacies of the jus civile and were deemed to be an improvement over the older rules "in generality of application, in simplicity and informality".[43] In an abstract sense jus gentium referred to the rules and institutions which were believed to be common to the whole human race. The source of this universal aggregate of laws was said by the Roman juris Gaius (c. 110–180 A.D.) to be the naturalis ratio, or natural reason of man, from which the jus naturale was derived; and thus the two became nearly identical in meaning. The jus gentium, it is said, tolerated slavery and was therefore the law common to all free men; the jus naturale was common to all men.[44] "The jus naturale or law of Nature", said Maine, "is simply the jus gentium, or law of Nations, seen in the light of a particular theory." [45]

The conception of a jus naturale identical with jus gentium enabled the medieval Civilians, commentators on the Roman law, to overcome the diversities of local customs and ordinances by an appeal to natural reason; and many of the concepts of Roman law came to be regarded as inherently reasonable and as having the power to override local positive laws or customs. At the same time the law of nature became an ideal of humane interpretation of positive laws, and so brought about their amelioration. Maine ascribes to this ideal the origin of Jefferson's ringing declaration that all men are, and of right ought to be, free and equal.[46]

Hugo Grotius (1583–1645), the founder of international law, in his famous treatise on the law of war and peace (1625) placed natural law upon a secular basis, the social nature of man, a conception which he derived primarily from the Stoics. Man has a natural tendency to the conservation of society which leads him to recognize the possessions of others, to fulfill promises and

---

43 See Jones, op. cit., 102. For slightly different versions of jus gentium see Bryce, Studies in History and Jurisprudence (1901), 558, 589; Bodenheimer, Jurisprudence (1940), 111–113.

44 Ibid., 103.

45 Maine, Ancient Law (1861), 52; Hall, p. 24.

46 Ibid., 83–85, 88, 94–96; Hall, pp. 56–58.

to make reparation for damage done by fault.[47] In these illustrations can be detected one of the common failings of natural law theorists, namely, to identify the "natural" and the "reasonable" in law with that which is familiar, established, antecedently given.[48] However, Grotius made an important contribution when he brought together two theories of the derivation of natural law, which may be called the rational and the empirical or sociological:

"That there is such a thing as Natural Law is commonly proved both a priori and a posteriori: the former, the more subtle, the latter, the more popular proof. It is proved a priori by showing the agreement or disagreement of anything with the rational and social nature of man. It is proved a posteriori when by certain or very probable accounts we find anything accepted as Natural Law among all nations, or at least the more civilized. For a universal effect requires a universal cause: now such a universal belief can hardly have any cause except the common sense of mankind." [49]

Grotius' appeal to the Europeans of his time was not in vain, for his followers, Vattel and Pufendorf, persuaded the nations of western Europe that there ought to be a law governing the conduct of states. From this recognition came the development of techniques of interpretation which gave to many conventions of international intercourse the characteristics of professional law (§ 2.35) rather than of popular morality. At the same time the basis of international law was found in consent, bilateral or multilateral compact (with the notion of reciprocity and exchange), custom and precedents (in which customs often originate). In these foundations of international law one can see the data of Grotius' a posteriori proof of natural law. They are similar to the sources of law enumerated in the Statute of the International Court of Justice (1945). On the other hand, the power to decide a controversy ex aequo et bono is conferred only by special agreement of the parties.[50] Deduction of norms from the social nature of man is still too uncertain a process to be entrusted at large to an international court operating as a court of law.

---

[47] De Jure Belli ac Pacis (Whewell ed., 1853), Vol. I, Prolegomena, pp. xli–xlii, sec. 6; p. xliv, sec. 8.

[48] See Dewey, "Nature and Reason in Law" in Philosophy and Civilization (1931), 172.

[49] Op. cit., supra, n. 47, Vol. I, ch. 1, XII, pp. 16–17; Hall, pp. 49–50.

[50] Art. 34; supra, § 2.35.

The Charter of the United Nations (1945) is a further attempt to establish a universal law for all mankind. Pursuant to a provision in the Charter, a Commission on Human Rights was created and directed to prepare a statement of fundamental human rights. The Commission reported a Universal Declaration of Human Rights which was approved by the General Assembly of the United Nations in 1948. This declaration emphasizes "the social nature of man" as calling for the recognition of fundamental human rights, which are set forth in twenty-eight articles. Nowhere is "natural law" referred to,[51] a circumstance which is rather fortunate in view of the historic associations and differences of opinion regarding that term. The provisions of the Declaration are sometimes stated in the idealist terms of a moral code, and sometimes in the more precise terms of a legal code. Except for a catch-all provision on duties [52] there is no indication of how the rights are to be implemented. The Declaration is to be followed by a Covenant which will make the implementation more definite. Meanwhile the Declaration stands as an idealistic moral code for the future.

§ 4.13—Natural Law and the Law of God; St. Thomas Aquinas

The theory of natural law set forth in the treatise, Summa Theologica, of St. Thomas Aquinas (1226–1274)[53] is a remarkable synthesis of Christian theology and Aristotelian philosophy, with some influences of other writers on natural law. His philosophy of law is generally accepted by Roman Catholic scholars and by some who are not members of that Church. While he revered Aristotle, whom he referred to as "the Philosopher", Aquinas constructed an original system of philosophy. The theory of natural law is only a part of his book on law, in which

---

[51] The only place where "natural" appears is in Art. 16(3): "The family is the natural and fundamental group unit of society . . .".

[52] Art. 27 of the Declaration states that everyone has duties to the community and shall be subject in the exercise of his rights "only to such limitations as are necessary to secure due recognition and respect for the rights of others and the requirements of morality, public order and general welfare in a democratic society." Mrs. Eleanor Roosevelt, the American delegate, defended this article as an essential limitation on the previous articles which unqualifiedly asserted human rights. N. Y. Times, Nov. 24, 1948, p. 8.

[53] He was born in the territory of Naples, of a noble distinguished family; he studied at Cologne and taught philosophy and theology at Cologne, Paris and elsewhere.

he sets forth the relation between Eternal Law, Divine Law, Natural Law and Human Law.

Aquinas begins his discussion of "the essence of law" by saying that he has now to consider "the extrinsic principles of acts." His initial statement is:

> "Law is a rule and a measure of acts, whereby man is induced to act or is restrained from acting: for lex (law) is derived from ligare (to bind) because it binds one to act. Now the rule and measure of human acts is the reason, which is the first principle of human acts . . . Consequently it follows that law is something pertaining to reason." [54]

Here law is used to mean a rule of human conduct. For the most part he adheres to this conception; yet sometimes he attempts a fusion of physical law and normative law like that which was characteristic of the Stoics. In his discussion of Eternal Law, he comes closer to a fusion of the two ideas:

> ". . . the whole community of the Universe is governed by Divine Reason. Wherefore the very idea of the government of things in God the Ruler of the universe, has the nature of a law. And since the Divine Reason's conception of things is not subject to time but is eternal, . . . therefore it is that this kind of law must be called eternal . . ." [55]

Eternal Law. The eternal law is the law of things as well as of persons; but Aquinas has separated the two in his distinction between the speculative reason and the practical reason. He then proceeds to define natural law, human law and Divine law. All things participate in the eternal law, in so far as they derive from its imprint their respective inclinations to their proper acts and ends.[56] Thus natural law, too, includes physical laws as well as normative rules of human conduct.[57] Man as a

---

[54] Summa Theologica, (Part II, first part), Q. 90, Art. 1; (Dominican Fathers trans., 2d ed., 1927), 1–2. The subsequent references in this section are to the Questions in this part (II–I).

[55] Ibid., Q. 91, Art. 1.

[56] Ibid., Art. 2.

[57] See Le Buffe and Hayes, The American Philosophy of Law (1947), 38. Yet jurisprudence is concerned only with the moral natural law. Ibid., 39. But Dabin, a distinguished Belgian Scholastic, excludes physical laws from natural law, on the ground that "law being a matter of reason", only the participation of the reasonable creature in the eternal law properly merits the

rational creature participates in the eternal law "in a most excellent way"; and "this participation of the rational creature in the eternal law is called the natural law." [58] The eternal law is also known to man through direct revelation; this is Divine law, as revealed in the Bible.[59]

What are the precepts of natural law? They are to be apprehended by the practical reason; and since the practical reason, which is directed to action, apprehends first of all the good as the end of action, the first principle of natural law is to seek the good and avoid evil. Except for a few suggestions,[60] he does not give any definite examples of natural law precepts. However, he introduces the view, which is most difficult to grasp, that all of man's natural inclinations are apprehended as good:

> "Since, however, good has the nature of an end, and evil, the nature of a contrary, hence it is that all those things to which man has a natural inclination, are naturally apprehended by reason as being good, and their contraries as evil, and objects of avoidance." [61]

Acquinas sets forth three levels of natural law precepts: The lowest is derived from the "inclination" which man has as a substance, and which inclines him to preserve his being (hence whatever is a means of preserving life belongs to the natural law). The second level is the set of inclinations which man shares with the animals, such as sexual intercourse and the education

---

name of law. The Legal Philosophies of Lask, Radbruch and Dabin (1950), 418, n. 3.

[58] Q. 91, Art. 2.

[59] The Divine law is designed to direct man to his "end of eternal happiness, which is inpropriate to man's natural faculty" (Q. 91, art. 4); it forbids and punishes all sins, though human law may be inappropriate to attain this end (ibid.); and it is divided into the Old law (of the Old Testament) and the New law (of the New Testament) (Q. 91, art. 5), which are discussed at length (QQ. 98–108).

[60] Theft is contrary to natural law, though Julius Caesar found that some German tribes were unaware of it. Q. 94, Art. 4. Homosexual lust is "the unnatural crime" because it is contrary to sexual intercourse, which is natural to all animals. Q. 94, Art. 3, Rep. Obj. 3.

[61] Q. 94, Art. 3. However, one of my scholastic-trained students has explained that since man's nature comes from God, man's natural inclination can only be good, even though the apparent good may be not good. This explanation brings out the inseparable connection of natural law and religion. See also infra, § 4.14, n. 94.

of offspring.[62] The third is his inclination to good, according to his reason, which nature is proper to him.[63] The third one seems to be the only one that merits the name of law as a measure of human conduct by reason.[64]

With respect to the certainty with which one can derive principles of natural law, Aquinas was more cautious than some of his followers have been. Here he introduces the difference between the speculative reason, which deals with necessary truths, and the practical reason, which deals with the contingent affairs of human conduct, and therefore may become defective as it descends into detail. If one takes the speculative reason to be that of physics or geometry and the practical reason to be that of ethics or law, the distinction accounts for the difference between physical laws and moral or legal norms. The latter is the sense in which Aquinas discusses the relation between natural law and human law. The limitations of the practical reason are thus illustrated: Since every one should act according to reason, it follows that goods entrusted to another should be restored to their rightful owner. Yet in a particular case this may be unreasonable, as where the goods are claimed for the purpose of fighting against one's country. The greater the number of conditions added, the greater the number of ways in which the principle may fail to be reasonable.[65] The conclusion seems to be that subordinate principles, such as the rule requiring restoration of trust property, cannot be formulated as unconditionally right for all cases; there will be exceptions. The only natural law principle which he states to be unqualifiedly right is: Seek good and avoid evil.

As to the unchanging character of natural law, Aquinas asserts that it can be added to both by Divine law and by human law. In its first principles, the natural law cannot be changed by subtraction; in its secondary principles, which are detailed and only proximate conclusions drawn from the first principles, it may be changed in some particular cases of rare occurrence (such as the illustration given above), though even its secondary principles will remain right for most cases. This is, in substance,

---

[62] Here he cites the passage from Ulpian referred to supra, § 4.12, n. 42.

[63] Q. 94, Art. 3.

[64] Professor Dabin includes only this last in his conception of natural law. Infra, § 4.14, n. 94.

[65] Q. 94, Art. 4.

the scholastic doctrine of the immutability of natural law. Since the natural inclinations of all men need to be directed according to reason, natural law is universal for all men.[66]

Human Law. The Thomistic conception of human law is given in his definition of "law":

"An ordinance of reason for the common good, made by him who has care of the community and promulgated." [67]

In discussing the question whether it is useful for men to make laws, he considers the argument that men have recourse to judges as "animate justice", which is better than the inanimate justice of laws; hence, one may argue, it would be better to let judges decide cases according to justice, without laws. To this Aquinas gives several good answers. First, it is easier to find a few wise men competent to frame right laws, than to find many judges who would judge aright in each case. Secondly the lawmakers can take time to consider many possible cases in making law before any single case has arisen, and are therefore better able to see what is right than the judge who must promptly decide a particular case. Thirdly, because lawmakers judge in the abstract and for the future, they are less affected by love, hatred or cupidity, by which the judge may be affected.[68] Now some of the *assumptions of fact* underlying these arguments are in modern states (at least) highly questionable: Rarely, if ever, are the members of the legislative body generally wiser, or more foresighted or more free from passion than are the judges of the higher levels. Yet Aquinas' arguments admirably support political principles—the supremacy of the legislature over the judiciary, the independence of the judiciary from political pressure and the dependence of the judiciary upon previously given legal norms—which are the fundamentals of "justice according to law".

The conflict between natural law and human law is one of the recurrent problems of legal philosophy. It is touched upon by Aquinas in several ways, which may be divided into two questions: 1. Is human law derived from natural law? 2. Is human law binding upon the conscience?

1. As to the derivation of human law, in the first place it is, in a sense, derived from eternal law, which is the plan of gov-

---

66 Q. 94, Art. 5, ad 3.

67 Q. 90, Art. 4. The elements of this definition are repeated in his discussion of human law.

68 Q. 95, Art. 1, ad 2.

ernment of the Chief Governor. All human laws, in so far as they partake of right reason, are derived from the eternal law, and in so far as they do not so partake, they are unjust laws: yet human laws need not endeavor to direct everything that Divine law directs.[69] The subordination of human law to eternal law *may* be taken to mean that state officials who are members of the Roman Catholic Church are under a peculiar duty to give effect to the law of God as interpreted by that Church;[70] yet such a conclusion does not, it seems, necessarily follow from what Aquinas says. The derivation of human law from natural law occurs in two ways: By deduction, a conclusion from premises, and by determination of particulars. An example of the first is: From the principle, "one should do harm to no man," one deduces the conclusion, "one should not kill a man".[71] Now the conclusion thus derived is not a rule of human law unless some sanction or legal consequence is implied by it; hence the illustration shows the derivation of a more concrete natural law principle from a more general one. By "determination of particulars" St. Thomas meant, it seems, the determination of the punishment or sanction; and those aspects of human law which are thus derived "have no other force than that of human law".[72] Since all legal norms (of human law) express or imply legal consequences, and since the principles of natural law do not, it follows that no human law can be logically deduced from natural law and likewise that no human law can be shown by deduction to *contradict* (logically) a principle of natural law—that is, not without bringing in some premise which requires that human law should implement a natural law principle in some particular way.[73] However, the *tendency or effect* of a human law may be such as to induce men to act contrary to a principle of natural law.[74] Thus, if respect for another's property is a prin-

---

[69] Q. 93, Art. 3.

[70] See examples of such interpretations cited in Wright, American Interpretations of Natural Law (1931), 274–276.

[71] Q. 95, Art. 2.

[72] Ibid. Cf. Aristotle's conventional parts of a political law. Supra, § 4.11, n. 19.

[73] Parenthetically, this arguement applies equally to other natural law theories and to other kinds of idealist legal philosophy. See Cohen (Morris), "Positivism and the Limits of Idealism in the Law" (1927) 27 Columbia L.Rev. 241, 243.

[74] See Dabin's similar view, infra, § 4.13.

ciple of natural law,[75] a political society which has no law against theft would make it more difficult, but not impossible, for a virtuous man to live in accordance with the natural law principle. Similarly a law permitting divorce may induce some spouses to violate the principle of the indissolubility of marriage; yet it does not compel them to do so. It seems, then, that human law can be contrary or opposed to natural law only if the latter is a *political* principle either prescribing what officials should do or not do or prescribing what citizens should do or refrain from doing.

2. To the question, does human law have the power to bind a man in conscience?—St. Thomas answers that just laws have this power, because of the eternal law from which they are derived. He mentions two kinds of unjust laws: Those that are contrary to human good (and therefore do not conform to the end of human law) and those that are contrary to the Divine good, such as a law inducing one to idolatry.[76] The latter must not be obeyed; the former are not binding in conscience, since they are acts of violence rather than laws; yet in Christian humility the citizen may observe them to avoid scandal or disturbance.[77] Since he says that a human law may be unjust because it is conducive, not to the common good, but to the "cupidity or vainglory"[78] of the ruler, or because, though made with a view to the common good, it imposes burdens unequally on the community, this passage seems to [79] open up possibilities of individual anarchy, in which each man's conscience would be a judge of the public good. In taking the position that an unjust law is no law he relies on St. Augustine, whose philosophy was Platonic. In other passages, which seem more Aristotelian in derivation, Aquinas argues that, except in dire emergencies, the citizen should obey the law, and look to the lawmaker to change it.[80]

The philosophy of law of St. Thomas Aquinas is the first comprehensive and systematic one. In stating that the function of human law is to promote the good (happiness) of the community

---

[75] See supra, n. 60.

[76] Q. 96, Art. 4.

[77] Ibid.

[78] Ibid.

[79] Seems to, because the citizen may still deem it better to obey an unjust law, for the sake of peace.

[80] Q. 96, Art. 6; 97, Art. 4.

by the use of reason and with the aid of sanctions, he gave a workable conception which need not have been tied to his conception of natural law nor to his theology. His natural law conception frequently confuses physical and biological generalities with ethics, and it is too closely related to his theology to serve as a common ground of reasoning and evaluation for those who do not belong to his church. His insights into the problems of human law [81] are valuable independently of his views of natural law.

§ 4.14—Modern Scholastic Natural Law: Gény, Duguit, Dabin

The influence of the natural law theories outlined in the preceding sections was shown in an extensive body of literature on natural law, some Protestant, some Catholic, and some professing to be independent of any religious faith. Many of the religious writers on natural law have been but little known outside their own theological circles. Three jurisprudents of the present century have, without departing from Thomism, presented legal philosophies with a wider appeal. These are Gény, Duguit, and Dabin.

Francois Gény distinguished between the factors *("données")* which influence the content of law and the professional technique *("construit")* which goes into law making. One can see in this a continuation of Aristotle's distinction between the natural and the conventional parts of a law; [82] yet Gény has added something, that the "artificial" element in law is not purely arbitrary but is the product of an art. The factors which enter into law-making (the *"données"*) are derived from four primordial elements. First, law is conditioned by certain stubborn facts which constitute the external world of man's environment (geography, climate, etc.) and his own physical and mental characteristics. A second is made up of traditions which yield slowly to change. A third is composed of the principles of conduct which commend themselves to the greater part of any community as being reasonable. Lastly, the law is influenced by the ideals of religion, morals and ethics which often strike the balance in any given conflict of interests.[83] This epitome of the so-

---

[81] For an excellent commentary, see Cairns, Legal Philosophy from Plato to Hegel (1949), 163–204.

[82] Supra, § 4.11, n. 19.

[83] This summary is based upon Jones, Historical Introduction to the Theory of Law (1940), 111–112. Dabin calls the four "givens" the natural

cial and ethical factors from which the lawmaker derives the content of his laws was found useful by Judge Benjamin N. Cardozo in formulating his outline of the four methods of the judicial process.[84]

The influence of Thomism upon Gény is shown in his ultimate appeal to some kind of existential natural law. In the last volume of his work on legal science and technique, Gény fervently urged the recognition of the "existence" of natural law, not as an ideal type of law but as a prototype of positive law having the same kind of objectivity that the latter has.[85] Yet he rejects the notion of a "natural law" in the sense of physical, biological or even economic or sociological laws, because these latter are "fatalistic." [86] He considers natural law a necessary presupposition of the juridical organization of men in society.[87] To Ripert's accusation that his (Gény's) belief in natural law is a disguised religious belief, Gény replies that he considers the doctrine of natural law established apart from religious conceptions, which only give it a not indispensable support.[88] In the end, however, he is unable to formulate doctrines of natural law.

Léon Duguit is best known for his conception of social solidarity. The sense of social solidarity which binds all men together, and a sense of justice common to all men, give rise to feelings of obligation, to reactions hostile to violations of these social senses, and so to the social rule *(droit objectif)*. When the members of the social group have become aware that the social reaction against infringers of the rule can be socially organized in a definite procedure, usually coercive, the social rule becomes a legal rule. At this stage the legislature or the judge may adopt and apply it, but whether these officials accept it or not, they cannot abolish it. This, as has been remarked, is the old overriding law of nature, in a new, sociological version.[89] Duguit rec-

---

"given", the historical "given", the rational "given" and the ideal "given". General Theory of Law, No. 128, in The Legal Philosophies of Lask, Radbruch and Dabin (Wilk trans., 1950), 347.

[84] See Cardozo, The Nature of the Judicial Process (1921) 30 et seq. Cardozo did not (as Gény did) try to separate the factors (data) from the method.

[85] Gény, Science et Technique en droit privé positif, t. IV (Paris, 1924) 216.

[86] Ibid., 217.

[87] Ibid., 220.

[88] Ibid., Preface, viii.

[89] Jones, op. cit. (supra, n. 83) 113. See Duguit, Traité de droit constitutionnel (3d ed., 1927), ch. 1.

ognized only a few basic normative rules of "objective law" in the French civil code; the rest were merely constructive rules, or technical implementations. In both Gény and Duguit can be seen the influence of modern theories of sociology.

Jean Dabin (1889– ——), a professor in the principal center of Thomistic philosophy in Europe,[90] has constructed a valuable and interesting general theory of law which unites the conception of political authority and coercion with the conception of an immediate juristic end, the maintenance of public order in society for the common good. He gives as his initial thesis the following definition of the law *(jus politicum):*

> "The sum total of the rules of conduct laid down, or at least consecrated, by civil society, under the sanction of public compulsion, with a view to realizing in the relationships between men a certain order—the order postulated by the end of the civil society and by the maintenance of the civil society as an instrument devoted to that end." [91]

How does Dabin reconcile the positive and the teleological elements of this definition? If one defines law as a rule of human conduct having political authority and sanction, then how can one say that any other characteristic, such as that the rule must be designed to promote the public good or even public order, is also necessary, without leaving open the argument that some authoritative and sanctioned rules are not so designed and hence, because they are "bad laws", are not law? His answer, as I understand him, would be that the making and application of law (what he calls "the elaboration of law") constitute an art, governed by prudence, which only the statesman-jurist is competent to practice; that the *meaning* of a legal rule is to be understood as a product of this art directed toward the end, the public good; and that no mere moralist or natural law theorist is competent to pass upon the product of the jurist's art. The legal rule is not just a mere implementation of natural law. Legal experience, as it comes from the general practice of legislation, case law and customs, clearly confirms this conclusion. In some cases, it is true, the professional formulation of the le-

---

90 A native of Belgium, educated at the University of Liége, he has been since 1922 a professor at the University of Louvain, and has served as exchange professor at the Universities of Paris, Poitiers, Nancy, Dijon, Lyon and Lausanne.

91 Dabin, Théorie générale du droit (1944), No. 6, translated in The Legal Philosophies of Lask, Radbruch and Dabin (Wilk trans., 1950), 234, (cited below as L.R.D. with section number and page of the translation).

gal rule begins with a principle of natural law and justice, yet it always subjects the principle to certain adjustments or exceptions. Frequently, to promote security, it sacrifices such principles (as when a thief is allowed to acquire title by prescription). Moreover, the principles of natural law do not and cannot provide a definite legal solution; they simply call for a search for the best legal solution, taking everything into account. The statesman-jurist, not the theorist of natural law and justice, makes the choice.[92] He rejects Gény's doctrine that law is partly "given" and partly "construed"; on the contrary, it is all "construed", a construct of prudent invention. He concludes that while there is a moral natural law and a political natural law, there is no juridical natural law:

> "Third, there exists no juridical natural law in the sense of solutions or even mere directives given in advance to the authority charged with the establishment of the civil (state) law according to the public good." [93]

The temporal public good includes many values of men in society which are not directly moral nor natural in character: Rules prescribing the effects of failure to register a conveyance of land; traffic rules; rules of negotiable instruments, etc. Only in a remote sense are these professional products derived from natural law or morality.

But when he comes to discuss natural law and morality he seems to equivocate on the question, whether a "bad" law, one which is "contrary" to natural law or morality, is something which is not law at all (and which the citizen is therefore not *legally* bound to obey), or is merely a law which does not bind the citizen's conscience and which the lawmaker *ought* to change. He defines natural law as a universal and immutable norm issuing from nature:

> "as the adjective 'natural' indicates without too great ambiguity, the rule of human conduct that is called natural law is deduced from the nature of man as it reveals itself in the basic inclinations of that nature under the control of reason, independently of any formal intervention by any legislator whatsoever, divine or human.[94]

This definition restricts natural law to a norm of human conduct, and it takes the inclinations of man to be subject to the con-

---

[92] L.R.D., Nos. 115, 116 (pp. 333–336).

[93] Ibid., No. 215 (p. 430).

[94] Ibid., No. 203.

trol of reason;[95] yet it does not explain how any conclusion can be logically "deduced" from the nature of man unless some a priori principle were first derived from man's nature. He then considers the relation of positive law:

> "Natural law, furthermore, dominates positive law in the sense that, while positive law may add to natural law or even restrict it, it is prohibited from contradicting it.[96] How could the legislator, or at least the human legislator, have the power to rebel against the 'given' of human nature?"[97]

Since Dabin has said that positive law depends upon "power",[98] an enactment that the legislature had no power to enact is not law, and once more natural law appears as an overriding superior norm. Again, in view of Dabin's careful definition of positive law as always including a legal sanction, while natural law does not include such a sanction, how can a rule of positive law ever (logically) contradict natural law? Moreover, if positive law can add to natural law, might not the principle thus added and implemented interfere in its effects with the effects of some prior prinple of natural law? Thus the principle that the conduct of delinquent minors should be controlled by a juvenile court partly contravenes the principle that the parent has a "natural" right to control the moral education of his minor child. However, Dabin gives no examples of contradiction, and he adds that the present tendency is to restrict natural law to the "minimal conception"; that is, that only the first principles, directly "given" by the inclinations of nature, are included in the term.[99]

The problem recurs when he considers the relation between morality and the temporal public good: "A legal rule positively contrary to morals must be condemned as contrary to the public good".[1] Further, "the law cannot command what morals

---

[95] Cf. excerpt from Aquinas, supra, § 4.13, n. 61 and comment. Curiously enough, Dabin quotes (No. 205) St. Thomas' three types of inclinations (supra, § 4.13, n. 63); the first he takes to mean that man owes duties to himself.

[96] Here he cites Aquinas, II–I, Q. 94, art. 5, summarized supra, § 4.13, before n. 66.

[97] Dabin, L.R.D., No. 203 (pp. 419–420). Here again the religious interpretation of human nature seems implicit. Cf. supra, § 4.13, n. 61.

[98] Ibid., Nos. 16 et seq.

[99] Ibid., No. 204 (pp. 420–421).

[1] Ibid., No. 245 (p. 456).

forbids nor can it forbid what morals commands.[2] Here he explains that the "contradiction" does not have to be immediate. A law which by its provisions *tends to discourage* the virtuous act in creating obstacles (formalities, delays, taxes) or to encourage the vicious act in setting up advantages (prizes, remissions) is, he says, also contradictory. As "historic or imaginable examples" he mentions laws *requiring* apostasy, dueling, abortion, euthanasia, and laws prohibiting acts of liberality inter vivos or by will.[3] Would a gift-tax law or an inheritance-tax law applicable to "liberal" testamentary dispositions, be contrary to morals?

Despite a few rather extreme statements, Dabin seems to regard natural law as ethical rather than legal in character, as constituting a part of the data which the lawmaker must consider, and as having at times a peculiarly strong claim upon his judgment. For the most part Dabin's lawmaker (whether by legislation or by case law) is concerned with the temporal public good, which, as Dabin outlines it, seems not very different from Bentham's greatest good of the greatest number, or from Pound's social interests (§ 4.61).

§ 4.15—"Natural Rights" and the Social Contract: Locke

The theory of "natural rights" is distinct from the theories of natural law previously discussed; its architect was the English philosopher, John Locke (1632–1704). Locke, the son of a country lawyer and small landowner who joined the parliamentary army in the English Civil War, studied science, philosophy and medicine. Though he never became a lawyer, his social compact theory bears some imprints of the English common law. His chief work on political theory [4] was written to refute the argument for the divine right of kings and to uphold the tolerant, democratic and egalitarian principles of the Puritan revolution.

Locke's objective was to justify the establishment of *a* government, to state the ends for which government is established

---

[2] Ibid., No. 246 (p. 457).

[3] Ibid.

[4] Two Treatises on Civil Government, first published 1690, though written several years earlier. The edition here used is Everyman's Library (ed. W. S. Carpenter), and the references are to sections of the Second Treatise. The First Treatise, a refutation of the divine right of kings, is not here important.

and the limitations upon the powers of government.[5] His argument is in three steps: 1. Man was originally in a State of Nature, a pre-political society. 2. The members of this society entered into a social contract by which they established a government. 3. The powers of this government are limited by the terms of the social contract which are implied from the two preceding steps.

In a state of nature all men are equal in that no one has more power or jurisdiction than his fellow man; yet each man's liberty is governed by the law of nature, a law of reason, which teaches that no one ought to harm another in his life, health, liberty or possessions; and every one is bound first to his own preservation and, subject to this, to do as much as he can for the preservation of other men.[6] Locke makes several important assumptions: That man's nature is basically good; that man has to live in social relationships; and that a pre-political society would be or at least might be a fairly good kind of society. Locke almost persuaded himself that such a society had existed historically, for he refers to the "golden age",[7] to an idyllic condition in which a man's only "property" was his labor,[8] and to a bargain struck between a Swiss and an Indian in the woods of North America.[9] Yet he regarded the state of nature as a fictitious assumption, not wholly contrary to fact, but expedient as a way of answering the question of men living in a political state: "How can the powers of government be justified?" Locke's answer begins by inferring the condition that would exist without a government.

In a state of nature every man would have a right to enforce the law of nature, to punish the wrongdoer in order to restrain him from future wrongs and to obtain reparation from him. This natural right, however, violates a basic principle that no man shall be a judge in his own cause. The enjoyment of one's natural rights, the protection of one's property rights, in a state of na-

---

[5] The Second Treatise is entitled: "An Essay Concerning the True Original, Extent and End of Civil Government". The conceptions of natural rights and of a state of nature were put forth earlier by the Spanish jurist-theologians, and the social contract idea is also much older. See Haines, The Revival of Natural Law Concepts (1930), Ch. 1, especially p. 18.

[6] Second Treatise, §§ 4–6.

[7] Ibid., § 111.

[8] Ibid., § 45.

[9] Ibid., § 14; also § 25 ("the wild Indian").

ture is insecure.[10] Thence it is necessary to establish a civil society in order to have an impartial magistrate.[11] The means of this establishment is a social compact between the adult members of society, whereby each agrees to give to the majority the "power necessary to the ends for which they unite into [civil] society." [12] An adult is bound by his promise, since promises are binding by the law of nature; he cannot bind his children. Locke reaches the strange (and legally erroneous) conclusion that "a child is born the subject of no country nor government".[13] But this anomalous situation is corrected by his doctrine that any man who possesses or enjoys any of the benefits of a government, even by traveling on the highway, gives his tacit consent to obey the laws of that government during such enjoyment.[14] This tacit compact smacks of the English doctrine of consideration, or of the older conception of an obligation based upon a quid pro quo.

The chief end for which men so unite is to preserve their "property"—a term which Locke used comprehensively to include their "lives, liberties and estates".[15] The original State of Nature was made unsafe by (1) the absence of an established, known and settled law, (2) the absence of a known and impartial judge, and (3) the absence of a power sufficient to execute and enforce the judgment. Hence the government established by the social compact has the power and is under a duty to govern by established laws, by upright judges, and by the use of force only in the execution of such laws and the prevention or redress of injuries by foreign enemies.[16] "And all this to be directed to no other end but the peace, safety, and public good of the people." [17] Locke's conception of the end of the state is, one might say, included in the basic concept of "the common good" which St. Thomas Aquinas found to be the end of human law.[18] Locke made the end more specific (and less sublime) by restricting it to the paramount interests

---

10 Ibid., § 123.

11 Ibid., §§ 87–88.

12 Ibid., § 99.

13 Ibid., § 118.

14 Ibid., § 119.

15 Ibid., § 123. Every man has a property in his own person and his own labor.

16 Ibid., §§ 124–126, 131.

17 Ibid., § 131.

18 Supra, § 4.13, n. 67.

of a mercantilist age: The protection of property by the impartial administration of justice according to law.

From the social compact theory Locke derived two further important implications: First, since by the law of nature no man can give another an arbitrary absolute power over himself, therefore he cannot alienate to the government any such arbitrary power, for no man can transfer any more power than he has.[19] From this rule of property law he derived the political conception of "inalienable rights", incorporated by Thomas Jefferson in the American Declaration of Independence. The next step, that a legislative act which purports to deprive a man arbitrarily of his property is beyond the *legal* power of the legislature, was implicit in some American decisions declaring legislative acts unconstitutional.[20] While Locke's argument is set in a legalistic framework, it seems that he was only stating political principles which were congenial to his age. Secondly, when the government so established goes contrary to the trust imposed in it (or, in other words, violates the social compact) [21] then the "people" have a right to revolt, to return to the pre-political state of nature, and to establish a new government by a new social compact.[22] Here again is the overriding "law of nature" but in a new form. The "right" of revolution is one to be exercised only as a last resort; citizens must put up with a great many mistakes and frailties on the part of their governors. Who is to decide when and how to exercise this right of revolution? Apparently Locke would say only a majority of the people could exercise it; otherwise the revolution would be merely a rebellion.[23] Hence it is not a legal right but a political right grounded in Locke's theory of political natural law.

While Locke's discussion of political and pre-political society frequently refers to God as the Creator of all and hence the Origi-

---

[19] Ibid., § 135.

[20] See Haines, op. cit., supra, 77–79; Haines, "The Law of Nature in State and Federal Judicial Decisions" (1916) 35 Yale L.J. 1026; infra, § 4.18.

[21] A pertinent analogy is the right of one party to a bilateral contract to rescind because of the other's material breach. However, this right was not recognized as one arising from a general principle until nearly a century after Locke wrote. Kingston v. Preston, 2 Doug. 689 (1773).

[22] Ibid., Ch. XIX.

[23] See Cairns, Legal Philosophy from Plato to Hegel (1949) 336. However, sometimes the natural rights doctrine was taken to mean that each individual's conscience was the final arbiter of both political and legal obligations. See Haines, op. cit., (supra, n. 5) 65 n. 2, 66 n. 3.

nator of the natural laws governing man's conduct,[24] yet his political theory is not, I think, dependent upon sectarian religious or theological doctrine. Locke depended rather too much upon contemporary English laws and conventions for the structure of his social compact and for the economic theory which he developed from the state of nature. In this he displayed a common weakness of natural law writers. Yet the political theory which he thus constructed was not insular; it had sufficient universality to make a widespread appeal to those who believed in religious tolerance, economic liberty and the rule of the majority of the people, throughout western Europe. It provided an ideological justification for two major revolutions, the English (1688) and the American (1776), and partly for the French Revolution (1789).

Locke's theory also provided the political framework of nineteenth century economic liberalism. The government was a civil society created by the consent of the governed to provide freedom under law, to protect men from the necessary inconveniences of the state of nature.[25] His conception of a community or society existing, even though fictitiously, apart from law and government, made plausible the view that economic activities should be left as far as possible to the control of "natural" economic laws. In this aspect Locke anticipated Adam Smith's theory of economic freedom; he also anticipated the conception of law as only one instrument of social control (§ 2.06).

§ 4.16—Natural Law and the Nature of Man

The ambiguity of "nature" has been the chief source of the fertility of natural law theories. Sometimes nature is physical nature in general, either as a model of the kind of order, stability and universality which men should seek to attain in their political laws (suggestions of this are found from Plato to Cardozo), or as a part of man's environment setting inexorable limitations upon what human laws *can* do. The latter conception has been recognized from Montesquieu to modern anthropologists; it is scarcely to be reckoned as a "natural law" theory, since under any theory the human legislator should recognize such limitations. Sometimes nature has meant the biological make-up of man, as in Ulpian's famous passage. One can scarcely conceive of a comprehensive body of human laws which would not take account of man

---

[24] Second Treatise, §§ 6, 24, 25, 77, 142 ("the law of God and Nature").

[25] Ibid., § 57.

as a two-sexed viviparous mortal animal. Not only the laws regulating (or purporting to regulate) marriage and the relations between the sexes, the protection of life and the succession to property after death but also the laws regulating the ways in which men can preserve life by seeking food, shelter, clothing, rest and health, are dependent on the biological traits of man. They are dependent in two senses: First, in that these biologocal traits create social conflicts which need regulation by instruments of social control, including law; and secondly, because legal regulations, in order to be effective controls, must be framed with man's biological traits in view as means and as limitations. This is far from saying, however, that from man's animal "nature" one can deduce any particular workable norms of human conduct. Anthropologists have shown too many variations in particular norms, legal or customary, in different societies to make any such view tenable. Indeed, an "animal-nature" law would resemble the régime of a successful cattle-ranch or a well ordered menagerie.

The peculiarly human attributes or qualities of man are the ones which most natural-law theories refer to and rely upon. Now men have long differed as to the basic traits of human nature, and assumptions about human nature often give a natural-law theory its basic slant. To illustrate this we may contrast the assumptions of John Locke (§ 4.15) with those of his contemporary, Thomas Hobbes (1588–1679). Locke regarded man as naturally good, hence in a state of nature men would seek the good of others as well as their own, and would need a government only as a convenience for the settlement of disputes. Hobbes thought that the life of man in a condition of nature would be a war of all against all, in which each would seek only his own good and fear his neighbor; the establishment of a political government was necessary to security, and man's desire for security was so profound that nothing could relieve men of their obligations of obedience under the social contract by which they established a political government—nothing but the government's failure to provide them with security.[26] Thus the Lockeian conception and the Hobbesian conception of the ends and limitations of politically organized society differed because of their different conceptions of human nature. Adherents of natural law theory have often ascribed to human nature some innate, immutable and uni-

---

[26] Hobbes, Leviathan (original ed., 1651), Chs. 13, 14; Hall, pp. 50–55. See Cairns, op. cit. (supra, § 4.15, n. 23), Ch. VII, especially p. 250.

versal characteristics and then ascribed to those who reject their
theories a rejection of these characteristics. Even the tolerant
Dabin seems to draw the conclusion that those who reject his conception of natural law must necessarily believe that might makes
right, that there is no norm of public good prevailing over individual interests, and that there is no place for a rational method
of elaboration of positive law.[27] Yet he nowhere explains what
are the universal, identical and invariant characteristics of human
nature which he categorically asserts.[28]

A further difficulty with natural law theories is the difficulty
of separating inborn human nature from human culture, or rather
from the characteristics manifested in human conduct which are
produced by the environment (physical and social). The varieties of social practices and conventions found among different
peoples indicate the adaptability of human nature, whatever its
basic traits may be, to different patterns of conduct and culture,
to different ways of life. Can one derive any such innate traits a
posteriori by inference from these cultural manifestations, or
should one assume certain fundamental characteristics a priori
and ignore all observations that do not conform to them? The
latter seems to have been the typical method of natural law men;
the former, of anthropologists, who are much more cautious in
their conclusions as to the immutable nature of man.

The contrast in method is exemplified in conflicting views as
to the husband's right to recover damages for the alienation of
his wife's affections. A statute abolishing the action for the
alienation of affections was declared in 1946 to be contrary to
"moral law" and on this ground, among others, was held to be
unconstitutional.[29] A prominent anthropologist, surveying the
problems of the relations of the sexes in contemporary American
society, said recently:

"Breach of promise cases are a silly excrescence in a world
in which women do half the proposing, and alienation-of-
affection cases between two men, which assume that the
woman is a gently pliant lily, ring just as false." [30]

---

27 Dabin, General Theory of Law (1944), § 200, in The Legal Philosophies of
Lask, Radbruch and Dabin (Wilk trans., 1950), 416–417. The conclusion that
no inescapable natural principles can be deduced from these broad assumptions
about human nature is presented in Neumann, "Types of Natural Law," 8
Studies in Philosophy and Social Science (1940) 338, 339.

28 Ibid., § 203.

29 Heck v. Schupp, 394 Ill. 286, 68 N.E.2d 464 (1946).

30 Mead (Margaret), Male and Female (1949), 299.

The illustration may be used to show another fallacy in the assumption that positive laws can be deduced from characteristics of human nature. The anthropologist's conception of "human nature" may be the descriptively correct one, that typically males are no more the aggressors than females in situations where alienation of a wife's affections is a result. Yet the lawmaker may seek to protect the stability of the monogamous marriage, as a highly important social institution, by creating legal remedies which impose on third persons (of either sex) a duty to refrain from conduct inimical to the marital relation—a duty that runs counter to some of the inclinations of human nature, and reenforces others. The effects of the legal remedy, in deterring such inimical conduct and in providing pecuniary reparation for the injured spouse, may be doubtful, and may be outweighed by the abuses of the legal remedy as a means of entrapment and extortion.[31] The legislature was, it would seem, within its province in deciding that the social disadvantages of the legal remedy outweighed the advantages. Such questions cannot be settled merely by an appeal to natural law nor merely by an appeal to descriptive cultural anthropology. The best method is a reasoned appraisal of fact and value, of means and ends and consequences.

That human nature is rational or reasonable is another view that determined the direction of many natural law theories. English lawyers in the sixteenth century (and perhaps earlier) were wont to argue that something was contrary to "Reason" rather than that it was prohibited by natural law.[32] Cicero regarded true law as "the highest reason implanted in nature"; [33] and Sir Frederick Pollock in the early twentieth century considered the Law of Nature to be "a living embodiment of the collective reason of civilized mankind." [34] From Nature to Reason is a leap from one slippery iceberg to another. For "Reason" was used in many different senses. In the seventeenth and eighteenth centuries it meant predominantly the exercise of human intelligence in improving upon older law and in establishing new law; and thus it contributed to many valuable improvements in the law.[35] Yet "reason" as well as "nature" can become identified

---

31 See further discussion in cases cited supra, § 3.16, n. 55.

32 St. Germain, Doctor and Student (first published in 1518), Ch. V (Muchall ed., 1874), p. 12; Hall, p. 43.

33 Supra, § 4.12.

34 Pollock, The Expansion of the Common Law (1904), 128.

35 Dewey, "Nature and Reason in Law" in Philosophy and Civilization

with what is familiar by custom or tradition, and thus become a means of preserving the status quo. Dewey has traced the influence of this type of "reasoning" upon the nineteenth century American law of master and servant.[36] If human reason meant no more than the capacity to understand geometry or grammar, one could well assert that it is necessary but not sufficient for the making and administration of law. For law must take account of passions, desires, evaluations, both of the subject of law and of the lawmaker. Hence "reason" in natural law theory means more than logic; it means wise or prudent evaluation. Of this human talent natural law theory has no monopoly.

The conception of the nature of man as that which he tends to become when he attains his fullest and best development is the teleological or functional conception of nature. Thus Aristotle said that the state is a creation of nature since man's nature is such that he attains his best end in the state.[37] Yet this is no more than saying that human beings, or some of them, have characteristics and capacities which lead them to seek human society and that with an intelligent appraisal of means and ends men are capable of maintaining a political society in which they can attain the highest good. The functional conception of human nature, thus interpreted, provides a worthy thesis for the ends of the law and the state.[38]

§ 4.17—Natural Law and Positive Law

Of the many aspects of the relations between natural law and positive law, as exemplified in legal and jurisprudential writings, two main types are here singled out for discussion. One is the *rhetorical* [39] use of natural law theory, as designed either to conserve positive law (conservative) or to improve it (ameliorative). The former includes not only justifications of the continuance of

---

(1931), 166 et seq., Hall, 230. On the meanings of "reason" in political philosophy, see Sabine, A History of Political Theory (1937) 599.

36 Ibid.; Hall, p. 234.

37 Supra, § 4.11, n. 25.

38 For similar statements as to the end of political society by writers who do not base their conclusions on natural law, see Dewey and Tufts, Ethics (2d ed., 1932), Ch. XVII; Pound, "How Far Are We Attaining a New Measure of Values in Twentieth Century Juristic Thought?" (1936) 42 W.Va.L.Q. 81, 96.

39 "Rhetorical" is not here used in a derogatory sense; it is equivalent, in Professor Morris' analysis, to the "pragmatic" dimension of meaning. Supra, § 3.26.

present positive laws but opposition to new ones. Thus natural law principles have often been derived from the customary, the familiar, the traditional. When Antigone, in Sophocles' drama, appealed to the "unwritten" law against Cleon's decree that she might not bury her brother, she invoked ancient Greek customs.[40] In Roman law the identification of jus naturale with jus gentium was an argument for the modification of the older jus civile, an argument for legal change.[41] Grotius used the law of nature as a basis for the acceptance of a (new) law governing the relations between states.

In the seventeenth and eighteenth centuries the appeal to natural law justified a good many legal innovations. In the nineteenth century natural law was invoked quite as often to resist legal change as to support it. Natural law has in modern times steadily played this role.[42] In the present century, likewise, it seems that natural law arguments have been more often used to prevent legal change.

The second aspect of the natural-positive law relation is that of legal method. Sometimes natural law is proposed as a basis from which positive laws may be or are derived. Sometimes natural law is regarded as a limitation or prohibition on positive laws, which, as long as they do not infringe natural laws, are indifferent or neutral. A third view is that natural law principles are to be used in determining the meaning of positive laws, though they do not wholly control that meaning.

The effort to deduce positive laws from natural law has produced some of the least satisfactory specimens of natural law writing. One eighteenth century lecturer on natural law argued that polygamy is contrary to natural law because by an implied term of the marriage contract each spouse gives the other an exclusive right in his or her person; and hence polygamy would be a violation of the marriage contract.[43] Since the contractual term is implied only because of the "nature" of the marriage re-

---

40 See Wormuth, op. cit., (supra, § 4.11, n. 18) 51.

41 See Jones, op. cit., (supra, § 4.12, n. 42) 102.

42 See Pound, The Formative Era in American Law (1938), 1–37, especially 16. In this lecture Pound uses natural law to mean any kind of legal ideals, including the ideal of order and system. A summary of the "two-faced operation of natural law in the social process" is given in Stone, The Province and Function of Law (1946) Ch. VIII, § 24.

43 Rutherforth, Institutes of Natural Law (2d Amer. ed. 1832; first published 1754), Ch. XV, 163, 167; Hall, 71–72.

lation, the circularity of the argument is scarcely concealed. Many excellent reasons can be given for maintaining monogamy by positive law in American society today without resorting to such fictitious arguments. Another writer who argued for the derivation of positive laws from natural law principles was the Protestant Scotchman, James Lorimer, whose treatise, subtitled "A treatise of the principles of jurisprudence as determined by nature", drew upon theology, ethics and previous writers on natural law.[44] The "rights" revealed by nature, "animate and inanimate", include a right to be, and therefore include a right to continue to be (from which he derives the right of self-defense and a duty of protecting from wanton destruction human, animal or vegetable life[45]); these imply "a right to the conditions of existence", from which he implies the right to the exclusive ownership and possession of property.[46] The right to be implies a right to develop our being and to the conditions of its development, from which he derives the conclusion that the individual has a right, against the state and the parent, to receive an education, and to enter any career for which he is fitted.[47] The right to be involves the right to reproduce and multiply our being, yet this right is limited by the duty of caring for offspring and by the duty to make marriage a means of human wellbeing.[48] This is a touch of Darwinism. The conclusion of this chain, derived ostensibly from the right to be, is that we have a right of transmitting to our offspring the conditions of existence which we confer, and the right to dispose of our property (here justified on the labor theory of Locke and Adam Smith) either by conveyance inter vivos or by testamentary disposition.[49] From this one might easily draw the further implication that a heavy inheritance tax would be contrary to natural law.[50] The "deduction" of positive laws from natural law principles is likely to lead to the

---

44 Lorimer, The Institutes of Law (2d ed., 1880).

45 Ibid., 212–214.

46 Ibid., 215. Professor Lorimer would probably have been surprised if someone had deduced, from his "right to the conditions of existence", the employee's right to be paid a minimum wage.

47 Ibid., 222–225.

48 Ibid., 226–228.

49 Ibid., 229–235.

50 The "natural right" of an owner to transmit his property to his "natural successors" was asserted by Marshall, J., in Black v. State, 113 Wis. 205, 223, 225 ff., 89 N.W. 522, 529 ff. (1902).

justification of positive laws as they are. "Nature" is mirrored in custom.

The second view of the relation between natural law and positive law is expressed by some scholastic writers who emphasize the prohibitions and limitations of natural law upon human law, but consider most human laws to be neutral or indifferent with respect to natural law.[51] The position taken by Professor Dabin of Louvain in his recent treatise seems consistent with this view.[52] It also accounts for the distinction in English law between malum in se, an act inherently wrong, and malum prohibitum, an act that is wrong only because it is legally prohibited.

The third view, that natural law principles are to be used in determining the meaning of positive law, seems to be the one that Aristotle referred to when he said that all political laws are partly natural and partly "legal" (conventional).[53] This means that legal norms should be taken as the expression of a policy or policies which the lawmaker chose to effectuate by means of the substantive and procedural norms which form its text and context. The Roman lawyers used their ideas of natural law in the interpretation of their "actual" law.[54] Professor Fuller seems to take a similar view when he defines natural law as "the view which denies the possibility of a rigid separation of the *is* and the *ought* and which tolerates a confusion of them in legal discussion." [55] However, the teleological or purposive interpretation of statutes or of case law is not dependent upon the acceptance of such a confusion, nor is it an exclusive property of natural law.

§ 4.18—Natural Law in English and American Case Law

The circumstances favorable to the use of principles of natural law or natural rights as justifications for judicial precedents in

---

[51] See Miltner, "Law and Morals" (1934) 10 Notre Dame Lawyer 9–10 (but he also says that "positive human laws are contained implicitly in the natural law").

[52] Supra, § 4.14.

[53] Supra, § 4.11, n. 19.

[54] Barker, Introduction to Gierke, Natural Law and the Theory of Society (1934), vol. I, pp. xxxvi–xxxvii; Hall, p. 25.

[55] Fuller, The Law in Quest of Itself (1910), 5. See also Fuller, "Reason and Fiat in Case Law", (1946) 59 Harv.L.Rev. 376, 379.

English and American law were twofold: First, the unsystematic character of case law and the absence of a comprehensive code left gaps in the law which courts felt obliged and authorized to fill; and secondly, the legal changes made by case law had to be justified by judges as mere declarations or applications of something antecedently given. For this purpose natural law and natural rights vied with common custom and what was sometimes called "reason". On the whole it seems surprising that natural-law arguments did not play a larger part in the judicial opinions of appellate courts both in England and the United States than they did.

Among the factors which limited the resort to natural law the chief one was the principle of legislative supremacy, which was taken to mean that natural law, as a body or a source of principles not to be found in statutes or case law, was a source of law for legislatures rather than courts. This view was expressed by Wildes, J., in 1871:

> "I would observe, as to these Acts of Parliament, that they are the law of this land; and we do not sit here as a court of appeal from parliament . . . The proceedings here are judicial, not autocratic, which they would be if we could make laws instead of administering them." [56]

The reluctance of American courts to resort to natural rights arguments in their opinions, with relatively few exceptions,[57] is all the more striking because most state constitutions have long contained explicit references to "inalienable rights".[58] A second reason was the feeling that conclusions drawn from "natural law" were too subjective, too open to doubt and dispute among honest and able men, to be solid support for a judicial innovation:

---

[56] Lee v. Bude & Torrington Junction R. Co., L.R. 6, C.P. 576, 582 (1871); Hall, p. 289. Here the court was asked to declare an act of Parliament invalid on the ground that it was fraudulently obtained. An argument like that of Wildes, J., was made by Cardozo, J., in Snyder v. Com. of Massachusetts, 291 U.S. 97, 122, 54 Sup.Ct. 330, 338 (1933).

[57] See McGovern v. Van Riper, 137 N.J.Eq. 24, 33, 43 A.2d 514, 519 (1945), where Vice-Chancellor Kays said the right of privacy was one of the "natural and inalienable rights" recognized by Art. 1, sec. 1 of the New Jersey constitution. The appellate court's opinion did not discuss this suggestion. 137 N. J.Eq. 548, 45 A.2d 842 (1946).

[58] Haines, The Revival of Natural Law Concepts (1930), 183. Resort to "natural law" is authorized by the Louisiana Civil Code (Art. 21) "where positive law is silent".

"The ideas of natural justice are regulated by no fixed standard: the ablest and the purest of men have differed upon the subject; and all that the court could properly say, in such an event, would be, that the legislature (possessed of an equal right of opinion) had passed an act which, in the opinion of the judges, was inconsistent with the abstract principles of natural justice." [59]

In a somewhat similar vein, the inadequacy of either natural law or natural justice to guide the court in solving the intricate problems of an orderly and predictable judicial process was expressed by Scrutton, L. J., in commenting upon Lord Mansfield's earlier statement that the action for money had and received was founded upon "ties of natural justice and equity":

". . . the whole history of this action has been what I may call a history of well-meaning sloppiness of thought".[60]

A fourth reason why both English and American judges since 1850 have not very often resorted to natural law or natural rights is that they have found ways of deriving general principles or policies from the syntactical or genetic meanings of the whole body of legislative and case law. Thus Andrews, J., in 1878, rejecting the view that laws may be declared void "when deemed to be opposed to natural justice and equity", said:

"Indeed, under the broad and liberal interpretation now given to constitutional guaranties, there can be no violation of fundamental rights by legislation which will not fall within the express or implied prohibitions and restraints of the Constitution, and it is unnecessary to seek for principles outside of the Constitution, under which such legislation may be condemned." [61]

Another example of a tempting situation for natural law or natural right theory was a case involving the power (or lack of power) of the Postmaster-General of the United States to refuse second-class mailing privileges to a publication deemed by him to be lacking in literary, artistic or scientific value; yet the opinion of the court, without relying on natural law or natural rights,

---

[59] Iredell, J., concurring especially in Calder v. Bull, 3 Dall. (3 U.S.) 386 (1798). Concluding his study of natural law concepts in the United States, Professor Haines said: ". . . natural law has had as its content whatever the individual in question desired to advocate". Op. cit., 339.

[60] Holt v. Markham, [1923] 1 K.B. 504, 513. See further comments, infra, n. 74.

[61] Bertholf v. O'Reilly, 74 N.Y. 509, 514–15 (1878); Hall, p. 294.

found the answer in a genetic study of the federal statute governing the official's power.[62]

What influence has natural law or natural rights philosophy had upon the development of case law? At the outset it may be asked, are the utterances in a court's opinion to be taken as reliably signifying the influences that led to the decision? The position here taken is that the opinion of the court and the opinion of each judge is significant both with respect to the public aspect of the motivations for the decision and with respect to the norms which judges express for guidance in future cases.[63] Yet the tenor of an opinion may well support the conclusion that a reference to natural law or to natural rights (or to any other ideal concepts) is a rhetorical flourish made to adorn an otherwise dull and technical opinion. Thus Professor Stone's conclusion that the judicial language of English Chancellors, invoking natural justice, was to a large extent rhetorical,[64] seems justified. A further question is, do judicial references to "natural law", "natural rights", "natural justice" signify the influence or the acceptance of natural-law or natural-rights philosophy in any of its definitive versions? Without more evidence (as to the particular case) the answer must be negative. Thus English chancellors during the seventeenth century often circumvented common law or statute by deciding cases in accordance with "reason" and "conscience", but unlike the "natural lawyers", they "refrained from formulating in advance the assumptions on which [they] proceeded." [65]

Yet sometimes the opinion indicates the kind of natural-law philosophy which is relied upon as justification. In Calvin's Case [66] the opinion of the English court contains a summary of the Thomistic philosophy of eternal, Divine and natural law, with citations of Bracton, Fortescue and Doctor and Student. On the other hand, the following passage from the famous dictum of Chase, J., in Calder v. Bull, seems to have been taken from the pages of Locke:

---

[62] Opinion of the Court by Douglas, J., in Hannegan v. Esquire, Inc., 327 U.S. 146, 66 Sup.Ct. 456 (1946). The opinion also invoked "freedom of the press" as a principle of interpretation.

[63] See Robinson, Law and the Lawyers (1935), Ch. X; infra, § 5.06.

[64] Stone, The Province and Function of Law (1946), Ch. VIII, §§ 14, 15.

[65] Ibid., § 15.

[66] 4 Coke 1, 77 Eng.Rep. 377 (K.B., 1610); Hall, p. 287. The court held that a Scotchman was not disabled to sue in an English court.

"An act of the legislature (for I cannot call it a law), contrary to the great first principles of the social compact, cannot be considered a rightful exercise of legislative authority. The obligation of a law, in governments established on express compact and on republican principles, must be determined by the nature of the power on which it is founded." [67] In American judicial opinions discussing the powers of the legislature with respect to natural rights, the argument is usually based upon the social compact [68] or upon the inherent nature of free governments and the inalienable rights derived from it,[69] that is, upon the Lockeian conception. The chief use of natural-law philosophy in the United States has been in connection with decisions declaring legislation unconstitutional as impairing "vested" rights. While the common technique was to interpret the constitution as necessarily preserving certain inalienable or vested rights, yet some judges went further and said that legislation was void if it violated either the Constitution or natural right.[70] The late Professor James Bradley Thayer, an expert on constitutional law, concluded that in no case within his knowledge had the doctrine of natural law or natural rights been "the single and necessary ground of the decision." [71] The discredit of the natural rights theory in the United States during the present century was due partly to its identification with conservatism and the protection of laissez faire as a natural economic law.[72]

The use of natural law theories in private law has been much less conspicuous and much less frequent. Reference has been made [73] to the development of English equity law during the sev-

---

[67] Calder v. Bull, 3 Dall. (3 U.S.) 386, 388–9 (1798); Hall, p. 291. The court declined to hold that a legislative act, setting aside a judicial decree and granting a new trial, was an ex post facto law.

[68] Miller, J., in Citizens Savings & Loan Ass'n v. Topeka, 20 Wall. (87 U.S.) 655, 663 (1874); Hall, p. 296. For other references to the social compact see Haines, The Revival of Natural Law Concepts (1930), 87, n. 1.

[69] Haines, op. cit., especially 216 ff.

[70] Field, J., concurring in Butchers' Union Co. v. Crescent City Co., 111 U.S. 746, 754, 4 Sup.Ct. 652, 656 (1883). Cf. Marshall, J., in Fletcher v. Peck, 6 Cranch (10 U.S.) 87, 139 (1810) ("the state of Georgia was restrained, either by general principles which are common to our free institutions or the particular provisions of the constitution of the United States . . .").

[71] Thayer, "The Origin and Scope of the American Doctrine of Constitutional Law" (1893) 7 Harv.L.Rev. 129, 133; Haines, op. cit., 75, n. 57.

[72] Field, J., cited Adam Smith's Wealth of Nations in his concurring opinion in the Butchers' Union case, (supra, n. 70). See Haines, op. cit., 219 ff.

[73] Supra, n. 64.

enteenth and eighteenth centuries as based on the chancellor's conscience rather than upon antecedent principles of nature. Lord Mansfield, who was primarily trained in Scotch law with its Roman law background of jus naturale, invoked conceptions of "natural justice and equity" [74] to bring under the principle of unjust enrichment certain judicial precedents which were still wrapped in the swaddling clothes of common law procedure.[75] Despite Scrutton's criticism, Mansfield's creative work has generally been praised. The influence of Ulpian's maxim, sic utere tuo ut alienum non laedas [76] upon the English and American law of torts may be ascribed to Roman jus naturale in the beginning, but it has long since become an accepted maxim of case law. The common law right of literary property has been justified by the principle, "one has a right to the fruits of his labor",[77] which could be taken from Locke's "natural law in a state of nature",[78] and probably from earlier sources.

Contemporaneous examples of reliance upon natural law in the creation of a legal right are found in several cases on the right of privacy. In a leading case upholding the plaintiff's right not to have his picture used in a public advertisement without his consent, the opinion of the court argued from the state-of-nature concepts of individual rights, that the individual had not surrendered his right of privacy (when he "entered" society), that the right of privacy had "its foundation in the instincts of nature" since every normal individual resents an invasion of his privacy, and that hence it was an "absolute" and "immutable" right.[79] The misleading consequences of the "natural right" technique as a means of justifying judicial innovations is shown in the subse-

---

[74] In Moses v. Macferlane, 2 Burr, 1005, 1012, 1 W.Bl. 219 (K.B., 1760); see also Sadler v. Evans, 4 Burr. 1984, 1986 (1766). Mansfield might have cited the Roman law principle of unjust enrichment (Dig. 12.6.14), but that would have aroused the hostility of English lawyers.

[75] See Jackson, The History of Quasi-Contract in English Law (1936); Dawson, Unjust Enrichment (1951).

[76] Ulpian, a Roman jurist and prolific text-writer who died about 228 A.D., gave three maxims which have often been taken as maxims of natural law: "Honeste vivere, alterum non laedere, suum cuique tribuere". (Dig. I, 1, 10, 1). ("Live honestly, do not harm another, render unto each his due.")

[77] See Baker v. Libbie, 210 Mass. 599, 604, 97 N.E. 109, 111 (1912).

[78] Locke, Second Treatise on Civil Government, secs. 24–26, 45.

[79] Cobb, J., in Pavesich v. New England Life Ins. Co., 122 Ga. 190, 194–195, 50 S.E. 68, 69, 70 (1905); Hall, pp. 299–300.

quent development of the law on this subject. The right of privacy is not "absolute" and "immutable"; an adult can release it for a compensation; and it is qualified by the public interest in the dissemination of information. The court could find no such extravagant claims in the leading law review article on the right of privacy.[80] A New Jersey Vice-Chancellor, following the Georgia opinion, declared:

> "It is now well settled that the right of privacy, having its origin in natural law, is immutable and absolute and transcends the power of any authority to change or abolish it." [81]

In his decree, however, he merely enjoined the defendant, a police official, from sending the plaintiff's photograph and finger prints to other police departments, but did not enjoin the taking of the photograph or finger prints. Thus the right of privacy was qualified or limited by the judge who declared it to be absolute. More recently a Nevada court reached a similar decision, but rejected the view that the right of privacy is absolute.[82] The individual's claim to privacy is generally respected in the mores of American society, and the legal protection of similar interests supports the conclusion that this individual interest should likewise receive some legal protection. The need for the legal protection of such a claim has been greatly enhanced by the growth of mass media of communication, such as newspapers, periodicals, movies and radio. Yet these media are also entitled to protection because of social interests in freedom of speech and of the press, in political and cultural progress. So the right of privacy "naturally" should be limited. The individual interest in privacy is no more "natural" in contemporary American society than are the social facts which show the need for limiting its legal protection. The delicate task of delimiting these conflicting policies or social interests through judicial decisions can be aided though never wholly supplanted by legislation.[83] The creative work of case-law (or legislative) development can be better achieved without the assumption of antecedently given immutable laws of nature and without the supposition of an idyllic pre-political society.

---

[80] Brandeis and Warren, "The Right of Privacy", (1890) 4 Harvard L.Rev. 193, 214, 217 (recognizing the limitations of public interests upon the right of privacy).

[81] Kay, V. C., in McGovern v. Van Riper, 137 N.J.Eq. 24, 33, 43 A.2d 514, 519 (1945).

[82] Norman v. City of Las Vegas, 64 Nev. 38, 49–50, 177 P.2d 442, 447 (1947).

[83] See N.Y.Civil Rights Law, secs. 50–51.

Chapter 14

REALITY AND VALUE: KANT AND THE
NEO–KANTIANS

§ 4.20—General Significance of Kant's Philosophy

Among the ideals of the present time is the exaltation of
broad universal human rights and the subordination of corresponding human duties and responsibilities.[1] During the present century the chief goal of law and government, at least in
practical politics, has been the maximum satisfaction of human
wants.[2] What place can be found in contemporary jurisprudence
for Kant's moral and legal philosophy, with its cardinal tenet
that law should protect the freedom of the individual to fulfill
his moral duty by acting disinterestedly, unhindered by any conflicting motive to satisfy his selfish desires? In this chapter we
shall try to answer the question by presenting the salient features
of Kantian and neo-Kantian philosophy.

The life of Immanuel Kant (1724–1804) partly explains the
stern and disciplined character of his philosophy. He was born
in Koenigsberg, then in East Prussia, and never traveled far from
his native city. He was a Protestant, of partly Scotch ancestry.
He was a bachelor, a recluse and (without any necessary connection) a professor of philosophy in the University of Koenigsberg. So precise were his habits, it is said, that when he came
from his study in the afternoon to take a walk, the neighbors
would set their watches at four o'clock. Though he did not remain wholly aloof from the philosophical polemics of his time,
during a long life he devoted himself wholeheartedly to the construction of a complete system of philosophy. It was the foundation of German idealism, and its influence is still manifest in
Europe and in North and South America. Both Nazis and
Fascists recognized Kantians as ideological enemies.

Kant profoundly shook natural law theories which tended to
confuse the physical and the normative, *reality* and *value*. He
sharply differentiated between the pure reason which deals

---

[1] E.g., the Universal Declaration of Human Rights (supra, § 4.12, p. 346; n.
51); the Four Freedoms of the Atlantic Charter.

[2] See Pound, "How Far Are We Attaining a New Measure of Values in
Twentieth Century Juristic Thought?" (1936) 42 W.Va.L.Q. 81.

with the phenomenal world of nature, and the practical reason, which deals with human action. "Ought" has no meaning in the empirical realm; there the mind has only to do with "Is".[3] While in developing his own moral theory he occasionally refers to the laws of nature, he makes it clear that he is speaking of physical laws and that he is using them by way of analogy or contrast. Kant also showed, as the late Professor Gustav Radbruch has said, that "reason" is not a storehouse of ethical or legal norms but only a power of constructing norms:

> "Kant's critique of reason has shown that reason is not an arsenal of finished theoretical cognitions, of ethical and aesthetical norms ready to be applied, but rather the mere power to arrive at such cognitions and norms; that it is not a complex of answers, but rather one of questions, of points of view from which what is given is to be approached. . . . Only the category of right, just law, but none of its applications, is universally valid." [4]

As Pound pointed out, the natural law of the eighteenth century was unable to meet the rigorous requirements of Kantian epistemology.[5]

Kant conceived of reason as the faculty of man to distinguish himself from all other things, from his own receptivity to sensations and even from his understanding, that which enables him to bring his sense perceptions under rules and thus to unite them in one consciousness. Reason is spontaneous in that it is not wholly governed by either the senses or the understanding; it transcends both. Hence man as a rational being can attain moral freedom, that is, freedom from the domination of his senses,[6] from the law of cause and effect which governs the clod and the beast. This is Kant's fundamental conception of human freedom.

---

[3] See Cairns, Legal Philosophy from Plato to Hegel (1949), 392. The earlier refutation of eighteenth century natural law theories by the English philosopher, David Hume, is summarized in Sabine, A History of Political Theory (1939), 601 ff.

[4] The Legal Philosophies of Lask, Radbruch and Dabin (Wilk trans., 1950), 60. A similar point was made by Garlan, Legal Realism and Justice (1941).

[5] Pound, The Formative Era in American Law (1938), 30; Pound, "The Revival of Natural Law" (1942) 17 Notre Dame Lawyer 287, 297.

[6] "Foundations of the Metaphysics of Morals" in Kant, Critique of Practical Reason (Beck trans., 1949), 106–7 (cited below as "Practical Reason").

A third conception of Kant's moral philosophy is "the will". This is the faculty of desire, which leads the individual to like and dislike and to make choices of action, *in so far as* the ground of liking or disliking lies in the reason. Thus the will is not mere impulse or desire, but a drive governed more or less by reason. When choice is determined by pure reason, the will is wholly free.[7] We shall try to explain what this means in the next section.

From the foregoing conceptions of man one can draw, as Kant did, what is perhaps his most important principle of moral and legal philosophy. Since man can choose to act by a reason which is not dominated by his senses, desires and aversions, and since his will can be autonomous and free, man is a rational being. Therefore he must never be treated merely as a means to an end, but always as an end in himself.[8] This principle found expression in the nineteenth century movements for the abolition of slavery. Even after the institution of slavery has been ended, the Kantian principle still gives meaning to the constitutional prohibition of "slavery" and "involuntary servitude" when a court invalidates some novel form of labor peonage.[9] Likewise it finds expression in the legislative maxim, "labor is not a commodity." [10] Indeed, this Kantian ideal that every man must be treated as an inviolable person and not a thing became a persistent twentieth century ideal of such American liberals as Lester Ward, Walter Lippman, and Henry Commager.[11]

§ 4.21—Kant's Moral Idealism; the Categorical Imperative

"Nothing in the world—indeed nothing even beyond the world" —said Kant, "can possibly be conceived which could be called good without qualification except a *good will*." [12] Thus he states the ideal on which his moral philosophy is founded. He begins

---

[7] Kant, Philosophy of Law (Hastie trans., 1887), 12–13 (first published 1797).

[8] Op. cit., supra, n. 6, 95.

[9] See Pollock v. Williams, 322 U.S. 4, 64 Sup.Ct. 792 (1944), applying U.S. Constitution, Amendment XIII.

[10] The Clayton Act of 1914 (38 Stat. 730), § 6, begins: "That the labor of a human being is not a commodity or article of commerce". The Act was designed to exempt labor unions from laws prohibiting restraint of trade in commodities. United States v. Hutcheson, 312 U.S. 219, 61 Sup.Ct. 463 (1941).

[11] See Commager, The American Mind (1950) 223, quoting Lippman.

[12] Practical Reason (supra, § 4.20, n. 6), 55.

with common rational knowledge of moral qualities. Do we not know of men of wit, intelligence and judgment, and men having riches, honor and power, whom we admire less than the man of good will, the man whose feelings toward others and whose motives of action are purely disinterested? This conception of ideal character is explicit in Christianity and is exemplified for millions of people, by the lives of such men as Buddha and Gandhi. Now you and I might say that we admire such a man because we can trust him to keep our money for us or to have political power over us. But Kant would say that a good will does not need to be justified on such practical grounds: since the function of reason is to produce a good will, and since nature has (here as elsewhere) distributed capacities suitable to the functions which they are to perform, the function of reason is to produce a will "good in itself and not merely as a means." [13] The conception of something "good in itself" is typically Kantian; one can see the same idea in sayings that something is "inherently" or "intrinsically" right or wrong. Kant has reserved it for the one thing in the world which he deems best: the good will. His "proof" that it is intrinsic, as set forth above, seems to be based on the assumption that "nature" never creates anything without a purpose. Now modern physiologists have found two dozen or more parts of the human body for which no purpose can be discovered. The "proof" rests upon a proposition which is only empirically probable.

Yet Kant would stick to his ideal, that the good will is the highest good, because he believed that morals was founded on a priori principles, that is, principles not derived nor justified empirically. The good will is not just sympathy or benevolence; these are human inclinations, and the gratification of human inclinations, even though it leads to happiness, does not produce the highest moral worth. The man of good will is one who, without feeling the slightest sympathy for another person in distress, would help him from a sheer sense of duty. Kant would feel surer of the purity of the benefactor's will if he found no pleasure in his benefaction. Such a cold ascetic altruist would scarcely be an admirable friend.

To have moral worth an action must be done from duty. The moral value of an action depends upon the principle of volition, the maxim on which the will acts, and not upon either the purpose of the actor in aiming to attain a given result or in his

---

[13] Ibid., 58.

success in attaining it.[14] This is another Kantian conception of intrinsic value which it is difficult to grasp. Does Kant mean that the attainment of ends is unworthy of consideration in the reasoning which precedes human action? He has been so interpreted. Yet he insists that the man of good will should treat all other human beings as ends and not merely as means. Thus he does not exclude intrinsically good ends but only those which are selfish or self-gratifying. Contrast Kant's doctrine that one should be honest because one cannot conceive of dishonesty as a universal maxim of human conduct, and therefore honesty is intrinsically right regardless of consequences, with Cervantes' well-known aphorism, "Honesty is the best policy." The latter may be expressed as a hypothetical (conditional) imperative: *"If* honesty is the best policy, *then* you should be honest." Whom do we admire (and trust) the more, the man who is honest because he believes that he will be better off by being honest (and who therefore might discard his maxim if he believed he would be better off by being dishonest) or the man who believes in honesty as intrinsically right, regardless of the consequences to himself? [15]

Kant recognizes that human conduct is motivated by many hypothetical imperatives. *If* you want to stay in business, be fair to your customers. *If* you want a raise in salary, do your job well. These may be prudent guides but obedience to them is not the highest moral worth. That can be attained only by obedience to the *categorical* (unconditional) *imperative:*

"Act according to a maxim which can be adopted at the same time as a universal law of human conduct".[16]

To understand this famous ethical doctrine one should have in mind the steps by which it was reached: the human reason as a power of creating maxims of conduct, the duty of man as a rational being to determine his conduct by creating maxims of conduct, and the view that man can attain moral freedom—freedom from control by his appetites—only by accepting the categorical imperative as unconditionally obligatory. Thus Kant reconciles the seemingly incompatible notions of moral freedom and moral duty.

---

[14] Ibid., 61; repeated in his Philosophy of Law (supra, § 4.20, n. 7), 17.

[15] Practical Reason, 63.

[16] Phil. of Law, 34; cf. Practical Reason, 80.

The categorical imperative is not by itself a maxim of conduct, but rather a guide to the reason in formulating such maxims. It is the queen of moral maxims. Hence the criticism that it is an empty formula from which no conclusions can be *deduced* misinterprets Kant's conception of it. The moral principle which the reason, confronted with a problem of conduct, formulates for that situation is the major premise. For example, a man in financial difficulties asks, may I make a false statement about my credit standing in order to obtain a loan which will (as I believe) enable me to carry on my business successfully and thus pay off all my debts? [17] The proposed conduct is lying. Can any rational being conceive of such a maxim as this as a universal principle of human conduct: "One should (or may) lie whenever one pleases"? Since one cannot, then the maxim enjoined by the categorical imperative for this moral problem is: "One must never lie." In his later years he defended this principle as one to which no exceptions can be allowed, even in such an extreme case as this one: Suppose A asks B whether his friend, C, is hiding in B's house and B knows that A intends to murder C: should B, believing that C is then in B's house, answer truthfully, or may he answer "No" in order to save C's life? Kant said B should answer A truthfully, because a lie violates an unconditional duty which everyone owes to all mankind.[18] If by telling the truth (where one *must* give an answer) one causes harm to another, this harm is "accidental"; it is not a moral wrong.

Kant's categorical imperative is, even as merely a guide for individual ethics, open to two serious objections. One is that either the formulated maxim is an intuitive and dogmatic emotional hunch, derived from experiences and indoctrinations which are not examined and analyzed, *or* that predictions and evaluations of *consequences* enter into the reasoning by which the maxim is grasped, tested and formulated. Indeed, Kant's own arguments bring in this latter kind of reasoning. Thus, in the case of B's answer to A, the prospective murderer, Kant argues that B might be mistaken (in saying that C is hiding in his house), that the murderer might by B's lie be led to seek C elsewhere and, finding him, consummate his evil intent.[19] Here B's

---

[17] This example is based on several which Kant gives. Foundations of the Metaphysics of Morals, in: Practical Reason, 63, 78–79.

[18] "On a Supposed Right to Lie" (first published in 1797) in Practical Reason, 346, 349–50.

[19] Ibid., 348.

moral problem becomes complicated with *probabilities:* how reliable (probable) is B's belief that C *is* hiding in the house? How probable is it that if B is mistaken, A will seek and find C elsewhere? If B may ask *such* questions of probability, may he not then ask: What is the probability that my lying to this prospective murderer will have the consequence of impairing the faith that men generally place in each other's utterances? [20] Kant himself suggests this question when he argues that truthfulness is a legal duty because it

> "must be regarded as the ground of all duties based on contract, and the laws of those duties would be rendered *uncertain* and *useless* if even the least exception to them were admitted." [21]

"Uncertainty" and "uselessness" are practical tests of consequences, and are thus "impure."

A modern example of Kant's problem is this: A applied to L, a life insurance company, for additional life insurance. He was examined by Dr. B, L's physician, who found that he had a heart condition which made him unacceptable and so informed him; but Dr. B also told him that his heart condition would probably not prevent him from living a long time—this last in order not to aggravate his condition. A thereupon decided to surrender his existing contract of life insurance to L. He died of heart failure shortly afterward, and a suit was brought to rescind the surrender of his life insurance policy. Kant apparently believed that such a suit would be successful.[22] However, an appellate court denied rescission, and Taft, J. (later Chief Justice of the United States) approved of Dr. B's conduct as "dictated by the most humane feeling and justified by the most stringent rules of professional ethics." [23] American law seems in accord with this conclusion, probably on the ground that the consequence was not foreseeable [24] when the "white lie" was told. Not every instance of making a knowingly false utterance will

---

[20] Kant would deny that he should, except on the inferior moral level of prudence; he would, apparently, say that his arguments about consequences were invoked merely to influence those who believe in that kind of argument.

[21] Ibid., 348; italics added.

[22] Ibid.

[23] Taft, J., in Wagner v. National Life Ins. Co., 90 F. 395, 406 (C.C.A.6 1898). The court refused to rescind the patient's release of his life insurance policy, which he claimed to have been induced by the physician's statement.

[24] See Restatement, Torts (1938) § 531; Prosser, Torts (1941) § 87.

have the consequence of making all human utterances "uncertain and useless."

A second difficulty with Kant's moral theory is this: How can one be sure that another (or even one's self) is motivated by a disinterested moral maxim formulated in accordance with the categorical imperative? Kant recognized that one cannot prove by any examination that the will is determined by the moral principle alone.[25] From this he argues that the supreme moral principle must be derived a priori and not from experience. Yet he also recognizes that perhaps only the occasional saint will act pursuant to the categorical imperative. Hence, like Plato before him, he accepts as "second best" criteria of valuation of conduct, the attainment of human perfection, and the attainment of happiness.[26] The latter is the third best criterion; it rests upon merely empirical principles, since what will make a person happy depends on the particular circumstances; it lacks universality. The concept of perfection is a rational one and therefore preferable; yet it lacks content, unless one puts into it that which one seeks to draw from it, and then it ends in circularity.

Kant's philosophy of individual ethics has significance chiefly because of three ideas which it sharply emphasizes. One is that moral decisions should not be made merely on the basis of moral feelings or emotions but should be guided by a transcendent power of the human mind, reason. A second is that a man attains his full stature as a rational being only when he frees himself from the domination of his sensual appetites and passions and acts from disinterested motives. This he exaggerates by regarding disinterestedness as the only pure worthy motive of conduct. A third is that moral decisions cannot be made solely on the basis of the facts of previous experience projected as predictions of probable future consequences; some rational ideaʲ which transcends the facts must enter into the evaluation. He overemphasized this by excluding as impurities all calculations of material consequences, though he doubtless recognized that imperfect human creatures do take account of them. His conception of the intrinsic good, at first limited to the pure will, seems to have been extended to such subordinate principles as the one against lying. His idealist philosophy thus overemphasized abstractness and inflexibility. Yet the importance of re-

---

[25] Practical Reason, 78–79.

[26] Ibid., 98–101.

liability in communications between individuals and groups in our present society and the readiness to justify distortions of truth on grounds of short-sighted economic or political expediency make one believe that some heavier doses of Kantian morality might well be administered to all mankind at an early age. The reasons for this reactionary statement are that the inculcation of maxims of conduct by trial and error has been only partly successful and that the child and the youth cannot test in their own experience the validity of moral maxims.

Kant's failure to distinguish between *kinds* of pleasures and desires seems to be an error which vitiates some of his basic assumptions. Thus a modest and sincere benefactor of the poor and the sick who enjoys making other people happier should not be placed in the same class, morally, as a man who prizes only the satisfaction of his sensuous desires. Moreover, the satisfaction of sensuous desires is not (as Kant seems to imply) an inherent evil; the altruist does not debase his character by enjoying a hearty meal. Kant's lasting contribution to man's moral ideas is that man can by the use of his reason raise himself above the level of sensuality.

§ 4.22—Kant's Philosophy of Law

Kant's short treatise on the philosophy of law, first published in his old age,[27] embodies the maturity of his thought and the culmination of his labors in the realm of practical reason. In making subordinate principles of the legal order into inflexible absolutes it seems at times to manifest the hardening of his arteries. For instance, his insistence that the penal law is a categorical imperative commanding punishment from which the violator should not be allowed to escape by any slippery arguments of expediency[28] (such as the present systems of suspended sentences may be taken to represent), shows a hardening of his thought as compared with his earlier idealist views of moral problems. We may represent his philosophy of law by three of his basic doctrines: 1. That which differentiates ethical duties from

---

[27] Metaphysische Anfangsgründe der Rechtslehre, dated 1797 (Koenigsberg), was the first part of his "metaphysics of morals." It is here cited as "M.A." The translation by Hastie, under the title "Kant's Philosophy of Law" (1887), is the volume cited here as "Hastie".

[28] Hastie, 195. Kant's use of the term "Strafgesetz" (M.A., 196) shows that he had definite statutory provisions in mind. The executive pardon, he said, should be limited to such crimes as treason. (Hastie, 204.)

legal duties. 2. That which assigns to law the role of protecting moral freedom. 3. That which assigns to the will of the individual a major role in private law.

1. *The Difference between Moral Duties and Legal Duties.* While both moral and legal rules (legislation) state what action is objectively necessary, they differ with respect to the *motive* which influences the human will to conformity. "Legislation" (i. e., any rule of human conduct) which makes the duty that it creates the motive of obedience is ethical; that which creates some other motive (e. g., sanction) is juridical (legal).[29] The man who fulfills his (legally unenforceable) promise because he is moved by his duty to do so, acts ethically. The man who obeys the law merely to escape punishment or some other legal sanction performs a legal duty but not a duty of virtue. Ethics depends upon the internal motivation of reason and conscience; ethical duties can have no external legislation. From this division several consequences follow. While ethical motivation is an ethically superior kind of motivation, Kant never suggests that ethics provides norms that are politically superior to legal norms. Whatever is juridically in accordance with external laws is just; whatever is not, is unjust.[30] On the other hand, legal norms may impose duties which the individual reason accepts as proper ethical maxims of conduct; in that case the individual by conforming can fulfill both an ethical and a legal duty. Indeed, Kant seems to recognize that a good many ethical maxims have been adopted from the law, such as the principle that agreements must be fulfilled (pacta sunt servanda).[31] The extent to which ethical philosophers as well as popular moralists have borrowed the content of their maxims from law and other authoritarian sources has been considerably underestimated. Kant does not, I think, make this mistake; but he makes another one in his philosophy of law, namely, the assumption that the legal concepts and principles with which he was familiar—those of the modern Roman law—were universal concepts and principles of right-law. Furthermore, in restricting ethical duties to those which had no (external) sanction, he tacitly ignored what Austin has aptly termed "positive morality," the prevalent moral beliefs of a community or group, which are sanctioned by overt but unorganized manifestations of disapproval.

---

[29] Hastie, 20–23; M.A., xiv.

[30] Hastie, 32; M.A., xxiii.

[31] Hastie, 22; M.A. xvi.

Kant's conception of an ethical duty led him to define unintentional transgression (e. g., negligence) as mere fault; crime (Verbrechen) is intentional violation of a duty.[32] This conception of crime, adhered to by some judges and writers of the present century, would lead to the conclusion that the requirement of intentional wrongdoing must be read into every penal statute,[33] and would make it impossible to enforce many legal regulations of business which are necessary to prevent social harm.[34] Holmes evidently referred to Kantian morality when he argued that legal duties should be tested by the criterion of the "bad man" who cares not a fig for your reason and conscience. In urging that the law should be based on considerations of social advantage he made the consequences of conduct rather than its motive the criterion of illegality.[35] Kant's separation of law and ethics was not rigidly maintained, since he grouped them both under the general heading of morals (Sitten). Each has its own criterion of moral conduct.

2. *The Role of Law is to Protect Moral Freedom.* Since law has to do only with the external relations of individuals to each other, it is concerned only with acts, and if one seeks the universal principle of all laws, it can be expressed thus:

> "The law (Recht) is the whole of the conditions under which the voluntary actions of any one person can be harmonized with the voluntary actions of every other person, in accordance with a universal law of freedom." [36]

Now Kant recognized that law was entitled to exercise compulsion against the individual, and that any such compulsion was an interference with that individual's freedom, that is, his freedom in the physical (phenomenal) world. Kant called this a hindrance to freedom and justified it on the ground that it was necessary to prevent some other hindrance to some other per-

---

[32] Hastie, 32; M.A. xxiii. See Cohen (Morris), in The Heritage of Kant (ed. Whitney and Bowers, 1939), 293; same in Cohen, Reason and Law (1950), 118–119.

[33] See further discussion supra, § 3.16; State v. Prince, 52 N.M. 15, 189 P.2d 993 (1948).

[34] See majority opinion (by Frankfurter, J.) in United States v. Dotterweich, 320 U.S. 277, 281, 64 Sup.Ct. 134, 136, 137 (1943) and dissent (by Murphy, J.), 286.

[35] Holmes, The Path of the Law, (1897) 10 Harv.L.Rev. 457; Collected Legal Papers (1920), 167; infra, § 4.54.

[36] M.A. xxxiii; cf. Hastie, 45, where "das Recht" is translated as "right".

son's freedom. Thus all law is a hindrance of a hindrance of freedom.[37] But further than this Kant did not recognize the merely physical aspects of freedom. The freedom which the law should ultimately aim to protect is freedom of the will, which, is, to the "practical" reason, the possibility of a moral choice which can have (mysteriously) consequences in the sensible world.[38] Kant's conception of freedom did not, indeed, seem to require any material content; a man of good will could exercise his moral freedom while starving in the depths of a filthy dungeon.[39] In this respect he resembled Hegel, but differed from other legal or political philosophers of the nineteenth century who postulated freedom as the basic purpose of the legal order. Bentham and Adam Smith exalted economic freedom and Herbert Spencer thought law should protect the freedom of every individual to attain his destiny as determined by the survival of the fittest (infra, § 4.34). The four freedoms of the Atlantic Charter (1942) are rather earthy [40] as compared with Kant's moral freedom.

3. *The Will of the Individual in Private Law.* When Kant came to apply his "universal principle" to private law, he insisted that the *content* of the will should not be considered (e. g. whether a merchant is making a profit out of a transaction) but only the *form* of the transaction as consisting of mutual acts of the will.[41] Now this was, in a sense, what was done in Roman law; and it is also applicable to legal transactions in Anglo-American law. For instance, the legal validity of a contract based upon an exchange of acts or promises is even now not dependent upon its being beneficial or profitable to one or the other party. While expanding conceptions of fraud and coercion have narrowed the scope of this principle, the Kantian conception of a contract as a union of wills still has considerable influence in American law. By a contract one person acquires a right over the person (i. e., the conduct, active or passive) of another. How can this right of one over another be reconciled with the sancti-

---

[37] Hastie, 47; M.A. xxxv.

[38] E. g., Hastie, 28, 36; M.A., xviii, xxvii.

[39] " . . . men like Kant and Hegel who make most of metaphysical freedom, leave us rather little of the freedom that we do care about . . . " Cohen (Morris) in The Heritage of Kant (1939), 300; same in Cohen, Reason and Law (1950), 126.

[40] Freedom of speech, of religion; freedom from want, from fear.

[41] Hastie, 45; M.A. xxxii–xxxiii.

ty of the individual?   Only because the individual obliged, in
alienating a power over himself, also acquires a right over the
other person.   Hence the union of wills must occur in an instant
of time;   the offer and acceptance must click together.[42] The
time when this conceptual clicking occurs becomes especially
important when the contracting parties are at a distance;[43] and
the place of clicking, as the locus contractus, is often an arbitrary test of choice of law, where a conflict of laws is involved.
Moreover, the union-of-wills conception of contract became the
"subjective" theory of American contract law, often expressed
in the saying that a contract is a "meeting of minds." The subjective theory supports the doctrine that if one party is led by
his mistake of fact to enter into a contract, even though the
other is not mistaken nor aware of the mistake, the former
has a right to avoid his obligation.   The objective theory, on
the contrary, would regard such a transaction as binding because the expectation of the other party must be protected.
American case law generally favors the latter view, but with
some dissents.[44]   On the other hand, in the commonly accepted
 doctrine that the death of the offeror, even though unknown
to the offeree, revokes an offer, the subjective theory triumphs;
no union of wills can occur when one party is dead.   The Kantian
conception of contract was taken over by the learned and influential Savigny, from which it was absorbed into early editions of Sir Frederick Pollock's treatise on contracts, and into
Bishop on Contracts, a popular American treatise of the late
nineteenth century.[45]   These examples show the influence of
Kantian philosophy upon both Continental and Anglo-American
law.   It was, perhaps, a mistake to draw any conclusions about
detailed legal rules (of risk or of convenience) from Kant's a
priori conception of a contract.   Kant treated all contracts as if
they were alienations of one's property;   even one's promise to
render service is, in a sense, a transfer of one's person.   To justify
this one must find (since slavery is obviously wrong) a consent
of the promisor, an act of the will, that curious mental catalyist

---

[42] Hastie, pp. 100 ff.;   M.A., 96 ff.

[43] See Patterson, "The Delivery of a Life Insurance Policy," (1919) Harv.
L.Rev. 198, 210–212.

[44] See Williston, Contracts (rev. ed., 1936), § 1579; Patterson, "Equitable
Relief for Unilateral Mistake," (1928) 28 Col.L.Rev. 859, 884.

[45] See Williston's Wald's Pollock on Contracts, Appendix, Note A; Bishop
on Contracts, § 313.

of reason and desire. Do we not still regard the freely-given consent of the obligor as a basic requirement of law for any good society?

Kant's conception of property as an extension of the will of the owner apparently required that every human should have some property; [46] but whether he had enough for his health, safety and general welfare was a question with which Kantian legal philosophy was not concerned. In a state of nature, men would own property; but such ownership would be only provisory (insecure) without the political state, which would make it secure. Hence Kant said it was man's *duty* to leave the state of nature and enter the political state. But when one comes to consider international law, one finds the nations of the world living still in a state of nature, and the external property of states is only provisional, so long as it may be taken away by war. Hence it is the duty of all nations to pass over into a "universal union of states analogous to that by which a nation (people) becomes a state." [47] It is only thus that a real state can become a peace state. On this timely theme we close our sketch of Kant's idealistic philosophy of law.

§ 4.23—Neo-Kantians: Stammler

A great system of philosophy is like a theatrical wardrobe, to which many actors playing different parts can resort for costumes suitable to their ideas. One can find in most European philosophies of the nineteenth century some of the borrowed apparel of Kantianism. His conception of law and his conception of a juristic act (supra, § 4.22) were taken over by the distinguished German jurist, Savigny (infra, § 4.31). During the twentieth century a rather significant group of European legal philosophers derived many of their basic ideas from Kant; yet they rejected some of Kant and added ideas derived from Hegel, Jhering and others; hence they were loosely designated as "Neo-Kantians." Of these the four most significant writers were: Rudolph Stammler, Hans Kelsen, Emil Lask and Gustav Radbruch. Each of them relied heavily on Kant's theory of knowledge and upon his rejection of a pre-existing discoverable universally valid natural law. All except Kelsen adopted Kant's basic conceptions of ethics (supra, § 4.21). Lask and Radbruch will be discussed in the following section.

---

[46] Hastie, 62 ff.; M.A., 56 ff.

[47] Hastie, 224; M.A., 226–27.

Since Kelsen's theory of law has been outlined and criticized above (§ 3.22), here we need only note the typically Kantian argument by which Kelsen supports his conception of the "basic norm." [48] Kant had developed transcendental principles of cognition which are presupposed by all scientific investigations. The basic norm is a similar principle. It transcends all positive legal norms just as the principles of cognition transcend all empirical laws.[49] One may paraphrase the analogy as follows: Just as the scientist in his work assumes the unity and uniformity of nature, so the lawyer in his work assumes the unity and validity of legal norms which were lawfully derived (supra, § 3.22) from the prevailing constitution. However, Kelsen's theory does not tell the lawyer or the official what should be aimed at in creating new law. It lacks a legal axiology, except in so far as any system of legal positivism implicitly emphasizes the values of order and stability.

Rudolph Stammler (1856–1938), a professor of law at Halle, Berlin and other German universities, is known today for his ideal of social justice, his four principles of just law, and his conception of a "natural law with changing content," an idea which he eventually gave up as misleading. His refutation of Marxist materialism in his first book,[50] by showing that economic materialism did not determine the content of laws, had a profound influence upon the German Social-Democratic party, in its conversion from a revolutionary into a reform party.[51] In the United States Stammler's ideas influenced Morris R. Cohen, Benjamin N. Cardozo, Roscoe Pound and other legal philosophers. The conceptions of social justice of the Progressive Party (1912–1916) and the New Deal reflected ideals like those of Stammler.

Stammler accepts Kant's conception of ethics as having to do with the intention of the actor, and his conception of law as a regulation of external conduct (§ 4.22). He also accepts positive law as a body of norms characterized by their sovereignty and their inviolability.[52] Neither ethics nor any feeling or conception

---

[48] Supra, § 3.22, pp. 262–63.

[49] See Kelsen, General Theory of Law and State (Wedberg trans., 1945), 436.

[50] Wirtschaft und Recht (1895).

[51] See Wu, "Stammler and His Critics," in The Theory of Justice (Husik trans., 1925), 564–565. For a more recent critique, see Ginsberg, "Stammler's Philosophy of Law," in Modern Theories of Law (1933), 38–51.

[52] Stammler, The Theory of Just Law (Husik trans., 1925), 17.

of justice is superior to positive law. However, since legal regulation is the determining form of social activity, the theory of law (as distinguished from legal technique) must consider every specific legal rule as a means to an end, and for this purpose must seek to find a "universal method" of just law. All law is an attempt to be just; even tyrants pretend to be giving justice.

Here we may stop to compare Stammler's conceptions of justice with those of Aristotle. The latter treated of justice in two senses: as an individual virtue, and as a principle of legal regulation.[53] In the regulatory sense he distinguished *commutative* (rectificatory) justice, which prescribes that one who has by a civil wrong (i. e., a tort or a breach of contract) caused harm to another should compensate the other in an amount equal to the harm thus caused. This kind of justice takes no account of the whole personality of the actor, his goodness or badness in general, but only of the actor's particular conduct and the resulting injury. There is another kind of justice, *distributive* justice, which is designed to distribute the honors or rewards of a society among its members in proportion to their merits: the greater the merit, the greater the honor or reward. Among the applications of this principle is that which occurs when men of different callings exchange their services and products with each other. Suppose the shoemaker wants a house and the house-builder wants shoes: how many shoes should be required to buy a house? Aristotle says the number must "correspond to the ratio of builder to shoemaker." [54] The medium of exchange, by which such values are reduced to a common scale, is money. Since the Greek term for money was derived from the same root as the word for law, Aristotle concluded that money "exists not by nature but by law." [55] A state by providing the exclusive medium of exchange, money, facilitates the operation of distributive justice even though it does not fix the prices of houses and of shoes.

Stammler, in saying that just law is not an ethical doctrine, pointed out that if justice is thought of as the virtue of the person who lays down and carries out the law, it pertains to ethics.[56]

---

53 Aristotle, Ethica Nicomachea (Ross trans., 1942), Bk. V, 1129a–1134a.

54 Ibid., 1133a–20–25.

55 Ibid., 1133a–30.

56 Op. cit. supra, n. 52, 67–68.

If justice refers to the objective content of definite norms, it is just law. Now law needs the support of ethics, for law "is in the last analysis an endeavor to compel justice," [57] and must therefore accept the support of that discipline which seeks to purify the will of injustice. Yet ethics will never be a substitute for law. Even if, some day in the sweet by and by, all people might be governed by principles of unselfish love and sincere devotion to right, still it would be necessary to have rules to guide the external conduct of co-operation in society. In typical Kantian fashion Stammler expresses the need for law in society by saying:

> ". . . law is necessary a priori, because it is inevitably implied in the idea of co-operation, which latter is the main object of our entire discussion."[58]

Since people can by co-operation carry on the struggle for existence better than they could in isolation, by joining the community each one is best serving his own interest.[59] Here Stammler is concerned with the age-old problem of the subordination of the individual to the law of the community. He meets it by defining the community "as the formal unity of all conceivable individual purposes." [60] This "formal" unity does not conceal the empirical conflict between individual purposes and the group aim or objective. Just law is designed to unify the "methodical adjustment of individual purposes in accordance with the one final purpose of the community." [61] This final purpose is not happiness, nor the greatest good of the greatest number, nor yet the perfection of the individual. Each of these is empirical and subjective (and hence inferior). The ultimate ideal is freedom of the will of the individual. The "social ideal" is therefore a *community of men willing freely,* as this comprehends all possible purposes of persons united under the law.[62]

Stammler then attacks another long-standing problem, the reconciliation of egoism and altruism. The social ideal is not itself a legal proposition. It needs to be supplemented with princi-

---

[57] Ibid., 68.

[58] Ibid., 55.

[59] Ibid., 152.

[60] Ibid.

[61] Ibid., 152–53. Compare the ethical theory of William James, infra, § 4.52.

[62] Ibid., 153.

ples of just law. Accordingly he develops four such principles, two principles of respect and two principles of participation. The former aim to enable the individual member of a legal community "to determine his own volition in freedom that accords with justice." [63] They are:

> "*The Principles of Respect.* 1. The content of a person's volition must not be made subject to the arbitrary desire of another.

> "2. Every legal demand must be maintained in such a manner that the person obligated may be his own neighbor." [64]

The first principle means, in effect, that anyone who interferes with another's choice of a method of pursuing his own interests must show a *reason* for so doing: individual freedom, even selfish freedom so far as the content of just law is concerned, is an end-in-itself. While the laissez-faire of Adam Smith's economic theory was a freedom for another end, prosperity or happiness, Stammler's freedom is for him, I think, an ultimate end. This idea is recognized in Pound's theory of Social Interests by the inclusion of a social interest in the individual human life (infra, § 4.61). However, in Pound's scheme this social interest is only one of many; the others may provide reasons why an invasion of the individual's freedom is not arbitrary.

Stammler's second principle brings in his peculiar notion of "being one's neighbor," which is basic in his principles of participation. These are:

> "1. A person under a legal obligation must not be arbitrarily excluded from a legal community.

> "2. Every ability of disposing that is granted by law may be exclusive only in the sense that the person excluded may be his own neighbor." [65]

These principles seek to express the idea of co-operation in a community, with its necessary implication that the individual must partly assume the burdens of others. So every one who assumes the legal obligations of a community (i. e., roughly, every mentally competent adult) acquires a right to participate in the community; and this right limits his obligations. The dispositive rights of others (e. g., contract and property rights) must

---

[63] Ibid., 161.

[64] Ibid.

[65] Ibid., 163.

recognize the right of those excluded. They mean that a member of the legal community must not be left to carry on the struggle for existence alone.[66] While Stammler is cautious about giving concrete illustrations, the idea of participation would seem to include, for example, a minimum wage law, and perhaps some unemployment insurance for those who are able to work. However, he was apparently not including any schemes of charity or philanthropy in his principles of just law.

Who is my neighbor? Stammler offers a method of answering this question when he comes to the third stage in the determination of just law: the *model* of just law.[67] To say that one should love one's neighbor does not mean that one should love all humanity alike, nor that one owes equal obligations to everyone. Hence we must arrange the persons living under the law in a series of concentric circles, thereby establishing special communities [68] of neighborship, among which the smallest and most intimate circle has priority. When he comes to give illustrations of correct judgments in particular cases, Stammler mentions a suit in a French court by a woman to enjoin her sister-in-law from excluding the plaintiff from the companionship of her brother, the defendant's husband. He remarks rather tersely that such an action would not be successful under German law, because (it seems) the husband-wife circle implies exclusive rights superior to those of the family (brother-sister) circle.[69] In the famous case of the Miller Arnold, which arose during the reign of Frederick the Great (1740–86), an upper riparian owner diverted all of the river water into his fish ponds and thus deprived Arnold of any water with which to run his mill. The Prussian supreme court held that Arnold was entitled to no redress; but the autocratic Frederick rejected this decision, imprisoned those who were responsible for it, and awarded Arnold damages to be paid out of the pockets of the errant judges. Stammler argues that the upper owner's right should not be exercised in such a way as to exclude Arnold entirely, and yet the former should not be obliged to bear the loss of refraining entirely, for Arnold's sake, from using the water. He then suggests a formula in which the combined loss of each

---

[66] Ibid., 164.

[67] Ibid., 220. The first two stages are, the social ideal and the principles of just law, discussed above.

[68] Ibid., 221.

[69] Ibid., 2?2.

riparian owner would be "divided between them in proportion to the amount of property contributed on each side." [70]   While the proposed solution has a delusive exactness, Stammler's conception of neighborship is used to extend the scope of legal relations—rights and duties—beyond the face-to-face conduct of early law to broader circles of causal relation between one man's conduct and another's harm.

More recently Lord Atkyn, in the House of Lords, asked the question, Who is my neighbor?   The case was an action for damages by a woman who bought an impure bottle of ginger beer, against the manufacturer who was not the immediate seller but whose negligence caused the impurity.   In holding the manufacturer liable, Lord Atkyn answered thus:

> "The answer seems to be—persons who are so closely and directly affected by my act that I ought reasonably to have them in contemplation as being so affected when I am directing my mind to the acts and omissions which are called in question." [71]

Thus Stammler's conception of neighborship can be used to break down the ancient citadel of privity.

Stammler's social idealism will, I believe, have some enduring gain for legal philosophy because it emphasizes values—especially the intrinsic worth of the individual human—which are common to occidental and Christian civilization.   His insistence that only an abstract method of determining just law can be devised, and that no law in its concrete content can be absolutely just, avoids the Scylla of dogmatic natural law but not the Charybdis of abstraction so empty as to be meaningless. [72]   The reasons why I consider Stammler's work still worthy of study are twofold: First, because like Kant he emphasizes the much-neglected conception of duty; and secondly, because his principles of just law are, in a way similar to Kant's categorical imperative, [73] suggestive guides to the discovery and creation of just law.

---

70 Ibid., 248.

71 In Donoghue v. Stevenson [1932] A.C. 562, 580, Lord Atkyn did not cite Stammler.   For fuller discussion, see Stone, The Province and Function of Law (1946), c. XII, § 6.

72 The emptiness of Stammler's formula is emphasized in Cohen (Morris R.), "Positivism and the Limits of Idealism in the Law," (1927) 27 Col.L.Rev. 241, 243 ; Hall, pp. 154–155, n. 2.   Another criticism is that of Stone, op. cit. supra, n. 71.

73 Supra, § 4.21.

§ 4.24—Neo-Kantians: Cultural Science and Relativist Philosophy; Lask and Radbruch

The line which Kant drew between natural science and ethics (supra, § 4.20) became the basis for the sharp separation between reality and value which is found in both Lask and Radbruch.

Emil Lask (1875–1915), first a law student and then a student of philosophy, became a distinguished professor at Heidelberg. His promising career was cut short by his death while a sergeant in the German army during World War I. In his only work on legal philosophy [74] he sought to present a "methodology" of legal science, by which he meant a general outline of the place of law in relation to the sciences. The critical philosophy of law by its separation of reality and value opens the way for a clear demarcation between natural law and a legal philosophy free of the metaphysics of natural law. There is only one kind of reality, empirical reality; it is the "scene or the substratum of trans-empirical values or meanings of general validity."[75] This is to say that values are *dependent upon* empirical reality and yet one cannot determine values having the stability and dependability that natural science, as well as our daily experience, finds in empirical reality. Since men through many ages have sought to find stability and security in their ethical, moral, political and legal beliefs, and since one persistent direction of this quest for certainty has been the search for imminent, immutable values in empirical reality, Lask's purported solution is worth exploring. A simple illustration of a value-situation will help to clarify even if it somewhat oversimplifies. A signs and delivers (to B) his negotiable promissory note for $1,000 payable to B and B delivers to A his check for $1,000 payable to A. Is A under an *ethical* or a *moral* obligation to pay B in accordance with his promise? Is A under such a *legal* obligation? Here are value questions, since the word "obligation" clearly means an "ought," and an "ought" implies a norm which expresses, or guides, a valuation. Now one might ask, is this value, this oughtness, to be

---

[74] Rechtsphilosophie (Heidelberg, 1905), also published in Germany in Die Philosophie im Beginn des 20 Jahrhunderts (1st ed., 1905, 2d ed., 1907). The references in this volume are to The Legal Philosophies of Lask, Radbruch and Dabin (Wilk trans., 1950), cited below, "L.R.D.".—A brief appreciation of Lask's essay is "Lask and the Doctrine of the Science of Law" by Professor Enrique Martinez Paz of the National University of Córdoba, Argentina, in Interpretations of Modern Legal Philosophies (Essays in Honor of Roscoe Pound) (1947), 574.

[75] L.R.D., 4.

found *in* the facts above set forth in my illustration; or is it something added on by human reason or by human convention or fiat? At this point a "realist" may interject: "But you have not given *all* the facts: Where did this note-check exchange occur? What were the conventions of this locale or of the group in which A and B operated?" My reply would be that one needs value-selectors to determine what additional facts to look for, even to recognize that additional facts are needed. As I understand Lask, he would say that values can be found in culture (conventions, laws, mores, religion, ethics), that empirical reality (the things and events that I have recited in the note-check situation) is on a level of meaning below that of value, which is in turn divided into levels of individual value (the value of a single concrete situation) and common or typical value, with which philosophy has to deal.[76] This static dualism of reality and value is rather satisfying because it accepts man's role as a creator of values without overlooking that the empirical realization of values is limited by and dependent upon empirical reality. To this one should add that, in the process of evaluating, which is the dynamic or pragmatic aspect of the relation, concepts or selectors from a realm of meaning known as value are used in choosing and processing "facts" which are the emotives or the reasons of evaluation, or both.

If the promissory-note situation is rather too simple and clear a case of both a moral and a legal obligation, then take more doubtful illustrations: Is the advertiser of a kind of article liable for his refusal to sell one on the terms advertised? Is a passer-by liable for not applying a tourniquet to a man, struck by a motor vehicle, who is bleeding to death? There is no more reason to believe that the answers to these atypical questions are *inherent in the nature of the facts*, than there is in the routine case of the promissory note.

For Lask legal philosophy, as the theory of the specific value of the law, can be, like other branches of philosophy, only a theory of typical values. He rejected Kant's view that law is concerned only with the externals of human conduct. From Kant's individualism also he departed in finding law to have specific social values: it maintains order in the community and, as G. Jellinek said before Lask, law maintains an "ethical minimum" for the society in which it prevails. Lask, following Hegel, gave law a place in cultural evolution.

---

[76] Ibid., 5.

Legal science, distinct from legal philosophy, is a systematic "cultural science," according to Lask.[77] Here we must note that German philosophers recognized, besides the natural sciences and quite distinct from them, disciplines or fields of knowledge which some called "spiritual sciences" (*Geisteswissenschaften*) and others called "cultural sciences" (*Kulturwissenschaften*), and which included the humanities, history, and the social sciences.[78] In this cultural legal science, law may be regarded either as a cultural reality, something that produces effects in the real world, e. g., as a rent-control law produces effects in society, or as a system of cultural normative meanings, which the lawyer must always compare with the prejuridical substratum of the law, the realities of culture and of "ordinary" life.[79] The latter cultural meaning is close to the "formal" law of the lawyer; the former cultural reality is not very different from legal sociology. Most revolts against the "formalism" of legal science are based on appeals to legal sociology.[80] Furthermore, legal science is teleological. It has ends of its own to fulfill:

"'Property' no more coincides with the physical thing than 'Person' does with the human being. In the same way all the subjects accessible to the law are covered, as it were, with a teleological web. . . ."[81]

Lask's short treatise is only a systematic sketch of a philosophy of law, with many details avowedly omitted and many others left obscure because of the abstractness of his terminology. Still it is one of the finer products of German idealism, with its struggle to reconcile the ideal man of humanity with the concrete brute world that he must live in.

---

[77] Ibid., 24–26.

[78] See ibid., 3, Prof. Wilks' note (b). On the "spiritual sciences" in Kantian philosophy transplanted to America, see Schneider, A History of American Philosophy (1946), 470–473.

[79] L.R.D., 27–28.

[80] See discussion of Ehrlich, supra, § 2.03. Another example is Pound's reliance upon jury verdicts, nearly always for the injured employee against his employer, as contrasted with the common law rules of the master-servant relation, in "Law in Books and Law in Action," (1910) 44 Amer.L.Rev. 13.

[81] L.R.D. 31. Lask's "teleological web" seems to include the policies or ends of property-law, as well as the more direct legal consequences which Hohfeld referred to in distinguishing "property" in the legal sense from "property" as a physical object. Hohfeld, Fundamental Legal Conceptions as Applied in Judicial Reasoning (1923).

Gustav Radbruch (1878–1949) was successively a professor of law at the universities of Königsberg, Kiel and Heidelberg; he was also (1920–1924) Minister of Justice of the German Reich in the cabinets of the Social-Democrats, Wirth and Stresemann, and was a member of the Reichstag. Because of his political views he was removed by the Nazi government from his position as professor at Heidelberg in 1933. He was restored to this position in 1945.

Radbruch's principal work, Legal Philosophy,[82] was based on Kant's critical philosophy, with profound modifications derived from Hegel's theory of cultural evolution and Rickert's theory of meaning, with direct personal influences from his friends, Emil Lask and Hermann Kantorowicz, and with a rich variety of literary and classical allusions. Here we can summarize only four of the highly suggestive and stimulating ideas of his slender volume: 1. The four attitudes toward values. 2. Relativism in legal philosophy. 3. The values of individual, collectivity and community. 4. The antinomies of the idea of law: justice, expediency and certainty.

1. *The Four Attitudes Toward Values.* In true Kantian fashion Radbruch derives his conception of value from the process of cognition by which the human mind (re)cognizes value in experience. Because experiences (sensations and perceptions) come to man colored by his evaluations, it is necessary for the ego to withdraw, as it were, from the immediacy of experience in order to distinguish reality from value.

> "The mind learns how its evaluating consciousness may be sometimes screened off and sometimes deliberately put in."[83]

The primitive man sees in the approaching thunderstorm a threat from the gods; the week-end picnicker sees in it a threat to his sport; but the meteorologist, viewing it with unevaluating detachment, gives a scientific account of it. Thus we find at the outset two attitudes toward (empirical) reality: The *value-blind* attitude of science, and the *evaluating* attitude of philosophy (logic, ethics and aesthetics). Two others are intermediary. The third is the *value-relating* attitude of culture (scientific efforts, artistic efforts, positive morality) which, though it con-

---

[82] Radbruch, Rechtsphilosophie (3d ed. 1932), in The Legal Philosophies of Lask, Radbruch and Dabin (Wilk trans., 1950). The references here ("L.R.D.") are to the sections (same in original and translation) and to the pages of the translation.

[83] L.R.D., § 1, p. 49. This seems to be a basic postulate of all social science.

tains truth and error, beauty and ugliness, humanity and barbarism, always has significance or meaning for the realization of value.[84] The religious attitude of mercy and forgiveness, above the law and beyond the merit of the individual forgiven (witness the parable of the prodigal son) is the *value-conquering* attitude. To these four attitudes he finds a corresponding fourfold formulation of what is given: 1. Existence. 2. Value. 3. Meaning. 4. Essence. Law as a cultural phenomenon is to be understood only within the framework of the value-relating attitude. Law may be "unjust" but it always means to be just.[85] The value-relating attitude toward law is that of legal science (Rechtswissenschaft), which is a cultural, not a natural, science.[86] The evaluating attitude toward law is that of legal philosophy. This division is substantially the same as the one, made above, between formal legal science and philosophy of law (supra, §§ 1.03, 1.04).

The age-old problem, how can one escape both brutal materialistic determinism and a futile dreamer's idealism?—troubles Radbruch as it had Kant and his followers. Radbruch accepts Kant's dualism of reality and value as a methodical dualism: from a statement concerning existence (a fact) one cannot *logically* derive any statement concerning what ought to be, a statement of value. From a "This is so" one cannot deduce a "That ought to be so." True, the judge will often, no doubt, have a "hunch" about a case as soon as he has heard the facts stated, just as Michelangelo may have had a vision of the statue of David as soon as he saw that rough-hewn marble block out of which he eventually delivered it.[87] But for the judge (however it may be for the sculptor) this is a case of lucky intuition and not a method of cognition. While the Is and the Ought are thus methodically divided, evaluations may well be *causally* derived from existing facts, including not only the facts of a legislative problem but also the facts of the social environment of those who do the evaluating. Here Radbruch seems to have left behind, as a futile ideal, Kant's "man of good will" whose will would not be causally determined (supra, § 4.20). Does he then walk into the parlor of Marxist determinism, the theory that law and government are determined by the selfish interests of the dominant economic class? No, because value-ideas are not mere lifeless

---

[84] Ibid., 50.

[85] Ibid., 52.

[86] Ibid., and see n. 78, supra.

[87] L.R.D., § 2, p. 54.

ideologies; they have an autonomy of their own, partly independent of material factors, and become powerful forces on the battlefield of politics.[88]

2. *Relativism.* Since statements about what ought to be can be formalogically derived only from other like statements, the ultimate statements about the Ought are axioms, incapable of proof. Between opposite ultimate views of values there can be no scientifically unequivocal answer. Yet scientific method can achieve three things in the field of the Ought: First, it may establish the means necessary to realize the end that ought to be attained. Guidance in the choice of the "right" means for a legal end is "legal *policy*"; [89] legal philosophy goes further in clarifying the end by showing the means necessary for its attainment and the incidental effects which those means will produce.[90] On these means-end relations turn most political debates about proposed legislation: "The end (e. g., fair prices for consumers of food and for farmers) is good but what will it cost?" This is the "lowest" (i. e., most concrete and variable) level of legal philosophy. Secondly, legal philosophy should clarify the ultimate value-presuppositions of a legal value judgment, up to the utmost generality of world outlook. These presuppositions would be statements from which the particular value judgment could, he believed, be logically deduced. In regarding these broader presuppositions as "logically" necessary, he seems to overlook the indeterminacy of induction from a conclusion to a major premise.[91] He says:

"He who evaluates is to be made conscious that in approving a particular end of the legal Ought he *must* accept not only the means connected therewith by causal necessity but also the more general evaluations involved therein by logical necessity." [92]

Does a legislature *necessarily* embrace socialism or any postulate thereof in adopting a subsidy for farmers, a protective tariff for manufacturers or a compulsory automobile insurance law?

Thirdly, one can systematically develop the *possible* systems of legal philosophy by an exhaustive presentation of various sys-

---

[88] Ibid., 55. See infra, § 4.35.

[89] Cf. supra, § 3.25.

[90] L.R.D., § 2, pp. 55–56.

[91] Supra, § 3.30(3).

[92] L.R.D., § 2, 56 (emphasis added).

tems of legal evaluation standing in opposition or in contrast with each other, even though one cannot establish *the* one and only system. This legal philosophy of relativism, though called by another neo-Kantian "a feeble and miserable philosophy,"[93] is typical of Radbruch's gentle and tolerant eclecticism. For that, no doubt (along with his idealist views), his book was burned.[94] Is not tolerance something worth fighting for?

3. *The Individual, the Collectivity, the Community.* Since justice determines only the form of the law, to get the content of legal rules a second idea must be added, expediency, or suitability for any purpose. Questions of the purpose of law and the purpose of the state are inseparable. Then he postulates three kinds of things as having "absolute" (ultimate) worth or value: Individual human personalities, human collective personalities (the state, the society) and human works (e. g., products of scientific and artistic effort). To these correspond three alternatives of world outlook: The individual, the transindividual and the transpersonal. The first is Kantian, and its slogan is "freedom." The second was represented by Hegel's and Mussolini's glorification of the state and its slogan is "nation." The third he represents by the aesthetes, such as the one (Treitschke) who said:

"A statue by Phidias counterbalances all the misery of the millions of slaves of antiquity."[95]

He might have added that we subordinate the "individual will" to the needs of the state for intelligent citizens and the need of the community for culture whenever parents coerce ("persuade" is the gentler word) a small boy to attend school. True, the coercion of the boy is "for his own good"; yet it can scarcely be denied that the individual is coerced into making sacrifices for the good of the nation and of the common culture—and rightly so, because these latter stand for other individuals, both those living and those yet unborn. Radbruch's synthesis of Kant and Hegel is valuable and suggestive. Yet we must never forget that the state and other human works exist for present or future individuals. After all the shouting about "nation" and "culture" is over, "there is nobody here but us humans."

---

93 Ibid., § 2, p. 58, n. 8, quoting Stammler.

94 This is inferred from the extreme scarcity of copies in Germany in 1945.

95 Ibid., § 7, p. 93. Cf. Dewey's statement that our material culture becomes collective and corporate while our moral culture, including legal concepts and institutions, remains feudally individualist. Individualism Old and New (1930), 74.

4. *Justice, Expediency and Certainty.* Radbruch finds three antinomic elements in what he calls "the idea of the law": Justice, expediency, and certainty. The essence of distributive justice (§ 4.23) is equality, "equal treatment for equal, and correspondingly unequal treatment of different, men and relationships." [96] Yet justice is not enough from which to derive the content of law: expediency, fitness for practical purposes, determines the specific content of laws. Now the exploration of the purposes of the law and of the state ends in relativism, a multiplicity of choices. The law of the state cannot be handed over to the disagreements of individuals; there must be one legal order over all. Hence we must postulate a third element: legal certainty. The law must be positive, it must be established by an agency which is capable of carrying it through. There is a constant tension between these three elements. Legal certainty is the most important in the sense of being indispensable to the existence of a legal order:

> "The existence of a legal order is more important than its justice and expediency, which constitute the second great task of the law, while the first, equally approved by all, is legal certainty, that is, order or peace." [97]

Radbruch's arguments for this position are similar to those which were urged above (§§ 2.04, 2.11) for the generality, authority and sanction of positive law. His conception of legal certainty does not include exactness of terminology, much less that stability of administration, certainty of "law in action" and predictability of fact-finding [98] which have been emphasized by American legal realists. Yet Radbruch's antinomic ideas of law can help us methodically to locate the tensions in our thinking about legal problems, even if they cannot give us the one formula that will solve them.[99]

---

[96] L.R.D., § 9, p. 107.

[97] Ibid., 108.

[98] See Frank, Courts on Trial (1949).

[99] In the volume above cited (supra, n. 82), Radbruch exemplifies his relativist analysis of values by his delightful discussions of special topics, such as ownership, contract, marriage, penal law, procedure, the law of nations, and war.

Chapter 15

HISTORICAL AND EVOLUTIONARY THEORIES OF LAW

§ 4.30—The Uses of History in Legal Evaluations

For many centuries men have appealed to history for guidance or support in legal problem-solving. Chiefly the reliance on history has had one of two bases. One was faith in our forefathers, the belief that our traditional, legal and social institutions should be continued unchanged. The other is evolutionary, the belief that history discloses a pattern of steady improvement, that future changes conforming to this pattern are likely to be both right and successful. Obviously these two beliefs can conflict. What is not obvious is the various meanings developed from them by the historical and evolutionary jurists of the past century and a half, and the deposit which their ideas have left in our legal culture. The present chapter will give a concise survey of the men and ideas of the German, English and American historical schools of jurisprudence and of the evolutionary theories of law and the state put forth by Spencer, Hegel and Marx. The evolutionary theory of Marx is an important part of the communist creed. While the need for seeking remote historical foundations no longer dominates American legal scholarship as it once did, the rejection of legal history in recent years from American legal education and legal writing calls for a re-appraisal of the various aspects of its significance. Hence this chapter begins with a brief survey of the five principal uses made of history, especially legal history, in legal evaluations, especially those on the level of generalization of legal philosophy. What are the uses of history in determining what the law ought to be? And incidentally, when does a legal historian become an historical jurisprudent?

The five chief uses of history in legal evaluations are as follows:

A. *Historical Meanings.* If history includes everything that happened both in the immediate and in the remote past and if learning the meanings of legal propositions is an indispensable step in solving every legal problem, then historical meanings are indispensable. If every inhabitant of a nation were by some biological weapon stricken with total loss of memory, no one would

404

know the meanings of statutes and case law, and these would cease to have any effects. But we need not adopt such a broad meaning of history to establish the point. Even if history be taken to mean the things that were said and done a long time ago, historical meanings of legal terms are still important. If legal history means the remote past—say, prior to 1600 in Anglo-American law—then historical meanings will need to be resorted to chiefly in the interpretation of legal norms whose terminology originated in that far-away period. Could one explain such common terms of Anglo-American property law as "fee simple" or "executory devise" or "heir" or "executor" without some slight dosage of legal history? "Equity" is another important term in Anglo-American law which has had a peculiar historical meaning due to the rise of separate "courts of equity" in England and in the United States. The need for teaching in law schools the historical aspects of modern judicial remedies and concepts that were derived from "equity" has been greatly exaggerated. The Federal Rules of Civil Procedure, adopted in 1938, carefully avoid the use of the term "equity" in order [1] to avoid carrying on the historical impedimenta of that term. Yet whether this effort to break with the past can be effective remains doubtful, since the term "equity" is used in the constitutional provision delimiting the scope of the jurisdiction of federal courts, and the statute which authorized the one form of action emphatically stated that the right of trial by jury "as at common law" should be preserved inviolate.[2] The historical meaning of equity must be preserved in order that we may know when jury trial is not demandable as of right.

The Federal Constitution as adopted in 1789 contains some provisions which call for historical interpretation. Such a term as "bill of attainder" [3] was used by the framers to refer to a specific evil, and a strong argument can be made for the view that the Supreme Court, exercising with due caution its power to declare acts of Congress unconstitutional, should adhere to the historic meaning of the term.[4] Thus whether a court should

[1] As reported by one of the draftsmen.

[2] U.S.Const., Art. III, Sec. 2; Act of Congress of June 19, 1934, 48 Stat. 1064, 28 U.S.C. §§ 723b–c.

[3] "No bill of attainder or ex post facto law shall be passed." U.S.Const., Art. I, Sec. 9(3).

[4] See separate concurring (but partly dissenting) opinion of Mr. Justice Frankfurter in U. S. v. Lovett, 328 U.S. 303, 66 Sup.Ct. 1073 (1946).

give a functional (policy) or genetic (historical) interpretation to constitution or statute is often a crucial issue in litigation. Can any reliable generalization about it be laid down? Holmes told a group of law students that the judicial reports of a given jurisdiction restate "pretty much the whole body of the law" in the course of a generation (about thirty years, I suppose) and that it could be reconstructed if all that went before were burned.[5] While this statement seems to me a rhetorical exaggeration, it is a prudent admonition for each new generation of lawyers. Would it not be reliable to say, then, that two generations of desuetude should be enough to bury (for the lawyer as distinct from the historical scholar) any legal meaning that is not embalmed in constitution or statute?

B. *Historical Correctives.* Legal history can be used to correct erroneous assumptions about contemporary law, especially case law. Sir Frederick Pollock in his urbane plea for the continued use of historical interpretation, gave the following justification:

> "No competent person will deny, surely, that the application of methodical historical criticism (from whatever school derived) to commonly accepted statements has exploded one baseless legend after another to the confusion of partisan writers and the relief of honest students." [6]

The best examples of this use of legal history are to be found in the late Dean John H. Wigmore's deservedly famous treatise on the law of evidence. One method was to show that a certain contemporaneous legal norm or concept was established in response to a situation (a legal or social institution or some phase of one) which has now disappeared or been greatly modified. Thus the strictness of the judicial rule limiting the admissibility of a confession of crime was emotionally caused by the one-sidedness of criminal procedure and the subservient attitudes of the "lower" classes toward the police[7] during a certain period in England. By the use of historical sources Wigmore was able to disentangle

---

[5] Holmes, "The Path of the Law" (1897) 10 Harv.L.Rev. 457, 458; Collected Legal Papers (1920) 167, 169. The Restatement of Law (American Law Institute) by framing its own definitions and minimizing the resort to genetic meanings has helped to make Holmes' statement true.

[6] Pollock, "A Plea for Historical Interpretation" (1923) 39 L.Q.Rev. 163, 168, reviewing Pound, Interpretations of Legal History (Cambridge, 1923).

[7] See Wigmore, Evidence (3d ed., 1940) §§ 817–820, 865, outlining the history of the rule.

the rational from the accidental in such confused topics as the privilege against self-incrimination, the so-called "best evidence" rule(s), the admissibility of regular entries and the like. Another use of legal history is to show that a contemporary legal rule now regarded as "established" is not of ancient lineage but originated in fairly recent times in the aberrations of a particular court or judge. As Wigmore showed, the nineteenth century rule that (with vague exceptions) a party to litigation against whom any error was committed by the trial court in the admission or exclusion of evidence, was, in case of an adverse verdict, entitled to a new trial as a matter of right, was an innovation of the English Court of Exchequer in the 1830's, and was contrary to the older English rule which took account of the effect of the error on the case as a whole.[8] That the rule denying recovery of money paid under mistake of law was itself the result of an early nineteenth century mistake of law[9] has doubtless made it easier for some American jurisdictions to reject the rule.[10] This use of legal history merely fulfills the negative function of clearing the way for arguments as to what the law should be now.

C. *Emotional Attachment to Old and Primitive Law.* The emotional pull of old customs and old laws, especially those regarded as primitive, has been strong in all ages and civilizations. Various kinds of emotions may be involved in different situations. Just as infants are frightened by the withdrawal of physical support, adults are quite commonly frightened by the threatened withdrawal of traditional cultural supports. Reverence and respect for parents and ancestors, just because they were ours, is transferred to the laws and institutions under which they lived. "What was good enough for father is good enough for me." Attachment to old laws and customs may be a part of loyalty to one's community or nation. Thus emotional attachment to past laws and usages is in some sense individual, arbitrary, irrational. The rationalist may scorn all local and nationalist ties; yet who is content to believe merely the product of a set of rational equations? Moreover, the common fear (it seems almost instinctive) of being dealt with arbitrarily or capriciously or even maliciously by one's political superior (judge or executive or legislator) makes resort

---

[8] Ibid., § 21.

[9] Bilbie v. Lumley, 2 East 469 (1802); Woodward, Quasi Contracts (1913), §§ 35–36.

[10] The most recent being New York: Civil Practice Act, § 112–f (enacted in 1942).

to a rule or an aphorism handed down from previous generations and hence not tainted by present personal bias, an emotional refuge. Antigone's famous appeal to the "immutable unwritten laws of Heaven" against Creon's harsh decree that she might not bury her brother was very likely an appeal to ancient Greek religious customs.[11] Some of these emotions were appealed to by a patriotic young man named Savigny in a famous little book which launched the historical school.[12] Old men are more likely to be strongly attached to old laws and customs than young ones. Sometimes because they are wiser, sometimes because experience has made them cynical about improvements, and sometimes from the inertia of habit.[13] Sometimes, perhaps, they commit the anachronistic pathetic fallacy of turning persons and actions of past centuries into symbols of what they love today.[14] The legal historian, whatever his nostalgic bias, will hardly tolerate this sloppy use of history.

D. *Historical Survival as the Test of Experience.* A rational argument for the use of legal history is that a legal rule, doctrine or concept which has survived for a century or more has met the test of experience and is therefore presumptively the best one until a better one can be produced. William James, no devout worshiper of the past, accepted such a presumption as a working rule for the moral philosopher.[15] Since no controlled experimentation in law and its social consequences is possible (as far as we know), the fact of survival is the next best thing. Now when one investi-

---

[11] Wormuth, "Aristotle on Law" in Essays in Political Theory Presented to George H. Sabine (ed. Konvitz and Murphy, 1948) 45, 53.

[12] See infra, § 4.31.

[13] See Wigmore, op. cit. supra, n. 7, I, 368, referring to the "inveterate professional instinct" of lawyers to venerate unduly the rules they work with daily. Dewey has continually emphasized the inertia of habit in Individualism Old and New (1930) 71; Human Nature and Conduct (1922), especially Ch. IV.

[14] Gilbert, "The Vital Disequilibrium in Croce's Historicism" in op. cit. supra, n. 11, at p. 211.

[15] See James, "The Moral Philosopher and the Moral Life" (an address delivered in 1891) in The Will to Believe and Other Essays in Popular Philosophy (1896) 184, 204–208; infra, § 4.52. Dewey also recognizes such a presumption. Speaking of moral principles, he says: "There is a long record of past experimentation in conduct, and there are cumulative verifications which give many principles a well earned prestige. Lightly to discard them is the height of foolishness." Human Nature and Conduct (1922) 239. Pound's "judicial empiricism" contains the same idea. The Spirit of the Common Law (1921), Lecture VII.

gates the numerous legal doctrines set forth in the judicial reports of the sixteenth and seventeenth centuries in England (for instance) and notes how many of them have expired without surviving issue, one is inclined to believe that those which survived were the better ones for the society in which they survived. Especially is this argument persuasive for the English rules and doctrines that came through the consciously selective judicial process in the United States during the early part of the nineteenth century.[16] The argument must not be pressed too far, of course, since stare decisis accounts for a good deal of survival of case law doctrines. Who can say that the doctrine of consideration (a central concept and a constellation of rules) has survived because of stare decisis or because on the whole it works well? The presumption means merely that until someone shows a better single criterion of the enforceability of promises, it seems better to patch it up and supplement it rather than to throw it out.

In a much broader context Professor Adolf A. Berle, Jr., has recently used the test of historical survival as a test of the success and the goodness of "political forces," by which he means the central idea of a political movement and its accompanying apparatus of means. He says:

"Let us consider that a 'good' political force is that force which demonstrates that it can survive and maintain itself—which necessarily includes the fact that it enables its followers, its adherents, the nations it organizes and international groups it brings into being, to survive likewise." [17]

Professor Berle relies upon the analogy of biological-natural selection, yet basically his theory consists of a new theory of ideal evolution operating in accordance with certain trends or principles.[18]

E. *Historical Evolution, Material and Ideal.* An evolutionary interpretation of the past is one which sees in it a trend or a line of development that will be projected into the future. Even though such an interpretation *may* be merely deterministic—"It *must* be this way"—it will usually end by being normative: "It *should* be that way—and we should all work to make it that way."

---

[16] See Pound, The Formative Era in American Law (1938), Ch. III, especially 124–125; Llewellyn, "How Appellate Courts Decide Cases" (1945) 16 Pa. Bar Ass'n Q. 220, 225; Hurst, The Growth of American Law: The Law Makers (1950) 185 ff.

[17] Berle, Natural Selection of Political Forces (1950), 50.

[18] Ibid., especially his statement of his thesis at p. 17.

Even evolutionary interpretations which purport to be neutral—
as with Spengler and Toynbee—tell us in effect that we *should*
not try to swim against the stream of history. The three most important evolutionary theories, with respect to law, were Herbert
Spencer's and those of Hegel and Marx, discussed below.

§ 4.31—The Spirit of the People: Savigny

The German historical school of jurisprudence was launched on
its way by Savigny's famous little book published in 1814.[19] Friedrich Karl von Savigny (1779–1861), a scholarly aristocrat, was
called to the professorship of Roman law at the newly established
University of Berlin in 1810, and in 1815 he published the first
volume of his monumental History of Roman Law in the Middle
Ages, still a work of pre-eminent legal scholarship.[20] Savigny
was one of the most famous and influential legal authors of the
modern world. His historical theory of law was as much a plea
for historical research as for anything else.

The "Vocation" essay appeared at a critical moment in the history of the German states, then not united in an empire. Napoleon I had imposed on the parts of Germany which he conquered
the adoption of the French Civil Code (Code Napoléon, 1804);
in other parts of Germany it was adopted more or less voluntarily.
With Napoleon's defeat (at Leipzig in 1813 and finally at Waterloo
in 1815) came the opportunity to throw off the Code as a part of
the conqueror's chains. But there were some who favored reten-
tion of the French Code (it remained in force in parts of Germany
until 1900), others who favored the adoption of a code based on
the Austrian Civil Code (1811), and still others, notably one Professor Thibaut, who urged the preparation and adoption of a code
of private law ("civil code") for all Germany as a new undertaking. Then came Savigny's "Vocation," dashed off in white
heat and bearing evidence of the rancorous Francophobia of the
time.[21] It was highly influential in deferring the adoption of a

---

[19] Savigny, Über den Beruf unserer Zeit fü Gesetzgebung und Rechtswis·
uenschaft (1814); 2d ed., 1828, translated by Hayward as: Of the Vocation of
Our Age for Legislation and Jurisprudence (London, 1831). The references
below, "Vocation," are to this translation. The originator of the German historical school was Hugo.

[20] Kantorowicz, "Savigny and the Historical School" (1937) 53 L.Q. Rev. 326,
341.

[21] As Savigny admitted in the Preface to the second edition, his historical
theory of law was stated more concisely and calmly in System des heutigen

code in Germany until 1896 (effective in 1900). Its arguments are still the chief arguments of historical jurisprudence.

The first is that the law of a nation, like its language, originates in the popular spirit, the common conviction of right, and has already attained a fixed character, peculiar to that people, before the earliest time to which authentic history extends. In this prehistoric period the laws, language, manners and political constitution of a people are inseparably united and they are the particular faculties and tendencies of an individual people, bound together by their kindred consciousness of inward necessity, "excluding all notion of an accidental and arbitrary origin." [22] This popular spirit (*Volksgeist*) is the foundation of all of a nation's subsequent legal development. Custom is its manifestation. The popular spirit is shown, for example, in the various symbolic acts by which legal transactions are solemnized.[23] In early law we find different ceremonials in different nations: The weighing of the price among the Romans, the handing over of the spear or festuca among the Germanic tribes, livery of seizin in early England. These symbolic acts do appear to be of prehistoric origin, but only a primitive faith could exclude the notion that they are partly accidental or arbitrary in origin.[24] Thus the origin of the popular spirit is veiled in mysticism, and its crude beginnings are colored with romanticism.

But Savigny knew as well as John Chipman Gray [25] that the popular spirit did not create the complex system of rights in land in Roman law or in any other advanced culture.[26] Accordingly, he supplemented his "popular spirit" origin with the theory that the

---

römischen Rechts, § 7, § 12. His follower, Puchta, developed an even more mystical conception of customary law. Puchta, Outlines of Jurisprudence as the Science of Right—a Juristic Encyclopedia (Hastie trans., 1887), 26, 30–32, 38, 39, 57, 58.

[22] Vocation, 24; Hall, 87.

[23] Ibid., 130.

[24] Savigny himself lets the cat out of the bag when he says that the ancient Italic peoples had more fixed and regular forms than the Germans, "which perhaps arose from their [Italian] city constitutions." Vocation, 26. In his System, § 12 (supra, n. 21), he recognized the arbitrary character of many customs.

[25] Gray said the *Volksgeist* carries a piece of sulphur in its pocket to ward off rheumatism. The Nature and Sources of the Law (1909) § 209.

[26] Savigny limited his discussion to the development of law "among nations of the nobler races." Vocation, 24.

jurists (legal scholars including professors and judges), who become legal specialists with the advance of civilization, are the representatives of the community spirit and are thus authorized to carry on the law in its technical aspects.[27]   Thenceforth law has a twofold existence: First, as part of the aggregate life of the community, and, secondly, as a distinct branch of knowledge in the hands of the jurists.[28]   Thus legal history has the "holy duty" of maintaining a lively connection between a nation's present and its primitive state; to lose this connection will deprive the people of the best part of their spiritual life.[29]   In explaining the role of legal history he invokes the organismic theory of legal development:

> " .   .   . its object is to trace every established system to its root, and thus discover an organic principle, whereby that which still has life may be separated from that which is lifeless and only belongs to history." [30]

Stripped of its metaphor this passage could be taken to state the role of the courts in Anglo-American law.

From the foregoing arguments (the primitive-popular-spirit and the jurist-representation) he arrived at his third, that the immediate codification of German private law would be futile or crude or dangerous or all three.   It would be useless to codify the law of marriage, for instance, until the public mind had shown a "decided and commendable tendency," since marriage belongs half to law and half to manners,[31] and thus comes closer to what he calls the "political" element in law.[32]   The "technical" element, which would predominate in a civil code, would require greater professional talent than could be found in Germany at that time; indeed, he argues that the code should be written by a single great law-giver, and where could one find such a man? [33]   (Germany was too poor in talent to draft a code, but was rich enough to engage in fruitful legal scholarship as a substitute.)   A code would purport to be comprehensive and gapless, yet it really could not be.   The recent codes of the eighteenth century were framed on

---

[27] Vocation, 28; Hall, pp. 87-88.

[28] Ibid., 136; Hall, p. 88.

[29] Ibid., 136; Hall, p. 88.

[30] Ibid., 137.

[31] Ibid., 63.

[32] Ibid., 62.   He referred to the clerical differences about divorce.

[33] Ibid., 179-80.

the assumption that a group of men by the exercise of reason could create a complete system of laws valid for all times and places.[34]   On the contrary, Savigny's *Volksgeist* theory was incompatible with that of a universal law of nature, the same for all nations.   He conceded that legislation (apart from "political" legislation, which he did not discuss) could be used to improve procedure and to record established customary law.[35]

Savigny's arguments carried an appeal to everyone who counted.   He was opposed to the "blind rage for improvement" [36] and to "political" or reform legislation; this pleased the princes.   The democrats were pleased to learn that law came from the people, not from the princes, and the Germanist romanticists like to believe that the middle ages was a legal paradise untainted by alien Roman law.[37]   The professors were doubtless pleased that they were to develop the law through legal scholarship and that the judges were to follow their expert findings, even though Savigny did say that German legal scholarship was still too undeveloped to prepare a civil code.   At Berlin he revived the old device by which law faculties served as Courts of Appeal.[38]   The judges were doubtless pleased that they were not to be tied down to the mechanical application of a code but were rather to have discretion in determining the law from scholarly sources.[39]   Rarely, if ever, has a theory so filled with romantic fallacies and implicit contradictions made so many people happy.   The theory of the popular spirit was in tune with the spirit of the times.[40]

What ideas in Savigny's theory still have value for twentieth century jurisprudence?   His distinction between the "political" and "technical" elements in law is essentially the same as that which Cardozo made in arguing for the establishment of a permanent commission to propose needed changes in "technical" law.[41]

---

[34] Ibid., 34.

[35] Ibid., 151–154.

[36] Ibid., 20.   This may refer to the Prussian Code (*Landrecht*) which Savigny eventually deigned to teach at Berlin as a set of footnotes to Roman law.   Kantorowicz, op. cit. supra, n. 20, 337.

[37] Here I paraphrase Kantorowicz, op. cit., 336, 337.

[38] See Vocation, 149.

[39] Ibid., 150–151.

[40] Kantorowicz, op. cit., 336.

[41] "Technical" here means professional.   The title of Cardozo's article, "A Ministry of Justice" (in (1921) 35 Harv.L.Rev. 115) may have come from Hay-

Law professors are increasingly engaged in the technical drafting of legislation. His view that the framing of a comprehensive code requires the highest order of talent, which Francis Bacon had asserted long before,[42] is indisputable. His argument that codification would put an end to careful investigation of pre-code law was not verified in Germany. As to the law of the popular spirit, he was right in believing that each nation has some peculiarities of custom and attitude which cannot be learned from their written codes or treatises or even wholly from their judicial decisions; and he was wrong, I believe, in supposing that the *primitive* customs and attitudes of a people *should* have primacy over later developments. As a legal sociologist one would have to recognize in most countries an emotional attachment not only among lawyers and officials but also among laymen, to long-established traditions; and in so far as this emotional attachment is a means to security and is in itself a source of happiness, it is a good which the legal philosopher must weigh against the competing goods, if any, promised by specific departures from traditional ways. To suppose that these traditions are tied to primitive modes of conveyancing, or even to conventional notarial practices, as Savigny appears to, is a romantic fallacy. The American traveler in England or in France can best verify the core of truth in Savigny's *Volksgeist* theory. The English are more precise in their transactions, more conscious of legal implications and more meticulous both in exacting and fulfilling legal duties. In the United States an amorphous "fairness," partly based on routine, is the primary criterion in ordinary affairs, with the law as a refuge which a "good sport" should not resort to. As to France, one quickly finds that there is a great deal of normative material not apparent in either the civil code or in an expert treatise. These national characteristics give individuality to a people and they would constitute at present serious obstacles to the adoption and usefulness of a comprehensive world code of laws for all peoples. We need to build a world community of interests before we can establish a world régime under law.

§ 4.32—English and American Historical Jurists

The German historical school had a profound influence upon jurisprudence and legal scholarship, and even some influence on

---

ward's translation, 151. Cardozo's proposal resulted in the creation of the New York Law Revision Commission in 1934. See infra, § 4.62.

[42] See Vocation, 37.

legal practice, in England and in the United States. England already had its own historical jurists in Coke, who glorified the English common law as at once the common custom of the realm and the embodiment of reason, and Blackstone, whose theory that judges only find the law is akin to the popular-spirit idea of Savigny. The chief representative of the historical school in England was Sir Henry Maine (1822–1888), who was for many years Regius Professor of Civil Law at Cambridge. Maine partly accepted Savigny's view of the importance of primitive legal institutions, when he said that the rudimentary ideas of early law are to the jurist what the primary crusts of the earth are to the geologist. "They contain," he said, "potentially all the forms in which law has subsequently exhibited itself." [43] While this may seem to be the *Volksgeist* garbed in a scientific analogy, Maine departed from Savigny in two important respects: He believed in stages of legal evolution, in which the primitive ideas might be discarded; and he sought to discover by comparative studies of different systems of law the ideas which they had in common. These two tenets account for the content of his first and most important book, Ancient Law (1861). The first he derived partly from Hegel and partly from Darwin, whose Origin of Species was published in 1859. The second, while not original with him (Montesquieu and Austin had both made comparative-law studies) was an extension of his belief that history could be a science and could have methods like those of the other sciences.[44] His work was a forerunner of legal sociology and sociological jurisprudence.[45]

Two of Maine's chief contributions to legal theory were his analysis of the methods of legal change and his status-to-contract generalization. After the stage of customary law and its embodiment (in most European societies) in a primitive Code, legal change to meet the emergent needs or demands of society becomes difficult because of a superstitious reverence for traditional rules. The "agencies by which law is brought into harmony with soci-

---

[43] Maine, Ancient Law (1st ed., 1861), Ch. I (Everyman ed.) 2; Hall, p. 113. The Everyman edition will be cited below.

[44] See Village Communities and Miscellanies (1865), 266: ". . . if indeed history be true it must teach that which every other science teaches, continuous sequence, inflexible order, the eternal law." Hall, p. 114.

[45] Infra, § 4.60. See Stone, The Province and Function of Law (1946) Ch. XIX, §§ 1–4 (pp. 451–463) where Maine is placed in the context of "law and society in retrospect." The Second Printing of Professor Stone's book (Harvard University Press, 1950) preserves the chapter, section and page numbers of the first printing.

ety" are, he says, three: Fictions, equity and legislation.[46] Legal fictions he found operating both in Rome and in England at similar stages of legal development. In Rome, foreigners were allowed to sue in Roman courts by making the plaintiff's allegation that he was a Roman citizen an indisputable and thus a fictitious one for the purpose of that case. The fictions by which the English courts of Queen's Bench and Exchequer usurped the jurisdiction of the Court of Common Pleas were similar. Maine included more than these procedural fictions. He even went so far as to treat as a fiction the assumption, by both counsel and judges, that a law-suit is to be decided solely on the basis of old principles and not new ones; for do we not admit as soon as the decision has been rendered that it has modified the law? [47] Roman law was developed by a similar fiction that the responses of the jurisconsults were merely "interpretations" of the ancient Roman Code, the Twelve Tables. Although fictions serve a useful purpose at an early stage of legal development, Maine thought they should be abandoned in a mature culture because they make the law more difficult to understand and to arrange in harmonious order.[48] While this conclusion seems sound as to the older procedural fictions, one should recognize differences in the kinds and purposes of fictions, and that some of them have limited and temporary usefulness for modern law.[49] For example, the "fiction" of adoption was, Maine says, indispensable to the development of society [50] from the family to the tribe, because it preserved the assumption of blood-kinship and the emotions attached to it. The modern legal device of adoption is still useful for thousands of childless couples; it treats the adopted child for the purposes of inheritance, family rights and duties and otherwise, "as if" he were a "natural" child; yet it involves no assumption of blood relationship for the purposes or in the context of legal relations.[51]

---

[46] Ancient Law, Ch. II, 15.

[47] Ibid., 19.

[48] Ancient Law, 16.

[49] See Cohen (Morris) "On the Logic of Fiction" (1923) 20 J. Philos. 477, 486–7. "Without fictions," said Jhering, "many profound changes in Roman law would not have taken place until a much later period." 3 Geist des römischen Rechts (3 aufl.) § 58, 297. That the use of legal fiction is by no means ended, see Fuller, "Legal Fictions" (1931) 25 Ill.L.Rev. 877 ff.

[50] Ancient Law, 16.

[51] See Fuller, "Legal Fictions" (1930) 25 Ill.L.Rev. 363, 392. The contextual theory of meaning (§§ 1.12, 3.26) fulfills a function similar to that of the fiction, and usually with more awareness of its limits.

Still, legal fictions are to be avoided as hindrances to clarity and effectiveness in legal terminology.

By "equity" Maine meant a body of rules existing by the side of the original law, founded on distinct principles and claiming to supersede the civil law in virtue of an inherent ethical superiority.[52] This sounds like the classical conception of the law of nature; Maine developed the two conceptions together.[53] Equity was relied upon in Rome by the Praetors and in England by the Chancellors. In each case, said Maine, the interference with the established law was open and avowed.[54] In England the scarcely concealed overriding of law by equity was glossed by the maxim that "equity acts in personam." The role of equity in protecting married women's and infants' property by the device of the trust and the separate estate is one example of the adaptation of law to the changing mores of the society. Legislation, the third instrument of legal change, comes relatively late in most societies. Maine regarded it as the preferable method of legal change; but he warned that the laws of a political sovereign would be futile if they conflicted with the deep-seated traditions of the community.[55] Maine's study of the methods of legal change pointed three ways: It helped to understand the meaning of present law; it showed that the Austinian conception of law was not enough to guide the lawmaker; and it provided a negative kind of valuation by showing that societal facts limited the practical effectiveness of laws.

Maine's status-to-contract generalization has been punched full of holes, yet it serves as a useful paradigm for the orientation of present-day legal changes. In the early stages of progressive societies, Maine said, the family is the legal unit; the paterfamilias is its head, and the other members—wife, children, slaves—are dependent on him and subject to his power. Only the paterfamilias has the power to contract; the rights and duties of the other members are determined by "status", which he used to mean position in the family. The abolition of slavery, the breakdown of the paterfamilias' power over the children and the emancipation of married women made possible greater freedom of all these persons in the making of contracts. From this he concluded:

---

[52] Ibid., 17, 26.

[53] Ibid., Ch. III.

[54] Ibid., 17.

[55] Maine, Early History of Institutions (1875), 359–360; Hall, p. 112.

" . . . the movement of the progressive societies has hitherto been a movement *from Status to Contract.*" [56]

Maine was careful ("hitherto") to state an historical summary, not a prophecy; and his generalization, using "status" to mean only *family* relations, is still true. The paterfamilias has gone with the dodo. But his famous epitome has been taken to mean that Maine supported freedom of contract as including freedom from governmental regulation—*laissez faire* [57]—and in this sense Maine's generalization was becoming less accurate at the time when he made it. He gave color to this economic interpretation when he pointed out that, in Western Europe, the status of the slave had been superseded "by the contractual relation of the servant to his master." [58] Today the individual employee in industry has little or no opportunity or power to bargain over the terms of his employment; these are determined by a labor union, in which he has a voice. The individual entrepreneur of Maine's day has to a considerable extent been swallowed up in the stockholder-management relation or the management-employee relation of giant corporations. Even that sturdiest of rugged individualists, the farmer, depends on a governmental subsidy. Does it follow, then, that the evolution will be cyclical, a return from contract to status? Not necessarily, I believe. The new economic relations above referred to are all consensual relations. The important thing is that the individual is not born into them and he may (though sometimes only at a prohibitive cost) renounce and leave them. Moreover, these relations are not *all-embracing;* the employee as consumer, as parent or spouse, as political voter, preserves more individual autonomy than the dependent members of the household ever had under the *paterfamilias.* History need not repeat itself.

United States. In the United States, as in Germany and England, the influence of the historical school has come about chiefly through the writings and teachings of law professors, a circumstance ascribed by Pound to the fact that professors distrust legislation and are averse to action.[59] The two men whose influence here was greatest were the two who initiated and propagated the

---

[56] Ancient Law, Ch. V, 100.

[57] See Stone, op. cit., supra n. 45, 463.

[58] Ancient Law, Ch. V, 99.

[59] Pound, Interpretations of Legal History (1930), 16–17; Hall, p. 103. He mentions Ames, Thayer and Bigelow (M. M.) in America. A newer generation of law teachers seems to be free from this aversion.

casebook and the case method of teaching law, and thus revolutionized American legal education. Christopher Columbus Langdell (1826–1906), a sturdy son of New Hampshire's hills, became dean of the Harvard Law School in 1870 and in 1871 published the first American casebook, Cases on Contracts. In its preface, he stated his reasons for adopting the casebook as a means of instruction. First, the law as a science consists of certain principles or doctrines; [60] secondly, each of these can be best understood as an historical growth:

> "Each of these doctrines has arrived at its present state by slow degrees; in other words, it is a growth, extending in many cases through centuries. This growth is to be traced in the main through a series of cases; and much the shortest and best, if not the only way of mastering the doctrine effectually is by studying the cases in which it is embodied. But the cases which are useful and necessary for this purpose at the present day bear an exceedingly small proportion to all that have been reported. The vast majority are useless and worse than useless for any purpose of systematic study." [61]

If law is a science and reported judicial decisions are the data of that science, then why should some be discarded as "useless"? Would a botanist discard specimens because they did not fit into his classification? However, if it be assumed that the doctrines and principles extracted by the law teacher from the earlier historical sequence of cases have an intrinsic superiority over later innovations, then Langdell's rejection of "useless" specimens is understandable. That Langdell did make this assumption is indicated by the preponderance of older English cases in his casebook, and by his other writings.[62] Yet Langdell did not become absorbed in early English legal history as did Ames.

James Barr Ames (1846–1910), a cultivated Bostonian who studied for more than a year at German universities, was among

---

[60] Langdell, Cases on Contracts (1871), Preface. Speaking many years later he compared the law library to the laboratory of the physicist or the botanical garden of the botanist. (1887) 3 L.Q.Rev. 121–122.

[61] Preface, op. cit., last note. Compare Savigny's organismic conception, supra, p. 412.

[62] Notably his Summary of Equity Pleading (1877) and Brief Survey of Equity Jurisdiction (1905). One story is that Langdell spoke to his class of "a comparatively recent case by Lord Hardwicke," who was Lord Chancellor of England, 1737–1754

the first students to use Langdell's casebook, and after his appointment to the Harvard Law faculty he became a prolific producer of casebooks which were widely used in American law schools. Ames dug deeper into Yearbook law than Langdell, and in his casebooks he frequently began a chapter or a topic with Yearbook cases in law French which few law teachers, let alone law students, could translate. His casebooks on trusts, equity jurisdiction, torts, bills and notes, etc., are still valuable collections of historical material. Ames was a brilliant and inspiring teacher. While he was by no means wholly devoted to historicism, he expressed his belief in the primacy of some early legal concepts. At the end of his brilliant historical essay on "The Disseisin of Chattels," he wrote:

> "In a subsequent paper, the writer will endeavor to show that this doctrine [of disseisin] is not a mere episode of English legal history, but that it is a living principle, founded in the nature of things, and of great practical value in the solution of many important problems.[63]

Ames' encomium has not, I believe, been justified, even by his persuasive insights into the principles or policies underlying a seemingly technical group of cases.[64] He was the leader of a generation of law teachers who made historical investigation, principally of legal cases and texts,[65] seem to be the only kind of legal scholarship. It is fortunate that this generation did its work of historical scholarship well and it is also fortunate that later generations of legal scholars were not dominated by this model. In legal education the sheer pressure of time has led to the dropping of large quantities of material formerly used to show historical sequence.[66] As Holmes said, with some rhetorical exaggeration in both parts of his aphorism:

> ". . . historic continuity with the past is not a duty, it is only a necessity."[67]

---

[63] Ames, Lectures on Legal History (1913) 191; first published in (1889) 3 Harv.L.Rev. 23, 40. But see Ames' views on contract law, infra, § 4.50.

[64] See Ames, "The Nature of Ownership" in Lectures in Legal History (1913) 192–209. He made a similar statement at the conclusion of his third article, (1890) 3 Harv.L.Rev. 345–46.

[65] I. e., they were rather short on what Pound calls "sociological legal history."

[66] This thesis was further developed in a book review of a casebook on equity. (1935) 48 Harv.L.Rev. 1261.

[67] Holmes, "Learning and Science" (1895) in his Collected Legal Papers (1920) 138, 139; Hall, p. 669.

§ 4.33—American Codification: The Field-Carter Controversy

The historical jurists were distrustful of legislation and generally opposed to codification of private law. For one thing, they were usually thorough legal scholars and were thus aware of the errors in legislation purporting to be declaratory of existing law. Savigny pointed out the crimes against Roman legal history which the French Civil Code committed,[68] and Ames pointed out numerous defects in the proposed Uniform Negotiable Instruments Law.[69] That such legal scholars have deterred hasty and ill-considered codification is a genuine service. Yet it needs to be said, as Pound has pointed out in his comment on Savigny,[70] that an historical error may make a valuable improvement in the law. To one who thinks of English case law as an organic growth a statute here and there may be necessary to correct minor errors or to provide added remedies for new evils; yet it should always be interpreted as designed to remedy a specific and narrowly defined evil, and must not be taken to have modified the common law in general. The maxim that "statutes in derogation of the common law are to be strictly construed" had such a narrowing and hampering effect on legislation during the nineteenth century and the early part of the twentieth, in the United States [71] that it became standard usage to insert in ameliorative statutes provisions that were designed to overcome the maxim, such as a preamble stating broadly the purposes of the act and a paragraph stating that the statute should be "liberally" construed. The late-nineteenth century judges were typically historical jurists. With the change in judicial attitudes during the past thirty years such precautions against historical sabotage are, I believe, unnecessary. On the contrary, there is some danger that the next generation of judges may extend the policy interpretation of statutes too

---

[68] Savigny, Vocation, Ch. VII, 69–99. See comment in Pound, Interpretations of Legal History (1930), 15.

[69] See his articles in (1900) 14 Harv.L.R. 241, 257; ibid., 442, 449; (1903) 16 Harv.L Rev. 255, 261: " . . . it is wiser to have no code at all than to adopt the Negotiable Instruments Law in its present form." The Law had then been adopted in twenty states.

[70] Supra, n. 68.

[71] "After 1920 it became hard to assemble from the Digest any substantial citations to so familiar a late-nineteenth century shibboleth as the rule that statutes in derogation of common law must be strictly construed." Hurst, op. cit. supra, § 4.30, n. 16, at p. 187. But even in 1952 they are not unknown. See Falls v. Employers' Liability Assur. Corp., 104 F.Supp. 256, 257 (D.C.La. 1952) ("in derogation of common right").

broadly and that a new standard section may have to be added: "This statute means just what it says and no more."

The adoption of a civil code is likely to be advocated in the United States during the next generation. Some of the arguments to be used or avoided in the debate over this proposal may be derived from a study of those made by David Dudley Field (1805–1894) in support of the adoption in New York of his civil code, and by James Coolidge Carter (1827–1903), a prominent New York lawyer who, as chairman of a bar association committee, led the attack against it. Field was a follower of the great English law reformer, Jeremy Bentham (Ch. 16) and his arguments for codification were substantially those of his master. Summarized briefly, they were: 1. Judges should not be lawmakers, as they are under case law. 2. Codification will make the law "cognoscible" to laymen, who cannot understand case law. 3. Codification will make the law systematic and clear, so that prediction will be more reliable. 4. A code will permit flexibility of interpretation and will not be a strait-jacket. 5. Even an imperfect code is better than none; no nation that has once adopted a code has ever gone back to uncodified law. 6. The code can be amended as imperfections develop.[72]

Carter's arguments against the adoption of Field's Civil Code may, with some interpretations, be summarized thus: 1. Judges will continue to make the law after the code is adopted, because they cannot apply it to novel situations without resorting to the case law that preceded the code. The judges will torture the language of the code to mean what they think it should mean. 2. The code will be no more accessible to laymen than is case law. 3. The code will not make prediction more reliable if the terms are general and vague, thus making possible different judicial constructions. 4. If the code is phrased in very specific terms, it will prove to be arbitrary and unjust as to new cases, and the judges will have to torture the language to cover them. 5. There is no short cut to the mastery of the law. The bulk of case law is greatly exaggerated. While public law and procedure have often been codified, there is no really successful code of private law. 6. A code will impede the growth of law, since amendments can come only after the mischief has been done; a code overgrown by amendments will be an incoherent mass. 7. Codifiers

---

[72] This is a condensation of Hall's excellent summary (pp. 119–20) of Field's article, "Codification," (1886) 20 Amer.L.Rev. 1; see also Field's reply to Carter in (1890) 24 Amer.L.Rev. 255.

assume the superhuman task of anticipating all future conditions.[73]

The arguments match each other roughly, except the last, which is reminiscent of Savigny.[74] Field might have retorted that it would be easier to find a small group of wise and far-seeing lawmakers than to continue to find a host of judges capable of reading, understanding and applying the amorphous body of case law. As to Carter's other arguments, No. 1 is reminiscent of Gray's position that statutes are not law but only sources of law.[75] Carter exaggerated the possibilities of judicial interpretation just as Gray did and just as the judges around 1890 did. The present realization that judges inevitably "make law" by adding to the sum total of legal meanings, but that they are limited in what they can add at any one time makes it possible to argue that codification would reduce the scope of judicial lawmaking even though it would never eliminate it. Carter's argument that the judges would resort to the case law which preceded the code was confirmed temporarily by the New York decisions interpreting Field's code of procedure,[76] which was for a half century after its enactment rendered partly ineffective by historical interpretations. In California and the states which borrowed most of its civil code, based upon the Field Civil Code, English and American precedents are blithely cited as if the code had never been adopted. But the civil procedure of New York today has been greatly improved, by legislation and judicial interpretation, as compared with that of 1840, before the Field Code. The improvements made by codification may not be immediately apparent, yet, given a reasonably adequate treatment, over a few decades it will count enormously. Carter's argument that the layman will not resort to the code for guidance seems correct, but neither will he resort to case law. Carter's arguments Nos. 3 and 4 state the dilemma of codification: either vague and futile or precise and

---

[73] See Hall's summary (op. cit., 120–121) of Carter, "The Province of the Written and the Unwritten Law" (1890) 24 Amer.L.Rev. 1. Carter's first attack, "The Proposed Codification of our Common Law," circulated as a pamphlet in 1883, had considerable influence in preventing the adoption of the Field Code, which was twice passed by the Legislature and vetoed by the governor. See "James Coolidge Carter" in (1909) 8 Great American Lawyers 19.

[74] Supra, § 4.31, n. 33.

[75] Gray, op. cit. supra, § 3.11, nn. 10, 11, 12.

[76] Adopted in New York in 1848, and subsequently in twenty-four states. Field's work for codification is outlined in (1908) 8 Great Amer.Lawy. 145–169.

harsh. Yet careful terminology and system can reduce both risks. As to Carter's statement that no "successful" code of private law has ever been drafted, Field pointed to codes in Europe and South America; and the more recent German and Swiss codes show improvement in drafting. France, approaching the sesquicentennial of the Code Napoléon, is engaged in a thorough revision of it, but would never dream of going back to its eighteenth century chaos of local custom and Roman law. Field's statement that no nation has abandoned codification is, I believe, still correct.

Carter's work in opposing the Field Code led to his preparing a series of lectures which, though never delivered, were published posthumously. Rejecting natural law as too vague and idealistic and Austin's positivism as making law rest upon fiat, he turns to history for the true meaning of law, and finds it in custom:
"Human nature is not likely to undergo a radical change, and, therefore, that to which we give the name of Law always has been, still is, and will forever continue to be Custom."[77]

Justice derives its supremacy among the moral sentiments from the profound convictions of custom.[78] No written law can ever inspire men's loyalty as can customary law. A statute which goes contrary to custom cannot be enforced, and an unenforced law is a "law" in name only.[79] The influence of the German historical school is apparent throughout Carter's book. It seems likely that he had been taught these ideas by his teacher, Cushing, who had been a pupil of Savigny.[80] The seeds of historical jurisprudence, planted in youth, blossomed in old age.

The arguments for and against codification will continue. The best argument of the antagonists has been the serious defects of the drafting. The California Civil Code, despite some amendments, still contains obscure or anachronistic provisions. To cite one example, it compels a Federal court, where California law governs, to apply a rule as to concealment by an insured, in non-marine insurance,[81] which case law elsewhere has made virtually

---

[77] Carter, Law: Its Origin, Growth and Function (1907), 120.

[78] Ibid., 159.

[79] Ibid., 3.

[80] Pound, Interpretations of Legal History (1930), 34-35. See also (1909) 8 Great Amer.Lawy. 5.

[81] See Gates v. General Casualty Co., 120 F.2d 925 (C.C.A.Cal.1941) (insured's innocent non-disclosure of a material fact made liability insurance contract voidable.)

obsolete. The uncertainty as to the scope of the case law change (that is *its* peculiar defect) could be partly obviated by legislation. Aside from a few state codes, the American substitutes for the European type of codification have thus far been threefold: 1. The Uniform Laws drafted and sponsored by the National Conference of Commissioners on Uniform Laws. 2. The Restatement of Law, a valuable systematic summary of fundamental portions of private case law, not enacted but having the unofficial authority of its able and learned redactors. 3. The amendments drafted by the New York Law Revision Commission (and similar bodies in a few other states) admittedly piecemeal improvements on case law.

§ 4.34—Biological-Cultural Evolution: Herbert Spencer

The publication in 1859 of Darwin's famous book on the origin of species gave a new turn to earlier nineteenth century beliefs in evolution and progress based on Christian theology, on Hegelian idealism or on Bacon's theory of man's power over nature. Darwin's central concept was that of natural selection, the "selection" of those individuals fittest to survive because of better adaptation to their environment. This theory was applied to contemporary human societies by Spencer.

Herbert Spencer (1820–1903), frail son of a Derby schoolmaster, was educated to be a philosopher and during a long life poured forth semi-popular works on biology, psychology, sociology and ethics. His political and ethical views were a mixture of Kantian theories of human perfectibility and freedom, combined with Darwin's theory of adaptation and survival. In one of his earliest works, Spencer adopted as a "first principle" that every man is entitled to "the fullest liberty to exercise his faculties" that is "compatible with the possession of like liberty by every other man." [82] His reasons for this conclusion were: The Divine will is that man shall attain happiness, and human happiness is best attained when men are free to exercise to the utmost the faculties that are given them. The ultimate perfection of man was logically certain because human history revealed a continuous progress from savagery to civilization which, unless interfered with, would eliminate all unfitness of man for his en-

[82] Spencer, Social Statics (1st Amer.Ed., 1865), Ch. IV, secs. 1–4 (first published 1850). In a later work he recognized the similarity of this principle to Kant's "universal principle of right," of which he was unaware when he first formulated it. Spencer, Justice (1892), Appendix A.

vironment and thus all his imperfections.[83] (The assumption of a fixed environment for man seems patently fallacious; yet "adaptation" can include man's alteration of his environment to fit his traits and needs.)   The state should do nothing to further nor to interfere with this progress, except to protect individual liberty as above formulated.   Hence Spencer was violently opposed to the English "poor laws," by which the sufferings of the indigent were mitigated, on the ground that these laws interfered with the operation of that "beneficent" but "severe discipline" by which the incompetent, the idle, the weak and the imprudent are eliminated from society, along with their unfortunate widows and orphans.[84]   On similar grounds Spencer opposed governmental support of public schools by taxation. To tax a capable person who can provide for his education is to reduce his power to develop his faculties to the fullest, in order to help a less capable person.   Spencer even argued that omitting to provide a child with instruction did not deprive him of his freedom to exercise his faculties.[85]   This is the same negative conception of freedom that sometimes resulted from Kantian idealism.[86]   His position on public education spoke for English tradition rather than for some more humane principles which Spencer at times expressed.   Thus he recognized that slavery belonged only in a state of savagery; in civilization it depraved the moral sense and rendered men unfit to act together.[87]   In a later work Spencer recognized that altruistic moral sentiments, such as the care of offspring by parents, were essential to the survival of the fittest.[88]   Still he might argue, as he had earlier, that for the state to educate children weakened the altruistic sentiments of parents.[89]   One may ask, why did he not consider the importance for the state of an educated citizenry?   Spencer, like most philosophers of evolution, vacillated between the Is and the Ought, between merely predicting the inevitable and trying to help it along.   Thus he defined "pure" ethics as consisting of the "absolute principles of right conduct," a system which ignores evil,

---

[83] Ibid., 78–79. See also Ch. XXX, sec. 4, pp. 454–455.

[84] Ibid., Ch. XXV, sec. 6, pp. 352–355. For a good criticism of Spencer's thesis, see Bodenheimer, Jurisprudence (1940), 50.

[85] Ibid., Ch. XXVI, sec. 1, pp. 360–361.

[86] See supra, § 4.22.

[87] Ibid., Ch. XXX, sec. 4, p. 457.

[88] Spencer, The Data of Ethics (New York, 1879), 19, 200.

[89] See citation supra, n. 84.

wrong, injustice and crime,[90] yet he made some impure arguments that the state *ought* not to support public schools.[91] He adopted the organismic conception of society:

> ". . . society is a growth, and not a manufacture— a thing that makes itself, and not a thing that can be artificially made." [92]

This conception of society had its counterpart in the historical jurists' theory of the growth of the law. In the United States, Spencer had numerous disciples, notably John Fiske.[93] On the whole, he was the philosopher of "rugged individualism," of William Graham Sumner's industrious and prudent "Forgotten Man." [94]

The reaction against Spencer's stern evolutionary theory came during his lifetime. Lester F. Ward, an idealistic sociologist, reversed for human society Spencer's principle of natural selection:

> "The dynamics of society is, in the main, the antithesis of the dynamics of animal life. . . . The survival of the fittest is simply the survival of the strong, which implies and would better be called the destruction of the weak. If nature progresses through the destruction of the weak, man progresses through the protection of the weak."[95]

This passage corrects one exaggeration by another; the loaded ambiguity of "weak" and "strong" makes analysis futile. William James, a founder of pragmatism and a believer in a kind of "survival-of-the-fittest" doctrine,[96] pierced the pseudo-scientific veil of Spencer's philosophy and declared that Spencer's "philosophy of evolution," as distinct from what is known about specific changes in biological evolution, was "a metaphysical creed and nothing else." [97]

---

[90] Op. cit. supra, n. 82 at p. 70.

[91] Supra, n. 85.

[92] Op. cit. supra, n. 82, 370. Compare the quotation from Langdell, supra, § 4.32, n. 61.

[93] See Schneider, A History of American Philosophy (1946) 351, 362 and Ch. 33, "Genetic Social Philosophy."

[94] Ibid., 382, 400.

[95] Ward, The Psychic Factors of Civilization (1893) 135, quoted in Schneider, op. cit., 386.

[96] Supra, § 4.30, n. 15; infra, § 4.52.

[97] James, The Will to Believe (1897), 253–254, quoted in Schneider, op. cit., 384.

Mr. Justice O. W. Holmes, another pragmatist, gave the *coup de grâce* to Spencer's evolutionism in a famous dissenting opinion. The State of New York enacted a statute making it a penal offense to employ a baker for more than ten hours a day. A bakery proprietor who had violated the law contended that it was invalid because contrary to the "due process" clause of the Fourteenth Amendment to the Federal Constitution. A majority of the Supreme Court upheld this contention, but Holmes dissented in an opinion which contained the following:

> "The liberty of the citizen to do as he likes so long as he does not interfere with the liberty of others to do the same, which has been a shibboleth for some well-known writers, is interfered with by school laws, by the Post Office, by every state and municipal institution which takes his money for purposes thought desirable, whether he likes it or not. The Fourteenth Amendment does not enact Mr. Herbert Spencer's Social Statics." [98]

What, if anything is worthy to survive in Spencer's theory of survival? Very little that is distinctively Spencerian, but much that he shared with his contemporaries. The belief in human progress through social co-operation is a common faith of western culture and is justified by a considerable body of fact, selected by evaluations shared by most occidental peoples. The view that survival is some evidence of good selection has been referred to above.[99] Spencer's grim reminder of the struggle for existence should not be forgotten even though some idealists and politicians like to promise pie in the sky for every one, regardless of individual effort or merit. The struggle for existence is not confined to the jungle, and the desire to compete, excel and win by individual effort is a persistent human trait. That the State should, along with various forms of social co-operation, seek to give each individual opportunity to develop his innate capacities in competition with others seems a basic political principle for present-day western societies.[1]

§ 4.35—Ideal and Material Evolution: Hegel and Marx

Hegel's philosophy of ideal-cultural evolution was one of the powerful mental constructs of the nineteenth century. It at-

---

[98] Lochner v. New York, 198 U.S. 45, 75, 25 Sup.Ct. 539, 546 (1904).

[99] Supra, § 4.30.

[1] Cf. Dewey and Tufts, Ethics (1932), 276.

tracted a host of followers, not only philosophers and professors but also men of action, politicians and statesmen. Among them was Karl Marx, whose dialectical materialism became the philosophic basis of Communism. In attempting to summarize these two philosophies we cross the imaginary line that separates legal philosophy from political philosophy. The importance of this set of ideas to the legal profession justifies the excursion.

Georg Wilhelm Friedrich Hegel (1770–1831), son of a petty German official, successively a professor at Heidelberg and Berlin, poured forth over a period of some twenty-four years a comprehensive philosophy of logic, science, psychology, art, religion, history, law and the State. He remarked that writings on philosophy could be understood by any educated man until Kant came along; but Hegel outdid Kant in obscurity of expression. Even writers who try to explain and paraphrase Hegel cannot escape from his fundamental obscurities.[2] Thus Hegel's work poses at the outset a problem in theory of meaning, or semiotics. To a plain man of the law, Hegel's philosophy in its constructive phases (Hegel was much clearer as a critic, but aren't we all?) seems like a mysticism concealing itself in logomachy. Take, for example, one of his basic utterances:

"Whatever is rational is real (actual); whatever is real (actual) is rational."[3]

In its semantic aspect,[4] the referents of the words used are scarcely imaginable directly; "rational" and "real" or "actual" are like "x" and "y",[5] variables to which different users may give quite different values to suit their needs. Followers of the most diverse political views have been able to ground their conclusions on some of Hegel's magnificent cloudy aphorisms. But the plain man of law should not overlook another, and to him quite famil-

---

[2] For example, Whitehead, Process and Reality (1930), 254; and even in places the generally lucid and valuable exposition of Cairns in Legal Philosophy from Plato to Hegel (1949), Ch. XIV, which has been used in this summary more times than it is cited.

[3] Hegel, Grundlinien der Philosophie des Rechts (2d ed. by Gans, Berlin, 1840), 17 (hereafter cited "Grundlinien"); same in Hegel, Philosophy of Right (Dyde's trans., 1896), xxvii (hereafter cited as "Dyde"); Hegel's Philosophy of Right (Knox trans., 1942), 10 (hereafter cited as "Knox"). Professor Knox contends that "actual," and not "real," is the accurate translation. But Hegel's meaning seems to sway between the layman's "actual" and the philosopher's "real."

[4] I.e., as a term supposed to have a definite object of reference.

[5] E.g., in the equation $x = 2y$.

iar, aspect of meaning, syntactics, or the relations of signs to each other.[6] Thus the passage quoted above can be understood only in the context of Hegel's system of metaphysics with its complex interrelated terminology. Perhaps "language, in its ordinary usages, penetrates but a short distance into the principles of metaphysics." [7] At any rate, Hegel's system and terminology is such a grand construct that those who master it are often mastered by it. A third aspect of meaning, called "pragmatics," [8] is the effect of language upon its interpreters, especially its emotive effect. This effect becomes blind faith when, as in the case of Marx's dialectical materialism, the words of the master are repeated as a primitive ritual.

Hegel's philosophy of law and of the state were united. The end of the law is to realize freedom of the human will; but freedom is not just arbitrary caprice; it must be compatible with order; and the state is the realization of order. How could Hegel glorify individual freedom, on the one hand, and the state, on the other? Because the individual finds his highest ethical development in the state. The individual can leave the narrow social restraints of his family and his small community, can find liberty to "live his own life" in the urban community which has marked the rise of the modern state.[9] In this Hegel parallels Aristotle's conception of human nature (§ 4.11) and resembles Jhering (§ 4.44). In private law Hegel's exposition of legal concepts—property, contract, crime, etc.—in terms of freedom of the individual will has not, I believe, left much of enduring value and need not be discussed here.[10] Hegel chided both Plato and Fichte (his predecessor at Berlin) for having tried to derive detailed rules from philosophy,[11] which can give only general principles. The philosopher who risks giving advice on exact rules is likely to incur the bitter contempt of later generations. Hegel has not, as far as I know, incurred any contempt on this score.

Hegel's evolutionary theory was grounded on three basic metaphysical ideas.

---

[6] See Morris, "Foundation of the Theory of Signs" in I Internat'l Encyc. of Unified Science, No. 2 (1938), 3, 6, supra, § 3.26(6).

[7] Whitehead, op.cit., loc.cit., supra, n. 2.

[8] Supra, n. 6.

[9] This is a rather free interpretation of Hegel's cloudy generalizations. See Grundlinien secs. 75, 260; Dyde, 79, 248; Knox, 242, 160.

[10] See Cairns, op.cit. supra, n. 2, for discussion of this part of Hegel.

[11] Grundlinien, 17; Dyde, xxviii; Knox, 11.

1. *The rational is the actual.* This proposition, even if one does not at once grasp its full meaning, suggests that Hegel was not concerned with an imaginary perfect world, such as Plato's Republic or Moore's Utopia, but with the use of reason in the activities of life. Secondly, if the rational *is to become* the actual, we must not get lost in the "brew and stew" of emotion and inspiration, we must not found upon the feelings what has been for centuries the labour of reason and understanding.[12]   Thirdly, Hegel built upon Kant's conception of reason but he greatly modified it. The categorical imperative calls for a universal rule of action [13] but it is empty of content; any general rule will satisfy Kant's requirement, said Hegel. So Hegel goes beyond the logical *Universal* which can function well enough as the subject or predicate term in a proposition of a syllogism, to the second stage, the *Conception,* which is the universal "in action," with all of its ambiguities and even its contradictions. The third stage is the *Idea,* which is the conception synthesized by the reconciliation of its contradictions.[14]   Reason is the process of synthesizing, of reconciliation of opposites, of dealing with universals in their relation to concrete particulars. So "whatever is rational" is for Hegel not merely a formal logical construct but something that conforms to reason in this concrete sense. Fourthly, the word "actual" or "real" (*wirklich*) seems to sway between "that which happens" and "that which is fundamental or ultimate." The former would mean, as applied to law, to politics and to ethics, "whatever is, is right." Hegel lays himself open to this interpretation. However, he meant to include the second notion, that reason grasps the fundamental aspects of the actual, the eternal in the present, the universal in the concrete purged of its accidental attributes. When Hitler's Nazism was "actual," was torturing and killing innocent German people, would Hegel have said: "This is actual, therefore it is rational?" I believe not.

---

[12] Grundlinien, 11; Dyde, xxii; Knox, 6.

[13] Kant's Philosophy of Law (Hastie trans., 1887), 45; supra, § 4.21.

[14] A modern illustration *might* be this: The *Universal* signified by "promise" enables a law student to understand the statement: "A contract is a legally enforceable promise or set of promises." But he could not apply this rationally to a concrete conduct-sequence without seeing some of the ambiguities of the word "promise." Is an advertisement a promise? Is a prediction a promise? A reasoned grasp of the concrete universal would be the *Conception* of promise. But promise as a part of the legal order implies obligation and its opposite, freedom, and so must be further synthesized in the *Idea* of Freedom.

Yet Hegel warned that philosophy might come too late to be of any use; it could at least interpret the past. There is a basic ambiguity in Hegel's philosophy of law: Does it merely purport to describe fundamentally the past or does it prescribe for the future? Hegel blurred Kant's sharp distinction between the Is and the Ought, between reality and value (§ 4.20).

2. *The Stages of Development.* One of Hegel's favorite devices is the use of stages of development. Sometimes these are merely *"logical"* stages, that is, a succession of steps in the sequence of the thinking process which Hegel calls reason or his own "logic." The sequence of Universal, Conception, Idea, given above, is an example. In his philosophy of history he presented at length *historic* stages of development which had been briefly outlined in his philosophy of law.[15] Each nation has a single natural principle comprised under its geographical and anthropological existence; when *its* principle coincides with one of the stages of the development of the *universal* spirit in world history, then to that nation is assigned the accomplishment of that stage. For a given epoch this nation is dominant; it has an absolute right to be the bearer of that phase in the development of the world-spirit. It can have the dominance of an epoch only once; when its principle "passes over" into some other principle, it then becomes merely the passive recipient of the new principle. He then names the empires that had been dominant down to date: The Oriental, the Greek, the Roman and the German. He tries to characterize the "single principle" of each, but the language is elusive if not illusory.[16] When the German Kaiser in 1914 thought the historic hour had come, he relied on Hegel's philosophy of history. When the Anti-Cominterm Pact was signed in 1940 by Germany, Italy and Japan, the newspaper of the Nazi party issued a grandiloquent statement that "the plutocratic world order is ripe for conquest" because "it corresponds to the logic of historical development."[17] Russian Communists await the hour when they may

---

[15] Grundlinien, §§ 341–350, pp. 423–432; Dyde, 341–350; Knox, 216–223.

[16] The "four empires" are treated at length in his Philosophy of History, where he deals separately with China, India, Persia, Assyria, Babylonia, Judea and Egypt, all under "the Oriental World." Some writers group them into three epochs: Oriental, Classic (Greek-Roman) and Teutonic. What is the use of ascribing a "single principle" to each of these great areas and periods in civilization?

[17] N. Y. Times, Sept. 28, 1940, p. 6, quoting the Völkischer Beobachter. The full sentence shows the Hegelian touch: "It corresponds to the logic of historical development, therefore, that the inheritance of the old powers is suc-

strike for the dominance of an epoch. Dominance by force was not what Hegel meant; he referred to the dominance of ideas. But since ideas are mere abstractions unless realized (made actual), Hegel's system cannot escape the charge of having inspired such perversions.

Hegel's view that reality can be found only in the whole and not in any of its parts leads to the thesis that the spirit of a people at any given time is a definite spirit which builds itself into a present world, which is comprised in its religion, its culture, its usages, its political constitution and laws, in the whole of its arrangements, its events and achievements. Who are the English? The people who sail the ocean, who possess world trade, who own East India with all its riches, who have a parliament and juries, etc.[18] Thus Hegel regarded each institution, such as the state and the law, as part of a nation's spirit at a given time. The spirit may change and pass over into a new spirit; but the new spirit will contain all the steps of the earlier one.[19] These two ideas have proved to be very attractive. The "spirit of the times" is regarded as a unity, something that controls (with some cultural lag) all phases of culture, from clothing fashions to contract law. Kohler, a Neo-Hegelian, explained the fact that contracts for future performance are used far more generally in occidental than oriental societies by the oriental belief in inexorable fate as contrasted with the occidental faith in ability to control the future.[20] Here the legal institution is seen as depending on a basic *spirit* rather than on economic needs. Professor Roscoe Pound's jural postulates of civilization, a part of his sociological jurisprudence, represent a deep insight into the expectations that civilization presupposes and civilized law tries to fulfill.[21] Like many of Hegel's other ideas, this one has produced consequences which he could never have anticipated. Along with Comte's philosophy of social science it has led during the present century to studies in comparative laws and cultures, and to attempts to "integrate" law and social science.

---

ceeded by those nations whose revolutionary force in Europe and East Asia has proved that they are destined for their great historic duty."

[18] Hegel, Philosophie der Geschichte (2d ed., by Karl Hegel), 91-92, in 9 Hegel's Werke (Berlin, 1840).

[19] Ibid., 98.

[20] Kohler, Philosophy of Law (Albrechts trans., 1914), 134. But Hegel considered Savigny's conception of the primitive "spirit of the people" too narrow and provincial.

[21] These jural postulates are set forth infra, § 4.60(3).

But Hegel's thesis is open to grave objections. Aside from the metaphysical and logical flaws pointed out by Bertrand Russell,[22] the attempt to see everything in its totality, in the qualities and relations which distinguish it from *everything* else, ends in futility. He who attempts this should be an expert in all knowledge; more likely he will be ignorant in many things. Hegel and his followers, Marx and Spengler, are said to exemplify this conclusion.[23] Again, the unity ("Spirit") of the culture of a given epoch or of a given nation at a given period, which Hegel postulated, is only a partial truth: In any given period and nation one finds many conflicting tendencies, ideas, "spirits." [24] The problems of legal evaluation are (among others) to choose which ideas or tendencies should be given effect, to what extent and by what means. Sometimes the law is called upon to counteract a prevailing tendency. When automobile owners first came before the courts and were held strictly liable for the injuries they caused, Kohler criticized this trend because, he said, "the future belongs to the automobile." But legal development has imposed ever stricter liability on the automobile owner. Finally the blurring of fact and value in Hegel's philosophy of evolution merely obfuscated any attempts to find empirical grounds for law-making.

3. *The Dialectic.* As Hegel never gave a definition of his dialectic, every writer has to make his own, with illustrations. The dialectic is a *process of reasoning* and also (since the world spirit is governed by reason and determines history) *a process of historical development.* The reasoning process is the resolution of the dramatic conflict of ideas; the first step is the understanding and defining of some simple thesis, then the realization that it has a contradictory (antithesis) and the reconciliation of the two in a third, the synthesis, "one ultimate, luminously self-evident insight . . . in which the original conflict of ideas is harmonized.[25] Here is a borrowed illustration of the dialectic. "The Absolute is Pure Being," says Hegel. But pure being would have no qualities assigned to it; it would be nothing. "The Absolute is Nothing." But this antithesis is partly false. Thence we pass on to the synthesis; "The Absolute is Becoming." [26] This syn-

---

[22] Russell, A Survey of Western Philosophy (1945), 743–746.

[23] Ibid., 735.

[24] See Frank (Jerome) in (1949) 16 Philosophy of Science, 3, 14.

[25] Hook, Towards the Understanding of Karl Marx (New York, 1933), 77, referring here to Plato's conception of the dialectic.

[26] Russell, op. cit., 733. See Cairns, op. cit., 506.

thesis is also incomplete, since there can be no "becoming" without something to become. So the process must go on. Its end is the Absolute Idea, Hegel's conception of God. The following illustration (mine own) seems implicit in Hegel's discussion of the problem of codifying law, which he strongly favored (in contrast with his Berlin colleague, Savigny). Two antithetical ideas are those of *certainty* in law and *change* in law. Hegel's discussion may be represented thus:

Thesis. The law should be codified because it needs to be certain.

Antithesis. The law should not be codified because it continually needs to be changed in detail.[27]

Synthesis. The law should be codified as to its general principles, which change very slowly, and not as to its details, which should be left to the judge's discretion.[28]

This illustration shows Hegel's logical dialectic at its best. The basic defect is that it requires one to find *just two* propositions which signify the contradictions and conflicts in a problematic situation. In any such situation there are likely to be (almost certainly are) *more* than two possible principles of action. Thus in the problem of codification there is another antinomy, mentioned by Hegel,[29] between the principle that the law should be universally made known (to laymen) and the principle that law should be developed by experts whose technical terminology will give it scientific exactness. In Dewey's instrumental logic (§ 4.-53) the dialectic becomes a choice between several or many.

Hegel's dialectic was also an account of historical development, since the rational realizes itself in human experience as the actual. This aspect of it was the one utilized by Marx.

Karl Marx (1818–1883), native of the Rhineland, educated at the University of Berlin and breaking away from his ancestral (Jewish) and religious (Protestant) heritage, became with Frederick Engels, the son of a wealthy German manufacturer, the (unsuccessful) leader of a workers' party movement in Germany, and died in London after thirty-four years of study and writing. Marx adopted Hegel's method but substituted for ideal evolution the material (economic) theory of evolution which became known

---

[27] See Savigny's arguments, supra, § 4.31.

[28] This argument is derived from Grundlinien, § 216, with § 211 (Add.) and § 215; Dyde, pp. 212–13, 206; Knox, 138, 134–136, 271–273 (Add.).

[29] Ibid., § 215.

as "dialectical materialism," or economic determinism.[30] As Engels said, Marx took Hegel's dialectic and turned it right side up. Marx said that in every age the ruling ideas are the ideas of its ruling class; and the chief factor in determining the ruling class was the method of economic production. Under slavery it was the slave-owners; under feudalism it was the feudal over-lords; under capitalism it was the bourgeoisie, or "middle class," a term which includes everything from millionaire bankers and manufacturers down to petty tradesmen who employ one or two helpers.[31] In contrast with the bourgeoisie is the proletariat, which means those who are dependent on their labor for their living. In capitalist countries, said Marx:

"Law, morality, religion are to him [the proletarian] so many bourgeois prejudices, behind which lurk in ambush just as many bourgeois interests." [32]

Without stopping here to point out the exaggerations, weasel words and obscurities in this and other Marxian pronouncements, we may note that it explains why Communists refer to any American newspaper (except their own) as "the Wall Street press"; it *must* be dominated by Wall Street bankers, because of Marx's law of economic determinism. By the same principle Soviet Russian law should be and is (or is said to be) created and administered in the interests of the "ruling" class, the workers.[33] In classic (Marx-Lenin) Communist theory the dictatorship of the proletarian class was to be merely a stage in the development toward a classless society, in which both law and the state would "wither away" because they would no longer be needed.

Marxist evolutionary theory, patterned on the Hegelian dialectic of history, provides the philosophic foundation and faith of its followers. The instrument of progress is class conflict, the conflict of opposites for which Hegel's logic provided the solution.

---

[30] For a brief account of Marxian theory, see the articles by Professor Sidney Hook and by Sherwood Eddy in The Meaning of Marx (ed. Hook, 1934), especially pp. 10 ff. (Hereafter cited as "Meaning.")

[31] See the Essentials of Marx (Lee ed., 1926), 66 (hereafter cited as "Essentials").

[32] Quoted from the famous Communist Manifesto of 1848, in Essentials, 42. The Manifesto displayed the exaggerations and misleading insinuations which have since characterized Communist propaganda.

[33] See Vyshinsky, The Law of the Soviet State (Babb trans., 1948), 50, 159–160; and comment in Fuller, "Pashukanis and Vyshinsky" (1949) 47 Mich.L.Rev. 1157, 1159; also supra, § 3.25.

In the feudal stage, the overlords were dominant, yet they were obliged to admit a third estate, a class who were not their subjects, i. e., the merchants and tradesmen. Thus the feudal society, chiefly because of its defective method of production, gave rise to its antithesis, which led to its destruction and the rise of capitalism. Capitalism exploits the proletariat, the workers, who will rise to destroy it, and thus it will pass over into the dictatorship of the proletariat.[34] Communists believe that this succession is inevitable: "History is on our side." Like many other believers in Destiny, they feel obliged to help it along.

But the dictatorship of the proletariat was deemed to be only an antithesis, a temporary stage necessary to prepare for the classless society. When that synthesis is reached, law and the state will slowly disappear, because all internal struggle will disappear. Such was the orthodox view of Pashukanis, who was from about 1925 to about 1938 the leading Soviet legal philosopher. However, the Soviet Communists and their followers have now discovered that Pashukanis' prediction of the withering away of the state and its law applied to the Soviet state, and was therefore subversive. Pashukanis was first made to recant and then vanished. In Vyshinsky's treatise the disappearance of law and the state is obscurely treated and seems a long way off.[35]

The Marxian evolutionary theory is inadequate and unsound in many respects. First, it ascribed all cultural phenomena to what is treated as a single cause, the method of production. In this it claims to be "scientific" and therefore infallible. But as Professor Dewey has remarked, only naïve people such as "literary persons" now believe that science offers a new kind of infallibility.[36] Moreover, the "single-cause" conception, borrowed from theology by natural science in its early stages, has long been discarded by science:

"There is a worldwide difference," said Dewey, "between the idea that causal sequences will be found in any given set of events taken for investigation, and the idea that *all* sets of events are linked into a *single* whole by *one* causal law." [37]

---

[34] Meaning, 21. A more extensive division of periods is suggested by Eddy at p. 24.

[35] Supra, n. 33.

[36] Dewey, Freedom and Culture (1939), 96.

[37] Ibid., 84. Communist theory even dominates biological science, music, and art in Russia.

One can very well believe that economic causes have important effects on government, law, literature, the press, etc., without believing that they are the *sole* causes. Moreover, a qualification that Marx admitted in his original formulation has often been ignored by his followers: When the effects of economic determinism on politics, law, science, etc., have once been produced, these become causes of subsequent events and are capable of modifying the forces that originally produced them.[38] For example, the bourgeoisie who overthrew the feudal lords in England (1600's) and France (1700's) established freedom of speech and of the press under laws which made them a protection for all classes of people, including the impoverished Marx who, by his own "scientific" theory, should have been hanged in England. To take intensified class conflict as a *method* of social progress is about as scientific as to say that, since every machine generates some friction, the way to eliminate it is to abolish lubrication and magnify the friction.[39] The Marxian theory is not a guide for the continued investigation of social phenomena; a generalization made at a particular time and place is deemed to have the nature of ultimate truth.[40] The chief threat of the Marxist evolutionary creed is in its mystical faith, its propaganda effects.

The uses of history in legal evaluations are partly methodical or technical, and partly they rest upon an emotional attitude toward the past. Even in using historic meanings and historic origins as guides and correctives one shares some attitude toward the wisdom or the folly of earlier generations. The belief in progressive evolution, characteristic of recent Occidental and especially American culture, is something more. It is not a fatalistic belief in recurrent cycles. It is based partly on an optimistic interpretation of past experience and a belief in the capacity of human societies to shape their futures for the better, as well as to predict them.[41] The resemblance of the Marxist evolutionary creed soon disappears when one penetrates into its inflexible dogmatic assumptions. One need not, just because one rejects the mystical absolutes of Hegel or the harsh absolutes of Marx, abandon to history all historical and evolutionary theories of law.

---

38 Ibid., 77.

39 Ibid., 86.

40 Ibid., 87.

41 Thus Professor Berle's interesting set of hypotheses about the "natural selection" of political forces provides an optimistic outlook for American society and yet the selection of political forces is at least partly within the control of individuals composing it. Op. cit. supra, § 4.30, n. 18, passim.

Chapter 16

UTILITARIANISM: BENTHAM AND JHERING

§ 4.40—General Significance of Bentham's Work

Utilitarianism is the body of doctrine which evaluates both human conduct and human law by the test of utility. If "utility" means merely usefulness in general, then utilitarianism is just a naïve philosophy of common sense. This it partly is, at least in the United States, where many of its ideas are now accepted as commonplace. Yet the chief dangers of reliance upon common sense are that unavowed or unconscious assumptions will be made controlling and that the remoter implications of avowed assumptions will not be explored or even perceived. When the man of common sense becomes aware of these dangers, he is likely (unless he is a supreme egotist like Adolph Hitler) to become rather confused and frustrated. At this point the patient philosopher is ready to take him by the hand and lead him to detect some unavowed assumptions and to explore and define his assumptions until a unified whole, or at least a more inclusive order, has been attained. Every philosopher, it is believed, will at some point, openly or surreptitiously, appeal to your common sense as a starting point for his imaginative flights. Common sense seems to have been left pretty far behind by some philosophers, such as Kant (§§ 4.20–4.22) and Hegel (§ 4.35), not to mention such esoteric great minds as Spinoza and Leibniz.[1] On the other hand, utilitarianism as a body of philosophic speculation never gets very far away from its common-sense origins. It has two sides, one as a theory of ethics (§ 4.41) and the other as a theory of legal evaluation. The latter is by far the more important because the founder of utilitarianism, Bentham, was less concerned with the ethics of individual conduct than with constructing a justification and a guide for his efforts to reform the English law of his time.

Utilitarianism as a theory of legal evaluation has the following four basic tenets:

1. The goodness or badness of human conduct *should* be judged by its consequences to the actor and to the other individuals in society. This principle makes utilitarianism a teleological legal

---

[1] See Cairns, Legal Philosophy from Plato to Hegel (1949), Ch. VIII (Spinoza), Ch. IX (Leibniz).

439

axiology (§ 1.13) and gives it a distinctive character even if the pleasure-pain test be rejected (§ 4.41). The consequences to be envisaged are potential as well as actual, remote as well as immediate.

2. The goodness or badness of a law, present or proposed, *should* be judged by its consequences to the aggregate of the individuals in society, present and future. While this was not an exclusive nor an original idea, it was emphasized by Bentham and his followers more than it had been previously.

3. The consequences to individuals, just referred to, *can* and *should* be determined by measuring their individual pleasures and pains and striking a balance, thus finding either an excess of goodness or of badness. This is the principle of Bentham's *felicific calculus* (§ 4.41).

4. In making this calculation, one individual's pleasure and pain should be counted as no more and no less than any other's. The interest of the society as a whole is not some mystical spirit or personification but merely the aggregate of individual interests.[2] The conception of interest, to which Bentham assigned a minor role, became a very significant one in the legal philosophy of the present century.

Of these four, the first and second are conceded to be essential tenets of utilitarianism. The third, the pleasure-pain principle, belonging to the ethical theories known as *hedonism*, is highly controversial; it is sometimes regarded as a merely accidental part of Bentham's philosophy,[3] which was discarded (virtually though not avowedly) by his principal follower, John Stuart Mill.[4] The fourth tenet stands for an aspect of democracy which was epitomized in "the greatest good of the greatest number" and which made utilitarianism the dominant legal philosophy of England and the United States during the nineteenth century. That utilitarianism was influential not only upon national policy but also upon legal method was due to the indefatigable labors of its founder.

Jeremy Bentham (1748–1832), precocious son of a prosperous English solicitor, attended a select preparatory school, entered

---

[2] Bentham, Principles of Morals and Legislation (Oxford Univ. Press, 1892, a reprint of 2d ed., 1823), 3. (This book is cited hereafter as P.M.L.)

[3] See Dewey and Tufts, Ethics (rev. ed., 1932) 263 ff., and critique of hedonism, 206–215; infra, § 4.41.

[4] Ibid., 268. See Mill, Utilitarianism (Everyman ed.).

Queen's College, Oxford, at the age of twelve, and received his bachelor's degree at the age of sixteen.[5] His education was chiefly classical, yet he did manage to squeeze in a few dull lectures on physics. Classical in his learning, conservative in politics, orthodox in religion, he reacted against his environment and yet partly succumbed to it. Acquiescing in his ambitious father's plans for a successful career at the bar, Bentham attended in 1763 Blackstone's lectures on English law, later published in the famous Commentaries. He was at once critical of the "frivolous" reasons that Blackstone gave for various rules of English law. His experiments in chemistry, which he performed in his bachelor quarters to the disturbance of his neighbors and the annoyance of his father, led him to seek a scientific basis for legal rules and procedures. At some turning point between 1766 and 1772 he determined to devote his life to legislation and jurisprudence and so informed his puzzled sire. Although Jeremy was called to the bar in 1769, he never took a brief. When offered one, he informed the contestants that litigation would prove profitable only to the lawyers and advised them to settle out of court.[6] No wonder that his father despaired of his ever putting his talents to any use! A crisis came in 1774 when he fell in love with a pretty girl of good country parentage but of no fortune. Bentham, confronted with the choice between his romantic love and his chosen career, worked feverishly to write a book that he could sell for enough money to finance his marriage. But the publisher was cold to the project, and the young woman became even colder. Bentham settled his problem of romantic love by the rationale of his felicific calculus.[7] The connubial manuscript, a digression from his great work on critical and penal jurisprudence, was not published until 1928.[8]

Where did Bentham get his ideas? Professor Everett has pointed pretty clearly to the sources of some of them. From John Locke he took his insistence upon clear and concise expression;[9] Locke's theory of the social contract (§ 4.15) he regarded as a

---

[5] For these and other biographical references I am indebted to Everett, The Education of Jeremy Bentham (1931), especially 23, 37.

[6] Ibid., 48.

[7] Ibid., Ch. V.

[8] Bentham, A Comment on the Commentaries—a Criticism of William Blackstone's Commentaries on the Laws of England (edited, with an Introduction, by Charles Warren Everett; Clarendon Press, 1928).

[9] Everett, op. cit. supra, n. 5, 73.

useless fiction.[10] From Locke he also derived his leaning toward nominalism [11] and an epistemological slant called "sensationalism" (§ 4.41). He first glimpsed the principle of utility in Hume's view that the moral sense bestows its approval upon whatever is *useful* or *immediately* agreeable.[12] Yet he overlooked or rejected Hume's conception of a moral sense. The theory of pains and pleasures he derived principally from Helvetius; and "the greatest happiness of the greatest number" came to him either from Priestley, the distinguished English scientist who was also a pamphleteer, or from Beccaria, whose famous book on the theory of punishments appeared in 1764.[13] Bentham was a warm admirer of Lord Mansfield, who sought to reform the English common law by introducing into it principles of equity and Roman law, mercantile customs and a strong infusion of Scotch common sense.

Bentham was endowed with a mind that was both acutely analytical and thoroughly systematic. His passion for thoroughness led him to neglect publication of the greater part of his manuscripts, now estimated at some 150,000 sheets, until after his death; a good deal remains unpublished. He worked at his writing habitually from six in the morning until ten at night, over a period of fifty-five years.[14] It is unfortunate that he did not stop to revise his work; much of his writing was repetitious and some was superficial. His Principles of Morals and Legislation, one of the great books of the nineteenth century, expounds his theory of pains and pleasures as an introduction to a penal code which Bentham proposed to draft but never did. He permitted his manuscripts to be used by Dumont, a Swiss clergyman, who had them published in French translations on the Continent.[15] Thus Bentham became famous on the Continent and in Spanish America before he did in England.

---

[10] See the Principles of Legislation, Ch. XIII, secs. 6, 9; in Bentham, The Theory of Legislation (Ogden ed., 1931), 72–74, 81–82.

[11] See his definition of law, supra, § 2.05; Patterson, "Bentham on the Nature and Method of Law" (1945) 33 Calif.L.Rev. 612, 620.

[12] See Cairns, op. cit., 366; Everett, op. cit., 47.

[13] Everett, op. cit., 38, 47.

[14] Ibid., 104.

[15] Dumont's French versions were translated and published in the United States, first by Neal in 1830, and secondly by Robert Hildreth in 1864. The Hildreth translation was used in Ogden's edition of The Theory of Legislation, supra, n. 10, and infra, § 4.41, n. 17.

Bentham's English followers included James Mill and his illustrious son, John Stuart Mill, John Austin (§ 2.04) and numerous liberal political leaders through whose efforts many of his proposed reforms were put into effect. Bentham's greatest service to the practical needs of his country and his time was in furnishing both a philosophical justification for re-examining many of the traditional rules and institutions of English law, and a rational plan for improving them. While Bentham's system of calculated individual hedonism has serious limitations, his political hedonism was, and still is, a rational basis for an attack on social problems and on the problems of legal and political technique. His ideas were an inspiration to liberals for many years after his death; and many of Bentham's specific proposals were adopted in English and American legislation. Sir Henry Maine (§ 4.32), though he found Bentham's conception of positive law inadequate for primitive societies, said in 1874:

> "I do not know a single law reform effected since Bentham's day which cannot be traced to his influence." [16]

§ 4.41—The Pleasure-Pain Principle in Ethics and in Legislation

Bentham's basic statements about the principle of utility equate good with pleasure and evil with pain.

> "Nature has placed men under the empire of *pleasure* and of *pain*. We owe to them all our ideas; we refer to them all our judgments, and all the determinations of our life. He who pretends to withdraw himself from this subjection knows not what he says . . . These eternal and irresistible sentiments ought to be the great study of the moralist and the legislator. The *principle of utility* subjects everything to these two motives. '*Utility*' is an abstract term. It expresses the property or tendency of a thing to prevent some evil or to procure some good. *Evil* is pain, or the cause of pain. *Good* is pleasure, or the cause of pleasure. That which is conformable to the utility, or the interest of an individual, is what tends to augment the total sum of his happiness. That which is conformable to the utility, or the interest of a community, is what tends to augment the total sum of the happiness of the individuals that compose it. . . . I use the words *pain* and *pleasure* in their ordinary signification, without inventing any arbitrary definition for the sake of ex-

---

[16] Maine, Lectures on the Early History of Institutions (7th ed., 1914) 397 (1st ed., 1874).

cluding certain pleasures or denying the existence of certain pains. In this matter we want no refinement, no metaphysics. It is not necessary to consult Plato, nor Aristotle. *Pain* and *pleasure* are what everybody feels to be such—the peasant and the prince, the unlearned as well as the philosopher." [17]

The dominance of pleasure and pain over our judgments, our actions and even our ideas is asserted as a fact. It is also asserted that good is pleasure or a means to pleasure; and it is implied that the sum of one's pleasures is one's happiness. Both the moralist and the legislator, it is implied, *ought* to take utility as the principle by which individual acts or legislative acts should be judged, because both the individual and the community *seek and ought to seek* happiness as the utimate end. Finally, he takes pain and pleasure empirically, that is, he judges by the actual pains and pleasures of men of all stations in life.

Bentham's utilitarianism was devised to serve both as a theory of individual ethics and as a theory of legislation, an instrument for the evaluation of laws. Most of its critics attack it in the former capacity rather than the latter. An appraisal of these two distinct aspects will clarify its present status.

I. IN ETHICS

The chief issues raised concerning utilitarianism as an ethical theory are indicated by the four questions discussed below, which also serve to bring out its relations to other leading ethical theories.

1. *Motivation in Fact.* Are all individuals in fact always governed *in all respects* by the seeking of pleasure and the avoidance of pain? Bentham, recognizing that some individuals are governed by the *ascetic* principle, the principle that leads hermits and martyrs to suffer pain or destruction, argued that they endured these sufferings for the sake of glory on earth or happiness in the hereafter—in short, for some remote happiness.[18] Or they shun all sensual pleasures because they might be tempted to do pernicious acts, those of which the evil consequences would exceed the good—a mistaken application of utility, but still an applica-

---

[17] Bentham, The Principles of Legislation (hereafter cited "Prins.Legis.") Ch. I in The Theory of Legislation (hereafter cited as "Theory") (1931), 2–3. This is Bentham slightly diluted by Dumont. The same ideas are in P.M.L. (supra, § 4.40, n. 2), Ch. I, written before 1781.

[18] Theory, 4–5; P.M.L. 8, n. 1.

tion.[19] However, it cannot be doubted that many human actions
are impulsive acts of heroism, without a moment's reflection as to
consequences, or are repetitions of useful habits, or else are performances of duties imposed by custom, a common sense of de-
corum or law.[20] It is no answer to these objections to say that
they *could* determine their actions by a rational use of the principle of utility. Nor is it an answer to say that a man *is* governed
unconsciously by pleasure-seeking and pain-avoiding, just as he
is governed unconsciously by the law of gravitation. If the principle of utility operated unerringly to lead men to act always for
the maximum of total pleasure (minus total pain), then the reply
would hold; but Bentham delights in pointing out that people who
act from ascetic or sentimental motives often err in the maximiz-
ing of pleasure.[21] Indeed, Bentham qualifies his factual statement
by saying that "by the natural constitution of the human frame"
men on "most occasions" embrace the principle without thinking
of it, "if not for the *ordering* of their own actions, yet for the *trying* of their own actions, as well as of those of other men." [22] Here
he shifts from motive to standard. Yet one may say, in support of
Bentham's assumption, that pleasure-seeking and pain-avoiding
are the *commonest* of mankind's motivations, and that they offer
a basis for political, moral and other *sanctions*.

2. *Norm of Motivation.* *Should* all individuals in all of their
conduct be guided by a deliberate choice of the maximum net sum
of pleasures? Bentham believed that men should govern themselves in accordance with enlightened self-interest; he conceived
of man (at his best) as a reflective calculating creature who acts
in each case after a careful estimate of the relative pains and
pleasures of what he is about to do. (Like the dyspeptic who
comes to a dinner party and has to calculate the effects of every
bite he takes.) Indeed, the calculation of pleasures and pains will

---

[19] Theory, 5; P.M.L. 12–13.

[20] William James, recognizing the importance of pains and pleasures as
stimuli but rejecting the view that they are the only stimuli, suggested the
term "interest" as "a single name for the condition on which the impulsive
and inhibitive quality of an object depends." Psychology (Briefer Course,
1892), 444, 448. More recently psychologists have measured various kinds of
hedonic tone, a technical name for feelings of pleasantness and unpleasantness. See Boring, Langfeld and Weld, Psychology, A Factual Textbook (1935),
Ch. 15.

[21] Theory, 4–13; P.M.L., Ch. II.

[22] P.M.L., Ch. I, 4 (italics added).

often frustrate the attainment of pleasure; in our most intense enjoyments there must be a feeling of careless rapture. But Bentham could meet this objection, in part, by saying that he is primarily concerned with the *judging* of our past conduct or that of others.[23] It is in this sense that Bentham's principle has generally been accepted or rejected, and we turn to it.

3. *Ethical Evaluation. Should* the goodness or badness of individual conduct be judged *ethically* by the principle of utility as defined by Bentham? Here the objectors are numerous. First, Bentham (and his disciple, J. S. Mill) have been accused of a logical fallacy in arguing that because men *are* moved by their desires *therefore* they *ought* to be. But Bentham was seeking a workable test of oughtness, one that would be more definite and more susceptible of measurement than Hume's moral sense or Blackstone's natural law.[24] The latter included, along with other borrowed raiment, the Thomistic conception (§ 4.13) of natural law as a rule of conduct deduced from the natural inclinations of man. Bentham sarcastically pointed out that, for example, if *all* parents were naturally inclined to support their children, and did so, it would be unnecessary to have a law telling them that they ought to.[25] Yet the same objection can be made to Bentham's hedonism: morals must provide a guide or a criterion of choice as between pleasures (and pains). Bentham did not overlook this point; he set about to devise a rational analysis which would enable one to classify and measure pleasures and pains so that the maximum net pleasure in the long run would be attained. This was his *felicific calculus*. By it he thought that an enlightened choice of conduct would be made. Pleasures and pains were classified, and the circumstances affecting their *values* were listed.[26] One circumstance, for example, was the *fecundity* of an act producing pleasure—its tendency to produce other pleasures later on. Thus to the claim that Bentham made no qualitative distinction between pleasures, that he put tossing pennies on a par with listening to a symphony concert, he might reply that the former would quickly be forgotten, while the latter would long afterward arouse

23 Supra, n. 22 (he says "trying").

24 In defense of Bentham and Mill, see Hall, "The 'Proof' of Utility in Bentham and Mill" (1949), 60 Ethics 1; Monro (D.H.) in (1950) 60 Ethics 285.

25 "Parents *are inclined* to support their children; parents *ought* to support their children; these are two distinct propositions." Theory, 83 (Prins. of Leg., Ch. XIII, sec. 10).

26 Theory, 20–27, 31–32 (Prins.Legis. Ch. VI, Ch. VIII); P.M.L., Ch. V.

pleasant memories and excite the imagination. But the latter statement would be true only for a person *capable* of such enjoyment. Bentham's evaluative scheme, which he tries to make "unbiased" by including the pleasure of malevolence, is weighted with the criterion of the man who is good already.[27] He dashed off his felicific calculus in order to clear up his own ideas on moral theory; but when he came to grips with the problems of a penal or civil code, he used only parts of it. Before turning to utility as a legislative criterion, we need to discuss another objection to the pleasure-pain principle.

4. *Happiness and the Good.* Is a surplus of pleasure over pain equivalent to happiness and also to the good? Bentham assumes that happiness is the ultimate rational end of both individual and governmental action, that the degree of attainment of happiness depends upon, can be measured by, and is equivalent to, the surplus of pleasures over pains, as determined by his calculus. On the contrary, it is said, happiness is not a transient condition, as pleasure is, but is one dependent on the standing disposition of the self in meeting situations; one can be happy in the midst of annoyances.[28] The mere pleasure-seeker may be selfish and greedy. Bentham might reply that he takes account of *enduring* pleasures, that he emphasizes the pleasures of benevolence and knowledge, and that his elaborate analysis of the circumstances affecting an individual's sensibility to pleasure and pain [29] includes the disposition of the individual along with climate, occupation, sex, age, etc. This reply is partly adequate but it emphasizes the use in Bentham's ethics of the theory of virtues (character), as well as the view that happiness is a condition of the *whole* self and not just the gratification of a particular appetite. The shades of Aristotle and Plato have not been banished from Bentham's feast. As to "the good", Bentham was exceptional in treating the good as including *means* of attaining pleasures, as well as pleasures. Most ethical philosophers treat the good as the ultimate end. Whether this ultimate end can be equated with happiness in ethical theory is a question too large to be treated here. In legal evaluations, the "greatest good of the greatest number" ought to be taken to mean, not just bread and circuses for the largest number of voters, but the well-being and the intellectual and moral

---

[27] Dewey and Tufts, Ethics (1932), 208. Thus he lists the pleasures of knowledge; but what about the pleasures of ignorance?

[28] Dewey and Tufts, op. cit., 213–214.

[29] Theory, Ch. IX; P.M.L., Ch. VI.

development of the (present and future) members of the society. For instance, the recent discoveries by astronomers of countless galactic systems like our own, and the body of knowledge connected with such discoveries, seem to be valuable goods even though they have no immediate usefulness and bring far less pleasure to most people than, for instance, a Disney film. The good must include the condition of future generations, intellectual and moral as well as physical.

Let us briefly compare the three types of ethical systems referred to earlier (§ 1.13). Kant's man of good will would not be doing his highest moral duty, selfless motivation, if he used Bentham's analytic table of enlightened self-interest; but if he turned to his second- or third-rate standards, human perfectibility or human happiness, he would find Bentham's table a valuable guide in formulating his maxims of conduct. Bentham's table tacitly presupposes a duty to formulate maxims of conduct which one is willing to apply to oneself and to others.[30] The man of good will would find that in order to attain his end his best means would be to cultivate those good habits which constitute virtues; and this would lead him backward in time to Aristotle or forward to Dewey. The three types of ethical theory are interdependent and no one is, I think, self-sufficient.

II. IN LEGISLATION

When the principle of utility is considered as a guide to legislative evaluations, that is, to the criticism of existing laws or to the framing of new laws, most of the objections that can be persuasively urged against it as an ethical theory either disappear or are minimized. The individual in choosing his own conduct cannot always be the prudent calculator, but the legislator is expected to act *always* with reason and deliberation. The objection that good character is more important for ethics than good calculation of pains and pleasures becomes less significant when one is testing the goodness of a law by its (predicted) consequences in relation to the greatest happiness or the general welfare. In the latter case a minute consideration of consequences is in order.[31] To this view of lawmaking must be added two cautions. The legislator who calculates the consequences of proposed laws

---

[30] E. g., Theory, 18 (Prins.Legis., Ch. V): "The obligation which binds men to their engagements [contracts] is nothing but the perception of a superior interest, which prevails over an inferior interest."

[31] Dewey and Tufts, op. cit., 265.

must be a man of good character in order that he may be able to choose the good consequences. Again, laws have consequences partly through being promulgated but chiefly through being administered; the character of the administrator has to be assumed in estimating consequences. Even with these reservations, the difference pointed out is still significant.

The important thing about Bentham's theory was that it proposed to judge laws by their consequences—a striking and even a radical proposal. How could one estimate consequences? For the *kind of consequences* that could be controlled by the law, pleasure and pain gave a readily understandable and fairly workable test, though it never attained the exactness that Bentham hoped it would have. His "calculus" was not a mathematical formula but only a highly ingenious classification of kinds and relations of pleasantness and unpleasantness. He aspired to be the Newton of the moral world but he came nearer to being its Linnaeus.[32]

Yet Bentham was more than a classifier; he invented theories of social causation as well as evaluations of social harm. In the development of his proposals for the penal code and the civil code he made little use of his analysis of pleasures and somewhat more of his analysis of pains. The latter was used for two distinct purposes: To determine the social harm of conduct as a guide to imposing legal sanctions; and to distinguish the kinds of sanctions, especially the difference between moral and legal sanctions. Of these in their order:

1. *The Social Harm of a Mischievous Act.* Bentham distinguished between the *primary* and the *secondary* consequences of a mischievous act. The former includes its effects upon a definite number of individuals (e. g., upon the the victim of a robbery, his dependent wife and children, his relatives who must help him), while the secondary effects relate to an indefinite number. The act may produce *alarm* among those who hear of it and fear that they will be robbed; and *danger*, the chance that others will suffer the same harm, from the first robber or from those who have been in some degree led on by knowing of the success of the first one.[33] Thus Bentham deals with the case of the starving poor man who steals a loaf of bread from a rich man (the case of Jean Valjean) by pointing out that while the poor man receives more

---

[32] See Mitchell (Wesley C.), "Bentham's Felicific Calculus", (1918) 33 Pol. Sci.Quar. 161, 182.

[33] P.M.L., Ch. XII, pp. 152–155; Theory, 48–59 (Prins.Legis. Ch. X).

good from the act than the rich man receives harm, yet the secondary evil of alarm and danger from letting such acts go unpunished would outweigh the good to the thief.[34] On the other hand, to permit a man to strike another in self-defense would not create alarm or danger to the community generally, since other men would have nothing to fear unless they commence an illegal attack.[35] While Bentham made consequences the basic test, yet the secondary consequences of an act were greatly enhanced if it was done intentionally, rather than inadvertently or carelessly, because of the greater likelihood that the intentional act would be repeated. By similar reasoning an act of vengeance against a particular individual creates less alarm and danger, and is less pernicious, than an act done for wealth or some motive more impersonal.[36] This reasoning seems rather formal, as does also his assumption that, since every individual is the best judge of his own pleasure or displeasure, his consent to a harm inflicted upon him signifies that no harm was caused and hence no punishment should be imposed.[37] His analysis of social harms led to some influential conceptions of property and contract (§ 4.42).

2. *Bentham's Theory of Sanctions.* His theory of sanctions was the most ingenious and fruitful of all of his contributions, even though he confusingly calls the "natural" consequences to oneself of one's doing a careless act, a "physical" sanction (§ 2.32). The other three sanctions are the moral, the political and the religious. The legislator must realize that he can operate directly only by means of the political (legal) sanction; yet if he neglects the others in his calculations, he will be deceived in his results. The political sanction has many advantages over the moral and the religious: It acts upon all men with equal force; it is clearer and more precise in its precepts. Yet it has not a sufficient hold upon "private conduct", and because it cannot be invoked save upon proofs which it is sometimes impossible to obtain, it is vulnerable to secrecy and stratagem.[38]

Two examples of the way in which he used a theory to justify a practical conclusion will suffice here. He argued that since

---

[34] Theory, 58 (Prins.Legis., Ch. XI).

[35] Ibid., 59.

[36] P.M.L., Ch. XII, 163–168.

[37] Ibid., Ch. XIII, 171–172. The community has an interest in the individual human life. § 4.61.

[38] Theory, 27–30 (Prins.Legis., Ch. VII); also partly in P.M.L., Ch. III.

punishment is a pain, an artificial pain, no more should be inflicted than was necessary to prevent the mischief; and that greater
certainty and *proximity* of the pain of punishment would make
it a more effective deterrent than would its greater *intensity*,
with less certainty that it would be speedily inflicted.[39] Bentham's
conclusions pointed to milder penalties, a more efficient police
force and more efficient and speedy trials, improvements made in
England during the nineteenth century. At the beginning of that
century more than a hundred offenses were, under English law,
punishable by death.[40] The movement for the reform of this
harsh system was carried on by Bentham's followers. The other
conclusion was longer in bearing fruit. In his analysis of pleasures and pains he discussed the circumstances affecting an individual's sensibility to pleasure or pain; and he argued that the
punishment to be inflicted on an offender should depend, in part
at least, on his sensibilities. Since, however, the inner sensibility
of an individual would be impossible to prove, he decided to fall
back upon the manifest circumstances affecting sensibility, which
he counted as sex, age, rank, race, climate, government, education
and religious profession.[41] This proposal anticipated the twentieth century "individualization of punishment".

3. *"The Limits Which Separate Morals from Legislation."*
Under this heading Bentham pointed out that law was more restricted in the area of misconduct with which it could deal, first,
because the evil of the punishment would in some cases be greater
than the evil of the offense, and secondly, because the difficulty
of defining the offense might "overwhelm the innocent in seeking
to punish the guilty." [42] Thus while public opinion, the sanction
of morality, may condemn hard-heartedness, ingratitude, perfidy,
yet the law should not make them punishable unless it can define
them as exactly as it does theft, homicide, perjury. This is a settled policy of modern penal laws. Even if the offense could be
defined, as in the case of drunkenness, he thought its enforcement
would require a host of informers and spies, thus making the

---

39 The conclusions follow from his table of values of a pleasure or a pain,
according to which "intensity" and "duration" are no more than "certainty"
and "proximity". Theory, Ch. VIII; P.M.L. Ch. IV; and see also P.M.L.
183–184.

40 C. K. Ogden in Theory, xxiv.

41 Theory, 33–48 (Prins.Legis., Ch. IX); P.M.L., Ch. VI.

42 Theory, 60 (Prins.Legis., Ch. XII); P.M.L., Ch. XVII.

secondary evils greater than the original ones.[43] His prediction was substantially verified by the results of the American prohibition law (1920–1933). Roscoe Pound extended Bentham's insight to civil remedies as a part of his sociological jurisprudence.[44] The present century is indebted to Bentham for devising a criterion of individual acts and a criterion of laws, in terms of their social consequences.

§ 4.42—Liberty, Equality and Security: Property and Contract

Freedom or liberty became the ultimate objective of the legal order in several of the more important legal philosophies of the nineteenth century. Locke's theory of inalienable rights (§ 4.15), which was carried over from an earlier period, was designed to protect the citizen from invasions of his property or his personal freedom. Kant thought the end of the law was to protect the moral freedom of each in harmony with the moral freedom of all (§ 4.22). Hegel found the system of right (law) was actualized freedom and the state was the embodiment of concrete freedom.[45] Spencer believed that freedom from legal regulation or aid would enable the fittest to survive (§ 4.34). Bentham was no exception, yet he always treated freedom *from* something as a means for the avoidance of particular evils or the attainment of particular goods.

His conclusion that freedom of the press was necessary was based on an analysis of the dangers of censorship.[46] He deemed freedom of inquiry essential to correct the errors of the past.[47] Legal limitations on official powers were necessary means of protecting the individual from oppression.[48] His presumption in favor of economic freedom was based on two arguments. First, every law that grants a right to one man imposes an obligation on another or others; every "coercive" law is an attack upon lib-

---

[43] Theory, 62; P.M.L. 320.

[44] See Pound, "The Limits of Effective Legal Action", (1917) 3 A.B.A.J. 55, 67; 27 Ethics 150.

[45] Hegel, Philosophy of Right (Dyde trans., 1896), § 4, § 260.

[46] Theory (supra, § 4.41, n. 17), 370 (Principles of the Penal Code, Pt. IV, Ch. II).

[47] Theory, 440 (Principles of the Penal Code, Pt. IV, Ch. XVIII). Progress in human knowledge Bentham regarded as both a direct enhancement of pleasure and a means to other pleasures.

[48] Ibid., 463 (ibid., Ch. XXI).

erty, and he who advocates the adoption of a new one must show that the specific reasons in favor of it outweigh not only the specific evils it may cause but also the *general* reason against every such law.[49]   This is good conservative political doctrine.   The second argument was that the best way in which the government can promote the greatest happiness of the community is by leaving the care of his enjoyments to the individual and guarding him against pains.[50]   This principle is still adhered to in the main by modern states, although state operas and state broadcasting systems represent a different policy.   At any rate with Bentham liberty is not ranked as one of the principle objects of the law, but is instrumental.

The Ends of the Civil Code.   The four subordinate ends that the legislator should seek, in his efforts to promote the greatest happiness, are: 1. Subsistence. 2. Abundance. 3. Equality. 4. Security.   The division was not wholly exact, he admitted, but it served to classify the objects of laws.   Security, he said, was the pre-eminent object, because only it *necessarily* relates to the future.[51]   The law cannot do anything *directly* to provide for the subsistence of the individual, whose needs and desires would impel him to provide for his own subsistence by his own labor.   The best way to provide subsistence is by protecting him while he labors and by making him sure of the fruits of his labor.[52]   The same is true of abundance, the surplus of goods which serves as a safeguard against bad seasons, wars and other calamities.[53]   To Bentham equality in the distribution of wealth was a worthy goal, but he would not undertake to bring it about at the expense of security.   The confiscation of a large part of the property of the wealthy, in order to distribute it among those who have less, would be a direct attack on security and would do more harm than good.   Men are more sensitive to pain than to pleasure; [54] it would hardly be possible to bring about sufficient pleasure (in the recipients) to equal the pains of the despoiled ones and of others who would fear confiscation.   But wait until the death of the owner, and then the law can require equality in its distribu-

---

[49] Theory, 94 (Prins. Civil Code, Ch. I).

[50] Ibid., 95.

[51] Ibid., 96–7 (Prins. of Civil Code, Ch. II).

[52] Ibid., 100 (Prins. Civil Code, Ch. IV).

[53] Ibid., 101 (Ch. V).

[54] Ibid., 108 (Ch. VI).

UTILITARIANISM

tion; those who are to succeed after death have formed no expectations, and no one's security is disturbed.[55] Bentham's argument supported the abolition of primogeniture and entails, and
the present laws of inheritance taxation.

Bentham, despite the detachment with which he tried to draw
his inferences of social causation, was not immune from the prevalent economic conceptions of his time. He was opposed to placing
shackles upon trade and industry, though he also opposed monopoly.[56] His Defense of Usury (c. 1787) was a vigorous attack
on laws limiting the rate of interest that money-lenders could
charge. In general he accepted the economic views of Adam
Smith, whose Wealth of Nations appeared in 1774. Bentham's
theory of pains and pleasures contained the marginal utility
theory of value,[57] long familiar in economics. He recognized that
there could be no such thing as an "absolute" property right: all
such rights are subordinate to the needs of the state in maintaining security, external and internal.[58] He examined the disadvantages of private charity as a means of providing a minimum of
subsistence for the poor, and decided that this should be done in
an orderly way through funds raised by taxation.[59] His economic
liberalism was basically instrumental to the fulfillment of his
"greatest happiness" principle, which *could* have justified extensive social welfare laws.

Bentham conceived of property and contract as both founded
on expectation:

"The idea of property consists in an established expectation; in the persuasion of being able to draw such or such
an advantage from the thing possessed, according to the
nature of the case." [60]

This expectation can only be the work of the law, which gives it
security. Poverty is the primitive condition of the human race,
from which it emerges only by establishing security and order
through law, and thus encouraging industry to produce subsist-

---

55 Ibid., 122 (Prins. Civil Code, Ch. XII).

56 Ibid., 123 (Prins. Civil Code, Ch. XII).

57 E. g., his application of the marginal utility theory to wagering. Theory,
106, note (Prins. Civil Code, Ch. VI).

58 Ibid., 124–126 (Prins. Civil Code, Ch. XIII).

59 Ibid., 132 (ibid., Ch. XIV). Compare unemployment benefits and old age
assistance under present laws.

60 Ibid., 112 (ibid., Ch. VIII).

ence and abundance. Like Hobbes he believed the life of man in a "state of nature" would be precarious and miserable. While property rights are creatures of the law, the maintenance of them against attacks depends on public opinion; "governments and the people are, in this respect, like tamed lions." [61] He opposed restraints upon the alienation of land, since the new owner would be likely to put it to a more productive use than the old one.[62] Bentham's conception of property was a considerable improvement over the conceptions of Kant and Hegel, who attached it to the human will rather than to expectation. Yet Bentham's discussion was limited in several ways: He regards land as an object of use by the owner rather than as a source of income; he misses the significance of intangible forms of wealth which are now important in many societies (savings accounts, insurance, pensions, stocks and bonds); and he could not be expected to foresee that "job security" would become an important objective of modern legislation—an objective which (except in the case of government employees) is aimed at indirectly by protecting the formation and proper functioning of labor unions. That men will need and will seek security in some form, in some legal device that will protect their well planned expectations and reward their useful efforts, is as true today as it was in Bentham's time.

Bentham's treatment of contracts, while more casual than his treatment of property, is still significant. The faith of promises is the basis of society; unless they have obligatory force, there would be no security, no commerce; we would have to "go back to the woods." [63] Alienation of property by consent always signifies that the grantor gains some advantage in pleasure or satisfaction and so does the acquirer. "Alienation imports advantage" is a safe maxim here, he says, as well as in the case of agreements by which one party is to render services to another.[64] Where the agreement is one of *exchange,* there are two alienations, of which each has its separate advantages. Bentham here makes no reference to the English law, which then required a seal or a "consideration" (exchange) as a prerequisite of the legal obligation of a promise. He does, however, give a long list of grounds for the invalidation of exchanges, among which are some that would impair the security of expectation of the promisee. Thus he was

---

[61] Theory, 145, and see 113 (Prins. Civil Code, Chs. IX, X, XV).

[62] Ibid., 174–175 (ibid., Pt. II, Ch. II).

[63] Theory, 82 (Prins. Legis., Ch. XIII (9)).

[64] Theory, 168, 192 (Prins. Civil Code, Pt. II, Ch. II, Ch. V).

inclined to allow a grantor (or promisor) to avoid his contract if he entered into it under an erroneous idea that the value of what he was giving was *less* than its true value and if the error was due to no fault of the grantor—even though this might impair the security of transactions.[65] Thus Bentham seemed to favor making all promises presumptively enforceable and correcting injustices by a broad set of grounds of avoidance and considerable latitude in excusing performance because of supervening circumstances.[66] There are some indications that Anglo-American law is moving in this direction. Bentham also recognized the principle of unjust enrichment at several places. For instance, he upheld the physician's claim to compensation for professional services rendered to an unconscious man (incapable of consent) [67] more than a century before an American court first upheld it.[68] While Bentham made enlightening comments on the law of contracts, his followers, Austin and Holland, who gave currency to the prevalent "expectation" (so-called "objective") theory of contracts, derived it from the writings of another utilitarian, Paley, who was a contemporary of Bentham.[69]

§ 4.43—Bentham on Codification and Law Reform: England and the United States

For the drafting of a civil code designed to regulate property and contract and thus to protect expectations, Bentham laid down a set of rules [70] which are still valuable guides for the legislative draftsman. First, a law should not upset settled expectations;

---

[65] Theory, 171 (Prins. Civil Code, Pt. II, Ch. II). It must be remembered that Dumont wrote this book in French from Bentham's notes, and may have substituted civil-law examples for English-law ones. The protection of the *seller* (not the buyer) is reminiscent of the Roman law doctrine of *laesio enormis*.

[66] Theory, 193 (Prins. Civil Code, Pt. II, Ch. V), where he mentions as grounds of discharge (of an agreement for services) "physical impossibility" and "intervention of a superior inconvenience".

[67] Theory, 191 (Prins. Civil Code, Pt. II, Ch. V). He did not overlook the dangers of the "officious meddler". Ibid., 192.

[68] Cotnam v. Wisdom, 83 Ark. 601, 104 S.W. 164 (1907). See Restatement, Restitution (1937), § 116.

[69] See Austin, Jurisprudence (4th ed.) II, 939, and I, 326; Holland, Jurisprudence (10th ed.), 253; Paley, Principles of Moral and Political Philosophy (first published 1785) (8 Am. ed., 1815), Ch. V. See Patterson, "The Delivery of a Life Insurance Policy", (1919) 33 Harv.L.Rev. 198, 213.

[70] Theory, 148–157 (Prins. Civil Code, Pt. I, Ch. XVII).

the legislator must respect settled laws and usages, especially in relation to property; thus he is constantly fettered in his efforts to make improvements, for he must give notice far in advance. The laws should be known in order that they may prevent contrary expectations. Bentham believed that a code could be drawn in simple plain language that laymen could understand; then, perhaps, it could be a manual of education, as among the Hebrews, or a knowledge of it could be made a prerequisite to the exercise of political rights. Probably no one today believes that real property law, for instance, could be codified in such simple language that a layman could understand it; yet commercial law and traffic laws, for example, have been made accessible to literate laymen. The layman's use of law is still a problem (§ 3.02). At any rate our laws are not posted so high that no one can read them, as was done by the fiendish Roman emperor, Caligula. Thirdly, the laws should be *consistent,* that is, they should conform to a principle generally accepted, and they would thus conform to expectation. And this should be the principle of utility, toward which all expectations have a "natural tendency".[71] The arrangement of laws should be such as to simplify their use. Laws should be certain to be executed, as otherwise they will arouse no expectation. Finally, the laws should be "literally followed"; they should be purged of ancient barbarisms so that it will be unnecessary for the judges, under the guise of a spurious "interpretation", to bring the law down to date, and thus introduce uncertainty of expectation. Bentham was vigorously opposed to law-making by "Judge & Co." and poured the vials of his wrath upon the obscurity and verbosity of case law, which he called "customary law".[72] In all this he greatly overestimated his skill as a draftsman and the difficulties of interpretation of a well-drawn statute. His devoted disciple, Austin, disagreed with him here and recognized that judicial law-making is inevitable. It seems curious that Bentham, seeing clearly that "consistency" within a statute would depend on its having a common principle of arrangement,[73] did not also recognize that principle (or policy) would be resorted to in applying the statute to novel situations, and that the undefined breadth of meaning of any principle would make some range of choice inevitable. Perhaps he would agree with the avowed practice of

---

[71] Theory, 151.

[72] See the passage, without Dumont's dilutions, in Bentham, The Limits of Jurisprudence Defined (Everett ed., 1945), Ch. 17.

[73] Theory, 150.

the English courts today, in never resorting to "policy" interpretation unless the literal meaning is ambiguous.[74]

Bentham's influence upon law reform, in England and the United States, and even in South America, was so extensive that it would be difficult to recount it all. His arguments for the reform of judicial pleading and practice and for the abolition of the separation between legal and equitable proceedings influenced David Dudley Field (§ 4.33) in drafting the first New York Code of Procedure (1848–50) which spread rapidly to other states, and also influenced the English Judicature Act of 1873.[75] Bentham's Rationale of Judicial Evidence, a work published in 1825 by J. S. Mill from Bentham's notes, was used again and again by Wigmore in his monumental treatise; yet the statutory reform of the law of evidence still lags behind other phases of procedural reform.[76] In penal law, the number of capital offenses has been greatly reduced, whipping and the pillory have been abolished, and criminal procedure has been improved. In Bentham's day a divorce could be obtained only by a special act of Parliament, at a cost of about £500; in 1857 a divorce court was established.[77] Bentham invented the Panopticon, a prison so arranged that each prisoner can live in individual seclusion and yet be kept economically under constant surveillance. The Joliet Penitentiary, erected in 1921 in Illinois, is a replica of Bentham's plan. In Central America, where Bentham's works had a wide vogue, it is said that the humblest jail is called a "Panopticon".[78] He has also been credited with the abolition of imprisonment for debt, the reform of representative government in England, the movement to codify international law (a term that he invented) and a system of registration of vital statistics. A recapitulation of his achievements by an ardent admirer sounds like the march of progress of the nineteenth century.[79]

---

[74] Supra, § 3.25. See Stone, The Province and Function of Law (1946), Ch. VII, § 27.

[75] Pound, "David Dudley Field: An Appraisal", in David Dudley Field Centenary Essays (1949), 1, 4, 5, 8.

[76] See Morgan, "Codification of Evidence", in ibid., 164.

[77] See Introduction by C. K. Ogden, The Theory of Legislation (1932) ix–x, and 540–541.

[78] Everett, The Education of Jeremy Bentham (1931), 178. Forty thousand copies of Bentham's works were sold in South America before England had absorbed one-tenth that number. Ogden, op. cit. supra, n. 77, xx.

[79] Ogden, op. cit. supra, n. 77, ix–x.

What is Bentham's place among the legal philosophers? Some would dismiss him as an opinionated law reformer of temporary fame. His most recent editor rates him high among the philosophers of modern times, especially for his ideas on the theory of language and the psychology of value.[80] Neither of these seems as important as his still living theory that laws should be evaluated by estimating their social consequences to the interests of individuals. No one before him had said this so well, and supported it with such cogent arguments and examples. His influence on law reform stands highest. One of his followers aptly remarked that the legal philosophies of the nineteenth century were divided into two groups, the Utilitarians and the Futilitarians.

§ 4.44—Jhering's Social Utilitarianism; the Jurisprudence of Interests

The basic ideas of Jhering's philosophy, called "social utilitarianism", stand for a connecting link between Bentham's individualist utilitarianism and two important philosophic movements of the present century: The "jurisprudence of interests" in Germany and the sociological jurisprudence of Roscoe Pound in the United States. We shall consider Jhering's work in this threefold aspect.

Rudolph von Jhering (1818–1892), following his family tradition in studying law, disdained the prevailingly Hegelian lectures on philosophy in his student days and, confronted with the need of a larger framework for the ideas he had developed at fifty years of age, constructed an original though rather lawbound philosophy of man in society. The occasion, he tells us, was his discovery, in writing the third volume of his great treatise, the Spirit of the Roman Law, that a legal right is a legally protected *interest*.[81] The conception of interests beneath rights led him to the search for purpose in the law; and finally to the conception that purpose is the creator of the entire law; every legal rule owes its origin to a purpose, that is, a practical motive.[82]

Here he began to build his system. From modern science and its liberator, Kant, he took the principle of sufficient reason,

---

[80] Ibid., by Ogden, xi.

[81] See Author's Preface, p. liii, of Jhering, The Law as a Means to an End (Husik trans., 1914). (This book, a translation of vol. I of Jhering's Der Zweck im Recht (vol. I, 1877; vol. II, 1883) will be cited: "L.M.E.") On the legal right, see Geist des römischen Rechts, III (I) § 60.

[82] L.M.E. liv, 330.

which in the mechanical world meant cause and effect. But he did not make the mistake of trying to apply this directly to *all* human conduct. The human will is free from mechanical causation but it is subjected to the law of purpose, it acts "because of" reasons and "in order to" achieve purposes.[83] The will can no more act without a compelling reason than Baron Munchausen could pull himself out of a swamp by his own hair. Every act is an act done for a purpose. How, then, can Jhering account for human acts that are done habitually, not in a trance or by the stimulation of a reflex, but without present deliberation as to the purpose? Habitual action, he says, is that which was originally called forth by a more or less consciously felt purpose, and which by frequent repetition for the same purpose has bound purpose and action together so that the act is done without consciousness of the purpose.[84] Here, it seems, he switches to another track, from the motivation of the individual actor's will by purpose, to the onlooker's conception of purpose, that is, how an onlooker would explain the usefulness of the habit. The habit may have been formed without the actor's conscious reflection on his purpose, as in the case of imitation or obedience to authority. We can now see that by "purpose in the law" Jhering means three things: The relations of individual purposes and habits to legal rules, the purposes of lawmakers who established these rules, and, above all, the purposes or ends which Jhering finds in these rules. Here he turned back to the historical development of Roman law and traced the rational unfolding of a purpose, in successive stages of its development, with a touch of Hegelian faith in evolution.[85]

His conception of human nature was different from Bentham's. Jhering recognized that most people on most occasions act from egoistic self-assertion. Yet man cannot live alone; he needs to live in society and his social impulses are the result of adaptation to his social environment. Men serve social purposes by the enlightened pursuit of their own purposes; here he follows Adam Smith. But he does not attempt, as Bentham did, to make benevolence and heroic sacrifice fit into the category of an egoistic pleasure. Men are also moved by altruistic motives.[86]

---

[83] L.M.E., 2.

[84] L.M.E., 15.

[85] E. g., L.M.E., 57, 181.

[86] L.M.E., 45–46, 73.

Law is a creature of the state, and it is law only if it is enforceable by compulsion.[87] Yet law is not the only means of social control. Thus he constructs his scheme of social mechanics:

I. Egoistic levers: a. Reward. b. Coercion.

II. Altruistic levers: a. Feeling of duty. b. Love.

Because he treats law in the broader context of society, rather than in Bentham's narrow context of individual pain and pleasure, Jhering is called a "social utilitarian".[88]

The social lever of reward is operated less effectively by law than by commerce. Since justice is the proportional reward of merit and the proportional punishment of fault, justice is most nearly achieved, he said, in business; the contract of equivalent exchange serves the diverse interests of the contracting parties so that neither loses.[89] Here he assumes equality of bargaining power between merchants; this assumption narrows the validity of his generalization. His suggestion that gifts were probably unknown in ancient Roman law and came in under the guise of exchanges [90] betrays his consistent distrust of altruistic motivations. His analysis of the Roman law of contracts in terms of exchange and gratuitous promise [91] provides a useful means of comparison with Anglo-American law. The binding force of a promise, he insists, cannot and should not be determined by attempting to apply an abstract formula; in each case one must consider the practical function of the promise. To say, as Kant would, that a contract is binding upon a party because it expressed his will, is wholly inadequate because it does not explain why he may not will today the exact opposite of what he willed yesterday. When we consider what the will must do in order to attain its purpose in society, we are brought to consider the practical function of contract.[92] The Roman law did not, he maintains, recognize the enforceability of gratuitous promises (except under the guise of an exchange) until the time of Justinian, who was moved to intro-

---

[87] Ibid., 240, 249.

[88] Merkl, his contemporary and admirer, called him that in an article published shortly after his death. L.M.E. (Appendix I), 444. So, Pound, Outline of Jurisprudence (1943), 16.

[89] L.M.E. 92, 157. Cf. Bentham's maxim, "Every alienation imports advantage," supra, § 4.42, n. 64.

[90] L.M.E., 209.

[91] L.M.E., 72, 203 ff.

[92] L.M.E., 200–201.

UTILITARIANISM § 4.44

duce them by the Christian conception of charity and liberality.[93]
The system of rewards in society is organized in two forms: Contract (in the widest sense) and association. The latter, unlike
the transaction at arm's length, involves *identity of purposes* of
the persons associated. Each of these devices is in effect a refined form of egoistic self-assertion.[94] But when egoism seeks to
overreach itself, as in the case of usury or other extortionate contracts, the law should curb these excesses of egoism.[95] How can
this intervention be justified? The purpose of the law, which determines its content, is to *secure the conditions of social life.*[96]

This conception leads him down a path of the law which eventually branches in two directions, that of social interests, and that
of the jurisprudence of interests.

Social interests; Pound. The conditions of social life include
not only those of physical existence but also ideal values, such as
honor, religion, art and science. What these will mean is relative
to the social order of a particular society; he recognized the
relativity of purpose to time and place.[97] The role of the law appears in "three forms of the functions of a thing as determined by
human need" : 1. Individual property. 2. State property. 3.
Public right. The latter refers to the rights of the public to the
use of public roads, rivers and other public places.[98] The third
category is expanded until it includes the social values which the
state protects through criminal law, rather than by conferring
legal rights on individuals or associations. These values are physical, economic or ideal. Jhering's inchoate scheme suggested to
Roscoe Pound his classification of interests into "individual",
"public" (here the right of the state as a juristic person) and social (§ 4.61). Each supported his scheme by numerous examples
drawn from mature legal systems, Jhering from Roman and German law, Pound from Roman and Anglo-American law. However suggestive to Pound Jhering's ideas may have been, they are
inferior to Pound's theory of social interests in three respects:
1. Jhering's discussion of his third class, which he sometimes
called "social", was prolix, discursive, and much less complete

93 Ibid., 214.

94 Ibid., 157–165.

95 Ibid., 104.

96 Ibid., 330.

97 Ibid., 331–334.

98 Ibid., 348–9.

than Pound's. 2. Jhering did not expressly recognize that individual interests merit legal protection only in so far as this protection will also act in furtherance of a social interest. 3. Jhering left implicit the compromise character of law, as a reconciliation of conflicting interests. This last conception was developed by the German school known as the "jurisprudence of interests".

Jurisprudence of interests. The group of German jurists who comprised this "school" of thought were aiming to find a theory of judicial interpretation of statutes, especially code provisions, which would free the judge avowedly (his surreptitious freedom they recognized) from the prevalent technical "construction" of law, give him some discretion, and yet keep him within the law by directing him to do two things: 1. To seek and find the interests involved in a litigated controversy. 2. To find in the legal texts the interests which it was the purpose of the law to protect. While Jhering was quite insistent upon the importance of the separation of powers, of the independence of the judiciary and of the requirement that the judge should intellectually and impartially apply the law,[99] the newer school sought to develop a method of analysis which would enable the judge to fulfill his duty to apply the law and also to arrive at a decision that would more nearly represent the true intention of the legislature. Philipp Heck, the leader of this school, said:

"The fundamental truth from which we must proceed is that each command of the law determines a conflict of interests; it originates from a struggle between opposing interests, and represents as it were the resultant of these opposing forces." [1]

The judge should discover what interests the legal rule protects *and* what were the opposing interests which were made to give way as far as the rule prescribes. Heck therefore rejects Jhering's original and simpler idea of discovering "the purpose" of a legal rule. For instance, the purpose of a tax law is to raise revenue, but a particular tax law owes its *special* character to the *way* in which the interests of taxpayers have been taken into consideration.[2] His position is similar to that taken above (§ 3.25), that is, rejection or distrust of the assumption that a statute has

---

[99] L.M.E., 289–309.

[1] Heck, "Jurisprudence of Interests", (a lecture delivered in 1932), translated in the volume, The Jurisprudence of Interests (Twentieth Century Legal Philosophy Series, vol. 3, 1948), 35. Heck was inspired by Jhering. Ibid., 126.

[2] Ibid., 36; also 137–8.

just *one* policy which is sufficient to guide its interpretation. Heck vigorously defended his theory of the judicial process from the charge that it was identical with the "Free-law" movement in Germany, which would permit the judge, instead of subsuming the facts of a case under statutory concepts, to decide the case in accordance with his own intuitive sense of justice. This movement, represented by Ehrlich and later by Isay, never got beyond the protest stage: It produced no constructive substitute for the logical process which it decried as fictitious.[3] The jurisprudence of interests presented a valuable theory of judicial interpretation. Besides the conflicts of private (individual) interests, there are conflicts between these and public (i. e., social) interests, and between different social interests as competing ends of legislation.[4] The judge should determine, not what *he* would do but what adjustment of conflicting interests the legislator has made. Despite this moderate view of the judicial function, at least one adherent as early as 1930 recognized the dangers of judicial subjectivism (the judicial "hunch") and the related danger of a "politicized" judiciary.[5] The jurisprudence of interests sought to recognize and limit judicial law-making by giving it a professional and rational method, and thus to maintain the independence of the judiciary from political non-legal controls such as those exercised by party leaders.

---

[3] Ehrlich's view was set forth in the volume, The Science of Legal Method (Modern Legal Philosophy Series, vol. IX), Ch. II, and in Die juristische Logik (1918). Heck sets forth and refutes Isay's theses in The Jurisprudence of Interests (1948), 185–187.

[4] The Jurisprudence of Interests (1948), 132, n. 6. The term "interest" includes "ideal" interests. Ibid., 133.

[5] Prof. Max Rümelin in ibid., 22.

Chapter 17

PRAGMATISM IN LEGAL PHILOSOPHY

§ 4.50—Basic Ideas of Pragmatism in American Legal Philosophy

In order to show the main trends in American legal philosophy during the first half of the twentieth century we shall need to distinguish between American law, American legal scholarship and American legal philosophy as of 1900.

As to American law, for the present purpose it can be said that the method of judicial decision (in appellate courts, at least)[1] was the logical application of traditional concepts historically defined, with a marked tendency to rest the decisions of cases on procedural defects and to avoid the discussion of substantive grounds wherever possible. Public discussions (in judicial opinions or in bar association addresses, etc.) of what the law should be (other than defenses of its traditional institutions)[2] were avoided as dangerous or at least immodest. In cases of constitutional interpretation the political theories of Locke and Adam Smith supplemented the traditional concepts of English common law and political theory. These generalizations, partially false though they may be (since late Victorianism was never as dull as its detractors have depicted it), will serve to show the significance of the "radicals" who appeared on the scene. The best American legal scholarship around 1900 was to be found in law reviews rather than in treatises, and it was of the analytical or historical type. Although criteria of justice and expediency were not ignored, the legal scholars of the turn of the century were nearly all fascinated by legal history and especially by the task of uncovering the procedural origins of substantive legal rules. Hence one could scarcely find any predominant American legal philosophy. A watered-down Blackstonian natural law theory was sometimes used to ornament a treatise; yet the implications of the prevailing historical scholarship were that the true guid-

---

[1] As far as my limited observation went, the same was true in *trial* courts in the early part of the century.

[2] A good example is the address by Joseph H. Choate, a leader of the New York bar, to the American Bar Association in 1898, defending "Trial by Jury," including the unanimous verdict requirement (Choate, American Addresses (1911) 197, 214) which sometimes favored corporation defendants in tort cases.

ance could be found in the historical origins of legal concepts. The requirement of consideration, for instance, was ascribed by each of several writers to a different single historical antecedent, a position which Professor Ames rightly rejected [3] for the view that it was a product of diverse legal influences. Legal scholarship was only occasionally utilitarian, as in Ames' theory of consideration.[4]

The two men who were the first to disturb the complacency of the *fin de siècle* philosophy of law (what there was of it) were Oliver Wendell Holmes, Jr., and Roscoe Pound. Holmes had fired the opening gun as far back as 1880, when he boldly told a distinguished Boston audience: "The life of the law has not been logic: it has been experience." [5] Yet the legal traditionalists were more shocked than hurt by what followed in the Lowell lectures. Holmes took a shot at formal logic by way of preparing his readers for his extensive and fascinating incursions into legal history. Not until 1897 did he break definitely with the historical school,[6] and definitely though rather apologetically advocate a legal axiology of social advantages. Pound shocked the American Bar Association in 1906 by taking seriously the evidences of popular dissatisfaction with the administration of justice (§ 4.60). Each of these men was greatly influenced by pragmatism, especially by the pragmatism of William James (§ 4.52). A slightly later generation of writers on jurisprudence was influenced by another pragmatist, John Dewey (§ 4.53). Now the legal rebels were not just "followers" of a school of legal philosophy, as was common in Europe. The thoughts that they struggled to express were congenial to the basic ideas of pragmatism. What were they?

The general ideas which have characterized the pragmatic and post-pragmatic philosophy (general and legal) of the twentieth century are: 1. Problematicism. 2. Probabilism. 3. Pluralism. 4. Ethical and axiological relativism. 5. Operational and contextual theories of meaning. These rather obscure terms are simpler than they sound, as a brief explanation will show.[7]

---

3 Ames, Lectures in Legal History (1913) 129, first published in 1887.

4 Ibid.; "Two Theories of Consideration," 323, 353 (first published, 1899).

5 Holmes, The Common Law (1881) 1; delivered as the Lowell Lectures in 1880. Further comment on this much-quoted passage infra, § 4.55.

6 Holmes, The Path of the Law, (1897) 10 Harv.L.Rev. 457, 467.

7 This analysis was partly suggested by a valuable summary of "the phi-

1. *Problematicism.* The belief, often implicit, that reality begins with a problematic situation which stimulates the mind to do something by way of resolving its indeterminacy, is, for legal philosophy, the most striking common characteristic of pragmatists. To practicing lawyers the troubled client's story is the initial problematic situation; and to the Anglo-American "common law" lawyer the problematic situation, with its resolution in a judicial decision, is the empirical reality from which inference to generalizations—or reasoning by analogy—begins. Thus pragmatism from the outset was congenial to the ways of thought of lawmen. What legal pragmatists did, for the most part, was to point out that the method of solving a legal problem, by finding an established legal rule and applying it logically to the facts, was not as "certain" as the formal statement of rules and facts in the judicial opinion, nor as the statement of rules in the treatise or the statute book, made it appear to be. At the turn of the century, the lawyer whose prediction of the outcome of a litigation turned out to be inaccurate either thought that he had missed the "true" path of logical method, or that the court had gone astray.[8] One thing that pragmatism did, then, was to "undermine" or "subvert" or cast doubt upon some supposedly established legal doctrines. The favorite targets were contributory negligence and assumption of risk in the law of employer's liability for injuries to his employees. Thus the impression was created that pragmatism was anti-conceptual and anti-rational, that it jumped from the frying pan of rationalism into the fire of intuitive sensationalism, the "facts" being regarded as stimuli of the immediate hunch. Perhaps some followers of pragmatism can be convicted of such utterances. Every now and then someone will create a nine-day wonder by pointing out that judges belong to the animal kingdom.

But the founders of pragmatism would emphasize instead the indeterminacy of the generalizations to be used in a problematic situation and the range of choice of hypotheses which would resolve the indeterminacy.[9] A *problem* does not confront one except in terms of *some* concepts or generalizations. Thus prob-

losophical legacy of the founders of pragmatism" in Wiener, Evolution and the Founders of Pragmatism (1949) c. 9.

[8] Judge Cardozo confessed to having such a belief when he practiced law. The Growth of the Law (1924) 57. I recall a similar feeling.

[9] Well brought out in Northrop, The Logic of the Sciences and the Humanities (1947) 12–14.

lematicism, as a kind of logical-metaphysical starting point of pragmatism, leads to the view that generalizations, to be genuinely useful in problem-solving, are necessarily contingent and probable, in the sense that they are subject to exceptions (probabilism); and likewise to the view that the generalizations used in one problematic situation may not be logically consistent with (form a systematic whole with) those used in another (pluralism). The other characteristics mentioned above—ethical relativism and theories of meaning—are also derived from the problematic starting point.

One weakness of problematicism is that it tends to produce results that are episodic, intuitive, individualist and in this sense "arbitrary." Judge Cardozo's first two books on the judicial process [10] are written from the problematic outset and they give the reader a sense of charming immediacy in the presence of an understanding and loyal mind, more than they give generalizations which one can treasure for future use. Yet this tendency prevails only if the method of resolving the indeterminacy resembles the immediate intuitiveness of an artistic decision rather than the reasoning of a science. This contrast is brought out by Dewey (§ 4.53) and emphasized by Northrop.[11] Another weakness of the problematic approach is the neglect of the creation of generalizations and of the systematic ordering of generalizations for future use. The avowed pragmatists have produced relatively little systematic constructive writing. The late Walter Wheeler Cook (to give one example) an admirable and popular law teacher at a half-dozen law schools, was more brilliant in criticizing Beale's conflict-of-laws theories than in his final effort to construct his own. Both of these examples may be controverted (for both Cardozo and Cook did construct coherent generalizations), yet the weakness remains.

A third weakness of problematicism is one that follows from the first two, namely, the difficulty of determining the scope of the indeterminacy. If the touring automobilist finds himself approaching a fork in the road and consults his map as an aid to the indeterminacy of which fork he should take, he need not, and ordinarily would not, regard as problematic the accuracy of his map or of the road signs; whether he should abandon the trip and go back home; whether he should abandon his car and proceed on foot, etc. Fortunately not even philosophers can make us

---

[10] The Nature of the Judicial Process (1921); The Growth of the Law (1924).

[11] Supra, note 9. Not to say that Northrop is a pragmatist.

overhaul our whole lives at every fork of the road. The area of indeterminacy in the tourist's problematic situation is ordinarily obvious.[12] With legal problems the limits of indeterminacy are not as easy to set. Every litigated case *may* be taken to open up questions as to the accepted rules or principles of contracts, torts, etc., or as to the acceptability of such classifications, or as to the ends of law and the state. Fortunately the doctrine of stare decisis limits, for counselor as well as judge, the area of indeterminacy; that is one of its important and often overlooked functions.[13] Even if the problematic situation is that of the legislator, the area of indeterminacy is not unlimited, for any proposed legislation must be compatible with some statutory and constitutional provisions that are not for the present to be disturbed. While I have called the indeterminacy of the indeterminacy a weakness of problematicism, it is no worse in this respect than other logical-metaphysical theories, which avowedly ignore it and thus remain aloof from the battleground of doubt.

2. *Pluralism.* Most philosophies have assumed reality to be of one kind (monism, usually either mind *or* matter) or of two kinds (dualism, usually taken to be mind *and* matter). In this metaphysical context pluralism assumes that there may be more than two kinds of reality. In a methodological sense, more congenial to pragmatism, pluralism is the piecemeal analysis of the diverse issues of diverse problems—physical, biological, psychological, linguistic and social—which resist solution by a single formula.[14] By attacking problems separately, without waiting for the revelation that will unify them, pragmatists and their followers [15] have accomplished many useful results. This ad hoc method is indigenous to the common law, which was never reduced to a system.[16] That liability in tort was (with exceptions) based on fault while liability for breach of contract was not, did not trouble nineteenth century lawyers and judges, although a rationalist philosopher, Kant, tried to bring both under the theory of autonomy of

---

[12] But both roads might lead to the same destination, one being shorter and the other scenically preferable.

[13] This is substantially the same as the like function of legal rules. Supra, § 3.24. See also the discussion of the unprovided case, § 5.05.

[14] Here I have paraphrased Professor Wiener's statement about "pluralistic empiricism." Op. cit. supra, n. 7, 191.

[15] However, other contemporary schools of philosophy—logical positivists, critical realists—have adopted pluralism in method. Wiener, op. cit., 192-3.

[16] Supra, §§ 3.20, 3.21.

the will. At the beginning of the economic depression of the 1930's when new types of "social legislation" were being proposed, Professor Dewey took pains to point out that it was not necessary to have a social science in order to make intelligent improvements in social control.[17] Most of the legislation of the New Deal was based upon legislative experiments in other countries—England, Germany, Australia—rather than upon "social science."[18] Pluralism means also that the pragmatist cannot accept a single overriding conception of the class struggle—the Marxist dogma—as explaining all social phenomena.[19]

But what of a unifying formula for all human law, such as "the greatest good of the greatest number" (Bentham) or "the common good" (Aquinas): Is not the unity of the legal system maintained by bringing all law under such a formula? In a formal sense, yes; but not significantly in a methodical sense. That is, such a formula is too abstract and empty to guide one in the interpretation or creation of norms to be used in problem-solving. The pragmatist calls for meanings that are "clear" in terms of "the literal details of the separate facts."[20] Yet this effort to attain concrete clarity will, unless checked, end in heterogeneity and ignorance. The dilemma is a general one:

> "Hence the unsatisfactoriness of all our speculations. On the one hand, so far as they retain any multiplicity in their terms, they fail to get us out of the empirical sand-heap world; on the other, so far as they eliminate multiplicity the practical man despises their empty barrenness."[21]

The only possible philosophy, then, must be a compromise between "an abstract monotony and a concrete heterogeneity."[22]

3. *Probabilism.* In physical or social science probabilism means that its laws are only probable or contingent.[23] When

---

[17] "Social Science and Social Control," in John Dewey's Philosophy (Ratner ed., 1939) 951; reprinted from The New Republic, July 29, 1931.

[18] Social science, however, contributed methods of computing consequences such as costs and benefits under social security laws.

[19] See Dewey's reply to the educators who urged that the "class struggle" be taken as the intellectual guide of teachers, in op. cit. supra, n. 17, 696–702, reprinted from The Social Frontier, May, 1936.

[20] James, "The Sentiment of Rationality," in Papers on Philosophy (Everyman Lib. ed., 1917) 128; first printed in Mind, 1879.

[21] Op. cit., last note, 129.

[22] Ibid., 128.

[23] Wiener, op. cit., 200.

pragmatism came to be applied to law this conception acquired several different meanings. To the extent that legal rules are based on assumptions as to the usual course of events in social life, they are based upon probabilities, not certainties.[24] When Holmes said that the law is a body of predictions of what courts will do (§ 2.20) he twisted the normative meaning of law into an empirical meaning and thus assigned it a probability-status. In yet another sense, it can be taken to mean that the *authority* of a legal proposition is more or less probable. For instance, on the evidence it is more or less probable that the highest court of New York will deem authoritative the rule that performance of a pre-existing duty to a third person is not a sufficient consideration to make a contract.

Two other pragmatist views resemble probabilism though they digress from it. Since no legal rule or principle is so clearly phrased that its application in all subsequent cases will be unmistakable, it may be rejected as not applicable by its terms or as subject to an exception. This last is, of course, a perversion (logically) of the meaning of probability as it applies to empirical propositions. Finally, we may include the view that all distinctions are distinctions of degree. An early legal pragmatist, Nicholas St. John Green, urged that the important legal distinction between "proximate" and "remote" consequences of tortious conduct meant "only the degree of certainty or uncertainty with which the connection between cause and effect might have been anticipated."[25] While many legal distinctions can be taken to imply a "more or less," it is erroneous to ascribe to pragmatism the view that *all* distinctions are distinctions of degree, and likewise erroneous to apply it to all legal distinctions. A court does not give three-fourths damages (or any at all) for the non-performance of a three-fourths contract, nor for the commission of a three-fourths tort. This uncritical common-sense notion expresses an emotional attitude rather than an aspect of probabilism.

4. *Ethical and Axiological Relativism.* By "axiological" is meant, as was pointed out above (§ 1.13), the range of value-

---

[24] E. g., the assumption that an offeree's acceptance, duly mailed, will reach the offeror in due course. See Patterson, "The Delivery of a Life Insurance Policy," (1919) 33 Harv.L.Rev. 198, 213.

[25] Wiener, op. cit., 159, quoting Green, Essays and Notes on the Law of Tort and Crime, 15-17. However, this is not the only significance of the distinction: The kind of harm (to person or property) foreseeable is also important and is not a distinction of degree.

theory which includes and goes beyond ethics as a theory of individual conduct. Although pragmatists ordinarily include the oughtness of social problems in ethics, they would also recognize that in transforming a social-ethical "ought" into a legal "shall" something importantly new has been added, and that any such proposed transformation raises value-problems that are peculiarly legal, that is, problems of legal axiology (§ 1.13). The term "relativism" is more than ambiguous; it probably has more meanings than the thirteen that Professor Lovejoy ascribed to "Pragmatism." [26] Perhaps the one common notion in all of the meanings of "relativism" is the exclusion of "absolutism", which also has different meanings. Let us then proceed by listing a few of the meanings of "relativism." In the first place, the concept of probabilism applicable to scientific truths was transferred to the validity of ethical principles. The "right" is only the expedient in the way of our behaving as the truth is the expedient in our way of thinking.[27] A similar transfer occurs in the writings of some legal pragmatists.[28]   Here "relativism" means contingent and probable rather than certain. Again, pragmatists and their followers have generally emphasized the dependence of value-propositions upon fact-propositions, and hence the contingency of the latter inheres in the former. This is the negation of Kant's position that moral laws are non-empirical (a priori) and hence absolute, while physical laws are only probable. The ethic of pragmatism is teleological, and any prediction as to the future consequences that will follow from social action pursuant to a given rule or principle is merely probable and contingent.[29] What will be the consequences of abolishing the action for breach of promise of marriage, or of establishing a proposed plan of old-age pensions, or of establishing a certain scheme of compulsory health insurance? Intelligent legislation calls for an appraisal of factual consequences.

A third meaning of ethical relativism is the most important: A social formula signifies different things, in its consequences and its practical meaning, under different social conditions.

---

[26] Lovejoy, "The Thirteen Pragmatisms," (1908) 5 Jour.Phil. 1–12, 29–39.

[27] James, Pragmatism—A New Name for Some Old Ways of Thinking (1925) 222; Hall, p. 228. For further discussion of this much-criticized statement, see § 4.52.

[28] See Harper, "Some Implications of Juristic Pragmatism," (1929) 39 Ethics 269, 280–281; Hall, p. 254.

[29] Not all pragmatists embrace a "naturalistic" ethics, one which identifies ethical and factual propositions.

"That which was on the side of moral progress in the eighteenth and early nineteenth centuries may be a morally reactionary doctrine in the twentieth century; that which is serviceable now may be injurious at a later time." [30]

This conception of relativism seems to involve two ideas: the belief in social evolution, which played an important part in pragmatic ethical theory; and the pragmatist theory of meaning. As to the latter, let us suppose a Thomist asking a pragmatist: "Do you not believe that the statement, 'Everyone should seek the good and avoid evil,' is absolutely right or valid in all cases?" To this the pragmatist would reply that such a formula is too vague in meaning to guide an ethical judgment, that its significance, being emotive (hortatory) or formal (as an axiom) would be uncertain relative to action, and not absolute. A fourth meaning of relativism is given by problematicism: In reasoning toward a practical evaluation (in law, for instance) as the solution of a problem, one has to compare and *balance* different values, so that no one is "absolute", i. e., entitled to unconditional control of a practical situation. Thus the pragmatist would agree that truth-telling is generally a duty, yet he would not agree with Kant that no exceptions be recognized, that is, that there should be no situations in which other values should outweigh this one. The physician who, when called upon, falsely denies to his patient that his ailment is incurable and fatal, where telling the truth would only do harm, fulfills an ethical duty and does what is legally permissible.[31] Another example is Cardozo's tentative scale of values in which, surely, human life will *always* be placed above property, convenience, commerce; yet he recognized that the law permits men to risk their lives in building skyscrapers [32] (even though it may require safety devices to reduce the risks). Pound's theory that law-making depends on a weighing of competing social interests (§ 4.61) expresses a similar conception of relativism.[33]

5. *Operational and Contextual Theories of Meaning.* Pragmatism originated with a group of Cambridge intellectuals of whom Charles S. Peirce was the leading spirit; and one of Peirce's chief problems was how to make our ideas clear:

---

[30] Dewey and Tufts, Ethics (1932) 373.

[31] Supra, § 4.21, n. 23.

[32] Cardozo, The Paradoxes of Legal Science (1928) 57.

[33] Professor Wiener has noted five kinds of relativism, some of which overlap the ones mentioned above. Op. cit., 198.

"Consider what effects that might conceivably have practical bearings we conceive the object of our conception to
have. Then, our conception of these effects is the whole of
our conception of the object." [34]

This conception of meaning is not very different from the operational one, mentioned above (§ 1.12). The contextual theory of
meaning followed from problematicism, since each term or proposition takes its meaning from the context (literary or situa-
tional) in which it functions (§ 3.26). These theories of meaning,
though not the exclusive property of pragmatists, appealed to
legal scholars and judges who were striving to make *their* ideas
clear, even though some of them would reject the label, "pragmatist". Hohfeld, Corbin, Cook and Kocourek were the leaders
in a juristic movement to clarify American legal terminology
which was one of the dominant influences in legal scholarship
during the period 1913–30. Of these men only Cook was a pragmatist. Yet pragmatism made the operational theory of meaning respectable.

In this general survey of pragmatism in its relation to jurisprudence I have generalized as broadly as I dared to. Pragmatism was, more than any other major philosophy, a product of co-
operative effort by a group of rugged individualists. This will be
brought out more fully in the next section. In the ensuing sections the chief contributions to legal philosophy of the leading
pragmatists and their followers will be outlined.

§ 4.51—Pragmatism: Origin and Chief Representatives

Pragmatism is a new kind of philosophy that originated in the
late nineteenth century. When William James, whom we may
justly call its creator, christened it in 1907 as "a new name for
some old ways of thinking," [35] the germinal ideas had already
been developed by a group of men in Cambridge, Massachusetts,
during the 1870's. Charles Saunders Peirce, son of a distinguished mathematician, initiated pragmatism in his essay, "How
To Make Our Ideas Clear." [36] Other members of the group were
William James, Chauncey Wright, mathematician and warm

---

[34] Wiener, op. cit., 92, quoting from Peirce's article, "How To Make Our
Ideas Clear," published in 1878 in the Scientific American.

[35] James, Pragmatism: A New Name for Some Old Ways of Thinking
(1907). James had used the term "pragmatism" earlier. Infra, n. 43.

[36] Supra, § 4.50, n. 34.

admirer of Darwin, John Fiske, follower of Darwin and Spencer and author of a work on cosmic philosophy, Nicholas St. John Green, a Benthamite and a philosophical lawyer, and Oliver Wendell Holmes, Jr., then a Boston lawyer. Fiske, Green and Holmes, as well as another regular attendant, Joseph B. Warner, were graduates of the Harvard Law School. Thus the originating group, sometimes called the "Metaphysical Club" in defiance of current skepticism,[37] contained representatives of natural science and of social problems, and these have ever since been the chief interests of pragmatists. Chauncey Wright (1830–1875), though he never attained first-rate academic status at Harvard, was the gadfly of the incipient pragmatists and seems to have influenced Holmes more than any of the others did. Wright embraced Darwin's theory of biological evolution with enthusiasm and yet he rejected Spencer's effort to extend it to social evolution.[38] This anticipated by thirty years Holmes' famous dissent in Lochner v. New York (§ 4.34). Wright assumed a position of neutral scientific skepticism that Holmes emulated and that James sharply criticized. Fifty years after Wright's death Holmes acknowledged his indebtedness to Wright for teaching him that "I must not say *necessary* about the universe, that we don't know whether anything is necessary or not."[39] Yet Wright's faith in the attainment of truth through experimental science was also shared by Holmes, with the same reservations. In this belief and in the belief that the fittest of ideas will survive, Holmes shared Wright's views.[40] Wright was, however, a precursor rather than a founder of pragmatism. Perhaps the absence of a label for Wright's philosophy may explain the mystery of Holmes' not remembering that he had ever heard of "pragmatism" until after 1891.[41] Wright enjoyed referring to the "cosmic weather", meaning the contingency and temporality of natural laws. One finds similar expressions in Holmes' extra-judicial writings.

----

[37] On the controversial history of the "Metaphysical Club", see Wiener, Evolutionism and the Founders of Pragmatism (1949), c. 2. The chief doubt is about the name. There is no doubt that the group met and talked with each other.

[38] Wiener, op. cit., 35 and n. 10, citing an article published by Wright in 1875.

[39] Ibid., 174, citing II Holmes-Pollock Letters (1941) 252, written in 1929.

[40] Ibid., 176.

[41] Ibid., 22 (letter to Morris R. Cohen in 1920).

Peirce was primarily interested in logic, semiotics and metaphysics. He rejected the nominalism of the British empiricists, at the same time using the evolution of human culture to explain his rather intricate theory of signs. His conception of scientific method was his most important contribution to philosophy.[42] Yet he was on the whole the most conservative of the Cambridge group, and when William James eventually came forth with his radical empiricism, Peirce felt unable to accept some of James' views and re-named his own philosophy, "pragmaticism." James had previously credited Peirce with giving the name, "pragmatism", to the early philosophical doctrine of the Cambridge group.[43] Peirce, differing from James, insisted upon a tendency of the universe to evolve toward a rational goal. Nicholas St. John Green, another member of the original pragmatic group, practiced law in Boston and was a part-time lecturer at the Harvard Law School. He was a follower of Jeremy Bentham. Pragmatist ethics in its testing of consequences showed a marked similarity to Bentham's. Green's articles on defamation revealed the often fictitious character of the "malice" required in actions of libel and slander. Holmes used this to point up the difference between law and morals: "Malice" in law must not be confused with a wicked mind.[44] It cannot be said, however, that this analysis led to anything more than the recognition of the formal character of "malice" in this context. Green's article on proximate cause, referred to above,[45] was the precursor of several debunking articles which served to clarify the evaluative aspect of legal cause, which many judges discussed as a purely physical concept. Green had but little respect for the doctrine of stare decisis and delighted to criticize judicial decisions.[46] Had he lived a half century later, he would have been called a "legal realist."

The "founders" of pragmatism were individualists, and recognized no authority over their ideas. Like all philosophic rebels, they agreed better on what they opposed than on what they believed. They did not so much reject traditional philosophic beliefs as deem them inadequate. Pragmatism, or parts of it, can still be used to supplement other philosophies. The original

---

[42] See Buchler, C. S. Peirce's Empiricism (1939).

[43] Wiener, op. cit., 18, citing James' public address of 1898.

[44] "The Path of the Law" (1897), in Collected Legal Papers (1920) 176.

[45] Supra, § 4.50, n. 25.

[46] This account of Green is based on Wiener, op. cit., c. 7, and App. F.

group of pragmatists were not skeptics nor cynics. They had a profound though often unexpressed faith (shaken at times, as all faiths are) in the capacities of men to solve their problems and to improve their societies. As Professor Wiener's book has neatly shown,[47] they shared a faith in ameliorative evolution, in "progress", whether it was Darwinian, Lamarckian or Hegelian. It appears in James' and Holmes' survival test of ethics, in Dewey's latent Hegelianism and in Pound's sociological jurisprudence.

§ 4.52—William James: The Radical Pragmatist

William James (1842–1910), born into a literary family, first studied botany, then medicine, then turned to psychology and ended his active career as a professor of philosophy at Harvard. Despite his genteel cultural background he cracked a good deal of philosophical crockery in his colorful and vigorous style. His work on psychology became a classic and gained him many "converts" to pragmatism, including John Dewey. He rejected hedonism as a comprehensive and exclusive theory of human motivation, and suggested "interest" as the comprehensive term for human motivation and striving [48]—a suggestion which was adopted and amplified by two of his ablest followers, Ralph Barton Perry [49] and Roscoe Pound (§ 4.60). We shall first discuss James' metaphysical theories, which always turned around method, and then his ethics.

Metaphysics and Method. James' metaphysical views seem to have had more influence on legal thinkers than his ethics. At any rate this seems to have been true in the case of Holmes and Pound. James stated the pragmatic method in its simplest terms as interpreting each notion by tracing its practical consequences:
> "What difference would it practically make to any one if this notion rather than that notion were true?" [50]

The idea here is similar to Peirce's [51] yet with this difference: James has focussed attention on the *choice* between concepts, on what I have called by the barbaric name of "problematicism" (§ 4.50). James carried this idea further than Peirce had in the

---

[47] Supra, n. 37.

[48] Supra, § 4.41, n. 20.

[49] See Perry, General Theory of Value (1926).

[50] James, Pragmatism (1925) 45; Hall, p. 227.

[51] Supra, § 4.50, n. 34.

direction of subjectivity and emotionalism. The formula for testing the truth of an idea is its agreement with reality, its harmony with other parts of our experience, and "this function of agreeable leading is what we mean by an idea's verification." [52] We find here, as in other parts of James' writings,[53] a belief like that of Descartes, that if one can think a thing through very clearly, it must be true. This kind of belief may, as James doubtless realized, call the most arrant dogmatist the greatest truthfinder. James, on the contrary, would find our best chances of getting the truth in the work and the report of a careful investigator who, though he believed in one answer to the problem, would be very nervous about making an error.[54] Much of this kind of talk in James arose from his interest in psychology and in explaining our belief-practices as having survival-value in the evolution of the race. He pushed this idea to the limit—or beyond—when he said:

" 'The true,' to put it very briefly, is only the expedient in the way of our thinking, just as 'the right' is only the expedient in the way of our acting." [55]

This joining of truth and right under the category of expediency leads to the belief that both truth and right are only contingent and probable, that is, to probabilism.[56] Such ideas encouraged the rising generation of legal doubters to question many of the established rules and concepts of Anglo-American law. In law, one may say, "the right" *is* more nearly what is expedient (on the whole) than in the ideal realm of ethics.

But to say that "the true," in a judicial trial (for instance), includes any facts which it is expedient to believe, *might* mean that the judge, prosecutor and jury could find as "true" whatever facts were necessary to convict a particular accused whom they found it "expedient" to imprison or hang. Such an interpretation would make a travesty of Anglo-American conceptions of a fair trial or "due process of law." This last sentence discloses one of the reasons of "expediency" which would have to be considered,

---

[52] Op. cit. supra, n. 50, 202; Hall, p. 228.

[53] E. g., in "The Sentiment of Rationality," in James, Selected Papers on Philosophy (Everyman Lib. ed., 1917) 126 (first published in 1879): When we are able to think with perfect fluency, the thing we think of seems pro tanto rational.

[54] Selected Papers, 116.

[55] Pragmatism (1925) 222; Hall, p. 228.

[56] Supra, § 4.50.

namely, that a proposed method of truth-finding would not be expedient for other cases. When James says "expedient" he means "expedient on the whole, in view of all future consequences." Now the future consequences of telling the jurymen that they should find that the defendant X killed Y with premeditation and malice aforethought, if they deem it expedient that X should be put to death, include these: That the reliable method of determining the truth of a factual proposition, on the basis of evidence, would be abandoned; and that without some other evidence on which to ground it a judgment as to the expedient treatment of X would be capricious and tyrannical. For these reasons alone neither James nor Dewey would accept the short-range conception of expediency. The reader who has not been exposed to the sophistical perils of philosophy will at this point, I hope, realize how difficult it is for a philosophy, even a legal philosophy, to be practical.

Lord (Bertrand) Russell, in one of his popular books on philosophy, has two more sophistical arguments against the pragmatist conception of truth as that which it is expedient to believe. One is that the truth of beliefs as to the past is to be determined by their *causes* rather than their effects. Suppose, for example, Miss A is about to take an examination in history in order to obtain a teaching position, and she knows that Mr. B, who will grade the papers, believes that Columbus discovered America (first crossed the Atlantic) in 1493. She finds the future consequences of this belief (i. e., her getting a better grade on the examination and thus having a better chance of getting the job) are expedient, and therefore the belief is true.[57] Accordingly she answers: "1493." Now another consequence that Miss A might well consider is whether it would be expedient to be a teacher in a school system employing such a dumb examiner as Mr. B.

However, pragmatists do not interpret truth in this way. James' emphasis on the importance of open-minded observation and search for data [58] refutes any such charge. Professor Dewey, replying in detail to Lord Russell's more technical attack on pragmatism, states emphatically that knowledge is warranted assertion. Such an assertion always requires some inference and the means of testing the inferential element in knowledge are "the

---

[57] See Russell, A History of Western Philosophy (1945), 817, where this type of argument is suggested though not made explicit; also 824–826.

[58] Supra, n. 54.

data provided by observation and *only* by observation."[59] The whole temper of pragmatism is empirical. So the warranted assertibility of an historical fact, such as the date of Columbus' first crossing, is to be determined by examining historical records, which involves, of course, drawing inferences as to their reliability. The pragmatist conception of truth serves to emphasize the degrees of probability (§ 4.50) of the correctness of factual statements. This conception is no less important in legal procedure than in natural science. In the latter factual statements, as to a particular occurrence or observation, can be checked more reliably than in the former. In a judicial trial of issues of fact all (or nearly all) the "evidence" is testimonial, that is, it consists of assertions of fact made by witnesses, and the credibility of the witness has to be taken into account in fact-finding, along with the credibility of the fact asserted on the basis of its correspondence with other evidence. The pragmatic conception of truth is therefore not a perversion of honesty and objective-mindedness but a recognition of fallibility and an incentive to better methods of fact-finding in judicial trials.

Russell's second argument against the pragmatic conception of truth [60] is that both James and Dewey boldly exaggerate the efficacy of human effort to *make* things true, as opposed to the inexorable brute realm of existence which limits man's achievements. In short, Russell accuses the pragmatists, especially Dewey, of a lack of humility toward the universe, of "cosmic impiety." [61] There is some justification for this charge, as one of over-emphasis or exaggeration: James was sometimes rather cocky about what man can do, and Dewey, through his primary interest in education, stresses the adaptability and latent capacity of mankind rather than its limitations. This exaggeration (for such I feel it to be) is chiefly rhetorical, that is, intended to emphasize what can be a basis for, or a means of, useful action. The emphasis formerly puzzled me. Once I asked Professor

---

59 Dewey, Problems of Men (1946) 336 (first published in 1941 as "Propositions, Warranted Assertibility and Truth," a reply to certain passages in Russell, An Inquiry into Meaning and Truth (1940). Neither of these is recommended for subway reading.

60 The "infinite regress" argument may be mentioned in passing: To know the truth of a statement (P shot Q) one would need to know the consequences of believing it; to know the truth of those consequences one would need to know the consequences of believing *them*; and so on ad infinitum. See Russell, op. cit. supra, n. 57, 817.

61 Ibid., 827–828.

Dewey,[62] "Why do you talk only of the influence of the social environment on the individual and not about his inborn traits, which limit and determine his destiny in life far more than his education or other environmental influences?" After a pause he replied: "I suppose it's because we can't do anything about them."

A few concluding remarks on James' metaphysics must suffice here. He was not a "materialist," for his "will to believe" was a justification for holding religious and supernatural beliefs outside the scope of empirical verification or disproof. He was vigorously opposed to the American "imperialism"—the expansion of territory in the Far East and the Carribbean—following the Spanish-American war.[63] His attitude toward law was sometimes casual or contemptuous. He contrasted the inquiry into truth about nature, in which the risks of believing an immature theory can be postponed until more evidence is available, with the need for prompt, hit-or-miss decisions of legal controversies:

> "Law courts, indeed, have to decide on the best evidence attainable for the moment, because a judge's duty is to make law as well as to ascertain it, and (as a learned judge once said to me) few cases are worth spending much time over: the great thing is to have them decided on *any* acceptable principle, and got out of the way." [64]

The fact that is established in the courtroom is, indeed, not the truth for all time; and yet the consequences of deciding cases hastily and superficially are not as trivial as he suggests. In another passage he anticipated the American Legal Realists (§ 4.63) in their skepticism of legal rules as controlling factors in judicial decisions:

> "Given previous law and a novel case and the judge will twist them into fresh law. . . . All the while, however, we pretend that the eternal is unrolling, that the one previous justice, grammar or truth are simply fulgurating and not being made. But imagine a youth in the courtroom trying cases with his abstract notion of 'the' law [or a censor of speech with his "mother-tongue," a professor with his Truth], and what progress do they make? Truth, law and

---

[62] In the Seminar in Legal Philosophy, which Professor Dewey and I gave jointly, 1925–1930, in Columbia University.

[63] Wiener, op. cit., 203.

[64] Selected Papers, 115 (from "The Will to Believe," an address delivered in 1896). The "learned judge" might have been O. W. Holmes, in one of his cosmic moods.

language fairly boil away from them at the least touch of novel fact. . . . Far from being antecedent principles that animate the process, law, language, truth are but abstract names for its results." [65]

This passage gives support to the theory of rationalization and to the charge that James was anti-rationalist. On the contrary it is believed that James was merely emphasizing the fluidity of antecedent principles when used in the problematic process with its unforeseen novelties. Elsewhere he said: "Concepts never change." New ones are continually being made out of the old ones. If one accepts this theory, then a court never *merely* applies its own precedents; it makes new law (molecularly, to use Holmes' description) when it "applies" its own established rules to a fresh case, since such a case will always contain *some* novel fact. This last is James' metaphysical assumption.

Ethics. James' ethics is of concern to us here chiefly in so far as it provided guidance for Roscoe Pound and other legal pragmatists. At the outset one must say that while James in his later years blurred the distinction between reality and value, by characterizing both the true and the right as the expedient,[66] in earlier writings he clearly recognized the importance of this distinction.[67] His ethical theory was most fully stated in his address of 1891.[68] The ethical philosopher cannot be a skeptic because that would mean giving up his aim of finding a stable system of moral relations; he cannot believe in a dogmatic ethical philosophy made up in advance nor in final truth in ethics, any more than in physical science; yet in the end he must recognize that, for his own system of ideals, the belief in an ideal impersonal universe that imposes obligations upon man is less acceptable than the belief in a divine thinker whose "ideal universe would be the most inclusive realizable whole." [69] Since, however, the divine thinker's thought is hidden from the mundane ethical philosopher, "our postulation of him serves only to let loose in us the strenuous

---

[65] Op. cit. supra, n. 50, 240–242; Hall, p. 229.

[66] Supra, n. 55.

[67] Selected Papers, 158–159.

[68] The essay is entitled "The Moral Philosopher and the Moral Life," first published in Ethics (1891) and reprinted in James, The Will to Believe and Other Essays in Popular Philosophy (1896), 184–215. (This volume is cited below as "The Will.")

[69] The Will, 214.

mood," [70] the heroic mood which makes us indifferent to present suffering if only some greater ideal is attained. These basic assumptions will circumscribe his affirmative ethical position.

As to the psychological origin of moral beliefs, he rejects the view of the intuitionist that they originate wholly in the "conscience," as well as the dogma of the evolutionist (or social scientist) that they originate solely in the teaching of the environment. The pain-pleasure principle (§ 4.41) will explain many of our cherished beliefs, but not all; as a psychologist he must recognize that some human moral beliefs are "brain-born," they fly in the teeth of the conclusions given by utility or habit.[71] To this extent the intuitionists are right. In any event good and evil can exist, can be found, only in a world of sentient human beings. Here he brings forth his first moral principle: There can be no obligation without a claim made by some concrete person; and every claim gives rise to some obligation. His argument for this principle is:

"Take any demand, however slight, which any creature, however weak, may make. Ought it not, for its own sole sake, to be satisfied? If not, prove why not. The only possible kind of proof you could adduce would be the exhibition of another creature who should make a demand that ran the other way. The only possible reason there can be why any phenomenon ought to exist is that such a phenomenon actually is desired." [72]

This basic principle exemplifies ethical relativism (§ 4.50) since one person's claim is to be judged in relation to others. The argument ("any [human] creature, however weak") suggests Christian ethics; yet it is consistent with that secular democratic individualism which, according to Professor Wiener, is a part of the legacy of pragmatism.[73]

Why does every person's claim import *some* obligation? Why does a Hitler's claim to conquer and despoil an innocent weaker nation such as Czechoslovakia import *any* (moral) obligation on any one? Only because every member of the human race has a right to have his claim heard and examined, even though it is immediately rejected because of the conflicting claims of others.

---

70 Ibid., 215. That is, religious belief furnishes emotional inspiration.

71 Ibid., 185.

72 Ibid., 194.

73 Wiener, op. cit. (supra, § 4.50, n. 7) 202 ff.

This is a kind of "due process of law" conception of moral judgments, yet one can see no other sense in which James' first principle is ethically valid.[74] Finally, *upon whom* does this obligation rest? Does the claim of a Borneo child for his daily rice, of which I have no knowledge except a bare surmise, impose any obligation on *me*? If so, is it cancelled out by my claim to have time to write a book on jurisprudence, which I cannot do if I must keep busy satisfying all of these other claims? James' theory of the primacy of *claims,* like the Stoic theory of universal rights (§ 4.12), leaves one unsatisfied as to who is supposed to take on the corresponding duties.

Upon what principle are these conflicting claims to be judged, satisfied or rejected? In an ideal world, says James, all claims could be satisfied, all conflicts eliminated. Do Tom and Dick both want to marry Bianca? Then a duplicate Bianca would immediately be created so that both claims could be satisfied. (Of course we should have to consult the claims of the two Biancas, and matters would grow complicated for even an idealist ethical philosopher.) Since the world we have to live in is a limited world, the ethical philosopher must be prepared to sacrifice some of *his* claims, even some part of his own cherished ideals. The second principle, which we may call "the principle of scarcity," is stated thus:

> "Since everything which is demanded is by that fact a good, must not the guiding principle for ethical philosophy (since all demands conjointly cannot be satisfied in this poor world) be simply to satisfy at all times *as many demands as we can?* That act must be the best act, accordingly, which makes for the *best whole,* in the sense of awakening the least sum of dissatisfactions. In the casuistic scale, therefore, those ideals must be written highest which *prevail at the least cost,* or by whose realization the least possible number of other ideals are destroyed." [75]

This second principle partly answers some of the questions raised by the first. The ethical philosopher is to be a kind of legislator or judge, approving some claims, cutting down others, rejecting others, arousing the least sum of dissatisfactions. Does this mean just *immediate* dissatisfactions or are remote ones to be considered? The reference to "ideals" indicates that he included ideal

---

[74] James uses "true" in reference to an ethical principle, where I would use only "valid" or "right."

[75] The Will, 204; Hall, p. 237.

values, such as the knowledge of future generations, as well as present material ones. So, for example, in budgeting for this poor world of scarcity, the ethical philosopher might well allow some funds for finding the remains of primitive man even though this would mean denying an increased allowance for the relief of the poor. Pound's theory of social interests (§ 4.61) shows how James' second principle can be developed for legal evaluations.

But what will make the best whole, arouse the least dissatisfactions and satisfy the most demands? James used no felicific calculus, as Bentham did. He falls back upon the belief in evolution, not the survival of the fittest in a biological sense but the survival of the fittest in the realm of ideas. For ideas must compete with each other in the "market place." Hence tolerance of all claims (at least initially), freedom of discussion and freedom of speech are of the essence of James' social ethics.[76] Whatever survives the scrutiny of reasonable men (of good will, Kant would say) has as good a claim to being right or just as anything can have on this earth. Hence the ethical philosopher must recognize the value of social experiments. One can see here the meaning and scope of the "liberalism" in O. W. Holmes' dissents. Still, the differences of James' day were not as abysmal as those which separate a twentieth century despotism from a slightly confused benevolent democracy; and some "social experiments" can be reversed only at a terrific cost to innocent bystanders. Besides, the ethical philosopher, in a world of scarcity of time and energy, cannot experiment over every ethical problem that arises. For several reasons "the presumption in case of conflict must always be in favor of the conventionally recognized good." [77] This is equivalent to the evolutionary conception of history mentioned above (§ 4.30). Custom, said James, not only enables us to pass fluently from a thing to another related one and thus creates a sentiment of rationality; it also satisfies expectancy. It is a mental sedative, whereas novelty is a mental irritant. The utility for the survival of the animal of this emotional effect of novelty leads to the conclusion that novelty *ought* to irritate the creature.[78] Yet the customs of today cannot be final:

---

[76] James' emphasis on freedom is brought out by his former pupil and follower, Professor Horace M. Kallen, in his essay "John Dewey and the Spirit of Pragmatism," in John Dewey: Philosopher of Science and Freedom (Hook ed., 1950) 3 ff.

[77] The Will, 204.

[78] Selected Papers, 137-138 ("The Sentiment of Rationality").

". . . as our present laws and customs have fought and conquered past ones, so they will in their turn be overthrown by any newly discovered order which will hush up the complaints that they still give rise to, without producing others louder still." [79]

So James takes account of the customary or conventional as sometimes a mental sedative and sometimes a moral irritant.

James' philosophy changed as he grew older, and his style became more radical than his ideas. His ethical theory took a good deal for granted: That individuals have decent ideals and respectable habits and that a society's customs are the survivors in a competition which has been on the whole rationally selective. The good is only a prima facie candidate for the best. The best, in this poor world, is a compromise, of claims and ideals, to be determined by the free discussion of reasonable men. This resembles the method of ascertaining "true" theory in modern science, yet the differences are profound.

§ 4.53—John Dewey: Instrumental Reasoning

The philosophy of John Dewey has far-ranging significance and has gained followers in many walks of life. For legal philosophy its chief importance is his instrumental logic and his empirical theory of valuation, or "scientific ethics." Along with these are several facets of his political and social philosophy which reflect upon law.

John Dewey (1859–1952) celebrated his ninetieth birthday in 1949, in the presence of nearly a thousand devoted admirers. Born and reared in Vermont, his literary style has some of the laconic tautness that marks the speech of its inhabitants. He was not one of the "founders" of pragmatism, yet through his profound influence on American public school education and its teachers he has probably done more than any of the founders to make it the typically American way of thinking. He taught philosophy at Hopkins, Michigan, Chicago, and finally at Columbia, where he formally retired in 1930. He became interested in education while at Chicago. His efforts to reduce the rote-learning in primary and secondary education and to adapt the curriculum and teaching methods to the needs and limitations of mass education helped to make it possible to enforce compulsory attendance laws with a minimum of violations. He was at

---

[79] The Will, 204.

one period a follower of Hegel, and even after he was attracted to pragmatism by James' treatise on psychology [80] he retained a good deal of implicit Hegelianism. He explained some of James' exaggerations and made pragmatism a more orderly philosophy than James had done. James believed that reason cannot control an impulse except by finding another impulse to counteract it.[81] Dewey believed that reason and feeling were equally basic in human conduct:

> "In truth, feeling as well as reason springs up with action." [82]

James' pragmatism provided more support than Dewey's ever did for the view that judicial decisions are the result of hunches and that the opinions written by judges are *mere* rationalizations of decisions arrived at on other grounds (§§ 3.31, 5.06). James placed a higher value on freedom and Dewey on order.[83]

1. *Instrumental Reasoning.* Dewey's instrumental logic is an account of how one *should* proceed in arriving at important decisions, in order to attain the best results. It is not an account of how human beings necessarily or even customarily act. Sometimes they act with a minimum of foresight, without examination of what they are doing and its probable consequences. They act from habit, from appetite, or from a blind hunch. This is the method of intuition or of instinct. In many situations it is good. The offhand appraisal of an expert may be better than the elaborate calculations of a duffer. Yet the unreflective intuitive action may also be arbitrary, capricious, careless. The other type of action follows from a decision which is the result of inquiry, comparison of alternatives, weighing of facts. This decision is *reasoned*. Dewey's basic proposition is that logic is the theory of the procedures followed in reaching reasoned decisions in those cases in which subsequent experience shows that they were the best procedures that could have been used under the conditions. And how can experience show the best pro-

---

[80] For the record, Dewey showed definite traits of ethical pragmatism before he had read James. See Mead, "The Philosophies of Royce, James and Dewey in Their American Setting," in John Dewey: The Man and his Philosophy (1930), 99–100.

[81] Wiener, Evolution and the Founders of Pragmatism (1949), 111.

[82] Dewey, Human Nature and Conduct (1922), 76.

[83] See Kallen, supra, § 4.52, n. 76; Perry, Characteristically American (1949) 51: ". . . whereas James stressed the force of the will by which obstacles are overcome, Dewey stresses the intelligence by which they are circumvented."

cedures? By the consequences. So instrumental logic is a logic relative to consequences rather than to antecedents.[84]

Of this general statement it may be said that Dewey's use of the term "logic" to designate the norms of a reasoning process has shocked some professors of philosophy who are accustomed to conceive of the subject matter of logic as the formal relations between propositions [85] and not thought-processes. However, usage had not been uniform. In the second place, Dewey's conception of logic here was normative or prescriptive, though it was stated in descriptive terms. Thirdly, his logical theory starts from his metaphysical assumption that the most important kind of reality is the act and especially the problematic act, as distinct from one that proceeds from routine or instinct. This characteristic contribution of pragmatism (§ 4.50) was congenial to the thoughtways of law teachers, judges and other lawyers during the 1920's. The liberals were pleased by a theory that served to explain the fallibility of the Supreme Court's 5-to-4 decisions (invalidating social reform legislation) and even conservative lawyers, puzzled by the frequency with which their predictions of appellate decisions went wrong, were receptive to a rational explanation of how judges think.

The logic of the syllogism, said Dewey, sets forth the *results* of thinking but it has nothing to do with the *operation* of thinking. "As a matter of fact," he says, "men do not begin thinking with premises", but rather with a "complicated and confused case, . . . admitting of alternative modes of treatment and solution." Premises, he continues, gradually "emerge" from analysis of the total situation.

> "The problem is to *find* statements, of general principle and of particular fact, that are worthy to serve as premises." [86]

The beginning of the thought-process is an indeterminate existential situation, and the end, if the process be carried through properly, is a modified existential situation, one that has been transformed by the process of inquiry.[87] One can understand

---

[84] See Dewey, "Logical Method and Law," (1924) 10 Cornell L. Q. 17–18, 25; Hall, pp. 343–44, 353.

[85] See Eaton, Logic (1931) 8; supra, § 1.11; Patterson, Logic in the Law, (1942) 90 U. of Pa.L.Rev. 875, 876.

[86] Op.cit. supra, n. 84, 20; Hall, p. 349.

[87] Dewey, Logic: The Theory of Inquiry (1938), 118; and see his defense of this conception in Problems of Men (1946), 322 ff.

bridge-building as such a transformation of one existential situation (a river, its banks, steel mills, bridge workers, etc.) into another (the completed bridge). One is inclined to think of the outcome of legal inquiry and reasoning as being a merely *mental* transformation, the ideational classification of stated facts and their arrangement in a "new" mental pattern. A certain exchange of correspondence between parties to litigation is presented to a judge; he decides that it does not constitute a "contract," and writes an opinion giving his reasons.[88] It appears that what the judge has done is to classify something in his own mind as being, for instance, "acceptance" or not. Dewey would point out, however, that the decision (motion granted) is publicly recorded and that it terminates the litigation unless other steps are taken; that the opinion becomes public; and thus the terminal and determinate situation is existential. Premises are tools to be used in the transformation of an indeterminate existential situation: They are "instrumental."

Now he does not deny the usefulness of the rules of formal logic. On the contrary he would have the human mind create out of a puzzling universe as much of the framework of a formal-logical order as the limitations of brute existence will permit. Again, Dewey's emphasis on consequences *rather than* antecedents does not mean that antecedent knowledge is to be ignored, that the reasoner is to begin with only the raw sensations of an existential situation, from which by profound cogitation premises will somehow "emerge." He denies immediate knowledge, either of raw sensations (empiricism) or ultimate universal principles (rationalism). Knowledge, i. e., that which we are warranted in asserting, always involves mediation, i. e., an inferential function.[89] Dewey's "public" conception of knowledge, as something that we are warranted in asserting (with respect to existence) is apt for judicial trials where most of the proof consists of human utterances, oral or written; and the unsymbolized data (demeanor of witnesses as evidence of credibility) are used inferentially. Thirdly, Dewey does not suppose that a lawyer or judge is going to construct a new legal code for every problematic situation.

Dewey's account of (good) legal reasoning has the simplicity of his earlier account of reasoning in ordinary affairs, as set forth in his widely read and influential little book, How We

---

[88] E. g., the case of U. S. v. Braunstein, 75 F.Supp. 137 (D.C.N.Y.1947).

[89] Logic, 139 ff.

Think.[90] In legal reasoning the existence of a body of concepts and generalizations having the characteristics of a special linguistic system (§ 3.21) differentiates it from commonsense reasoning. Now the man who first sees the legal problem in a confused and complicated situation untainted by legal coloring matter (if possible) is the counselor who first hears the story of the client and witnesses, rather than the judge, who is acquainted with them only after they are to some extent processed (selected, characterized and presented in sequence) by the legal reasoning of counsel (§ 3.01). In the early English common law the counsellor was required to state his client's claim in a prescribed formula, and the defense counsel was limited to a single issue. This kind of procedure made the judge's problematic situation much narrower than the total situation of the client's claim, and thus exaggerated the consequences of counselor's mistakes in choosing the incorrect formula; e. g., of plaintiff's counsel in choosing to commence an action of trespass instead of trover. The object and effect of successive pleading reforms ("fact" pleading and now "claim" pleading) has been to minimize the harm of counsel's mistakes in legally characterizing his client's claim and its factual situation, and to bring the judge closer to the "raw facts" (i. e., the layman-processed facts) that came in the office door. These procedural changes and others have imposed greater responsibilities on the judges, both trial and appellate, and increased their opportunities for doing justice in the individual case.[91] Still neither the trial judge nor the appellate court is an inquisitor; it is dependent on the "facts" presented to it by counsel.[92] The judicial process is limited by the scope of the judicial function.

Dewey spoke of premises as "statements of general principle and particular fact," [93] thus recognizing, somewhat indefinitely, the correspondence of legal rule and proven fact to the major and minor premise, respectively, of the syllogism. Such a correspondence has long been recognized in the analysis of pleadings; the claimant's pleadings were expected to set forth the

---

[90] Published in 1910; revised edition, 1933.

[91] See Clark (Judge Charles E.), "The Dilemma of American Judges: Is Too Great 'Trust for Salvation' Placed in Them?", (1949) 35 A.B.A.J. 8.

[92] This was well brought out by the majority opinion in the second-electrocution case. Louisiana ex rel. Francis v. Resweber, 329 U.S. 459, 67 Sup.Ct. 374 (1947).

[93] Supra, n. 86.

propositions of fact which provide an adequate minor premise for some legal (major) premise that is left implicit, i. e., is not stated in the written pleadings. Dewey's account of legal reasoning explains the "uncertainty" as to what rule will be applied to proved facts; it does not go into the other uncertainty of the judicial process in trial courts, the process of fact-finding.[94] He was, of course, aware of the intricacy of a judicial trial, and of the inferences of fact called for at various temporal stages. The final (legal) judgment of a court is the outcome of a series of intermediate (logical) judgments.[95]

The imagined experimentation with alternative or multernative premises and their consequences, which gave the theory its earlier name, "experimental logic," [96] is the crux of the method. It is a kind of dialectic which the inquirer carries on with himself, except that he does not look for just two opposites or contradictories (as in Hegelian logic) but rather for alternatives. When a doubtful fact or a missing fact stops the dialectic, a further factual inquiry is called for. The counselor tries to ascertain and prove the fact. The judge can only await further proof by counsel, draw inferences of fact or apply legal rules as to burden of proof. In many situations the lawyer and the judge will find the interplay of rule and proof, particular fact and legal concept, an ongoing process: First the testimony, then the cases and statutes, then another search of the record in the light of both, is a common pattern of legal thinking. Now one may ask, what *are* the consequences that the pragmatist would have the inquirer consider in his imagined experimentation and weighing of alternatives? The answer has been partly given in discussing James' notion of expediency.[97] The counselor would consider one set of consequences (to his client), the advocate another, the judge still others. The first consequence to be considered by the latter is the correspondence or non-correspondence of the proved facts to the legal meanings of proposed norms.[98] It is necessary to repeat here, pragmatism does not

---

[94] Which is the leit-motif of Frank, Courts on Trial (1949).

[95] Logic, 120–122.

[96] See Dewey, Essays in Experimental Logic (1903).

[97] Supra, § 4.52, pp. 478–480.

[98] Logic, 120–122. In two essays I discussed Dewey's theory of legal reasoning: One in The Philosopher of the Common Man (1940), 172 ff.; the other in John Dewey: Philosopher of Science and Freedom (1950), 118 ff., also published as "John Dewey and the Law," (1950) 36 A.B.A.J. 619.

mean that the proved facts should be distorted to attain consequences deemed for the moment expedient. Beyond this, within the limits of choice of the tribunal, the consequences within the legal system (in upsetting expectations), in government and in society, of the selection of one law-fact combination rather than another, would be quite relevant.

The building of law into a logical system with a view to the utmost consistency and generality of propositions is indispensable yet it is not ultimate; it is an instrumentality for improving, facilitating and clarifying the inquiry that leads to concrete decisions.

> "It is most important that rules of law should form as coherent logical systems as possible. But these logical systematizations of law in any field, whether of crime, contracts or torts, with their reduction of a multitude of decisions to a few general principles that are logically consistent with one another while it may be an end in itself for a particular student, is clearly in last resort subservient to the economical and effective reaching of decisions in particular cases." [99]

The logical process in law over a considerable period, says Dewey, is the same as in other fields: Some methods are found not to work well in subsequent cases, and are discarded. There is a kind of "natural selection of the methods which afford the best type of conclusion." [1] This is another instance of an evolutionary interpretation of history (§ 4.30). It also resembles Pound's conception of judicial empiricism. In *this* meaning of logic, O. W. Holmes could find no antitheses between logic and experience.[2]

Courts not only reach decisions: They often state the justifying reasons in their opinions. Dewey never accepted the view that the opinion of the court is a mere rationalization of a conclusion arrived at by some occult, Freudian or other non-rational process. He distinguished the logic of search and inquiry, wherein the conclusion is problematic, from the logic of exposition, which implies that a definite decision has been reached and

---

[99] Op.cit. supra, n. 84, 20; Hall, pp. 345–46.

[1] Ibid.; Hall, p. 346.

[2] Ibid. The Holmes quotation is given supra, § 4.50, n. 5. Dewey's conception of experience was said, by one of his pupils, to be "all that the anthropologist includes as belonging to human culture." Randall, "John Dewey, 1859–1952" (1953) 50 Jour. of Philosophy 5, 10.

seeks to justify it and to indicate a rule for dealing with similar cases in the future. Indeed, if men had not had to account to others for their decisions, conceivably logical operations would never have developed.[3] Why do judicial opinions often assume a mechanical, abstract didactic form? Because the personal element cannot be wholly excluded, judges tend to make the opinion as impersonal and rational as possible; and the social need for certainty and stability in judicial decisions likewise calls for emphasis on logical connections. Dewey had more concern for the routine case than had James,[4] who was fascinated by the heroic and the enigmatic. In this difference one can see Dewey as the philosopher of the goal of order rather than of freedom to invent.

Dewey's faith in logic as an instrument of orderly control was made explicit in his treatise on logic:

"An operation not formulated in a proposition is logically uncontrolled, no matter how useful it may be in habitual practice." [5]

By "operation" is meant a logical step, a portion of the process of transformation of an existential situation. He is talking about the formulation of *operational* rules or principles, the kind that are used in control of operations. So it could be true under this analysis that a court might utter a proposition as an explanation of its decision and yet that proposition had nothing to do with the mental process by which the decision was reached. Two types of cases may occur. One may suppose that the judge or judges (or a majority of them) were led to the decision by one value-generalization ("labor unions should be curbed") and justified by another ("every employer has a constitutional right to choose his employees.") The early twentieth century liberals suspected that this was what happened in a good many Supreme Court decisions on constitutional law.[6] Dewey would merely

---

3 Ibid., 21–22; Hall, pp. 350–351.

4 See quotation supra, § 4.52, n. 64.

5 Logic, 274; supra, § 2.12.

6 E. g., a Kansas statute which imposed a penalty upon an employer who discharged an employee because he had joined a labor union was held to be unconstitutional on the ground that it violated the liberty of the employer. Coppage v. Kansas, 236 U.S. 1, 35 Sup.Ct. 240 (1914). Holmes, J., dissented, on the ground that the legislature could reasonably believe that only by belonging to a labor union can the employee obtain a contract that is fair to him. Ibid., 26 ff.

say that the judge might better control his bias or prejudice if he were to formulate for himself the most persuasive or moving ("real") reasons for his decision. However, it seems unlikely that the reasons given in these opinions were *wholly* unrelated to the mental processes of the judges in reaching the decision. In the second type of case, one may suppose that a trial judge in the course of a trial quickly sustains an objection to the offer of certain evidence, not formulating in his mind any rule or "proposition" by which the operation is controlled. Later, on a motion for a new trial, he files an opinion setting forth the "reasons" for his ruling. Now it may well have been that some of these reasons were latent in his trained intuition, which enabled him to use previously learned generalizations without explicit formulation. Dewey's theory of inquiry supports this view:

> "A map is no less a means of directing journeys because it is not constantly in use." [7]

Only in the first type of case, if at all, could one say that the reason publicly given was a "rationalization."

In his little book for teachers, Dewey stressed the fundamental importance of conceptions, as standard meanings, and said that they are instruments (i) of identification, (ii) of supplementation and (iii) of placing in a system.[8] Suppose that a writing is presented to a court as a last will and testament: By the standard meaning of this legal concept one can identify the instrument as being a case of a "will." Thereupon supplementation may take place: A will has the legal characteristics of being revocable and hence this instrument may have been superseded by a later expression of deceased's will. Finally, the "will" is a type of "transaction," a class which are rendered voidable by fraud or coercion. The concept is a part of a larger system.

§ 4.54—John Dewey: Scientific Ethics

Dewey's ethical and political theories have never been far apart because he views ethics as the systematic account of judgments of moral conduct; moral conceptions and processes grow naturally out of the conditions of human life; and men live nat-

---

[7] Logic, 136.

[8] Dewey, How We Think (1910), 126. For a more profound account of legal system and the "essences" of juridical institutions, see Dewey, Experience and Nature (1926), 197–200.

urally and inevitably in society. The basic conceptions of morals —good, right, duty, virtue, etc.—constitute the *formal* side, while the study of the moral aspects of social problems constitutes the *material* side.[9] The individual, however, is still the ultimate end of society and its institutions; not just the individual's wants or needs (which are basic causes of moral problems) but rather his opportunity to satisfy them by his own efforts:

"Social conditions should be such that all individuals can exercise their initiative in a social medium which will develop their personal capacities and reward their efforts." [10]

This statement of the end of the good society seems to avoid the weaknesses of Bentham's "greatest good of the greatest number" and of Stammler's principles of participation and respect, and resembles Dabin's neo-scholastic conception of the public common good.[11] His books on social psychology [12] and on political theory [13] contain frequent comments on law in relation to ethics and the institutions of government.

Professor Dewey's most important contribution to ethical theory is his controversial view that valuation can be an empirical process, that ethics can be "scientific." [14] As his analysis is tautly constructed with exact terminology and with almost no illustrations, and as the present work is concerned only with the bearing of Dewey's theory upon legal evaluations (legal axiology), a summary of the principal points will be presented, in their bearing on legal philosophy, on law and the legal order. The general nature of the problem, let it be recalled, is the one felt by Judge Cardozo when the cry escaped him, "They do this thing better with logarithms." [15]

---

[9] Dewey and Tufts, Ethics (rev. ed., 1932) 3, 343, 347. "At the present time, almost all important ethical problems arise out of associated life." Ibid., 352.

[10] Ibid., 276.

[11] Dabin, General Theory of Law, No. 136, in The Legal Philosophies of Lask, Radbruch and Dabin (Wilk trans., 1950) 355; supra, § 4.14.

[12] See Logical Conditions of a Scientific Treatment of Morality (1903), reprinted in Problems of Men (1946) 211–249 (cited below as "Problems"); Human Nature and Conduct (1922).

[13] The Public and Its Problems (1927); Freedom and Culture (1939).

[14] "Theory of Valuation" in International Encyclopedia of Unified Sciences (1939) (cited below as "Valuation").

[15] Supra, § 1.26, n. 31.

(1) *Logical Uniformity of Scientific and Moral Judgments.*
Scientific statements are hypothetical universals that depend upon individual judgments for their origin and that have their function only as instruments for other individual judgments. This is,
of course, the pragmatic problematicism and probabilism (§ 4.50)
which serves to characterize the meanings of scientific statements. Professor Dewey has remarked that only a certain type
of (ignorant) literary person believes in the infallibility of (physical) science. For Dewey "science has its life in judgments of
identification," [16] that is, in judgments (e. g., *this* is a glacial deposit) for which scientific statements are instruments. Moral
judgments are likewise capable of control through logical universals, which are derived from prior individual experiences.
To deny this, says Dewey, is to deny the "continuity of moral experience," [17] and thus to say *either* that moral judgments express merely isolated momentary likings [18] *or* that they depend
upon transcendental conceptions, religious or otherwise. Dewey
rejects these alternatives and thus finds an empirical base for
moral judgments in moral experience. The argument is persuasive though not demonstrative.

(2) *Scientific (Physical) Judgments Exclude the Attitude of
the Judger; Moral Judgments do Not.* This is a recognition of
an important difference, and should serve to show that Dewey's
ethical theory is not "materialistic" in the sense that it *identifies*
moral judgments with scientific judgments. The statement of
scientific universals *excludes all reference* to the attitude of
the judger; yet the attitude of the judger is a fact, both in the
formation of the universal and the singular judgment to which
it leads.[19] In cases of moral judgment, the identification of the
singular as a case of the universal ("that is wrong") is consciously dependent on the attitude or disposition of the judger.[20]
At this place one may note what Dewey has pointed out elsewhere, that judicial decisions inevitably involve a personal element, hence the effort to make the reasons given appear as impersonal as possible (§ 4.53). The conclusion drawn from this
difference is that since the character or disposition of the judg-

---

16 Problems, 247 (1903).

17 Ibid., 213.

18 See his comment on Russell, ibid., 178.

19 Ibid., 228.

20 Ibid., 230.

er entered into every moral judgment, the ability to control such judgments depends upon our power to state character in terms of generic relations of conditions, conditions detachable from the pressure of circumstance in the particular case. The means is psychological analysis.[21] Now this theory, useful though it is in education, seems to have only limited usefulness in law. One can predict (prediction is a kind of control) that *because* a certain judge (or any judge) is a member of a certain church he will *probably* be influenced to deny divorces, and hence the plaintiff's attorney in a divorce case should avoid a trial before such a judge, if possible. The proportion of litigated cases in which such a disposition, of a judge to decide a particular way, can be generalized,[22] does not seem to be very large. The method does not, it seems, give any answer to the question, on what grounds should divorces be granted at all?

Such a question relates to the *content* of a moral judgment, in abstraction from its bearings upon a singular action; this depends upon the development of an ethical science which will be primarily social.[23] Although more than four decades have elapsed since that theory was published, not much progress has been made in developing a "science" of psychological analysis of the character of jud*gers* (or jud*ges*) or of social-ethical relations. Yet the interest, among legal scholars and law teachers, in the relevance of facts to value-judgments has steadily increased, and has produced useful results.

(3) *Meaning of "Scientific."* By "scientific" in this context Dewey means "methods of control of formation of judgments." [24] This is, it seems, an attenuation of the conception of (physical) science. A "science" of palmistry may provide a method of control over the judgments ("You have a long heart-line and will meet a tall, dark man") of palm-readers, yet neither the propositions nor the judgments have reliability.[25] Later Dewey agreed that the "objectivity" of evaluative judgments resides in "the publicly observable conditions and consequences of value-

---

[21] Problems, 237. As the context shows, he did not mean "psychoanalysis," the Freudian term.

[22] I. e., as distinct from the lawyer's knowledge of the peculiarities of a particular judge, his pet peeves and sentimentalities, etc.

[23] Problems, 241–245 (1903).

[24] Ibid., 247 (1903).

[25] The palmistry example is, of course, not a fair application of Dewey's logical theory, which requires an existential transformation.

experiences." [26] Legal evaluations, it seems, generally satisfy this requirement.

(4) *Value-Propositions and Propositions-About-Valuations.*[27] Propositions of value are "lying is wrong" or "a written offer is irrevocable if it so states;" propositions-about-valuations are, it seems, such as these: "Kant *said* all lying is wrong; " "the State of New York *has enacted* that a written offer," etc. In the usual discourse of judicial opinion and legal treatise these two are often fused. The importance of maintaining the distinction is that one needs to know by whom and under what conditions a valuation has been made, not merely because the personal authority of the judg*er* is persuasive (§ 2.30) but also because the meaning of the stated value-proposition is thus affected. The Anglo-American case-law system provides a good deal of information about the conditions of making particular evaluations, and these give meaning to the valuation-propositions [27a] stated or inferred from the cases.

(5) *Standardized Ends.* Standardized ends provide more or less blank frameworks within which definite ends must fall.[28] This is a recognition of the role of such ends as "health," "knowledge," "happiness" or "human perfection" in the determination of evaluations: They are not just slogans, yet they have no meaning content from which a particular end can be definitely evoked.

(6) *Valuation-Propositions Empirically Grounded.* Dewey's statement that valuation-propositions must be grounded in physical generalizations,[29] that is, upon temporal and causal relations, is one that is easier to accept than to interpret. First, some men have often urged that *their* valuation-propositions were of mystical or transcendental origin and *need not* be grounded on physical generalizations. Hence Dewey's statement is normative; it tells how valuation-propositions *ought* to be grounded. Secondly, in what way are valuation-propositions grounded in physical generalizations? In the sense that prior valuation-experience is temporal and causal, the statement seems correct. For instance, many customs probably originated in the making of arbitral or

---

[26] Ibid., 253 (1943).

[27] Valuation (supra, n. 14), 19–20.

[27a] The term "valuation-proposition" is used as synonymous with "value-propositions".

[28] Ibid., 45.

[29] Ibid., 53, 57.

judicial decisions in particular cases,[30] that is, in temporal and causal events. In what way were such decisions causal? In that subsequent experience showed them to have been satisfactory, just, good. Yet this is not all that Dewey means.

Every valuation-proposition ought to be grounded in physical generalizations in the sense that it can be justified logically only as a means to an end, i. e., a means by which an existential situation is transformed so that it conforms with a given end; and the control of the means to attain the end depends upon physical generalizations. "Reckless driving" of an automobile is such driving as will create exceptional danger of physical harm to the driver and to others. "Lying is wrong" is grounded (in part) on generalizations as to the physical consequences of an utterance upon the overt conduct of others. In this sense a statement such as "every one should live according to nature" seems not to be a valuation-proposition, because it is too vague in meaning to point to any physical generalization as justification or consequence.

But the difference between scientific propositions (as physical generalizations) and valuation-propositions remains: The end to be attained (or avoided) is not *given* in the existential situation. Only in so far as people can *agree* upon ends (avoidance of physical suffering, avoidance of deception, etc.) can rules of conduct be made acceptable by proving facts. Dewey knows quite well that an "Ought" proposition cannot be formally derived from "Is" propositions alone. His ethical or evaluative theory does not show us any way to persuade every one that a given valuation-proposition is wrong, merely by producing physical facts.

When Einstein's theory implying that light was bent by gravitational pulls was denied by some astronomers, several crucial observations during eclipses settled the question *among astronomers* and the rest of us accept the conclusion on authority. More recently the Soviet theory of Lysenko (Michurin) that acquired characteristics are inherited (in plants) has been shown erroneous by the overwhelming weight of experimental evidence of English and American biologists. The Russians claim that it is supported by certain experiments which, however, they refuse to submit to scientific scrutiny. For instance, the reliability of the experiment depends on the purity of the original strain

---

[30] Supra, § 3.15, n. 94; Allen, Law in the Making (1939), 115–117.

(scion).[31] So even the physical generalizations of natural science cannot be proved true to those who refuse to accept a rational mode of testing truth. Can it be said, then, that given a rational-empirical mode of testing value, one can prove a valuation-proposition, such as: "Political dictation of scientific propositions to scientists is bad."? With some qualifications, yes. That is, assuming that the relation of means to ends becomes capable of empirical proof, as in highway safety, factory safety and public health legislation. That is why the facts developed by legislative committees are often quite persuasive.

One critic has argued that Dewey's theory applies only to *instrumental*, not to *intrinsic*, values.[32] Professor Dewey's argument is that even ultimate values (i e., subjective valuations) are not necessarily, by their being value-facts, impervious to rational argument, but that the belief that they are is (or at least, may be) only a socio-cultural belief, which may thus be changed.[33] By education in a given society, it would seem, one could produce an attitude of willingness to submit one's innermost preferences to rational scrutiny and empirical testing. An empirical theory of valuation thus rests upon a common cultural framework. In this conclusion is a warning and a hope: A warning that societies of diverse socio-cultural strains should not be hastily forced into a tight legal bond; and a hope that in another ten thousand years these differences may have been reduced or eliminated.

§ 4.55—O. W. Holmes: Pragmatist, Liberal, Realist

The legal philosophy of Justice Oliver Wendell Holmes, Jr., could better be told biographically than formulated analytically. Several biographies have been written and more will come.[34] He

---

31 See Huxley (Julian), Heredity East and West (1949) c. 3, esp. p. 68: "The Michurinites [Lysenko followers] do not carry on discussion in a scientific manner."

32 Pap, "The Verifiability of Value Judgments," (1946) 56 Ethics 178, 180.

33 In Problems of Men, 289 (first published 1944) he *suggests* that it *may* be socio-cultural.

34 Catherine Drinker Bowen's Yankee From Olympus (1945) (cited below as "Bowen"), an absorbing story constructed with imaginative skill, is the best all-around. Max Lerner's The Mind and Faith of Justice Holmes (1943) is a selection of Holmes' writings, with a short biography and valuable comments (cited below as "Lerner"). Other biographies are by Bent (1937) and Biddle (1942). The "authorized" biography by Professor Mark De Wolfe Howe (Harvard) is in course of preparation.

spoke of one collection of his essays and addresses as "little fragments of my fleece that I have left upon the hedges of life." [35] He left an unassembled philosophy of law as his legacy to posterity. It was not a sytematic or integrated philosophy; not only does it lack the apparatus of definitions and postulates of the professional philosopher but also it contains unresolved paradoxes which are deeper than semantic difficulties. He wrote only one complete book,[36] yet his speeches, judicial opinions and letters [37] make up a formidable volume of provocative literature. He is best known for his views on American Constitutional law,[38] a subject which cannot be explored here. His place in contemporaneous American legal philosophy can be shown by outlining, after a brief sketch of his life, the origins of his thinking in pragmatism and its effects in twentieth century liberalism and American legal realism.

Oliver Wendell Holmes, Jr. (1841–1935), descendant of cultivated New England patricians, son of a famous author and lecturer whom he twitted with delight, was educated at Harvard College, voluntarily enlisted in the Massachusetts Militia, was thrice wounded in the Civil War and came home a captain.[39] Perhaps his war experiences seared his soul with those beliefs in the physical power of law, and in the ruthlessness of the struggle for survival which sometimes appeared in his discussions of law; yet the cause lay rather in Holmes than in his experiences. Enticed by philosophy, he chose, or was pushed into,[40] the law. After graduation from the Harvard Law School he joined a Boston law firm. Friendship with "Bill" James blossomed about this

---

[35] Holmes, Collected Legal Papers (1920), Preface. (This volume is cited below as "C.L.P.")

[36] Holmes, The Common Law (1881).

[37] Holmes-Pollock Letters (Howe ed., 1941), 2 vols.; Justice Holmes to Dr. Wu (no date); letters to the late Professor Morris R. Cohen, "The Holmes-Cohen Correspondence" (F. S. Cohen ed.), (1948) 9 Jour.Hist.Ideas 14; also letters to William James in Perry, The Thought and Character of William James (1935).

[38] See Frankfurter, "Mr. Justice Holmes and the Constitution," in Mr. Justice Holmes (by Cardozo and others, 1931), 46 ff.

[39] He was mustered out in 1864 as a brevet lieutenant-colonel. Bowen, 203.

[40] So he said at ninety or later: "I was rather shoved than went into the law when I hankered for philosophy. I am glad now and even then I had a guess that perhaps one got more from philosophy on the quarter than dead astern." Frankfurter, in Dictionary of American Biography XXI, Supp. 1 (N.Y., 1944), 419.

time; philosophy and legal scholarship absorbed more of his interest than client care-taking. As the editor of a new edition of Kent's Commentaries, completed in 1873, Holmes had the invaluable experience of making a survey of American Law. During the seventies he joined in discussions with Peirce, James, Wright and others, a group which Peirce, the founder of pragmatism, afterward designated as the "Metaphysical Club." [41] For ten years Holmes worked on his book, The Common Law, which he read as the Lowell Lectures for 1880–81. Then came the law professorship at Harvard, September (1882), which he relinquished all too soon (December, 1882) for an appointment to the Supreme Judicial Court of Massachusetts. His judicial opinions on this court, most of them in the fields of private law, were learned and incisive; some of them are still landmarks on crucial issues. His views on public questions were of more concern to President Theodore Roosevelt who, after cautious inquiry, appointed Holmes in 1902 an Associate Justice of the Supreme Court of the United States. Here he became the Great Dissenter. He retired from the Court in 1932 and died in 1935.

Holmes' literary style was matched, among modern legal authors, only by Maitland's; he had a gift for apt metaphor which Cardozo nearly matched (but used with less restraint), and a clarity of expression excelled only, in this country, by Judge Learned Hand. Holmes turned out aphorisms that illumined, persuaded and yet conveyed meaning. "The life of the law has not been logic: It has been experience." Here he wished to emphasize the following sentences, in which he set forth his view that public opinion, custom and even judicial prejudices have helped greatly to shape the law. [42] Doubtless Holmes, working at his high desk, enjoyed the sheer artistry of creating these verbal intaglios. Yet he used them as rhetorical devices to *emphasize* some sober and less spectacular conclusion. The temptation to quote them out of context, without the ideas that he intended to emphasize, has led some of his interpreters astray.

1. *Pragmatism.* Holmes took part in the beginnings of pragmatism, though he did not hear that name until many years later. He belonged to the James wing, to the heroic mood, "full steam ahead and damn the syllogisms," rather than to the orderly-logical wing which was originally Peirce's and later Dewey's. Yet Holmes did not share James' tender-mindedness, his

---

[41] Supra, § 4.51.

[42] The Common Law, 1.

sentiment of rationality, his leaving room for "the interstitial miracle." He got from Chauncey Wright (§ 4.51) his skepticism of "necessary truths" and a belief in probability which he called "bet-abilitarianism"—what I am willing to bet on. His theory of evolution when applied to ideas, that is, to customs and political laws, resembles the ethical theory of William James.[43] Thus in his famous dissent from a Massachusetts decision to enjoin even peaceful picketing by employees of the employer's place of business, he argued that free competition leads inevitably to combination; whether good or bad, it is a necessary means in the struggle between capital (which is society) and the laborer.[44] The argument here is based on social evolution. The test of the survival of ideas was cogently stated in the famous Abrams case, involving a conviction of sedition for distributing leaflets in 1918 vilifying the Federal administration because of its policy toward the Bolshevik government in Russia:

> "But when men have realized that time has upset many fighting faiths, they may come to believe even more than they believe the very foundations of their own conduct that the ultimate good desired is better reached by free trade in ideas—that the best test of truth is the power of the thought to get itself accepted in the competition of the market, and that truth is the only ground upon which their wishes safely can be carried out." [45]

The "market" metaphor has been invoked by Holmes' critics to show that he was a materialist,[46] a blood brother of both Karl Marx and Adolf Hitler. Now Holmes was a "materialist" in the sense that he believed that both truth and goodness, at least in the legal and political realms, are dependent upon physical reality; yet he also believed profoundly in the value of ideas and ideals that man can choose and control. Holmes did not mean that the non-fiction best-seller of the week has the highest claim

---

[43] Supra, § 4.52(2).

[44] Vegelahn v. Guntner, 167 Mass. 92, 104 ff., 44 N.E. 1077, 1079, 1080 (1896).

[45] Abrams v. U. S., 250 U.S. 616, 624, 40 Sup.Ct. 17, 20 (1919) (Holmes dissenting). Dewey quoted this passage as Holmes' most significant utterance: Dewey, "Justice Holmes and the Liberal Mind," in Mr. Justice Holmes (ed. Frankfurter, 1931), 33.

[46] See, for example, the comparison of Holmes' "test of the market place" analogy to the materialism of Marx by Mr. Justice O'Halloran in (1950) 8 The Advocate 106, 111, commenting on In re Martin [1949], 1 W.W.R. 903, a decision of the Supreme Court of British Columbia upholding the refusal to admit a Communist to membership in the Law Society.

to truth, that a book purporting to turn a comet into a planet
overnight has a better claim to truth than the professionally
recognized astronomical treatises and journals. His use of the
market metaphor expressed a kind of intellectual humility toward
political ideas. These are not established in the talks of philosophers or learned societies, but in the hurly-burly of politics under
representative government. Holmes was skeptical of the power of
analytic reason, the reason of the philosopher or the professional, to control the "unreasoning mass of the public's will and emotions." [47]   Yet he deeply respected the net product; what survived embodied the story of a nation's development through many
centuries. The competition of ideas in a primitive democracy,
such as a New England town meeting, would have been a micro-
cosmic analogy for Holmes; he was, however, seeking a metaphor. "Competition of the market" belittled unduly what he was
seeking to praise.

How can one reconcile Holmes' survival test for ideas with his
famous aphorism that the Fourteenth Amendment does not embody Mr. Herbert Spencer's Social Statics? [48]   Primarily, I believe, this passage expressed Holmes' conception of the *limited
function of the Supreme Court* on constitutional issues rather
than his approval of government control of big business.[49]   Indeed, he recognized the grimness of the biological-survival test
and urged the need for preventing the continuance of the unfit.[50]
He disapproved of Spencer's harsh method of eliminating them.

The spectrum of Holmes' legal philosophy is best shown in his
famous essay, "The Path of the Law." [51]   First he told his law-
student audience that the object of their study was to predict
what courts would decide; that they should not be misled by
moral terminology in law; their job was to look at law for
the bad man, who only wants to keep out of the law's clutches.
His prediction theory of law (§ 2.20) and his bad-man analogy
have led critics (who will not read the rest of his essay) to charge
him with moral nihilism, a charge which is untrue and unfair.[52]

---

[47] Wiener, op. cit., supra, § 4.53, n. 81, 176.

[48] Supra, § 4.34, n. 98.

[49] Professor Wiener's statement that Holmes "certainly supported the growing control of big business by government in the Lochner case" (Wiener, op. cit.,
177) does not adequately represent Holmes' personal conviction.

[50] Ibid., 176, 177, quoting letter to Dr. Wu, 1925.

[51] 10 Harv.L.Rev. 457; C.L.P. 167–202; Lerner, 71 ff.

[52] See Wiener, op. cit., 183; Howe, "The Positivism of Mr. Justice Holmes"

Holmes was emphasizing the distinction between the law that "Is" and the law that "Ought" to be. This distinction every conscientious judge (at least, Anglo-American) tries to maintain, and rightly so. That Holmes also intended to shock his youthful hearers with the grim realities of law practice (as Professor Parsons had done when Holmes was a student at Harvard)[53] seems not unlikely. Yet he was thoroughly convinced both that law "is the witness and external deposit of our moral life" [54] and that the legal implementation of moral principles changed them into something different—a view shared by both Dewey (§ 3.15) and Pound (§ 4.60). Then Holmes turns abruptly from "the limits of the law" to "the forces which determine its content and growth." [55] Logic is not the *only* force at work in the development of the law; it has been exaggerated because it satisfies the longing for certainty and repose which is in every human mind. Then comes one of his famous sentences:

> "But certainty generally is illusion, and repose is not the destiny of man." [56]

This Delphic utterance has been cited to support various heterodoxies. Perhaps "certainty generally is illusion" means that not everything in the cosmos can be connected with everything else in a definite way—there is always some play for chance and the heroic deed: a passage like one from James in his "strenuous mood." At any rate Holmes seems to contradict his prediction theory of law; for a prediction that turned out to be an illusion would not bring back the client for a second consultation.

Holmes then sets forth his view that law is determined by a choice between "competing legislative grounds," that the judges should adequately recognize "their duty of weighing considerations of social advantage." [57] This is Holmes' adaptation of the utilitarianism of Bentham and John Stuart Mill, which he had come greatly to admire. Now if the bad man wants a prediction

---

(1951) 64 Harv.L.Rev. 529; Hart, "Holmes' Positivism—An Addendum" (1951) 64 Harv.L.Rev. 929; Howe, "Holmes' Positivism—A Brief Rejoinder" (1951) 64 Harv.L.Rev. 937.

[53] Parsons regularly told his first class: "If a young lawyer pays for his sign the first year and his office rent the next, he can tell himself he is doing very well." Bowen, 205.

[54] C.L.P., 170.

[55] C.L.P.,179.

[56] Ibid., 181.

[57] Ibid., 184.

as to what the law will do to him, his counselor will have to consider the public good as a part of his prediction-data, even if his client would scorn it. This is one of the paradoxes in Holmes. The only reconciliation apparent is that Holmes (like Pound) believed that courts are continually balancing competing social advantages; predictability and security are sometimes given effect and sometimes the law's ideals.[58] Aside from its professional uses (by counselor or judge) the search for the remoter rational explanations of the law satisfies a basic human longing; through it you may "connect your subject with the universe and catch an echo of the infinite." [59] The man who wrote this was no crass materialist.[60]

2. *Liberalism.* Holmes' views on freedom of speech and on the judicial function gave him a reputation for economic liberalism or radicalism that was largely undeserved. First, he believed that the Court had only a limited function in reviewing the constitutionality of legislation: The judges must not read their predilections into the Constitution as untouchable principles; they must respect with due humility the work of the elected legislators.[61] When Brandeis and Stone joined the Court they shared this view. Secondly, the preservation of free speech and a free press was a value that ranked high with Holmes for several reasons: Because it fell within those broad provisions of the constitution which safeguarded the fundamentals of limited government, because without free discussion of political issues (and a free ballot) all other freedoms would be precarious, and because the survival test fitted his pragmatic-evolutionary theory as outlined above. Thirdly, Holmes' personal views on economic questions, expressed off the bench, were pretty conservative. In a letter to Dr. Wu he disagreed with Laski's socialist trend:

> "I think it a manifest humbug to suppose that even relative universal bliss is to be reached by tinkering with property or changing forms of government so long as every social improvement is expended in increased and unchecked propagation." [62]

---

58 On "the ideal" toward which law tends, see C.L.P., 185–194.

59 Ibid., 202.

60 Of Holmes' oscillation between a subjective and objective theory of truth, see Wiener, op. cit., 187.

61 See Frankfurter in op. cit. (supra, n. 38) 59–64; Otis v. Parker, 187 U.S. 606, 608–609, 23 Sup.Ct. 168, 169, 170 (1903). This was Holmes' first Supreme Court opinion. Lerner, 136.

62 Wiener, op. cit., 177; Lerner, 428.

His economic views were expressed in other letters: It makes no difference, practically, that a few rich people are able to spend money lavishly on luxuries; nearly all of the goods produced (ninety-nine per cent or more) are distributed among the masses of the population, and if private ownership increases production it is doing what is economically desirable.[63]

> "The real problem, under socialism as well as under individualism, is to ascertain, under the external economic and inevitable conditions, the equilibrium of social desires. The real struggle is between the different groups of producers of the several objects of social desire.[64]

His belief that production should come first is basic. His ideas about distribution were, it seems, more conservative than those prevalent today. His political liberalism has already been found too "conservative." [65] His "clear and present danger" test [66] has, however, been sufficiently flexible to survive two major wars.

3. *Realism*. The aggregation of ideas which came in time to be known as American Legal Realism (§ 4.63) contained many which were either genuinely derived from Holmes' or were inspired by his ripped-out aphorisms. For Legal Realism the two most influential of Holmes' ideas were his prediction concept of law and his view (not uniformly adhered to), that policies and prejudices have more to do with judicial decisions than the logical application of rules. Yet these were not all. When Holmes said that "the first requirement of a sound body of law is that it should correspond with the actual feelings and demands of the community, whether right or wrong," [67] he stated a doctrine that could be either radical or conservative. Moore's search for the correlation between banking law and banker's usages, and Cook's

---

[63] C.L.P., 279 ff. (letter of 1904).

[64] Letter to Franklin K. Lane, Mar. 17, 1912, in The Letters of Franklin K. Lane (Cambridge, 1922), 92.

[65] I. e., Holmes' view that executive regulation of making speeches in a public park does not infringe the right to freedom of speech (Com. v. Davis, 162 Mass. 510, 39 N.E. 113 (1895)) was silently rejected in Hague v. C.I.O., 307 U.S. 496, 59 Sup.Ct. 954 (1939) ; Lerner, 106.

[66] "The question in every case is whether the words used are used in such circumstances and are of such a nature as to create a clear and present danger that they will bring about the substantive evils that Congress has a right to prevent. It is a question of proximity and degree." Schenck v. U. S., 249 U.S. 47, 50, 39 Sup.Ct. 247, 248 (1919).

[67] The Common Law (1881), 41.

search for a "scientific method" in law derived inspiration from Holmes. Llewellyn found in Holmes support for his cleavage between "paper rules" and "working rules." Frank found Holmes' recognition that certainty is not attainable, the chief sign of his maturity and wisdom.[68] An example of the aphorism-sprinkling is the frequent misuse of Holmes' phrase, "intuitions too subtle for any articulate premise," [69] which was said in reference to a board assessing property for taxation, not in reference to a court.[70] Holmes was rather careful to say that the judges should have the end which every rule of law subserves "stated or ready to be stated in words." [71] Holmes expressed the hope that social issues could be resolved by quantitative methods,[72] and this influenced some realists. Above all, Holmes had a gamin-daredevil streak which sometimes made him want to twist the tail of the cosmos, and so did many of the legal realists.

---

[68] See Frank, Law and the Modern Mind (1931), Part III, Ch. II, "Mr. Justice Oliver Wendell Holmes, The Completely Adult Jurist." Further discussion, infra, § 4.64.

[69] The nearest equivalent is in Chicago, Burlington, & Quincy R. Co. v. Babcock, 204 U.S. 585, 598, 27 Sup.Ct. 326, 329 (1907): "an intuition of experience which outruns analysis and sums up many unnamed and tangled impressions. . . ." This passage justified judicial restraint in reviewing the decisions of lay administrators.

[70] Cf. Cook, "The Logical and Legal Bases of the Conflict of Laws," (1924) 33 Yale L.J. 457, 487; Hall, p. 365.

[71] C.L.P., 186, 238–9.

[72] ". . . the man of the future is the man of statistics and the master of economics." C.L.P., 187; see also 231. "An ideal system of law should draw its postulates and its legislative justification from science." C.L.P., 139; Lerner, 35.

Chapter 18

SOCIOLOGICAL JURISPRUDENCE AND AMERICAN LEGAL REALISM

§ 4.60—Roscoe Pound: Program of Sociological Jurisprudence

Pound's sociological jurisprudence is the most comprehensive, coherent and original philosophy of law yet produced in the United States. Most of its basic beliefs are grounded on pragmatism, much of its constructive apparatus resembles Hegel's dialectical idealism (§ 4.35) and many of its valuable insights were derived from the Roman and civil law. It is true that Pound has built upon the work of many others, but he has built. The growth of sociology from Comte to Lester Ward, Ross and Small gave support to the belief that legal theory could be based on social science. Pound greeted with enthusiasm Ehrlich's sociology of law.[1] He later distinguished sociological jurisprudence (from legal sociology) as a discipline designed to utilize the social sciences for the development of law in the imperative sense [2] (§ 2.04), a discipline which had its beginning with Holmes. Concisely, sociological jurisprudence is prescriptive, while sociology of law is descriptive. This difference will serve to indicate the chief criterion by which selection has here been made of Pound's principal ideas.

Roscoe Pound (1870– ——) was born in Lincoln, Nebraska, at a time when the western frontier civilization had not disappeared. From his father, a successful lawyer, he seems to have derived his political conservatism; from his mother, a college graduate, the habit of satisfying a widely ranging intellectual curiosity. Roscoe was torn between the classics and botany. Entering the University of Nebraska at the age of thirteen, he "concentrated" on both, and eventually obtained a Ph.D. in botany. Some of his critics have claimed that his legal theory is merely taxonomic; this is untrue, yet his tendency to classify legal ideas as botanists classify plants sometimes obscures the originality and force of

---

[1] In his lectures on Jurisprudence of 1919–20 (which the present writer attended) he gave Ehrlich's Grundlegung der Soziologie des Rechts (1913) far more significance than it deserved. Supra, § 2.03.

[2] Pound, "Sociology of Law and Sociological Jurisprudence," (1943) 5 Univ. of Toronto L.J. 1, 2–3, 12 (retaining the imperative conception).

his ideas. He attended the Harvard Law School (1889–90) but left without graduating because the faculty would not let him complete the three-year course in two years. Even so, he was digging into Roman law during his first year. Returning to Lincoln, he practiced law (1890–1901) until his appointment as a Commissioner (an auxiliary judge) of the Supreme Court of Nebraska, for which he prepared opinions in more than 200 cases. He became Dean of the law school of the University of Nebraska in 1903. He moved on to Northwestern, Chicago and Harvard, where he was Dean (1916–1936) and Carter Professor of Jurisprudence. His non-academic work included important practical aspects of law: international arbitrator, member of President Hoover's Committee on Law Observance (1929–31), consultant on crime surveys and administrative procedure, and in 1948 as adviser to the ill-starred Chinese Nationalist government.[3] The book is not closed.

Even though he rejected the Populist radicalism of his youth, Pound early became a reformer in jurisprudence and in professional law. His first major law review article [4] was a warning that the procedural fusion of equity and law might be like that of the lady and the tiger. His criticisms of American law and procedure before the American Bar Association in 1906 [5] aroused a storm of protest in that staid body. Yet he came back the next year as chairman of the Section on Legal Education of the Association to announce the need for a sociological jurisprudence.[6] His provocative articles showed what such a legal philosophy would mean: "Mechanical Jurisprudence," in which he acknowledged his indebtedness to William James' pragmatism,[7] "Liberty of Contract," [8] in which he contrasted the theoretical Hegelian liberty of the industrial employee with his actual liberty, and "Law in Books and Law in Action," [9] where he contrasted the legal rules

---

[3] These facts may be gleaned from Sayre, Life of Roscoe Pound (Iowa City, Iowa, 1948) (cited "Sayre").

[4] Pound, "The Decadence of Equity," (1905) 5 Col.L.Rev. 20 (a bar association address of 1903).

[5] Pound, "The Causes of Popular Dissatisfaction With the Administration of Justice," (1906) 29 Rep.A.B.A., Pt. I, 395–417; 40 Amer.L.Rev. 729. See Wigmore's dramatic comment in Sayre, 147–151.

[6] Pound, "The Need of a Sociological Jurisprudence," (1907) 19 Green Bag 607–615.

[7] (1908) 8 Col.L.Rev. 605, 607, 608, 621.

[8] (1909) 18 Yale L.J. 454.

[9] (1910) 44 Amer.L.Rev. 12.

about personal injuries resulting from negligence with the verdicts of juries. Then, settled at Harvard, he launched the series of articles on sociological jurisprudence.[10] A bibliography of Pound's writings to 1940 shows fifteen books and 241 major articles.[11]

Would he have written better had he written less? Yes and no. His omnivorous reading, his prodigious memory and his vast learning [12] have led him to summarize and comment upon the views of others, sometimes too fully and sometimes in repetition of previous summaries, before giving his own views. Had he written more compactly he might have displayed less of his learning and more of his insight. Yet most of his books, and many of his law review articles, were delivered as addresses: Had he written less he would have reached fewer audiences. Pound's style lacks the grace of Holmes' and Maitland's, and the sententious quality of Cardozo's and Judge Learned Hand's. Yet his diction is colorful, and he has a nice eye for the enlightening anecdote. More important, he gives not only stimulating flashes of insight but also sustained illuminations. Of the latter we shall speak in this and the following section.

1. *Program of Sociological Jurisprudence.* Pound's writings are hard to summarize because they are themselves mostly summaries. He outlines the program of sociological jurisprudence under eight headings,[13] four of which deal with the relation of law to society. First, there should be study of the social effects of legal institutions and legal doctrines. As examples of such study he referred to Ehrlich's research in living law (§ 2.03), Moore's studies of banking practices and the Douglas study of bankruptcies, the last two the work of legal realists (§ 4.63). Here the reference is to a sociology of law, undertaken without having in mind any specific societal evils or legal changes. "Sociological study in preparation for law-making" is now a commonplace of enacting social legislation, but this was not always so. "Study of the means of making legal precepts effective in

---

10 Pound, "The Scope and Purpose of Sociological Jurisprudence," (1911) 24 Harv.L.Rev. 591; (1911) 25 ibid. 140, (1912) 25 ibid. 489.

11 Setaro, A Bibliography of the Writings of Roscoe Pound (Cambridge, 1942), with an appendix, giving references to published comments on Pound and his work. The count was taken from Sayre, 331.

12 Holmes wrote Pollock that it made him tired just to read the titles of what Pound "knows." The Holmes-Pollock Letters (Howe ed., 1941), II, 115.

13 Pound, Outlines of Lectures on Jurisprudence (5th ed., 1943), 32–34.

action" produced some of Pound's best work, notably his excellent address on "The Limits of Effective Legal Action," [14] which stressed the inadequacy of an award of damages to make reparation for intangible injuries. Nor is specific redress always effective: Even an injunction cannot make a man's wife love him. Other examples were studies of small-claims procedures and of legal-aid bureaus. "A sociological legal history," his fourth item, had this principal object: Find out the social situation in which a legal doctrine originated and you can better tell whether it is worthy to survive. Wigmore did some of this in his treatise on evidence.[15] Pound amusingly explained the exemption laws of the middle western states, with their liberality to farmer-debtors, as survivals of a time when an influential part of the frontier population consisted of noble pioneers who had fled from their eastern creditors.[16]

Pound included in his program the study of juridical method: Of the psychology of judicial decisions, of the factors that influence them and of the ideals that judges strive to attain by them. This was represented in Cardozo's books, and in realist literature about the judicial process. The establishment of a Ministry of Justice to draft legislation correcting anachronisms in private law, as advocated by Cardozo (§ 4.62), was another item in the program. "Recognition of the importance of reasonable and just solutions of individual cases" covered several diverse trends. One was the "individualization of punishment", the court's investigation of the convicted individual (in juvenile cases, before "conviction") and the use of suspended sentence or parole as a means of reformation. This change has not, it seems, realized the expectations of its sponsors; the experiment needs to be re-appraised every thirty years. Another instance of individualization in the application of law is the administrative application of legal standards (§ 3.23) established by the legislature, such as "reasonable rate" or "unfair labor practice." On this Pound delivered a basic statement.[17] He also included the art of judging, which he con-

---

[14] A bar association address reprinted in (1916) 27 Int.Jour.Ethics 150. It is delightfully complemented by Cohen, "Positivism and the Limits of Idealism in the Law," (1927) 27 Col.L.Rev. 237.

[15] Supra, § 4.30(B), nn. 7, 8.

[16] "The Pioneers and the Law," in The Spirit of the Common Law (1921), 126–27.

[17] "The Administrative Application of Legal Standards," (1919) 44 Rep.Amer. Bar Ass'n 445.

ceived of as the application of law to individual cases.[18]   These instances of individualization were all more or less in derogation of Pound's basic view that the best kind of justice, judicial justice, should be "justice according to law" (§ 2.11).   These items are, he concludes, only *some* of the means to "make effort more effective in achieving the purposes of law." [19]   The program is not closed.   It may include many more procedures of "social engineering." [20]

Of Pound's program it may be said that he did not claim to have originated the studies and legal changes which he listed, yet in many instances his influence encouraged their protagonists and mollified their opponents.   His insights brought them together under a common ideology, a loose theory created by an imaginative mind looking at legal phenomena with the aid of pragmatism, mid-western shrewdness, Hegelian and native American idealism, and a touch of sociology.   Here was a down-to-earth jurisprudence that could point to practical results.   It suffers the inevitable fate of all concrete programs, that they are adopted and become commonplace, or are discarded as outdated.   Yet apart from the special projects, Pound's sociological jurisprudence included ideas of enduring value as means of social engineering.   It also includes, as a part of its theoretical structure, three other contributions: The five stages of legal evolution, the jural postulates of civilization, discussed below, and the theory of social interests (§ 4.61).

2.   *The Five Stages of Legal History.*   Pound's basic conception was to detect the end or ends of the law at each of the stages of its development, as revealed in its rules and doctrines,[21] in contrast with the history of juristic or philosophical thought.[22]   To a thorough Hegelian these two must coincide (the rational is the actual) (§ 4.35), but Pound discovered a definite parallelism only in the last two stages.   The first stage is "primitive law," in which

---

18 See Llewellyn, "Some Realism about Realism," (1931) 44 Harv.L.Rev. 1237, 1240–41.

19 Outlines, 34.

20 See Spirit, 195–96.

21 See Pound, "The End of Law as Developed in Legal Rules and Doctrines," (1914) 27 Harv.L.Rev. 195–234.   An independent but somewhat similar historic-philosophical survey in terms of stages of development is given in Potter, The Quest for Justice (London, 1951).

22 See Pound, "The End of Law as Developed in Juristic Thought," (1914) 27 ibid. 605–628.

the end of what legal ordering there is, is to keep the peace, especially to prevent the blood-feud by setting up a tariff of compositions for the redress of injuries. This stage of law was found among literate peoples of the Near East (Hammurabi), in southern and western Europe and in England. The early laws commonly prescribed a definite penalty for a definite injury: an eye for an eye and a tooth for a tooth; or so much money for striking a commoner, and so much (more) for striking a nobleman, whose vengeance had to be bought off at a higher price. The rules were sporadic and incomplete; they were literally construed. While not all the same characteristics have been found by the primitive-law studies of anthropologists (who have investigated non-literate living societies), this does not affect Pound's thesis, which relates to the oldest historic stage of (Occidental) civilized legal systems. In England this stage is represented by the Anglo-Saxon laws and the Welsh laws.[23]

The second stage is that of "strict law," in which the end is certainty and uniformity in the legal ordering of society. The means to this end are rule and form. He ascribes such a period to Roman law, the period when the law recognized only the free Roman, a citizen and a pater-familias.[24] It was the period of formal actions for redress and of formal transactions. In the corresponding English stage, the sealed instrument was binding on its maker, even though he was induced by fraud of the other party to execute it. The plaintiff must allege and prove his claim within the limits prescribed by the formula he chose, or suffer dismissal of his suit. In England this stage is represented by the fourteenth and fifteenth centuries, by Littleton on tenures and Coke on Littleton. Rule and formula, both in substance and procedure, were intended to minimize the tyranny made possible by judicial discretion.[25] The stage of equity and natural law came in both Roman and English law with the loosening of strict law by moral ideas, such as the requirement of honesty and good faith in transactions. Human beings, rather than merely the head of the family, became the "subjects" of legal rights. Unjust enrichment became a ground for legal redress. In England this was the period of equity of the seventeenth and eighteenth centuries. By

---

[23] See King Ethelbirth's Dooms (c. XXI) and Laws of Howell Dda (c. XXII) in Kocourek and Wigmore, Sources of Ancient and Primitive Law (1915).

[24] See Pound, "A Theory of Social Interests," (1921) 15 Papers & Proc. Amer. Sociological Soc. 16 ff; Hall, p. 240.

[25] Pound, An Introduction to the Philosophy of Law (1922), 111–113.

Lord Eldon's time equity had hardened into a system and the nineteenth century in England and the United States was the stage of the "maturity of law." Once more, as in the strict law, certainty becomes a paramount end, but now it is enlarged to include security of expectations, and is accompanied by equality, a carryover from the equity stage. The fifth stage, the "socialization of law," is marked by a new infusion of morals, this time a sociological conception of morals. Among the signs of this stage are limitations on the antisocial use of property (e. g., spite fences, zoning laws), limitations on freedom of contract (e. g. by insurance companies, common carriers), limitations on the powers of creditors to exact satisfaction (wage exemption statutes), liability without fault as a device for spreading the burdens of industrial risks from employees to consumers, protection of dependents, and recognition of legal groups such as the corporation and the labor union as units representing the individual. This stage has been reached in the United States, in Great Britain and in most of the nations of Western Europe.

Is Pound's evolutionary scheme accurate? Is it significant? The first question cannot be fully explored here. It seems to me that he has rightly interpreted the dominant end of the legal order during each of his roughly-indicated periods. True, one can probably find some signs of a *later* stage during each *earlier* stage: some signs of equity and natural law in the two earlier stages, and some signs of legal standards (a mature conception) in the strict law period.[26] Yet the deviations appear to be a-typical. Conversely, one should expect to find, and does find, survivals of each *earlier* stage in each *later* stage.[27] This accords with the parallel principle in Hegel's philosophy of history (§ 4.35). Indeed, the chief significance of Pound's synthesis is that it helps us to roll back the layers of history in our present law, to deter-

---

[26] "From the earliest times until now much of the law is expressed in terms of what is reasonable. A widow shall have reasonable dower; she may have reasonable estovers; a party shall give reasonable notice; he shall act reasonably, etc., etc. The pages of Glanvill and Bracton are as full of this sort of thing as those of our latest volume of reports." Thayer, A Preliminary Treatise on Evidence at the Common Law (1898) 213–14. The last sentence seems an exaggeration.

[27] Examples: Current property and commercial law contain rules intended to promote certainty; criminal law and procedure still contain rules designed chiefly to limit the discretion of the court. Workmen's compensation laws, with their schedules of payments, resemble the tariffs of compositions of primitive laws.

mine when and why a curious survivor got its start, and perhaps to determine whether its continued survival would be compatible with our *Zeitgeist,* the dominant ideological postulates of contemporary culture.

3. *Jural Postulates of Civilization.* Pound's conception of the jural postulates of civilization was derived from Kohler, a German Neo-Hegelian, who stressed the ideals of the civilization of a given period rather than its chancy and non-rational elements.[28] Pound formulated a set of jural postulates in his endeavor to explain the law to laymen attending a labor union school. They were first published in the outline of these lectures.[29] Each of them begins with the phrase, "In civilized society men must be able to assume." Each of these postulates has a threefold aspect: It is a kind of implicit *Volksgeist,* it is a requirement for a society *to be* civilized, and it is a principle to guide courts in applying law. Condensing the latest revision [30] we have:

[In civilized society men must be able to assume]

"I.   That others will commit no intentional aggressions upon them.

"II.   That they may control for beneficial purposes what they have discovered and appropriated to their own use, what they have created by their own labor, and what they have acquired under the existing social and economic order.

"III.   That those with whom they deal in the general intercourse of society will act in good faith and hence

   "(a) will make good reasonable expectations which their promises or other conduct reasonably create;

   "(b) will carry out their undertakings according to the expectations which the moral sentiment of the community attaches thereto;

   "(c) will restore specifically or by equivalent what comes to them by mistake or unanticipated situation whereby they receive, at another's expense, what they could not reasonably have expected to receive under the actual circumstances.

---

[28] See Kohler, Philosophy of Law (Albrecht trans., 1909), and excellent comment, Stone, The Province and Function of Law (1946), c. XIII, §§ 3–7.

[29] Pound, An Introduction to American Law (pamphlet outline of lectures at Trade Union College under the auspices of the Boston Central Labor Union, Spring Term, 1919).

[30] In Outlines of Lectures on Jurisprudence (1943), 168, 179, 183–84. (Reprinted by permission of the author.)

"IV.   That others will act reasonably and prudently so as not, by want of due care under the circumstances, to impose upon them an unreasonable risk of injury.

"V.   That others who maintain things or employ agencies, harmless in the sphere of their use but harmful in their normal action elsewhere, and having a natural tendency to cross the boundaries of their proper use, will restrain them or keep them within proper bounds."

While a lay audience would not grasp the last four without some explanation and illustration, it seems that with such understanding most of the audience (in the United States, in Great Britain, in Western Europe and probably in the western hemisphere) would agree that these postulates state some of the fundamental expectations of reflective men.   They are grounded in human na·ture and conduct.[31]   A philosopher has said that they not only state the characteristic American ideals of the present time but also embody absolute values of all time.[32]   Pound would not claim for them any eternal verity.   Professor Stone, while giving them due respect, believes they are already partly outmoded by social changes, e. g., the postulates about labor relations.[33]   If an employee has a claim to job security that is legally protected, to that extent the employer's property is impaired.   However, this criticism merely shows that the postulates are "principles," that they overlap and conflict and claim more than they govern (§ 3.24). Pound does not assert that they are a complete set of axioms for a deductive system.   Indeed, one can recognize the empirical (positive-law) origin of each of them.   The first is from the law of torts and crimes, a necessary survivor from the stage of primitive law.   (Some labor union practices, tolerated by local police, have made exceptions to this postulate, too.)   The second is the postulate of property law, closely resembling Locke's theory of the origin of property (§ 4.15).   Here again one might note deviations: In modern industry the "creator" of the product is, in one sense, the group of employees of all grades; yet the product belongs to the employer, the owner of the means of production, whose claim is based upon the third mode of acquisition listed by

---

31 ". . . all conduct is *interaction* between elements of human nature and the environment, natural and social."   Dewey, Human Nature and Conduct (1922), 10; see also cc. IV–VI.

32 Hocking, Present Status of the Philosophy of Law and Rights (1926) §§ 41–48.

33 Stone, op. cit. (supra, n. 28), c. XV, § 9; c. XXI, § 10.

Pound. (In another sense, the creator of the product is the one who invented the plan and process of production.) Postulate III states succinctly the basis of the law of contract and of restitution. Postulates IV (negligence) and V (liability without fault) complete the basic principles of torts. Now each of these can be shown to be inaccurate in detail as a statement of present rules of law, or at least inadequate. Again their significance as statements of general principle, both of present civilization and of present law, is not substantially impaired. Others may be added. On the whole Pound's jural postulates constitute one of the important contributions to jurisprudence of the first half of this century.

They supplement and are compatible with the five stages of legal evolution. Can these two be reconciled with Pound's program of action by using social engineering, as outlined above? If legal history is going to evolve because of inherent rational contradictions or even because of non-rational accidents, then why is any program of action needed to help it along? The charm of Hegelianism modified by American optimistic progressivism is that one cannot be sure whether Pound is actualizing the rational or rationalizing the actual.

§ 4.61—Roscoe Pound: Theory of Social Interests

Pound's theory of social interests, his most important contribution to legal philosophy, is one of the significant ideas of the century, not only because it preserves that continuity with the past which is inevitable and valuable, but also because it stands for the method of reason and compromise which is essential to the development of a democratic and free society. His table of social interests seems to embrace all of the public policies of which legislatures and courts should take account in their respective spheres of lawmaking and interpretation; or at least it can serve, as Mendelejeff's table of chemical elements has done, in looking for the missing ones. It is not composed of value-propositions, such as the jural postulates (§ 4.60), but of values, as ends and as means, for the construction of legal norms. Yet choices will remain. To illustrate: If the social interest in public safety and health ("general security") calls for the elimination of advertising billboards obstructing the view at highway intersections, the social interest in the security of acquisitions (property rights, also classified under "general security") must give way to some extent; but whether the owner's loss of advertising revenue shall be compensated depends in part upon factors not covered by Pound's table.

Indeed, the survey or inventory of social interests is only a part of his general plan for determining the scope and subject matter of a legal system. The plan includes also four other steps or processes: To determine the interests which the law should seek to secure; to determine the principles upon which such chosen interests should be defined and limited; to determine the means by which the law can secure them; and to take account of the limitations on effective legal action [34] (§ 4.60).

Pound was working on his theory of interests as early as 1913,[35] and brought it to fruition in an inaccessible publication of 1921.[36] He revised it and republished it in 1943.[37] The earlier draft is interesting because it showed that Pound tried to find in sociology, in theories of social instincts, the basis for a theory having the down-to-earth quality which Holmes had urged him to seek.[38] The law had to reckon with the instincts of self-assertion, of acquisitiveness, of gregariousness. However, he concluded that the jurist could not safely use social instincts as a basis of classification because sociologists were not agreed about them. Indeed, Dewey's work on social psychology showed that instincts were inadequate to explain human conduct and attitudes, without the mediation of custom and habit.[39] He then turned to a less pretentious method of finding a classification of social interests: By the study of legal phenomena as social phenomena. The lawyer can contribute to social science generally as well as to legal science, by surveying legal systems "to ascertain just what claims or wants or demands have pressed or are now pressing for recognition and satisfaction and how far they have been or are recognized or secured."[40] The data of the survey are chiefly judicial

[34] Pound, Outlines of Lectures on Jurisprudence (5th ed., 1943) 96 (cited below as "Outlines"). For a longer commentary, see Patterson, "Pound's Theory of Social Interests," in Interpretations of Modern Legal Philosophies (1947), 598.

[35] Letter of Pound to Holmes, Feb. 22, 1913, in Sayre, The Life of Roscoe Pound (1948) 270.

[36] Pound, "A Theory of Social Interests," (1921) 15 Proc.Amer.Sociological Soc. 16; Hall, pp. 238–246. However, the survey of interests appeared in the 1914 edition of his Outlines of Lectures in Jurisprudence (2d ed.) 56–59.

[37] "A Survey of Social Interests," (1943) 57 Harv.L.Rev. 1–39 (cited below as "Survey" with page number).

[38] See letter, supra, n. 35.

[39] Dewey, Human Nature and Conduct (1922), esp. Pt. II, secs. V, VI, where he cogently argues that there are no separate instincts.

[40] Hall, p. 243; 57 Harv.L.Rev. 13.

decisions and legislation; that is, for the most part they are propositions about valuations (to use Dewey's terms (§ 4.54)) as
facts, from which the surveyor abstracts or generalizes values.

But this is getting ahead of our story. The term "interest" was
used by Bentham as an indefinable or primitive term.[41] Pound
combined Ihering's conception of the legal right as a legally protected interest (§ 4.44) with James' conception of a claim or demand as the source of ethical obligations (§ 4.52) to define individual interests as "claims or demands or desires involved immediately in the individual life and asserted in title of that life." [42]
It is an alloy of social ethics and a social analysis of law. Alloys
are often highly useful because they are stronger and more dura-
ble than the elements of which they are composed. Now two
questions may be asked about Pound's conception of an individual
interest. First, is it necessary that the claim or desire be actually and continuously asserted? Does the one-year-old infant who
has just inherited a tract of land (which his deceased father
owned) have an "interest" in the land? No, if interest means an
asserted claim or desire. Yes, if interest means the kernel of a
(primary) legal right. A radical operationalist, as Holmes was at
times, might say that there is no legal right to the property until
an action at law is brought in which that issue is adjudicated. A
primary right is only a prophecy of what a court will do *if* certain
things occur.[43] Yet this view recognizes a primary right as having a potential status even though no present claim or demand is
being asserted. So the conception of individual interest includes
the cases of *potential* claims or demands, such as those of the infant when he grows up, or of the idiot through his guardians or
of the private corporation through its directors.[44] This extension
is based not only upon law-buttressed customs and attitudes but
also upon the need for maintaining an orderly society by channeling conduct in advance of controversy. Secondly, are indi-

---

[41] An Introduction to the Principles of Morals and Legislation (Oxford,
1892), 3. A thing promotes the individual's interest when it increases his happiness. Ibid. But James used it in a broader sense. Supra, § 4.41, n. 20.
"Value" has been defined as "the object of any interest." Perry, General
Theory of Value (1926), c. V.

[42] 57 Harv.L.Rev. 1.

[43] Holmes, "The Path of the Law," in Collected Legal Papers (1920), 168.

[44] Similarly, Bentham had to extend his simple conception of pain and
pleasure to include potential and remote pains and pleasures. Supra, §§ 4.41,
4.42.

vidual interests "facts" or "values"? As Professor Dewey has protested against this contrast by asserting that values *are* facts,[45] the question may be rephrased, are individual interests the mere claims or demands of men, what Dewey calls their "prizings," regardless of an "appraisal" by someone else, *or* is the latter necessarily included? The answer is the first alternative. A pickpocket in the subway has (under certain circumstances) an "interest" in my watch (which is in my pocket), though not one that the law will legally protect.[46] Thus one function of law is to discriminate (a word having the same root as "crime") between the interests that will be and those that will not be protected. Pound has written valuable articles on the legal protection and means of protection of interests of personality and interests in the domestic relations.[47] A third class of individual interests he calls "interests of substance," property and contract rights.[48]

Pound's inventory includes two other classes of interests, public and social. In defining these he adheres to the basic notion of interest and changes the connections:

> "Public interests are claims or demands or desires involved in life in a politically organized society and asserted in title of that organization. They are commonly treated as the claims of a politically organized society thought of as a legal entity. Social interests are claims or demands or desires involved in social life in civilized society and asserted in title of that life. It is not uncommon to treat them as the claims of the whole social group as such." [49]

The state as a juristic person has "interests of substance," since it is a property owner. The interest of the United States in a post-office building is such an interest. It also has "interests of personality," in the sense that national dignity and honor are recognized in international law, and under recent statutes the state is suable in tort as well as in contract. The conception of public interest does not correspond to res publicae in Roman law [50] nor to

---

45 Dewey, Problems of Men (1946), 278–279 (first published 1944).

46 I. e., not against anyone before the thief has gained possession.

47 "Interests of Personality," (1915) 28 Harv.L.Rev. 343; "Equitable Relief against Defamation and Injuries to Personality," (1916) 29 Harv.L.Rev. 640; "Individual Interests in the Domestic Relations," (1916) 14 Mich.L.Rev. 177.

48 "Individual Interests of Substance—Promised Advantages," (1945) 59 Harv.L.Rev. 1.

49 57 Harv.L.Rev. 1.

50 Which referred to property open to use by people generally, such as

"public policy" in Anglo-American law. The terminology is at
first confusing. Yet Pound made a considerable advance over
Ihering when he separated public from social interests. The
state's property interests are not the same as the public policies
which it enforces for the public good; the latter are the social
interests.[51] They are the claims of the whole society, of which
the political state is the guardian. Pound pointed out that the
English common law had long recognized public policy as a ground
for declaring contracts invalid, that English and American judges
generally distrusted public policy because it had not been clearly
worked out, and that the reasons for this distrust were upon analysis other public policies, such as the policy that private property
rights must be protected against confiscation or impairment.[52]
So the very same judges who in the nineteenth century and early
twentieth century regarded "public policy" as an "unruly steed,"
had all along been riding another steed, called "freedom of contract" or "vested property rights" or "no liability without fault,"
which was only a different public policy, a horse of another color.
Once it is recognized that policy-weighing goes on in the judicial
process, the next step is to devise a method of balancing interests
that will place them on the same plane. This is to be done, under
Pound's plan, by subsuming the respective competing individual
interests in a controversy under the social interests which support them and by weighing the consequences, in relation to social
interests, of alternative modes of action. Thus the public policy
against involuntary servitude was infringed *in fact* by a Georgia
statute that imposed a penalty upon an employee who obtained
money or property pursuant to a contract of employment and
then failed to perform the contract; though the statute was apparently aimed at fraudulently obtaining money, in effect it could
be used to hold employees in peonage.[53]

---

roads, bridges and rivers. Ihering, The Law as a Means to an End (Husik
trans., 1914), 348–9.

51 57 Harv.L.Rev. 3.

52 Pound's examples include the dissent by McKenna, J., from a decision
upholding the constitutional validity of an Arizona statute making an employer liable without fault for injuries to his employees in their employment.
McKenna, J., viewed the decision with alarm as a menace to all rights, "sub-
jecting them unreservedly to conceptions of public policy." Arizona Employers' Liability Cases, 250 U.S. 400, 439, 39 Sup.Ct. 553, 562, 563 (1919), 57
Harv.L.Rev. 2.

53 Taylor v. Georgia, 315 U.S. 25, 62 Sup.Ct. 415 (1942).

Pound's survey of social interests was intended to end the chaotic and episodic character of discussions of public policies by listing all of the main headings or classes of policies recognized in mature systems of law. He found six classes and several subclasses: [54]

I. *Social interest in general security.* This interest was protected in the period of strict law under the policy promoting certainty, later under the policy promoting individual liberty. The subdivisions are:

    a. Safety from aggression, external and internal. (E. g., crimes of homicide, mayhem, assault and battery, and tort liability).

    b. Health, a concern of mature legal systems.

    c. Peace and order. In mature systems, not only suppression of mobs but also of excessive noises.

    d. Security of transactions, including the enforcement of contracts and giving effect to conveyances.

    e. Security of acquisitions, the protection of property rights.

II. *Social interest in security of social institutions.*

    a. Domestic, i. e., the domestic relations.

    b. Religious, as indicated in penalties for blasphemy and other conduct injurious to religious feelings; but sometimes outweighed by the interest in free speech.

    c. Political, i. e., the state and its subdivisions, and the political practices necessary to their maintenance, such as freedom of speech and freedom of the ballot; also protection against bribery of officials.

    d. Economic, i. e., the convenience of commerce affecting commercial law (Mansfield). Overlaps "security of transactions," supra, I(d).

III. *Social interest in general morals,* that is, protection of the moral sentiments of the community. Includes policy of penalizing *dishonest* conduct in various ways; sexual immorality; obscene literature; other moral standards of the community.

IV. *Social interest in conservation of social resources.*

    a. Physical resources. Conservation of forests, of gas and oil, of irrigation water, riparian rights, game laws.

---

[54] Outlines, 104–111; 57 Harv.L.Rev. 14 ff.

b. Human resources. The protection and training of dependents and defectives, as represented in the English Chancellor's jurisdiction over infants, lunatics and idiots, and in juvenile court laws, reformation of delinquents; also in Social Security legislation, small loan legislation.

V. *Social interest in general progress.*

a. Economic: free trade, free competition, encouragement of invention and freedom of property from restrictions on alienation or use. (Note the similarity to II (d).)

b. Political: free criticism; free opinion. (Note similarity to II(c).)

c. Cultural: free science, free letters, encouragement of arts and letters and of higher education.

VI. *Social interest in the individual life.* Individual self-assertion, physical, mental, economic; individual opportunity, political, physical, cultural, social, economic; individual conditions of life (as expressed in Fair Labor Standards Act and state minimum wage laws, and earlier in bankruptcy acts and exemptions from execution).

This summary is inadequate to represent the richness and variety of his illustrations drawn from Roman, Continental, English and American law, both statutory and case law. A more thorough summary of the ends of a mature legal order, all directed to the common good or the greatest good of the greatest number, can scarcely be conceived.

Whether Pound's inventory of social interests is the best for its purposes is debatable. His plan of classification has been affected by various factors, including the attitudes of judges and lawyers toward certain ends, and the historical development of others. Thus "general security" includes the primitive and still basic needs of public and individual safety from aggression, and peace and order. To these public health has been added in modern times. However, the security of transactions and the security of acquisitions (contract and property), while given top importance in nineteenth century case law, are frequently made to yield to other social interests; these two might well have been grouped under economic institutions (II(d)). The class of "general morals" could be broken down by criteria of social consequences so that it would come under other headings: sexual immorality is usually regarded as impairing domestic institutions (II(a)), and dishonesty or fraud or corruption impairs other social institutions. Yet "general morality" stands for the popular mores, traditional and conservative, accepted intuitively and not in terms of consequences. Pound is trying to keep his inventory from being merely a survey of a philosopher's cloudy ideals.[55] Putting the conservation of forests and water in the same class with the conservation of defectives and delinquent minors seems odd now, yet in 1914 the juvenile court movement needed some such analogy to support it in public discussions. The social interest in the individual life may be thought broad enough to include all the others; for what is the end of the state if not to protect and promote the good of the individual? Pound recognizes that argument in support of (for instance) minimum wage legislation for women, is sometimes based on the evil effects upon the health and morals of women, and sometimes upon the individual's claim to a minimum enjoyment of life.[56] The six social interests overlap in the sense that an individual claim can ordinarily be subsumed under (or supported by) more than one. That is the way things are in contemporary social discourse.

One question that may be asked about Pound's inventory and his method of using it is, does it provide an "objective" criterion of value and, if so, in what sense? Each of Pound's social interests is anchored three ways, that is, it must satisfy three requirements: First, it must be a measuring or testing device for individual interests; second, it must be inferred from the positive law and legal processes of a given society; third, it must conform to a widespread set of demands or convictions of the members of that society. Perhaps there is a fourth requisite that a social interest must be a means to the maintenance of a civilized society, one having a mature level of culture. Now the relation of the individual claim to the social interest is that the general qualities or attributes of *such* a claim are used to predict what will be, in case the claim is recognized and protected generally or in a particular way, the social consequences which a social interest designates as significant, and as good or bad. So the claim to enforce a contract in restraint of marriage is supported by the social in-

---

[55] Pound said: "I doubt the ability of the jurist to work out deductively the necessary jural presuppositions of society in the abstract." 57 Harv.L. Rev. 15.

[56] E. g., in the Appendix to Brief of Appellant in Adkins v. Children's Hospital (first minimum wage decision), 261 U.S. 525, 43 Sup.Ct. 394 (1923) and in Appendix to Brief of Defendant-in-Error in Bunting v. Oregon, 243 U.S. 426, 37 Sup.Ct. 435 (1917); cited by Pound, n. 185.

terest in the security of transactions and is bad when tested by the social interest in domestic institutions. Such causal relations are, of course, only more or less probable. Where Bentham speaks of the "tendency" of a wilful invasion of one property owner's claim to cause pain to all property owners (§ 4.42), Pound would speak of the social interest in the security of acquisitions. Pound's theory of social interests thus represents a teleological axiology, like that of Bentham and Ihering.

It is "objective" in the sense that the value-propositions implicit in the table are based upon the propositions *about* valuations that are found in the legal system, case law and legislation (and even in proposals for legal change). It is not "objective" in the sense that any value is absolute (must always prevail over all others) nor in the sense that the use of the method will supply either a unique deductive demonstration (if there be any such) nor an unambiguous experimental verification of a particular valuation. Judges will differ on such questions as, does the allowance of any tort action by a minor child against his parent unduly impair family life, or may *some* such actions be allowed without undue harm? [57] Judicial prophecies of consequences have often been proved fallible. One recalls Lord Abinger's prophecies of the dire consequences of making a master liable to his employee for a fellow-servant's negligence, and the Wisconsin court's prediction that the admission of women to practice law would demoralize them.[58] On the other hand, Pound's inventory is sufficiently comprehensive and enduring that a Soviet jurist, for example, could recognize in his own legal system some similar claims or demands and could construct, on Pound's model, a similar inventory of social interests in the Russian legal order. However, the Soviet jurist would be handicapped by the necessity of treating all deductions arrived at by Marxist dialectical materialism (§ 4.35) as beyond dispute.

Pound's social interests are not transcendental values that purport to override or supersede the positive law. Hence to say that his theory is only another name for natural law or natural rights is erroneous. The referents (semantically) of social interests are the values aimed at by public policies, which are a part of

---

[57] Pound, 57 Harv.L.Rev. 21, n. 87. Cf. Cannon v. Cannon, 287 N.Y. 425, 40 N.E.2d 236 (1942) with Dunlap v. Dunlap, 84 N.H. 352, 150 A. 905 (1930) (where an insurer would pay the bill).

[58] In (respectively) Priestly v. Fowler, 3 M. & W. 1, 5–6 (1837) and In re Goodell, 39 Wis. 232, 245–6 (1875).

the legal system.[59] In this sense Pound may accurately speak of a "survey." Yet the table of social interests is an imaginative construction of the ends of a civilized legal order.

Pound's theory, like Bentham's utilitarianism, is useful in framing legislation, and is much more useful in the judicial process of appellate courts. Most American judges, like nearly all the English ones, will prefer to find precise rules to guide their problematic thinking as well as their opinion writing. They will hesitate to rely upon and even more to put into published opinions the vague propositions represented by Pound's broadest categories of social interests. They will, for instance, quote the rule that "clear and convincing proof" of mutual mistake in integration is required for reformation of a written instrument,[60] without adverting to the social interest in the security of transactions as an important reason for this rule (and others). Still the increasing manifestations of the judicial urge to look for the policies or objectives that justify and limit a legal rule, to use these in the thinking stage and (more reluctantly) in the expository stage, constitute a significant trend of the present century.

One further question about Pound's policy-method, raised a generation ago,[61] is, how can one "weigh" or "balance" against each other social interests which are not translatable into some common scale of value? Such expressions as "weighing" and "social engineering," like Bentham's "felicific calculus" and Holmes' "accurately measured social desires," may hold out a misleading hope of quantitative exactness. Yet men do make choices between things of imponderable value and express the choice in quantitative terms, as the use of money continuously shows. One may "weigh" a contribution to charity against a splurge on pleasure. Judges are unavoidably called upon to make some crucial choices. Pound's table of social interests is well adapted to make such choices reflective, reasoned, and in keeping with the dominant values of the prevailing legal order. They represent the need of the social order for both stability and change.

---

[59] See supra, § 3.25.

[60] E. g., Amend v. Hurley, 293 N.Y. 587, 59 N.E.2d 416 (1944).

[61] See Lepaulle, "The Function of Comparative Law with a Critique of Sociological Jurisprudence," (1922) 35 Harv.L.Rev. 838, 844.

§ 4.62—Benjamin N. Cardozo: The Judicial Process

The chief contributions of Benjamin Cardozo to jurisprudence were his revelations of the methods of the judicial process. Since his analysis of these methods was designed to guide the search for premises, of law and fact, in dealing with a problematic situation, he might appropriately have been discussed with the pragmatists, yet he was also a follower of Pound. His judicial opinions exemplified in part his account of the process and contributed in many fields to the improvement and clarification of American law. Added to these was his personal influence among judges, lawyers and law professors as a wise and revered leader of twentieth century legal change.

Benjamin Nathan Cardozo (1870–1938), some of whose ancestors emigrated from the Spanish peninsula and settled in New York city before the American Revolution, was born and reared in that city and attended Columbia College. There he became an admirer of Matthew Arnold, of his style and of that combination of reason and morality, of Hellenism and Hebraism, which Arnold deemed characteristic of Western civilization.[62] The youthful Cardozo's commencement oration of 1889 [63] contains vigorous arguments against Communism couched in florid Victorian language. His literary style, luminous, metaphorical, graceful, never lost this early influence. The use of metaphor, sometimes so finely wrought as to be fine writing, became more restrained with the New York Bar Association address of 1932.[64] Cardozo's style, both in his opinions and in his extra-judicial writings, places him in the distinguished company of O. W. Holmes and Learned Hand.

After two years of study in the Columbia Law School,[65] Cardozo was admitted to the New York bar in 1891. His work as a prac-

---

[62] See Cardozo's Columbia College essay, "The Moral Element in Matthew Arnold" in Selected Writings of Benjamin N. Cardozo (1947), 61 ff. (This collection will be cited as "Sel. Wr.")

[63] "The Altruist in Politics," Sel. Wr., 47 ff.

[64] "Jurisprudence," Sel. Wr. 7–46 (1932 N. Y. State Bar Ass'n Rep. 263).

[65] With the coming of Dean William A. Keener to that law school came also the lengthening of the course of study from two to three years, a change which was, unfortunately, made applicable to those who had already entered the school under the two-year program. Cardozo was one of these, and joined with his classmates in refusing to take the third year. Hence he never received an LL.B. degree, though eventually a certificate was awarded to the members of his class. This will serve to explain why one of our greatest

titioner, unexciting, honorable and highly respected, ended with his election to the bench in 1913 on a Fusion ticket. Soon afterward he was appointed to the Court of Appeals and continued on that Court, by election, until 1932. During this period of some eighteen years he made his distinguished contributions to private law—the law of contracts and torts, of trusts and restitution —with which that Court is chiefly concerned. After his elevation to the (Federal) Supreme Court, where his work was chiefly in public law and statutory interpretation, he looked back wistfully upon those happy years. Yet his work on the Supreme Court, where he was regarded as Holmes' successor both in learning and in liberality of outlook, was scarcely less distinguished.[66] Pound rightly included him, along with Holmes, in his list of the ten most distinguished judges in American judicial history.[67] Of his work as a judge more will be said later. Here we are concerned with his writings in the field of jurisprudence.[68]

What ideas did Cardozo contribute to jurisprudence? Very few, perhaps, that can be regarded as original and significant. One of these, the conception of a ministry of justice, will be discussed below. Likewise, very few that were systematic, or comprehensive; his four methods of the judicial process are considered below. Yet his continued emphasis upon pressing moral values in the law, along with the demands of reason and order and political stability, was original in its wholeness, in its recognition of inner struggle, in its mediation between the nineteenth century love of security and the twentieth century love of progress. In an era of transition he was the great mediator.

1. *The Ministry of Justice.* In one of his earliest public lectures [69] Cardozo urged the need of a permanent governmental

---

judges never obtained his professional degree. Columbia University was the first (1915) of many to award him the honorary LL.D.

[66] Cardozo's frail health reduced his judicial activity in his later years. For a collection of excerpts from his judicial opinions, with a valuable commentary, see Levy, Cardozo and Frontiers of Legal Thinking (1938).

[67] Pound, The Formative Era in American Law (1938; four lectures delivered in 1936), 4, 30, n. 63.

[68] For a fuller treatment, see Patterson, "Cardozo's Philosophy of Law," (1939) 88 U. of Pa.L.Rev. 71–91, 156–176 (cited below by volume and page alone). See also the present writer's Foreword to Selected Writings, supra, n. 62.

[69] "A Ministry of Justice," (1921) 35 Harv.L.Rev. 113; Lectures on Legal Topics (Ass'n of the Bar of the City of New York) 1921–22; Sel. Wr. 357; Hall, 1132.

body to aid the courts in correcting the anachronisms of private, man-to-man law. Formerly, he said, legal change was brought about by fiction and by equity (§ 4.33). These methods are no longer sufficient. The modern method is legislation. The courts need liberation from precedents which have become anachronisms, which they revile and yet are obliged to follow. Why are they obliged to follow them? For one thing, the requirement of legal certainty, of giving effect to expectations which have been created by the prevailing rule, checks their zeal to reform. Again, the judges are divided as to the appropriate time and the appropriate case for making the change; such divisions would distract them from their principal tasks, if they were to attempt legal reform by the process of overruling their precedents. Furthermore, the latter process would be sporadic and piecemeal. For instance, the rule that a sealed contract can be modified only by another sealed contract (which was affirmed and applied by the New York Court of Appeals as late as 1921) [70] could be overruled only when a case came before the court in which the rule was involved. Other incidents of the sealed instrument, such as the rule that an undisclosed principal is not bound by a sealed instrument executed by and *in the name of* his agent, might not come before the same court for several years, and the court might then decline to overrule its precedents on the ground that to do so would upset settled expectations.[71] A statute could wipe out all of these rules, for future transactions, and at the same time substitute others designed to accomplish the same purpose.[72]

Who is to present to the legislature proposals for such changes? The state administrative officials, even including the Attorney-General, will present proposals to amend existing *legislation,* such as the Workmen's Compensation law. No one is charged with the duty of keeping private *case law* up to date. The legislatures are too busily engaged with "political" legislation, what Cardozo gently called "issues more clamorous than those of courts," [73] to

---

[70] Harris v. Shorall, 230 N.Y. 343, 130 N.E. 572 (1921) cited by Cardozo, Sel. Wr., 361.

[71] The Court did so refuse in Crowley v. Lewis, 239 N.Y. 264, 146 N.E. 374 (1924), and Cardozo explained why in The Paradoxes of Legal Science (1928), 70.

[72] Thus, seals no longer have any effect whatever on the obligation of a written instrument. N.Y.C.P.A. § 342. Yet a gratuitous modification of a contract in writing is binding only if itself in writing. N.Y.Pers.Prop.Law, § 33.

[73] Sel. Wr., 358.

find time to overhaul the law of contracts, torts, etc. The courts themselves are in no position to draft and submit legislation. Thus we can understand the cry that escaped Cardozo:

"The courts are not helped as they could and ought to be in the adaptation of law to justice." [74]

What the courts needed was a body that would study present law and discover the anachronisms and inadequacies which the courts were practically powerless to correct, would draft legislation and would present it to the legislature. This body Cardozo called a Ministry of Justice, after the European analogues; it eventuated in New York as the Law Revision Commission. One final touch showed Cardozo's view of the judicial process, and of the kind of legislation needed to modify the grand compartments of case law ("common law"). The courts need only enough legislation to free them from precedent, to start them on a new path. "Often a dozen lines or less will be enough for our deliverance." [75] The legislation need not be lengthy and detailed; it need only state a principle.

The New York Commission, created many years later as a direct result of Cardozo's recommendation, has generally followed his suggestion as to method. Its statutes are usually brief, and ordinarily they do not purport to lay down an affirmative rule, but rather to negate a factor which was heretofore decisive in case law. Thus the several statutes modifying the English-American requirement of consideration declare that certain agreements shall not be invalid because of the absence of a consideration; [76] the statute "abolishing" the mistake-of-law rule provides that relief for mistake shall not be denied merely because the mistake is one of law rather than of fact.[77] This means that the New York court is invited to overhaul its precedents on mistake of law and determine in what types of cases of such mistake relief should be given. This process will call for an exploration of the grounds and principles underlying the granting (and the denial) of similar relief for mistake of fact.

Cardozo claimed no originality for his proposal; he pointed out that Pound, Bentham and others had made similar proposals, and that continental European countries had long had similar govern-

---

[74] Ibid., 357.

[75] Ibid., 361.

[76] N.Y.Pers.Prop.Law, § 33.

[77] N.Y.C.P.A. § 112-f (enacted 1942).

mental devices.[78] Yet his own proposal was cogent because it displayed a basic respect for legal stability as well as legal change, and for the conservative attitudes of courts toward law-making. Cardozo went further and suggested that the ministry of justice should have not less than five members, of whom at least two should be chosen from faculties of law or political science and at least one should represent the bar. The New York Commission, created in 1934, has conformed to these suggestions. Members of the legislature have always been included in its make-up. The Commission employs research assistants or special consultants (frequently law professors) who prepare thorough studies of legal questions, including often a comprehensive survey of English and American law and some account of Roman and civil law.[79] These studies are presented to the Commission with or without recommendation, and the Commission has not infrequently decided that it could not make any recommendation for legislation as a result of such a study. Sometimes the Commission's recommendations are rejected because of definite opposition. However, a great many valuable improvements in New York law have been made as a result of the Commission's work. Cardozo's plea for liberation from tradition has been partly realized.

2. *The Four Methods of the Judicial Process.* In his most important book Cardozo outlined four "methods" of the judicial process which provided the framework of that work,[80] were repeated in his second book [81] and were ignored in his third.[82] They were sometimes called "directive forces" and sometimes "methods," as in the following passage:

----

[78] Sel. Wr., 358. In France the Minister of Justice can and does not only recommend corrective legislation, but he can also appeal a judicial decision, in civil litigation, which he deems to involve a question of public concern. This latter feature was not included in Cardozo's plan.

[79] Unfortunately, these studies are available in permanent form only in the official Reports of the Commission, of which only a limited number are obtainable outside of New York official circles. The first report was issued in 1935, pursuant to N. Y. Laws 1934, Ch. 597.

[80] Cardozo, The Nature of the Judicial Process (Yale Univ. Press, 1921), 10, 30–31 and *passim.* This volume, containing the Storrs Lectures at Yale, is cited below as The Nature (reprinted in Sel. Wr. with original paging).

[81] Cardozo, The Growth of the Law (1924), 62, 73, etc. This volume, cited below as The Growth is reprinted in Sel. Wr.

[82] Cardozo, The Paradoxes of Legal Science (1928), containing his Carpentier Lectures at Columbia; cited below as The Paradoxes (also in Sel. Wr.).

"The directive force of a principle may be exerted along the line of logical progression; this I call the rule of analogy or the method of philosophy; along the line of historical development; this I call the method of evolution; along the line of the customs of the community; this I call the method of tradition; along the lines of justice, morals and social welfare, the mores of the day; and this I call the method of sociology." [83]

These are methods to be used by the judge after he has extracted from the judicial precedents the underlying principle, the ratio decidendi. His task is not yet done. He must determine the path along which the principle is to develop.[84] Logic and history would seem to be the routine lines of development. Either one feels bound by the inexorable logic of an inescapable ratio decidendi, or one is hemmed in by the pressures of legal history from cutting a new path. The four methods are not simply guides for the rare case; they are guides for the commonplace case as well. The first two are the ones most commonly used. The third is resorted to normally in that mercantile customs determine how to apply established rules, and occasionally create new ones.[85] The fourth method, though of paramount authority once it is invoked, is least often called into play.[86] Then "justice" is the last idea that a judge should resort to? Yes, according to Cardozo's conception of "justice" and of the judicial function. He adhered firmly to the view that only in rare instances should even the highest appellate court, empowered to overrule its precedents, venture to innovate. Law making is primarily for the legislature. And "justice" or "social welfare" are vague terms, about which judges will differ as well as other men. Rarely should they impose their ideas of justice upon the community as law. Here logic and social welfare may concur: [87] Adherence to the logic of established law and legal history will normally have greater social value than trying out a new legal doctrine created by the judge's sense of justice.

Of these four methods the second and third are the most clearly intelligible. The method of history reconciles the judge to the necessity of applying rules of real-property law descended from

---

[83] The Nature, 30–31.

[84] Ibid., at 30.

[85] The Growth, 60–61.

[86] The Nature, 40–41, 98.

[87] Ibid., 65.

the system of feudal tenures, which was not created by a rational modern law-giver; [88] so as to the law of sealed instruments. Here one may ask, does the court *really* exclude considerations of policy or social welfare in following established conventional rules; does it not, in effect, prefer the values of stability and certainty to those of piecemeal and chaotic judge-made change? No doubt one can use Pound's theory of social interests (§ 4.61) to formulate the judicial problem, and thus make all four of Cardozo's methods applicable in all cases. However, Cardozo did not think of the choice that way. In the vast majority of cases (before an appellate court), he thought the result is predetermined by established rules and principles and by the canons of the art of judging. The judges, loyal to the traditions of the office, have no choice. That is, prevailingly, Cardozo's doctrine. In many of his most famous judicial opinions he shows how the aim of justice or social welfare guided the interpretation of the facts in the record and enabled him to escape from the application of a rule which his official loyalty would not permit him to contradict. That is why a good many of them, though they are brilliant specimens of judicial dialectic in the formulation of the factual (minor) premise, left historically established doctrines untouched or at most questioned.

A few examples must suffice here. In the famous Hynes case [89] a boy who had trespassed on railroad property adjoining a river and who was about to dive from a springboard affixed to that property and extending seven feet over public waters (the Harlem River) was struck and killed by the falling of the railroad company's defectively maintained electric wires. The lower courts, applying inexorably the rule that no duty of care [90] is owed to a trespasser, had denied his mother's claim for damages. In the Court of Appeals Cardozo by persuasive rhetoric and ingenious casuistry changed the boy's situation from that of a trespasser on railroad property (the springboard) to that of a bather lawfully in public waters (the river below), thus convincing three of his colleagues that the defendant owed the boy a duty of care. What effect does the holding have on the rule, sometimes harsh in application, that a landowner need not keep his land in a safe condition for trespassers? Not that it is rejected or

---

[88] Ibid., 64.

[89] Hynes v. New York Central R. Co., 231 N.Y. 229, 131 N.E. 898 (1921). Further discussion infra, § 5.05.

[90] I. e., the only duty to a trespasser is not to injure him wilfully.

even modified; only that the Court will seek to exclude marginal cases from its operation. Again, in a noted contract case,[91] Cardozo avowed adherence to three precedents of his own Court establishing an unpalatable corollary of the doctrine of consideration [92] and circumvented it by so construing the facts of a marriage settlement and the ensuing marriage as to make out a different consideration for the promise of the bride's father to pay her an annuity. Here again it is hard to say what effect the decision had on the unwanted rule, since it was merely found to be inapplicable and therefore irrelevant. In each of these cases Cardozo stayed within the logical application of well-settled law to the facts as he construed them. Arguments of justice and policy were used as makeweight arguments to support his conclusion. His skill was in constructing a factual rather than a legal premise.[93]

Cardozo's four methods were not clearly labelled, nor were they clearly conceived. Logic must be used in all four methods; analogy is not the only method of logic, and it is misleading to call this the "method of philosophy." Custom and tradition, though loose terms, are by no means equivalent; a recent mercantile custom may upset established tradition. Why "history" should be separated from "tradition" is hard to understand. Yet Cardozo's outline served two purposes: First, to show that a court engaged primarily in applying or creating law should seek conservative stability most of the time; and that reasons of policy or social welfare can be stated in words, to justify rare or close decisions, without impairing the stability of normal procedure.

3. *The Great Mediator.* Cardozo was the great mediator, both in his work on the New York Court and in his jurisprudence. Judge Lehman, his colleague on that Court, has said that "from boyhood until death he walked steadily along the path of reason, seeking the goal of truth." [94] This is true and yet it is not all. Cardozo was moved by his feelings and revealed more clearly than

---

[91] De Cicco v. Schweizer, 221 N.Y. 431, 117 N.E. 807 (1917).

[92] I. e., that a promise by A to B to perform what A is already under a contractual duty to C to do, is insufficient consideration to buy a binding promise from B to render a performance to A. (Pre-existing duty to third party.)

[93] He employed the same technique in finding that the college, by accepting a completed gift, had impliedly promised to devote the entire donation, completed and promised, to a memorial for the donor, and in thus avoiding a holding on promissory estoppel, in Allegheny College v. National Chautauqua County Bank, 246 N.Y. 369, 159 N.E. 173 (1927).

[94] Lehman (Irving) "A Memorial," Sel.Wr., xii.

most judges have done his inner struggle with conflicting emotions. His revelation in classical prose of his struggle between the desire for stability as a means for legal order and the quest for justice or social welfare as the goal of legal change made his opinions, as well as his writings, appealing to a larger audience of conservative judges and lawyers than those who could follow Holmes or Brandeis. After discussing Stammler's theory of just law (§ 4.23) which attracted him emotionally yet left him with no instruments of legal thinking, he concludes that justice as a jural norm, in contrast with the justice of ethical theory, is " . . . so much of morality as juristic thought discovers to be wisely and efficiently enforcible by the aid of jural sanctions." [95] "Juristic thought" includes the "authoritative technique" of the courts. Thus Cardozo's limitation on the implementation of moral principles by law resembles that of Jean Dabin (§ 4.14), though Cardozo did not envisage any situation in which law would be invalid because it conflicted with moral principles. One might think that always, in this enlightened age, the safety of the person should be preferred to property interests. Yet "we run railroads, though lives might be saved if we were satisfied to travel slowly." [96] To his own generation of judges and lawyers Cardozo was loyal both to the past and to the future; he was a wise man and a prophet.

But the limits to his compromise and tolerance were revealed in the Bar Association address of 1932 [97] in which he repulsed the assaults of the legal realists upon his citadel of reason, symmetry and order. What troubled him most was the view that the judge's intuitive hunches were the crucial factors in the judicial process, that legal rules and principles had little (or nothing, in the extreme view) to do with the decisions, and that the opinions of courts were relatively unimportant post-rationalizations. Oliphant's theory of judicial precedents (§ 3.31) and Judge Hutcheson's exaggeration of the judicial hunch [98] were disturbing because he, Cardozo, had pointed to the creative role of the judge and to the need for shaping by reason the development of legal doctrines. At first he tried to disregard these realist views as mere excrescences.

---

[95] The Paradoxes, 35. It is typical of Cardozo's eclecticism that a little further on (p. 48) he transforms this into something resembling Duguit's "social rule" (supra, § 4.14).

[96] Ibid., 57.

[97] Supra, n. 64.

[98] Hutcheson, "The Judgment Intuitive: The Function of the Hunch in Judicial Decisions," (1929) 14 Cornell L.Q. 274, discussed Sel.Wr., 26.

Then he took a new line: Legal certainty need be maintained only as laymen's certainty, not as lawyer's certainty, since it is from the laymen, primarily, that conformity is due. The law will seldom disappoint the laymen's expectations if it conforms to the customs or mores of the times, even though it does not follow from previously established formulas.[99] The idea is attractive as a limitation upon the nineteenth century exaggeration of legal certainty. Perhaps no stockholder rushed to sell because the automobile manufacturing company was held liable to the remote purchaser for injuries resulting from defects in manufacture; no investments had been made in reliance on the old requirement of privity.[1] Yet in so far as laymen rely on lawyers' predictions (§ 3.02), lawyers' certainty counts even for laymen. Despite a conciliatory attitude, Cardozo had no tolerance for a "jurisprudence of mere sentiment or feeling," [2] for a "doctrine of undisciplined surrender to the cardiac promptings of the moment, the visceral reactions of one judge or another." [3] He found comfort in Professor Morris Cohen's support of a rational order in law, even though it had twilight zones, and of the importance of the reasons given in judicial opinions.[4] Still the mediator, Cardozo argued that, to satisfy the urgent need for legal change, courts of final resort should adopt the method of prospective overruling, of giving judgment in the instant case in conformity with the old rule but announcing that a different rule will be followed in cases arising hereafter.[5] So, leaving the door open for a reconciliation with the realists, he ended his last important public address on a note of patient optimism.

§ 4.63—American Legal Realism: Origins and Methods

The term "legal realism" emerged about 1930 as a label for the lively and somewhat heterodox legal theories of a group of American law teachers and lawyers who diverged from each other in many respects and yet had much in common. The origins of this

---

[99] Supra, n. 66, 29.

[1] Supra, § 3.30 (2); The Nature, 146; Sel.Wr., ("Jurisprudence") 34.

[2] Sel.Wr., 28.

[3] Ibid., 15.

[4] Sel.Wr., 25 (discussing Cohen's principle of polarity) and 31–32 (discussing Cohen's defense, and Goodhart's (§ 3.32)), of the significance of judicial opinions.

[5] Sel.Wr., 35–37.

movement are to be found chiefly in pragmatism, especially the pragmatism of O. W. Holmes (§ 4.55). Perhaps the one view that all legal realists shared was expressed by Holmes in his "cynical acid" passage:

"You see how the vague circumference of the notion of duty shrinks and at the same time grows more precise when we wash it with cynical acid and expel everything except the object of our study, the operations of the law." [6]

The legal realists differed a good deal among themselves as to the desirable degree of corrosiveness of the cynical acid, and as to the constructive substitutes which they proposed; nor would all agree that they were concerned solely with "the operations of the law," leaving out the operations of society. Some legal realists were influenced by, or borrowed from, nearly every novel contemporary twentieth century theory or trend: Behavioristic psychology, statistical sociology, psychoanalysis, psychology, and even the "stream-of-consciousness" technique of novelists, such as Proust and Joyce. Taken all together this caldron of ideas was a witches' brew that revolted such moderate pragmatists as Pound and Cardozo along with such moderate rationalists as Morris R. Cohen, Hermann Kantorowicz and Professor Lon Fuller.

Who were the realists and what were their ideas? Professor Llewellyn answered the first question, at least partly, in his reply to Pound's criticism of some of the excesses of the realist movement.[7] He included Bingham (formerly of the Stanford law faculty) and Lorenzen (formerly of Yale) because Pound regarded them as realists. The leaders of legal realism, after Holmes, were, in my opinion, six men: Underhill Moore, Herman Oliphant, Walter W. Cook, Karl N. Llewellyn, Charles E. Clark and Jerome Frank. The others mentioned by Llewellyn were: Arthur L. Corbin, T. R. Powell, Leon Green, Max Radin, Joseph E. Hutcheson, Samuel Klaus, Wesley Sturges, W. O. Douglas, Leon Tulin, Joseph F. Francis, Hessel E. Yntema and Edwin Patterson. All

---

[6] Holmes, "The Path of the Law" in Collected Legal Papers (1920), 167, 174 (first published in (1897) 10 Harv.L.Rev.).

[7] Llewellyn, "Some Realism about Realism—Responding to Dean Pound", (1931) 44 Harv.L.Rev. 1222, 1226, n. 17, n. 18. (Hereafter cited as "Some Realism.") Llewellyn and Frank made a survey of the writings of all of the legal realists they could think of, in order to determine by evidence whether Pound's charges (which mentioned no names in the printed article) were substantiated. See Pound, "A Call for a Realist Jurisprudence", (1931) 44 Harv. L.Rev. 697. To Llewellyn's list might be added, with justification, Thurman Arnold and Felix Cohen.

of those listed were law teachers except Judge Hutcheson, Judge Frank (then with the Securities and Exchange Commission) and Klaus, a New York lawyer. Some of their writings will be referred to below.[8]

Everyone, doubtless, wants to be a realist. No one cares to admit that his serious effort to think through to a conclusion any social or legal problem is only shadow-boxing, mere grasping at ghostly unrealities. What is reality? To some it is found in tangible things and events, in "facts" of which ideas are only pale ghosts or statistical summaries. To others, wearied or distrustful of sensational experience, reality is to be found in the eternal verities, the essential concepts of which transient sensed experiences are but wavering reflections. The second is Platonic realism, as symbolized in the famous cave-simile of The Republic.[9] One can find signs of Plato's conception of reality among the American legal realists: In Holmes' rhetorical hope that through jurisprudence one may "catch an echo of the infinite," [10] and in occasional passages of other realist writings.[11] But for the most part the legal realists sought reality in human behavior, in judicial and other official conduct, in concrete operations rather than in essences. This trend is exemplified in their conceptions of law.

1. *Conceptions of Law.* Perhaps the commonest conception of law among the legal realists was that it consisted of a body of descriptive generalizations about official conduct, or about the conduct of judges. Thus Cook, laying down the postulates for a scientific method of studying law, said:

"This past behavior of the judges can be described in terms of certain generalizations which we call rules and principles of law." [12]

These descriptive generalizations are, he says, used by practicing lawyers in trying to forecast future events, that is, future decisions of courts on certain sets of facts. But whereas Holmes had treated the rules as "prophecies" of future decisions, Cook treats

---

[8] A Selective Bibliography of legal realism is to be found in Garlan, Legal Realism and Justice (1941), 135 ff.

[9] The Republic of Plato (Lindsay trans., 1935), Bk. VII.

[10] Holmes, Collected Legal Papers (1920), 202.

[11] Rather in what Llewellyn has called the "afterglow" than in specific passages.

[12] Cook, "Scientific Method and the Law", (1927) 13 A.B.A.J. 303, 308; Hall, p. 784.

them as descriptions of past decisions, and gives them a somewhat lower status. From the descriptive generalization to the conception that law is what officials do, the "do-law" concept (§ 2.10), is a transition made easy by the conventional practice of referring to case-law propositions as "rules *of* law" rather than "laws"; hence legal rules are rules of official action, and the latter is "law":

"Rules, whether stated by judges or others, whether in statutes, opinions or text-books by learned authors, are not the law, but are only some among many of the sources to which judges go in making the law of the cases tried before them. . . . The law, therefore, consists of decisions, not of rules. If so, then, whenever a judge decides a case he is making law." [13]

"What these officials do about disputes is, to my mind, the law itself." [14]

Yet Llewellyn has said elsewhere that law includes not only "all that lawmen *do*, as such," but also predictions, rules for the doing, and ideologies.[15] While Cook mentioned only judicial doing, Llewellyn includes also the doings of prosecutors and sometimes of policemen. Now these views of law seem to regard it as a set of social phenomena, as the materials of that projected sociology of law [16] which has not been written. In another passage Llewellyn has referred to law as a "social science" [17] and Oliphant was wont to refer to it that way.[18] Moore, whose terminology was carefully chosen, referred to a "legal institution" as "a group of persons . . . acting in some way" [19] and to a "statement of law" as

---

[13] Frank, Law and the Modern Mind (1930), 127–128. In a later book, Judge Frank expressed his intention of avoiding the use of the word "law." Courts on Trial (1949), 3.

[14] Llewellyn, The Bramble Bush (1930), 3.

[15] Llewellyn, Behind the Law of Divorce, (1932) 32 Col.L.Rev. 1281, 1297. See also his essay in the volume, My Philosophy of Law (1941).

[16] See Llewellyn, "The Theory of Legal 'Science'," (1941) 20 N.C.L.Rev. 1, 17.

[17] "But one concerned with law as a social *science*, a science of observation, must center his thought on behavior, on the interactions between the behavior of law-officials and behavior of laymen." Llewellyn, "Legal Tradition and Social Science Method—A Realist's Critique" in Essays in Research in the Social Sciences, (1931) 90; Hall, 789–90.

[18] Oliphant, "Facts, Opinions and Value-Judgments", (1932) 10 Tex.L.Rev. 127 (" . . . the study of law or any other social science. . . . ")

[19] Moore, "Rational Basis of Legal Institutions", (1923) 23 Col.L.Rev. 609.

a forecast which results from the application of legal method.[20] Moore and Oliphant wanted to establish a conception of law as descriptive or factual in order that a scientific method of dealing with it might be invented or discovered.

Of this aspect of American legal realism the best criticism was made by the late Professor Hermann Kantorowicz, himself a former leader of the rebellious "free-law" movement in Germany. These realists, he says, have the "sociological prejudice"; they believe they can study social phenomena by themselves without regard for the rules that govern them. But this cannot be done. One cannot, for example, *determine what is* the Congress of the United States without having regard for its being the body established and continued pursuant to the rules (directions, norms) contained in the Constitution.[21] The attempt to leave out the normative element in law always results in distortion; the result is not merely that the writers talk about different things but that they talk inadequately about what they do purport to discuss. The exclusive concern with prediction of the outcome of a litigated dispute-about-law shows the "professional prejudice," the overemphasis on the training of counselors.[22] The social phenomena that are influenced by law include behaviors conforming to legal rules (without official action directly applied) as well as non-conforming behaviors. As he rightly concluded, a legal science that ignores the normative or prescriptive character of law will be incomplete.

2. *The Judicial Process.* The leading realists centered upon the judicial process. Oliphant sought to develop a theory by which one could predict the reaction of a judge or judges to the stimuli of a given set of facts (§ 3.31). Moore's elaborate study of the debiting of direct discounts was designed to verify the following hypothesis: The decision of a court on a given set of facts, which cannot adequately be predicted by the use of legal rules or precedents, can be predicted by reference to external factors, the local and contemporary institutional practices in the type of situation involved and the kind and degree of deviation from the in-

---

[20] Moore and Sussman, "Legal and Institutional Methods Applied to the Debiting of Direct Discounts—I. Legal Method: Banker's Set-off", (1931) 40 Yale L.J. 381.

[21] Kantorowicz, "Some Rationalism About Realism", (1934) 43 Yale L.J. 1240, 1246.

[22] Ibid., 1246–47.

stitutional pattern which the instant case presents.[23] While neither Moore nor Oliphant believed that sexual drives or similar
psychoanalytical factors had important influences upon judicial
decisions, yet each believed that the "hunch" played a significant
part and that the decision in a close case could be better explained
by extra-legal factors—the patterns of social institutions or practices—than by the legal rules laid down in statutes or in judicial
opinions. Thus each of these realists sought to find the real or
ultimate basis for judicial decisions outside the law-in-books,
often outside the legal order of officialdom, located somewhere in
the social-cultural matrix of inquiry.[24] A concrete example
would be this: A judicial decision (by the Supreme Court of the
United States) that a statute forbidding an employer to exact
from his employees agreements not to join a labor union, is contrary to "due process of law," is not determined by just the meanings of the Constitution and the judicial precedents construing it,
but rather by the views of social policy held by the social and
professional groups from which the judges came. In this sense
the hunch theory was not a flat rejection of rational modes of
solution but an effort to find new premises for legal reasoning.
On the other hand, the "hunch" theory of Judge Hutcheson [25]
seems to have been somewhat simpler, a discovery that judges do
not think through to their conclusions solely (or even usually) by
formulated syllogisms, that flashes of intuitive insight are important and that there is what Graham Wallas aptly called an "art
of thought." [26]

3. *Logic and Semantics.* O. W. Holmes sounded off the realist
attack on logic when in 1881 he startled a sedate audience attending his Lowell lecture with the statement that the life of the law
has not been logic but experience.[27] Later realist attacks on

[23] Moore, op. cit. supra, n. 20, at p. 564; Moore and Hope, "An Institutional
Approach to the Law of Commercial Banking", (1929) 38 Yale L.J. 703, 705.
This may be called "the institutional—correlation" hypothesis.

[24] See Dewey, Logic (1938), Ch. III.

[25] Hutcheson, "The Judgment Intuitive: The Function of the Hunch in
Judicial Decision", (1929) 14 Corn.L.Q. 274–276, in which Judge Hutcheson
reveals his earlier conception of judicial thinking as rather mechanical.
Later he expressed views reminiscent of Bergson's vitalism, in reviewing
Rueff's book. (1931) 17 A.B.A.J. 185–188. Still later he hedged a bit. Infra,
§ 5.03, n. 46.

[26] Wallas, The Art of Thought (1926), Ch. IV. Yet generalizations have
at least an implicit part in the process of thinking, even in an "art."

[27] Holmes, The Common Law (1881), 1.

logic or conceptualism were negations of the exaggerated pretenses of nineteenth century rationalism exemplified in Holmes' eminent judge who said he never let a decision go until he was absolutely sure it was right.[28] Prof. Walter Bingham began the attack on the sufficiency of legal generalizations to account for judicial decisions by pointing to the vagueness of legal terms, such as "legal possession." [29] Yet he did not deny what he had said in his earlier realist article:

> "The intelligent direction of human action necessarily involves the use of generalizations." [30]

What he sought to emphasize in this pioneer article on realism was that legal generalizations are significant only in so far as they *do* influence human action, especially official action. This leads in its extreme variation to the "do-law" theory discussed above. In these instances logic is found *inadequate* to explain the thought-processes of judges—a view which any formal logician would concede.

Another attack on logical formulations came from the (somewhat belated) discovery by legal realists that two non-Euclidean geometries had been invented in the nineteenth century, and that one of these proved useful in the space-time theory based upon Einstein's theory of relativity. Since a basic axiom of Euclidean geometry, that parallel lines do not meet,[31] which had long been regarded (at least among laymen who had their noses rubbed in geometry) as a self-evident truth, was now shown to be merely a postulate of a traditional system of geometry, it might well be that many of the basic principles or concepts of our legal system are only postulates which can be modified or dispensed with. The contemporaneous attack on classical economic concepts and maxims was used to strengthen this argument.[32] In retrospect

---

[28] Holmes, "The Path of the Law", in Collected Legal Papers (1920), 180. Judge Hutcheson remarked that as a young lawyer he thought experienced judges had the legal rules and principles all ready for a prompt solution of any legal controversy. Op. cit. supra, n. 25, at p. 274–276.

[29] See Bingham, "The Nature and Importance of Legal Possession", (1915) 13 Mich.L.Rev. 535, 537.

[30] Bingham, "What is the Law?", (1912) 11 Mich.L.Rev. 1, 12.

[31] More accurately, the Euclidean postulate that through any one point outside a given line only one parallel line could be drawn. For a brief discussion, see Cohen and Nagel, An Introduction to Logic and Scientific Method (1934), 144.

[32] See Oliphant and Hewitt, Introduction to Rueff, From the Physical to the Social Sciences (1929).

the non-Euclidean line of argument seems to this writer less per-suasive than it did when it was first propounded. For one thing the number of fruitful geometric systems that can be developed has not been shown to be unlimited. Again, the mathematical analogy does not signify that an unrestricted assortment of axioms or postulates can be employed in building a legal *system*, a coherent and fruitful body of legal propositions designed to avoid internal contradictions. Thirdly, since even the so-called "a priori" or "self-evident" legal principles are in some sense based on experience, the difference between "deductive" and "induc-tive" methods in law is easily exaggerated.

Oliphant used his "inductive" theory of law to discover in judi-cial precedents "new" major premises, already implicit there, which would better explain and justify the decisions on grounds of social policy than would the traditional generalizations which the courts gave as "reasons."[33] For example, the judicial deci-sions generally enforced limited promises not to compete which the seller of a business made to his buyer, but refused to uphold similar promises made by an employee to his employer not to compete with the employer after a term of employment.[34] The principle by which Oliphant perceived this distinction in the cases was in a sense a priori, i. e., derived from other experience than the immediate facts of these cases. Here, again, was no attempt to reject logic but rather to use it with different premises.

Judge Jerome Frank has picked a different weak spot in the use of formal logic by hammering away for twenty years and more at the *minor* premise of the legal syllogism. The chief rea-son why legal rules do not more adequately perform the principal tasks they are supposed to do—guide and predict the decisions of trial courts—is, he maintains, because of the uncertainty as to what *facts* the trier of fact (especially the jury) will "find" as the ones to which the legal rule or principle is to be applied.[35] A man in possession of real property has a right (privilege) to use "rea-sonable" force in repelling wilful intruders, but how can he tell, when confronted with an intruder, what a jury will subsequently find to be "reasonable" force? Thus one of the supposedly

---

[33] Supra, § 3.31.

[34] Oliphant, "A Return to Stare Decisis", (1928) 14 A.B.A.J. at p. 159.

[35] See Frank, "Are Judges Human?", (1931) 80 U. of Pa.L.Rev. 17, 27: "The jury system is the Cadi system at its maximum. We use twelve unin-structed haphazardly selected Cadis instead of one." Frank, Courts on Trial (1950), esp. Ch. III, "Facts are Guesses."

securest of legal rights in American law, a basic part of the ownership of real property, is rendered insecure by the uncertainty as to what the trier of fact will find.[36] What is the use of constructing precise major premises if the process of constructing minor premises (findings of fact) is so lacking in precision as to nullify the predictive value of the major? One answer to this question is, legal rules need not and cannot be any more precise than the instruments used in measuring the facts to which they are applied. Another answer is that fact-finding in litigation should be made more accurate and reliable. In part this fact-uncertainty is due to the practice of letting juries find general verdicts without bothering to specify facts, and in part to the prevalent attitude of the American juror that he is called in to decide the whole case, both the law and the facts. Judge Frank's somewhat drastic proposal is to "abandon jury trials except in major criminal cases." [37] Much can be said in its favor, yet it should be accompanied by measures which would reduce the influence of political patronage in the selection of judges. The merits of this proposed reform cannot be fully discussed here. Eventually Judge Frank made a useful classification of American legal realists into "rule-skeptics," those who doubt that legal rules are effective to predict or to guide judicial decisions after the facts have been determined, and "fact-skeptics," who trace the major cause of legal uncertainty to trial uncertainties.[38] Some of Judge Frank's earlier statements about logic in law were aimed at exaggerated claims of rationalism.[39]

Llewellyn, whom Frank classifies as a "rule-skeptic," stated that realists were distrustful of broad rules that purported to include dissimilar situations, and preferred to work with narrower categories.[40] A careful survey of realist writings reveals that

---

[36] The example is not Judge Frank's yet it illustrates his thesis. The vagueness of the norm relating to the use of force by a private individual may express a policy of discouraging its use by discouraging any one from coming close to the line, and also a policy of letting each jury decide where that line is on the basis of vague community standards.

[37] Frank, Courts on Trial (1950), 423.

[38] Frank, "Cardozo and the Upper-Court Myth", (1948) 13 Law and Contemp.Prob. 369, 384.

[39] See Frank, "What Courts Do in Fact", (1932) 26 Ill.L.Rev. 645, 662–663, 648, aimed at Adler's "law in discourse" (supra, § 3.00); Hall, pp. 1103–4. A statement similar to that in the text is made for the realists generally in Garlan, op. cit., n. 8, at pp. 8–10.

[40] "Some Realism," 1237; supra, § 3.24.

they were not denying the need for logical reasoning in law but were asserting the insufficiency of logic to account for legal processes.

Semantics attracted many legal realists, because the requirement that every term shall have a concrete referent helped them in their efforts to show that such conventional legal terms as "privity" and "due process of law" were virtually meaningless as explanations of decisions, and also because the newer conceptions of meaning put some of them to work inventing new terminologies for narrower categories. The influence of Ogden and Richards' book [41] was considerable. It introduced two useful words into legal writing: "Referent," that to which a term refers, and "emotive," an adjective applied to such words as "liberty," which have no definite referent but will in some circumstances arouse the emotions of persons to whom they are addressed. Thurman Arnold's satirical works [42] implied the extreme position that a word has no meaning unless it has an *immediate* reference to experience, and that if a word has an emotional appeal, it therefore can have no value as an intellectual instrument.[43] Such an extreme position not only ignores the historical dual function of language [44] and the levels of meaning in a complex linguistic order,[45] but also would render meaningless some of Mr. Arnold's views expressed in such terms as "benevolence" and "practical and humanitarian attitude." [46] Still the realist word-baiting, aided by Hohfeld's operationalism and Dewey's contextualism (§ 1.12), led to some determined efforts to improve legal terminology and thus to make it a more useful instrument of social control.

4. *Scientific Method in Law.* The chief end of some of the leading realists—Oliphant, Moore, Cook, Yntema, at least—was to develop, if not *the* "science of law," at least scientific method in the solution of legal problems. For this reason, primarily, Oliphant, Cook and Yntema left their law teaching positions and es-

---

[41] Supra, § 1.12, n. 18.

[42] See Arnold, The Symbols of Government (1935), satirizing the anti-trust laws, and compare his own views as stated in Ch. X; Arnold, The Folklore of Capitalism (1937).

[43] Garlan, op. cit., n. 8, 108.

[44] Supra, § 1.12.

[45] Supra, § 3.26, notes 54–57.

[46] Garlan, op. cit., 109.

tablished the Institute of Law, a research institute, at The Johns Hopkins University in 1929, and Moore began his fruitful connection with the Yale Institute of Human Relations. The publications of the short-lived Hopkins Institute, on divorce proceedings and other phases of judicial procedure, revealed the empirical-statistical bent of its founders.[47] Moore's chief studies were aimed at two diverse factual problems of the legal order: What is the correlation between judicial decisions and institutional practices related to the facts of those decisions? What is the relation between legal symbols and lay obedience to those symbols, as exemplified by the traffic (parking) signs?[48] The precise conclusions of these laborious investigations are at the present time of trifling significance; yet the insight and analysis revealed by Moore and his assistants was of a high order and may well prove useful to later investigators in the sociology of law. One other example is noteworthy, the investigation of the causes of business failures by W. O. Douglas and his associates.[49] The efforts to obtain information by interviewing bankrupts as to the adequacy of their books of account, if any, their gambling habits and many other matters, were only partly successful owing to the lack of coöperation from bankrupts and officials. One may question whether Douglas' ultimate recommendations for changes in the bankruptcy act[50] could not have been made just as well by his reading the English bankruptcy act and the well-analyzed English reports on its operation, without going through his elaborate and expensive procedure of factual investigation. Yet the answer is, I believe, negative. The investigators learned about the people and events with which the recommended changes would have to do, and were thus better able to predict the operation of the legal formulae they chose.

---

[47] One example of many is: Oliphant and Hope, A Study of Day Calendars (The Johns Hopkins Press, 1932), which revealed, among other things, the sloppy habits of lawyers (or clients?) in New York courts in postponing the settlement of cases until they are announced "ready" for trial. Other field studies involved litigation in Baltimore and in Ohio.

[48] As to the former, see n. 20, supra; as to the latter, see supra, § 3.02, and Moore and Callahan, "Law and Learning Theory: A study in Legal Control (1943, The Yale Law Journal Co., Inc.).

[49] See Douglas and Thomas, "The Business Failures Project—A Study in Methodology", (1930) 39 Yale L.J. 1013; (1931) 40 Yale L.J. 1034.

[50] See Douglas (W. O.), "Some Functional Aspects of Bankruptcy", (1932) 41 Yale L.J. 329, which summarizes the statistics on bookkeeping and proposes more frequent denial or suspension of discharges in bankruptcy.

Of course no lawmaker, as Aristotle long ago pointed out (§ 4.11), can foresee all cases that will arise, all consequences that will follow from the application of the legal norms that he enacts or adopts. Yet the human fallibility of the legislator does not excuse him from the obligation to foresee as best he can the more-probable-than-not consequences of proposed legal norms or procedures. The lawmaker can better foresee those consequences by a fair sampling of the present situation in which the legal consequences will have social effects (or fail to have intended effects). On the whole, the realists were on the right track in seeking to establish (invent and find) techniques of empirical-legal investigation.[51]

§ 4.64—American Legal Realism: Psychology, Ethics and Education

1. *Psychological Theories.* Some of the Legal Realists used one or more of the newer psychological theories of the early twentieth century as instruments of investigation or as grounds of justification of their views. Three such theories may be mentioned here: Behaviorism, Freudianism and Abnormal Psychology (rationalization).

The most important was the *behaviorist* theory, that a scientific study of human conduct should be confined to external behavior and should make no assumptions about the consciousness of the individual under observation. This theory, developed out of the conditioned reflex as exemplified in Pavlov's experiments with the bell-slobbering dog, was stated in its extreme form by Watson,[52] first a professor of psychology and then a successful advertising consultant. If an advertising agency can by careful field work ascertain which advertising slogan will best appeal to the twelve-year-old mind, then why cannot legal research determine the effects of legal prohibitions in society? Moore used some such theory in his traffic study, and even in his investigation of bankers' practices (§ 4.63). Oliphant found in behaviorism support for the so-called "objective" or expectation theory of contracts, and for his method of interpreting a judicial de-

---

[51] The use of factual investigations in connection with legislation long antedated the American legal realists; yet their influence was partly responsible for the extensive Congressional investigations during F. D. Roosevelt's administration; e. g., the T.N.E.C. report.

[52] See Watson, Psychology from the Standpoint of a Behaviorist (1919). Watson founded the behaviorist school around 1913.

cision as the response of the judge(s) to the stimuli of all the facts in the record (§ 3.31). As a protest against the introspective method (sometimes called "the armchair method") of acquiring information about human conduct, the behaviorist theory was a valuable corrective. However, as the present writer believes he has sufficiently shown, the attempt to describe conduct-situations of the type known as fraud or mistake, without using words that refer to the state of consciousness of the actor, ends in absurd clumsiness.[53] A legal system which would consistently refuse to take any account of the states of mind, the inferred motivations and foresights of its subjects, would produce results shocking to the sense of justice of most men as we have known them thus far. Behaviorism, though it is now outmoded as a formal systematic position, had a tremendous influence upon modern psychology,[54] as it also had upon jurisprudence, in America.

Freudianism had far less influence upon legal realism than some detractors of the latter have supposed. Frank introduced a touch of it into his literary bombshell, Law and the Modern Mind (1930) and thus increased the shock. He sought to explain the "basic myth" of the legal profession, the belief that the law is stationary and certain. Day by day, lawyers argue cases in appellate courts as if the law were certain and established, and appellate court judges write opinions which state the logical grounds for their decisions in legal rules or principles that are treated as if well settled. Yet in every such case, one lawyer was wrong; one lawyer's law was not as certain as he thought it to be.[55] Lawyers and judges (as well as laymen) seek to find or to attain in law a degree of certainty that is, according to Frank, utterly unrealizable. Why do they do so? As a "partial" explanation he turns to the psychology of childhood, to the childish fears and beliefs that are carried along by the mature man. The child

---

[53] See Patterson, "Equitable Relief for Unilateral Mistake", (1928) 28 Col. L.Rev. 859.

[54] See Boring and others, Psychology: A Factual Textbook (1935), 7.

[55] This is a partial summary of Ch. 1, Pt. I, of Law and the Modern Mind (second printing, 1931). His argument has merit; yet it would have been more realistic to note that sometimes a case is appealed *in order to have* the law settled, rather than on the assumption that *it is*. Still this modification does not affect Judge Frank's basic argument as stated in the next sentence of the text. By "certainty" he seems to have meant reliability in predicting how courts would decide on given facts.

"strives to retain something like pre-birth serenity." [56] The childish craving is satisfied for a time by his belief in the omnipotence and infallibility of his father; when this illusion is shattered, as it must be, often the individual carries over into maturity a basic craving for a father-substitute and the law is one such substitute. Hence the basic legal myth that the law is or can be made "unwavering, fixed and settled." [57] By this analysis O. W. Holmes, Jr., was one of the few mature legal thinkers, because he recognized the inevitable uncertainty of judicial decisions. Since Mr. Frank submitted fourteen other explanations of his "basic myth" [58] and has emphasized the provisional and limited nature of his explanation in the same text and in later works,[59] it may seem unnecessary to discuss its merits. However, the present writer is not impressed by an appeal to an "unconscious" or a "subconscious" to explain human conduct and human strivings which can be quite well explained by explicit statements based on reason and experience, just as the failure to attain perfect legal certainty can be explained by other reasons.[60] Judge Frank has more recently rejected the view ascribed to Professors Lasswell and McDougal, that a psychoanalytic technique will have a high predictive value with respect to the outcome of trials.[61] The subconscious may be something with which, like man's animal nature, all judges and lawyers are tainted along with other men and women; if so, it has not been shown to have any distinctive bearing on law or its administration. However, the theory of subconscious hidden motivations of judicial decisions re-enforced the theory of rationalization.

---

[56] Op. cit. supra, n. 55, 18.

[57] Ibid., 20. His account of child development, taken principally from Piaget, "derives chiefly from the Freudian school," who take account of "other factors." Ibid., 326.

[58] Ibid., Appendix I. Among them are the religious impulse, the aesthetic impulse, professional habits, a human instinct to seek security and certainty, imitation, inertia, laziness, etc. Most of these seem better than the Freudian one.

[59] See, If Men Were Angels (1942).

[60] Among them the uncertainty of jury trials, as ably presented by Judge Frank. Supra, § 4.63, n. 35.

[61] Frank, Courts on Trial (1950), 204. An attempt to apply psychoanalysis to the explanation of judicial decisions was made in Schroeder, "The Psychological Study of Judicial Opinions", (1918) 6 Calif.L.Rev. 89. It does not appear to have produced any fruitful results.

Abnormal psychology revealed that when a person confined to an insane asylum so acted as to upset the routine of the asylum and was questioned by his supervisors as to his conduct, he commonly invented "good" reasons which he thought would appease them and which were not the "real" reasons for his conduct.[62] A distinguished historian, the late James Harvey Robinson, in an earnest, diffuse plea for intelligent social improvement, gave currency to the terms, "rationalizing" and "rationalization" [63] as meaning a kind of thinking by which we invent or discover "good" reasons for what we already believe, without inquiring about the "real" reasons:

> "The result is that most of our so-called reasoning consists in finding arguments for going on believing as we already do." [64]

This astounding statement was limited, in its context, to the reasons given by political officeholders for their acts and beliefs and to the reasons commonly given by individuals for their cherished political or religious beliefs, whenever these are challenged. Robinson's chief point was that the "real" reasons for such beliefs are the accidents of birth, nurture and propinquity; "we unconsciously absorb them from our environment." [65]   As a plea for *better* reason-giving, J. H. Robinson's argument had merit. However, in applying it to the reasons given by courts in their formal opinions, some legal realists extended it, out of its context, to the rather sophisticated and self-conscious search for "reasons" which judges go through with in writing (and approving) opinions. The Dewey theory that the process of finding reasons is different from the process of making up one's mind what to decide (§ 4.53) seems sufficient without ascribing the "real" or ultimate "reasons" to some inscrutable savage drive in the "unconscious." These new ideas were placed in their proper perspective

---

[62] Prof. John Dewey gave as citations for the origin of this theory: Hart, The Psychology of Insanity (1910), 66, and Tansley, The New Psychology (1920), 159, 160, 168. See Patterson, "Dewey's Theories of Legal Reasoning and Valuation" in John Dewey: Philosopher of Science and Freedom (1950), 118, 126.

[63] These terms had been used in the 19th century, sometimes to mean the giving of reasons and sometimes to mean the giving of formal or spurious reasons. See Murray's English Dictionary.

[64] Robinson (J. H.), The Mind in the Making (1921), 41; and see pp. 40–48. He referred to "modern psychologists" yet cited (p. 43) only Trotter, Instincts of the Herd.

[65] Ibid., 43.

by the distinguished Yale psychologist, the late Edward S. Robinson.[66] Nevertheless the theory of rationalization must be counted, for better and for worse, as a part of the realist contribution.

2. *Ethical and Axiological Theories.* The ethical and axiological theories (§ 1.13) of the legal realists were among the most elusive of all. Having known personally nearly all of those who were listed above (§ 4.63) as realists, the present writer can say that he has not known any group of men who were more earnestly concerned than they were for the discovery of the true and the good and for the development of means of promoting ultimately the welfare of their fellow men. The realists were (are) not cynics. Yet they were skeptical of traditional or "self-evident" truths for determining wherein human welfare consists, and they were also skeptical of the traditional means of allegedly promoting that welfare. Professor Llewellyn stated accurately that most of them believed in the temporary divorce of the Is and the Ought for the purposes of studying the Is.[67] The "Is" here referred to was not "what the law is," a conventional summary of propositions and instances of legislation and case law; rather it included the observed effects of legal rules and doctrines upon official behavior and upon laymen's behavior, and a study of societal facts in which law operates or from which conceptions of legal change may be derived. The realists were seeking primarily to discover or invent the methods of a sociology of law. In these respects their aims and evaluations were not very different from those of Pound's sociological jurisprudence, which included in its proposed program both a study of the social effects of legal institutions and team work in the social sciences.[68] Few, if any, critics have questioned the intended ethical and political idealism of Pound's philosophy of law. Why, then, did the legal realists evoke such violent reactions in some quarters? And were these reactions justified.

First, some of the realists (especially Moore, Cook and Radin, it seems) deliberately chose to shock their hearers or readers out of a supposed moral complacency about "established" legal rules.

---

[66] See Robinson, Law and the Lawyers (1935), 171–181. "But psychologists are becoming increasingly suspicious of the instincts and urges which are supposed to be the underlying reality of overt behavior." P. 175.

[67] Llewellyn, "Some Realism", § 4.63, n. 7, at p. 1236.

[68] Supra, § 4.60; and see Pound, "How Far Are We Attaining a New Measure of Values in Twentieth Century Juristic Thought?", (1936) 42 W.Va.L.Q. 81, 90–92.

They therefore concealed their own evaluations, though these were often fairly conventional. Witness Radin's listing, in reply to his book review critics, of fourteen or fifteen propositions which he believed and with few of which one could quarrel.[69] Another example is found in Fuller's well-known article on legal realism. Professor Fuller was justified in saying that the bankers' practices of New York, Pennsylvania and South Carolina did not necessarily show that the respective courts of those states should regard the norms derived from those practices as the most desirable basis of decision.[70] Moore realized this, too, and he also believed that an investigation of bankers' practices was a better way to determine what the law should be than postulating one or four or eight vague and general "goals" of the law, as some rationalists have done. Moore, instead, made a table of the values which he perceived in a banking transaction-sequence (such as cashing a check at a bank) and in various types of deviations from it: Familiarity, certainty, efficiency, and five types of risks (harms to be avoided); each with regard to the interests of the bank and the customer.[71] For instance, if a customer were to demand orally (without a check or written memorandum) payment of an amount less than his deposit, most of the negative values would be properly ascribed to this deviational conduct. So Moore's initial study did not even temporarily divorce the Is and the Ought. By means of his valuation-analysis he reached the conclusion that a certain banking procedure was "reasonable, fair and just." [72]

Of the other realists, similar evidence of evaluative theories may be produced. Oliphant's article on value-judgments [73] and Llewellyn's work on the Uniform Commercial Code, are only two of many examples of the drive for improvement in law through the creation of new theories of valuation, which basically motivated most of the legal realists.[74] Among the changes which may be partly ascribed to the legal realists is the greater frequency

---

[69] See Radin's reply to the adverse criticisms of his book, Law as Logic and Experience (1940): Radin, "In Defense of an Unsystematic Science of Law", (1942) 51 Yale L.J. 1269, 1270.

[70] Fuller, "American Legal Realism", (1934) 82 U. of Pa.L.Rev. 429, 459; Hall, 999.

[71] Op. cit. supra, § 4.63, n. 20, (1931) 40 Yale L.J. at pp. 1228–1229.

[72] Ibid., 1241.

[73] Op. cit. supra, § 4.63, n. 18.

[74] See Garlan, op. cit., Ch. V.

with which judges today try to state in their opinions the immediate value-propositions on which their decisions rest.

3. *Influence on Legal Education.* The most important immediate consequences of legal realism were in the field of legal education. While outside of academic halls the realists seemed to many to be merely cynics or iconoclasts, within those halls legal realism was a vital constructive influence.[75] At Columbia, the hotbed of academic realism, a distinguished economist-educator, Leon Marshall, was called in to guide a faculty survey of the curriculum; and Oliphant's summary of these studies [76] is still a significant document.[77] At Yale a nucleus of realists augmented by Moore in 1930 produced more striking changes in the law school curriculum than occurred at Columbia, yet the outpouring of teaching materials by the Columbia faculty after 1928 was largely stimulated, and partly guided, by the realist studies. To claim for legal realism all of the innovations in legal education after 1930 would be an exaggeration; to restrict the influence of legal realism to those who became its avowed followers would be no less misleading. A good many law teachers who rejected the extreme positions of legal realism were moved to incorporate more moderate versions of its ideas in their own work. The effects of legal realism may be grouped under three headings: The case method of instruction, the curriculum and personnel.

"Cases and Materials" became the standard heading for the classbook, revised to include, besides the traditional collection of reported judicial decisions, "materials" showing economic or social theory or fact, relevant business practices, excerpts from works on psychiatry, forms of contracts, and frequently just straight legal text from law reviews or treatises.[78] The realist drive for "factual" or "extra-legal material" to be studied in connection with reported cases, as a means of "integrating" law and the social sciences, or as a means of showing the place of law in

---

[75] But cf. McDougal, "The Law School of the Future: From Legal Realism to Policy Science in the World Community", (1947) 56 Yale L.J. 1345.

[76] Oliphant, Summary of Studies in Legal Education (1929) (out of print).

[77] See, for example, the tribute to this summary in Lasswell and McDougal, "Legal Education and Public Policy", (1943) 52 Yale L.J. 203; and see Currie, "The Materials of Law Study", (1951) 3 J.Leg.Educ. 331, 332 ff.

[78] The changes are partly summarized in Patterson, "The Case Method in American Legal Education: Its Origins and Objectives", (1951) 4 Journal of Legal Education 1. See, also, Ehrenzweig, "The American Casebook: 'Cases and Materials'", (1944) 32 Georgetown L.J. 224.

society (which incidentally helped to make the law students into better client-care-takers), concurred with a movement toward the use of textual material in casebooks, a heterodoxy to Langdell's earlier followers. The claims made for visual education may have led two distinguished Harvard scholars to include in their monumental casebook on Equity a picture of the lovely heroine of that leading case, Lumley v. Wagner.[79] How could the jaded second-year student better be made to realize the effect of the court's stern decree, for though Joanna might choose not to sing for Lumley, she might not (for the period of her contract with Lumley) choose to sing for anyone else?

The inclusion of extra-legal materials in a casebook still leaves the teacher with a pedagogical problem: How can it be used as interesting material for class discussion? Or should it be merely assigned reading which prepares the student to read the cases? Clearly no one answer will do. The realists made other changes in casebook construction. Something had to be squeezed out, and it was often the earlier practice of presenting historical development by reprinting a sequence of cases. Cases were chosen for their interesting facts, for the business situations or practices that they dealt with rather than for the accuracy or clarity of their opinions. The use of "classroom cases" [80] as illustrations has given way to the posing of more concrete and plausible situations that raise problems of meaning and policy. A further change in casebooks has been the "functional" grouping of cases and materials, rather than a doctrinal, chronological or historical grouping. Thus a casebook on contracts contains such headings as "Gifts," "Bailments," "Services" and "Building Contracts."[81] A casebook on the law of insurance has four main headings: "The Insurance Carrier," "The Interests Protected," "The Selection and Control of Risks," "The Marketing of Insurance." [82] However, the old bottles are still more commonly used for the new wine.

In curriculum revision legal realism pushed toward greater student participation in class discussion and in research and hence toward small-group instruction (seminars) or individual supervi-

---

[79] Chafee and Simpson, Cases on Equity (1934), vol. I, 424.

[80] E.g., "A says to B: 'I'll give you $10 if you walk across Brooklyn Bridge,' " etc. The realists deprecated the use of such academic illustrations.

[81] See Havighurst, Cases on Contracts (1934; 2d ed., 1950).

[82] Patterson, Cases and Materials on the Law of Insurance (2d ed., 1947).

sion (essays or other legal writing) in the second and third years. Some topics which deal with the rare bird have been dropped. The ownership of wild animals is omitted or subordinated, and many students now miss that fascinating problem, when A takes B's corn and makes corn-liquor, who owns the whiskey? There will always be some law for students to learn after they are graduated. One further effect of the realist thesis has been the appointment to law faculties of men having special competence in related fields of knowledge. Thus (to give only three examples) Walton Hamilton, an economist, joined the Yale law faculty in 1928, Robert L. Hale, lawyer and economist, became a lecturer in legal economics at Columbia in 1922 and Sheldon Glueck, primarily a criminologist, moved from the department of Social Ethics to the Harvard Law School in 1929. The realist movement, supplementing sociological jurisprudence, broke down some of the barriers between faculties of law and other university scholars.

• • •

These seven phases of American legal realism show that it was a true child of the period (1919–1940) between the World Wars, when skepticism of tradition, reverence for science and faith in man's ability to make his world better by inquiry and effort were articles of the American academic creed. In these respects legal realism was not very different from pragmatism and sociological jurisprudence. These two, along with legal realism, constitute the first native American philosophy of law.

§ 4.65—Some Conclusions

Although this book is not intended to construct a philosophy of law, the author's views have been stated from time to time and are implicit in some aspects of the selection and treatment of subject matter. Here a few concluding comments may tie together these scattered lines of thought.

My own philosophy of law is eclectic because I recognize that each of the major philosophers has begun his system with several appealing self-evident principles, and I cannot reject it as wholly wrong. Moreover, even those philosophies which appeal to me least in their basic maxims, such as Kant's ideal of the disinterested and cheerless saint, contain valuable correctives (in this instance, the emphasis on duty) of those which have a greater over-all appeal, such as William James' ethical theory of claims. My eclecticism in legal philosophy is based partly on my belief in tolerance, partly on my belief in pluralism, and partly on the inertia of habit. In the modern state it is too much to expect that all men (all human adults) will agree on either basic principles or specific measures, and so a philosophy of law intended for the public view (as distinct from private and secret individual ethical or religious beliefs) should be tolerant of a wide variety of basic principles. Yet there must be a limit to such tolerance, as democratic liberals have discovered during the present century. Some limits must be fought for. One of the uses of legal philosophy is in exploring and defining these limits. Pluralism to me means no more than that principles, good persuasive principles well grounded in experience, will conflict. They may not contradict each other but they will lead in divergent directions or they will sideswipe each other. I doubt if it is semantically possible to construct a system of legal philosophy in which all such potential conflicts are abolished. Hence I am not disposed to try to build a "pure" philosophy of law like Dr. Kelsen's pure analytic theory. The inertia of habit has led me to carry along, without great discomfort, pieces of legal philosophy which I have absorbed over a period of some forty years.

The generalizations of legal philosophy are, I believe, very influential, directly or indirectly, upon the attitudes and conduct of officials and citizens in the Western world (probably in the East also). When men's differences are settled by reason (and not by force or violence), experience indicates that conceptions of a highly inclusive and far-ranging order are genuinely persuasive. So general statements of goals, such as "liberty, equality, fraternity" or "the common good" or "the greatest good of the greatest number", are useful motivations of social action. Yet, paradoxically enough, these vague goals have only a slight *guidance* value in working out governmental implementations. It is significant that quite recently somewhat more precise statements of the ends of a legal order—those which the best one should have, I suppose—have been worked out independently by Professors Lasswell and McDougal,[83] Lon L. Fuller [84] and Edmond Cahn.[85] Since all three of these seemed to me to be still tentative, I did not venture to comment upon them here.

Legal philosophy should be concerned with the means of implementing the ends of a politically organized society, and should

---

[83] One version is given in the citation supra, § 3.25, n. 9 at p. 283.

[84] Fuller, The Problems of Jurisprudence (temporary ed., 1949), ch. VI.

[85] Cahn, The Sense of Injustice (1949).

thus not be confined to idealistic criticism of existing legal orders or ideal statements of ends. While philosophic saints in their ivory towers construct ideal societies, "burly sinners rule the world." Thus the assumption that seems to underlie many public discussions of the foreign policy of the United States, that that nation is and must be wholly disinterested and altruistic, has done some harm to our foreign relations. Similar dangers of naïve idealism appear in discussions of our internal political affairs. This leads me to add that I have tried to draw a line (for the purpose of writing this book and of teaching its subject matter) between legal philosophy and the political philosophy of the state, on the one hand, and programs of political reform, such as the welfare state, on the other. While a philosophy of law cannot and should not exclude these other two, as a job done by a lawyer it ought to take account of the great mass of work of the legal profession which calls for professional skills.

With these predilections in mind, I regard Roscoe Pound's theory of Social Interests (§ 4.62) as the best constructive philosophy of law that I can find. While its categories are largely derived historically and could be made more symmetrical by an imaginative reconstruction, yet it reveals the struggles and conflicts of a mature legal system. I would not venture to propose it as *the* legal philosophy for all time. Yet it seems that with some modifications it could serve as a structural guide for a good legal order in any good society that is practically conceivable.

Part V

THE JUDICIAL PROCESS *

Chapter 19

THE JUDICIAL PROCESS

§ 5.00—The Judicial Process: Why a Focal Point

American jurisprudential discussions of the first half of this century were chiefly centered upon the judicial process. Cardozo's delightful lectures, published in 1921,[1] gave a name to the theme and added some new themes to the name. Although both Pound and Wigmore had applied the term to the exercise of reasoning in deciding cases,[2] Cardozo's books revealed the struggles and doubts, the freedom of choice and its limits and something of the ethics and logic of the judges engaged in deciding cases in appellate courts. Yet these themes were by no means new. Holmes' prediction theory of law (§ 2.20) centered upon the judicial decision; he recognized that the felt necessities of the times and other influences outside the books had shaped judicial decisions (§ 4.55). Some of Pound's earliest articles were criticisms of prevalent mechanical methods of judicial decision and justification (§ 4.60). Hohfeld defined rights and duties in terms of judicial actions. After Cardozo's first book had gained both a professional and an academic audience, many of the legal realists took up the study of the judiciary, the judicial process and the judicial precedent as the focal point of discussion. What were the reasons or causes of this concentration of interest?

---

* When this book was first outlined, Part V, The Judicial Process, was intended to have a much larger place than it now has. The treatment of this theme in earlier portions (especially Chapters 8, 11 and 18, supra), and the waning enthusiasm for it as a catch-all of jurisprudential problems, serve to explain why there is only one chapter in Part V.

[1] Cardozo, The Nature of the Judicial Process (1921); supra, § 4.62.

[2] See Frank, "Cardozo and the Upper-Court Myth," (1948) 13 Law and Contemp.Probs. 369, 373, where earlier uses of "the judicial process" are cited.

Partly they were peculiar to the development of American law at this period, and partly they were due to other cultural influences.[3] The following factors represent a fair sampling of the causes and reasons:

1. The predominance of case law as the chief form of American law, to the professional lawyer, the judge and the law teacher, continued over from previous centuries of Anglo-American legal history and was accentuated in the present century by many factors. Despite the increase in state and federal legislation, case law reports multiplied and the sheer volume of available precedents led to a fresh examination of the value of such publications. At the same time the dominance of the casebook in legal education started some unorthodox theories about the methods of the judiciary and the interpretation of their results. The distinction between holding and dictum was sharpened as never before by Oliphant's theory of stare decisis (§ 3.31).

2. Faith in the judicial branch of the government as honest, impartial and objective, in contrast with the partisan prejudice, political favoritism and occasional corruption of the legislative and executive branches, has led a large and important segment of the American public to support strongly the independence of the judiciary and to resist the attacks of its critics. The rejection of President F. D. Roosevelt's proposed Supreme Court "packing" legislation of 1937[4] showed how powerful was this belief in judicial independence even as against the Chief Executive who had just won an overwhelming victory at the polls. It was commonly assumed by conservative laymen that because the judges were more scrupulous (than other officials generally) in avoiding even the appearance of favoritism or partiality, therefore they were wholly objective in determining questions of constitutional law. This belief was opposed to that aroused by the liberal disillusionment.

---

3 In Germany a movement for freedom of judicial decision, which eventuated in the Jurisprudence of Interests (supra, § 4.44), influenced some American legal scholars, notably Roscoe Pound, John H. Wigmore and Charles G. Haines. Representative excerpts of the German literature were published in the volume, The Science of Legal Method (1917).

4 I.e., a bill to increase the number of judges from nine to fifteen, allowing President Roosevelt to appoint six additional judges who would be favorable to "New Deal" legislation and would thus, with previously appointed "New Deal" judges, outvote the conservative judges in cases involving the constitutionality and the liberal interpretation of such legislation.

3. The liberal disillusionment was brought about by decisions of the United States Supreme Court, often sharply divided, on the constitutionality of state legislation regulating big business, or protecting industrial employees, or on the interpretation of civil liberties. The decision invalidating the New York statute which purported to limit the hours of labor in bakeries to ten hours a day was perhaps typical of the line of cases here referred to.[5] How could one conclude that such a law contravened the "due process of law" clause unless one read into that provision a transcendent principle of laissez faire, like that of Adam Smith or Herbert Spencer? If this reasoning were correct, then such decisions were really governed by the economic and political beliefs of the judges rather than by the words of the Constitution. If so, then it was proper and even necessary for the President to nominate for membership on the Court men who were in sympathy with his political views; and by the same reasoning the Senate could (and did) refuse confirmation of a nominee on the ground that his political beliefs were too conservative or too radical. These conclusions were not radically new, since earlier appointments to the Supreme Court had involved similar considerations, and the popular election of judges in many states was based in part on like assumptions; yet during the 1920's and 1930's they became more respectable in academic circles and more widely known, especially among labor leaders. The constitutional cases, limited in number though they were, touched off a series of studies and theories about the mental processes of judges, which came to be dignified by the title, "the psychology of judicial decisions" (§ 5.06). Unfortunately, exaggerated conclusions were sometimes drawn as to the influence of individual personality factors upon the run-of-the mine judicial decisions in appellate courts.[6]

4. The arid and formal opinions of appellate courts near the close of the nineteenth century gave their decisions an appearance of apodictic certainty, which often failed to reveal the more basic reasons. At the beginning of this century an appalling proportion of appealed cases were decided on errors in procedure rather than on issues of substantive law; there was a marked tendency (by no means universal [7]) to avoid decisions on the merits. Eng-

---

[5] The case is discussed supra, § 4.34, p. 428.

[6] See Clark (Judge Charles E.), "The Dilemma of American Judges: Is too Great 'Trust for Salvation' Placed in Them?" (1949) 35 A.B.A.J. 8, 9.

[7] The present writer's early practice included a case in which the appellate court had an easy "out" on a fatal slip in appellate procedure, but based its decision wholly on substantive law.

lish judicial reports frequently set forth, even in the nineteenth century, the colloquy between judge and counsel which was often more revealing of the "real reasons" for the decision than the judge's formal opinion. American judicial reports rarely provided any such clues. From the conclusion that the "real reasons" were to be found elsewhere than in the opinion two types of inquiry resulted: One, a search for principles or policies which could satisfactorily serve as logical grounds for the decision and the rules enunciated; the other, a search for secret or subconscious motivations or psychic influences.

5. The logical theory of Pragmatism (§ 4.54) provided a theoretical basis for inquiry into the mental processes of judges as rational procedures rather than as emotional mysteries; and the emphasis on consequences, taken to mean the decision of the court, led to a devaluation of the judicial opinion which has often been carried to extremes.

6. Psychological theories, especially behaviorism, abnormal psychology and psycho-analysis provided opportunities for some fascinating speculations which have been partly explored above (§ 4.64), and will receive further attention below (§ 5.06).

7. The increasing importance of counseling for business men made the prediction of judicial decisions seem more and more important; and it was often assumed that clients were concerned only with results (judgments) and not with reasons. This was an exaggeration, to say the least, since only by the study of reasons could one foresee the recurrence of results.

8. The growth of administrative tribunals during the early part of the twentieth century led to a broader conception of the adjudicative process as exemplified in many of these tribunals. Some warm controversies over the scope of judicial review of administrative agencies served to enliven the theme of the judicial process.

Two able and realistic judges have recently stated the importance of the judiciary in American society. Judge Charles E. Clark, after commenting that judges rarely declare statutes unconstitutional today, said:

> "But so strong is the popular tradition of judicial omniscience and power that the general public still looks to the courts for its protection against all sorts of feared dangers and oppressions from those in authority." [8]

---

[8] Op. cit. supra, n. 6, at p. 8.

Judge Simon Rifkind, discussing the prejudicial effects on judicial trials of some types of newspaper and radio comments, said:

". . . the judicial process is the central pivot around which a free society revolves. I sometimes marvel at the fact that in over 5,000 years of history we have invented no other institution for the disposition of human conflict without violence." [9]

These words of praise are well deserved. In England and the United States (and in Western Europe, perhaps), the courts have the confidence of the public because they determine specific controversies by a procedure and a mental process which is impartial as between litigants, pure in its intention to attain a just result if possible and objective in that it is guided and limited by an expertly formulated body of law. Yet the results attainable by the judiciary are limited by the scope of the judicial function.

§ 5.01—The Judicial Function: Separation of Powers

The faith of the American public in its judiciary has been manifested in various ways. The power of the courts to declare legislation invalid on the ground that it conflicts with the constitution is so exceptional that it has been called "the American doctrine of judicial supremacy." No other nation has permitted its highest court to veto legislative proposals for changes in national policy and even in local (state) policy, to the extent that ours has done.[10] Furthermore, in times of internal crisis Americans turn to judges, if not to courts, to restore confidence in the integrity of governmental processes. A bitter dispute over the Presidential election of 1876 was settled by referring it to a commission of Supreme Court judges. When a bribery scandal of 1919 threatened to undermine confidence in the honesty of professional baseball games, the shrewd owners of the professional clubs persuaded an able and fearless Federal judge to become the dictator of the chief professional leagues. When a public and impartial investigation of the culpability of official personnel for the national disaster produced by the Japanese attack at Pearl Harbor in December, 1941, was sought, an Associate Justice of the Supreme Court was chosen to head the inquiry. The blocking of a popular president's effort to "pack" the Court in 1937 has been mentioned above (§ 5.00).

---

[9] Rifkind, "When the Press Collides with Justice," (1950) 34 J.Am.Jud.Soc. 46, 48.

[10] Although in several other federated republics the highest federal court has a similar power.

Other examples might be given of the public confidence reposed in the judiciary.

Yet the judicial process cannot be transferred to other areas of controversy in the same way that the Ford automobile assembly line has been adapted to the manufacture of other kinds of machines. The essential qualities of the judicial process, those that are prized by lawyer and layman alike, depend upon the framework of the judicial function. The scope of the judicial function is primarily the decision of controversies involving conflicting claims of individuals or of collective juristic persons, and its framework is the body of norms of procedural and substantive law that limit and guide the extrication of issues of law and fact, the scope and method of proof, the grounds of relief and the kind of relief. This is the core of the judicial function, and its scope may be even more narrowly conceived. In the English tradition, of the last two centuries at least, the courts were maintained primarily to administer private (i. e., "man-to-man") law, and the opinions of England's highest court in a recent case involving a striking invasion of civil liberty in wartime [11] sound more like a discussion of property law than one of our Supreme Court opinions on a comparable question. Indeed, this conservative view represents the rule rather than the exception even over here. Contrasting the functions of administrative agencies with those of courts, Mr. Justice Frankfurter said:

"Unlike courts, which are concerned primarily with the enforcement of private rights although public interests may thereby be implicated, administrative agencies are predominantly concerned with enforcing public rights although private interests may thereby be affected." [12]

With the emphasis upon "primarily" one can accept the contrast. When courts as such *or* judges as individuals go beyond this scope some of the prized qualities of the judicial process are diluted or disappear. Thus the power to declare legislation unconstitutional goes beyond this traditional scope and its exercise has aroused more hostility to courts than any traditional English exercise of judicial power. Another example, derived from the partly executive qualities of the English Lord Chancellor, is the appointment of receivers and guardians by courts; here political favoritism and even corruption are found to a far greater extent than in the hum-

---

[11] Livesidge v. Anderson (1942) A.C. 206 (House of Lords, 1941).

[12] Dissenting opinion, Federal Communications Commission v. National Broadcasting Co. Inc., 319 U.S. 239, 248, 63 Sup.Ct. 1035, 1039 (1943).

drum work of private litigation.[13] Moreover, the justices who served on the Electoral Commission of 1876 were not, it is believed, free from partisan bias. While judicial experience seems almost universally to produce habits of thought and motivations which are distinctly judicial, yet they are not wholly transferable to the determination of new policies or to the appointment of personnel; and there is some risk that attempts to use the judiciary for non-judicial functions may impair its usefulness for the judicial function.[14]

American courts recognize certain limitations upon the scope of the judicial function. A court is called upon to decide only a genuine controversy between the persons before it as litigants; it will not decide a "moot" controversy and this term has been taken to include one that became moot after the commencement of litigation.[15] Fortunately this principle no longer prevents the giving of declaratory judgments, where there is a real controversy over legal rights or duties which the court is asked to determine on the facts submitted, though no execution of the judgment is sought.[16] The granting of a license to operate a radio broadcasting station is not a judicial function and hence Congress cannot require the Supreme Court to review on appeal a determination by an administrative body that such a license be or be not issued.[17] The scope of the judicial function is *implied* in the constitutional separation of powers and is thus a limitation on the power of the legislative branch. On the other hand, the Supreme Court's jurisdiction over a criminal case properly before it cannot be ended through a confession of error by the executive branch, the Attorney-General; the court still has the duty of determining whether or not its decision (reversal) is in accordance with the public in-

---

[13] The most striking instance of judicial corruption in a higher court during the past generation was the conviction of a Federal appellate judge for accepting bribes in connection with the appointment of a receiver; yet the decisions in which he had taken part were not disturbed.

[14] For this reason the Justice who presided over the Pearl Harbor investigation later expressed his regret at having done so. Roberts (Owen J.), "Now Is the Time: Fortifying the Supreme Court's Independence," (1949) 35 A.B.A.J. 1, 2.

[15] See Cover v. Schwartz, 133 F.2d 541 (C.C.A.2 1943), where the Court refused (by 2 to 1) to review the validity of a patent because plaintiff had conceded that defendant was not infringing it anyhow.

[16] See Borchard, "Justiciability," (1936) 4 U. of Chi.L.Rev. 1.

[17] Federal Radio Commission v. General Electric Co., 281 U.S. 464, 469, 50 Sup.Ct. 389, 390, 391 (1930).

terest.[18] The limitations upon the judicial function are chiefly those imposed by the judiciary itself, since constitutional provisions seldom prescribe with exactness any such limitations. The most important limitation, the extent to which an appellate court of last resort will follow its own precedents, is likewise self-imposed and subject to no direct [19] control. Because they realize that moderation is essential to judicial independence, judges admit reluctantly or not at all that they and their colleagues "make law."

Without understanding the limited scope of the judicial function a layman or even a moderately dumb lawyer, especially one who has just lost his case, may criticize the courts for being "hidebound," "conservative" and "technical," when the court has merely determined to stay within the lines of precedent and leave change to the legislature. On the other hand, the nineteenth century conception of the separation of powers made the judicial function appear too narrow and the judicial process appear unduly mechanical. Alexander Hamilton, arguing for the adoption of the Federal Constitution, and especially supporting the proposal for life tenure of the judges ("during good behavior"), argued that while the executive has force and the legislature may impose its will in the form of legislation, on the contrary, the judiciary

> "can take no active resolution whatever. It may truly be said to have neither *FORCE* nor *WILL*, but merely judgment; and must ultimately depend upon the aid of the executive arm for the efficacious exercise of even that faculty." [20]

Now Hamilton did not say that courts do not make law; yet his picture of judicial impotence became highly dubious when Field, J., and his followers were riding rough-shod over ameliorative state legislation. The movement referred to in the last section (§ 5.00) was partly a reaction against the Hamiltonian type of conception of judicial power. Before exploring the problems of judicial law-making we need to point out some other aspects of the judicial process.

---

[18] Young v. U. S., 315 U.S. 257, 258, 259, 62 Sup.Ct. 510, 511, 512 (1942) (prosecution under Harrison Anti-Narcotics Act, 40 Stat. 1132).

[19] A capricious refusal of a state supreme court to follow its own precedents might be a denial of due process and hence subject to control by the Federal Supreme Court. Otherwise impeachment by the legislature, legislation correcting the overruling or refusal to re-elect or to re-appoint the judges, seem the only deterrents.

[20] Hamilton in The Federalist, No. LXXVIII; (Masters Smith & Co. ed., 1852) 355.

§ 5.02—Same: The Law Settling Function

The judicial function includes a good deal more than the settlement of issues of law. Since recent discussions of the judiciary have usually been concerned with the extent to which courts make law or follow precedent, and with the motivations of their decisions and opinions, it is well to note that the process thus referred to occurs as a part of the work of disposing of litigation. Besides settling disputed questions of law, courts are called upon in litigation to do two other jobs: Settle disputes of fact (either directly or by presiding over a jury trial) and give judgments which are to be used to coerce recalcitrant defendants.[21] In several large classes of cases the third function alone is involved: The court is merely an aid to a collection agency. Judgment for the plaintiff is usually entered by default; the defendant has no defense of law or fact. Examples are suits to collect ordinary consumer-retail debts, to recover goods sold on conditional sale contract where the buyer's payments are in arrears, and to recover unpaid rent or rent and possession of premises. Such suits are usually filed in courts of limited jurisdiction and never appear in a judicial report. They make up in bulk what they lack in professional interest. They constitute an important part of the exercise of the judicial function but do not intrigue students of the judicial process (as above defined).

The fact-settling function of courts has likewise been generally ignored by jurisprudents as distinguished from experts on judicial procedure. The chief exception is Judge Jerome Frank, who regards the uncertainty of fact-finding of a court as more pervasive and disturbing to expectations than the uncertainty of law-settling, that is, the reliability of pre-trial forecasts as to what norms of law the courts (trial and appellate) will accept and apply (§ 4.63 (3)). This conclusion seems to the present writer to be substantially correct. Judge Frank's proposals for amelioration,[22] especially the complete abolition of jury trials in civil cases, and special training for trial judges, seem beyond the scope of this book.

However, a thorough-going analysis of judicial proof seems to involve some assumptions about metaphysics and epistemology (§§ 1.14, 1.15). Among these is the assumption that reliable in-

---

[21] See Llewellyn, "Administration of Law" in (1937) 6 National Encyclopedia 176.

[22] Frank, Courts on Trial (1949) 422 ff.

ferences (conclusions) of fact can be drawn from (based upon) evidential facts. In a criminal prosecution for homicide, for instance, where the evidence is all circumstantial (i. e., no eye-witness of the act causing death is produced in court) it is a cynical view of the judicial process to say that under such circumstances the accused, if convicted, is convicted *of* the circumstantial evidence rather than *of* the inference which could be drawn therefrom, namely, that he did a specific kind of act that caused the death. More concretely, was Hauptman executed *because* he unfortunately occupied a house in the Bronx (New York) in the attic of which were boards that matched exactly the grain of boards in a crude homemade ladder found at the site of Colonel Lindbergh's home in New Jersey, seventy-five miles away, and in which house were found nails that peculiarly matched those used in the same ladder, etc., etc., or was he executed *because* it was inferred by the jury (with the opinion of two courts that such an inference was permissible from the evidence presented) that he kidnapped the Lindbergh child and caused its death? The latter is a correct statement of the judicial process, the mental processes of judges and jurors.[23] The former is "cynical" since it seems to imply that the connection between the evidence produced in court and the jury's verdict was merely conventional or ritualistic, rather than based upon more fundamental grounds of reason and experience. To take the latter view does not make the tribunal's inferences of fact infallible nor sacrosanct; on the contrary, it points out the risks of the process and the ways of detecting errors. The cynical view, ignoring these, is at best a sophomoric and misleading rhetorical device for criticizing the judicial process.[24]

The distinction between law-settling and fact-settling, in the trichotomy derived from Professor Llewellyn, is clear in gross but difficult in detail. One need not be a lawyer to recognize the difference between "what happened?" and "what's the law?". Yet what should one say about such conclusions as the following? —"This is an offer." "These facts show sufficient premeditation to kill." In the traditional syllogistic analysis of pleadings and

---

[23] The Hauptman case was a striking example of the cogency that circumstantial evidence can have; this reference to it does not imply any reasonable doubt of the correctness of the verdict of guilty.

[24] It was a part of the table-talk of some realists during the 1920's but no assertion of it in print has been found. It is mentioned here chiefly because Judge Frank in criticizing a statement about it in an earlier edition of this book, *seems* to have misunderstood my point. See Frank, Courts on Trial (1949), 60–61; and discussion supra, § 1.15.

proof such propositions appear as minor premises, the major premise being a statement of a legal consequence predicated on there being an "offer" or "premeditation to kill." Being in this formulation minor premises, such propositions are designated as "statements of fact." For instance, under a code of procedure which requires that the plaintiff's statement of his claim ("complaint" or "petition") shall contain only (statements of) facts, such statements as "the defendant agreed to sell to plaintiff," etc., are usually regarded as statements of "fact." However, the attempt to adhere strictly to "fact-pleading" has not been successful. The preferable view is that such statements as were presented above ("This is an offer," etc.) are *legal characterizations of facts*, in that they assign the factual propositions pointed tc by "this" to a legal category (e. g., "offer"), which connotes legal consequences (§ 3.26). This is a crucial step in many litigated cases, and much of the case lawyer's legal search is spent in finding in the precedents analogies that support or refute such legal characterizations. A good deal of uncertainty about the outcome of litigation arises from the unreliability of predictions as to how the judge and jury will characterize known and provable facts. This uncertainty is considerably reduced when the judge firmly takes charge of the decision as to legal characterization, rather than where, as under the procedure of some American states, he merely instructs the jury by giving them "abstract" generalizations of law which they are to "apply" to the facts. The rule which says that the trial judge has not done his duty as a law-settlor until he has, in his charge to the jury, applied the "abstract" rule to the facts of the case [25] seems the better one. Under the practice of taking general verdicts of juries they exercise a considerable amount of "law-settling" for particular cases, though their verdicts are not precedents to be cited in other cases.

This leads to the observation that the law-settling function of courts is twofold in character: One function is to determine the legal consequence (judgment, etc.) on the proved facts; to the extent that it is guided by legal norms it may be called the *"law-applying"* function. The other is the pronouncement of a norm (rule, principle, policy) which will be applied in the future to similar type-situations; this may be called the *"law-establishing* function." Most litigants, it seems, will be satisfied to have the

---

[25] See Lachman v. Pennsylvania Greyhound Lines, 160 F.2d 496, 501 (C.C.A. 4 1947); opinion by Dobie, J. A legal characterization of facts is not the same as giving an opinion on the credibility of certain testimony or on the weight of the evidence on certain issues. Cf. Botein, Trial Judge (1952) 203.

court apply the law; yet an appellate court, at least, feels itself under an obligation to write an opinion in many cases for the future guidance of lawyers, laymen and subordinate courts. The deplorable length of many judicial opinions has been ascribed to the court's conscientiously trying to answer all of the arguments of losing counsel—a laudable but somewhat quixotic effort. Hence comes the suggestion that the court should prepare two opinions, a lengthy one to be given only to the counsel, and a shorter one that will state concisely the legal propositions which the court lays down or adheres to for the purposes of this case.[26] Yet the longer ones would probably be published unofficially (since they would be public records and printers would find a market for them) and thus would merely add to the lawyer's burden. A better conclusion is that bench and bar should co-operate in reducing judicial opinions to statements that add to or modify the sum total of legal meanings, and are not mere reiterations.[27]

The law-establishing function is in the Anglo-American scheme a by-product of the settlement of disputes between litigants. The settlement of legal questions is left to the initiative of litigants and is therefore rather sporadic. A good many gaps result from the fact that on some questions of law no private litigant was sufficiently interested to carry a case involving it to an appellate court. In France a representative of the Ministry of Justice can intervene and have private litigation carried to an appellate court because of the general interest of the questions involved. With us, as Pound has said, John Doe must suffer for the commonwealth's sake. Cases involving small claims are usually not worth appealing; many types of quasi-contractual claims are typically small (e. g., the officious meddler, the unordered and unwanted chattel) and the law on such topics remains a thing of shreds and patches. On the other hand, the legal consequences of certain correspondence-school subscriptions is in many states well settled because the school appealed adverse judgments on its small claims for unpaid tuition. Such unevenness provides arguments for the would-be codifiers.

---

[26] See "Torrent of Judicial Opinions Can Be Checked," (1942) 25 J.Amer. Jud.Soc. 132. The Mississippi legislature required its Supreme Court to write an opinion in "cases settling important principles." See Yazoo & M. R. Co. v. James, 108 Miss. 852, 67 So. 484 (1914).

[27] See the report of the Committees on Duplication of Reports and Publications (Roscoe Pound, Ch'mn.), (1936) 61 Rep.Am.Bar.Assn. 848, 851–852. The report states that there is a "general and strong feeling" among the profession that the state's highest court "should pronounce definitely upon every point raised by counsel."

§ 5.03—Judicial Law-Making in Appellate Courts

When an appellate court in the United States enters judgment after full argument in a case brought before it on appeal and unanimously or by a majority approves and files an opinion by one judge giving the reasons for the judgment in statements of fact and law, does the court merely "declare" the law as "found" by it, or does it "make" law? Put in this general form, the question may be answered in three different ways: 1. That courts always (merely) find and declare the law. 2. That appellate courts "make" law in many cases. 3. That every appellate decision (judgment plus opinion) under the circumstances above stated is law-making in that it adds at least a new legal meaning to well-settled legal propositions. The first two of these represent the classic conflict between the Hale-Blackstone tradition and the Bentham-Austin-Gray position. The third view is here suggested as a semantic interpretation.

Sir William Blackstone in his famous Commentaries on the Laws of England (1765–68) set forth the declaratory theory and gave its rationale.[28] He constructed the latter out of Coke's theory that the common law was the common custom of the realm and Hale's view that judicial decisions were "evidences" of the common law. Yet the latter view was, according to Holdsworth, getting pretty thin by the end of the eighteenth century, when the modern theory as to the authority of decided cases had become substantially established.[29] With the obligation to follow precedents tightened the declaratory theory assumed greater importance. Blackstone said that judges are not to determine cases according to their own private judgments; they are "not delegated to pronounce a new law, but to maintain and expound the old one." [30] Can one reconcile this view with the acknowledged power of courts to overrule their precedents? Blackstone recognizes one exception to the rule that a court must follow precedent, namely, where the precedent is "contrary to reason." He also recognized that a judge could make a mistake about the common law. Hence the overruling of a precedent and the pronouncement by the court of a contradictory legal proposition is not a change in the law but merely the discovery of what the true law was all along and the correction of an erroneous declaration of it.

---

[28] I Blackstone, Commentaries, 69. The theme of this section was briefly discussed above from a different viewpoint. Supra, § 3.30, pp. 300–302.

[29] Holdsworth (W. S.), "Case Law," (1934) 50 L.Q.Rev. 180, 183.

[30] Op. cit. supra, n. 28.

Jeremy Bentham (§ 4.40) took Blackstone's theory to pieces in a youthful work: Judges do exercise private judgment in the cases brought before them, and when they follow precedents they merely determine that, in view of what courts had previously decided, and the uncertainty that would be caused by deciding differently, it is now expedient to decide in conformity with such a prior decision or decisions.[31] By this line of reasoning, every judicial decision might be deemed law-making, since it at least gives a new affirmation of what was said before. Bentham added that the decision was "new," though made "upon the pattern of the old." [32] Bentham is, it seems, to be classed with those who believe that judges make law only sometimes. Even in his old age he denounced English judge-made law as it was introduced into Ireland and Bengal.[33] His follower, Austin, deplored the uncertainty of judge-made law but regarded it as inevitable and even salutary.[34]

Another vigorous attack on the declaratory theory was made by a distinguished law teacher and legal author, John Chipman Gray. Confronted with the argument of James Coolidge Carter (§ 4.33) that the rules laid down by the judges are law and are so laid down because they are law (an argument made also by Pollock and other historical jurists), Gray states the Austinian positivist position:

> "The great gain in its fundamental conceptions which jurisprudence made during the last century was the recognition of the truth that the Law of a State . . . is not an ideal but something which actually exists." [35]

The "existence" of law is to be found in the rules laid down by courts.[36] With this as his premise, he supposes that in the state of Utah the facts and the claim of Rylands v. Fletcher [37] are, for

---

[31] Bentham, A Comment on the Commentaries (Everett ed., 1928), 190.

[32] Ibid.

[33] See Bentham, Introduction to the Principles of Morals and Legislation (2d ed., 1823) 14, n. 1. In writing to Americans, however, he spoke of the "matchless blessing" of the English common law. See Ogden's notes to The Theory of Legislation (Ogden ed., 1931), 522–23.

[34] Austin, Lectures on Jurisprudence (4th ed., 1873), 224.

[35] Gray, The Nature and Sources of the Law (1st ed., 1909), § 213; (2d ed., 1921), 94.

[36] Supra, § 2.05, n. 75.

[37] (1868) L.R. 3 H.L. 330 (landowner held liable where without negligence he built a reservoir on his land which burst and injured neighbor). Ameri-

the first time in that jurisdiction, presented to the highest court, which decides that the landowner is liable to pay damages to the injured party, and so lays down the rule. Now, what was the law in Utah one week before? Either it was the ideal rule which some ideal mind would find to be the right one (but no one can prove what that was) or it *was* the same that it is now that the court has spoken (but no one can prove that either) or there was no law at all on the subject. Gray concludes that the latter is the correct answer, and that the reluctance to admit it is due to the unwillingness to recognize that "courts are constantly making law *ex post facto*." [38]

Gray's argument oversimplifies the question and exaggerates judicial law-making by overlooking the process of reasoning by analogy and the logical indeterminacy of a judicial precedent. Surely the state (of Utah) would have some analogies on liability without fault (e. g., liability of an owner and keeper of a wild animal) which would help to guide the court or at least would provide a logical justification, a not unimportant part of judicial reasoning (§ 4.53). In short, courts make law, but they do not make it out of whole cloth. Yet Gray argued more cogently when he asked: What was the law in the reign of Richard I on the liability of a telegraph company to the addressee of a message? [39] Such a question points to the undeniably great extent of judicial law-making over a period of seven centuries. The moderate position of Cardozo, Holmes and Pound is, it seems, that courts change the law in some cases and, with the exception of rare overrulings, only in small ways. They are confined as Holmes said, from molar to molecular motions. At the midpoint of the twentieth century the Blackstonian declaratory theory of law seems to have been routed from the battlefields of jurisprudence.

But it seems to have a considerable vitality in the language of courts and advocates. Thus in an opinion upholding a Washington minimum-wage law for women employees a Chief Justice of the United States explained the overruling of the Adkins decision given by the same Court thirteen years previously by saying:

----

can state courts were, when Gray wrote, fairly evenly divided on following the liability-without-fault theory of this case. Gray chose Utah, presumably, because as one of the newer states it had, when he wrote, fewer judicial precedents.

[38] Op. cit. supra, n. 35, (1st ed.) § 224; (2nd ed.) p. 100.

[39] Ibid., § 222; p. 99.

"We think that the views thus expressed [in other precedents of the same court] are sound and that the decision in the Adkins Case was a departure from the true application of the principles governing the regulation by the state of the relation of employer and employed. Those principles have been re-enforced by our subsequent decisions." [40]

Is not this the "finding" of the true law and the correction of the earlier court's error? It seems likely that Hughes thought of the Adkins holding as being contrary to basic "principles" established *as of the date of that decision*. This is the *historical* technique of overruling, as stated by Blackstone: The court now discovers that the true law has always (as far back as history goes) been what it is now pronounced to be. The *evolutionary* technique of overruling is to find that by reason of intervening decisions and legislation the precedent has *become* incompatible with present principles established by the court and therefore is at present an error to be corrected. This view seems closely akin to Mr. Justice Douglas' reasoning when after reviewing analogous decisions of the Court since the much-criticized case of Ribnik v. McBride,[41] he said:

"The drift away from Ribnik v. McBride, supra, has been so great that it can no longer be deemed a controlling authority. . . . The Ribnik case, freed from the test [i. e., dedicated to a public use] which it employed, can no longer survive." [42]

Even the House of Lords, despite its austere rule of conformity to its precedents, would, it seems, recognize that the justification for homicide has changed since Blackstone wrote.[43]

The declaratory theory has permeated judicial techniques in other ways. When courts are authorized to exercise discretion it is often said that such discretion is "not the judge's sense of moral right, neither is it his sense of what is just" but rather

---

[40] Hughes, C.J., for the court, in West Coast Hotel Co. v. Parrish, 300 U.S. 379, 57 Sup.Ct. 578, 583 (1937). The Adkins case held a similar statute to be unconstitutional.

[41] 277 U.S. 350, 48 Sup.Ct. 545 (1928) (holding unconstitutional a state statute regulating fees of employment agencies).

[42] Olsen v. Nebraska, 313 U.S. 236, 244, 61 Sup.Ct. 862, 864, 865 (1941) (upholding constitutionality of statute regulating fees of employment agencies).

[43] See opinion of Lord Simon in Holmes v. Director of Public Prosecutions, [1946] A.C. 588, 600, 601.

"principles of law are to be ascertained and followed." [44] When a court gives effect avowedly to a novel legal right or principle it usually connects the decision with analogies in precedents or with some general principle of statute or constitution (§ 3.16). The retrospective operation of a judicial holding, even of an over-ruling, seems more compatible with Blackstone's view than Gray's; if the court's ruling is analogous to legislation, it would take effect only prospectively.[45] One cannot easily find admissions by judges in office that courts make law; even Judge Hutcheson corrected the impression that he had intended (in his article on the judicial hunch) to say that judges make law while pretending they are only finding it.[46] Would any forensic advocate (even one addressing Douglas, J.)[47] argue to an appellate court that it should decide a case merely on the basis of its sense of justice or injustice or on ethical principles alone? The speech of justice is in many respects compatible with the declaratory theory.

Cardozo's popular books contained a good many moderate views on the creative character of the judicial function. To say that judges only give effect to the law is but a half-truth.[48] Judges make law by evolution rather than by revolution.[49] The judge's power of innovation is insignificant in comparison with "the bulk and pressure of the rules that hedge him on every side." [50] Holmes was careful to say that courts make law only "interstitially", though in the course of a generation they take up most

---

[44] Rugg v. State, 278 App.Div. 216, 104 N.Y.S.2d 633, 636 (1951), quoting from an earlier case.

[45] The declaratory theory was stated by Taft, C. J., in an opinion holding that a state court's overruling decision did not constitute a violation of the clause in the Federal Constitution that "no state shall pass any law impairing the obligation of contracts," (Art. I, § 10). Fleming v. Fleming, 264 U.S. 29, 44 Sup.Ct. 246 (1924).

[46] Hutcheson, J., "The Status of the Rule of Judicial Precedent" (a symposium), (1940) 14 U. of Cincinnati L.Rev. 203, 272; and see his criticism of Gray's doctrine because it makes the judge "too big". Ibid, 248. Cf. supra, § 4.63, n. 25.

[47] Who said that while the judges should not write their own predilections into law in disregard of constitutional principles, yet the judge should let his conscience cast the vote. See Douglas, "The Dissent: A Safeguard of Democracy," (1948) 32 J.Amer.Jud.Soc. 104. See also his "Stare Decisis," (1949) 49 Col.L.Rev. 735.

[48] The Nature of the Judicial Process (1921), 169.

[49] Ibid. at 26–28.

[50] Ibid. at 136–137.

of their law and "restate it from the present point of view." [51] A judge whose brilliant opinions have greatly enriched American law said more than a generation ago that the courts have a modest complementary power to express "the social will." [52] These are moderate views of the proper scope of judicial law-making.

The third view, that every appellate judicial decision is law-making in character, is based on a semantic argument. For example, in a recent case of judicial innovation, the court declared that a minor child has a right of action to recover damages from the enticer of his parent, and cited in support of its position a vague and equivocal state constitutional provision.[53] True, one can formulate a logical argument with a major premise drawn from this provision and a minor premise subsuming the principal facts of this case under the middle term, which will justify the conclusion. Surely, however, no such meaning was apparent in the language of the provision, "all injuries and wrongs which he may receive in his person." Hence the decision adds a new authoritative [54] meaning to this Illinois constitutional provision. But then does not every appellate decision, even one which seems to be a routine application of well settled law, increase or decrease the scope of the referents (§ 1.12) of some term of that law, and thus "make new law"? The careful lawyer's exhaustive search for precedents (to cite in his brief) on even "established" legal rules or concepts seems to support such an interpretation; and law-book publishers obligingly publish for sale to the profession all appellate decisions, even those that the court labels "not to be officially published." So the semantic theory reduces judicial "law-making" to the commonplace.

Since it makes no distinction between a daring judicial innovation which may have important consequences and a routine application of predetermined law, it is less significant than the moderate view of Cardozo, Holmes and Learned Hand. In the long run this view represents a sound political principle, that every judge should take a modest view of his power to "legislate" in order that he may maintain his independence of the political pressures of the

---

[51] Supra, § 4.30, n. 5.

[52] Learned Hand, "The Speech of Justice," (1916) 29 Harv.L.Rev. 617–621.

[53] See supra, § 3.16, n. 51.

[54] How much "authoritative" is a Federal court's holding in a novel case falling within state law? At any rate an Illinois appellate court followed the Federal case. Johnson v. Luhman, 330 Ill.App. 598, 71 N.E.2d 810 (1947).

moment and be able to protect individuals against oppression by other officials, even when the latter are acting with the approval of majority groups. Alexander Hamilton's statement that the judiciary has no "force" nor "will" of its own (§ 5.01) is both descriptive of the way judges ordinarily think and normative in that it tells how they can best fulfill their governmental function.

§ 5.04—Retrospective and Prospective Overruling

A phase of judicial law-making that has been often discussed during the present century is the retroactive effect of a judicial overruling, its hardships and ways to avoid them.[55] An illustration of the probable hardship of an overruling with retrospective operation is Cardozo's comment on Crowley v. Lewis,[56] in which a mortgagee of land sought to hold an undisclosed principal liable on a sealed obligation executed only by his agent. The Court had in other situations sought to abolish the distinction between sealed and unsealed written contracts, and if Cardozo's feeling was shared by his colleagues, would have been glad to see it swept away. Yet there were contrary precedents of recent date, and "deeper grounds of policy." The judges knew of the practice, common in the city of New York, by which a land title was placed in the name of a "dummy" who executed a mortgage on it to secure a sealed bond for the payment of money to a mortgagee who fully understood that the owner, to whom the land was later conveyed by the "dummy", would not be personally bound to pay the debt. By overruling its precedents on the sealed instrument rule the court would hold liable not only this undisclosed principal but countless others who had taken advantage of the same device, probably following the advice of counsel who had relied on the older decisions; and it would confer on the corresponding mortgagees an unexpected windfall. These were reasons behind the scenes for adhering to outmoded precedents. When in 1941 the New York legislature completely abolished the effect of the seal the statute was applicable only to an "instrument hereafter executed." [57]

Early in the present century a number of American courts adopted a device which may be called "prospective overruling":

---

[55] This problem was discussed from a slightly different point of view supra, § 3.30, pp. 304–306.

[56] 239 N.Y. 264, 146 N.E. 374 (1924); Cardozo, The Paradoxes of Legal Science (1928), 70–71.

[57] N.Y.Civil Practice Act § 342, as enacted in 1941.

The highest court applies the old rule to the litigants before it but announces that it will apply a different rule to transactions or other conduct *occurring after* the date of the pronouncement. The device has been used principally in cases where property or contractual rights would be affected by a retrospective overruling, or where it would impose a criminal penalty for conduct that was lawful when it was done.[58] This procedure has been commended by legal scholars,[59] and one of them drafted a model statute to authorize its use.[60] Judge Cardozo, addressing a bar association in 1932 approved the practice [61] and as a Justice of the United States Supreme Court he shortly afterward wrote the opinion of the Court which held that prospective overruling, employed by the highest court of Montana on a question of local law, did not violate the "due process" clause of the Federal constitution.[62] Yet the device is not everywhere recognized. An Ohio statute evidently intended to authorize its highest Court to adopt the practice was declared to be an invalid attempt to confer non-judicial powers upon that Court.[63] Moreover, one may have mental reservations as to whether in a later case a court which has announced a prospective overruling will conform to its announcement, especially where the ruling was adopted by a closely divided Court.[64] Again, the precise scope of the prospective overruling may be difficult to ascertain unless the court takes the time to formulate

---

[58] E.g., State v. Bell, 136 N.C. 674, 49 S.E. 163 (1904). When an appellate court decides to ignore precedent and change a rule *in favor* of an accused, it has no similar scruples about disappointing several prosecuting attorneys. See Jones v. U. S., 175 F.2d 544 (C.A.Alaska, 1949).

[59] One of the earliest advocates was the late Professor George F. Canfield (Columbia) who addressed the South Carolina bar association in 1917. See Freeman, "The Protection Afforded Against the Retroactive Operation of an Overruling Decision," (1918) 18 Col.L.Rev. 230, 248, n. 63; Snyder, "Retrospective Operation of Overruling Decisions," (1940) 35 Ill.L.Rev. 121; Spruill. "The Effect of an Overruling Decision," (1940) 18 N.C.L.Rev. 199.

[60] Kocourek, "Retrospective Decisions and Stare Decisis and a Proposal," (1931) 17 A.B.A.J. 180.

[61] (1932) Proc. N.Y. State Bar Ass'n at 294–298; Selected Writings (1947), 35.

[62] Great Northern R. Co. v. Sunburst Oil & Refining Co., 287 U.S. 358, 53 Sup.Ct. 145 (1932).

[63] Eastman v. State, 131 Ohio St. 1, 11–12, 1 N.E.2d 140, 145 (1930). But cf. Bingham v. Miller, 17 Ohio 445 (1848).

[64] E.g., the 4 to 3 decision in Mutual Life Ins. Co. of New York v. Bryant, 296 Ky. 815, 177 S.W.2d 588 (1943).

its new doctrine in statutory form.   The drafting of legislation by a Law Revision Commission (§ 4.62) seems a much better way to bring about such changes.

§ 5.05—Judicial Techniques: The Hardship Case; the Unprovided Case

From the time when the law student begins to cut his professional eye teeth on into his years of professional advocacy and counseling he is engaged in observing judicial techniques (i. e., types of arguments) as employed in the official opinions of Courts [65] justifying their conclusions.   Pound has long emphasized the importance of judicial techniques.[66]   Llewellyn has explored judicial reasons and pseudo-reasons with the enthusiasm of an anthropologist studying the behavior of a savage tribe.[67] Professor Paton has recently presented a thorough and well-balanced account of judicial method.[68]   Professor Julius Stone's valuable exploration of the "fallacies of the logical form" in English judicial opinions [69] is more critical of judicial techniques and more skeptical than those others of the influence of avowed legal premises on the mental process by which the decision is reached.   Thus if a court decides a case supposedly by relying upon a legal category of meaningless reference, "it must be obvious that the real determinant of the decision must lie elsewhere." [70]   At any rate the court has not stated its reasons clearly.   The influence of legal arguments on official conduct is discussed elsewhere in the present book.[71]

---

[65] I.e., of majority rather than dissenting judges, since the latter are less restrained by the need of so shaping their opinions that other judges will concur.

[66] See The Spirit of the Common Law (1921), Ch. VII, "Judicial Empiricism"; An Introduction to the Philosophy of Law (1922), III.

[67] This objectivity seems to me to be implicit in his comments on seven varieties of equivocation in the use of precedents.   Citation supra, § 3.30, n. 14.   See also his report on a study of the cases decided by the New York Court of Appeals on a single day in 1940.   (1940) 14 U. of Cincinnati L.Rev. 203, 208–217.

[68] Paton, A Text-Book of Jurisprudence (1946), Ch. VII; (1951) Ch. VIII.

[69] Stone, The Province and Function of Law (1946), Ch. VII.

[70] Id., § 15 (1st ed., pp. 171–174).   An example of such a category is the alleged distinction between a case excluded by definition from a rule and one falling within an exception to the rule.

[71] Supra, §§ 3.00–3.01; infra § 5.06.

One of the favorite arguments of the nineteenth century was reductio ad absurdum. *Assuming* that a certain proposed decision of the instant case would imply a certain proposition, the judge would then subsume other facts under this proposition and derive a conclusion which was patently untenable or absurd, from which it followed that the initial proposition, and hence the proposed decision should both be rejected. Lord Ellenborough used this argument to support the rule that an offer by mail is ordinarily accepted by the mailing of a letter of acceptance; for if the acceptance is not effective until it is received by the offeror, then why should not the offeree be entitled to receive notice of such receipt?—and so on ad infinitum.[72] Here the argument leads to *practical* consequences which would be absurd. In arguing (unsuccessfully) against the rule of that case Baron Bramwell later argued that it would produce inconsistency in the legal system, since in other situations of fact a notice is not legally effective until received.[73] In the famous (eventually infamous) case first holding that a master is not liable to pay damages to his servant for injuries resulting from the negligence of his fellow-servant, Lord Abinger argued that to hold the master liable in such a case would make him pay damages to the footman because the carriage-maker had made a defective carriage, and other absurd consequences.[74] This example and several others were cases in which the master would not be liable even if the fellow-servant rule were rejected: The carriage maker is not a fellow-servant of the footman but an independent contractor for whose faults the master would not be vicariously liable. These inaccuracies on the part of a careful and conscientious judge indicate that he was emotionally upset. Still the rule of "common employment", despite these errors of technique in its origin, continued to be the law in England until modified by statute. In Adams v. Lindsell the argument to absurd consequences was used to justify a right-creating rule; in Priestly v. Fowler, it was used to negate a right. Usually it seems to have been used for conservative ends. The way to refute it was shown in two recent cases in which the court rejected the contention that a certain interpretation of a complex written contract would lead necessarily to certain absurd interpretations in reference to other situations, by saying that it would

---

[72] Adams v. Lindsell, 1 B. & A. 681 (1818).

[73] Household Fire, etc., Co. v. Grant, 4 Exch.Div. 216, 234 (1879).

[74] Priestly v. Fowler, 3 M. & W. 1 (1837).

deal with these other situations when they arose.[75]   This argument, too, has its limitations, for some foresight of the future consequences of its holdings is an essential part of the reasoning of an appellate court in English and American law.   The reductio ad absurdum argument when cloaked in sarcasm or rhetoric is often a crushing blow.   Its vulnerability can be unmasked by stating it in syllogistic form, so that its premises can be attacked separately.

Two types of cases bring out the ingenuities of judicial argument: The hardship case and the "unprovided" case.[76]

1. *The Hardship Case.* As the term is here used this type of case is one in which the legal doctrine applicable to the facts is clearly established and yet the consequences of its application are felt to be harsh and unjust or highly inexpedient.   Three questions arise as to the hardship case: How does the court recognize a hardship case?   By what techniques does it seek to relieve the hardship?   What effect does an appellate court's reported decision in such a case have on previously recognized legal doctrine?

Since every appellate judicial decision tends to impose a burden on or deny a claimed benefit to someone, is not every case a hardship case?   A sensitive layman might have twinges of conscience on making every decision, no matter which way he decided it.   Not so an experienced judge.   Even as sensitive a judge as Cardozo concluded that nine-tenths of all the cases that come before an American appellate court are predestined to be decided just one way.[77]   In other words, it seems that in this judge's experience nine-tenths of the cases were in the groove and evoked no feeling of hardship.   Some of the others are hardship cases: The feeling of decency or the sentiment of rightness [78] or the sense of injustice [79] of one or more of the judges arouses in them a drive to prevent the consequences that would follow from the routine application of established law to the facts.   Why should a judge,

---

[75] Sarnia Steamships, Ltd., v. Continental Grain Co., 125 F.2d 362 (C.C.A. 7 1941) (shipping contract); Johnson v. Maryland Casualty Co., 125 F.2d 337 (C.C.A.7 1942) (liability insurance).

[76] See Dickinson, "The Problem of the Unprovided Case," in II Recueil d'Etudes sur les Sources du Droit en l'honneur de Francois Gény (Paris), 503.

[77] The Growth of the Law, (1924) 60.

[78] Riezler, Das Rechtsgefühl (1946).

[79] See Cahn, The Sense of Injustice (1949), 13.

trained to reason like a lawyer, feel outraged by the results of that reasoning in particular cases? Professor Cahn regards the sense of injustice as partly rational and partly emotional,[80] and so it is in the sense that it includes "the capacity to recognize oppression of another as a species of attack upon himself." [81] Here it is considered to be primarily emotional. In many of the hardship cases some characteristic of the individual claimant's situation which indicates weakness (but which is legally irrelevant in private law under the principle of "equality before the law") arouses sympathy for him or her: The widow who bought from the banker her deceased husband's worthless note, giving her valuable promise; [82] the poor city youth who found his precarious recreation on the springboard projecting over the river from the wealthy railroad's right-of-way; [83] the poor manual worker who loyally crippled himself for life in order to save his employer from injury; [84] a veteran of a recent war, seeking a desperately needed home for his family and himself, made a contract on Sunday for the purchase of a house.[85] Now these special circumstances were not legally relevant in the first three cases; and in each of them the rule that denied the claim was one which aroused no emotional appeal: The requirement of consideration (in the first and third); the rule that a landowner's only duty to a trespasser is not wilfully to injure him; and the Sunday statute. One might explain the court's sense of injustice in the first three cases rationally by saying that the court saw in the strict award of commutative justice a violation of distributive justice (§ 4.23). Yet these courts do not give judgment for plaintiffs just because they are hard up—as rural justices of the peace are said to do. So the hardship case, as our illustrations reveal it, is jolted out of the judicial groove by some emotional drive caused by facts which

---

[80] Ibid., 26.

[81] Ibid., 25. Cf. Kant's categorical imperative, supra, § 4.21.

[82] Newman & Snell's State Bank v. Hunter, 243 Mich. 331, 220 N.W. 665 (1928).

[83] Hynes v. New York Central R. Co., 231 N.Y. 229, 131 N.E. 898 (1921) (a 4 to 3 decision). The poverty of the deceased was not mentioned in the opinion and is inferred by the present writer from the place where he went swimming.

[84] Webb v. McGowin, 27 Ala.App. 82, 168 So. 196 (1935), certiorari denied 232 Ala. 374, 168 So. 199 (1936). The poverty of the plaintiff does not appear in the official report; it is inferred from his being a manual laborer.

[85] Chadwick v. Stokes, 162 F.2d 132 (C.C.A.Pa., 1947). That the plaintiff was a war veteran with a family was here a legally relevant fact.

are in many instances legally irrelevant, according to the prevalent norms.

How does the court know about these legally irrelevant facts?
If the bits of evidence in the record were carefully purified of all
logically irrelevant facts and if the opinion of the court were as
desiccated as that of a French court, the court would never know
and the reader of its reports would never know of the hardship
factor. Indeed, when the court sternly rejects the appeal of hardship, it usually reduces the dramatic appeal of the facts, as in the
North Carolina case where the kind neighbor woman saved the
defendant from having his head split open by his irate wife and
yet was denied recovery on defendant's gratuitous promise to in-
demnify plaintiff for injuries sustained.[86] The moral obligation to
make recompense sufficiently appears from the bare facts. At any
rate the looseness of trial procedure plus inferences from facts of
common knowledge make it possible in some cases for these extraneous facts to get in. The troublesome thing about relieving
such hardship cases is that the production of emotive facts is necessarily somewhat chancy, and the risk of unequal treatment of
different litigants at different times is a substantial one.

Now as to techniques: The widow's promise was held not binding because her deceased husband's worthless note was not "consideration" for it.[87] The court resorted to the equivalency concept
of consideration which was ordinarily rejected during the nineteenth century.[88] This technique involved no torturing of the
facts, yet it was not a good professional job because it gave reasons which the court later could not adhere to. The self-sacri-
ficing employee was allowed to recover judgment on his employer's promise to pay him a small pension, on the ground that the
moral obligation of the employer to the employee was a sufficient
consideration.[89] Here again the technique would hardly be deemed respectable by most English and American courts. The decision can scarcely be quarreled with, for the emergency left the
employee no time for bargaining; a better professional job could
be done by quasi-contract arguments.[90] Judge Cardozo's tech-

---

[86] Harrington v. Taylor, 225 N.C. 690, 36 S.E.2d 227 (1945); cf. Webb
v. McGowin, supra, n. 84.

[87] Supra, n. 82.

[88] E. g., Haigh v. Brooks, 10 Ad. & E. 309, 323 (1839–40).

[89] Supra, n. 84.

[90] The opinion referred to the right of a physician to be paid for his services rendered in an emergency to a man accidentally rendered unconscious.

nique in the springboard case [91] was far more subtle: The railroad company did owe a duty of ordinary care to a passerby on the public waters of the Harlem River; and the boy standing at the end of the springboard poised to dive was over the public water and not a trespasser when the railroad's electric wires (negligently maintained, or so the jury might find) fell upon him and killed him. Cardozo's later explanation of the case also emphasized the policy of protecting the person as against the policy of leaving landowners free to take no precautions for the protection of trespassers. In the Sunday law case the court found the veteran's purchase of a home for his family was a "work of necessity" and hence within an exception to the Sunday statute.[92] The statute itself provided an exception for hardship cases of "necessity or charity"; yet some stretching of the exception appears.

What effects do hardship cases have on the law? The common maxim, "hard cases make bad law," expresses the view that they establish precedents for legal propositions that do not work well when applied in other cases, or that conflict with other propositions in the legal system. Yet the ratio decidendi of a case can be narrowly or broadly interpreted (§§ 3.30–3.32) and if the material facts, using Professor Goodhart's method (§ 3.32) are construed narrowly enough the hardship case will be readily distinguishable. Professor Paton ascribes the narrow interpretation that English courts place on their precedents to the necessity of distinguishing inconvenient cases which they do not have power to overrule.[93] Under this view of precedent and even under the looser American method the court's technique of justification in the hardship case would determine the material facts as viewed by the court, and would thus limit the scope of the precedent. Thus if the emergency requiring instantaneous action to save human life were made a part of the material facts in the case where the workman saw his employer below just as he pushed the huge block of wood over the edge,[94] then the precedent would be narrowed to such emergency situations. Cardozo's technique in the Hynes case [95] limited the scope of that case to a narrow inter-

---

See Cotnam v. Wisdom, 83 Ark. 601, 104 S.W. 164 (1907); Restatement, Restitution (1937), § 116.

[91] Supra, n. 83.

[92] Supra, n. 85.

[93] Paton, Jurisprudence (1946) or (1951), § 44, p. 161.

[94] Supra, n. 84.

[95] Supra, n. 83.

pretation of trespasser. Likewise his technique in the marriage settlement case tortured the facts into an agreement not to rescind [96] and left the precedents on pre-existing duty avowedly undisturbed. Yet this hedging-in of prior legal doctrine indicates probable further limitations by the same court on future legal doctrine; in short it increases uncertainty. The technique of the widow's-note case [97] seems the worst of those cited, since it places no limit on the scope of judicial supervision of the equivalence of exchange in bargains. Does it apply only to a widow, or to a widow vis-à-vis a banker, or to other kind-hearted relatives? On the whole it would seem better that courts, whether trial or appellate, should not write opinions in hardship cases.

2. *The Unprovided Case.* The term "unprovided case" has been used to refer to a situation of fact for which no law is provided in the present legal system which is jurisdictionally controlling.[98] At the outset it may be asked, how can there be such a case under a mature legal system? Either there are principles, policies or analogies which can guide the court to a decision and provide it with justifications, or, if this be not so, then the procedural rule that the claimant has the burden of establishing his claim in both law and fact would suffice to deny the claim. The term "unprovided case" is here used to mean one for which no close analogy on the facts can be found. Now a modest-violet type of court might deny the claim on the basis of the procedural rule suggested above; yet ordinarily in appellate courts other reasons are given. An example is the claim of a mother to recover damages from one who alienated the affections of her minor son.[99] The court could find no precedent in American or in English law for enforcing such a claim; yet it said the absence of a precedent was not conclusive. Analogies there were, such as the father's right to recover damages for the seduction of his minor daughter; yet there a claim of loss of services was conventional even if often fictitious. The Court concluded that it could find no good reason for enforcing such a claim. Is this "unprovided case" now provided for? The decision denying it established a negative precedent for that jurisdiction.

A more recent unprovided case was the claim of a minor child to recover damages from a woman who had enticed away the

---

[96] De Cicco v. Schweizer, supra, § 3.30, n. 11, and § 4.62, n. 91.

[97] Supra, n. 82.

[98] See Dickinson, supra, n. 76.

[99] Pyle v. Waechter, 202 Iowa 695, 210 N.W. 926 (1926).

father from the family home. The court could find no precedent
for enforcing such a claim either in Illinois (whose law was controlling) or in any other Anglo-American court of last resort.
However, the court held the claim enforceable, relying formally
on an equivocal provision of the Illinois constitution.[1] There
were some remote analogies: The liability of one who unjustifia-
bly induces another to break his contract with a third person, or of one who induces another to commit a tort which
harms a third person.[2] The opinion does not rely upon them but
rather upon the Court's belief that the claim ought to be allowed.
This was judicial law-making scarcely disguised. A later case in
Minnesota which enforced the minor child's claim against a man
who enticed away the mother did a somewhat more cautious professional job.[3] The courts that denied the claim found the case
was otherwise provided for in existing law.

The question of "gaps in the law" which was much discussed
in European literature during the first part of this century is virtually the same as that of the unprovided case: *Logically* there
are no gaps and no unprovided cases, since a logical justification
can always be found in the legal system for deciding the case one
way or another. *Semantically* there *are* gaps in the law and
unprovided cases, in the sense that no rule nor analogy can be
found whose terms have such direct reference to the instant facts
that the conclusion to be drawn is practically apparent. The gap
problem is thus one of meaning and mental process [4] rather than
of logic. Even a lengthy detailed code would leave some gaps.
Case law precedents tend to cluster along certain grooves; the
careful advocate does not want to assert that his case falls outside of any precedent or statute just as the cautious judge is reluctant to innovate. Nevertheless the gaps in meaning between
precedent grooves are frequent and they have to be filled in by the
application, in large measure creative, of principles and policies
and other guides which can be found within the legal system. The
gap problem in this sense is not peculiar to the tempered chaos

---

1 Daily v. Parker, supra, § 3.16, n. 51.

2 See (1947) 12 Mo.L.Rev. 358, commenting on Johnson v. Luhman, 330 Ill.
App. 598, 71 N.E.2d 810 (1947).

3 Miller v. Monsen, 228 Minn. 400, 37 N.W.2d 543 (1949). The court examined the policy arguments of decisions that had rejected such a claim. (There
were five decisions contra).

4 The part played by emotional drives is not overlooked: A judge may feel
impelled to narrow established precepts in order to make a gap for the instant
case.

of case law. Modern European codes also have to employ provisions [5] that are semantically as thin as a comet's tail.

§ 5.06—The Psychology of Judicial Decisions

The title of this section is an overworked cliché, often used to refer to common sense observations about the mental processes of judges rather than to anything that would be recognized by a psychologist as falling within his science. In the last section the feeling of rightness or the sense of injustice was referred to as the emotional drive in the recognition by a judge of a hardship case,[6] and yet this discussion employed no techniques of psychology. Nor were any employed in drawing the inference that Lord Abinger was emotionally disturbed from the circumstance that he used clearly inaccurate analogies in his reductio ad absurdum.[7] A skillful advocate, about to argue before an appellate court a case that will likely divide the court, and aware that a certain doubtful judge will respond favorably to a certain argument, will make that argument unless it will be likely to alienate other judges who are believed to be favorably predisposed because of other arguments. A judge's attitude toward marriage and divorce may have some bearing upon his decisions in some cases.[8] No course in psychology is needed to observe such influences on judicial behavior. While the law student should have his attention called to instances of various kinds of influences on judicial decisions, it remains doubtful whether any useful set of generalizations about them can be made in a law school. Perhaps two exceptions must be made: A course in professional ethics can deal with the permissible limits of advocacy and a course in forensic advocacy can develop the generalizations of an art.

Still, common sense observation can go sadly astray, and psychology has made some discoveries about human nature and conduct and about the technique of observing it. The trained psychologist may prevent the law-trained observer from making some mistakes; and psychology may give the latter some clues by which to interpret and analyze his observations. Three examples

---

[5] Supra, § 3.16, n. 57. See Dawson, Unjust Enrichment (1951), 108.

[6] Supra, p. 582.

[7] Supra, p. 580.

[8] A judge who had for years suffered a heavy matrimonial burden was avoided by lawyers representing wives in matrimonial matters, yet these alleged prejudices may well be exaggerated. Botein, Trial Judge (1952), 189.

of such use were discussed above (§ 4.64). We shall try to compress our present discussion of the subject under five headings:

1. *Reason and Emotion in the Judicial Process.* American legal realism, like its counterpart in Europe, the "free-law" movement of the early twentieth century, was a revolt against the prevailing belief that judicial decisions resulted inexorably from the logical application of the law to the facts. To show that choices of value were involved in this process and that the preferences of a judge or judges for one value over another were often decisive and were in some sense "emotional" was not very difficult. The movement went further, however, and asserted the dominance of emotion over reason, or made reason a mere ritual. Thus Ehrlich, arguing for judicial freedom of decision, uttered the half-truth:

"There is no guaranty of justice save the personality of the judge." [9]

Now it is true that a crooked judge or a biased judge can often find ways of circumventing legal norms; yet it is also true that he can sometimes be caught, and that pure-hearted judges sometimes make bad decisions as well as bad law. The anti-rational revolt was strengthened by the view, put forward by Rignano, that all concepts, even those of geometry, are determined by affectivity, a psychologist's attenuated name for emotion.[10] Such a generalization does not help beyond pointing out that one cannot think about anything or make decisions and take action without something that *moves* one. The nature of the mover is still open to question. The English philosopher Hume contended that "reason is, and ought only to be the slave of the passions, and can never pretend to any other office than to serve and obey them." [11] Now it is true that "reason," in the sense of formal logic, is empty of content, that its conclusions are determined by its premises and that in moral reasoning the ultimate major premises are not chosen merely by logic nor merely by observation, but partly by emotion or by authority. Still the question remains, is it possible that a judge's loyalty to the judicial

---

9 Ehrlich, (E.), "Judicial Freedom of Decision: Its Principles and Objects" in The Science of Legal Method (1917), 65.

10 See Rignano, The Psychology of Reasoning (1923), 81, 109: "Every common noun, every concept, is essentially merely an *affective* grouping."

11 Hume, A Treatise of Human Nature (Oxford, 1896), 415, quoted and discussed in Cairns, Legal Philosophy from Plato to Hegel (1949), 365. Cf. views of James and Dewey, supra, § 4.53, n. 81, n. 82.

technique in which he has been trained and to the law which he has sworn to uphold can overcome the contrary emotional pulls of particular factual situations or of his political or ethical beliefs which run contrary to prevailing legal doctrine? It seems not only possible but fairly common that this occurs.[12] To the cases of conscious emotional tension may be added the great bulk of litigation in which the judge has no strong feeling one way or another,[13] in which his principal drive is to do a good professional job. In another sense, too, reason can control emotion: The "cardiac promptings of the moment," to use Cardozo's caustic phrase,[14] can be overcome by reflection and search for long-range and distant consequences of a decision one way or the other. Reflective thinking (§ 4.53) can be backed by emotions which dominate other emotions. Yet one need not go so far as to expect that the judge will, like Kant's saintly man of pure will, decide in accordance with reason *and not* take satisfaction in so doing.

2. *The Prediction of Judicial Decisions.* The stimulus-response analogy of behaviorism gave Oliphant the clue to a mode of interpreting judicial precedents (§ 3.31), which has considerable value, even though it requires one to ignore the opinions of the judges. Given a case involving some genuine doubt about labor unions or monopolies or freedom of speech, during most of the past thirty years, and a shrewd counselor could guess how four to six Supreme Court justices would *vote* on the case with a probability value better than even. (This is, of course, the present writer's estimate.) That is not to say that the justices would all give the same reasons or concur in the same opinion. For clients who expect to have further litigation (such as large corporations and large labor unions) reasons are still important. More recently Professors Lasswell and McDougal have put forward the thesis that a technique of prediction of judicial decisions can be developed. "As scientist, the legal scholar will conceive that the response of any court is affected by two sets of factors:

---

[12] My elderly law partner used to dread trying a case before a Federal judge who was a good friend of his, because the judge always leaned over backwards to avoid partiality. Judges who have talked to me about their cases *before they had decided* exemplified the statement of the text. See also Botein, Trial Judge (1952), 309–10.

[13] See statement by Judge Charles E. Clark, supra, § 5.00, n. 6.

[14] In the 1932 bar association address: Selected Writings (1947), 15.

environmental and predispositional." [15] The former refers to what goes on when a case is tried; the latter to factors that existed before the case came before the judge. Here the authors reveal their own predilections by including in the predisposing factors the judge's biases and his attitudes toward the commerce clause or the opinions of Mr. Justice Brandeis, and by omitting the fact that the judge has studied, practiced and read something called "law". They seem to regard "legal norms" as mere conventional justifications contrived for losing counsel and higher courts or as having similar perfunctory uses.[16] Since this nascent science of prediction has been presented publicly only in the terminology stage, one could only conjecture what it would eventually be. As to the trial of issues of fact before a jury (especially under the general verdict plan), Judge Frank's prediction that the outcome will never be predictable [17] seems correct. Even if the predisposing factors of judge and jurymen could be ascertained, could be assigned accurately their quantitative values and placed in a mathematical determinant or similar complex formula for solution by a computing machine, the judge and the jury might assert their independence by responding differently. On the other hand the case that comes before a multiple-judge appellate court (where several judges can read the record) has its factual issues drawn and settled and its legal issues drawn; the vagaries of witness-proof and jury-response and trial-judge-response are all past. If, as seems correct, eighty to ninety per cent of the cases taken to appellate courts [18] are predestined to be decided just one way,[19] then it seems that a shrewd and expert counselor, presupposing a skilful advocate on each side, could predict the outcome of appellate litigation with a probability much better than half.

3. *The Relations of Legal Norms to the Mental Processes of the Judge.* The prior discussions of this theme [20] exemplify its

---

[15] Lasswell and McDougal, "Legal Education and Public Policy," (1943) 52 Yale L.J., 203, 238–241.

[16] Ibid., 240.

[17] Frank, Courts on Trial (1949), 202–204.

[18] This figure would include, I suppose, those in which no opinion is written.

[19] Cardozo said nine-tenths are predetermined (The Growth of the Law, 60) and Judge Frank has said this was "perhaps not too wide of the mark." (1948) 13 Law & Contemp. Probs. 369, 374. Cf. Llewellyn in (1940) 14 U. of Cincinnati L.Rev. at p. 219: "something more than 80 per cent of those cases were clearly predictable in outcome."

[20] Supra, §§ 3.00, 3.01; § 3.31; Dewey's instrumental logic, § 4.53; Cardozo's account of the judicial process, § 4.62.

difficulties and suggest the answers which here need only be summarized. Legal norms are used as fact-selectors in pleadings and proof and thus set the framework of litigation. They are used to narrow the issues of fact and law so that these become manageable in scope. This framing process reduces the need and the opportunity for judicial creativeness, and increases predictability. Furthermore, the statement of legal issues in terms of competing rules, principles or policies aids in the crucial decision. How does one know that legal norms play any such important parts in the mental processes of judges? Only by what honest men have said. The "hunch" theory of judicial decision [21] was at one time thought to have disposed of the thesis just stated; yet the chief protagonist of that view has corrected that impression.[22] Expert intuition employs generalizations which are not made explicit in consciousness (§ 4.53). Now judges do not, it seems, formulate complete syllogisms, and the judicial stream of consciousness, one may venture to suppose, contains a good deal of non-legal flotsam and jetsam. Men are not transformed psychically when they don judicial robes but they are transformed morally, i. e., in their dominant loyalties. Some judges decide on the whole case first and then proceed to the analysis of reasons; others by analysis build slowly toward a decision. The flash of insight that brings conviction may occur in an instant; yet the preparatory steps are none the less important.[23]

4. *The Relations of the Opinion to the Decision.* The view that the opinion of an appellate court is (typically or always) a mere post-rationalization of a decision arrived at on other grounds has been discussed above.[24] Now it seems true that the opinion of a court, even a rather poor specimen, is orderly and clear as compared with the turbulent stream of consciousness of a judge who is thinking toward the decision of a case: The opinion is not a replica of the mental process. Who would want a judicial opinion to imitate the literary style of James Joyce or even of Marcel Proust? In a multiple-judge court, *whose* stream of consciousness should be exhibited in the opinion? The public functions of a judicial opinion call for selection of reasons and for conciseness and clarity in the formulation of them. That the more recent justices of the Supreme Court have been more pro-

---

[21] Supra, § 4.62, n. 98.

[22] Supra, § 5.03, n. 46.

[23] Wallas, The Art of Thought (1926), Ch. IV.

[24] Supra, § 4.64.

lific in opinions, both concurring and dissenting, than their predecessors is due to their desire to be candid with the bar and the
public about their mental processes on important public issues.[25]
The opinion of the court may give as "reasons" such vague or
garbled concepts as to justify the inference that it does not adequately express the "real" reasons for the decision; [26] yet this
does not necessarily signify some dark secret prejudice or sin or
frustration of the judge: He may be a poor opinion-writer, or
he may have been hurried. Still, a judge's opinion occasionally
betrays his emotional disturbance. Lord Abinger, whose opinion in the leading case that originated the fellow-servant rule
(a boon to nineteenth century industrial employers) gave evidence of his agitation,[27] was, it seems,[28] concerned about his
position as head of the household of a suburban country estate
rather than about his investments in industrial enterprises.

The late Professor Edward S. Robinson, a distinguished psychologist who familiarized himself with judicial opinions, gave
the best account of the rationalization theory that has yet appeared. Whether the reasons given for the defense of a decision
are accurate statements of motivations or are fictitious is a question of fact that cannot be answered "by the loose, lazy and frequently cynical use of such terms as *unconscious complexes* and
rationalization." [29] "Psychologists are becoming increasingly
suspicious of the dark secret urges that are supposed to underlie
overt behavior." [30] One can look back into one's motivations and
discover "reasons" which were implicit in the mental process;
these are not mere post-rationalizations. The individual self is
not a lone wolf; its content is "largely social," and so the feeling that a critic will be examining one's conduct makes one prepare a defense. Especially with the appellate judge the need for
writing an opinion (not universal) brings the search for justifi-

---

[25] See, for example, Mr. Justice Jackson's statement that his "first impression" was to concur in the parochial school-bus case. Everson v. Board of
Education of Ewing Tp., 330 U.S. 1, 18, 67 Sup.Ct. 504, 513 (1947).

[26] See Stone, supra, § 5.05, n. 69.

[27] Supra, § 5.05, n. 74.

[28] The present writer made a study of the life of Lord Abinger some years
ago, with a view to determining whether he represented industrialists. All
of the evidence that I could find indicated a negative answer.

[29] Robinson, Law and the Lawyers (1935), 174.

[30] Ibid., 175.

cations into the process of deciding, and thereby both guides and clarifies it.[31]

5. *Individual Personality Factors and Group Pressures.* That some individual personality factors of judges have some influence upon some decisions is a statement which will not here be denied. One of the early proofs of this thesis was Professor C. G. Haines' study of the decisions of New York city magistrates. In 1916, for instance, 17,075 persons were charged (before the magistrates) with intoxication and 92 per cent were convicted; yet one judge discharged 79 per cent of those accused.[32] From these and like statistics Haines drew the conclusion that something else besides "the law" [33] and "the facts" was motivating some magistrates' decisions, though he did not determine what it was. From these cases he went on to the conclusion that the social and economic beliefs of some justices of the United States Supreme Court had more to do with their votes on the regulation of employer-employee relations than the words of the Constitution or the Court's precedents. Neither of these examples necessarily shows that the beliefs of judges on politics or any other theme have significant influences in the decision and justification of the vast majority of appellate decisions.

An additional ground for this belief is to be found in the tendency of consultation and discussion among the members of the court to reduce the extreme positions which individual judges might take at the outset. This view, put forward by Oliphant, found some confirmation in experiments conducted by Professor F. H. Allport.[34]

The judicial process will continue to be of great interest to lawyers, to judges, to law teachers and to law students. Case law will continue to be the staple diet of legal education; the method of casuistry can be introduced into the teaching of sub· jects that are codified. The legal profession can contribute to the improvement of the judicial process in many ways: By not waiting until the last minute to prepare their cases for trial; by not hurling at an appellate court every legal rubric and every

---

[31] Ibid., Ch. VIII, Ch. X.

[32] Haines, "General Observations on the Effects of Personal, Political and Economic Influences in the Decisions of Judges," (1922) 17 Ill.L.Rev. 96, 106.

[33] The chief examples he used were "intoxication" and "disorderly conduct," neither a model of legal clarity.

[34] See Allport, Social Psychology (1924), 277–278.

citation that has a remote bearing on the case and by not expecting an appellate court to discuss thoroughly every point made. Judges of appellate courts can improve the judicial process by ruthlessly reducing the number of cases in which opinions are written, in order to have time to write opinions selectively and concisely. The public (meaning the voters) could help by getting more able men into judicial office. The law teachers can help by teaching their students that the judicial process must keep on trying to be reason without passion, even though they know that it will never quite make it.

Patterson Jurisprudence F.P.Inc.

TABLE OF CASES

BOOKS AND PERIODICALS CITED

The books, articles in periodicals and symposia, and other works cited are listed below under the name of the author wherever possible; otherwise under the name of the periodical or other publication. The titles of articles in periodicals or symposia are listed in quotation marks; unquoted titles refer to books. The Collected Readings of Hall, and of Cohen and Cohen (see p. 5, n. 3), are not listed here.

The Index (infra) lists the names of authors and their ideas which are discussed at length.

[The references below are to pages]

ABRAHAMS, "The English Legal Assistance Plan, 36 A.B.A.J. 31 (1950), 192.

ADLER, "Legal Certainty", 31 Columbia L.Rev. 91 (1931), 182.

ALLPORT, Floyd H., Social Psychology (1924), 56, 57, 593.

ALLEN, Carleton K.
Law in the Making (1st ed., 1928), 229.
Law in the Making (1935), 261, 262.
Law in the Making (3d ed., 1939), Chs. I–II, 223, 224, 225, 226, 231, 499.

AMES, James B.
14 Harv.L.R. 241 (1900), 421.
16 Harv.L.Rev. 255 (1903), 421.
"Law and Morals" in Lectures on Legal History, 438 (1913), 235.
Lectures on Legal History (1913), 466.
"Lectures on Legal History" (1913), first published in (1889) 3 Harv.L.Rev. 23 (1889), 420.
"The Nature of Ownership" in Lectures on Legal History (1913) 3 Harv. L.Rev. 345 (1890), 420.
"Two Theories of Consideration," (first published, 1899), 466.

AMOS, Sheldon, Science of Law (1874), 10, 147.

AQUINAS, St. Thomas
Summa Theologica (trans. by Dominican Fathers, 1927), 191, 347.
(Part II, first Part) Art. 2, 347.
Q. 90, Art. 1, 347.
Q. 90, Art. 4, 350.
Q. 91, Art. 1, 347.
Q. 91, Art. 2, 348.
Q. 91, Art. 4, 348.
Q. 91, Art. 5, 348.
Q. 93, Art. 3, 351.
Q. 94, Art. 3, 348, 349, 357.
Q. 94, Art. 3, Rep.Obj. 3, 348, 352.
Q. 94, Art. 4, 348, 349.
Q. 94, Art. 5, 357.
Q. 94, Art. 5, ad. 3, 350.
Q. 95, Art. 1, ad. 2, 350.

BENTHAM, Jeremy—Continued
Principles of Legislation, Ch. XIII, 333.
The Theory of Legislation (Ogden ed., 1931), 33, 333, 442, 458, 459, 572.

BERGSON, 17 A.B.A.J. 185 (1931), 542, 575.

BERLE Adolph A., Natural Selection of Political Forces (1950), 409, 438.

BERMAN, Justice in Russia (1950), 286.

BIENENFELD, Rediscovery of Justice (1947), Pt. I, 334.

BINGHAM, Joseph Walter,
"Legal Philosophy and the Law" 9 Ill.L.Rev. 96 (1914), 38.
"What is the Law?" 11 Mich.L.Rev. 109 (1912), 38.
My Philosophy of Law, 12 (Symposium, 1941), 38.
"The Nature and Importance of Legal Possession", 13 Mich.L.Rev. 535 (1915), 543.
"What is the Law?" 11 Mich.L.Rev. 1 (1912), 543.

BISHOP, Contracts, 388.

BLACKSTONE, William, Commentaries, 72, 75, 159, 300, 571.

BOAZ, Franz, Anthropology and Modern Life (1928), 55.

BODENHEIMER, Jurisprudence (1940), 344, 426.

BORCHARD, "Justiciability," 4 U. of Ch.L.Rev. 1 (1936), 565.

BORING, LANGFELD and WELD, Psychology: A Factual Textbook (1935), 27, 549.
Ch. 15, 445, 477, 520.

BOTEIN, Trial Judge (1952), 188, 299, 328, 569, 587, 589.

BOUVIER'S Law Dictionary (1914), 67.

BOWEN, Catherine Drinker, Yankee From Olympus (1945), 500, 501, 505.

BRANDEIS, Louis D. and Warren, "The Right of Privacy" 4 Harv.L.Rev. 193 (1890), 222, 375.

BRAYBROOKE, E. K., "Custom as a Source of English Law" 50 Mich.L.Rev. 71 (1951), 82, 229.

BRECHT, "The Myth of the 'Is' and the 'Ought'", 54 Harv.L.Rev. 811 (1941), 41, 140.

BRINKMANN, Carl, "Economics," 5 Encyc. of Soc. Sci. 381-385 (1931), 54.

BROAD, Five Types of Ethical Theory (1930), 34.

BROWN, "Customary Law in Modern England", 5 Col.L.Rev. 561 (1905), 229.

BROWN, William J., The Austinian Theory of Law (1931), 135.

BROWNE, Douglas G., and TULLETT, E. V., The Scalpel of Scotland Yard (1952), 61.

BRYCE, Studies in History and Jurisprudence (1901), 344.

BUCHLER, C. S. Peirce's Empiricism (1939), 476.

BUCKLAND, William W., and McNAIR, Arnold D., Roman Law and Common Law (1936), 169, 207.

BUCKLAND, William W., Some Reflections on Jurisprudence (1945), 125, 161, 163.

CAHILL, Judicial Legislation (1952), 56.

CAHN, The Sense of Injustice (1949), 557, 581, 582.

CAIRNS, Huntington
Law and the Social Sciences (1935), 52, 78.
Legal Philosophy from Plato to Hegel (1949), 10, 83, 249, 336, 337, 340, 342, 343, 353, 361, 377, 588.
     Ch. VII, 363.
     Ch. VIII (Spinoza), Ch. IX (Leibniz), 439, 442.
     Ch. XIV, 429, 430, 434.
The Theory of Legal Science (1941), 11, 12, 52, 308.

CARDOZO, Benjamin
"A Ministry of Justice," 35 Harv.L.Rev. 113, 115 (1921), 413, 529.
"Jurisprudence," in Selected Writings of Benjamin N. Cardozo (1932 N. Y. State Bar Ass'n Rep. 263), 528, 536, 537.
Lectures on Legal Topics (Ass'n of the Bar of the City of New York, 1921–22), 529.
Selected Writings of Benjamin N. Cardozo (1932 N. Y. State Bar Ass'n Rep. 294) (1947), 578, 589.
"The Altruist in Politics," in Selected Writings of Benjamin N. Cardozo (1947), 528, 529.
The Growth of the Law (1924), 100, 120, 181, 281, 467, 468, 532, 533, 581, 590.
"The Moral Element in Matthew Arnold," in Selected Writings of Benjamin N. Cardozo (1947), 528–532, 536, 537.
The Nature of the Judicial Process (1921), 48, 256, 302, 305, 354, 468, 532, 533, 534, 537, 559, 575.
The Paradoxes of Legal Science (1928), 63, 234, 305, 473, 495, 530, 532, 536, 577.

CARNAP, Rudolf, Philosophy and Logical Syntax (1935), 28.

CARTER, James C.
"James Coolidge Carter," 8 Great American Lawyers 19 (1909), 423, 424.
Law: Its Origin, Growth and Function (1907), 424.
"The Proposed Codification of Our Common Law," (Pamphlet in 1883), 423.
"The Province of the Written and the Unwritten Law," 24 Amer.L.Rev. 1 (1890), 423.

CASTBERG, Problems of Legal Philosophy (c. 1948), 6, 38, 42, 43.

CHAFEE and SIMPSON, Cases on Equity (1934), Vol. I, 555.

CHASE, The Tyranny of Words, 295, 546.

CHESHIRE, Private International Law (1935), 221.

CHOATE, "Trial by Jury," American Addresses (1911), 465.

CHOUMENKOVITCH, "Insurance under Communism," 11 Casualty & Surety Journal 24 (1950), 287.

CICERO, Marcus Tullius
  De Legibus (Keyes trans., Loeb Classical Library. 1928), Bk. I, VI, 75,
    83, 342.
  Bk. I, XVI, 75.
  Bk. II, IV, 343.
  Bk. II, V, 75.
  De Re Publica (Keyes trans., Loeb Classical Library, 1928), Bk. III,
    XXII, 343.

CLARK, Charles E.
  "The Dilemma of American Judges: Is Too Great 'Trust for Salvation'
    Placed in Them?" 35 A.B.A.J. 8 (1949), 490, 561, 562, 589.
  "State Law in Federal Courts: The Brooding Omnipresence of Erie v.
    Tompkins," 55 Yale L. J. 267 (1946), 322, 323.

CLARK, John M., Social Control of Business (1926), 93.

CLARK, William, DOUGLAS, William O., and THOMAS, Dorothy S.
  "The Business Failures Project—A Study in Methodology", 39 Yale L. J.
    1013 (1930); 40 Yale L. J. 1034 (1931), 547.

CLARK and CORSTVET, "Untapped Legal Business in New Haven: The
    Economics of the Legal Profession," 47 Yale L. J. 1272 (1938), 192.

CLOE and MARCUS, "Special and Local Legislation," 24 Ky.L.J. 351 (1936),
    114.

COFFEY, The Science of Logic (1912), 306.

COHEN, F. S.
  Ethical Systems and Legal Ideals (1933), 308.
  "The Holmes-Cohen Correspondence," 9 Jour.Hist.Ideas 14 (1948), 501.

COHEN, Julius, "Towards Realism in Legisprudence," 59 Yale L.J. 886 (1950),
    243.

COHEN, Morris R., and NAGEL, Ernest
  An Introduction to Logic and Scientific Method (1936), 70, 107, 132, 257,
    543.
  Ch. II, "The Traditional Analysis of Propositions," 288.
  Ch. VII, 248.
  Ch. XIV, 306.

COHEN, Morris R.
  Editorial Preface to Tourtelon, Philosophy in the Development of the
    Law, 9.
  "Justice Holmes and the Nature of Law" 31 Columbia L.Rev. 352 (1931),
    39.
  "Law and Scientific Method," in Law and the Social Order (1933), 42.
  Law and the Social Order (1933), 39, 308.
  "On the Logic of Fiction," 20 J. Philos. 477 (1923), 416.
  "Positivism and the Limits of Idealism in the Law," 27 Columbia L.Rev.
    237 (1927), 36, 351, 395, 512.
  Reason and Law (1950), 386, 387.
  Reason and Nature (1931), 44.
  "Should Legal Thought Abandon Clear Distinctions?" 36 Ill.L.Rev. 239
    (1941), 68.
  The Heritage of Kant (ed. Whitney and Bowers, 1939), 386, 387.

COHEN, Morris R.—Continued
"The Place of Logic in the Law," 29 Harv.L.Rev. 622 (1916), 5, 22, 23, 100, 245.
"The Process of Judicial Legislation," in Law and the Social Order (1933), 49.

COLIN ET CAPITANT, Droit Civil Francais (1914), 73.

COLUMBIA LAW REVIEW
"Factors Relied on By Arbitrators in Determining Wage Rates," 47 Col. L.Rev. 1026 (1947), 294.
42 Col.L.Rev. 1030 (1942), 294.
30 Col.L.Rev. 360 (1930), 243.

COMMAGER, The American Mind (1950), 378.

COOK, Walter Wheeler, "The Associated Press Case," 28 Yale L. J. 386 (1919), 132.
"The Logical and Legal Bases of the Conflict of Laws," 33 Yale L.J. 457 (1924), 508.
"Scientific Method and the Law," 13 A.B.A.J. 303 (1927), 11, 120, 539.

CORBIN, Arthur L.
"Conditions in the Law of Contracts," 28 Yale L.J. 739 (1919), 40.
Contracts (1951), 29, 40.
"Legal Analysis and Terminology," 29 Yale L.J. 163 (1919), 15, 28, 90, 91, 120, 131, 140, 142, 145, 254.
"The Laws of the Several States," 50 Yale L.J. 762 (1941), 321.

CREIGHTON and SMART, An Introductory Logic (5th ed., 1932), Ch. IV, 294, 546.

CURRIE, "The Materials of Law Study," 3 J.Leg.Educ. 331 (1951), 554.

DABIN, Jean
General Theory of Law, in The Legal Philosophies of Lask, Radbruch and Dabin (Wilk trans., 1950), 348, 354, 355, 356, 357, 358, 364, 495.
La Philosophie de l'Ordre Juridique Positif (1929), 9.
Le droit subjectif (Paris, 1952), Ch. 1, 74.

DAWSON
"Economic Duress and the Fair Exchange in French and German Law," 12 Tul.L.Rev. 42 (1937), 268.
Unjust Enrichment (1951), 43, 374, 587.

DE LA MORANDIÈRE, "The Reform of the French Civil Code," 97 U. of Pa.L.Rev. 1 (1948), 201, 208.

DEALY, The State and Government (1921), 53.

Decretals of Gregory IX, Lib. I, Tit. IV, cap. 11, 169.

DEWEY, John
Allen, Law in the Making (1927), in 28 Columbia L.Rev. 832–833 (1928), 160, 229.
Characters and Events (Joseph Ratner ed., 1929), 148.
Essays in Experimental Logic (1903), 491.
Experience and Nature (1926), 494.
"Force, Violence and Law," in Intelligence in the Modern World (Joseph Ratner ed., 1939), 148.

EHRLICH, Eugen
   Die stillschweigende Willenserkärung (1893), 79.
   Fundamental Principles of the Sociology of Law (Moll trans. Harvard
      Univ. Press, 1936), 79, 148, 241, 334.
   Grundlegung der Soziologie des Rechts (1913), 79, 509.
   "Judicial Freedom of Decision: Its Principles and Objects," in The Sci-
      ence of Legal Method (1917), 464, 588.
   "Sociology of Law" (Isaac trans., 1922) 36 Harv.L.Rev. 130; 16, 80, 190.
   Die Juristische Logik (1918), 464.

EVERETT, The Education of Jeremy Bentham (1931), 441, 442, 458.

EVERETT, Helen, "Social Control," 4 Encyclopedia of the Social Sciences,
   344, 345 et seq. (1931), 93.

FIELD, David D.
   "Codification," 20 Amer.L.Rev. 1 (1886), 422.
   24 Amer.L.Rev. 255 (1890), 422.
   8 Great Amer. Lawy. 145 (1908), 423.

FRANK, Jerome
   "Are Judges Human?" 80 U. of Pa.L.Rev. 17 (1931), 544, 550.
   "Cardozo and the Upper-Court Myth," 13 Law and Contemp.Prob. 369
      (1948), 187, 274, 298, 545, 559, 590.
   Courts On Trial (1949), 47, 68, 99, 100, 298, 335, 336, 403, 491, 540, 544,
      545, 550, 567, 568, 590.
   Fate and Freedom (1945), Ch. X, 98.
   If Men Were Angels (1942), 550.
   Law and the Modern Mind (1930), 26, 99, 203, 540.
   Law and the Modern Mind (second printing, 1931), 549, 550.
   Law and the Modern Mind (1931), Part III, Ch. II, "Mr. Justice Oliver
      Wendell Holmes, The Completely Adult Jurist", 508.
   "Mr. Justice Holmes and Non-Euclidean Legal Thinking," 17 Cornell
      L. Q. 568 (1932), 124.
   16 Philosophy of Science (1949), 434.
   "What Courts Do in Fact," 26 Ill.L.Rev. 645 (1932), 43, 545.

FRANK, Hans, Rechtsgrundlegung des Nationalsozialischen Fuhrerstaates,
   (2d ed., 1938), 240.

FRANKFURTER, Felix
   Dictionary of American Biography XXI, Supp. I (N.Y. 1944), 501.
   "Mr. Justice Brandeis and the Constitution," 45 Harv.L.Rev. 33 (1931), 243.
   "Mr. Justice Holmes and the Constitution," in Mr. Justice Holmes (by
      Cardozo and others, 1931), 501, 506.
   The Commerce Clause (1937), 23.

FREEMAN, "The Protection Afforded Against the Retroactive Operation
   of an Overruling Decision," 18 Col.L.Rev. 230 (1918), 578.

FREUND, Legislative Regulation (1932), 285.

FRIEDMAN, W., Legal Theory (1st ed., 1944; 2d ed., 1948), 10.

FULLER, Lon L.
   "American Legal Realism," 82 U. of Pa.L.Rev. 429 (1934), 136, 553.
   "Legal Fictions," 25 Ill.L.Rev. 363 (1930), 416.
   "Legal Fictions," 25 Ill.L.Rev. 877 (1931), 132, 416.

FULLER, Lon L.—Continued
"Pashukanis and Vyshinsky: A Study in the Development of Marxian
Legal Theory", 47 Mich.L.Rev. 1157 (1949), 155, 436, 437.
"Reason and Fiat in Case Law", 59 Harv.L.Rev. 376 (1946), 369.
"Reason and Fiat in Case Law", 59 Harv.L.Rev. 381 (1946), 304.
The Law in Quest of Itself (1940), 68, 132, 333, 369.
The Problems of Jurisprudence (1949), 337, 557.
"Williston on Contracts," 18 N.C.L.Rev. 1 (1939), 25, 221.

FUNK and WAGNALL'S New Standard Dictionary (1930), 7, 8.

GALLAGHER, "The Lawyer Reference Plan", 36 A.B.A.J. 24 (1950), 192.

GARLAN, Legal Realism and Justice (1941), 377, 539, 545, 546, 553.

GÉNY, Science et Technique en droit prive positif, t. IV (Paris, 1924), 354.

GILBERT, "The Vital Disequilibrium in Croce's Historicism", 408.

GINSBERG, "Stammler's Philosophy of Law," in Modern Theories of Law
(1933), 390.

GLASSON, 3, Morel et Tissier, Traité théorique et pratique d'organisation
judiciaire de compétence et de procédure civile (3 ième ed., 1929), 208.

GLUECK, The Nuremberg Trial and Aggressive War (1946), 177.

GOBLE, "Affirmative and Negative Legal Relations," 4 Ill.L.Q. 94 (1922),
132.

GOODHART, Arthur L.
"Case Law in England and America" in Essays in Jurisprudence and
the Common Law (1931) 65 (reprinted from 15 Cornell L.Q. 173).
304.
"Determining the Ratio Decidendi of a Case," 40 Yale L.J. 161 (1930).
280, 300, 315.
"Determining the Ratio Decidendi of a Case," in Essays in Jurispru-
dence and the Common Law (1931), 315.
Essays in Jurisprudence and the Common Law (1930), 300, 301, 304, 315.
317, 318, 319.
"The Importance of a Definition of Law," 3 Jour. African Admin. 106
(1951), 68, 71.
"Precedent in the Court of Appeal," 9 Camb.L.J. 349 (1947), 208.
"Precedents in English and Continental Law," 50 L.Q.Rev. 40 (1934), 208,
211.
Quoting Codex 7.45.13 (A.D. 533), 50 L.Q.Rev. 56; 207, 308.

GOODRICH, "The Story of the American Law Institute," Wash.U.L.Q. 283
(1951), 222.

GRAY, John C.
The Nature and Sources of the Law (1st ed., 1909), 89, 90, 171, 189, 197, 199,
200, 210, 213, 230, 232, 239, 300, 411, 423, 572, 573.
Chap. XI, 217, 219.
The Nature and Sources of the Law (2d ed., 1921), 572, 573.
The Nature and Sources of the Law (2d ed., 1927), 89, 90, 572.

GREEN, Leon, Essays and Notes on the Law of Tort and Crime, 471, 476.

GREENLEAF, Evidence, 61.

GRINNELL, Frank W.
    25 J. Amer.Jud.Soc. 10 (1941), 222.
    35 A.B.A.J. 648 (1949), 265.

GROTIUS
    De Jure Belli ac Pacis (Whewell ed., 1853), Vol. I, Prolegomena,
        pp. xli-xlii, sec. 6; 345.
        p. xliv, sec. 8; 345
        Ch. 1, XII, 345.

GSOVSKI, VLADIMIR, 1 Soviet Civil Law (1948), 196, 238, 268, 286, 587.

HAINES, Charles G.
    "General Observations on the Effects of Personal, Political and Eco-
        nomic Influences in the Decisions of Judges," 17 Ill.L.Rev. 96 (1922),
        593.
    "The Law of Nature in State and Federal Judicial Decisions," 35 Yale
        L.J. 1026 (1916), 361.
    The Revival of Natural Law Concepts (1930), 334, 370, 373.
        Ch. 1, 359, 361.

HALE, Sir Matthew, History of the Common Law (1820 ed.), 300.

HALE, Robert L., "Economics and Law" Ogden and Goldenweiser, The Social
    Sciences (1927), 54.

HALSBURY, The Laws of England, "Judgments" (Vol. 18, p. 210), 316.

HAMILTON, Alexander, The Federalist, No. LXXVIII; (Masters Smith &
    Co. ed., 1852), 566.

HAND, Learned
    "Restitution and Unjust Enrichment," 11 Harv.L.Rev. 249 (1897), 295,
        546.
    "The Speech of Justice," 29 Harv.L.Rev. 617 (1916), 302, 576.

HANSON, Reform of Consideration, 54 L.Q.Rev. 233 (1938), 272.

HARPER, "Some Implications of Juristic Pragmatism," 39 Ethics 269 (1929),
    472.

HART, Bernard, The Psychology of Insanity (1910), 551.

HART, Henry M., "Holmes" Positivism—An Addendum," 64 Harv.L.Rev.
    929 (1951), 505.

HARVARD LAW REVIEW
63 Harv.L.Rev. 541 (1950), 237, 267, 576.
"Judicial Abrogation of the Obsolete Statute: A Comparative View," 64
    Harv.L.Rev. 1181 (1951), 169.
"Predictability of Result in Commercial Arbitration," 61 Harv.L.Rev. 1022
    (1948), 211.

HAVIGHURST, Cases on Contracts (1934; 2d ed., 1950), 555.

HECK, "Jurisprudence of Interests" (1932), translated in The Jurisprudence
    of Interests (Twentieth Century Legal Philosophy Series, Vol. 3, 1948),
    202, 463, 464.

HURST, Willard
"Law and the Balance of Power in the Community," 22 Okla.B.A.J.
1223 (1950), 59.
The Growth of American Law: The Law Makers (1950), 409.

HUTCHESON, Joseph C., Jr.
"The Judgment Intuitive: The Function of the Hunch in Judicial Decision," 14 Corn.L.Q. 274 (1929), 536, 542, 543, 575, 591.
"The Status of the Rule of Judicial Precedent," 14 U. of Cincinnati L.Rev.
203, 259 (1940), 316, 575, 591.

HUXLEY, Julian, Heredity East and West, ch. 3 (1949), 500.

HYDE, 1 International Law (2d ed., 1945), 174.

JACKSON, Richard M., History of Quasi-Contract (1936), 43, 270, 374.

JAMES, Fleming, Jr., and PERRY, Roger F., "Legal Cause," 60 Yale L.J. 761.
(1951), 44.

JAMES, William
Pragmatism: A New Name for Some Old Ways of Thinking (1907), 474.
Pragmatism—A New Name for Some Old Ways of Thinking (1925), 472,
477, 478, 482.
Psychology (Briefer Course, 1892), 445, 477, 520.
"The Moral Philosopher and the Moral Life," first published in Ethics
(1891), 482.
"The Moral Philosopher and the Moral Life" (an address delivered in
1891), in The Will to Believe and Other Essays in Popular Philoso-
phy (1896), 408, 427.
"The Sentiment of Rationality," in James Selected Papers on Philosophy
(Everyman Lib. ed., 1917), 470, 478, 479, 481, 482, 485, 493.
The Will to Believe (1897), 427.
The Will to Believe and Other Essays in Popular Philosophy (1896),
482, 483, 484, 485, 486.

JESSUP, "The Subjects of a Modern Law of Nations," 45 Mich.L.Rev. 383
(1947), 174.

JHERING, Rudolf
Der Zweck im Recht (Vol. I, 1877, Vol. II, 1883), 459, 460, 461, 462, 463.
Geist des Romischen Rechts, III (I) § 60, 459.
The Law as a Means to an End (Husik trans., 1914), 459, 460, 461, 462,
463, 522.

JONES, Harry W., "Extrinsic Aids in the Federal Courts," 25 Iowa L.Rev.
737 (1940), 203, 204.
"Statutory Doubts and Legislative Intention," 40 Col.L.Rev. 957 (1940),
202.

JONES, John W.
Historical Introduction to the Theory of Law (1940), 10, 262, 335, 343,
344, 353, 354, 367.

JUDLOWSKI, "Le Nouveau Droit de la Famille en Pologne," 1 Révue International de Droit Comparé 67 (1949), 251.

JUSTINIAN, Codex, 7.45.13 (A.D. 533), 207.

KALLEN, Horace M., "John Dewey and the Spirit of Pragmatism," in John Dewey: Philosopher of Science and Freedom (Hook ed., 1950), 485, 487.

KANT, Immanuel
"Foundations of the Metaphysics of Morals," Critique of Practical Reason (Beck trans., 1949), 377, 378, 379, 380, 381.
Metaphysische Anfangsgründe der Rechtslehre (1797), 384.
"On a Supposed Right to Lie," in Practical Reason 346 (first Published in 1797), 381.
Philosophy of Law (1797), translated by Hastie (1887), 32, 76, 378, 380, 384, 385, 386, 387, 388, 389, 431.
Practical Reason, 78, 383.

KANTOROWICZ, Hermann U.
"Legal Science—A Summary of Its Methodology," 28 Columbia L.Rev. 679 (1928), 109, 124, 239, 240.
Rechtswissenschaft und Soziologie, 182.
"Savigny and the Historical School," 53 L.Q.Rev. 326 (1937), 410.
"Some Rationalism About Realism," 43 Yale L.J. 1240 (1934), 541.

KARDINER, The Psychological Frontiers of Society (1945), 57.

KELSEN, Hans
General Theory of Law and State (Wedberg trans.) (1945), 15, 87, 92, 113, 136, 171, 228, 229, 260, 261, 262, 263, 264, 265, 390.
"The Pure Theory of Law," 50 L.Q.Rev. 474 (1934), 15, 136, 190, 260.
51 L.Q.Rev. 517 (1935), 92, 110, 260.
Modern Theories of Law (1933), 171.

KEYSER, C. J.
"On the Study of Legal Science," 38 Yale L.J. 413 (1929), 10, 279.
Thinking about Thinking (1926), 24.

KING, B. E., "The Concept of a Lawyer's Jurisprudence," 11 Cambridge L. J. 229 (1952), 68, 125, 229.

KLINEBERG, Social Psychology (1940), 57.

KOCOUREK, Albert
An Introduction to the Science of Law (1930), 10.
"Classification of the Law," 11 N.Y.U.L.Q. 319 (1934), in 2 Law: A Century of Progress 195 (1937), 15, 257, 258.
"Retrospective Decisions and Stare Decisis and a Proposal," 17 A.B.A.J. 180 (1931), 578.

KOCOUREK, Albert, and WIGMORE, John H., Sources of Ancient and Primitive Law (1915), 269, 514.

KOEHLER, The Place of Value in a World of Fact (1938), 41.

KOHLER, Josef
Einführung in die Rechtswissenschaft (1902), § 1 (trans. Pound, Outlines, 70), 74.
Philosophy of Law (Albrecht trans., 1914), 433, 516.

KORKUNOV, General Theory of Law (Hastings trans., 1909), 10, 127, 136.

KRECH and CRUTCHFIELD, Theory and Problems of Social Psychology (1948), 58.

LAIRD, An Enquiry into Moral Notions (1936), 31.

LANDIS, James M., "Statutes and the Sources of Law," Harvard Legal Essays (1934), 217.

LANGDELL, Christopher C.
A Selection of Cases on the Law of Contracts (Boston, 1871), 244, 256, 419.
Brief Survey of Equity Jurisdiction (1905), 419.
Harvard Celebration Speeches, 3 L.Q.Rev. 123 (1887), 419.
Summary of Equity Pleading (1877), 419.

LASERSON, Russia and the Western World (1945), 154.

LASK, Emil, Rechtsphilosophie (1905), also published in German in Die Philosophie im Beginn des 20 Jahrhunderts (1st ed., 1905, 2d ed., 1907), 396.

The Legal Philosophies of Lask, Radbruch and Dabin, (Wilk trans., 1950), 396, 397, 398.

LASKI, Harold, "The Personality of Associations," 29 Harvard L.Rev. 404 (1916), 58.

LASSWELL, Harold D., and McDOUGAL, Myres
"Legal Education and Public Policy: Professional Training in the Public Interest," 52 Yale L.J. 203 (1943), 245, 283, 284, 287, 554, 557, 590.

LASSWELL, Harold D., and KAPLAN, Abraham, Power and Society: A Framework for Political Inquiry (1950), 70, 150, 158, 162, 179.

LAWSON, The Rational Strength of English Law (1951), 244.

LEBOUTILLIER, American Democracy and Natural Law (1950), 333.

LE BUFFE and HAYES, The American Philosophy of Law (1947), 347.

LEHMAN, Irving, "A Memorial," Selected Writings of Benjamin N. Cardozo (1947), 535.

LEPAULLE "The Function of Comparative Law with a Critique of Sociological Jurisprudence," 35 Harv.L.Rev. 838 (1922), 527.

LERNER, Max
The Mind and Faith of Justice Holmes (1943), 500, 504, 506, 507.
"The Shadow World of Thurman Arnold," 47 Yale L.J. 687 (1938), 39.

LEVY, Beryl, Cardozo and Frontiers of Legal Thinking (1938), 529, 537.

LLEWELLYN, Karl N.
"Administration of Law," 6 National Encyclopedia 176 (1937), 567.
"A Realistic Jurisprudence—the Next Step," 30 Columbia L.Rev. 432 (1930), 142.
Behind the Law of Divorce, 32 Col.L.Rev. 1281 (1932), 540.
"Case Law," 3 Encyc.Soc.Sci. 249 (1930), 101, 206.
"How Appellate Courts Decide Cases," 16 Pa.Bar Ass'n Q. 220 (1945), 409.
"Legal Tradition and Social Science Method—A Realist's Critique," in Essays in Research in the Social Sciences (1931), 540.
My Philosophy of Law (1941), 82, 99, 540.
"On the Good, the True and the Beautiful in Law, 9 U. of Chi.L.Rev. 224 (1942), 49.

MEAD, George H.
"The Philosophies of Royce, James and Dewey in Their American Setting," in John Dewey: The Man and his Philosophy (1930), 487.

MERTON, Robert K., "The Role of Applied Social Science in the Formation of Policy: A Research Memorandum," 16 Philosophy of Science 161 (1949), 284.

MILL, Utilitarianism (Everyman ed.), 440.

MILLER, William G., Lectures on the Philosophy of Law (1884), 98.

MILTNER, "Law and Morals," 10 Notre Dame Lawyer 9–10 (1934), 369.

Missouri Law Review, 12 Mo.L.Rev. 358 (1947), 237, 586.

MITCHELL, Wesley C., "Bentham's Felicific Calculus," 33 Pol.Sci.Quar. 161 (1918), 449.

MONRO, D. H., 60 Ethics 285 (1950), 446.

MOORE, My Philosophy of Law (1941), 191.

MOORE, William U., "Rational Basis of Legal Institutions," 23 Col.L.Rev. 609 (1923), 540.

MOORE, William U., and CALLAHAN, Charles C., "Law and Learning Theory: A Study in Legal Control," (1943, The Yale Law Journal Co., Inc.), 547.

MOORE, William U., and HOPE, Theodore S., "An Institutional Approach to the Law of Commercial Banking," 38 Yale L.J. 703 (1929), 542.

MOORE, William U., and SUSSMAN, Gilbert, "Legal and Institutional Methods Applied to the Debiting of Direct Discounts—I. Legal Method: Banker's Set-off," 40 Yale L. J. 381, 1228 (1931), 541, 542, 547, 553.

MORGAN, Edmund M.
An Introduction to the Study of Law (1st ed., 1926), 316.
"Codification of Evidence", 458.
Introduction to the Study of Law (2d ed., 1948), 301, 310, 312.

MORRIS, C. W., "Foundation of the Theory of Signs," 1 Internat'l Encyc. of Unified Science, No. 2 (1938), 27, 295, 296, 430.

MORROW, "Plato and the Law of Nature," in Essays in Political Theory (ed. Konvitz and Murphy, 1948), 336, 343.

MURRAY, English Dictionary, 551.

NEUMANN, "Types of Natural Law," 8 Studies in Philosophy and Social Science (1940), 364.

NEWCOMB, Social Psychology, Ch. 5 (1950), 58.

NORTHROP, The Logic of the Sciences and the Humanities (1947), 26, 467, 468.

OGDEN, Charles K., and RICHARDS, I. A., The Meaning of Meaning (2d ed., 1927), 27, 287, 546.

O'HALLORAN, 8 The Advocate (1950), 503.

OLIPHANT, Herman
"A Return to Stare Decisis," 14 A.B.A.J. 71 et seq. (1928), 310, 311, 312,
313, 544.
Ass'n American Law Schools, 1928 Proceedings, p. 76, 310.
"Facts, Opinions and Value-Judgments," 10 Tex.L.Rev. 127 (1932), 540,
553.
Summary of Studies in Legal Education (1929), 554.

OLIPHANT and HEWITT, Introduction to Rueff, From the Physical to the
Social Sciences (1929), 543.

OLIPHANT, Herman, and HOPE, Theodore S., A Study of Day Calendars
(The Johns Hopkins Press (1932), 547.

PAGE, William H.
Handbook of the Association of American Law Schools (1920), 132.
"Terminology and Classification in Fundamental Legal Relations," 4 Am.
L.Sch.Rev. 616 (1921), 132.

PALEY, Principles of Moral and Political Philosophy (first published 1785)
(8 Am. ed., 1815), Ch. V, 456.

PAP, "The Verifiability of Value Judgments," 56 Ethics 178 (1946), 500.

PARK and BURGESS, Introduction to the Science of Sociology (1930), 93.

PATON, George W., Textbook on Jurisprudence (1st ed., 1946; 2d ed., 1951),
10, 218, 219, 220, 221, 232, 262, 272, 292, 332, 334, 579, 584.

PATTERSON, Edwin W.
"Bentham on the Nature and Method of Law," 33 Calif.L.Rev. 612 (1945),
137, 141, 172, 442.
Book Review of a Casebook on Equity, 48 Harv.L.Rev. 1261 (1935), 420.
"Cardozo's Philosophy of Law," 88 U. of Pa.L.Rev. 71, 156 (1939), 100,
256, 529.
Cases and Materials on the Law of Insurance (2d ed., 1947), 555.
"Dewey's Theories of Legal Reasoning and Valuation," in John Dewey:
Philosopher of Science and Freedom (1950), 551.
"Equitable Relief for Unilateral Mistake," 28 Col.L.Rev. 859 (1928), 388,
549.
"Hans Kelsen and His Pure Theory of Law," 40 Calif.L.Rev. 5 (1952), 260.
"Illusory Promises and Promisor's Options," Selected Readings in the
Law of Contracts (1931), 214, 218.
"John Dewey and the Law," 36 A.B.A.J. 619 (1950), 491.
John Dewey: Philosopher of Science and Freedom (1950), 491.
"Logic in the Law," 90 U. of Pa.L.Rev. 875 (1942), 20, 21, 488.
My Philosophy of Law (1941), 178.
"Pound's Theory of Social Interests," in Interpretations of Modern Legal
Philosophies (1947), 519.
"The Case Method in American Legal Education: Its Origins and Ob-
jectives," 4 Journal of Legal Education 1 (1951), 554.
"The Delivery of a Life Insurance Policy," 33 Harv.L.Rev. 198 (1919), 388,
456, 471.
The Philosopher of the Common Man (1940), 491.
27 Georgetown L.J. 999 (1939), 221.

PAZ, Enrique Martinez, "Lask and the Doctrine of the Science of Law," Interpretations of Modern Legal Philosophies (Essays in Honor of Roscoe Pound) (1947), 396.

PEIRCE, "How To Make Our Ideas Clear", in Scientific American (1878), 474, 477.

PERRY, Ralph B.
Characteristically American (1949), 487.
General Theory of Value (1926), 477.
General Theory of Value (1926), Ch. V, 520.
The Thought and Character of William James (1935), 501.

PHILBRICK, Language and the Law (1949), Ch. II, 296.

PLATO
The Republic, II, 377 (Everyman ed.), 330.
Republic (Lindsay trans., 1935), Bk. VII, 539.

PLUCKNETT, A Concise History of English Law (2d ed., 1936), 224.

POLLOCK
"A Plea for Historical Interpretation", 39 L.Q.Rev. 163 (1923), 406.
Essays in Jurisprudence in Ethics (1882), 126.
Essays in Jurisprudence and Ethics (1882), 205, 244, 247, 296, 335.
Essays in Jurisprudence and Ethics (1882), 244, 247.
The Expansion of the Common Law (1904), 333, 365.
"The Science of Case Law" (1882), 205.

POLLOCK and MAITLAND
History of English Law (1st ed., 1895), 73.

POLLOCK, Frederick, WILLISTON'S, Samuel, WALD'S, Gustavus H., Contracts, Appendix, Note A., 388.

POPE, "The English Common Law in the United States", 24 Harv.L.Rev. 6 (1910), 212.

POTTER, The Quest for Justice (London, 1951), 513.

POUND, Roscoe
"A Call for a Realist Jurisprudence," 44 Harv.L.Rev. 697 (1931), 538.
"Administrative Application of Legal Standards," 44 Rep.Amer.Bar Ass'n 445 (1919), 273, 275, 278, 512.
An Introduction to American Law (pamphlet outline of lectures at Trade Union College under the auspices of the Boston Central Labor Union, Spring Term, 1919), 516.
An Introduction to the Philosophy of Law (1922), 74, 268, 269, 270, 271, 272, 514, 579.
"A Survey of Social Interests," 57 Harv.L.Rev. 1 et seq. (1943), 519, 520, 521, 522, 523, 525, 526.
"A Theory of Social Interests" 15 Papers and Proceedings of the American Sociological Society, 16 (1921), 94, 514, 519.
"Classification of Law," 37 Harv.L.Rev. 933 (1924), 257.
"Common Law and Legislation," 21 Harv.L.Rev. 383 (1908), 217.
"Courts and Legislation," in the Science of Legal Method, 206 (1917), 182.
"David Dudley Field: An Appraisal," in David Dudley Field Centenary Essays (1949), 458.

POUND, Roscoe—Continued

"Equitable Relief against Defamation and Injuries to Personality," 29 Harv.L.Rev. 640 (1916), 521.

"Fifty Years of Jurisprudence," 50 Harvard L.Rev. 557 (1937), 132.

"For the Minority Report," 27 A.B.A.J. 664 (1941), 281.

"Hierarchy of Sources and Forms in Different Systems of Law," 7 Tul. L.Rev. 475 (1933), 268.

"How Far Are We Attaining a New Measure of Values in Twentieth Century Juristic Thought?" 42 W.Va.L.Q. 81 (1936), 34, 366, 376, 552.

"Individual Interests in the Domestic Relations," 14 Mich.L.Rev. 177 (1916), 521.

"Individual Interests of Substance—Promised Advantages," 59 Harv.L. Rev. 1 (1945), 521.

"Interests of Personality," 28 Harv.L.Rev. 343 (1915), 521.

Interpretations of Legal History (Cambridge, 1923), 74, 215, 406, 418, 421, 424.

"Juristic Science and Law," 31 Harv.L.Rev. 1047 (1918), 229.

"Justice According to Law," 13 Columbia L.Rev. 696 (1913), 105.

Law and Morals (1924), 30, 231, 239.

Law and Morals (2d ed., 1936), and Bibliography, 230.

"Law and the State—Jurisprudence and Politics," 57 Harvard L.Rev. 1193 (1944), 17, 153.

"Law in Books and Law in Action," 44 American L.Rev. 12 (1910), 118, 398, 510.

"Liberty of Contract," 18 Yale L.J. 454 (1909), 510.

"Mechanical Jurisprudence," 8 Col.L.Rev. 605 (1908), 11, 25, 510.

"The Need of a Sociological Jurisprudence," 19 Green Bag 607–615 (1907), 510.

Outlines of Lectures on Jurisprudence (5th ed., 1943), 68, 72, 74, 76, 89, 117, 125, 230, 332, 334, 461, 511, 513, 516, 519, 523.

Report of the Committees on Duplication of Reports and Publications, 61 Rep.Am.Bar.Assn. 848 (1936), 570.

"Sociology of Law and Sociological Jurisprudence," 5 Univ. of Toronto L.J. 1 (1943), 93, 509.

"The Causes of Popular Dissatisfaction With the Administration of Justice," 29 Rep.A.B.A., Pt. I, 395–417 (1906), 510.

"The Decadence of Equity," 5 Col.L.Rev. 20 (1905), 510.

"The End of Law as Developed in Juristic Thought," 27 Harv.L.Rev. 195, 605 (1914), 513.

The Formative Era in American Law (1938), 74, 212, 213, 220, 367, 377, 409, 529.

"The Ideal Element in American Judicial Decision," 45 Harv.L.Rev. 136 (1931), 214, 218, 333.

"The Limits of Effective Legal Action," 3 A.B.A.J. 55 (1917), 452.

"The Limits of Effective Legal Action," 27 Int.Jour.Ethics 150 (1916), 452, 512.

"The Pioneers and the Law," in The Spirit of the Common Law (1921), 512, 513.

"The Revival of Natural Law," 17 Notre Dame Lawyer 287 (1942), 333, 377.

"The Scope and Purpose of Sociological Jurisprudence," 25 Harv.L.Rev. 591 (1911), 94, 511.

POUND, Roscoe—Continued
The Spirit of the Common Law (1921), 94, 195, 237, 312, 408, 427, 579.
The Task of the Law (1944), 74.

POWELL, Richard R. B., Real Property, Vol. I (1950), 212.

PROSSER, Torts (1941), 235, 382.

PUCHTA, Outlines of Jurisprudence as the Science of Right—a Juristic
Encyclopedia (Hastie trans., 1887), 16, 79, 411.

RADBRUCH, Rechtsphilosophie (3d ed. 1932), in The Legal Philosophies of
Lask, Radbruch and Dabin (Wilk trans., 1950), 377, 399, 400, 401, 402, 403.

RADIN, Max
"Early Statutory Interpretation," 38 Ill.L.Rev. 25 (1943), 15.
"In Defense of an Unsystematic Science of Law," 51 Yale L.J. 1269 (1942),
553.
Law as Logic and Experience (1940), 46, 102, 553.
"Statutory Interpretation," 43 Harvard L.Rev. 863 (1930), 99, 202.
The Lawful Pursuit of Gain, Ch. III (1931), 235.

RANDALL, "John Dewey, 1859–1952," 50 Jour. of Philosophy 5 (1953), 492,
493.

RESTATEMENT OF LAW
Conflicts (Amer.Law Inst. 1934), 67, 89, 90, 250, 572.
Contracts (American Law Institute, 1932), 29, 107, 108, 144, 145, 279, 291,
292, 294, 316.
Property, Vols. IV, V (American Law Institute, 1944), 144, 145.
Restitution (American Law Institute 1937), 124, 143, 238, 456, 584.
Torts (American Law Institute, 1934, 1938), 141, 145, 382.

REUSCHLEIN, Harold, Jurisprudence: Its American Prophets (1951), 10.

RIEZLER, Das Rechtsgefuhl (1946), 581.

RIFKIND, "When the Press Collides with Justice," 34 J.Am.Jud.Soc. 46
(1950), 563.

RIGNANO, The Psychology of Reasoning (1923), 588.

ROBERTS, Owen J. "Now Is the Time: Fortifying the Supreme Court's Independence," 35 A.B.A.J. 1 (1949), 265, 565.

ROBINSON, J. J., Cases on Criminal Law and Procedure (1941), 113.

ROBINSON, Edward S., Law and the Lawyers (1935), 201, 372, 552, 592, 593.

ROBINSON, J. H., The Mind in the Making (1921), 551.

ROSS, Alf, Towards a Realistic Jurisprudence (1946), 38, 68, 71.

ROSS, Edward A., Social Control (1901), 93.

RUSSELL, Bertrand
History of Western Philosophy (1945), 61, 186, 341, 434, 479, 480, 496.

RUTHERFORTH, Institutes of Natural Law, Ch. XV, (2d Amer.ed. 1832; first
published 1754), 367.

RUTLEDGE, Wiley, "Declaration of Legal Faith," quoted in 71 Sup.Ct.
xxvii (1951), 77.

SABINE, A History of Political Theory (1937), 342, 366, **377**.

ST. GERMAIN, Doctor and Student, Ch. V (first published in 1518) (Muchall ed., 1874), 365.

SALMOND, John W.
  Jurisprudence (1902), 71, 89.
  Jurisprudence (4th ed.), 72.
  Jurisprudence (7th ed., 1924), 71, 89, 98, 104, 105, 117, 122, 127, 132, 196 199, 218, 223, 231, 269, 302, 303.

SAPIR, "Language," 9 Encyc. of Soc. Sciences 158 (1933), 27.

SAVIGNY, Friedrich Karl von
  Of the Vocation of Our Age for Legislation and Jurisprudence (Hayward trans., 1831), 16, 78, 410.
  System des heutigen römischen Rechts (1840), 117.
  Uber den Beruf unserer Zeit fur Gesetzgebung und Rechtswissenschaft (1814); 2d ed., 1828, translated by Hayward as: Of the Vocation of Our Age for Legislation and Jurisprudence (London, 1831), 16, 78, 410.
  Vocation, Ch. VII, 421.

SAYRE, The Life of Roscoe Pound (1948), 510, 519.

SCHEFFEL and McGARAH, Jurisprudence for Nurses (3d ed., 1945), 7.

SCHLESINGER, "Justice in Russia: A Dissent," 60 Yale L.J. 976 (1951), 286.

SCHNEIDER, Herbert W.
  A History of American Philosophy (1946), 56, 398, 427.

SCHROEDER, "The Psychological Study of Judicial Opinions," 6 Calif.L.Rev. 89 (1918), 550.

SCIENCE OF LEGAL METHOD, The (by various authors; 1917), 560.

SCOTT, "Judicial Logic as Applied in Delimiting the Concept of 'Business Affected with a Public Interest'," 19 Ky.L.J. 16 (1930), 292.

SCOTT, Austin W. and SIMPSON, Sidney P., Cases on Judicial Remedies (1938), 113.

SEAVEY, "Principles of Torts," 56 Harv.L.Rev. 72 (1942), 280, 281.

SELIGMAN, E. R. A., "Economics," 5 Encyc. of Soc.Sci. 344 (1931), 53.

SETARO, A Bibliography of the Writings of Roscoe Pound (Cambridge, 1942), 511.

SHARTEL, Burke, Our Legal System and How It Operates (1951), 10.

SIDGWICK, The Methods of Ethics (1930), 232.

SMITH, Adam, Wealth of Nations, I, Ch. 2, 54.

SMITH, Reginald H.
  "The English Legal Assistance Plan," 35 A.B.A.J. 453 (1949), 192.
  Justice and the Poor (Carnegie Foundation for the Advancement of Teaching, Bulletin No. 13, 1919), 192.

SMITH, T. V., "Ethics," in Encyc. of Soc. Sciences, 30.

SNYDER, "Retrospective Operation of Overruling Decisions," 35 Ill.L.Rev. 121 (1940), 578.

SPENCER, Herbert
Justice (1892), Appendix A, 425.
Social Statics (1st Amer.Ed., 1865).
    Ch. IV, 425, 427.
    Ch. XXV, 426.
    Ch. XXVI, 426, 427.
    Ch. XXX, 426.
The Data of Ethics (New York, 1879), 426.

SPRUILL, "The Effect of an Overruling Decision," 18 N.C.L.Rev. 199 (1940), 578.

STAMMLER
The Theory of Just Law (Husik trans., 1925), 390, 391, 392.
Wirtschaft und Recht (1895), 390.

STONE, Harlan F., in The Future of the Common Law (1937), 217.

STONE, Julius
The Province and Function of Law (1st ed., 1946), 10, 68, 222, 232, 262, 290, 458.
    Ch. II, 88.
    Ch. VII, 101, 204, 273, 274, 278, 308, 579, 592.
    Ch. VIII, 332, 334, 367, 372, 373.
    Ch. XII, 395.
    Ch. XIII, 516, 517.
    Ch. XV, 517.
    Ch. XIX, 197, 415, 418.
    Ch. XX, 284.
    Ch. XXI, 517.
    Ch. XXV, 241.

SUMNER, William G., Folkways (1906), 56, 224, 499.

TANSLEY, The New Psychology (1920), 551.

THAYER, James B.
A Preliminary Treatise on Evidence at the Common Law (1898), 515.
"The Origin and Scope of the American Doctrine of Constitutional Law," 7 Harv.L.Rev. 129 (1893), 373.

THOMPSON, Floyd E., Review of Professor Glueck's Book, 32 A.B.A.J. 506 (1946), 178.

TIMASHEFF, "Petrazhitsky's Philosophy of Law," in Interpretations of Modern Legal Philosophies (Essays in Honor of Roscoe Pound) (1947), 81.
"Torrent of Judicial Opinions Can Be Checked," 25 J.Amer.Jud.Soc. 132 (1942), 570.

TOURTELON, Philosophy in the Development of the Law (Read trans. 1922), 9.

TREUSCH, "The Syllogism," in Hall, Readings in Jurisprudence, 539–560 (1938), 20.

TROTTER, Instincts of the Herd, 551.

TUFTS, America's Social Morality: Dilemmas of the Changing Mores (1933), 240.

VYSHINSKY, The Law of the Soviet State (Babb trans., 1948), 155, 196, 287, 436, 437.

WALLAS, The Art of Thought, Ch. IV (1926), 542, 591.

WAMBAUGH, The Study of Cases (2d ed. 1894), 300, 301, 302, 307, 308, 309, 312.

WARD, The Psychic Factors of Civilization (1893), 427.

WATSON, Psychology from the Standpoint of a Behaviorist (1919), 548.

WEBER and PERRY, History of Philosophy (1925), 341.

WHITEHEAD, Process and Reality (1930), 429.

WIENER, Philip Paul
Evolution and the Founders of Pragmatism (1949), 487, 504, 506, 588.
Ch. 2, 475, 476, 477, 481, 483.
Ch. 9, 467, 469, 470, 474.

WIGMORE, John H.
Cases on Torts, II Appendix A, § 3 (1911), 89, 147.
Evidence, (1st ed., 1904), 61, 227.
Evidence (3d ed., 1940), 406, 407, 408, 512.

WILK, "Law and the State as Pure Ideas," 51 Intern.J.Ethics 158 (1941), 261.

WILKIN, Eternal Lawyer (1947), 343.

WILLIAMS, Glanville
"Language and the Law," 61 L.Q.Rev. 71, 179, 293, 384 (1945); 62 id. 387 (1946), 28.
"The Controversy Concerning the Word Law," 38 Archiv. für Rechts-und Sozialphilosophie 50, 59 (1949), 70.

WILLISTON, Samuel
Contracts (1st ed., 1920), 221.
Contracts (rev. ed., 1936 by Williston and Thompson), 130, 131, 221, 227, 388.
Some Modern Tendencies in the Law (1929), 25, 283.

WILLOUGHBY, Principles of Judicial Administration (The Brookings Institution, Washington, 1929), 192.

WINDELBAND, A History of Philosophy (Tufts trans., 2d ed., 1926), 97, 335.

WINFIELD, "Ethics in English Case Law," 45 Harv.L.Rev. 112 (1931), 283, 329.

WISE, Outlines of Jurisprudence (6th ed., 1948), 84.

WOODWARD, Quasi Contracts (1913), 407.
Words and Phrases, (West Publishing Co., 1940), 67.

WORMUTH, "Aristotle on Law," in Essays in Political Theory Presented to George H. Sabine (ed. Konvitz and Murphy, 1948), 337, 367, 408.

WRIGHT, Benjamin F., American Interpretations of Natural Law (1931), 351.

WRIGHT, Robert A. W., Baron, "Public Policy," in Legal Essays and Addresses, p. 66 (1939), 282.

WU, "Stammler and His Critics," in the Theory of Justice (Husik trans., 1925), 390.

INDEX

[References are to pages]

See also Books and Periodicals Cited; Table of Cases.

STAMMLER, RUDOLPH
Conception of justice, and Aristotle's, 391–392
Theories of just law, 389–395

STARE DECISIS
See *Case Law; Judicial Precedents; Judicial Process*

STATE
Coercive power, differentiates, 162
Dependence of law upon, 52, 92, 101, 147, 148, 152–156, 259–263
Enables men to attain good life, 338, 339
Enforceability of law by, 16
Enforcement of permissive rules, 127, 133–134
Individual ethical development in, 338–339, 430
Legal service to be provided by, 192
Meaning of, 152–154
Ranks of official authority in, 259

STATUTES
See *Legislation*

STOICS
See also *Cicero, Marcus T.; Natural Law*
Origin of philosophy of, 341, 484

SWISS CIVIL CODE
Provision on abusive exercise of right, 238

SYMBOLS
See *Semantics; Semiotics*

SYSTEM, IN LAW
A law in isolation is incomplete, 23, 279, 308–309
Compartmentalization and classification in law, 257–258
Conflict between co-ordinate bodies, 264
External and internal relations of legal, 2–3
"Gaps" and "unprovided cases", 267
Genetic system, in law, 256–257
Hierarchy of authority, 198, 259–265
Law tends to become a, 23
Levels of meaning, 281, 294–295
Linguistic system, in law, 252–255

SYSTEM, IN LAW—Cont'd
Minimum logical tests of legal, 265–268
Perfect legal-philosophical, 557
Perfect logical, meaning of, 23
Proposed aesthetic significance of, 48
Reasons for, and for lack of, 246–249
Systemic significance of precedents, 309, 313, 317, 323
Types of order in the law, 249–257
Uses and limitations of, in law, 244–249, 492, 494

TECHNIQUES, JUDICIAL
See *Judicial Process*

TERMINOLOGY
See also *Corbin, Arthur L.; Hohfeld, Wesley N.; Semantics; Semiotics; System*
Popular, differs from legal, 252
Popular, influence on legal, 249, 296–299

THOMISTS
See *Aquinas, St. Thomas; Neo-Scholasticism*

TORTS
Conversion, sanction or legal consequence, 163–164
Elevator accident, liability, 278
Jural postulates of, 516–517
"Malice" in defamation cases, 119
Negligence liability, as social control, 95
Proximate cause, evaluative aspect, 44, 476
Right of privacy, 374–375
Standard of prudent man, 272

TRADE UNIONS
See *Labor*

TRESPASS
Indirect existential reference of, 40, 140
Liability for trespassing animals, 212
Metaphysical status of, compared with walking, 41–43

UNITED STATES CONSTITUTION
See *Constitution, of United States*

End of Volume